W9-CBE-393

THE KENNEDYS ALWAYS ELICITED CONTROVERSY.

HERE'S HOW THEY WERE REVIEWED BY SOME OF THEIR CONTEMPORARIES:

"JFK was a lout, a cad, a boor, an oaf, a schemer, a liar, a blackmailer, and a reckless gambler with the nation's security, its integrity and its institutions. Kennedy was a man thoroughly out of control, thoroughly out of his depth, and maybe thoroughly out of his mind. Kennedy wasn't just a hoodlum Prince of Camelot, he was the incarnation of Sodom and Gomorrah."

Seymour Hersh, *The Dark Side of Camelot*

"During the Thousand Days, Kennedy arrogantly and irresponsibly violated his covenant with the people. While saying and doing appropriate things in the public light, he acted covertly in ways that seriously demeaned himself and his office. With the appointment of his brother as attorney general, he tried to found a political dynasty, abhorred by the founding fathers. The metaphor of Camelot, after all, is ultimately un-American and undemocratic, conjuring up images of crowns and dashing young princes and noble birth."

Professor Thomas Reeves

"Kennedy did not have incisiveness and he was out of his depth where he was. I hate to say this because I know it's going to be misunderstood, but his reputation is greater because of the tragedy of his death than it would have been if he had lived out two terms. He did not seem to me to be in any sense a great man."

Dean Acheson, former Secretary of State

"Jack told me he wasn't through with a girl till he'd have her three ways."

Traphes Bryant, Veteran White House staff member

"I found the president very penetrating."

Marilyn Monroe

"He never said a word of importance in the Senate and never did a thing."

Lyndon B. Johnson

"Why should I go back? What good would it do?"

John F. Kennedy on the stillbirth of his child in 1956
when he was sailing the Mediterranean
with a boatload of females.

"Joe Kennedy was one of the biggest crooks who ever lived."

Mob boss Sam Giancana

"Listen, honey, if it wasn't for me, your boyfriend wouldn't even be in the White House."
Sam Giancana to Judith Campbell Exner

"Maybe Marilyn, had she lived, her back stooped from osteoporosis, munching carrot sticks and sipping Dom Perignon, would sink into her sofa one autumn evening, slide in one of those tapes made-for TV movies and smile at just how wrong the filmmakers had gotten it all. Still, she might have mused, it made a lovely story."

David Marshall

"I never had Addison's disease."

John F. Kennedy

"That's a lie—he looked like a spavined hunchback."

Lyndon B. Johnson

"The dog will keep biting you if you only cut off its tail. You must cut off the dog's head."
Carlos Marcello, mob chief of New Orleans who controlled Texas,
vowing revenge when JFK had him deported
and dropped in a Guatemala jungle.

"A vulgar slut, a publicity seeker, an egomaniac, a self-promoter, a vicious bitch, an unbalanced drug addict, an alcoholic whore, a dime-a-dance floozie."
Jacqueline Kennedy on Marilyn Monroe

"Bobby Kennedy was human. He liked to drink and he liked young women. He indulged that liking when he traveled—and he had to travel a great deal."
Historian Arthur Schlesinger

"Sex to Jack Kennedy was like another cup of coffee, or maybe dessert. For this Kennedy, evidently, sex was not to be confused with love."
Journalist Nancy Dickerson

"The Kennedy story is about people who broke the rules, and were ultimately broken by them."
Christopher Lawford

"God, I hate Camelot. I've begged Jackie to tell them to play something else, but it's like talking to a goddamn brick wall."
John F. Kennedy, on the Marine String Orchestra
playing at the White House.

"The point is, you've got to live every day like it's your last day on Earth. That's what I'm doing."
John F. Kennedy

"I don't think there are any men who are faithful to their wives. Men are such a combination of good and bad."
Jacqueline Kennedy Onassis

"Joe Kennedy represented the height of vulgarity. He was horny—that's all he was."

Columnist Doris Lilly

"JFK was one of the great cunt men of all time—except for me."

Jerry Lewis

"Jack always had his mind between his legs."

Lady May Lawford

"Kennedy was the frequent recipient of nonreciprocal fellatio from longtime close friend LeMoyne Billings."

Mart Martin

"Is it not possible to be an effective president of the United States without necessarily being personally virtuous?"

Alice Leavenbrook

"John F. Kennedy was the most overrated public figure in American history."

American Heritage

"According to our poll, John F. Kennedy was the most popular president in U.S. history—75% rate him good to great, 30% wish he were still president."

Newsweek

"Lifting us beyond our capacities, he gave the country back to its best self, wiping away the world's impression of an old nation of old men, weary, played out, fearful of the future; he taught mankind that the process of rediscovering America was not over. He transformed the American spirit."

Arthur Schlesinger Jr.

"I'm afraid he's going to grow up to be a fruit."

Jacqueline Kennedy, discussing JFK Jr.

"We want winners. We don't want losers around here."

Joseph P. Kennedy Sr., to his sons

"I don't think Jack Kennedy was a ladies' man. He always felt they were a useful thing to have when you wanted them, but when you didn't want them, put them back."

Charles Houghton, JFK's roommate at Harvard

"Well, JFK Jr. is kinda naïve, like a young boy."

Madonna

"In the brief time Jack had, he touched our hearts with fire, and the glow from that fire still lights the world."

Senator Ted Kennedy

"Granny-O, they called her in the later years. She had become the dowager First Lady, the last American Queen, editing books, escorting the Clintons on a cruise. People had long since stopped gossiping about whether she knew of Jack's infidelities, if Warren Beatty had once been a beau. It didn't matter. She was a survivor. It was almost impossible to separate her from the myth of Camelot. After all, she actually invented it. In the end, she liberated herself from the Kennedys and became the last real Kennedy--glamorous, desirable, mythic."

Reggie Nadelson, describing Jacqueline Kennedy Onassis

"If there's anything I'd hate in a son-in-law, it's an actor. And if there's anything I think I'd hate more than an actor as a son-in-law, it's an English actor."

**Joseph P. Kennedy to his daughter, Patricia,
about her upcoming marriage to Peter Lawford**

"The old man [Joseph P. Kennedy] had an eye out for every woman that walked. In the Kennedys' sense of morality, that was all right."

Fashion designer Oleg Cassini

"Women keep calling to invite me to dinner, and I keep turning them down."

John F. Kennedy Jr.

"The greatest twenty seconds of my life."

Angie Dickinson, describing JFK

"Jack lost his virginity when he was seventeen years old in a Harlem whorehouse to a black prostitute."

LeMoyne Billings, JFK's homosexual friend

"Jackie related to men by flirting with them. She loved to have male admirers around her, including FDR Jr. She used to tease Franklin. She was horrid. She was so dreamy that he'd be floating on air. I didn't realize it myself at the time, but that was simply Jackie's style with men."

Suzanne Roosevelt

"When John F. Kennedy Jr. was named by People Magazine as The Sexiest Man Alive, he was subjected to merciless ribbing from his friends, which he endured graciously. Eager to poke fun at himself, John went to one Halloween party as 'The Golden Boy' clad only in a loincloth and gold glitter. He attended another bash as Michelangelo's David, wearing something akin to a fig leaf."

Author Christopher Andersen

"Peter Lawford was not a model father. With his children he was, I always felt, essentially ill at ease. He considered them more Kennedy than Lawford—or at any rate they had been, in his opinion, 'brainwashed' to be. He worried about what other Kennedy family members told them about him. He was humiliated to the point of hysteria by the rumors and writings and mouthing that he had 'pimped' for Jack and Bobby Kennedy with Marilyn Monroe and that he had been instrumental in helping to speed her death. He felt it all made him look like a 'court fool' he said to me."

Author Lawrence J. Quirk

"If all the stories about JFK's women are to be believed, as president he turned the White House into a Deer Park, like the Sun King at Versailles. He was like Nietzsche's rope-dancer. In the end, the danger line became a death line. Like Jack, Ted was drawn to danger but more in his private than his public life. He had Jack's attitude toward women: To triumph as often as possible, but to keep from yielding his heart and commitment. They both had difficulty in relating with any emotional depth to a woman, or seeing her as other than a sex object and a field for conquest."

Max Lerner

"Ari [Aristotle Onassis] told me that Teddy Kennedy was just like his brother Jack. He wanted me to organize a party to welcome him to Greece. I was instructed to round up some good-looking broads."

Johnny Meyer, pimp to Onassis

"Ari [Aristotle Onassis] was able to keep his growing intimacy with Jackie a secret for a very long time. Rumors that she'd taken up with Bobby after Jack's death were believable...and even understandable. But the American public just could not believe that she'd tumble for a beast like Ari. It was truly the mating of The Beauty and The Beast."

JFK aide David Powers

"People keep telling me I can be a great man. I'd rather be a good one."

John F. Kennedy, Jr.

"Marilyn would tell me breathlessly about Jack, though she never mentioned Bobby. Most of the stories involved how sexually obsessed Jack was with her, how many times and where they made love, from the suites at the Plaza in New York to broom closets at the Sands. I knew how horny Jack was, so nothing she said surprised me, except her belief in his promises that he would leave Jackie and that she would be his First Lady for his second term. That guy would say anything to score."

George Jacobs, valet to Frank Sinatra

THE KENNEDYS

All The Gossip
Unfit to Print

BLOOD MOON
Productions, Ltd.

OTHER BOOKS BY DARWIN PORTER

BIOGRAPHIES

Humphrey Bogart, the Making of a Legend
Howard Hughes: Hell's Angel
Steve McQueen, King of Cool, Tales of a Lurid Life
Paul Newman, The Man Behind the Baby Blues
Merv Griffin, A Life in the Closet
Brando Unzipped
The Secret Life of Humphrey Bogart
Katharine the Great: Hepburn, Secrets of a Lifetime Revealed
Jacko, His Rise and Fall (The Social and Sexual History of Michael Jackson)
and, co-authored with Roy Moseley
Damn You, Scarlett O'Hara, The Private Lives of Vivien Leigh and Laurence Olivier

COMING SOON:

Frank Sinatra: The Boudoir Singer
J. Edgar Hoover and Clyde Tolson, Investigating the Sexual Secrets of America's Most Famous Men & Women
and, in collaboration with Roy Moseley
Olivia de Havilland and Joan Fontaine, Twisted Sisters: To Each Her Own

FILM CRITICISM

50 Years of Queer Cinema--500 of the Best GLBTQ Films Ever Made (2010)
Blood Moon's Guide to Recent Gay & Lesbian Film--Volumes One (2006) and Two (2007)
Best Gay and Lesbian Films- The Glitter Awards, 2005

NON-FICTION

Hollywood Babylon-It's Back!
Hollywood Babylon Strikes Again!

NOVELS

Butterflies in Heat
Marika
Venus (a roman à clef based on the life of Anaïs Nin)
Razzle-Dazzle
Midnight in Savannah
Rhinestone Country
Blood Moon
Hollywood's Silent Closet

TRAVEL GUIDES

Many editions and many variations of *The Frommer Guides* to
Europe, the Caribbean, California, Georgia and The Carolinas, Bermuda, and The Bahamas

THE KENNEDYS

ALL THE GOSSIP
UNFIT TO PRINT

A Myth-Shattering Exposé of a Family Consumed by Its Own Passions

DARWIN PORTER AND DANFORTH PRINCE

THE KENNEDYS, ALL THE GOSSIP UNFIT TO PRINT

Copyright © 2011, Blood Moon Productions, Ltd.

ALL RIGHTS RESERVED.
WWW.BLOODMOONPRODUCTIONS.COM

Manufactured in the United States of America

ISBN 978-1-936003-17-4
First printing June 2011

Cover designs by Richard Leeds (www.bigwigdesign.com)
Videography and publicity trailers by Piotr Kajstura
Distributed in North America and Australia
through the National Book Network (www.NBNbooks.com)
and in the U.K. through Turnaround (www.turnaround-uk.com)

Blood Moon acknowledges the National Book Network
for its savvy guidance in the presentation and marketing of this book.

DEDICATION

THIS BOOK IS DEDICATED TO THE KENNEDYS,
BECAUSE OF THEIR CHARM AND THEIR CHARISMA,
AND BECAUSE NO OTHER POLITICAL CLAN
HAS EVER PROVIDED US WITH THE POSSIBILITY OF
SO MUCH ENTERTAINMENT.

REST IN PEACE

"So, with many hundreds of books about the Kennedys published over the years, you think you've heard all the deep dish, sizzling gossip and sexual intrigue surrounding America's royal family of politics and power?

"Think again. This buzz-rich exposé, culled from decades of intense research by a devoted team of Kennedy-philes, carefully documents the mind-boggling chain of triumph and calamity that has dogged generations of a dynasty both idolized and reviled by a nation. Pick it up and you'll be hard-pressed to put it down."

Richard LaBonté, Book Marks, Q Syndicate

CONTENTS

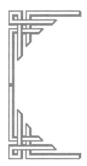
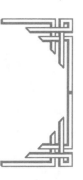

"Black Jack" Bouvier

And His Young Daughter Jackie

Photofest

Jacqueline Lee Bouvier *(center)*, as a little girl in gloves and hat, hardly looked like the fabled beauty that would enchant the world. In the usual scenario, she, like her mother, Janet *(left),* would marry someone in the Social Register and settle down in a Southampton estate, getting her name in the papers only on her wedding day and on the day of her death.

Jackie's father, **"Black Jack" Bouvier**, protectively holds her hand. Janet once accused him of being far too intimate with his daughter than he should be.

Jackie adored her father and was fascinated by his bluish-black skin, which according to the wisdom of the time was caused by some disease he had, Black Jack would get along with his future son-in-law, a senator from Massachusetts. Both of them had the same cavalier attitude about women, neither believing that a husband had to be faithful to his wife.

Florida Senator George Smathers claimed that both JFK and Black Jack wanted to be bachelors-at-large, even though each wore a wedding ring. The scene above was taken at the Southampton Horse Show in 1934.

JACKIE AND
THE BLACK SHEIK

The first love of young Jackie's life, **Black Jack Bouvier**, became the model for her future loves. He liked horses and women, but not in that order. When he wasn't at a race track or in a woman's boudoir, he was at the gambling tables.

He told Jackie, "You are the most beautiful daughter a man could ever hope to have." He later resented it when Jackie began to mature and to go out on dates. In a drunken scene, he once told her, "I can see I'm not the main man in your life anymore."

In Kathleen Bouvier's 1979 remembrance, *To Jackie With Love*, she wrote: "Throughout New York and the Hamptons, his notorious seductions, his cars, and his horses left an incredible impression. After his death, they are like fingerprints in the dust, the lingering last notes of a sonata."

Born to a wealthy Manhattan construction mogul, Janet Lee was barely twenty-one years old when she married the handsome and dashing "Black Jack" Bouvier (actually John V. Bouvier III). The date was July 7, 1928. By almost any judgment, the marriage would be a disaster, ending in a scandalous divorce.

Yet it would produce two daughters who each became world famous.

One year and three weeks after the wedding, Jacqueline Lee Bouvier entered the world on July 28, 1929. Her mother, Janet, turned her over to an English nanny, as Janet wanted to regain her figure. Against her doctor's advice, she took up riding again and won third place in the annual East Hampton riding competitions, although recently having given birth.

Alexandra Webb, a socialite who was familiar with the relationship and marriage of Janet and Black Jack, had strong opinions about the pair. "Janet married Black Jack because his name appeared in the Social Register. He married her because her father operated a bank. She was a bitch and he was a bastard, and in the end both were disillusioned. From such a union emerged Jackie, who inherited all the bad traits of both her mother and father, but hid it with such charm and grace she enchanted the world."

Taking time out from his boyfriends and girlfriends, Black Jack had managed to impregnate Janet again, which led to the birth of Caroline Lee Bouvier on March 3, 1933.

She would live forever in the shadow of her soon-to-be more celebrated sister, Jackie. In time, Lee would grow up to compete with Jackie for the same man, Aristotle Onassis himself.

From their shared East Hampton childhood through their high-profile adulthood, Lee and Jackie would be engaged in a jealous rivalry, evocative of those Hollywood sisters, Olivia de Havilland and Joan Fontaine, both Oscar winners.

Jackie always claimed that Black Jack "was the first man I ever loved." Although he was a rake, a womanizer, a bisexual, a fun-loving trendsetter, a gambler, and an extravagant wastrel, she adored him.

He adored her, too, perhaps too much so. He taught her to love horses and to make life carefree and fun. As such, he evoked life on the pages of F. Scott Fitzgerald's *The Great Gatsby.*

Black Jack's friends called him either "The Black Sheik" or "The Black Orchid."

He got the nickname because of his dark skin pigmentation, which looked most unusual. Joseph Kennedy privately told his clan, "I think somewhere along the way there was a nigger in the woodshed."

Janet objected to Black Jack bathing in the nude with young Jackie, and she was repulsed when she heard her daughter's squeals of delight.

"What is he doing to her now?" she asked the maid.

In spite of her objections, he kept taking baths with her even when she was ten years old.

His mother, Maude Bouvier, learned about this and saw nothing wrong with it. She told a friend, "It shows how loving my son is to his Jackie." To Maude, Black Jack could do no wrong.

One night Janet grew suspicious about what was going on between her daughter and Jackie. She entered his bedroom, turned on the light, and pulled the bed covers off Jackie and Black Jack. To her horror, she discovered his body with a large erection pressed up against Jackie. She yanked a screaming Jackie from Black Jack's bed and refused to let him bathe or sleep with her ever again.

What Jackie didn't inherit from Black Jack were his prejudices. When he drank, his hatred bubbled to the surface. It was "this kike and that kike." He hated the Irish, calling them "this mick and that mick." Italians were "wops" and the French were "frogs." A friend said, "When he drank, he was filled with nothing but hatred, most of it directed at himself."

Suggesting only a hint of the fabled woman she was to become, **Jackie Bouvier** would lead a life of great wealth but one tainted by tragedy. Her entrance into the world on July 29, 1929 would soon be followed by one of the greatest crises, the Wall Street crash of 1929, in which her father lost a lot of his family fortune.

Jackie later recalled, "My father would have been competition for Rudolph Valentino had he wanted to become a movie star. In the 1930s, he was often compared to Clark Gable. He had a great love for women, and women had a great love for him, including me, his oldest daughter."

None of that hatred was directed at Jackie. He worshipped his daughter. The love was returned. "She virtually swooned every time he came to see her," Janet said.

They partnered in father-daughter tennis tournaments, and he went to see her compete in horse shows. When she saw *Gone With the Wind*, she told Lee, "Clark Gable as Rhett Butler looks like our father. I want to sit through the movie again."

Even when Jackie tossed a chocolate cream pie into the face of one of her most despised teachers, Black Jack never disciplined her. "She's got a free and independent spirit—that's all," he told his mother, Maude. Consequently, she bragged to her socialite friends, "Jackie is going to grow up to become the female image of my son."

Later when Jackie started dating in college, she told Black Jack her escorts were "beetle-browed bores. I'll never get married until I find a man as exciting as you."

"Style is not how rich you are, but a state of mind that puts quality before quantity," he told young Jackie. "That's what makes you a Bouvier."

On September 30, 1936, Janet separated from her husband, who moved out of their Park Avenue duplex into the Westbury Hotel in New York. But he still visited Jackie on weekends.

She waited for hours to hear a series of long and short honks on the horn of his car. She ran to him screaming, "Jacks, Jacks" (her nickname for him) and into his arms. It would be lunch at Schrafft's, horse-and-buggy rides in Central Park, shopping expeditions on Fifth Avenue.

It would be years later before young Jackie learned that her beloved Black Jack also had affairs with men. According to author Edward Klein, "When Jackie was a young girl, she heard her father heap contempt on 'faggots.' The nuns and priests taught her that homosexuality was a sin." Fortunately, Jackie didn't inherit any of her father's prejudices, and she later became a friend and confidant of many homosexual such as Truman Capote. Klein claimed, "She started to accept the fact that, like homosexuals, she herself was not what most people considered 'normal.' In a way, she was 'almost normal,' just like her gay friends."

Charles Schwartz, in his biography of Cole Porter, revealed that "Some of Cole's most intense affairs were with men from distinguished families. Cole, for instance, was reported to have been very much taken at one time with Black Jack Bouvier."

"I'm just mad about Jack," Cole told his gay friends. Both men were in the same class at Yale.

Somehow the Bouvier family became aware of the affair of Black Jack with Cole. "Jack was very bi," claimed Schwartz. "He joined, from time to time, Cole and actor Monty Woolley during their hunts for working-class males. And not for bridge purposes."

Franklyn Ives, an insurance executive in New York, claimed that Black Jack had trouble keeping his fly zipped. One of his favorite Manhattan watering holes was Cerutti's, a gay bar on Madison Avenue. In those days, gay bars were not legal, so many homosexuals invited their gay-friendly women friends to accompany them to the bar so the police would not raid it, which they sometimes did when they found only men drinking at a tavern.

It was here at Cerutti's that Black Jack first encountered the original Archibald Leach who would ultimately become the movie legend Cary Grant, according to Ives.

Cary liked to sing Cole Porter songs, including "You're the Top," which for homosexuals had a double meaning not often understood by straight audiences of that day. Ironically, he would end up playing Cole Porter in the movie *Night and Day* (1946) although references to the composer's homosexuality could not be presented on the screen. The film's plot had to be almost totally fabricated.

Black Jack and Cary met around the piano where musician Garland Wilson entertained nightly.

When Black Jack met Cary, Cary was living as the lover of George ("Jack") Orry-Kelly, the costume designer, a relationship explored in Marc Eliot's biography, *Cary Grant*. To support himself, Cary was a paid escort, his handsome features making him highly desirable as a gigolo. Cary made it clear to all his clients that he was employed just for his "social services but not boudoir duty."

Black Jack, or so it is said, advised Cary about his clothes and even helped him get rid of his lingering British "singsong lilt," as Black Jack called it. "If you want to go to Hollywood you've got to speak like a radio announcer, without any accent at all."

Black Jack later recalled that "I taught Archie how to walk. Before that he walked with acrobatic rubber legs because of his former life as a street acrobat."

When Orry-Kelly kicked Cary out of his apartment, he went to live in a rented room at the

NVA Club in the Times Square area. Black Jack paid his rent. Janet became aware of this, and told her family and friends, hoping to discredit Black Jack.

Cary later dumped Black Jack when Cary took up with Reginald Hammerstein, the younger brother of Oscar Hammerstein II. He was casting a big new musical for the autumn, *Golden Dawn*. Archie and "Reggie" soon became a frequently spotted-together item in the nightclubs. Black Jack often encountered them but by then both men had moved on. At one point Black Jack was rumored to be dating a young married couple, socialites from East Hampton.

Years later, in 1953, Black Jack was bitterly disappointed to learn that he might be excluded from Jackie's wedding to John F. Kennedy. He told friends that Jackie "had crossed over to the other side, into the camp of Joseph Kennedy, who is nothing but a traitor and a crook."

To sabotage the possibility of his appearance at the church, Janet vindictively ordered Michael Canfield, Lee's husband at the time, to stock his room with plenty of liquor and champagne—"and lots of ice." Black Jack took the bait, proceeding to get so drunk that he knew it would be impossible to walk Jackie down the aisle without stumbling and "embarrassing myself in front of the world."

In his drunken state, Black Jack managed to show up at the wedding anyway. JFK's friend, Charles Spalding, one of the ushers, had been assigned to look after him if he turned up, which he did.

Spalding ushered Black Jack to the rear of the cathedral and seated him in a far corner. He was sitting there as the new bride passed by, escorted by her stepfather, Hugh D. Auchincloss. Jackie spotted Black Jack, but gave no sign of recognition.

As she left the church to start a new life with the groom, Spalding noticed tears in Black Jack's eyes. "I've lost my little girl forever."

Suffering from cancer of the liver, Black Jack died in July of 1957. Only days before, Jackie had met with him, finding him depressed and confused. Rushed to Lenox Hill Hospital in New York, he lapsed into a coma. But right before he died, he rallied and said one word, "Jackie."

Accompanied by JFK, Jackie arrived at the hospital but her father was already dead. She stood in stony silence holding her husband's hand until a nurse asked them to go.

On the way down in the elevator, Black Jack's doctor confronted her. "Your father had the most unusual pigmentation. His skin was extraordinary. Would you give me permission to dissect his skin?"

Stepping onto the elevator with JFK, Jackie let the door close on the doctor, ignoring him and his bizarre request.

She arranged Black Jack's funeral at St. Patrick's Cathedral, inviting only immediate family and a few of her father's business associates.

She was startled when eight older women, each dressed entirely in black with heavy veils, entered the cathedral and sat in the same row at the rear of the cathedral.

Later she learned that each of these mourners had been a mistress of Black Jack. Jackie ignored these women, whom she sarcastically denounced as "my father's fan club."

At the end of the services, JFK approached each of them and expressed his sympathy for their loss. One of the mourners told him, "After you've been with Black Jack Bouvier, no other man will do."

Three years later, after JFK became president, he sometimes called Cary Grant, just to hear the sound of his voice. One afternoon he bluntly asked him, "Are all those tales about you and Black Jack really true?"

Cary answered, "Please don't ask for the truth. I always believed it's wrong to lie to the President of the United States. Let's close the case."

A bisexual actor, **Cary Grant** was the lover of both **Cole Porter** and **Black Jack Bouvier.**

In spite of the image he projected on screen, he was alcoholic, brutal, and suicidal, as detailed in *The Lonely Heart* by Charles Higham and Roy Moseley. As documented by these biographers, there are many pages in Grant's life that were never filled in. A lot of his life was lived in shadows.

The killer, Charles Manson, claimed, "My greatest thrill I ever had was sleeping in the bed Cary Grant slept in."

Manson spent several nights in Grant's bungalow on the Universal lot when he was having an affair with a male studio hand.

According to Higham and Moseley, Grant almost got to know the Manson gang more intimately than he wanted. He lived near Roman Polanski and Sharon Tate. He was in a garden talking to a young man he wanted to seduce when he heard blood-curdling screams coming from the Polanski/Tate house. He fled the scene.

Pictured with reigning movie diva **Kay Francis,** the costume designer, **George Orry-Kelly,** was a lover of Cary Grant's, although he later turned on him.

"I knew him when his name was Leach, and that's all he ever was—a goddamn leach!" Handsome but effeminate, Orry-Kelly, during happier days, had fallen in love with Archibald Leach, the man who would eventually evolve into Cary Grant. The designer was barely making a living as a tailor's assistant when he met the dashing Englishman. It was love at first sight.

Archie was only seventeen when he came to live with Orry-Kelly. After the designer kicked him out, and after Archie changed his name, he pursued love affairs in Hollywood during the 1930s with matinee star Randolph Scott and the billionaire aviator and film mogul, Howard Hughes, but he always retained fond memories of Black Jack.

In time Cary Grant would sustain a series of affairs with everybody from Gary Cooper to Grace Kelly, from Noël Coward to Ginger Rogers.

Grant could be romantic, generous, and kind, until his mood changed violently.

Throughout his life, he tried to hide his Jewish past.

Cary Grant ended up playing **Cole Porter** *(above)* on the screen in *Night and Day* (1946) at the end of World War II.

After seeing it, the composer said, "Oh, well they made me look like Cary Grant—and that was a bonus. The picture was so sanitized it was ludicrous. They say I'm a practicing homosexual. That's a damnable lie. I'm perfect as a homosexual."

When not seducing Black Jack Bouvier or Cary Grant, Cole retreated to a notorious male brothel in Harlem staffed by young black men. On some nights he preferred a chorus boy, but other nights he sought out soldiers, sailors, truck drivers, and, his special favorite, longshoremen.

Like Black Jack, Cole was a Yale man of the class of 1914. "I'm mad about the boy," Cole told his homosexual friends about Jackie's father.

When Cole and Black Jack tired of each other, they often attended secret "fucking parties." Even though their love affair was relatively brief, they remained intimate friends throughout the rest of their lives.

JFK & the Man Who Loved Him

Lem Billings

On a summer vacation in 1937 **Jack Kennedy** *(left)* toured Europe with "best friend for life," **Lem Billings**, his roommate from prep school. Lem was a homosexual and in love with Jack.

In France, Lem proposed to Jack that they become "lovers for always" and live together after graduation.

But Jack told him, "I'm hopelessly heterosexual." He also told Lem that he planned to follow his father's advice and seduce every beautiful woman he could in life. "If you can still stay with me and still love me through all that, then welcome aboard. But it's going to be one god damn rough ride for you. Are you sure you don't want another boyfriend who will be more fulfilling?"

Lem responded, "Dreams die hard. I'm in for the duration, and I'm willing to put up with anything to be beside you."

It was a promise Lem would keep. Only a world war temporarily separated them. *(Photofest)*

"FIRST FRIEND"—
A STRAIGHT POLITICIAN'S LOVE
FOR A GAY MAN

"The only man I ever loved totally and completely and for all my life was Jack Kennedy."
—Lem Billings

Romping in the snow, **Lem Billings** *(here, the man on top)* has fun with his newly minted friend, **John F. Kennedy**.

After a few days of their initial meeting, Lem wanted to make their relationship sexual, but Jack turned him down. However, he did not turn down the offer of friendship.

Most teen friendships fade with the passing of school semesters, but this one would endure for decades, eventually reaching the White House.

There, Lem was assigned his own room, which was visited frequently by the president, who always locked the door and asked not to be disturbed unless there was a nuclear attack from the Soviet Union.

It is said that Pennsylvania-born Kirk LeMoyne Billings—affectionately known for decades within the Kennedy family as "Lem"—fell in love with the very young JFK as they showered together at the Connecticut-based Choate School for Boys in 1933. The bond they formed at Choate lasted a lifetime. Jackie Kennedy once claimed, "The love between those two lasted even beyond the assassination at Dallas."

It certainly lasted until Lem's death in 1981. "Lem died of a heart attack, but he really died of a broken heart," Jackie claimed. On hearing the news of Lem's death, Rose Kennedy said, "Lem has gone to Heaven to look after Jack."

Lem was 17 years old when he met the 16-year-old Jack, who was in a class behind him. The first day they came together, they talked until four o'clock that morning. A bond was formed, and they would become virtually inseparable.

When the dawn came, they applied for reassignment and became roommates. They also emerged with new names for each other, "Billy" for Billings and "Johnny" for John Kennedy. Over the years they would adopt other affectionate nicknames for each other—Lem, Lemmer, Leem, or Moynie, or Jack, Ken, or Kenadosus.

As author David Michaelis in his book, *Best of Friends,* put it, "For Lem, Jack was the best thing about life at school. Jack knew how to create the kind of fun that lightened the mood of everyone around him. His innate gaiety and zest for living challenged even the most caustic, passive members of their class. His high spirits were contagious. For Kennedy, Billings was more than just a partner in school crimes. He was the first intimate friend Kennedy had found outside his own family. And he was more fun to be with than anyone Kennedy had ever known. Lem's passionate readiness to experience the world enhanced Kennedy's cool curiosity. Lem's unfailing loyalty matched his own. In Billings, Kennedy had a unique ally."

Friends who knew both Lem and Jack claimed that Lem was in love with Jack all his life. On the other hand, Jack "was in love with Lem being in love with him." Every night at school, Lem even polished Jack's shoes.

As a teenager, Jack was oversexed. Lem discovered that during their first night as roommates. Jack urged Lem to masturbate with him. By the third night, Lem made his gay proclivities known. He asked Jack to become his lover. Until that point, Jack may not have known that his newly acquired friend was gay.

Reportedly, Lem was rejected. In many more or less equivalent cases in American boarding schools, one roommate has tended to move out into other lodgings soon afterwards. But not in this case. Even though Jack told Lem that he was "100 percent heterosexual," that did not totally deter or discourage Lem.

One night when Jack was masturbating, Lem came over to his bed and plunged down. At that point, JFK was too worked up to protest. Lem was content with servicing Jack with no reciprocation expected. From that night on, and up until Dallas, Lem became Jack's fellator.

Several years after the assassination in Dallas, after Lem ran out of money—Jack had provided nothing for him in his will—he tried to hawk a book project, first as a co-authored arrangement with writer Lawrence J. Quirk, who at the time was the dean of Hollywood biographers. Later, he developed a detailed sales pitch for the project and articulated it to the notoriously flamboyant New York-based literary agent, Jay Garon.

If such a book had ever been configured and published as a high-profile tell-all, replete with sexual details, it would have been a sensational but widely reviled best seller. But later, Lem lost his nerve and pulled the plug on both projects. He later mused, "Jack made a big difference in my life. Because of him, I was never lonely. He may have been the reason I never got married." Insiders fully realized, however, that the reason he never got married involved his having no interest in women, except as friends.

***

That summer of 1933, and for many other summers to come, Jack invited Lem to stay with his family at Hyannis Port. Having worked for years as an insider in the movie colony, Joseph Kennedy was well aware of homosexuality and its implications. He didn't approve of it, but he didn't denounce it either. Nonetheless he assured Rose, "All of my boys will grow up to be heterosexuals."

Throughout the years, however, as Jack was repeatedly accompanied during holidays and vacations at the family homestead with Lem, Joe became suspicious. When he was eventually confronted with some of the

In 1955, the love between **Lem Billings** *(left)* and **JFK** was still strong at Hyannis Port in the wake of Jack's marriage to Jacqueline Lee Bouvier.

She told her sister, Lee Radziwill, "From the beginning I realized that marriage to Jack also meant having to accept Lem, who was like a hungry puppy hanging around for a crumb tossed from his master's table."

In time, she came to like Lem and establish her own relationship with him. "You don't have a lot of choice," she told Kennedy aide David Powers. "If you love Jack, you've got to learn to love Lem. It's a package deal with those two."

9

We're puttin' on our top hat,

Tyin' up our white tie,

Brushin' off our tails,

In order to

Wish you

A Merry Christmas

Rip,   Leem,   Ken.

Ralph (Rip) Horton was assigned to room with Jack and Lem at Choate, although Lem may have resented his presence because he wanted to be alone with Jack.

Although Jack and Lem tried to keep the homosexual aspects of their relationship secret from him, it became obvious to Rip.

"Jack didn't much care if Lem were gay or not," Horton recalled. "He was a very forgiving guy, very understanding. Lem's homosexuality never interfered in my relationship with him. Lem and I became friends, so much so that it made Jack jealous. One night he called Lem 'a complete shit,' because he wanted to go do something with me and not with him."

This fading Christmas card was from 1935 and was found in Lem's apartment when he died. **Horton** (left), **Lem** (center), and **Jack** were sharing a tuxedo, with Horton getting the top hat, Lem a giant white bow tie, and Jack the jacket.

A copy of the card was sent out to all their friends and family, with this note: "We're puttin' on our top hat, tyin' up our white tie, and brushin' off our tails."

details about their relationship, he tried to find something good in it.

"My boy is oversexed," he said. "He's liable to go and knock up some girl, and then we'll be in the shithouse. You know, the Cardinal preaches against abortion. At least Lem gives Jack some relief. As for Lem, I don't know what he does for relief, and I don't much care. But at least he keeps my boy under control."

Joe tolerated Lem. As quoted within Lawrence Quirk's *The Kennedys in Hollywood,* "He did not want Jack impregnating any of the girls he dated, and he was of the old-fashioned school that held that masturbation was sexually wasteful, so if Jack allowed Lem to pleasure him, worse things could conceivably happen to anyone as undisciplined, rowdy, tomfoolery-perpetrating, and cynical as Jack was during his teen years and indeed into his twenties."

For Jack, spending holidays with Lem became a tradition. Eventually, almost with an air of inevitability, Joe said to JFK, "I guess you're bringing that queer to spend Christmas with us."

In an interview, Ted Kennedy later recalled, "I was five years old before it dawned on me that Lem wasn't one more older brother. So often did Lem come home with Jack that he kept more clothes in the closet than Jack did."

Lem was so dazzled by Jack's company that he stayed back a year at Choate so that he could be part of the same graduating class as Jack. The young men would graduate as seniors together in 1935.

Years later, their classmate, Rip Horton, was interviewed by Nigel Hamilton for publication in *JFK Reckless Youth*. He was also interviewed by other publications and quoted as saying, "In Lem, Jack found a slave for life. It was amazing how Lem was abused. He did Jack's laundry. Late at night he'd run out in the cold weather to buy him a pizza. Jack's back was always hurting, and Lem became his unpaid masseur, a job he relished." As future masseurs have testified, including Frank Sinatra's valet, Jack always became aroused when massaged by men or women.

While at Choate, Jack and Lem were still virgins, at least with women. Then one day Jack heard through Horton about a whorehouse in New York City's Harlem, where each of them could get laid for only three dollars. Lem was reluctant to join Jack on this quest, but ultimately, Jack persuaded him to go.

First the madam of the whorehouse showed them porno films "to get them in the mood."

For some reason, Jack insisted that both he and Lem should lose their virginity to the same prostitute. Jack went first. Always a quick man on the draw, he was back in only ten minutes.

Lem followed him and gave the prostitute three dollars. But he had another way of getting off. He later confessed in a book proposal he circulated after JFK's death that, "I closed my eyes, thought of Jack, and jerked off."

After that session, Jack became infected with gonorrhea, a disease that plagued him for years, according to historian Robert Dallek, who wrote *An Unfinished Life*. JFK managed to get a doctor to supply him with creams and lotions, but because of his rampant promiscuity, he may have carried some sort of venereal infection for the rest of his life

* * *

After his graduation from Choate, Jack went to England for a brief and vaguely defined stint at the London School of Economics as part of his first trip abroad. Just before the debut of the LSE's school year, in September of 1935, he sailed to England with his parents and his sister, Kathleen, aboard the SS *Normandie*.

Many of JFK's letters to Lem have subsequently been published, within such sources as Nigel Hamilton's *JFK Reckless Youth,* and in David Pitts' *Jack and Lem.* Jack wrote to Lem during the transatlantic crossing to England, telling him there was "this fat Frenchie homo aboard who is trying to bed me." He told Lem that "the frog followed me into the shower room and invited me several times to his cabin for a drink where he put the make on me." What JFK didn't explain was why he accepted all those invitations to the Frenchman's cabin. Lem chastised Jack, "That's what is known as prick teasing."

But soon after the beginning of classes at the LSE, Jack checked himself into a local hospital with symptoms associated with one of his many mysterious illnesses that doctors could not diagnose. In October of that year, he wrote to Lem from his hospital bed in London: "They are doing a number of strange things to me, not the least of which is to shove a tremendous needle up my cheeks. Today was the most embarrassing, as a doctor came in just after I had woken up and was reclining with a semi-erection. His plan was to stick his finger under my pickle and have me cough. His plan quickly changed when he drew back the covers and there was JJ. Maher quivering with life."

Previously, Lem and Jack had jointly nicknamed his penis "JJ. Maher."

A few weeks after his arrival in the UK, with inconclusive results from both the British hospital and the LSE, and with his academic plans in disarray, Jack returned to America.

Although Joe Kennedy was tolerant of Lem around the house much of the time, **Rose Kennedy** was much warmer and more affectionate with him.

Here they are seen together in Palm Beach in 1939, just before the outbreak of World War II. Rose made Lem a part of the family, whether at Hyannis Port in the summer or at Palm Beach in the winter.

Lem grew close not only to her, but to Eunice and especially Bobby as well.

One winter Rose wanted her family to herself and called Jack with a mandate—"no visitors this year." He told her he had a wonderful surprise Christmas present for her. When he arrived on Christmas Eve in '39, that gift turned out to be Lem.

11

***

During the previous summer of 1935, Jack had been accepted for enrollment at Harvard. But after learning that Lem would be attending Princeton, Jack prevailed upon Joe to let him enroll there instead. Princeton, however, turned out to be a disappointment to him. He later asserted that at Princeton, "they hate Jews and Catholics. The campus reeks with Presbyterian chapels."

Plagued with health issues, Jack stayed as a student at Princeton for less than two months. Lem later asserted, "He was sick the entire time. He just wasn't well." In a letter to Lem, Jack claimed, "I do not have sif, as they gave me a Wasserman. They have not found out anything yet except I have leukemia. I took a peak (*sic*) at my chart yesterday and could see that they were mentally measuring me for a coffin."

Midway through these inconclusive academic turmoils and medical uncertainties, Lem was invited to spend Christmas of 1935 in Palm Beach with the Kennedys. Since Lem had almost no money, Jack donated "fifteen smackeroos," half of the bus fare.

But during and after the Christmas holidays, Jack's illnesses continued. Joe said, "The boy is sick all the time."

From his hospital bed, Jack wrote Lem that a beautiful nurse came in to give him a rubdown "and I got this hard-on. They discovered I do not have sif." This was the second hospital where doctors had tested him for syphilis.

When Jack suddenly withdrew from Princeton, much to Lem's sorrow, a rumor spread that he'd secretly gotten married because "he knocked up some dame," and was forced to withdraw. The rumor turned out to be false. As Jack later recalled, "I was there long enough to be cured of wanting to be a Princeton man. It was Harvard for me."

In July of 1936, from Hyannis Port, in a state of renewed health, Jack once again applied for admission to Harvard—a school he'd eventually graduate from *cum laude* in 1940—stating that he'd had to leave Princeton that previous December "due to sickness."

In July of 1937, during vacation from their respective studies, Lem experienced the most intimate and romantic period with Jack that he'd ever known or would ever know again. That summer, they went on a tour of Europe together. Jack paid half of Lem's fare but claimed that he expected the money back after Lem graduated

Lem *(left)*, seen here relaxing with Jack on a chaise longue in Palm Beach during the winter of 1937, "looked after Jack like a protective mother hen," said Rose Kennedy. Lem was healthy and strong, but Jack's health was always precarious. In fact, he was chronically ill, always coming down with viral ailments.

He appeared vulnerable to all kinds of infection; a knee skinned on the tennis court became so infected he was in the hospital for nearly a month. There was always something wrong with him that was usually passed off as a "blood condition." Bobby Kennedy mockingly said, "Any mosquito that samples Jack's blood will die instantly."

In 1960, after JFK became president, he demanded that the full details of his illnesses be kept from the public. But Lem teased him, "I'm working on your biography," he told Jack. "I'm calling it John F. Kennedy: A Medical History."

Jack teased him right back, "You do and I'll cut off your balls—not that you have much use for them."

from Princeton. Joe agreed to pay for the transport of Jack's Ford convertible as extra baggage aboard the same ship that carried them to Le Havre in France, so they could jointly and conveniently tour Europe together. Since Lem had little money, Jack agreed to stay with him in cramped lodgings throughout the course of their trip, usually in rooms without plumbing. "We ate frightful food and slept for forty cents a night."

Before he'd left for Europe, Joe had encouraged Jack to "get laid as often as possible." Jack later claimed, "I can't get to sleep unless I've gotten off. If I go for twenty-four hours without an orgasm, I suffer these crippling migraine headaches." Fortunately, Lem was there night after night to provide relief.

Lem later revealed in his book proposal that whatever hotel they'd checked into would often assign them a single bed, "and I got to hold Jack in my arms all night. It was wonderful. He was very horny, and I took full advantage."

Lem cried when they returned to the States on September 16, 1937. "I was so sorry that the trip was over. I knew in my heart I'd never have Jack all to myself like that ever again."

Jack and Lem endured long separations during the war. After the Japanese attack on Pearl Harbor, both Lem and Jack tried to enlist, but both were at first rejected, Lem because of poor eyesight, Jack because of his chronically bad health. In 1942, Lem joined the Ambulance Corps, which didn't care about his bad eyesight, and saw action in North Africa. Later, through his receipt of a commission in the U.S. Naval Reserve, he got involved in wartime maneuvers in the South Pacific.

Lem had survived in the military as a closeted homosexual during the darkest days of World War II when the mili-

Even though **Jack** (left) loved **Lem**, he also made fun of him and constantly taunted him. After these photo booth pictures were taken, Jack studied them and called Lem "*Pithecanthropus Erectus*" (the walking ape man), a jab about Lem's high forehead and his clumsiness, including his "simian walk."

Even though from the first he'd known that Lem was a homosexual, Jack continued to poke fun at him because of his failure with the opposite sex. At one point, he told Lem, "The only reason a gal speaks to you is just so she can get close to me."

The Muckers Club at Choate was formed by close friends who had shared a hatred of the school's headmaster and resented all the restrictions placed on them by this prep school. From left to right are Ralph ("Rip") Horton, Lem Billings (resting his elbows), Butch Schriber, and JFK in an ill-fitting top coat. This picture was taken in the late autumn of 1935.

The school's headmaster designated Jack as "Public Enemy Number One" and Lem as "Public Enemy Number Two." One of their smelliest exploits involved dumping horse shit all over the floor of the school gym.

The schoolmaster wanted to separate Lem and Jack as roommates, but eventually wrote in his report, "Those two are bonded at the hip. God only knows what they are up to."

Above is Lem's naval portrait in 1944, and below is a soldier's first reunion in 1941, when **Jack** *(left)* and **Lem** resumed their relationship.

In 1944 when Jack arrived at Palm Beach during a break from active military duty, with Lem in tow, he dropped his suitcase, kissed Rose and Joe and the odd sibling, and that evening, headed for the nearest nightclub.

As expressed by Charles (Chuck) Spalding, "I guess when he was hanging onto that wrecked half of a PT boat in the South Pacific, Jack thought he would never see a pretty girl or hear dance music again."

The next day, in the privacy of a beach house, Jack allegedly gave Lem "what you've been waiting for."

tary was discharging, because of their homosexuality, thousands of men during a crisis when America was struggling merely to survive. Gays were officially defined as mentally ill "sexual psychopaths."

At the time of his enlistment, Lem had been asked if he were homosexual. Wanting to serve his country, he answered, "No."

Jack had learned through dialogues with his father that the military leader of Britain's war effort, Field Marshal Bernard Montgomery, was a closeted homosexual. Even so, Montgomery attacked the legalization of homosexuality in Britain. "This sort of thing may be tolerated by the French, but we're British, thank God."

Honorably discharged in 1946, Lem went on to attend Harvard Business School. After his graduation, he held a variety of jobs, including a stint as an executive at Lennen & Newell, a Manhattan-based advertising firm. He invented the 1950s candy drink, "Fizzies," for the company, adding fruit flavor to disguise the sodium citrate taste of Bromo Seltzer.

Lem continued in his devotion to Jack, although it was painful to watch him making love to a series of young women. Lem could only dream that Jack's lovemaking be directed at him.

But Jack never deserted Lem, and reserved time every week for them to get together. Their lovemaking became a ritual. Jack would strip completely naked for one of Lem's prolonged massages, which always led to a sexual climax on Jack's part. Lem later told Truman Capote that he "got off by going into the bathroom and jerking off with Jack's semen still in my mouth. At my climax, I swallowed his offering."

Truman Capote later claimed that "Lem at Studio 54 was always bragging about fellating Kennedy in Lincoln's Bedroom."

When Jack started dating Jacqueline Bouvier, Lem tried to discourage her from marrying him, according to several sources at the time. "I told her about all the mysterious illnesses that plagued Jack, including Addison's disease. I also told her that Jack put up a brave front but was in constant pain because of his back. Not only that, but I claimed that he wanted to be President of the United States, and she did not strike me as wanting to become the wife of a politician. I also warned her about Jack's roving eye, and told her he was too set in his ways to change."

When Jack wed Jackie, Bobby Kennedy quipped, "Jack is taking another wife."

Based partly on the discussions they shared regarding the publication of a tell-all biography about JFK, Lem developed an intimate relationship with Lawrence J. (Larry) Quirk. As stated by Quirk, "Lem confided in me that theirs was a friendship that included oral sex, with Jack always on the receiving end. Lem believed that this arrangement enabled Jack to sustain his self-delusion that straight men who received oral sex from other males were really only straights looking for sexual release."

As regards JFK's political career, Lem campaigned vigorously for the man he loved, helping him win both the Wisconsin and West Virginia primaries in 1960. He was also instrumental at the Democratic Convention in luring Democratic delegates away from Lyndon B. Johnson.

Beginning in 1961, after Jack became president, Lem became a permanent fixture at the White House, advising Jackie about redecorating the White House, and JFK about how to deal with Russia. He was assigned a permanent bedroom on site.

At the White House, the staff referred to Lem as "First Friend." As Jackie recalled to Democratic Senator George Smathers (Florida), "Just one weekend in my life, I'd like to have my husband to myself, but Lem is always there, bathing and massaging him, even putting on his shoes and socks."

"I never had to have a pass to get into the White House," Lem recalled. "All of the Secret Service men knew who I was."

Some people resented Lem's presence within the White House. That deeply cynical and always provocative distant relative of Jackie's, author Gore Vidal, referred to Lem as "the resident queer."

Historian Herbert S. Parmet claimed, "Lem subordinated his own life to his friend. Members of the president's staff thought of him as a handy old piece of furniture."

Even members of the press learned about Jack's homosexual liaison with Lem, but never printed any stories about it during JFK's presidency. Prior to the late 1960s, homosexuality in print was the love that dared not speak its name. Jack was also protected because the press almost never ran stories about his extramarital affairs.

It was painful and humiliating for Lem, but Jack forced him to arrange liaisons for him with some of the world's most alluring women. Lem was also assigned the often unpleasant task of getting rid of a woman after Jack was finished with

In the wake of his father's assassination in 1968, **Lem** became like a second father to **Robert Kennedy Jr.** They're seen together during a trip he took with the boy to Egypt in 1968.

As author David Pitts put it, "They hacked their way through the Columbian bush with machetes, rode horses across Latin American llamas, confronted poachers in Kenya, sampled ranch life in Mozambique, and navigated a previously unexplored Peruvian River."

"David Kennedy and Christopher Lawford often went with them. "Bobby [Junior, that is] got a lot of magnetism from Lem's fixation on him," said Chris.

Somewhere along the way, Lem decided that Bobby Jr. (not JFK Jr.) was the next best shot for carrying the torch of Camelot.

her. Lem didn't try to get rid of Marilyn Monroe. The stakes associated with that particular affair were so high that Jack entrusted the task to his chief troubleshooter, Bobby.

Charlie Bartlett, a Washington correspondent for the *Chattanooga Times*, recalled, "It was a tense time in the Cold War. If the Russians had found out that the president's best friend was a homosexual, it would have been valuable information to them."

Vidal said, "I think Jack felt quite comfortable in the company of homosexuals as long as they were smart enough to hold his interest. Jack was interested in women for sex, but for company he usually preferred men."

According to Lem's biographer, author David Pitts: "For Lem, Jack's death in Dallas was the end of the world. It wasn't so much that he never got over it. He didn't *want* to get over it. By all accounts, it took months for him to resume even the appearance of a normal existence. He just couldn't let go of the man who had been the most important person in his life since he was seventeen years old. Consumed by his memories, he talked about Jack constantly to his friends, and especially to the younger generation of Kennedys for whom he was the repository of so much information about the president in his younger days. For Lem, it was as if John Kennedy was not completely gone. Almost everything he said and did for the rest of his days was somehow connected to Jack."

After the loss of JFK in 1963, **Lem** drew very close, even intimately so, to **Bobby Kennedy**. Jackie felt that Lem was trying to replace Jack with Bobby, as she was doing herself.

Since 1934 Bobby and Lem had always been friends. Drawn together by their mutual sorrow, Lem and Bobby bonded as never before in the years leading up to Bobby's run for presidency in 1968,

Bobby and Lem even took vacations together as they did in 1967 at Waterville, New Hampshire *(see above)*. The year before, at the exclusive Lyford Cay in The Bahamas, they were seen together "in and out of their swimming suits."

A maid found them sleeping together in the nude, but Lem never commented on whether his relationship turned sexual or not. He did say, however, that "Bobby is our best hope for resurrecting Camelot."

Then, according to those who knew him, Lem "went to pieces in the worst way" after Bobby, too, was assassinated.

Although he tried to become a surrogate father to the children of RFK, he made all the wrong moves. He turned his apartment into a "candy store" of illegal drugs, with ongoing inventories of pot, cocaine, hash, LSD, even the more dangerous heroin. After 1968, according to Quirk, during the peak of flower power and its socially violent aftermaths, he often plied Robert Kennedy Jr. and Christopher Lawford (son of Peter Lawford and Patricia Kennedy) with drugs and became a dedicated user himself.

After RFK's assassination, according to Quirk, "These boys developed severe drug habits. Instead of firmly helping them to combat their addictions, Lem joined them and became as big an addict as they were."

Perhaps Bobby Jr. was the second man Lem truly loved. Lem was devoted to him, and they traveled the world together, most visibly in trips to exotic and obscure corners of South America. Through young Bobby, Lem was perhaps reliving some of his school days with Jack. The bedroom next to Lem's in his apartment on the Upper East Side of Manhattan was always referred to as "Bobby's room."

Lem lived to see New York City's Stonewall

Riots of 1969 and the advent of the gay revolution, but he never participated. He remained in the closet all his life, and ultimately, he refused to be associated with any book about the Kennedys wherein a publisher would insist that he preview the sexual aspects of his relationships. "I couldn't do that to Jack," Lem said to the literary agent Jay Garon, who politely informed him that without revelations of his sexual relationship with JFK, he could not get "a super advance." Garon, perhaps accurately, feared that without the description of sex, the memoirs would evolve into "just another one of those thousands upon thousands of 'friendship with the Kennedys' books."

Upon his death in 1981, Lem's will specified that his cooperative apartment at 5 East 88th Street in Manhattan be left to RFK Jr. A New York realtor, called in to evaluate its worth, found it piled high, almost to the ceiling, with old newspapers and magazines. He later reported that he also discovered an arsenal of drug paraphernalia. Surprisingly he found scattered human feces on the floors and carpets. Insiders surmised they resulted from Lem's drug and alcohol abuse during his final days.

It was appropriate that Bobby Jr. be designated as the mourner who would deliver Lem's eulogy, and part of it stated, "He felt pain for every one of us, pain that no one else could have the courage to feel. I don't know how we'll carry on without him. In many ways, Lem was a father to me and he was the best friend I will ever have."

John Kennedy was away with **Lem Billings** when JFK Jr.—soon to be called "John-John,"—entered the world prematurely, on November 25, 1960, at Georgetown University Hospital, weighing little more than six pounds.

Jack & Lem were in Palm Beach, with the newly elected president patronizing high-priced prostitutes ("they don't talk") but coming home for sleepovers with Lem.

Hearing that John Jr. had been born, Jack and Lem flew back to Washington. John-John was too young and Jackie was too protective of her boy to allow him to spend much time with Lem. Her friend, author Truman Capote, called it "Jackie's homosexual panic."

On occasion, Lem was allowed to take the beautiful, long-haired boy on an outing, such as when they visited Warner Brothers' Jungle Habitat Wildlife Preserve in West Milford, New Jersey, in 1972 (see above).

But when Jackie feared that Lem was taking far too much of a sexual interest in John-John, she cut off the relationship.

Eunice Kennedy Shriver ended the funeral by saying, "I'm sure the good Lord knows that Heaven is Jesus, Lem, Jack, and Bobby loving one another."

GORE VIDAL'S POINT OF VIEW ABOUT THE "RESIDENT FAG" AT THE WHITE HOUSE

One night at a White House party, author Gore Vidal, one of Jackie's distant relatives, came "face to face with a non-fan, Lem Billings." Lem chastised Gore for not attending meetings of the Council of the Arts. Gore did not think this was any of Lem's business, but JFK's best friend seemed to want to pick a fight with him.

"As the principal fag at court, Lem felt that he should eliminate any potentially controversial figure from the scene," Gore claimed. "My temper—no gentle affair at best—was certainly being tested." Gore claimed that he was tempted to confront Lem with the accusation that he'd "picked up a friend of mine, anonymously, in Times Square. But I refrained."

In happier times in 1980, one year before Lem's death, he is sandwiched between two handsome young men he adored, **Robert Kennedy Jr.** *(left)* and **Christopher Lawford** *(right)*, son of Peter Lawford and Patricia Kennedy. At the far left is a young **Caroline Kennedy** in need of a hairdresser.

When Lem began to spend days at a time with Chris and Bobby Jr., rumors swirled around Manhattan and Washington. By then, Lem was well known as a homosexual, and the fear was that he would attempt to seduce one or both of the young men.

Lawrence J. Quirk, the biographer, wrote that there was a particularly vicious rumor toward the close of Lem's life "that he was in love with the decades-younger Robert Kennedy Jr. and had aided and abetted his drug habit as to personally control and use him sexually."

In Lem's book proposal made to agent Jay Garon, he confessed, "Of course I was in love with Bobby Sr. and Jr. Who wouldn't be? They were adorable. But I swear I never touched Bobby Jr., at least not sexually."

Lem refused to divulge any hint of a private relationship with Bobby Sr. "From what he said—or didn't say—I suspect he gave Bobby Sr. blow-jobs, like he had done with his older brother," claimed agent Jay Garon.

Lem is seen here in his New York apartment during the twilight of his life. He is pictured in 1977 with that same happy smile he turned to the world, even though his heart was often breaking.

Author Gore Vidal, no friend of Lem's, claimed, "He's the guy who carries the coat, the guy who runs the errand. To Jack, Lem was a kind of idiot friend."

However, the evidence is overwhelming that Lem was so much more. Intimate friends maintained that Jack and Lem represented an enduring love between two men, one of whom just happened to be the most powerful man in the world.

"To Jack, Lem's friendship was priceless," Jackie claimed.

KIRK LeMOYNE
BILLINGS
APRIL 15, 1916
MAY 28, 1981

WITH RESPECT AND AFFECTION FOR

LEM BILLINGS
REST IN PEACE

Allegheny Cemetery,
Lawrenceville, PA

Much of the world was at war when the photo above was taken at Palm Beach during Christmas of 1940. The candid shot of the young beach lovers included, from left to right: **Harry Dixon, John Coleman, Charlotte McDonnell, Jack Kennedy, Kathleen Kennedy** (JFK's sister, nicknamed "Kick") and the ever-faithful **Lem Billings**. Lem always showed up for the Palm Beach holidays, even though Jack's parents, Joe and Rose, often expressed objections to his invasion of the family's privacy.

Charlotte and Kick were known for sharing "beaux." At the time, Jack was closer to Kick than to any of his other siblings, Rose claiming that both of these children had a rebellious streak. In Palm Beach, Jack was always chasing after girls, and Lem was always chasing after Jack.

Lem *(left figure in photo, above)* hoists a very young **Robert Kennedy** with some help from his older brother **Jack** *(right)*.

Lem and Jack couldn't spend all their time at the beach. They had to get ready for dinner by reading the editorials and columns in *The New York Times*. Joe Kennedy at the dinner table didn't suffer fools lightly, and he wanted both of them to be up on current affairs, especially news from Europe, which was being invaded by Hitler.

In the photo above, **Lem Billings** poses on the north lawn of the White House in 1962. He'd worked hard to get his best friend, Jack Kennedy, elected.

During Jack's occupancy of the White House, Lem came and went whenever he wanted to, as he had his own bedroom there. Around the White House, he was jokingly referred to as "First Friend." Behind Lem's back, some members of the Secret Service referred to him as "the President's second wife" because of his intimate relations with JFK.

Peek-a-Boo!

Guess Who?

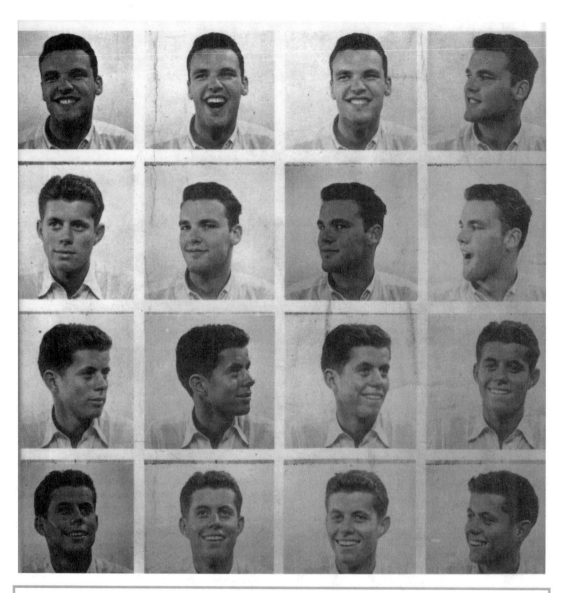

When a playful **Lem Billings and John F. Kennedy** posed for these photo booth shots while attending school in the 1930s, neither of them would have found it believable how their lives would go. Having breakfast with Lem, shortly after his election as president in 1960, JFK asked his best friend, "Did you think you'd ever be breakfasting with the newly elected leader of the Free World? And aren't you impressed?"

"Hell, no!" Lem countered, joking of course. "Kings sit on thrones. You sat for half an hour on your own throne last night, and I had to wipe your ass because of your back."

Whenever someone made a derogatory remark about Jack, that person became Lem's enemy for life. In 1960, when he was running for president, Adlai Stevenson told *Newsweek* that JFK was "somewhat arrogant." Lem hated him from that moment on. That very same year, columnist Drew Pearson quoted General Douglas MacArthur as having claimed that "Kennedy should be court-martialed for having let a Japanese destroyer mow him and his crew down in that PT boat." The general made another enemy in Lem.

MacArthur may have had a point. Many navy planners wondered how it was possible for Jack as the skipper to have gotten such a small maneuverable craft into the hazardous position to be slashed in two by the bow of a Japanese destroyer, all in Allied-controlled waters. No other torpedo boat suffered such a disaster in any of the world's oceans during WWII.

The Joseph Kennedys (Father and Son) Meet

Pamela Harriman,

"The Most Successful Courtesan of the 20th Century"

PLUS Their Sexual Involvements With

Deborah Kerr and *Princess Marina,*

the Duchess of Kent

Even though she married Randolph Churchill, Sir Winston's son, **Pamela Digby Churchill Hayward Harriman** was said to be "intolerant" of British men. She told friends that Americans were far better to their women than British men, accusing Randolph of "acting like a pasha."

"Britons take women for granted—sexually and intellectually—and treat them like pieces of furniture, even calling them old girl, regardless of their age." She gravitated to international men. In London she seduced Joseph P. Kennedy Sr., then America's ambassador to the Court of St. James's and later his handsome young son, Joseph P. Kennedy Jr. "Old Joe for the money," Pamela told director Peter Glenville, "young Joe for the sex." After divorcing Churchill, she privately confided, "I can no longer stand British men. Never again for me."

Boudoir Games at the Court of St. James's

Joseph P. Kennedy Jr., who except for his early death might have become the President of the United States, was the eldest of the nine children born to Joseph P. Kennedy Sr. and his wife, Rose Fitzgerald Kennedy. After the birth of her first son on July 25, 1915, Rose denied her husband "sexual favors" until it was time to give birth to another child.

His father wanted young, strong, handsome Joe Jr. to get the best education possible. He sent him to Choate, a boy's preparatory school in Wallingford, Connecticut, which his younger brother, John F. Kennedy, would later attend as well.

After graduation, Joe Jr. entered Harvard, where he may not have been the brightest student, but excelled in sports.

Joe Jr.'s Harvard tutor, Ken Galbraith, described him as "slender and handsome, with a heavy shock of hair and a serious, slightly humorless manner." Classmates found Joe Jr. "pushy and a bit of a bully." In college, he played for the Harvard football team and was considered a good athlete, unlike Jack whom Joe, Jr. described as "always sickly."

At Harvard, Joe became engaged to Athelia Fetter, a beautiful model and actress, but for reasons unknown, he suddenly broke off the engagement. Departing from New York, he sailed with his father to England where he studied in the London School of Economics.

> Call it puppy love: Joseph P. Kennedy Jr. went from girl to girl, one short lived infatuation after another until he became more serious about the widowed Duchess of Kent.
>
> Joe Jr. and his brother Jack were rivals. Rose weighed in on the respective sex appeal of her sons. "Jack didn't have the same sense of rhythm that Joe Jr. had when it came to dancing. Joe was, I think in a way, better looking but Jack had that sort of rugged face and then he photographed better than his older brother. Joe was so good looking, but the camera didn't capture how remarkably handsome he really was, whereas the camera made Jack better looking than he was."

In 1938, Joe Jr., along with his brother Jack and their sister, Kathleen (nicknamed "Kick"), were each eager to taste the worldly pleasures of London. Doors were thrown open to all three of them because Joe Sr. had been named U.S. Ambassador to the Court of St. James's by President Franklin D. Roosevelt.

Sidelined by an attack of appendicitis, Rose would follow later with the rest of the Kennedy clan—Robert (Bobby), Jean, Edward (Teddy), and Patricia. The ambassador's eldest daughter, Rosemary, was also to follow later, accompanied by her sister Eunice.

Joe Sr. wanted Joe Jr. to learn about affairs of state, with the understanding that one day he'd be President of the United States. He also wanted him "to get laid as often as possible, even if I have to seduce the gal first and then pass her on to you."

Joe Jr. was very independent-minded. Author Ted Schwarz, who wrote *The Mogul, the Mob, the Statesman, and the Making of an American Myth* about Joseph P. Kennedy, called Joe Jr. "arrogant, belligerent, and inappropriately aggressive with some of his siblings, especially Jack."

Joe Jr. didn't go over well with some women in British society, who viewed him as "the Ugly American—sexually aggressive and having a violent temper." Parroting his father, much to the alarm of whatever host whose party he was attending, he maintained that America should remain neutral if Britain went to war with Nazi Germany.

Joseph P. Kennedy Sr., father of three sons who each aspired to become president of the United States, was the much-loathed U.S. Ambassador to the U.K. But he had friends in high places, including Henry Luce, founder of both *Time* and *Life*. The publisher hated Roosevelt but considered Joe Sr. a possible candidate to replace Franklin D. Roosevelt in the 1940 election.

FDR had serious reservations about naming Joe to the post, although he claimed that he was one of the few men in America who could afford the expense of being an ambassador. Joe Sr. finally was awarded the post, but it turned into what he defined as "an endless series of nightmares."

Joe Jr. shared his father's political sentiments, expressing—at least in the beginning—an admiration for Nazi Germany. Joe Sr.'s stridently undiplomatic opinions angered his boss, President Roosevelt, and even more so, Winston Churchill, who would become the British Prime Minister in 1940.

Joe, Jr. attracted lower class girls from throughout London, a raft of dancers, models, actresses, and—his preference—older married women. He considered the latter category "safe." He was not interested in young women looking for husbands.

In contrast, Jack at this time in his life was driven by his testosterone. Unlike his older brother, he had not quite mastered the art of seducing young women he met at social functions.

According to Edward J. Renehan Jr., author of *The Kennedys at War*, Jack's "sexual adventures during the first years of his amorous life most often involved prostitutes. He told friends that he defined whores as plentiful, economical, and convenient. He was busy, he said, and he liked the idea of being able to go to a professional on his own schedule for some brisk and businesslike sex on demand."

Not surprisingly, considering the rank of Joe, Sr., the Kennedys were presented at the Court of St. James's. "Joe Kennedy Jr. is the apple of my husband's eye," Rose Kennedy told Queen Elizabeth (wife of George VI) at a reception at Buckingham Palace in 1938.

This vivacious woman, who ultimately became world-renowned as Pamela Digby Churchill Hayward Harriman and the doyenne of America's Democratic Party, became involved with the Kennedy family beginning in June of 1938, during the last of London's elaborate pre-war spring parties. She attended a dance at Prince's Gate, the official residence of the American Ambassador to the Court of St. James's. Joe Kennedy staged it in honor of his two daughters, Rosemary and Kathleen ("Kick"), who had each been presented at Court in May.

The Kennedys had invited three hundred guests who headed up a walkway bordered with lupins before mounting an elegant staircase leading to a paneled French-style ball-room on the second floor. Champagne awaited them, as did nightclub singer Harry Richmond, who with his band was generating an evening of swing music.

The embarrassment of the evening occurred when Rosemary Kennedy sexually propositioned two of the wait-ers. (It was such acts of overt sexual lewdness, some of them blatantly displayed in public, that prompted Joe Sr. and Rose to eventually authorize a frontal lobotomy on their errant daughter.)

In visible contrast to her sister, the hit of the ball was the more effervescently charming and more socially savvy Kick. As the star of the event, the press defined her after-wards as "the most exciting *debutante* of 1938."

***

In her 496-page memoir of Pamela, *Reflected Glory*, author Sally Bedell Smith, quoted an unnamed American journalist: "Pam liked to go around with men, and she liked sex and she was attractive, and they liked her. She said no to some and yes to some. The whole life in London was reason-ably casual. It was the mood of the time. It was carefree. Most American men who came were married but had girl-friends, and nobody cared. It was a fact of life."

The Kennedys soon learned two nicknames for Pamela, "Spam" and "Porcupine."

When the two Joes met Pamela, she was a long way from earning her reputation as "the courtesan of the centu-ry." The red-haired young woman was not the most beauti-ful woman in *le tout* London, but she was considered the most voluptuous, the sexiest, and the most pleasing to a man. When she focused on a man, as she did on Joe Sr., she devoured his every word as if it "were the Ten Commandments being read for the first time," claimed the well-known British actor and director, Peter Glenville.

She could also tell amusing stories. She fascinated Joe Sr. by describing her meeting with Adolf Hitler in Berlin. "The Führer made a pass at me, and I had always thought he was a homosexual," she claimed.

Joe Jr. found Pamela stunning in her *décolleté* gown of emerald-colored silk. "She could have converted all the fairies at your party to the straight-and-narrow path," he later told Joe Sr.

"I'll tell you one thing," Joe Sr. said, "That whoring bitch knows how to cocoon a man. She's after both sex and money, and I think she thinks I can provide both."

Joe Sr. was the first to seduce Pamela, right in the ambassador's residence when Rose had gone on a sightseeing trip to Oxford. Pamela would return to his bed several more times before the end of 1939.

One night over dinner at London's Ritz Hotel, Joe Jr. was invited to join Pamela and Joe

Sally Bedell Smith wrote *Reflected Glory: The Life of Pamela Churchill Harriman*, in which she revealed anec-dotes about most of the Kennedys.

As exposed in the biography, when Pamela hit New York in 1946 after divorcing Randolph Churchill, she was seen out on the town, rather blatantly, with Joe Sr. She also was seen dating Franklin D. Roosevelt Jr., even though at the time, she was secretly involved with Averell Harriman, who aspired to be Governor of New York and then President of the United States.

"When it came to men, Pamela always dated from the A-list," claimed gossip columnist Cholly Knickerbocker (actu-ally Igor Cassini).

Sr. It was a set-up, and Pamela seemed perfectly aware of what was about to happen.

At ten o'clock Joe Sr. excused himself, announcing that he had to return to the Embassy, leaving Pamela and his son alone. Joe Sr. had decided to "pass along" Pamela to his oldest son, and he'd already reserved the best suite at the Ritz for them.

The director, Glenville, who happened to be gay, had been an intimate friend and confidant of Pamela's, gossiping with her about various indiscretions within London's social landscape and theatre world for many years. He provided author Darwin Porter with many of the details of Pamela's connection to the Kennedys.

"Pamela just didn't give a fuck what stuffy English society said about her," Glenville claimed. "She knew Joe Kennedy would never divorce Rose and marry her, but she figured he might be of help to her in some way. Pamela loved two things: Money and sex. She slept with Joe Sr. but for real sex she turned to Joe Jr."

She confided to Glenville, "Joe Jr. got excited whenever he perceived that he was making a woman squeal when he penetrated her. Years later, I heard stories that he had the largest penis of all the Kennedys, including Papa."

At the debutante ball, Pamela, in addition to mesmerizing two of the Kennedy men, became "fast friends" with Kick, eventually having lunches with her, going shopping with her, and showing the Kennedy daughter her secret addresses in London.

In 1939, Joe Sr. and Kick invited Pamela to join their family for a vacation at their estate in Palm Beach, and she accepted. Pamela stayed at La Guerida, the Kennedy's oceanside villa at 1095 North Ocean Blvd, which would later be informally designated as JFK's "Winter White House." Originally built in 1923 for the heirs to the Wanamaker Department Store fortune, and designed by celebrity architect Addison Mizner, it had been bought in 1933, during the depths of the Depression, by Joe Kennedy, Sr., for the rock-bottom price of $120,000. A newpaper columnist described its style as "Bastard Spanish-Moorish-Romanesque-Renaissance-Bull Market-Damn-the-Expense."

At that time, Pamela was having a secret affair with the world's most famous news broadcaster, Edward R. Murrow, who had promised to ask his wife, Janet, for a divorce so he would be free to marry Pamela.

Murrow despised the Kennedys and pleaded with Pamela not to go. "Staying with old Joe Kennedy is like staying with Hermann Göring," he told her. Murrow had bitterly attacked Joe for his "hatred of the British, of Jews, and his devotion to Hitler."

In Palm Beach, Pamela received the cable she'd been dreading. Murrow wired her that their affair was over, and he was returning to "home and hearth" with Janet. Pamela was devastated. She poured out her dilemma to Kick, who violated her confidence and told her father.

That night Joe Sr. slipped into Pamela's bedroom after Rose had fallen asleep. Allegedly, he told her, "I'll fuck that

British director Peter Glenville (standing) seen here with his companion, American author Stanley Haggart (sitting), was Pamela Churchill's closest male confidant. "I can talk about men with him in a way I can't talk with other men."

When not in London, Peter and Stanley lived together in a cottage retreat in Essex. Pamela often retreated to their home for gossip and a place to liaise with an "off-the-record" boy friend. Peter said that sometimes Pamela didn't date just for the power, prestige, and money. "Sometimes she wanted pure sex. She brought some of the best looking R.A.F. pilots in Britain for weekend visits. She sure knows how to pick 'em."

bastard Murrow right out of your system."

He didn't quite succeed in that, but Joe Jr., taking "sloppy seconds," almost did. "I love having sex with that boy," she later told Glenville after her return to London. "Unlike his father, he's great in bed, but he's years away from having the power and money I need when I go looking for a man to marry."

***

With Florida suntans, both Joe Sr. and Joe Jr. arrived back in London, as did Pamela. War clouds loomed larger than ever, but Prime Minister Neville Chamberlain assured the British that he had appeased Hitler. Winston Churchill didn't believe the Prime Minister. But Joe Sr. did.

Joe Sr.'s days as U.S. Ambassador to the U.K. were numbered when it was learned in Washington that on two separate occasions he had tried to arrange a meeting with Adolf Hitler to discuss ways "to bring about a better understanding between Germany and the United States."

Back in pre-War London, Pamela opted to transform her affairs with two Kennedy men into friendships, and she went looking for bigger game. After being introduced to Randolph Churchill, son of Winston, he proposed marriage to her that very night.

She had been just one of eight English beauties that he'd proposed to that year. It was rumored that on one drunken night Randolph had proposed to three different young women.

The very year that Randolph proposed, Pamela was already on her way to becoming "a world expert on rich men's bedroom ceilings," according to author Max Hastings.

On October 4, 1939, four weeks after Britain went to war with Nazi Germany, Pamela married Randolph Churchill, First Lord of the Admiralty, at St. John's in Smith Square (a prestigiously located masterpiece of the English baroque style) in London.

When the Battle of Britain began during the summer of 1940, and when Joe Sr. said that the claim that the British were fighting for democracy was "just bunk," he was finished. A public outcry for his replacement arose both in England and in America.

Joe Sr. had never been fond of the Jews, referring to them for

At St. John's Church on Smith Square in London, Pamela Digby married her first husband, **Randolph Churchill**, the uncouth son of Britain's wartime prime minister. In *Reflected Glory*, the American journalist William Walton is quoted as saying: "Randolph was notorious. He was physically repellent. He used to pick his nose in public. He thought nothing of urinating on an open road in front of a group of women."

Lady Diana Cooper wrote: "His coughing is like some huge dredger that brings up dreadful sea-changed things. He spews them out into his hand." The press dubbed Pamela's husband "Randy" Churchill.

As a husband, Pamela, according to the author of *Reflected Glory*, found Randolph "noisy, opinionated, tactless, philandering, unpredictable, extravagant, and unreliable—unfit for marriage in every way." *(Associated Press)*

decades as "kikes and sheenies." "Some Jews are okay," he told Harvey Klemmer, his aide at the London Embassy, "but as a race they stink, they spoil everything they touch."

After a trip to Germany before the war, Klemmer had reported on the vandalism and assaults on the Jews by the Nazis. The ambassador had responded, "Well, they brought it on themselves."

Months before, Pamela had migrated from the Kennedy beds for quarters within 10 Downing Street after her father-in-law, Winston, became the wartime Prime Minister of Britain. Joe Sr. and Joe Jr. went looking for other conquests.

At the American Embassy, Joe Sr. entertained the Duke and Duchess of Kent, otherwise known as Prince George and Princess Marina. They took delight in each other's company, and both the Duke and Duchess seemed charmed by Joe Jr. They also met the young JFK but seemed to view him as a mere child not worthy of serious conversation.

The Duke of Kent—the younger brother of the exiled Duke of Windsor—was the fourth son of King George V and Mary of Teck.

Before their involvement with the Duke and Duchess of Kent, Pamela had filled in both

A big event in August of 1934 was the engagement of **Prince George**, uncle of the present Queen Elizabeth II, to **Princess Marina of Greece and Denmark**, a cousin of Queen Elizabeth's consort, Prince Philip. Later they became known as the Duke and Duchess of Kent. London was ablaze with pageantry for their wedding on November 29.

Theirs was to be no ordinary marriage. The Duke was bisexual and the Duchess had a roving eye, as Joseph P. Kennedy Jr. learned when he was invited as a house guest to their opulent country home. When Marina learned that her husband had seduced Joe Jr., she told him, "What's good for the Duke is also good for the Duchess."

Joes with lowdown information about the royal couple: Married in 1934, they had maintained an open marriage before that term was invented. The Duke was a notorious bisexual, and his wife (who, thanks to the interconnected genealogies of the royal bloodlines of Europe, was also known as the Princess of Greece and Denmark) "slept around," according to Pamela.

The Duke had sustained a long string of romances with both men and women, from socialites to actors from both the Hollywood film community and the London stage. The Duke's affairs included a dalliance with the young British actor, Laurence Olivier. The Duke's most memorable romance with a male involved Noël Coward.

He'd also seduced Fred Astaire, the African-American cabaret singer Florence Mills, socialite Margaret Whigham (later Duchess of Argyll), musical star Jessie Matthews, and banking heiress Poppy Baring. He'd also had sexual liaisons with his distant cousin, Louis Ferdinand, Prince of Prussia.

Soon Joe Sr. was having a secret affair with the Duchess of Kent, and she is now numbered among the list of famous women he seduced. Others included actresses Gloria Swanson, Marlene

Dietrich, Constance Bennett, Evelyn Brent, Nancy Carroll, Betty Compson, Viola Dana, and even Marion Davies, the mistress of press baron William Randolph Hearst.

The Duke and Duchess seemed to have become equally enamored with Joe Jr., and one weekend invited him as an overnight guest to their country home. Joe Jr. later shared memories of that weekend with Pamela, who proceeded to confide every juicy detail to her gay pal, Glenville.

Joe Jr. asserted that all three of them had had one or two too many before retiring. In the middle of the night, Joe Jr., still a bit drunk, became vaguely aware that someone was fellating him. When he revived, he decided at first that it must be the Princess Marina.

But when he reached down to clutch her head for his climax, he discovered a man's hair. It was the Duke of Kent. "At that point," he told Pamela, "I was too far gone to kick him out of my bed. He was really good at it, too. I find that girls don't know how to do it. The Duke and I became very close after that. I figured that if Jack could have his Lem Billings, I can have George. Incidentally, that blow-job led to an even more satisfying arrangement: three ways with him and the Princess."

Later, since the Duke and Duchess of Kent couldn't service Joe Jr. whenever he needed it, he turned his attention elsewhere. At Joe Sr.'s grand ball at the American Embassy, he'd met what he called "a demure English rose," and was very attracted to her. When her escort, perhaps her agent, was speaking to someone else, he took down her phone number, which she willingly offered. All he knew about her was that she was an aspiring actress and that she was unmarried.

Unknown to biographers, Joe Jr. slipped in a 1939 affair under the radar screen. Even his own father did not find out about it at first. Joe Sr. privately said, "I have to know the women my sons are fucking, at least their names."

The name in this case would become world famous. The Scottish-born actress, Deborah Kerr, and Joe Jr. became lovers. She was often wrongly described. Laurence Olivier called her "unreasonably chaste." Gabriel Pascal, the legendary Hungarian film producer, once approached her by saying, "Sweet virgin, you have a very spiritual face."

Joan Crawford had been slated to co-star with **Burt Lancaster** in *From Here to Eternity* (1953), but a dispute led to her walking off the picture. Consequently, the coveted role went to that "demure little mouse," English actress **Deborah Kerr**. She turned out to be a hot tamale not only on the beach with Burt but in his bed at night. Their love scenes on the beach, with water rushing over them, is considered a "high water mark of screen eroticism." Never again would either star be depicted in such reciprocal sexual activity on screen.

But before WWII, Joseph P. Kennedy Jr. got to Deborah long before Burt. As Joe told both his father and his brother, Jack, "She came to my bed a virgin but as sure as hell, she didn't leave until after I plugged her with my mighty hymen buster."

28

When Hollywood later beckoned, Kerr specialized in playing ladies on the screen. (No, not that kind of "ladies"). However, her breakthrough role, a portrayal most associated with her true character, was her actualization of a nymphomaniac in *From Here to Eternity* (1953). That love-making on the beach with Burt Lancaster is one of the most famous movie scenes of all time. Off-screen, she and Burt heated up the sheets.

Deborah later told Cecil Beaton that when Joe Jr. invited her to the U.S. Embassy for dinner, Joe Sr. propositioned her during an interval when his son was absent from the room. She said she turned him down. "I knew he was cheating on his wife, and I had no moral objection to that. I just didn't find him attractive. After all, I was only a teenager and he looked like my father or even my grandfather."

Eventually, Joe Jr. was eager to share his conquest of Deborah with his younger brother Jack, who was still patronizing London prostitutes. "I bagged her the first night," Joe, Jr. claimed. "She looks prim and proper, but once you get her panties down, she's one wild gal."

When Joe Jr. allegedly complimented her on her pelvic movements, Deborah claimed, "I originally trained as a ballet dancer."

Another of her lovers, Michael Powell, cast her as three women in his *The Life and Death of Colonel Blimp* (1942). In his autobiography, he admitted that he became her lover, finding her "the flesh-and-blood woman I had been searching for."

Joe Jr. had a reputation of falling in and out of love every few weeks or so. Usually, he was the one who dumped the woman, moving on to his next conquest. But in the case of Deborah, she dumped him when she fell for the handsome and dashing British actor, Stewart Granger, who was already married.

"Whether a man was married or not did not concern Deborah," said James Mason, who appeared opposite her in *Hatter's Castle* (1942). "When she saw a man she wanted, she went for him. She even came on to me." Privately the bisexual Mason confided to his co-star, Robert Newton, "I told Debbie if she'd invite me to the bed with Granger and her, I'd go for a *ménage à trois*."

Granger, in his memoir, *Sparks Fly Upward*, claimed that Deborah seduced him in the back of his chauffeur-driven car at the time he was making *Caesar and Cleopatra* (1945), with Vivien Leigh, who was also pursuing him.

Actually he was wrong about that. He'd begun his affair with young Deborah when she was still in her teens, the same as he'd done with his future wife, Jean Simmons.

He later told his sometimes lover Michael Wilding and his wife, Elizabeth Taylor, "I didn't want to admit that I was going around London deflowering virgins like Deborah. Yes, I can lay claim to taking the virginity of Deborah Kerr, although Joseph Kennedy Jr. at the time also made the same boast. I think she told both me and that Kennedy boy that we were the first."

After his affair with Deborah ended, Joe Jr. returned to America to enroll in the Harvard Law School but dropped out in his final year to begin officer and flight training in the U.S. Navy, earning his wings as a naval aviator in May of 1942. He returned to Britain in September of 1943, where he piloted Liberator patrol bombers on anti-submarine details during the winter of 1943 and 1944. In all, he completed more than thirty-five successful combat missions. Collectively, they entitled him to return to the States.

But he had opted not to return to the relative safety of the U.S., remaining instead in England flying combat missions. He had told his father that he wanted to be in England when D-Day came. He also believed that he might be of great use to the Navy during the inevitable and oncoming Allied invasion of Nazi-occupied France.

That was, of course, a heroic agenda to pursue, but he had another reason. He'd fallen in love. Rumors floated around London at the time that the ambassador's son had fallen in love with a married woman. Actually he'd fallen for a widow, whom he had already seduced while she had been married.

Born in 1906, the Princess Marina was nine years older than Joe Jr. but still a great beauty. Her notorious husband, the Duke of Kent, had been killed in an airplane crash off the coast of Scotland on August 25, 1942, while on active duty with the Royal Air Force.

Seeing her every time he went on leave, Joe Jr., from all reports, was "wildly, madly, enraptured with the Duchess." After only three weeks, he proposed marriage to her. She didn't say yes, but, on the other hand, she didn't exactly say no. Somehow, word of Joe Jr.'s proposal leaked back to Buckingham Palace.

Both King George VI and Queen Elizabeth detested the Kennedys and were shocked and completely opposed to the involvement of the Duchess with the Kennedy family. They had heard about how, after the first time that Joe Sr. had been invited to Buckingham Palace to meet the king and queen, he had later referred to Queen Elizabeth (later the Queen Mother), as "a cute trick."

Joe Jr. shocked his father when he told him that he wanted to marry the Duchess of Kent, his dad's former mistress. Father and firstborn son had passed women between them before. Normally, Joe Sr. would have opposed such a marriage, but in this case, he seemed thrilled that "an Irish mick" like his son might marry into the House of Windsor. He encouraged his son to pursue her.

Meanwhile, Britain, especially London, was being hammered by nightly assaults from Nazi V-bombs, and Churchill wanted their launch pads destroyed. With that in mind, and despite Marina's objections, Joe Jr. volunteered for a dangerous aerial mission called Operation Aphrodite/Project Anvil. It involved Joe's piloting of a small plane overloaded with explosives, setting the automatic pilot on a remote-controlled trajectory towards a ground-based target, and parachuting from the plane before it crashed. Based on the unpredictability of many technical factors associated with the operation, it was highly dangerous--the equivalent of a Kamikaze attack but with (albeit flawed) provisions for the escape of the pilot and his crew.

In the midsummer of 1944, Joe Jr. set off from a base in southern England within a small low-flying plane armed with 374 boxes of high explosives, collectively weighing more than 20,000 pounds. His co-pilot was Lt. Wilford John Willy.

It was anticipated that Joe Jr. and Willy were to parachute from their plane before the robot-guided plane

If Joe Kennedy Sr., had had his wish, his first born, **Joe Kennedy Jr.** *(left),* would by 1960 have become President of the United States. But in 1944, just as victory in Europe seemed near, he died in a plane crash.

Details of his mission were suppressed for decades. This picture was taken two hours before he boarded his plane for his final flight, heading for France.

Looking regal in her crown jewels, **Princess Marina, the Duchess of Kent**, was a recent widow when Joe Jr. fell madly in love with her and wanted to marry her. Before the war, he'd already become familiar with her charms.

nose-dived into its target, which in this case was a guided missile launcher at a V-3 Nazi cannon site in Mimoyecques, in northern (Pas-de-Calais) France.

Ironically, Elliott Roosevelt, son of the late president Franklin D. Roosevelt, was in a de Havilland Mosquito aircraft tailing the Kennedy plane.

Shortly after takeoff, flying low above the heaths and forests near Blythborough in Suffolk, and two minutes after switching on the automatic pilot, the robot plane exploded, creating a "fiery ball of fire," as Roosevelt later claimed. Three square miles of heathland was set on fire, hundreds of trees were felled by the explosion, and Joe Jr. and his co-pilot were vaporized.

The date was August 12, 1944. Joe Jr. was only twenty-nine years old.

On hearing the news that day, Princess Marina went into mourning at her country home.

Joe, Jr. never got to see his son marry into the royal family. Ironically, and through other means, he lived long enough to see his own family referred to as "American Royalty."

Joe Jr. was the first death-related tragedy to strike the Kennedy clan. Many tragedies lay ahead for this ill-fated family, so many, in fact, that the concept of a "Kennedy curse" eventually grew widespread.

Thanks to the U.S. government's order of an immediate cover-up of Operation Aphrodite, the details of Joe Jr.'s mission were shrouded in secrecy for almost sixty years.

The military had a reason for the cover-up. Joe Jr.'s mission was pointless, representing a massive intelligence failure. It was later disclosed that the target launch had been severely damaged by RAF raids seven days earlier, and that the bomb site had already been rendered inoperable after massive "Tall Boy" bombs were dropped almost directly on it.

Shortly after the death of the scion of such a prominent family, rumors spread rapidly. Actually, the source of some of these rumors was Josef Goebbels, the Nazi propaganda minister. He falsely claimed that German anti-aircraft guns had shot the plane down. Spinning out from that original rumor, there were other claims, including one surmising that Joe Jr. had parachuted down and was captured by the Nazis.

One story had him fatally shot during an escape attempt. Another rumor claimed that he, along with his co-pilot Willy, parachuted to earth where they were captured by a Panzer division. According to one report, both Joe Jr. and Willy were later executed by a Nazi general after undergoing vicious torture.

The wildest rumor, circulated around 1947, involved Joe being still alive and living in Germany as an victim. It was (falsely) rumored that he never recovered his memory, and that he was living in a suburb of Hannover, never knowing who he was.

Elliott Roosevelt tried to squelch these many rumors. "I was in the air, and I saw what happened," he said. "Both Joe and Willy died in an explosion. Joe's death was a complete waste and totally unnecessary, we learned later. His father told me that he was grooming Joe Jr. to become a future president. Of course, chances were he'd never become a president as fantastic as my father, but Joe Jr. was a great American, and we might have expected much from him."

As Thomas Maier expressed in *The Kennedys: America's Emerald Kings*, "Young Joe's death forever added tragedy into the family's equation of success, money, and achievement. The golden aura of the Kennedys, the air of invincibility that had permeated their lives in London and New York, seemed no longer to exist with Joe gone."

Joe Jr.'s death did not dim the fighting spirit of Joseph P. Kennedy Sr. Two days after his son's death, and much to the shock of Jack Kennedy himself, Joe Sr. called a family conference. "Joe is gone," he told the clan, "and we can never replace him. But life must go on. *We* must go on. Our political future now resides in Jack here. We'll get him elected to Congress, then the Senate. We'll see that he runs with the presidential nominee in 1956 as the Veep. In 1960, I predict Mr. John F. Kennedy, my fine son, will be on the way to sitting in the Oval Office."

A military officer (name unknown) later said, "It may be felt, perhaps, that Joe Jr. should not have pushed his luck so far and should have accepted his leave and gone home. But two facts must be borne in mind. First, at the time of his death, he had completed probably more combat missions in heavy bombers than any other pilot of his rank in the Navy, and therefore he was preeminently qualified. Secondly, as he told a friend early in August, he considered the odds at least fifty-fifty, and Joe never asked for any better odds than that."

In 1946, a destroyer, the USS *Joseph P. Kennedy Jr.*, was launched as the Navy's final tribute to a "gallant officer and his heroic devotion to duty."

***

Although after Joe Jr.'s death, Princess Marina faded from the Kennedy family's life, Pamela did not. She remained friends of the family until the end. Ironically, another Kennedy brother would attempt to seduce her.

Pamela, in her role as his daughter-in-law, spent many a wartime night with Winston Churchill in his bunker in London, as Nazi bombs rained down during the Blitz. She stayed close to the seat of a world power throughout the war.

One night she even enlisted the help of General Dwight David Eisenhower to help her in the kitchen of an officers' club in London. "He kissed me real deep," she later confided to Peter Glenville, "but we didn't go much farther that night. Besides, I heard he was impotent."

It hardly rivaled the Kennedy mansion in Palm Beach, but the **J.F. Kennedy Homestead** *(pictured above)* was where the Kennedy clan originated in Ireland.

Patrick Kennedy, John F. Kennedy's great-grandfather, lived in this modest homestead prior to his sailing with his family to find new life in America. As he sailed in steerage, with barely enough money for his fare, he could hardly imagine that he would be planting a seed in New England that would lead to the growth of America's greatest political dynasty.

The ancestral home lies at Dunganstown, New Ross, in Ireland's County Wexford.

Kick Kennedy *(above, center)* had married Billy Harrington against her parents' wishes. He died when he was shot through the heart by a German sniper in Belgium on September 10, 1944. He'd been married to Kick for only four months.

Pictured above is **Lord Peter Fitzwilliam** *(left)* with Kick. She fell in love with the married thirty-seven-year-old British lord, and they sneaked away for a weekend together in Cannes, They had rented a two-engine De Havilland Dove eight-seat plane in London for the ill-fated trip. They were killed in a fatal plane crash in the south of France in 1948. The Kennedy family disapproved of the relationship but nonetheless, **Joe Kennedy Jr.** *(far right)* seems to be looking on approvingly.

In 1947, a year after her divorce from Randolph Churchill, Pamela went to a house party at Lismore Castle in County Wexford in Ireland. She was invited to the castle by her close friend, Kick Kennedy, and Kick's lover Peter Fitzwilliam. At the steering wheel of Kick's American station wagon, Jack Kennedy drove the party to Lismore.

Once there, Jack was introduced to Anthony Eden, who had been the U.K.'s foreign secretary during World War II, and who later, from 1955 to 1957, became prime minister of England. During his first night in Lismore Castle, Jack learned that Eden and Pamela were slipping around, obviously engaged in an affair.

"I had met young Jack before," Pamela told Glenville. "I got to know him a lot better at Lismore. He was three years or so older than me—I think that's right—but he seemed like such a kid. I was used to dating older men. To me, Jack was like a boy and very skinny and scrawny."

"Joe Jr. was much more developed," she said. "Jack was just Kick's brother but he pursued me constantly when Anthony wasn't doing his duty. Jack really wanted to bed me. He claimed that his father and his older brother, who had died in a plane crash, had told him all about me, and that he was hot to trot and to prove to me he was just as much a man as his older brother was. He was not eligible as far as I was concerned, and he seemed really hurt when I said no."

She did agree to drive with Jack one morning on an expedition to discover where "the original Kennedys" had lived around Dunganstown near Ross. The location was about fifty miles from Lismore Castle in Ireland, where they were staying. "We took Kick's big station wagon across those bumpy country roads to nowhere," Pamela said. "We finally found a dump with chickens in the front yard. There seemed to be a dozen Kennedy look-alikes in this horrible compound. I told Jack it looked like *Tobacco Road*, and that really pissed him off."

Even though she'd trivialized the place of his origin, Pamela came to Jack's rescue when they returned to London. On September 21, 1947, she summoned her doctor to tend to an ailing Jack. He was immediately hospitalized at the London Clinic, where her own doctor, Sir Daniel Davies, told Pamela that he was suffering from Addison's disease.

Jack was in such bad shape that Joe hired a registered nurse to accompany him on the sail back to the port of New York. There was even a priest aboard who gave Jack last rites (extreme unction). Dr. Davies had privately told Pamela that "the boy has only a year or so to live."

After the ship's arrival in New York, Jack was flown on a stretcher to Boston where Joe received him. "Pathetic," he told Rose and his family. "And this is the boy I want to groom to become President of the United States."

Sixteen years later, on the occasion of his return to Ireland in 1963, the year of his death, President Kennedy recalled his earlier visit, asserting that the Kennedy cottage "was filled with magic and sentiment." This, of course, was in contrast to Pamela's view that the Kennedys were descended from "shanty Irish."

Pamela later befriended Jack's new wife, Jackie, and they became friends. Jack and Jackie watched as Pamela slept or married her way across Europe and America. She seduced generals, rich playboys, and titans of industry, including shipping tycoon Stavros Niarchos, Jock Whitney, Prince Aly Khan, Gianni Agnelli, and Elie de Rothschild. In 1960 she married Leland Hayward, one of the producers of the 1959 Broadway hit *The Sound of Music*.

Divorcing Hayward in 1971, she married the fabulously wealthy Averell Harriman that same year. The former ambassador to Russia, governor of the State of New York, and former presidential candidate, was 79 years old at the time. Since he was not capable of satisfying the oversexed Pamela, she amused herself with a number of other men, notably Frank Sinatra.

The aging Harriman was very jealous when Pamela went gaga over Sinatra. It even appeared in print that Pamela was going to marry the singer. When contacted, Sinatra denied the rumors. "Nah," he said, "she's too old for me, and besides she's got no sense of humor."

When funds started running low and her accountant advised her she was spending too much money, she told her aides, "I'll just have to marry Aristotle Onassis."

"But, Pamela, he's already married to Jackie Kennedy."

"That won't stop me," she said. "You surely don't think Jackie and Onassis will be together 'till death do us part.'"

For years Pamela sheltered the Democratic Party "in exile," and raised millions to ensure that Bill Clinton was elected president in 1992. In gratitude, he appointed her as U.S. Ambassador to France.

Pamela died on February 5, 1997 at the American Hospital in Paris' suburb of Neuilly-sur-Seine, after suffering a cerebral hemorrhage while swimming in the pool of the Ritz Hotel in Paris. President Clinton dispatched Air Force One to France to retrieve her body and fly it back to Washington, where he spoke movingly at her funeral at the Washington National Cathedral.

Teddy Kennedy privately told friends, "We have buried America's Madame de Pompadour. I have a unique distinction separating me from dad, Jack, and Bobby. I was the only Kennedy brother Pamela didn't seduce, although she tried one night."

The Biography of Pamela Digby Churchill Hayward Harriman

CHRISTOPHER OGDEN

One of the biographies of this remarkable woman was authored by Christopher Ogden. It elicited a lot of press commentary, "Suzy" in *The New York Post* writing "a *femme fatale* of the first order, catnip to men, a fascinating woman who has been loved by some of the world's most powerful men, she would make a delicious, page-turning subject."

Vanity Fair wrote, "Georgetown's political doyenne signed Bill Clinton to the board of her Democrats for the 80s committee. Now, at seventy-two, she's presiding over *le tout* Washington for the 90s."

People said, "The French sent us the Statue of Liberty, Brie, and Bordeaux. We are sending them Pamela Harriman. This is what is known as a fair trade agreement."

In London, the *Daily Express* claimed, "The formidable Pamela Harriman, once the daughter-in-law of Sir Winston Churchill, now the queen mother of the Clinton court, is the second most powerful woman in Washington after the president's wife."

New York magazine claimed that, "Some say that as much as any other private individual, Harriman is responsible for the Democratic party's 1992 victory."

PAMELA ON BOBBY: "THE RUNT OF THE LITTER"

In his biography of Pamela Harriman, Christopher Ogden quotes a RFK volunteer who remembered Pamela as being "very anti-Bobby Kennedy." After RFK was assassinated in 1968, Pamela told one of those "terrible, terrible jokes" about the shooting, which brought a strong reprimand from her husband, Averell Harriman.

The book also reveals how, during the mid-1960s, following a time-honored tradition of socially prominent ladies who open shops, Pamela recycled many of her own house gifts, antiques, and decorative accessories in the Jansen shop, a boutique at 42 East 57th St. in New York City. Ogden's biography reveals how she had trouble getting Ethel Kennedy to pay her bills that ran into the thousands.

Averell lent the RFK family his cottage in Sun Valley, Idaho, for a ski vacation, but after their departure, Pamela found it was left filthy, its carpets pitted with cigarette burns, dishes broken, and furnishings ruined. "Those Kennedys crammed nearly three dozen people into that little cottage," Pamela complained to Averell.

Howard Hughes, Billionaire

And His Infatuated Lust for Young JFK

IT'S FLAG DAY!

When a young man in 1940 was handsome, tall, rich, and on the prowl, it was perhaps inevitable that he would mesmerize the bisexual king of debauchery in Hollywood. When mogul **Howard Hughes** went after someone, he usually got his woman, or man as the case might be. Although Cary Grant was his main squeeze, no one dated from the A-list like Hughes. Hollywood columnist James Bacon called him the "greatest swordsman."

Among the women, Jean Harlow, Katharine Hepburn, Susan Hayward, Rita Hayworth, Marlene Dietrich, Kathryn Grayson, Veronica Lake, and Hedy Lamarr had fallen for his charm, or his money. Among the men, leading attractions in his bed included Robert Taylor, Gary Cooper, Errol Flynn, and Tyrone Power—Hughes went only for the best—"Grade A meat," as he called it.

Eventually, young **John F. Kennedy** became his target, and the mogul plotted his moves like the Japanese did their attack on Pearl Harbor months later. *(Photofest)*

35

Photofest

JFK AND ROBERT STACK:
HOLLYWOOD BACHELORS WHO SWING

Before meeting young JFK, Howard Hughes had his pimp Johnny Meyer check out his background rather thoroughly. Hughes never could stand rejection, and he wanted to figure in advance if "the ambassador's son" would be open to a sexual suggestion. Meyer concluded that he would, based on the fact that JFK had had an ongoing and long-term affair with his best buddy from prep school, Lem Billings.

In his report to Hughes, Meyer wrote: "Young Kennedy has a big ego, and often refers to himself—at least in one letter—as a 'God-like Casanova.' He appears to be girl-crazed but doesn't object to having a little homosexual action on the side, providing his partner does all the work. He's only into that kinky stuff for his own satisfaction, he doesn't care how his partner gets off."

"My conclusion: He's up for grabs, but you might want to entice him with a beautiful woman beforehand and then, at the right moment, move in for the kill. Okay, boss man?"

In the early 1940s, before his stint in the military, actor Robert Stack accepted an invitation from the eccentric billionaire, Howard Hughes, to go sailing, and asked if he could bring a friend along.

Howard reluctantly agreed, thinking it might be one of Robert's young starlet girlfriends. In those days, the extraordinarily handsome actor was making the rounds, seducing "a starlet a minute," as he put it. Howard would have preferred to enjoy the actor's charms alone but agreed to play host to whomever Robert brought along for their weekend sail to Catalina.

On the deck of the rented *Sea Queen*, Howard was introduced to the young John F. Kennedy, who was dressed like a sailor, all in whites. "He's Ambassador Kennedy's son," Robert said, introducing the young man who was twenty-three years old and a recent graduate of Harvard. He'd just published a book, *Why England Slept*, which had been ghostwritten for him and loosely based on his senior thesis at Harvard.

Howard detested the young man's father, Joseph Kennedy, their feud stemming from when the liquor dealer had been a power broker in Hollywood. On a few occasions, both men had seduced the same women, notably actresses Constance Bennett and Nancy Carroll.

When Howard later thanked Robert for inviting the young man for the weekend, Robert realized that Howard was smitten. John soon became "Jack." Howard confided to Robert, "He has the most perfect blue eyes I've ever seen on a man."

The moment Jack flashed his soon-to-be-famous smile at Howard, the tall, thin Texan bonded with the New Englander, and with his natural charm and grace. It was as if Howard had waited all his life to meet the perfect Prince Charming. The only problem was that the gleam

36

in the eyes of this young man from Massachusetts wasn't directed toward Howard, but at every beautiful woman in Hollywood. Over dinner that night, Jack told Howard that, "I want to fuck every woman in Hollywood." He called it "celebrity poon-tang."

A lifelong lover of gossip, Jack admired Howard and was eager for anything he might reveal about the many legendary stars he'd seduced. Jack wanted to use Howard as his role model for how to behave in Hollywood. "You're the swordsman out here," Jack told Howard. "No doubt about that. Even dad admits it's true, and he's bedded a few beauties—not just Gloria Swanson. I'm the new boy in town and I want to follow in your footsteps."

Robert and Jack had become almost immediate friends after a mutual friend, Alfredo de la Vega, had introduced them at Robert's studio. Over Howard's champagne and lobster dinner aboard the yacht, Robert told Howard about his secret hideaway, called "the Flag Room."

It was within a small flat that lay at the end of a cul-de-sac, Whitley Terrace, between Cahuenga and Highland in the Hollywood Hills. Here stood a jumbled mass of apartments stacked one on top of the other like a set of warped building blocks about to tumble over. Many of them opened onto balconies dripping in wisteria.

Robert claimed that within the Flag Room, he learned "about the birds, the bees, the barracudas, and other forms of Hollywood wildlife." Both Robert and Alfredo had convinced their parents that they needed this small hideaway to pursue their studies quietly and without interruption from their families. Their parents fell for this deception and agreed to pay the rent. "We studied all right," Robert confessed. "Female anatomy."

Robert Stack *(above)* was considered a bit conservative by his dates, Judy Garland calling him "stuffy." He later claimed that it was Jack's free-wheeling "bawdiness" that first attracted him. "Jack would even turn a medical procedure into something suggestive," Stack claimed.

Jack told his friend, Lem Billings, that he was turned on when surrounded by a bevy of nurses. "A doctor first stuck his finger up my ass and rolled it around suggestively," Jack said. "I told the doctor he had a good motion, and it broke everybody up. Out goes the finger and in goes an iron tube a foot long. Right in front of those nurses, I got a god damn hard-on."

In the corner of the apartment was a small bedroom with space for only one double bed, with a very narrow space (about two feet wide) on either side of it. Alfredo and Robert turned this into their "chamber of seduction." The ceiling was only five feet high, so both men had to bend over whenever they tried to stand up within the room. On the ceiling they pinned flags of various nations, strictly avoiding any symbols associated with Nazi Germany.

Whenever either Robert or Alfredo took a young woman here, they demanded that she memorize the order of the flags for a later quiz—or else she'd have to "Pay the Piper." Since the victim was already spread out horizontally, she was in a convenient position for the receipt of "punishment" for flunking the exam. "All the girls flunked," Robert said. "There were too many flags to remember." One blonde beauty, who looked like a future Marilyn Monroe, was so enticing and alluring to Robert, that he claimed to have "penalized" her three times in single night.

Many young starlets were repeat visitors to The Flag Room. "Horny bastards that we were," Robert said, "Alfredo and I rearranged the flags every night so that some foxy lady on her fourth or fifth visit would not be able to memorize the order and would flunk one more time."

Robert amused Howard by telling him that Jack, although he'd just arrived in Hollywood, had visited The Flag Room a total of eight times, each time with a different woman. Years later in his memoirs, Robert facetiously claimed that he'd helped Jack in his geopolitical studies by teaching him which flag belonged to which country.

"I've known many of the great Hollywood stars, and only a few of them seemed to hold the attraction for women that JFK did, even then," Robert said. He noted that before his handsome friend entered politics, he'd just look at a woman and she'd "tumble."

"I had a fixation on Carole Lombard," Robert admitted years later when he agreed to talk candidly about his life with Howard and his friendship with Jack. "Except for posing for some pictures with me, she never gave me the time of day. I guess she was settling for Gable's less than prepossessing inches instead of my fine tool. Actually, Gable became a great friend of mine, and I wouldn't have betrayed him anyway. Nonetheless, in those days I sought out starlets who looked like Carole Lombard, at least the dime store version."

Actress **Margaret Sullavan** liked to tell her conquests how they performed in bed. She never used the scale of one to ten, but would compare them to other conquests she'd had.

After seducing Jack, she told him he was far better in bed than her former husband, Henry Fonda, "but not as good in the sack as James Stewart," her co-star.

"Unlike me, Jack had completely versatile taste in women— blondes, brunettes, redheads, young ones, mature ones, gals with large breasts, gals with lemons for breast," Robert said. "Regardless of the girl, he always insisted on shapely legs."

Even in later life, valet George Jacobs in his autobiography, *Mr. S: My Life with Frank Sinatra*, admitted this was true. Jack, by then president, was still fascinated by women with shapely legs, notably dancers Cyd Charisse and Shirley MacLaine.

Aboard his yacht, Howard seemed eager to learn about young Jack's string of conquests, no doubt planning to conduct raids on the women himself if their seductions sounded enticing enough.

Robert later said that through "the humble portals" of the Flag Room passed a "guest list that ran the gamut from the chorus line to an Academy Award winner." In his memoirs, the actor asserted that "since I still live in California, I can't name names."

But in private conversations, Robert was much more forthcoming. When pressed, he cited Betty Grable as one of Jack's early conquests. Robert himself had struck out when he'd pursued "America's pinup with the dimples on her knees," but Jack scored big.

Jack claimed that Grable told him that child actor Jackie Coogan had taught her "more tricks than a whore learns in a whorehouse." She also confessed to him that she'd "seduced the unseductive" aspiring young actor Ronald Reagan.

For some reason, known only to himself, Howard didn't pursue Grable himself, even though he'd go after—and win over—all the leading pinup girls of World War II: Lana Turner, Veronica Lake, Rita Hayworth, and Ava Gardner, among others.

Robert amusingly confessed that even though Grable and Howard didn't make it with each other, they shared some of the same lovers, especially Tyrone Power and later Victor Mature. "Even that discovery of Henry Willson, Rory Calhoun, when he wasn't otherwise occupied with Marilyn Monroe and countless others," Robert claimed. "Rory once complained that the trouble with Hollywood was that there were no good cocksuckers, with the notable exceptions of Betty Grable and Howard Hughes."

Pert young actress Barbara Britton was another conquest for both Jack and Robert. Robert claimed that the actress has "luscious tits." Britton had arrived in Hollywood straight out of college to decorate a Hopalong Cassidy western, *Secrets of the Wasteland*. She is remembered today mostly by senior citizens, if at all, for her dominating image as "the Revlon Lady" on TV.

Margaret Sullavan, the sometimes caustic ex-wife of Henry Fonda, is famous in Hollywood history for her steamy affairs with the likes of James Stewart, Humphrey Bogart, and dozens of handsome young actors and studly men, many of whom she'd pick up in her car while cruising the streets of Los Angeles and Hollywood. Although not admitting to any personal appearances within the Flag Room, Sullavan later told her biographer, Lawrence J. Quirk, that Jack was "a beautiful, beautiful man. Even in his early twenties, he had all that cocky masculine charm."

When he appeared with Mickey Rooney in *My Outlaw Brother* (1951), Stack shared his memories of Judy Garland. Robert claimed that he and Judy had always been "great chums," although many insider Hollywood gossips thought this "cute couple" were enjoying an aggressively sexual aspect of their outwardly squeaky-clean, well-publicized dates. Robert said that much of the intimacy occurred in spots other than within an actual bed. He told Rooney, "When I introduced Judy to Jack, she fell madly in love with him. It was a friendship that would last for all their lives. Even when he was in the White House, the president would call Judy in Hollywood and have her sing 'If birds fly over the rainbow, why, then oh why can't I?' those words, and not anything from *Camelot*, were his favorite lines from any song."

Lana Turner was an emerging blonde bombshell who would share her favors with both Jack and Robert—and later with Howard himself. Robert remembered her as "so vulnerable . . . so lost!"

Before they reached Catalina Island, Robert realized that both Howard and Jack were true sailors, "born to ride the waves. The men quickly bonded," he claimed. Robert said to Rock Hudson during their filming of *Written on the Wind* (1956) that he never told Jack about Howard's homosexual streak. "I figured Jack could take care of himself. Many gays had come onto him. Besides, Jack told me that his best friend was a devoted cocksucker and always finished him off for the night when he didn't score with a girl."

That reference was to LeMoyne Billings, affectionately called "Lem" by Jack. The two men were considered as bonded at the hip. Their friendship would endure throughout the course of his marriage to Jacqueline Bouvier; through countless affairs with such stars as Marilyn Monroe and Gene Tierney; and throughout the Bay of Pigs fiasco, ending only by an assassin's bullet in Dallas.

Howard and Jack struck a harmonious note with each other during their respective descriptions of their sexual conquests. At that point, the only woman that both Howard and Jack had each had some form of sexual contact with was Marlene Dietrich. "That didn't surprise me since Marlene did anything in pants or skirts, although she never got around to me," Robert said. He later admitted he felt left out of the friendship that seemed to be blossoming between Howard Hughes and JFK.

On Catalina Island, Jack wandered off for about five hours," Robert said, "so Howard and I just assumed he'd gotten lucky. We know for a fact that he boarded another yacht in the harbor. The following Sunday we went for a nude swim. I couldn't help but notice Howard checking out Jack's equipment. Of course, Howard himself had all of us beat."

Robert said that he wasn't surprised when another invitation for another weekend was extended by Howard. "This time I was excluded, and it was all right with me. I had gotten mixed up with Howard in the first place because I thought he was going to advance my career. By 1940, I'd come to realize that Howard wasn't going to do a god damn thing for me. He just wanted Hollywood's handsomest boy—namely me—to hang out with him."

"Jack told me he was going to Palm Springs for the weekend with Howard," Robert continued. "He said that Howard had promised him 'a pleasant surprise,' whatever that meant. I didn't warn Jack not to go. Why shouldn't he go? He dropped a bomb on me when he told me that Howard had convinced him that he should pursue a career as a motion picture star, even though the ambassador, Jack's father, wanted him to go into politics one day. Two days before Jack left to join Howard in Palm Springs, I noticed that he kept looking at himself in every mirror he passed. I think every good-looking guy and beautiful gal in the world dreams of becoming a movie star. Why should Jack be an exception? He said, 'I can just hear dad shouting at me: No Kennedy becomes a movie star.'"

Ironically that same line would be uttered years later by Jacqueline Kennedy to her son, John F. Kennedy Jr., when he came to her and told her the startling news that he wanted to be an actor and had actually been offered the starring role in an upcoming movie.

Howard Hughes seduced the handsome hunk **Victor Mature** *(left)*, pictured here in his most famous role in *Samson and Delilah* (1949). But Hughes' favorite was **Tyrone Power** *(right)*.

To the shock of Hollywood, Power managed to intrude on the action when JFK started dating his favorite girl of the moment, Gene Tierney.

BUT WOULD ANY OF THEM ACTUALLY <u>VOTE</u> FOR JFK?

The pin-up girl of World War II, **Betty Grable,** seduced two future U.S. presidents—both of them when they were very young and new to Hollywood.

First came Ronald Reagan—"I just called him up and asked him for a date"—and next came JFK.

Grable found Jack satisfactory as a lover and called him for another date, but he turned her down. "I couldn't get beyond the smell," JFK told Stack.

Later Grable found out that a condom had become attached to the lining of her vagina, creating a repulsive odor. She had it surgically removed.

Judy Garland (center) "adored" JFK right from their first seduction, and they became lifelong friends. In 1960, three days before his nomination as president on the Democratic ticket, Judy and JFK had sat laughing, talking, and whispering to each other at a $100-a-plate dinner with Eleanor Roosevelt.

When asked about JFK in later life, Judy said "he was the man who got away," evoking her famous song.

On separate occasions, both Robert Stack and JFK brought the perky young actress, **Barbara Britton,** to the Flag Room. Hopalong Cassidy (William Boyd), and Joel McCrea got to her before them.

JFK found it a "hoot" when Britton became more famous on TV as "The Revlon Lady" than she did for any of her movies.

As president, he once invited her to the White House for a "sleep-over," but she politely turned him down.

JKF TO HEDY LAMARR:
"YOU SAVED THE WORLD."

"I like oversexed people like Jack Kennedy. The few I knew were always talented and sensitive. I'm oversexed: and I've never kept that a secret."
　　　　　　　　　　　　　　　　　　　　　　　　　　—Hedy Lamarr

A young John F. Kennedy had always admired screen goddess Hedy Lamarr. He'd seen her scamper through the Vienna Woods, nude, in *Ecstasy* and had vowed to seduce her whenever the chance arose. She was one of the Hollywood goddesses at the top of his list.

On the night that Robert Stack introduced him to Hedy at a party in Hollywood, he asked for her phone number and called her the next day.

"It was a night of pure Ecstasy for me," he later told Stack. "She's incredibly adept in bed, a real nympho that a whole load of sailors couldn't satisfy. But I had fun until she completely exhausted me, but only after hours had gone by. She's a stunner and will do things to a man that a lot of gals won't do."

After a few more dates, JFK told Stack, "I'm very disappointed. Our love-making has been great. Some of the best pussy I've ever had. But last night she told me she can't see me any more."

"Why in hell, if you guys like balling each other so much?"

"She claimed she was falling in love with me, and knew in her heart that I would desert her. She said she couldn't stand the pain of losing me, and wanted to end it before she plunged in more deeply." Jack also told Stack, "I was standing at the door kissing her perhaps for a final time. Suddenly, I did something wild. I unzipped and asked her to give me a blowjob right in the foyer as a farewell gift. Would you believe me if I told you she obliged?"

JFK was aware that Hedy had helped the U.S. Navy during World War II, coming up with an idea for a radio-directed torpedo, a technology she'd learned sitting with her former husband, Fritz Mandl, the Austrian munitions mogul, discussing Hitler's plans for wireless communication.

Years later, when JFK was president, after the Cuban Missile Crisis, he called Hedy and thanked her for her WWII intervention. In highly exaggerated praise, the president told her, "Had it not been for you, we might have gotten our asses blown off the planet."

Hedy's biographer, Stephen Michael Shearer, in *Beautiful: The Life of Hedy Lamarr,* wrote "The missile crisis was averted in no small part because of the advancement of technology and the use of the idea behind the original Hedy Lamarr patent. The Navy was able to develop her frequency-hopping into an overall strategy for a secure communications network by using sonobuoys and surveillance drones."

This technology that originated in Hedy's beautiful head provided secure communications between ships deployed during the U.S. blockade of Castro's Cuba.

Two views of **Hedy Lamarr**
(lower photo) Running naked through the
Vienna Woods in *Ecstasy* (1933)

Howard Hughes and JFK

PRELUDE TO AN ORGY
Starring Ingrid Bergman & Marlene Dietrich

Four American icons, each with a voracious sexual appetite, are pictured above. In the pilot's seat is **Howard Hughes**; in naval uniform a young **John F. Kennedy**. Top photo *(right)* is the Swedish film star **Ingrid Bergman**, who before the end of the 1940s would be driven from the screen in disgrace because of an adulterous affair with Italian director Roberto Rossellini.

Bottom right is the sultry **Marlene Dietrich**, arguably never looking more ravishing. So far as it is known, three of these icons had same-sex contacts, albeit in Jack's case as a non-aggressive and passive participant in the encounters.

When these four personalities agreed to a rendezvous in the desert resort of Palm Springs, their weekend became the scandal of insider Hollywood.

Not all of them got high marks in the sack, however. William Heller, pioneer Hollywood publicist, said, "Two of Howard's girlfriends told me he wasn't worth a damn as a lover."

"Jack was terrible in bed," said a former lover. "He did not perceive women as human beings or even as objects of affection."

Director Alfred Hitchcock claimed Ingrid "would do it with a doorknob." Of Marlene, critic Kenneth Tynan claimed, "She had sex without gender."

HOWARD AND INGRID
AND MARLENE.....
AND JACK

In the early 1940s, John F. Kennedy and actor **Robert Stack** were two of the most desirable males in Hollywood, according to Judy Garland. "Both men and women, including Howard Hughes, pursued them."

In the summer of 1940, from a base within his Hollywood Hills apartment, Stack kept JFK supplied with a bevy of beauties. "To my regret, most of them went for Jack and not me, although in my conceited way I thought I was more handsome, even better as a swordsman."

Jack later told his friend Lem Billings, "I called Robert my libidinous buddy. He threw down the red carpet. Crossing it were beautiful stars, lovely starlets, and so-so wannabees."

Growing up in Hollywood, Stack lost his virginity at the age of sixteen to a petite redhead "with a big smile and boobs" to match. Both of them took tap-dancing lessons at the Ernst Belcher School of Dance.

After WWII, when the treasured possessions of the late Anne Frank were inventoried, among her souvenirs was an eight-by-ten glossy of Robert Stack.

Years after its passage, the details of one particular weekend in Palm Springs in the late 1940s remain sketchy. The only source of what happened was Robert Stack, who wasn't even there. He later reported that he "learned a little bit from Jack and not a lot more from Howard Hughes."

According to Stack, Howard had obviously set up the weekend to impress Jack. He seemed to bask in the flow of Jack's admiration for him. Jack had been bragging about his conquests to Howard, but the older man wanted to show the younger one that he too could round up two "hot dates" for the weekend.

Howard had flown his own plane to Palm Springs with his "two surprises." Since Hughes's invited guest Jack had not been free to travel with them at the time, Howard arranged for a long black limousine to pick him up later that day and drive him out to a desert setting where Howard either rented a villa or owned it—no one was ever certain which.

Jack later claimed to Robert that he was completely flabbergasted when he arrived at the villa to learn the identity of the two "dates" Howard had arranged. The young New Englander, it turned out, had been intimate on some level with Marlene Dietrich. "In Marlene's case, it was no big deal to get her to accept an invitation to Palm Springs," Robert said. Over the years, she became a frequent visitor to Palm Springs. George Jacobs, Sinatra's former valet, reported in his memoirs that he caught Dietrich swimming nude in his boss man's pool, kissing an equally nude Greta Garbo.

The other star was Ingrid Bergman. "I think Howard wanted to impress Jack that even though he was an older Lothario, he could still round up two world-class beauties and stars," Robert said. At the time, Howard was promising that he was going to buy a studio and make her the queen of the lot. And indeed, when he bought RKO in 1948, the first half of that promise, at least, did indeed come true.

Robert said that Jack later reported that he was confused at first "about the pair-offs." Had Howard arranged for him to pair off with Ingrid or with Marlene? At first, Jack assumed that because of the differences in the ages of this quartet, that he and Ingrid would be the young lovers, and that Howard and Marlene would be the more mature romantic duo. But right from the beginning, Howard whispered to him that he planned to seduce Ingrid himself.

Marlene, therefore, was to be Jack's date. "She was quite a bit older than me," he said. "We'd made out together on the French Riviera when I was just a kid."

He told Stack that the star's first words to him were, "It looks like we have some unfinished business," no doubt referring to their sexual tryst near Antibes years before. "I bet you've known so many women since then, and are so much more experienced," Marlene had told him.

Robert claimed that Howard's ultimate plan for the weekend had been foiled. What he'd hoped to do on the following night was arrange a four-way with Jack, Ingrid, Marlene and himself. "I think Howard voyeuristically wanted to see young Jack in action," Robert said. "From what I was told, Jack and Marlene both agreed to it."

In later life, Jack, as president, would become notorious for three-ways. But Ingrid was the lone hold-out that weekend. The woman loved sex, and plenty of it. But, as she told Howard, "I'm not into orgies." Robert also believed that Ingrid preferred not to be on the receiving end of Marlene's lesbian affection. "*That one's* [meaning Marlene] reputation has already preceded her," Ingrid told Howard.

Howard may not have been entirely pleased with Ingrid's sexual performance in Palm Springs. He was even less pleased when he learned that their notorious weekend in the desert had become the talk of Hollywood. Nonetheless, he continued to pursue Ingrid for a few weeks, but ever so discreetly. He didn't want any more scandal.

"There must have been something he liked about Ingrid," Robert said, "although he complained to me about her preference for the missionary position. From what I gathered, the Swede refused to indulge Howard in his passion for oral sex."

Even Ingrid's second husband, Roberto Rossellini, the Italian director, complained about this to several of his friends. "She doesn't do the things a whore does," Rossellini claimed, telling his cronies that she always refused to fellate him. For that, he had to go frequently to one of the bordellos of Rome or other cities.

It is not exactly certain how Howard introduced himself to Ingrid, or how he persuaded her to travel that weekend to Palm Springs. Robert didn't know. "I knew that Howard had put her at the top of his list. In those days he was going down his list, crossing off one beautiful star after another when he'd had his way with her. I think I know how they met. Howard was a friend of David O. Selznick and would later try to marry his wife, Irene Mayer Selznick, after she divorced David. I heard that Howard got himself invited to a party at the Selznick home. There Howard met Ingrid, who at the time was having an affair with Selznick. He once told me that the reason he liked Ingrid so much was 'because she was the only actress in Hollywood who didn't want to play Scarlett O'Hara.'"

After many years had gone by, Howard would resume seeing Marlene, but only briefly, in 1952. Her longtime friend, director Fritz Lang, had cast her in a Technicolor Western, *Chuck-a-Luck* for Fidelity Pictures. Howard got involved when, as chief of RKO, he agreed to release and distribute the film.

He demanded an immediate title change. He told Lang, "What movie-goer in Europe will know what in the fuck *Chuck-a-Luck* means?" Howard's new title was *Rancho Notorious*. His time with Marlene was brief. The star was by then aging, although still "a beautiful antique," as Lang described her to Howard.

After the resumption of his brief affair with Marlene, Howard informed Lang, "the thrill is gone." Their boudoir performance had been lackluster, and so were the box-office receipts on *Rancho Notorious*. Most critics found it a poor man's version of *Destry Rides Again*.

Old friends since the 1930s, Howard would never see Marlene again. "Each of them would watch the other decay from afar," said Orson Welles, who cast Marlene in a guest appearance in his 1958 film, *Touch of Evil*.

After the Palm Springs weekend, Howard continued his hopeless pursuit of Jack, who'd soon be heading back to the East Coast. Howard never got to see Jack in action with Ingrid and Marlene, but he did take him to the private studios of a tall, black, muscular masseur who called himself "Nobu." During the war years, Nobu, from some unknown country, was famous in Hollywood for his thorough massages, which involved masturbating his clients, both male and female, to the "mother of all climaxes." His patrons included Errol Flynn, Lana Turner, Paulette Goddard, Joan Crawford, and even Howard himself.

Although it later became fashionable for certain masseurs in New York and California to give massages that involved sexual climaxes, in Nobu's time no one did that except prostitutes hired for that purpose.

Jack told Robert that Howard took him to be worked over by the "magic hands" of Nobu. Both men lay nude on separate beds in Nobu's studio while sensual music played. "I got this big erection," Jack later confided to Robert. "By the time he was finished with me, I was splattering the ceiling. I've never seen anything like it. He really knows how to touch the right spots."

Although Nobu may have been a peak experience in Jack's life, other masseurs have reported that JFK always got an erection when being massaged, even by a man. Sinatra's valet, George Jacobs, wrote in his memoirs, that he gave Jack a massage in Palm Springs when he was the guest of his boss. "By the time I rolled him [meaning Jack] over to do his trunk and thighs, he had an enormous erection."

From all reports, Howard never got to experience Jack's erection first hand. Robert speculated that Howard made one attempt and failed to win Jack over. Such an occurrence may have happened during Jack's final weekend in California before his departure for the East Coast. This time Jack was picked up and delivered to a beach house in Santa Monica which was owned by Marion Davies.

"I knew Jack was looking forward to it," Robert said, referring to this final weekend during the late 40s. "He thought that Howard, as part of his ongoing campaign to impress him, would come up with two more A-list film queens. How Howard planned to top Marlene and Ingrid I don't know. But he was an amazing man. I fully anticipated that he'd have Rita Hayworth, Lana Turner, and Betty Grable there. To Jack's disappointment, when he got to Santa Monica, he found that he was the only invited guest."

"I don't know exactly what happened that weekend because Jack never told me everything." Robert said. "And Howard abruptly changed the subject a week later when I inquired."

"The following Monday morning, however, when I was telling Jack good-bye, he told me that he 'never wanted to see Howard Hughes again—that guy's too much of a creep for me.'"

The Two Hottest Dates in Town

Robert Stack and JFK in mid-1940s Hollywood

In 1946 Hollywood, the hottest two dates in town were **Robert Stack and Jack Kennedy,** or so claimed Judy Garland, who found both of these handsome young men "adorable and more." Stack served as [his words] "Jack's guide to the hottest pussies in Hollywood."

When JFK became president and saw very little of Stack, the actor talked about the time he had spent with Jack during the 1940s. "I think he inherited all this womanizing from his father, Joseph P. Kennedy. He bragged about his father's conquests—not just Gloria Swanson, everybody knew about that—but Constance Bennett, Evelyn Brent, Nancy Carroll, Betty Compson, Viola Dana, Phyllis Haver, even Marion Davies and, surprise of surprises, Greta Garbo."

Stack claimed that "Old Joe's ways rubbed off on his son. Joe sorta denigrated Rose and rubbed her nose in his affairs. I think Jack did that to Jackie, even after he got to the White House. There was a big difference, though, between Joe and Jack. After a few weeks of philandering, Joe always came back with expensive presents for Rose. Jack didn't even bring Jackie flowers."

Handsome, Rich, Horny, and On the Make in Tinseltown

In an interview, gossip maven Hedda Hopper, to **June Allyson**'s (above) annoyance, asked her, "Are your breasts real?"

June smiled demurely. "Yes, ma'am."

"America's sweetheart," as she was dubbed in the 1940s, could have brought in witnesses—including two future presidents (Ronald Reagan and JFK, and even a presidential brother-in-law, Peter Lawford) to testify.

Of Peter, June later said, "We were more girlfriends than boyfriends."

June dated JFK when he was a handsome twenty-nine year old soon-to-be congressman. He was carrying on an affair at the same time with Gene Tierney, but neither woman found out about the other one.

In the mid 1940s and early 1950s, during the debut of his acting career, the charismatic actor Robert Stack was widely acknowledged as a hip, well-connected, and very popular "swinging bachelor of Hollywood."

When Stack was joined by young Jack Kennedy during one of his so-called "pussy expeditions" to Hollywood, it was spread through the grapevine that there had suddenly emerged a second swinging bachelor on the scene, a scion of the rich and powerful Kennedy clan of Massachusetts.

For a brief chapter in his ambitious life, Stack had been a toy boy of the bisexual Hollywood mogul, Howard Hughes. But for the most part, the actor spent much of his energy seducing, one by one, the leading starlets of Hollywood. And whenever he was in town, his long-time pal, JFK, joined him in the search for beautiful women.

June Allyson, known at the time as "America's Sweetheart," met Robert Stack at a party within the home of Peter Lawford, where he was living with his parents, Sir Sidney and Lady Lawford. Stack asked for June's phone number and called her the next day for a date.

"On our first date, we made love all night," June told her frequent co-star, the gay actor Van Johnson.

Robert and June dated for two months. One night he called her and asked her if a friend of his, visiting from Boston, could accompany them on their Saturday night date. "The more the merrier," June told him. That night, Robert introduced June to the handsome young visitor, John F. Kennedy.

"I could not imagine that Jack would one day become the President of the United States," June later recalled. "When I met him, I didn't even know that his father had been ambassador to England. And, of course, I had no idea that Peter would one day become Jack's brother-in-law after marrying Patricia."

June ended up spending the entire weekend with both Stack and the future president of the United States. "It was the wildest weekend of my life," she told Van. "All three of us in the same bed. I found Jack a god-like Casanova, with tremendous sex appeal."

"I wish I could have joined you in that bed," Van told her.

"Jack could literally charm the pants off a gal," she claimed. She revealed some very personal details. The dashing young man called his penis his "implement," and seemed obsessed with sex. He wanted to enter a girl through both the back and front door. "I'd never had anal sex before until I met him," she said. "At first I resisted, but he overcame my reluctance. Frankly, it's not my favorite thing, and it hurts."

June evaluated Stack as far more romantic than JFK. "I think Jack doesn't really like women," she later said. "He wants to seduce them and then wants them out of his way while he reads and talks endlessly on the phone. He was sort of a 'Slam, Bam, Thank You, Ma'am' kind of lover. Robert told me that Jack likes the chase more than the conquest. 'He's only a plunger,' Robert said. 'Once the act is over, Jack wants to move on to the next conquest.'"

After that weekend, JFK never called June again. Or so she said at the time.

Later, after he became president, she revised her story. "Jack got very serious over me. Before he married Jacqueline, he proposed marriage to me. I turned him down, preferring to stay married to Richard." [She referred to Dick Powell as "Richard." She had long since married Powell by the time Kennedy became president.]

"I know I broke Jack's heart," June later claimed, perhaps falsely. "He married Jackie on the rebound. She was definitely his second choice. I was the first choice. He told me that repeatedly. Perhaps it's just as well. Jackie made a far better First Lady than I ever could."

June, who later in life bedded Ronald Reagan after his breakup from actress Jane Wyman, had a unique perspective in her comparison of the lovemaking techniques of two future U.S. presidents. She was a bit coy in her "between the sheets" descriptions of the two fabled politicians.

"Neither would ever be what is called a great lover," she told Peter Lawford. "But both of them were the cleanest men I've ever encountered. Jack insisted on taking five showers a day. Ronald took at least three, one when he got up in the morning. He always insisted on having a shower before sex and after sex. Ronnie told me that sexual smells linger on the human body, and 'I don't want to leave your bedchamber smelling like I've just visited a cathouse.'"

Robert Stack *(left)* formed an immediate friendship with young **John F. Kennedy** when he first arrived in Hollywood.

Stack jokingly said, "Jack was the only man in Tinseltown better looking than me, and all the hot tamales on the West Coast took notice. He really needed a date book. I've known him to have sex in the afternoon with a woman, sex at cocktail time, sex after dinner, and even a sleepover after midnight. Each each with a different woman."

"Most of the great male stars of Hollywood, including Clark Gable, have passed through my life," Stack said. "Gable was a man's man, but liked a lot of different women on the side. But he was nothing compared to Jack. I was also introduced to Bobby Kennedy, but he didn't need the number of gals Jack did. One gal a day was enough for Bobby."

LAURA
JFK's Girlfriend Got It Right; Radziwill Bombed

"Sometimes I think Jack was making love not to me, but to Laura," said **Gene Tierney**, pictured above in a tense scene with **Dana Andrews** from her most famous movie, *Laura*.

Jennifer Jones had turned down the 1944 role, but Darryl F. Zanuck at Fox convinced Gene to film *Laura* as her comeback picture after she'd taken a year off because of her pregnancy.

When Jones saw *Laura*, she said, "God damn it, I turned down the role of a lifetime to give to Buck Teeth"

Author **Truman Capote**, at the time a close friend of Lee Radziwill, told Robert Stack that as an actress, "The Princess is a natural. It will be the casting coup of the year. Your ratings will be celestial."

Capote was supposed to have written the screenplay, but after his enthusiastic endorsement of Lee, he fled the scene, breaking all his commitments. Lee was furious.

He was later seen in the intimate company of a six-foot, four-inch, very good-looking black man on one of the Out Islands of The Bahamas.

"Perhaps he knew somthing about the film that the rest of us didn't," Stack concluded.

Robert Stack had the dubious honor of reprising the overly romantic detective role, the one originally played by Dana Andrews, in two different remakes of *Laura*. The first of these was for a made-for-TV version.

When Fox executives saw the final version of the first reprise, they realized that they had crafted merely a cheesy version of the 1944 original, and opted to re-release the original.

Amazingly, Stack went on to film yet a second version of *Laura*, this one starring Jackie's sister, Lee Radziwill, in the Gene Tierney role

(photo, left)

In the second re-creation of *Laura*, **Farley Granger** embraces **Lee Radziwill**.

According to Stack, the princess told him that he kissed better than Farley. "Of course I do," said Stack. "I'm into women. I'm not much of a cocksucker like Farley, although I don't have anything against it."

When he saw the finished version of the film, Stack said, "I don't think Godzilla at his worst could have broken down Princess Radziwill's café-society cool. In one scene, after twenty-two botched takes, I lost my voice, since it called for shouting...Lee sounded like she was reading 'the gray cat jumped over the spotted dog.'" *(Photofest)*

JFK's Affair with Sonja Henie

Skating on Thin Ice with a Nazi Collaborator

Sonja Henie

Queen of the Ice

Norwegian-born **Sonja Henie** (1912-1969) won the World Figure Skating Championship at the age of 11, and followed with gold medals at the 1928, 1932, and 1936 Olympics. She eventually went to Hollywood, where she skated so brilliantly in movies that few noticed that she could act.

Perky, blonde, blue-eyed and a Nordic beauty of sorts, she delivered her lines stiffly. But American audiences in the late 1930s and 40s found her appealing. Perhaps that was because they didn't know her that well. Those who knew her intimately claimed that she was possessed by an insatiable passion for money, diamonds, furs, and men.

Her sexual conquests ranged from a matinee idol politician (JFK) to a real matinee idol, Tyrone Power. She knew three husbands and dozens of lovers, including every man from bigtime stars to the lowest extras. She told Ethel Merman, with whom she starred in the 1938 *Happy Landing*, "I don't care what a man does for a living, just so long as he packs the right tool in his trousers."

51

SNOW QUEEN NYMPHO TAKES BERLIN, THEN HOLLYWOOD

Associated Press

In Berlin in the 1930s, Sonja Henie dazzled the Nazi high command, especially Adolf Hitler himself. To him, she represented the feminine ideal of the Nordic woman. At her first exhibition in 1932 in front of **Adolf Hitler** (*central figure, above*) and Nazi propaganda minister **Josef Goebbels** (*right figure, above*) in a skating exhibition, she'd shouted HEIL HITLER!

The reaction to that in her native Norway was so violent that she subdued herself when she appeared once again before Hitler at the Berlin Olympics in 1936.

Publicly, at least, she was much more subdued during other presentations in front of the Führer, although Hitler had personally called her and wished her luck. Sonja won many medals prior to her migration to Hollywood, and no one cheered louder than the Führer.

Before leaving the World Championship Competition, Sonja visited Hitler's Eagle Nest for an intimate lunch. Rumors reached Norway the next week that Sonja had come sexually intimate with Hitler.

The stigma of that allegation would remain with her throughout the rest of her life. In fact, many Norwegians referred to her as "a female Quisling."

When John F. Kennedy met the ice-skating champion, Sonja Henie, she was a ripe thirty-six and he was only twenty-nine. Just after World War II, the blonde Norwegian beauty was to ice skating what Esther Williams was to swimming.

Although she couldn't act, she became a movie star. She could skate, however, as proven by her winning gold medals at the 1928, 1932, and 1936 Olympic Games.

Jack was immediately fascinated by her Nordic charms, "I didn't have to seduce her; she seduced me," he told his best pal, a jealous Lem Billings.

When Jack first met Sonja, her career was starting to fade, although she had made a number of box office hits during the war years. But her most recent film, *It's a Pleasure* (1945), had bombed, even though it was the only feature film ever shot of her in color.

What she didn't tell her hot-to-trot new beau was that in the 1930s she'd sustained a brief but torrid fling with his father, Joseph Kennedy.

Jack later confided to actor Robert Stack, "Sonja is a great fuck, sexily adaptable to any position requested. Because of all that ice skating, she's developed vaginal muscles from hell. She not only drives a man wild, she drains him dry. Give her some Norwegian aquavit, and she becomes a dynamo in bed."

Sonja's devastatingly handsome lover, actor Tyrone Power, agreed. He'd had a torrid affair with her when they'd co-starred together in *Thin Ice* in 1937. He even bragged to a jealous future lover, Lana Turner, about Sonja's vaginal muscles.

Milton Sperling, a Hollywood screenwriter, remembered Sonja and Tyrone on the set of *Thin Ice*. "They were conducting a love affair throughout the filming," he claimed. "It was almost impossible to pry them out of her dressing room. When we did get them to the set, Ty always looked like he was about to collapse. She was one of the most voracious sexy broads in Hollywood, and really loved to fuck."

Tyrone and Sonja even adopted nicknames for their genital parts. She called her vagina "Betsy," and he nick-named his penis "Jimmy." But during her affair with JFK, she called her vagina "Sally" and labeled his penis "Wolfgang" for reasons not immediately apparent.

Her other affairs ranged from Desi Arnaz to the famous Hollywood attorney Greg Bautzer, from crooner Dick Haymes to Van Johnson (even though he was gay). She once announced to the press that she and Liberace had fallen in love and were about to be married. Other lovers included many ice-skaters, ski instructors, and studio employees at 20th Century Fox.

Sonja's producer, Darryl F. Zanuck of Fox, chastised her for slowing down production while she conducted an affair with a studio grip. "It is the irresistible lure of making love to a star that has him under my spell," she claimed. Zanuck himself tried her out. He, too, experienced "Hollywood's most powerful vaginal muscles. Slap some keys on her and we'll have a grand piano."

By the time Sonja hit the hay with JFK, she was far more experienced than she'd been when Tyrone seduced her.

When 20th Century Fox cast **Sonja** in *One in a Million*, she quickly developed a reputation at the studio for being "a bitch." Any time anyone criticized her, she attacked them for being "jealous" of her ability.

When studio head Darryl F. Zanuck saw the first rushes, he feared he had thrown away a million dollars launching a star with no talent. "But the cunt can skate, so I ordered the director to have her spend more time on ice," Zanuck claimed.

One day a rising young star, Tyrone Power, came onto the set. She called him "the most gorgeous man I've ever seen." He was linked to such Hollywood stars as Loretta Young, Alice Faye, Betty Grable, and Lana Turner. "I will make him forget all those cows," she told Zanuck. What Zanuck didn't' tell lovesick Sonja was that every day during their steambath together, he was already letting the bisexual actor "go down on my big pole. He can do it without choking."

Having heard of the Sonja/Jack romance, Tyrone met Jack at a party. "I understand you're going for my sloppy seconds."

"That's right," Jack shot back. "I never did like to break hymens—a messy affair."

After that, Tyrone and Jack became better acquainted.

When Joe Kennedy learned of Jack's affair with the ice-skating queen, he called him at once, demanding that he break up with the star. "Drop her at once," Joe told his son. "It's the Nazi thing."

That afternoon Jack learned more about Sonja's involvement with Adolf Hitler. She first met him in Berlin after her performance in a 1936 ice-skating exhibition attended by Hitler, Hermann Göring, and Josef Goebbels. The show was a prelude to the 1936 Winter Olympics. Minutes before she entered the arena, she was informed of the Nazi Leader's presence in the audience.

With the spotlight on her, she skated over to Hitler's party, coming to an ice-spraying stop in front of the Führer's box. She gave him the Nazi salute and proclaimed HEIL HITLER. The all-German audience rose in thunderous applause.

Hitler stood up and tossed her a kiss. She later dined with him at his Eagle's Nest in Berchtesgaden. She accepted his autographed portrait from a *Führer* who considered her "the perfect embodiment of a Nordic woman."

Even after migrating to Hollywood, Henie kept up her Nazi connections, arranging with Goebbels for the release, in Germany, of her first film, *One in a Million* (1937). Made by 20th Century Fox, it co-starred Don Ameche and the Ritz Brothers.

Returning to Oslo in 1936, Sonja was greeted with the headline: IS SONJA A NAZI?

In response, she said, "*Nazi-schmatzy*, I don't even know what a Nazi is." Her friendship with Hitler, such as it was, lasted until the Nazi invasion of her homeland of Norway.

When the Nazis occupied Norway, dozens of Nazi administrators witnessed the family's prominently displayed autographed photo of Hitler. None of the real estate owned by the Henie family was confiscated or damaged by Nazi troops.

Despite these links, in 1941, Henie became a naturalized citizen of the United States, partly because she was unpopular with the occupied Norwegians who resented her pro-Hitler stance. During the war, she never made an effort to support the Norwegian resistance movement, and she never took a public stand against the Nazis.

JFK was not aware of her link to Hitler. But he promised his father that he'd "drop the bitch at once," and he did. But he lamented, "I don't think I'll ever encounter vaginal pelvic muscles like that ever again.

"I know," Joe said nostalgically. That was the first indication Jack had that his father, years before, had melted The Queen of Ice.

Even though she was a rich woman, Sonja appreciated a piece of jewelry at the end of an affair, regardless of how brief it had been. When Jack told her he couldn't see her again, she demanded a "trinket" for the affection she'd shown him. After his exit from her life, he never sent her anything, not even a postcard.

Sonja later recalled that Jack Kennedy seemed in a "rush to have it all before he died, because he feared he would die young." He explained to her that for most of his life, he'd been the puny one of the family and was constantly in bed looking out the window as his siblings played touch football.

"He told me, 'I want to get it all in while the getting's good.' He said he had rather die than be trapped for years in a wheelchair being pushed around Palm Beach. Regrettably, his father did end up in a wheelchair unable to speak."

Marshall Beard, one of Sonja's skating partners, summed up her character. "She was miserably greedy. She could get down and dirty better than any woman I ever met in my life. She had the balls of a brass monkey. She once told me that she planned to marry Jack and, perhaps, one day, 'inherit the Kennedy millions.' Instead she latched onto the Norwegian multi-millionaire, Niels Onstad."

Sonja Henie
Goes to Hollywood

Sonja Henie Tyrone Power

THIN ICE

At a party in Beverly Hills, **Sonja Henie**, world acclaimed ice skater and movie star, came face-to-face with young John F. Kennedy. Though he was a bit puny by her usual standards, his boyish quality appealed to her. She also found him "young, eager for love, and with a certain sexy appeal."

They spent the first five minutes talking about Joe Kennedy, whom Henie had met before in New York. She expressed her great admiration for his father. Jack seemed thrilled that a bigtime star and Olympic athlete would be so obviously taken with him. Both Henie and Jack were extremely flirtatious with each other.

Joe Kennedy told young JFK that if Sonja ever became a Hollywood star she would need his expertise as a producer and mentor. Sonja told Joe, Sr., "I'm told that Hollywood is full of sharks, and I'm likely to be devoured."

A keen judge of women, Joe quickly retorted, "That will never happen to you. No shark would dare swim near you."

Joe unceremoniously dropped her when he decided that she was nothing but a gold-digger. "With that accent she won't make it in Hollywood," he said. When he heard that Sonja was later mocking his sexual prowess, he called Darryl F. Zanuck at Fox.

"Old Joe could out bitch a bitch," Zanuck recalled. "He warned me that Henie would be a box office liability and he told me if I used her at all, I should give her the lowest salary and never more than third billing."

"Put Alice Faye and Tyrone Power in the leads and bring Sonja on only for the skating," Joe said, vindictively. "That she can do. You can fuck her if you want to, but if you do, know that you're taking Hitler's sloppy seconds."

Ice Queen Sonja Henie warms up **Tyrone Power** in
Thin Ice (1937)

"He fucked me the first day he came onto the set of *One in a Million*," Sonja claimed. "He was a big star, Tyrone Power, and I was on my way to becoming the Queen of Fox. Why waste time?"

Her brother, Leif Henie said, "Power invited her to lunch, and they began a torrid affair. They saw each other before shooting in the mornings, at lunch, during breaks, and after work. Sonja felt no need to sit patiently through the preliminaries of courtship. When she saw something she wanted, she wanted it right away."

The title was apt when Sonja was cast opposite Tyrone once again in *Second Fiddle* (1939). Tyrone was already involved in affairs with Howard Hughes, Errol Flynn, and the French actress, Anabella, who would later become his wife. He told Sonja that he was in love with another, but "I always want to be your friend."

She would later say privately, "He threw me for another woman. In spite of that, I will always love him. In fact, he is the only man I've ever loved."

Associated Press

Although **Sonja**, on the extreme right of the photo above, at first looks like she's leading a troupe of Nazi storm troopers, appearances are deceiving. In Lake Placid, New York, on February 4, 1932, she lead the Norwegian contingent as they paraded past the reviewing stand. This was one of the opening exercises for that year's Winter Olympics.

Rumor spread quickly that she'd performed fellatio on eight of the handsomest of Norway's athletes. She called in a reporter, claiming, "The press is outrageous to me. Rumors but worse. Downright libel! Word is spreading across the American continent making me look like a whore. Everyone is jealous of my success—hence, all these lies. I'm a virgin."

Actually, she'd lost her virginity to Jackie Dunn, a young British skater whom she considered marrying. Jackie was ruggedly handsome and, from all reports, very well built in the right places. His handsome face and dark hair bore a strong resemblance to Tyrone Power, who would in the future figure so prominently in Sonja's romantic life.

Sonja made a big mistake with Dunn. After coming to America, she skated with him for two years. One night she introduced him to her other lover, Tyrone. Later, to her regret, she learned that Tyrone and Dunn had disappeared to Palm Springs. together. "They look so much alike," Sonja told Don Ameche, her co-star in *One in a Million*. "It must be like making love to yourself."

Dunn died of rabbit fever in 1939, which broke the hearts of both Sonja and Tyrone.

Hollywood Actors at War

For the Command of *PT 109*

Hollywood Dragon-Diva,
Miss Joan Crawford

PT 109 Commander JFK in 1943

"Would you like to fuck a returning naval hero?" **John F. Kennedy** in a self-mocking tone asked **Joan Crawford** after his return to Hollywood after a long absence. He'd long ago been introduced to the star by his father. Imitating Mae West, she invited him to "come up and see me sometime."

"How about at eight sharp?" he asked.

"It's a deal, big boy," she said. "But don't wear any underwear."

In this grainy, blurred photograph from 1943, John F. Kennedy *(far right)* is seen sailing the cobalt blue waters around the Solomon Islands in the South Pacific on August 2, 1943. Little did he know that his heroism as commander of a dozen men aboard United States Patrol Torpedo Boat 109 would one day help propel him into the role of President of the United States after the election of 1960.

Suddenly, seemingly out of nowhere, a Japanese destroyer emerged in the dark waters off Kolombangara Island. The destroyer rammed PT 109, virtually cutting it in half.

The day before, JFK had written to his brother Bobby, "The fun goes out of war in a fairly short time." After the sinking of his small plywood vessel, he later recalled, "Now I know what it's like to be killed."

THE COURSE OF WORLD HISTORY MIGHT HAVE CHANGED THAT NIGHT

Two of JFK's crew were killed instantly in the collision, their bodies never found. With six crew members, JFK clung to the hull of his PT 109. Then he swam out to lead survivors back to the floating wreck. He also towed Pat (Pappy) McMahon back to the hull. He was the boat's engineer and was seriously burned. Finally, JFK dived into the murky waters to rescue two more of his men.

After about nine hours of staying afloat, JFK led his men on a five-hour swim to the deserted Plum Pudding Island. Swimming on his stomach, Jack towed the wounded McMahon by clenching the ties of his life jacket (known at the time as a "Mae West") between his teeth, the engineer floating on his back. Finally after they swan to the larger Olasana Island nearby, they found two native islanders.

JFK scrawled a message on a coconut: NATIVE KNOWS POSIT. HE CAN PILOT 11 ALIVE NEED SMALL BOAT KENNEDY. He told the natives, "Rendova, Rendova," the site of the nearest PT base.

Thus, the future President of the United States was rescued, and history was made.

Partly as a means of glorifying the family name, and partly as a public relations lure in the political packaging of his son, Joseph P. Kennedy wanted a film made about the heroic exploits of his son in command of a gunboat that was fired upon in 1943 by the Japanese in the Pacific. Long a veteran of the Hollywood scene, Joe worked relentlessly to bring the story of his son's exploits—real or imagined—to the screen. "America loves a military hero," he told Hollywood producers.

Paul Newman became intrigued with the idea of playing JFK against the backdrop of the American campaign in the Pacific. It brought back memories of his own less-than-heroic service in the Navy.

Using his connection with JFK's close friend, Robert Stack, Newman arranged a meeting between the president and himself when JFK flew into Los Angeles. The president had a very rushed schedule, which included a rendezvous with Marilyn Monroe. Out of loyalty to Stack, Kennedy agreed to meet with Newman, but he could only grant him an audience of fifteen minutes.

The Secret Service ushered Newman and Stack into Kenedy's suite, where the relatively young, handsome president greeted Newman warmly and embraced his long-time friend, Stack. Newman was only mildly surprised when the two men kissed each other on their cheeks a total of four times.

Kennedy talked briefly about his wartime mission, which he hoped the film would dramatize. "You're handsome enough to play me," Kennedy said to Newman. "Everybody in the press writes about how good looking I am. Actually, the best looking guy in the family was Joe Jr. He had not just me, but my brothers beat on all counts. Dad would have run him for president if he hadn't been killed."

He was referring to Joseph P. Kennedy Jr., the eldest of the nine children born to Joseph and Rose Kennedy. The president's brother died on August 12, 1944 in a doomed flight during

World War II known as "Operation Aphrodite."

Newman later told friends that he was almost certain that the role of JFK was his. The next day the president called Stack with the bad news. "I don't want Newman to play me," JFK said to Stack. "Definitely not. There are two problems here. First, Newman is far too old for the part. Maybe if they did a movie about Dad, that would be different. Actually, Jackie wants Warren Beatty in the role. You know how she's always getting crushes on movie stars. There's another reason. I hesitate to bring it up. Newman looks too Jewish, not Irish at all. He just wouldn't do. Convey my apologies to him, would you?"

The popular singer, Edd Byrnes, was considered, even Peter Fonda, before the Kennedys decided on Cliff Robertson. As for playing a twenty-six-year-old JFK, Robertson was born in 1925, the same year as Newman. On hearing that his "forever competition," Robertson, had contracted for the part, Newman was furious.

He got over his anger when he saw a screening of *PT 109*, "What a disaster!" he said. Actually, he'd walked out of the film about half an hour before it ended.

Long after the film's release, the mystery about the whereabouts of PT 109 continued to intrigue explorers. Robert Ballard, the discoverer of the *Titanic*, set out to find the wreck somewhere on the Pacific Ocean's floor.

In 2002, using maps, historical accounts of the sinking, sophisticated sonars, and probes of the seabed, he eventually found the bow, but not the stern, lying 1,200 feet below the ocean's surface.

Navy historians later confirmed that the wreckage came from a PT boat, most likely JFK's PT 109.

Later, after days combing through the Solomon Islands in a dugout canoe, Ballard encountered the two islanders—Biuku Gasa and Eroni Kumana—who had discovered JFK's starving crew.

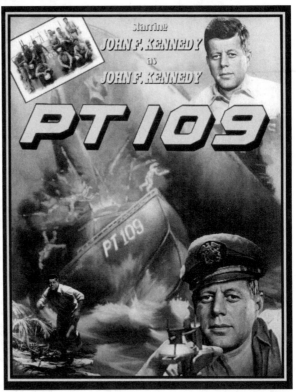

PT 109, a 140-minute biography and war drama, was released across America on June 19, 1963.

Around six months before he died, JFK as president saw it twelve times. The advertisement replicated above was completely misleading, claiming that the film "starred" John F. Kennedy playing himself.

Actually, it was Cliff Robertson who starred as JFK, the patrol boat's commander.

The 1943 patrol boats were actually about 85 feet long. PT 109 had been engaged in continual combat for five months when the young JFK took command. It was not the derelict, inoperative hulk depicted in the movie.

In the film, the vessel was painted gray; but actually it was painted dark green when JFK commanded it. That way, the boat could be camouflaged when it was moored along the bushes of the shoreline during daylight.

BUT WHICH ACTOR WAS GOOD-LOOKING ENOUGH FOR THE ROLE OF JFK?

Paul Newman (*upper left*) lost out on the coveted role of JFK, the part going to **Cliff Robertson** (*upper center*), although Jackie wanted **Warren Beatty** (*upper right*), on whom she had a crush. **Peter Fonda** (*lower right*) was briefly considered because he resembled the young JFK in both looks and build.

Edd ("Kookie") Byrnes is the only actor rejected who protested openly about the casting. "I lost out on PT 109, because, thanks to Kookie, I was typecast. (Edd's role as the jive-talking, hair-combing "Kookie" on TV's *77 Sunset Strip* had made him television's first teen idol.)

"I studied long and hard trying to perfect Jack Kennedy's Boston accent. I thought I gave a very good test. I really looked and sounded like a young JFK. Then I heard through the grapevine that President Kennedy had called from Washington to Jack Warner's office stating 'I don't want Kookie to play me.' He obviously knew me from the series, and he didn't want to be associated with my character."

The lower center photo represents Hollywood's casting of JFK's torpedo boat crew, with Cliff Robertson in command. **Robert Culp** played JFK's good friend, Ensign George Ross. **Ty Hardin** was cast as Ensign Leonard J. Thorn. Later in life he, too, would pursue a "political" career, but a bizarre one.

Years after his experience aboard PT 109, Hardin formed a militia group known as the Arizona Patriots, which taught that the sovereignty of the people was supreme and that citizens were not bound by the rules or regulations of any government. The group advocated stockpiling weapons and ammunition to protect people from the government, including the Internal Revenue Service.

Robert Blake was cast in the film as Charles ("Bucky") Harris. On March 16, 2005, Blake was found not guilty of the murder of Bonnie Lee Bakley, his wife, and not guilty of one of two counts of solicitation of murder. The other count was dropped after it was revealed that the jury was deadlocked 11-1 in favor of an acquittal.

Los Angeles District Attorney Steve Cooley, called Blake "a miserable human being" and the jurors "incredibly stupid."

Blake was forced into bankruptcy when Bakley's three children filed a civil suit against him. Initially they won a judgment of $30 million, which was cut in half to $15 million on appeal.

Peggy Cummins and JFK

Marital Yearnings of a B-List Hollywood Actress

In 1940, the bisexual mogul Howard Hughes pursued JFK in an attempt to seduce the handsome young man. But the aviator struck out.

Ironically, when **JFK** returned to Hollywood after the war, he found himself competing against Hughes for the attention of a blonde beauty, British actress **Peggy Cummins.**

At the age of fifteen, she'd made her movie debut in *Dr. O'Dowd* (1940), shot in London.

She didn't attract the attention of either JFK or Hughes until both of them (separately) had seen *English Without Tears* in 1944, a movie Cummins had made with Lilli Palmer (future wife of Rex Harrison) and Michael Wilding (future husband of Elizabeth Taylor).

She had several suitors in Hollywood and dated from the A-list. Her beaux included Huntington Hartford, the heir to the A&P supermarket fortune. He told Cummins, "If you marry me, you'll never go hungry again," like that promise Scarlett O'Hara made to herself in *Gone With the Wind.*

"Peggy sure dated high on the hog," said columnist Sheila Graham at a party, "Both Hartford and Hughes, two of the richest men in the world. And I hear that horny upstart, John F. Kennedy, son of that bastard, old Joe Kennedy, ain't exactly po'."

Although well known in England, **Peggy Cummins** *(two photos above)*, who once aroused sexual interest in JFK, is known mainly today for her portrayal as a gun moll in the 1950 film *Gun Crazy*. Its original title was *Deadly Is the Female*.

In it, she starred opposite **John Dall**, who is also remembered for interpreting the role of a homosexual killer in Alfred Hitchcock's film *Rope* (1948).

Dall first came to the attention of movie goers when he starred opposite Bette Davis in *The Corn Is Green* (1945). Dall and Cummins played the Depression-era bandits, Bart Tare and Laurie Starr, who were modeled on the infamous Clyde Barrow and Bonnie Parker.

"JFK Just Isn't the Marrying Kind"

In 1946, with a gleam in his eye and fresh from the battles of World War II, a handsome young Navy lieutenant arrived for a return visit to Hollywood. He told best pal Chuck Spalding, "I'm not here on a hunt for sex *per se*. I'm here to knock a name."

When Spalding asked for a translation, Jack said, "That means I want to knock up A-list actresses like Lana Turner, Joan Crawford, and Gene Tierney."

Eventually, Jack inaugurated sexual flings with all three of those screen beauties, and also found time to work in an affair with Peggy Cummins, a beautiful Welsh-born actress.

Today, Peggy is best known to movie buffs for her starring role in *Gun Crazy* (1949), in which she played a trigger-happy *femme fatale* who robs banks with her accomplice, as played by John Dall. Call it an early version of *Bonnie and Clyde*.

When Jack first met Peggy, she was recovering from the wounds inflicted upon her by Darryl F. Zanuck of 20th Century Fox, who fired her after she'd been cast as Amber in the Kathleen Winsor best-selling bodice ripper *Forever Amber*. Zanuck dismissed Peggy as being too young and not sexy enough.

Jack found her plenty sexy, but not willing to jump in the hay. "What is it with these gals from Wales? She's the only one I've met so far that wears a chastity belt."

"Peggy Cummins and Jack Kennedy are a surprise twosome around town during the Congressman from Boston's visit here," wrote columnist Sheila Graham, former lover of novelist F. Scott Fitzgerald.

As JFK admitted to his pal, actor Robert Stack, "I'm in Hollywood for sex, not searching for a bride."

Stack said, "Jack was just a care-free, happy-to-lucky kind of guy in those days. Peggy—and I could be wrong about this—was focusing on rose-covered cottages and settling down with a handsome beau. Jack was perhaps the greatest catch of the year in Hollywood of 1946. But marriage was the last thing on his mind. He was just sampling the wares out here on the coast."

If Jack was hoping for a quick roll in the hay with Peggy, he was disappointed. She was well bred and well educated. But she was not the type to jump into bed. From all reports, she was holding out for a wedding ring.

Betty Spalding, a friend of Peggy's, was an eyewitness to the romance. She suspected that Jack was interested in pursuing Peggy only as long as it might be possible to seduce her.

In Nigel Hamilton's *JFK Reckless Youth,* Betty claimed, "She was just a girl to date. Jack was quite thin and sickly at that time and he got out of Boston, deliberately, because he didn't want to be sucked into paying off a lot of election debts. He never had any money with him, and he was very tight with his money, too. He was parsimonious. Just a funny habit he had. I have no idea why this was so."

While in Hollywood pursuing Cummins, Jack also went to several homosexual parties. Back on the East Coast, his best friend, Lem Billings, was still in love with him. But he also enjoyed gay gatherings in Los Angeles.

"Jack may have been a phenomenal womanizer, but I think he felt quite comfortable in the company of homosexuals, as long as they were smart enough to hold his interest," said Gore Vidal.

"He mainly went to homosexual parties because he was narcissistic," said gay actor Clifton Webb. "At these parties, he was treated like the biggest movie star there ever was. He loved hearing directors and other actors tell him, 'You should be in pictures. After all, your father did well in Hollywood.' At many of these gatherings, often on a Sunday afternoon at some Beverly Hills mansion, he was often propositioned. I never saw him go off with any man, but frankly, I think he really liked being the center of attention. In some respects, he was just like the future Marilyn Monroe entering a crowded room and wanting to be noticed."

Eventually, Peggy sadly came to realize that Jack was not the marrying kind, at least not where she was concerned. "I don't plan to get married until 1960, perhaps to Barbara Hutton or Doris Duke," he said. "Neither of those two rich old bags will be marrying me for my money."

Stack, rightly or wrongly, claimed that what really drove the nail into the coffin of the Kennedy/Cummins affair "was the night he bragged to Peggy that he'd fucked Sonja Henie."

Reportedly, Peggy once told a friend that, "Jack never sent a box of candy, not even some flowers. Even though he seemed like a little boy at the time, he had big plans."

Eventually Peggy confided to friends that she feared Jack did not think her a worthy candidate for marriage. She might have been in love with him at the time.

"Jack wasn't in love with Peggy," Stack claimed. "He was in love with life."

Many movie stars or starlets were eager to go to bed with young JFK when he hit Hollywood in 1940 and again in 1946. "It was his charm and his boyish looks," confessed Gene Tierney. "But he was a sort of slam, bam, thank you ma'am type of lover, unlike Oleg Cassini."

Jack formed a close friendship with a Yale athlete, Henry James, who gave Nigel Hamilton a detailed interview in his 1992 book entitled *JFK Reckless Youth.*

JFK confessed to James, "I'm not interested—once I get a woman, I'm not interested in carrying on, for the most part. I like the conquest."

James claimed, "I think Jack had far more of the feminine in him than he'd ever admit. He was not real macho. He pretended to be. All this chasing after women was compensation for something that he hadn't got. He was very narcissistic, which is characteristic of a gay person—incredibly so."

JFK AND THE BOMBSHELL FROM BUDAPEST

Among the notches drilled into Jack Kennedy's belt in the months preceding his marriage to Jacqueline Lee Bouvier was Zsa Zsa Gabor. Before Paris Hilton, there was her step-great-grandmother.

She was a witty and ravishing blonde beauty who married nine times and made a multi-million dollar fortune and lurid headlines generated by her many affairs, including one with Porfirio Rubirosa, the heavy-hung "Playboy of the Western World."

Ironically, one of Zsa Zsa's affairs that managed to avoid a lot of publicity at the time involved sexual trysts with a young Jack Kennedy during the early 1950s.

"There was never any talk of marriage." Zsa Zsa claimed. "Joe Kennedy wanted his handsome young son to become president. There was no way that Joe would consider me a suitable bride or a future First Lady."

On June 14, 1952, Zsa Zsa found herself sitting in the first-class compartment of an Air France plane leaving from Paris' Orly Airport heading for Boston.

"A young girl, sort of prim and proper, had the seat opposite me," Zsa Zsa said. "She rudely kept staring at me throughout most of the flight. She wasn't very attractive and had this kinky hair and bad skin. As the hours dragged on, she finally got up the courage to speak to me. She complimented me on the beauty of my porcelain skin, and had the nerve to ask me how I took care of it. There was no way in hell I was going to give her my beauty secrets. Because I was Zsa Zsa, the customs men cleared me at once—not this ugly little duckling with the pimpled skin. To my surprise, I found Jack in the waiting room. He rushed to me, hugged me, and lifted me off the ground. Obviously, he wasn't in back pain that day."

"Oh, *dollink,*" Zsa Zsa said to him. "You seem in the mood for a repeat performance." She was referring to his seduction of her during his previous visit to Hollywood.

"Can't now," Jack told her, "But I'd love to. You'll always be my sweetheart. You know I've always been in love with you."

"At that moment, the Little Wren from the airplane appeared," Zsa Zsa said.

"Zsa Zsa, I want you to meet my *fiancée,* Jacqueline Bouvier. Jackie, this is Zsa Zsa Gabor, the best thing to come out of Hungary since goulash."

"I'm honored, I'm sure," Jackie said in a tiny, almost meek voice.

"Miss Bouvier shot daggers at me," Zsa Zsa claimed. "For the first time, I think she realized that I had been having an affair with her future husband. I told Jack what a beautiful girl he had. I also warned him, 'Don't you corrupt her morals.'"

Jackie looked straight into Zsa Zsa's eyes. With a little smirk, she replied, "He's already been there, done that."

As Zsa Zsa entered the valley of the shadow of death in 2011, her last husband, Frederic Prinz von Anhalt, showed prospective buyers around her 28-room Bel Air mansion.

He stopped in the living room and pointed out an oil painting of an olive-colored satin canopied bed. "That was the site of most of her great love affairs." the prince said, "Her first seduction in that bed was of a young man named John F. Kennedy."

Zsa Zsa Gabor

Gene Tierney

Rejected In Her Bid for the Role of First Lady

"I had heard in New York that the casting couch was a way of life in Hollywood; it posed no threat to me."

At least that is what the beautiful **Gene Tierney** (1920-1991) said. Ironically, at 20th Century Fox, she landed on the couch of studio head Darryl F. Zanuck.

The screenwriter and director Joseph L. Mankiewicz also chased and caught up with her. She was passed around from actor to actor, including Kirk Douglas ("I left my bedroom window open so he could sneak in"). She was pursued by the aviation and cinema mogul Howard Hughes. Playboy Prince Aly Khan went for her but ultimately settled for Rita Hayworth.

Lining up at her bedroom door were pint-sized Mickey Rooney, Greek God Tyrone Power; and suave George Sanders when Zsa Zsa Gabor didn't occupy his nights. When Spencer Tracy starred with her in *Plymouth Adventure* (1932), he said: "Although she was beautiful in her films, they couldn't quite capture all of her. Fortunately I did, even if it was late in my life."

"Of them all, I had the most bittersweet memories of a young naval lieutenant, JFK," she recalled.

Gene Tierney will be forever remembered as the beauty in *Laura* (1944), the most famous of her 36 films.

She also played the unwashed Ellie May in *Tobacco Road* (1941), the murderous Ellen Berent in *Leave Her to Heaven* (1945). She starred with and seduced many of her leading men, including Henry Fonda, Humphrey Bogart, and Rex Harrison.

She was famously married to fashion designer Oleg Cassini, who once proposed marriage to Jackie Kennedy.

Tumbling into mental illness, Gene recalled her stay in a hospital: "I was wrapped from the neck down in icy bedsheets, my arms strapped to my sides. Tears poured down my cheeks. I couldn't move. I lost the feeling in my hands and feet. My mind was in a panic."

TIERNEY:

HER ROLLERCOASTER RIDE FROM THE PINNACLE TO THE DEPTHS

On the set of the 1946 movie, *Dragonwyck*, the directorial debut of Joseph L. Mankiewicz, its star, the very beautiful (in spite of her overbite) Gene Tierney looked up.

In her own words, she claimed, "I turned and found myself staring into the most perfect blue eyes I had ever seen on a man. He smiled at me. My reaction was right out of a ladies' romance novel. Literally, my heart skipped. A coy thought flashed through my mind: I was glad I had worn a lavender gown for my scene that day. Lavender was my best color."

Thus, began the romance of a young JFK, who at the time was out of the Navy and running for Congress.

"Jack was tall and thin," she claimed. "He had the kind of bantering, unforced Irish charm that women so often find fatal. He asked questions about my work. The kind that revealed how well he already knew the subject."

On their first date together, both Gene and Jack talked about retardation in their families. He spoke sympathetically and frankly about his sister Rosemary who had been born retarded. "We loved and protected her," Jack told Gene.

He mentioned Rosemary in the past tense and failed to note that his parents, Joe and Rose, had insisted his sister have a lobotomy.

At the time, Gene was trying to make a decision about placing her daughter, Daria, her retarded child, into an institution. "Jack understood what I was going through."

The subject of retardation was painful for both of them. After a long silence, Jack said, "In any large family, you can always find something wrong with somebody."

Daria was not only retarded but deaf and blind. Years later a fan confessed to Gene that she had risen from her sick bed during a wartime event. She carried the germ of German measles contracted from soldiers in the army. Impulsively, she kissed Gene, who was pregnant at the time. Gene came down with German measles. Daria was born retarded.

Mystery writer Agatha Christie heard of this horrific moment in Gene's life, and loosely based the theme of her mystery novel, *The Mirror Crack'd,* on the star. It was turned into a 1980 movie, with Elizabeth Taylor starring in the role inspired by Gene's own life, along with Rock Hudson and a very campy Kim Novak.

That night on their first date, Jack shared his political ambitions with Gene. He told her he was going to be elected to Congress. From there, the Senate, then vice president on the Democratic ticket, and then president.

She wrote her family, "I have met the most wonderful man. He is going to become our president one of these days."

When Gene met this dashing young naval officer, she was on the threshold of a divorce from Oleg Cassini. But the famous designer had not quite released her yet. Even though he was having other affairs, he still seemed to want to hold onto Gene.

The bisexual **Oleg Cassini** (1913-2006) was a French-born American fashion designer who created the costumes worn by his wife, film and stage actress **Gene Tierney**. His designs appeared in almost a dozen of the films she made in the 1940s and 50s.

His brother, Igor Cassini, became the famous gossip columnist "Cholly Knickerbocker."

Oleg's marriage to Gene, his second, occurred on June 1, 1941. Life for the couple was volatile, plagued with infidelity on both sides and mental illness for her.

JFK arrived to dislodge their marriage even more. During a brief period after his divorce from Gene, Cassini was briefly engaged to actress Grace Kelly, who incidentally was another one of JFK's lovers.

Cassini tells his side of the story in *In My Own Fashion: An Autobiography* (1987), but he left out most of the juicy details, including those associated with his "secret life."

Just as Gene began to fall in love with Jack, the devastatingly handsome Tyrone Power had begun a love affair with her when they were cast together in *The Razor's Edge* (1946).

Their studio, 20th Century Fox, fanned the rumors of an upcoming marriage between two of its hottest stars. Tyrone had already divorced Annabella, his French movie star wife.

Both of the gossip mavens, Louella Parsons and Hedda Hopper, were pushing for Gene to marry Tyrone. Parsons gushed, "They are the most beautiful couple in Hollywood. Imagine the kids they will spawn."

As biographer Lawrence J. Quirk noted, "Gene Tierney was not one of Kennedy's easy Hollywood lays. She was no overly accommodating starlet or all too willing bimbo, and JFK let old Joe Kennedy know that in no uncertain terms." His father had urged him not to get involved. "Her family is Republican," Joe said. "Not only that, they're Episcopalians to boot."

Joe finally gave in to his son's demands that he keep seeing Gene. "I understand the bitch is going through a divorce from that Cassini faggot. Better watch yourself around him. He was once caught sucking off Victor Mature. Okay, so Tierney needs a few good lays, and you're the man to do that. A chip off the old block."

To strike back at the cavalier way Joe was treating Gene, Jack told him, "You know Gene has a retarded child that may need lobotomizing."

"Dad, you've certainly had far more actresses than I have," Jack told him. "I still remember that summer in 1929 when I was only twelve. I wandered into the wrong cabin on our family yacht and caught you and Gloria Swanson making out like bandits."

When Oleg heard that Gene was dating Jack, he met privately with her.

Oleg, who would figure so largely in the *haute couture* life of Jack's future bride, knew the Kennedy family and was acquainted with Jack superficially.

"You've got to face reality," Oleg told Gene. "I've come to talk some sense into that pretty head of yours. Jack's going into politics, maybe big time. Old Joe will never let him marry you. They are staunch Catholics. If he marries a divorced woman, it will ruin him politically. Many voters won't support him because he's Catholic. Add divorce to the batch and you've got a witch's brew. His family would never let you join the clan."

She rose to her feet and started shouting at Oleg. "He will marry me! He will! He's told me so!" Then she ran screaming from the room.

Oleg wavered back and forth about whether he should let Gene go or not. He felt humiliated that she'd left his bed and had jumped between the sheets of both Tyrone and Jack, two of the most desirable bachelors in the

Associated Press

Fashion designer **Oleg Cassini** presents his sketches for First Lady Jacqueline Bouvier Kennedy's inaugural wardrobe to chicly dressed fashion editors in New York on January 12, 1961.

Jackie's allegiance to his clothing designs led to floods of publicity. Women from 18 to 80 copied his recurrent theme of simple, geometric dresses in sumptuous fabrics with pillbox hats designed to set off elegant coiffures.

Cassini designed some 300 outfits for the First Lady, including a much copied coat made of leopard pelts, and a heavy satin gown for the inaugural balls in January of 1961. The designer outfits were usually paid for by Joseph P. Kennedy, Sr.

On occasion, Cassini also serviced Mrs. Kennedy in other ways.

world, so quickly after leaving him.

Oleg still had the key to the door of Gene's home. One night he decided to discuss two pressing items, including what to do with their daughter Daria. He also wanted to see if there was still any chance of saving their faltering marriage.

What happened next became the scandal of *tout* Hollywood. Oleg knew that Gene was home, but she wasn't answering the door. He let himself in and searched for her. He heard sounds coming from the bathroom. He figured she must be in the shower with Tyrone, and he decided to confront the lovers.

To his shock, he barged into the bathroom to discover that indeed, Tyrone and Gene were together in the shower. But they were not alone. He pulled back the shower curtain to discover the bisexual Tyrone on his knees, performing fellatio on Jack while Jack kissed Gene and fondled her breasts.

As he later reported to his brother, Igor Cassini, "Jack was nearing a climax in Power's mouth. He pulled back the curtain for privacy, and shouted at me, 'Let us alone, Cassini. I'm coming!'"

Oleg barged out of the house. His mind was made up. Gene and he were getting a

According to his most ardent fans, matinee idol **Tyrone Power** never looked better or showed more skin than he did in the *Son of Fury*, a 1942 adventure film.

Less than four years later, Tyrone and Tierney would later become lovers when they made *The Razor's Edge*, which was released in 1946, but during filming of *Son of Fury*, they played it chaste, since Tyrone was settling into his marriage with the French actress Annabella, and Tierney was still in love with her husband, Oleg Cassini.

The deeply troubled actress Francis Farmer played the fourth lead in *Son of Fury*. One of the most beautiful actresses of the 1930s, with golden hair, Farmer was a very talented stage star who often expressed her belief that movies cheapened her. Almost like a preview of her own impending mental illness, Gene watched Frances as she frequently became unraveled on the set.

"It reached a point where, if a man offered her a drink at lunch she would snap, 'I know. You want me to have a martini so I'll get loaded and you can take me to bed,'" Gene said about Frances.

Frances would go on to spend a total of eight years in state asylums for the insane, at one point reduced to making pies.

divorce.

In 1946, only insider Hollywood knew about Tyrone's bisexual life. His co-star, gay Clifton Webb, knew all about it, but most other people, including Gene and Tyrone's future lover, Lana Turner, were not yet aware that Tyrone liked men even more than he liked women.

After that night when Gene had first introduced Tyrone to Jack, she had anticipated that it might spark some jealousy between two jealous lovers. But when Tyrone came on to Jack, she was startled but went along with the venue more out of curiosity than passion.

The next day, Oleg was even more furious, wanting revenge on both Jack and Tyrone, perhaps Gene as well. He didn't know where Jack was, but in his search for Tyrone, he headed for the set of *The Razor's Edge* at 20th Century Fox.

LIFE

I FIGHT THE FIGHT MOB
BY INGEMAR JOHANSSON
THE FLOP THAT GAVE
MOSS HART HIS START

JACKIE KENNEDY:
A FRONT RUNNER'S
APPEALING WIFE

AUGUST 24, 1959

Imagine Gene Tierney's regret when she picked up the August 24, 1959 edition of *Life* magazine to see her former lover, Jack, on the cover with his stunningly beautiful wife, Jackie Kennedy. The headline read, "A Front Runner's Appealing Wife."

When the magazine was published, Gene was at a low point of her career. Her last movie, *The Left Hand of God*, co-starring Humphrey Bogart, had been released four years before, in 1955.

At the time Gene's mental health was deteriorating, and she was undergoing electric shock treatments. She would tell her nurses, "If I had played it right, I would be on the way to the White House now. I would be on that cover of *Life*. Jackie stole from me the role I was destined to play."

When he found that no one was in Gene's dressing room, he went at once to Tyrone's dressing room, where he encountered three men playing cards. Oleg demanded to know where Gene was. One of the men wisecracked, "She's probably in the shower with Ty." Obviously he'd heard about the incident from the previous night.

As Gene Tierney's biographer, Michelle Vogel, related,

"If ever there was a red-flag-to-a-bull moment, that was it. Oleg was the bull and that comment was the reddest of flags. Oleg flew across the room, ripped the guy from his chair and threw him against the wall.

He then proceeded to destroy Tyrone's dressing room. He was picking up chairs and swinging them above his head, sweeping items from tables and throwing anything he could in an uncontrolled rage. He later said of the incident, 'I was out of my mind.'"

While all this violence was occurring, Tyrone and Gene were lunching peacefully in the studio's commissary.

Oleg felt betrayed, not only by Gene but by Jack and Tyrone. He wanted to strike back at them. He spread the word, even telling Darryl F. Zanuck at Fox, who feared that the news would harm box office receipts of *The Razor's*

Edge. Jack's political career could be destroyed before it had really begun, and Tyrone's diminished sex appeal at the box office might mean the end of his career.

Clifton Webb was an evil gossip, and he spread the word at dinner parties. Even Oleg's brother, Igor Cassini, got in on the act. He wouldn't dare mention such a scandalous story in his gossip column, which he wrote under the *nom de plume* of "Cholly Knickerbocker." But he spread the word in New York and among Palm Beach society. "People needed a hot topic to gossip about in 1946, and this was it," Igor said.

Jack invited Gene to Cape Cod, where he met her at the train station. As Gene later recorded in her autobiography, *Self-Portrait,* "He was wearing patched blue jeans. I thought he looked like Tom Sawyer. He was like a little boy lost, gazing at me with a wistful smile. I knew I was madly in love with him, but I was also in love with Tyrone. And I still was in love, a bit, with Oleg. And with the problem of Daria, it was one of the most confused periods of my life."

For the sake of appearances, Gene, throughout the course of her visit to Cape Cod, stayed with her friends, Mr. and Mrs. Hal Wright.

She later remembered her days on the Cape as the most romantic moments of her life—walking on the beach in the moonlight, swimming, sailing, and "just taking pleasure in each other's bodies."

After a romantic interlude with Gene on Cape Cod, Jack and Gene met for lunch after both of them returned separately to New York.

He was due shortly thereafter back in Washington, and their final rendezvous was viewed as a sort of farewell luncheon. At the time, she still felt that their love affair was in full swing, especially after the passion he'd shown for her in Hyannis Port. But before departing that day, he delivered the blow. "You know, Gene, I can't marry you."

All she could say at the end of the lunch was, "Bye, bye, Jack."

"What do you mean by that?" he asked her. "Those words sound . . . like final."

"It is," she said. "It is."

She later said, "He just walked out of my life as my lover and future husband."

The controversial film, *Advise & Consent* (1962), marked Gene's return to the screen in this Otto Preminger movie that starred Henry Fonda, Charles Laughton, Walter Pidgeon, Don Murray, and Peter Lawford. Lawford was JFK's brother-in-law at the time. He played Lafe Smith, a senator from Rhode Island.

Preminger offered a cameo role to Dr. Martin Luther King Jr., to play a U.S. Senator from Georgia. No African-American senators were serving at that time. King turned it down.

Don Murray, playing a senator, is implicated in a homosexual affair and commits suicide. Lawford was instrumental in getting Gene invited to the White House where she had a reunion with JFK again.

Before she left, he offered to privately show her the Oval Office. Once inside, he held her in his arms and kissed her. "Had fate been different, Gene," he told her, "you and I could be sitting at this desk trying to defuse a nuclear war."

Despite having ended their relationship, she sent him a letter of congratulations when, in 1947 at the age of 29, he was elected as U.S. Congressman from Massachusetts, winning by a margin of 78,000 votes.

That was not the final climax, however, the way it might have happened in a romantic novel. In 1952 in Paris, Gene was dining with her friend, the actress Michele Morgan.

Still a bachelor, Jack was mapping out a campaign to run for the Senate. He came up to Gene's table and asked her to dance. She accepted. As he held her close, he asked her, "Isn't it time we started all over again?"

"No, Jack," she said. "Not this time. It's over."

Less than six months later, she read of his marriage to Jacqueline Lee Bouvier.

When he ran for president, Gene, who came from a staunch Republican family, voted for Richard Nixon.

In 1962, months into the Kennedy presidency, Gene was invited to the White House to celebrate the release of her new picture, *Advise and Consent*. Perhaps with a sense of mischief, Jackie seated her next to the president.

Gene was accompanied by her latest husband, Howard Lee, the Texas oil millionaire. Jack had heard that she'd been in and out of mental institutions, where she'd undergone electric shock therapy treatments and had made three attempts at suicide.

All he asked was, "Have you been okay?"

She reached for her husband's hand. "I'm lucky to have Howard in my life now. He loves me even when I go nuts."

"That was my moment of closure," she later said. "Jack and I were through. I'd become a footnote in the history of the president. Had things been different, I could have become the First Lady."

It took Oleg a long time to get his revenge on Jack, even though on the surface they remained friends. Jack was especially pleased that Oleg was supplying the First Lady with expensive *haute couture* dresses free.

One night, he visited Jackie in the White House to show her his new designs. Jack was out of Washington at the time.

As Oleg later related to his brother, Igor, "I got my revenge fuck. I seduced Jackie. The First Lady has had a few revenge fucks against Jack in her lifetime. Maybe we both were doing it for revenge—not for passion."

In one of her final interviews, Gene claimed that she had no regrets about not marrying Jack and defying both of their families, religion, and public opinion. "It was not to be," she said. "Just think of what a burden my later illnesses and my daughter's retardation would have done to Jack. He still felt great sorrow for his poor sweet retarded sister, Rosemary."

"With its many wounds the heart, hopefully, becomes full and deep, and compassionate and loving—in the true meaning of loving," she said. "In a way, I never stopped loving Jack. All lives are filled with a 'what might have been.'"

Suspicions of Bigamy

JFK's First Wife

Durie Malcolm, pictured above, was the reputed first wife of a young **Jack Kennedy.** He married her in 1947. On orders of Joe Kennedy, evidence of their marriage was removed from the courthouse at Palm Beach.

Joe often urged his son to chase after women, following in his own footsteps. But when it came to picking a wife, Joe was adamant that Jack make a calculated choice—"not related to your groin. You've got to marry a beautiful woman who will be gracious and charming. One without a lot of baggage, including previous husbands. Also, a woman who is Catholic."

Durie did not fit any of Joe's qualifications for the perfect wife. "Durie's made more for fucking than marrying," Joe Sr. told Jack. "I've on occasion even gone after her myself. When the right gal comes along, I'll tell you when to marry. Don't you ever pull that stunt again, or else you can kiss the presidency goodbye."

How Not to Marry
a Millionaire

During the heyday of Joe and Rose Kennedy's child-rearing years, back in the 1930s, weathly industrialist George H. Malcolm, who was married at the time to Isabel O. Cooper, lived in a sprawling house across from the Kennedy compound in Palm Beach. From her previous marriage to a man named Frederick Kerr, Isabel had produced a daughter, Durie Kerr, who had been born on December 30, 1917, the same year as JFK.

Shortly after Isabel's marriage to Malcolm, the girl was adopted by her new stepfather and her name was changed to Durie Malcolm. She was referred to this way by her Palm Beach friends throughout the rest of her life, despite her subsequent marriages to different men, possibly to John F. Kennedy himself.

By 1939, Durie had evolved into the most popular woman in Palm Beach society, pursued by a series of what she called "beaux." "I felt like Scarlett O'Hara in the opening scene of *Gone With the Wind*," she later recalled. "But of all my pursuers, the one who caught my eye was the very handsome and charming Joseph Kennedy Jr. He was very dashing. Frankly, I didn't care for his family of micks, especially the ambassador."

"I knew Durie in Palm Beach over many a year," claimed author Truman Capote. "When we'd had one too many--and when wasn't that so?--Durie often talked to me about her brief marriage to Jack. She claimed that with a bad back and all those illnesses, he still had stamina."

Also according to Capote, "If Durie is to be believed, he assaulted her six times in a period of twenty-four hours. She told me that 'Jack made love like I could have been any woman under him. He was a pig about hogging all the fun for himself and didn't seem to give a fuck whether I enjoyed it or not. Yes, there was an abortion, but I'll be god damned if I'm going to talk about that.'"

She was referring to Joseph P. Kennedy, appointed by Franklin D. Roosevelt as ambassador to England from 1938-1940. In those days, the Irish were still regarded as low class by much of Palm Beach society. "I was willing to overlook his background and that awful father of his—a bootlegger, no less—because Joe Jr. was so fascinating to me."

Actually JFK first dated Durie in 1939 when Joe Jr. was away. Jack was always very competitive with his older brother. Durie told friends at her country club, "Joe Jr. is a man, but Jack is still a little boy."

Durie was quite beautiful and had an engaging personality that had been evident since her childhood days in Lake Forest, Illinois, an upmarket suburb north of Chicago. As she grew older, she evolved into a well-coordinated athlete and became an exceptional tennis player. "She'd even play ice hockey in the winter and basketball with the guys," close friend Charles (Chuck) Spalding claimed. "She attracted rich men to her like bears to honey. One of those rich boys was Jack Kennedy himself."

When JFK first met Durie in Palm Beach during the late 1930s, she'd already been married twice, first to F. John Bersback of Illinois in 1937, that marriage lasting 14 months. She then married Firman Desloge IV of St. Louis in 1939. That marriage was short, but she didn't file for divorce until 1947.

Before he entered the Navy in World War II, Durie dated Jack, and she also resumed her affair with him when he returned home after heroic service as a PT-boat commander. She had seemed to favor Joe Jr. over Jack, but regrettably, she learned he'd died in a plane over France.

In 1946, when JFK returned to Palm Beach after his service in the Navy, he and Durie resumed their dating, which they had left off in 1939. She told him how saddened she was to have learned about his brother's death in an airplane crash two years earlier.

The high-profile romance between Durie and JFK did not go unnoticed. A society writer, Charles Ventura, covered Palm Beach for the now-defunct *New York World-Telegram*. In an article published on January 20, 1947, he wrote that Palm Beach's "annual Oscar for achievement in the field of romance" went to Jack Kennedy for winning the much-coveted hand of Durie Malcolm. "He gave her the rush of the season, coming on real strong," Ventura said. "But Jack couldn't stay around to accept his Oscar, because he was called back to Washington."

Photofest

Two handsome brothers, **Joe Jr**. *(left)* and **Jack** *(right)*, each scored a bull's eye with Durie Malcolm, whom Jack later married. But **Papa Joe** *(center)* struck out with the Palm Beach socialite, though he tried hard on more than one occasion. He believed that women should be passed on, perhaps from father to son but it could work the other way, too, from son to father.

Joe Sr. even discussed the sex rituals he shared with Rose with both of his sons. "After Teddy," Joe told Joe Sr. and Jack, "your mother said there will be no more kids; therefore, no more need for intercourse."

In an attempt to explain Rose's rationalization of her husband's infidelities, author Ted Schwarz in his biography on the founder of the Kennedy clan, *Joseph P. Kennedy, The Mogul, the Mob, the Statesman, and the Making of an American Myth* theorized, "If she were not having sex with Joe, then he could not be committing adultery."

John F. Kennedy and Durie Malcolm were married early in 1947 before a Justice of the Peace in a ceremony conducted right after dawn at Palm Beach. They had been partying all night.

Durie was known among her friends in Palm Beach and Illinois for her wild sense of adventure. When her crowd heard rumors of the marriage, it was dismissed as a "lark, a wild night that got out of hand." Later on, friends gossiped that the marriage had a far more compelling reason than that.

Spalding, who had been one of JFK's oldest and most trusted friends, broke five decades of silence when he granted an interview to Seymour M. Hersh, one of America's leading investigative reporters. In 1997 Hersh released his shocking exposé, *The Dark Side of Camelot*, giving details and back-up support to the validity the Malcolm/Kennedy marriage.

Hersh claimed that Joe had a "hemorrhage" when he learned about the marriage.

"When Jack told me about it, I accused him of being crazy," Spalding said. "I knew that Joe wanted to run him for President one day, and here Jack goes and pulls off some dumb shit like this."

"Jackie would make the perfect wife for you," Joe Sr. told Jack. "She's got class, and I like that." He often used the word class.

"The good news is that she's Catholic," said Joe Sr. "You can't marry outside your religion if you want to make it to the White House. Being Catholic itself is burden enough."

His son protested getting married. "I'm having too much fun, dad," he said.

In response, Joe Sr. answered, "Was I ever faithful to your mother? Getting married doesn't mean you have to play dead." *(Photofest)*

As a twice-divorced woman and an Episcopalian, Durie would not be acceptable as a First Lady, and Joe knew that.

"When he found out, he struck his son in the face and called him a fool," Spalding claimed. "Joe called me and got me to agree to destroy all traces of that marriage."

Joe told Jack, "This Malcolm bitch is a whore." He cited as evidence gossip he'd heard in the locker room at the tennis club in Palm Beach. "There were at least fifteen guys there, and it seems that every last one of these buck-assed naked bastards had had your Miss Malcolm. One told us that she gave great head; another said she took it up the ass, and a third said she'd trained her vaginal muscles 'to milk a man dry.'"

"I personally went to the Palm Beach County Courthouse and removed the marriage documents," Spalding later claimed. "I had help from a lawyer. Joe had me do this."

No record of a divorce has ever been found for a marriage which, in essence, would make both JFK and Durie bigamists.

George Smathers, Democratic Senator from Florida, was also a close friend of JFK's. Later he functioned as best man at John's wedding to Jacqueline Lee Bouvier. Smathers also confirmed that JFK told him the details of his 1947 marriage to Durie.

Both Smathers and Spalding later asserted that they were under the impression "that a kid was in the oven," as Smathers so colorfully put it.

According to their suspicions, that was the real motivation for the hasty marriage. If that were true, then it wasn't on the level of some college prank. According to Florida law at the time, the couple did not have to take a blood test, but would have to apply for a marriage license three days in advance.

Hersh's book claims that a missionary, Father James J. O'Rourke, shared a bottle of Scotch late one night with Cardinal Richard Cushing, who was in Bolivia on missionary work with O'Rourke. O'Rourke quoted Cushing as saying, "Kennedy was married before, but it got taken care of."

Suspicion has always centered on Cushing, who allegedly interceded with the Vatican in Rome to have JFK's marriage to Durie annulled.

O'Rourke's point of view was that since JFK and Durie were married in a private civil ceremony in Palm Beach, and not in a Catholic church, an annulment was not necessary in the eyes of the Vatican.

Approximately six months after her marriage to JFK, on July 11, 1947, Durie then married a wealthy Palm Beach socialite, Thomas Shevlin. Shevlin was a former Yale football star and scion to a lumber fortune. It was her third marriage and it lasted until her husband's death in 1973. According to reports, the details of Durie's marriage to JFK were widely known within the Shevlin family.

Morton Downey Jr., a Kennedy friend who had been a radio and TV performer during the 1950s, reported that during a summer visit to the Hyannis Port compound, he overheard the Kennedy family talking about "Jack's stupid marriage in Palm Beach."

Later, when John F. Kennedy ran for and won the Senatorial seat for Massachusetts, J. Edgar Hoover of the Federal Bureau of Investigation sent agents to Palm Beach to verify the claims about JFK's first marriage. He was determined to prove that JFK was a bigamist. Hoover knew all about JFK's womanizing, but the charge of bigamy was a potentially explosive issue. It meant that any children born to Jacqueline and John Kennedy would be illegitimate.

The FBI agents got some members of the Palm Beach elite to admit that they knew about the marriage. Agents directly interviewed Spalding, who admitted that the marriage had occurred. Hoover's agents agreed to grant him anonymity if he would give them the information they wanted.

He was also promised that this information would never be made available during Kennedy's lifetime.

Spalding also confessed to the FBI that he, working on the orders of Joe Kennedy, had bribed a staff member at the Palm Beach Courthouse to remove all records and evidence of the mar-

"Jack and I were partners in crime," Senator **George Smathers** *(top photo and left figure in photo with bathing trunks)* told his cronies in Palm Beach.

"Jack and I could never keep our zippers up. He had a smorgasbord of women, and sometimes found it hard deciding what to put on his plate. I did too. The girls were really crazy for both of us back then. I fell for Durie too, and she gave me a tumble here and there.

"Jack was not above stealing my wife, so I went after his—and later, that included Jackie too."

"His daddy liked girls. He was a great chaser. Jack liked girls, and girls liked him. He had just a great way with women. He even taught me a few lessons."

riage.

More than a dozen years later, when JFK made his bid for the presidency in 1960, he and Bobby feared that news of his marriage to Durie would leak out and cost him the election.

Senator Smathers later claimed that JFK was extremely worried that Richard Nixon's "people" had learned of his first marriage and planned to release all the details of the marriage to the press in October of 1960, right before the November elections.

Smathers confirmed that he later learned that the Nixon camp did indeed learn this information. For reasons known only to Nixon himself, he chose at the last minute not to have his campaign staff release the story of the marriage.

There has long been speculation that it was a trade off. Apparently, Joe Kennedy had gathered information so damaging to Nixon that it would have cost him the election had it been released. Joe used to brag about his "Mexican stand-off" with Nixon. As to what clandestine information Joe had on Nixon, there is only speculation, no smoking gun. Smathers always claimed "it was something dreadful having to do with Nixon's finances."

The American public only became aware of the potential scandal on September 2, 1962 when news of it was published in Walter Scott's *Personality Parade*, written by Lloyd Shearer. The columnist was asked about the rumor that the President had been married before Jackie. Based on his aggressive and heated denial, Shearer gave the rumor its widest dissemination.

After that, JFK called in his close friend, Benjamin Bradlee, bureau chief in Washington for *Newsweek*. Bradlee, as requested, revealed the rumor in print, then denied it. The *Newsweek* story was picked up by the national press, but still made little impression on the American public.

The press had long speculated about JFK's first marriage. On January 24, 1997, London's *Daily Mail* ran a provocative headline: WAS SHE JFK'S SECRET FIRST BRIDE? The paper also published a photograph of Durie wearing a wedding dress.

Throughout the course of her long life (she died in 2008), Durie always denied the story. "I wouldn't have married Jack Kennedy for all the tea in China," she said. Of course, if indeed she had married Jack, she wouldn't have admitted it, since it would have made her a bigamist, too. She told London's *Sunday Times* in 1996, "I didn't care for those Irish micks, and old Joe was a terrible man."

One of Durie's remaining friends, Betty Howard Ritter, who died in 1986, always claimed that Durie "told me that she was married to Jack. She also told me even a more shocking story—the reason for her marriage. She was two months pregnant. She claimed old Joe arranged for her abortion of the Kennedy kid and settled $750,000 on her. She wanted a million but he got her down on her

Richard James Cushing (1895-1970), the longtime archbishop of Boston who was elevated to the status of cardinal in 1958, was the keeper of secrets for the Kennedy clan—and he had a lot of them to keep.

Born the third of five children to a pair of impoverished immigrants from County Cork and County Waterford, Ireland, he was torn between a career in politics or the church.

He became close to the Kennedy family and officiated at the marriage of Jack and Jackie in 1953, even though he knew that Jack had previously married Durie Malcolm and had never divorced her.

"The saddest day in my life," as he later recalled, "was when I had to celebrate President Kennedy's funeral mass at St. Matthew's Cathedral in Washington."

As part of the extended funeral rites, he delivered a televised eulogy for the assassinated President.

Cushing later publicly defended Jacqueline Kennedy after her marriage to Aristotle Onassis in 1968.

Subsequently, Cushing received many bundles of hate mail, and his defense of Jackie's second marriage was "contradicted" by Church officials in Rome.

price."

In his memoir, *Counsel to the President*, Clark Clifford—who Kennedy had appointed to, and later made chairman of, his Foreign Intelligence Advisory Board—wrote about his investigation of the Durie Malcolm incident. The attorney remembered being called to the Oval Office, where JFK presented him information about a scandal that was close to breaking into the mainstream media. He said that rumors of a marriage to Durie Malcolm had surfaced because of a privately printed book, a genealogy of all the descendants of a 17th-century Dutch Hudson Valley settler named Blauvelt. Louis Blauvelt, a retired General Electric toolmaker from New Jersey, had compiled the work in 1957. One of his books is on file at the Library of Congress. The entry in the otherwise dry genealogical listings read like this:

(12,427) Durie, (Kerr), Malcolm. . . . She was born Kerr, but took the name of her stepfather. She first married Firmin Desloge IV. They were divorced. Durie then married F. John Bersbach. They were divorced, and she married third, John F. Kennedy, son of Joseph P. Kennedy, one time Ambassador to England.

The names of her first two husbands were reversed, and Firman's name was misspelled. But the dry, factual nature of the entry into the otherwise nonsensationalist genealogical record sent shock waves through both the Kennedy clan and the media.

JFK was neither honest nor forthcoming when he told Clifford, "All I know is that some years ago, I knew very briefly a young woman named Durie Malcolm. I think I had two dates with her. One may have been a dinner date in which we went dancing. The other, to my recollection, was a football game. Those were the only two times I ever saw her. My brother, Joe, also dated her a few years earlier. I remember that she was quite attractive."

Clifford told JFK, "Mr. President, I think she was one of the most attractive women I ever met." The President was startled that his counsel knew Durie.

Clifford called Durie in Palm Beach, and she denied ever having married JFK. "Imagine being married to President Kennedy. That's a laugh."

He pressed her further. "Was there anything serious between the two of you?"

"Absolutely not," she said. "We hardly knew each other. There were those two casual dates. We did not seem to click, and that was all there was to it."

"I told her I would repeat all this back to the president, and we would look for ways to stop the story from spreading any further," Clifford said.

Durie would spend the rest of her life asserting, in public, that she'd never married JFK, although few people within her inner circle were convinced

Morton Downey Jr., the singer, songwriter and controversial 1980s TV talk show host, grew up next door to the Kennedy clan at Hyannis Port, Massachusetts. He was not only an intimate friend of the Kennedys, but privy to many of their secrets, including Durie Malcolm's marriage to JFK.

His aunts included the Hollywood film goddesses Constance Bennett and Joan Bennett.

During his Hollywood years, Joe Sr., involved at the time in a torrid affair with Gloria Swanson, also fell for Constance, "a beautiful slim blonde," when she appeared unexpectedly on the set.

One day Swanson returned early from her studio to discover the younger, stunningly attractive Constance in Joe's bedroom wearing a *negligée*.

JFK brought good looks and self-confidence to the televised presidential debates of 1960, and insisted on having sexual intercourse immediately before each session. In contrast, **Richard Nixon** looked sweaty and jowly, as commentators asked the question, "Would you buy a used car from this man?"

Television viewers, it was revealed, were more inclined to vote for JFK, whereas radio listeners favored the deep-voiced Nixon. In one debate, JFK's advocacy of open intervention in Cuba brought out the hound dogs from the press, who chased after him.

Journalist Murray Kempton, always acidic, asserted in the *New York Post*: "I really don't know what further demagoguery is possible from Kennedy on this subject, short of announcing that, if elected, he will send Bobby and Teddy and Eunice to Oriente province to clean Castro out."

Nixon had already been nicknamed "Tricky Dickie," but he felt the label should have pertained to JFK instead. He claimed that the Kennedy clan had unlimited money and were "the most ruthless group of political operators ever mobilized for a political campaign. Kennedy's organization approached campaign dirty tricks with a roughish relish and carried them off with an insouciance that captivated many politicians and overcame the critical faculties of many reporters."

Charles (Chuck) Spalding, JFK's friend, later claimed that in addition to having sex before making an appearance on TV, JFK also received amphetamine injections from Dr. Max Jacobson (aka "Dr. Feelgood").

"After a visit from Max and his needle, Jack could jump over a twelve-foot fence," Spalding claimed. "When Bobby tried to persuade his brother not to take the shots, JFK told him, "I don't care if it's horse's piss. It's the only thing that works."

she was telling the truth.

***

There was a problem with JFK's many denials, especially as regards their transmission to members of his staff. At various times, JFK told different people different stories about Durie. Even though he denied it publicly, even to his own lawyer, JFK admitted the existence of and details associated with the marriage to Smathers. As for Spalding, he was by his own admission the cover-up man.

Prior to his assassination in 1963, after which it didn't matter anymore, JFK had greatly feared the upcoming elections of 1964. News of various scandals past and present were lurking beneath the surface, seemingly everywhere. It was widely anticipated that JFK, running for a second term as a Democrat, would face off against the very popular Republican, Nelson Rockefeller.

During strategy planning for the electoral contest to come, JFK was urging his campaign staff not to attack Rockefeller for his divorce, which some Democrats wanted to make an issue. In later presidential elections, of course, that didn't prove a problem for Ronald Reagan.

According to Smathers, "Jack told me 'better a divorced man than a bigamist. This might even go nuclear' Jack said, 'The tabloids might be writing about my two bastard kids in the White House.'"

On the evening of Valentine's Day, February 14, 1962, at a small party that Durie was hosting in Palm Beach, her guests crowded around a television to watch Jackie Kennedy take America on a tour of the White House. Three out of four television viewers nationwide were tuned in and watching. Durie had been drinking heavily.

At one point she cursed Jackie's image on the TV. "If it hadn't been for that fucking mick asshole, old Joe Kennedy, I would be the First Lady conducting the White House tour and getting plugged in the Lincoln bedroom with Jack's much overused dick."

How Jackie Lost Her Maidenhead

In a Creaky Paris Elevator

In December of 1951, Jackie Lee Bouvier accepted a position as "inquiring photographer" for the *Times-Herald* of Washington, D.C., a newspaper no longer published. Her editor told her to interview both known politicians and "the unknown man" on the street. Of course, she had to take a photograph of each of her subjects, which she is pictured doing in the photo above with JFK.

In some ways, many of her questions foreshadowed her future life in the White House. At a social gathering, she encountered the stern, grim, and supremely judgmental Bess Truman, wife of the then-sitting president, Harry S Truman. "Mrs. Truman, if you had your choice, which First Lady would you like to have been?"

"None," Bess snapped at her before walking on.

Jackie also asked Julie, the six-year-old daughter of the newly elected vice president Richard Nixon. "What do you think of your father's new office?"

The girl looked despondent. "He's always away. If he's famous, why can't he stay at home?"

Her questions to a rising new politician, JFK himself, were more pointed:

1. "Do you think Irish men make great lovers?"
2. "Do you believe that wives of politicians should go on the campaign trail with their husbands?"
3. "If you were elected president of the United States in the years to come, what qualities would you look for in a First Lady?"

"THE QUEEN OF THE DEBUTANTES" EAGER TO GET DEFLOWERED

In 1947, **Jacqueline Bouvier** made her debut at the Hammersmith Farm Estate of the Auchincloss family, formally "presented" to 300 A-list guests as an eligible and available newcomer on the social scene. A formal dinner and dance was staged at the Clambake Club in Newport, Rhode Island.

Writing under the pen name of Cholly Knickerbocker, Igor Cassini, gossip columnist for the Hearst Newspapers, covered the event. He was the brother of Oleg Cassini, who during Jackie's White House years became not only her favorite fashion designer, but her lover as well.

In his column, Igor wrote, "The Queen of the Year of 1947 is Jacqueline Bouvier, a regal brunette who has classic features and the daintiness of Dresden porcelain. She has poise, is soft-spoken and intelligent, everything the leading debutante should be. Her background is strictly 'Old Guard.'"

The jury has decided: Jacqueline Lee Bouvier did not go to her wedding night bed a virgin—far from it. Her affair with the handsome young senator from Massachusetts, Jack Kennedy, began long before she walked down the aisle to meet him at the altar.

"Jackie said she was going to Paris to study at the Sorbonne, but she really went to have a good time and lose her virginity," said author Gore Vidal.

During her junior year abroad, Jackie perfected her French and fell in love with both Paris and John Phillips Marquand Jr., son of the famous novelist.

He was the perfect WASP, with his tweed jackets, steel-blue eyes, and pale blue Oxford shirts from Brooks Brothers on New York's Fifth Avenue.

Jackie and Marquand were seen dancing together at the chic L'Elephant Blanc where all the rich young expats hung out. She viewed him as a dashing war hero, as he was in the second wave of U.S. Army troops that routed the Nazis out of Paris.

His friends called him "Jack." As Jackie later recalled, "He was the first Jack in my life. Maybe I should have married him," she later recalled. "We had the same tastes in literature."

Together, Jack and Jackie frequented Left Bank bistros such as Chez Allard (41 rue St.-André-des-Arts, Paris 6e), where they dined with Jean-Paul Sartre and Simon de Beauvoir. On another night they were seen drinking French cognac at the Deux Magots (6, place St-Germain-des-Prés, Paris 6e) with author William Styron.

She loved talking art and literature with Marquand, telling him that of all the people who'd ever lived, she most wanted to meet "first and foremost," Oscar Wilde (1854-1900), the French poet Charles-Pierre Baudelaire (1821-1867), and the ballet impresario, Sergei Diaghilev (1872-1929).

It was rumored that Jackie helped Marquand write his novel, *The Second Happiest Day*, which he published in 1960 under an abbreviated version (John Phillips) of his name, because his father feared readers would otherwise think it was "daddy, not the errant son, writing the blasted thing."

The distinguished John P. Marquand Sr., that chronicler of American aristocratic WASPs, became known at first for his stories about the Japanese detective "Mr. Moto." In 1938 he won the Pulitzer Prize for his biography, *The Late George Apley.*

Evenings at "The White Elephant" found Jackie lighting one *Gauloise* after another and downing Grasshoppers (made from equal parts crème de menthe, crème de cacao, and either fresh cream or vodka, or both, shaken with ice and strained into a chilled cocktail glass), which that summer was her favorite cocktail.

Seduction was slow in coming. Marquand told his friends, "Jackie will not go all the way. She'll give me a blow job, but she won't let me screw her in the missionary position."

Perhaps Jackie had too many of those Grasshoppers at the White Elephant, but one night Marquand got lucky. In fact, as he later told some male friends, "She was so hot to trot she couldn't wait until I got inside my apartment. I figured I'd better go for it before she changed her mind."

And so he did, as related in Edward Klein's book, *All Too Human, The Love Story of Jack and Jackie Kennedy.* "In the creaky French elevator, Jackie let herself get carried away. She was in Marquand's arms, her skirt bunched above her hips, the backs of her thighs pressed against the decorative open grillwork. When the elevator jolted to a stop, she was no longer a *demi-vierge*" meaning of course a "half virgin."

The elevator had stalled on the second landing. Actually, it was in good working order. Marquand had used the deliberately stalled elevator as a seduction technique on many an unsuspecting young woman he'd previously invited upstairs for a drink.

Jackie later told confidants that she surrendered her virginity "only on my wedding night." That was hardly true. Jack Kennedy himself confessed to several people, including his brother, Bobby, and to Florida Senator George Smathers, that he and Jackie were having an affair months before their wedding.

According to her gossipy friend, author Truman Capote, "Virginity was something Jackie wanted to get rid of as soon as possible. She knew her sister had lost hers, and, as the older sister, she didn't want to be the last to sample what a man had to offer. If my calculations are correct, she went to bed with at least five guys before Jack sampled the honeypot. Certainly John P. Marquand Jr., takes the honors as the first in a string of get-lucky beaux."

After the "love-in-the-lift" seduction, Jackie and Marquand began a passionate affair that

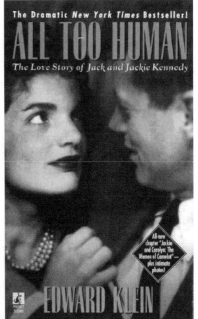

One of the best and most penetrating books written on the love story of Jack and Jackie Kennedy was Edward Klein's *All Too Human.*

Klein was editor-in-chief of the *New York Times Magazine* and covered John F. Kennedy's 1960 campaign.

A longtime friend of Jackie's he wrote: "Of all the great love stories that have had an impact on our times—Eleanor and Franklin, Winston and Clementine, the Duke and Duchess of Windsor— none has remained as shrouded in secrecy and misunderstanding as that of John and Jacqueline Kennedy."

He answers a lot of questions, many revealed for the first time, including:

1. To what extent was Jackie aware of Jack's compulsive womanizing, and how did she react?; and

2. Did Jackie have affairs of her own?

lasted until she returned to America.

Janet Auchincloss, Jackie's mother, had trained her daughters "to grow up, look chic, behave yourself, and marry a rich man."

When her mother discovered that Jackie was having an affair with Marquand, she violently objected. "Writers are always poor as church mice."

For a while, Jackie broke up with Marquand, but resumed her love affair with him upon her return to Paris. Back in Paris, the romantic couple was seen at fashionable places around the city, eventually returning to their former haunt, the White Elephant. "I was still in love with Jack, and he was passionately in love with me," Jackie recalled. "I chose not to listen to mother. After all, I was grown up and wanted to live my own life. Besides, isn't a woman supposed to take a husband for richer or poorer?"

In 1978, Kitty Kelley published a pioneering biography called *Jackie Oh!* that was highly controversial. The public at the time, although fascinated with Jackie, knew virtually nothing of her affairs, only her marriages to John F. Kennedy and later to Aristotle Onassis.

Kelley was the first author to write of Jackie's first love, John P. Marquand, Jr., who was alleged to have been the first man to deflower Jackie. In fairness to Kelley, she admitted that the story might be more "apocryphal than authentic." As the tale goes, Jackie, upon losing her virginity, said in disappointment, "Oh, is that all there is to it?"

When the book appeared, Marquand was ridiculed by his friends, one of whom asked him, "Did Jackie have to ask you if you were in yet?" Marquand denied the taking of Jackie's virginity. By this time, there were additional links that bound him to his memories of Jackie: His wife Sue Coward, had roomed with Jackie during her sojourn in Paris at the Sorbonne, and Sue's first cousin, Michael Canfield, had been the first husband of Jackie"s sister, Lee Bouvier (later Radiziwill).

"The Kelley story reflected on me a hell of a lot more than it did on Jackie?" Marquand said. "What kind of asshole would make claims on the maidenhead of Jacqueline Bouvier and go around bragging about it? Not only that, but the rumor made me sound less than manly. The story became so prominent that when I was having lunch one day with Jackie, I brought it up," Marquand recalled. "She completely dismissed it and asked me to drop the subject."

"It's pure bullshit" she said. "I don't know where on earth Kelley got such a story. I certainly

Photofest

In this photo from 1947, **Jacqueline Bouvier** poses in front of her first postwar car. She could have been any attractive housewife in America, from any typical suburb at the time. She had yet to discover her distinctive style and had not yet learned to set off her distinctive look and beauty that would enchant the world.

She was extremely proud of her 1947 black Mercury convertible, believing that it gave her a freedom she didn't have before. She told her sister, Lee—jokingly or not—"I plan to lure many a man into the back seat of my car."

"Jackie back then was just beginning to sharpen her nails on the road to becoming the number one *femme fatale* in the world," said her distant kin, author Gore Vidal.

Charles Pearson, a navy veteran and cohort of JFK, told his politican friend that "the best way to get Jackie was to mix up a batch of lethal martinis and get her really tight. Her inhibitions will fall away. She's really hot, but doesn't yet know how hot she is. When you take down her panties, you'll find out."

didn't tell her, and I know you didn't either. It's categorically untrue. But I'm too much of a lady and you're too much of a gentleman to sue. Besides, the press would have a field day with a lawsuit like that. Kelley would sell five million books in hardcover alone."

But apparently, Marquand made up this story about his reaction and Jackie's reaction to Kelley's revelations. To his close friends (all male), he told a very different story, claiming that Kelley had been right all along.

Vidal dismissed their denials. "Jackie did lose her virginity to John in that elevator. He was a friend of mine and he told me the truth."

After the resumption of her affair with Marquand, Jackie returned to America to confront Janet once again. This time her mother slapped her hard on both cheeks, "trying to knock some sense into you."

As Jackie later told her sister, Lee, "Mother never hit me before. She's also withdrawn my allowance. I'm going to have to figure out a way of making money myself."

Jackie continued to see Marquand whenever she could," claimed her friend, author Truman Capote. "But she was also screwing a guy named Demi."

Capote was referring to John Gates, nicknamed "Demi," a young CIA operative who fell madly in love with Jackie. She also started hanging out with a Yale man, John G.W. Husted Jr., a Wall Street broker. They seriously considered marriage even though Husted was not a Catholic. Husted came into Jackie's life in 1951, following his serving with the American Field Service in WWII. She was introduced to him by a friend of her stepsister, Yusha Auchincloss.

After only a month, Husted proposed to Jackie at the Polo Bar in the Westbury Hotel in New York. She reluctantly accepted.

Hugh Auchincloss threw an engagement party at Merrywood, his nine-bedroom, seven-acre estate in McLean, Virginia, where Husted presented her with a diamond-and-sapphire ring that had once belonged to his mother.

Ormande de Kay, another of Jackie's beaux serving at the time in Korea, thought Jackie was going to marry him. They had had "an affair of the heart," as she put it, in Paris. She wrote him, telling him, "I will always remember our walks along the Seine. But I want you to be the first to know that I've found the love of my life, the man I want to marry."

Mail delivery was erratic in Korea. When Ormande received her "Dear John" letter, Jackie had already broken

Tall, rich, and handsome, aspirant politician **John F. Kennedy**, age 29 in 1946, parades through the streets of working class Boston.

From the very beginning, women voters were attracted to him. At many a luncheon, women actually swooned when he mounted the stage. His close friend, Charles (Chuck) Spalding, claimed, "The temperature went up a hundred and fifty degrees when Jack walked in."

In Nigel Hamilton's *JFK Reckless Youth,* a biography of young JFK, the author wrote, "Rose Kennedy was a cold, unmotherly, and distant woman, leaving him emotionally crippled in his relations with women; a young man who disliked people embracing him, who showered compulsively—often five times a day—and yet perpetually craved the most symbolic and intimate of all touching: sexual union."

Photofest

In 1947, **Jackie** herself gave a description of how she appeared to the world, or, more accurately, to herself:

"I am tall, 5'7", with brown hair, a square face, and eyes so unfortunately far apart that it takes three weeks to have a pair of glasses made with a bridge wide enough to fit over my nose. I do not have a sensational figure, but can look slim if I pick the right clothes. I flatter myself on being able at times to walk out of the house looking like a poor man's Paris copy, but often my mother will run up to inform me that my left stocking is crooked or the right-hand top button is about to fall off. This, I realize, is the Unforgivable Sin."

off her engagement to Husted and was engaged to a politician named Jack Kennedy.

Husted and Jackie became so "hot and heavy," that on January 21, 1952, *The New York Times* ran a story announcing their engagement.

According to some reports, Lee Bouvier, her sister, urged her not to marry Husted. Lee was quoted as saying, "I don't think Jackie was in love with John, and he would probably have bored her after one month of marriage."

When Janet learned that Husted was making less than $20,000 a year on Wall Street, she again intervened, threatening Jackie with disinheritance if she continued her latest relationship.

When Janet finally convinced her daughter that Husted would never be a rich man, she began to date other men, including John White who worked in Washington for the State Department, and Godfrey McHough, a former major in the U.S. Air Force who had a reputation of being "a ladies' man." She also dated a journalist, William Walton, but Janet said, "newspaper reporters are among the poorest breed on earth."

In Washington, Jackie needed a date for the ball thrown by the Dancing Club at the end of the social season of 1951-1952. She asked her friend, Martha Bartlett, what to do. "I know you love money, and Jack Kennedy has a lot of it—or at least old Joe Kennedy does. Why don't you call Jack? He's very handsome. I understand he knows how to show a gal a good time."

"I just might call him," Jackie said enigmatically. She did an hour later, and he accepted her invitation.

Once at the ball, and, as a harbinger, he more or less deserted her. She spotted him with a married woman she knew, Wendy Burden Morgan, whose looks were evocative of Jackie's. Jack didn't want to dance with Wendy but to sneak away with her onto the terrace.

While he was coming on strong to Wendy in the moonlight, Jackie suddenly appeared and tapped him on the shoulder.

"Jack," she said, as he spun around. "The Meyer Davis Orchestra has struck up 'From This Moment On,'" she said. Looking at Wendy, then at Jack, she said, "Your date for the evening wants to dance." She pulled him away, in the middle of his conquest. Such a scene would become a familiar refrain in their lives.

To make money to support herself, Jackie in December of 1951 took a job working for the now defunct *Times-Herald* in Washington D.C. She went from a stint as a "gofer" to city room receptionist and finally rose to the rank of a columnist producing a regularly scheduled "inquiring photographer" feature. One of the first subjects she interviewed was a young John F. Kennedy. Thanks to her promotion to a new job as a photographer, her pay went from $42.50 a week to $56.75.

While working at the *Times-Herald*, Jackie's boss asked her who would be ideal as a man for her to marry.

"I look at a male model and am bored in three minutes," she said. "I like men with funny noses, ears that protrude, irregular teeth, short men, skinny men, fat men. Above all, he must have a keen mind, and he must weigh more and have bigger feet than I do."

Jackie later recalled how she started dating Jack. "I met him at the home of friends of ours [probably Charles and Martha Bartlett]. They had been shamelessly matchmaking for a year. Usually those things don't work out. But when I first met Jack, we clicked."

Although she was still engaged to Husted, Jackie began secretly to date "the other Jack in my life," a reference, of course, to Kennedy.

The romantic new couple was seen dancing at the Shoreham Hotel in Washington, D.C. Jackie told her sister, Lee, "I find him dangerous, just like our father, Black Jack."

Jack, now in his mid-thirties, was preparing to run for the Senate seat from Massachusetts, and his father, Joe Kennedy, was urging him to settle down and find a presentable wife. "You've got to stop this whoring around, knocking up women, and sending them off to have abortions. Of course, we both know that abortions are necessary from time to time, although opposed by the Holy Father."

By the spring of 1952, Jack's wooing of Jackie became more pronounced, as related by Jack's jealous homosexual friend who wanted to walk in Jackie's shoes. Lem Billings said, "On some nights they would simply go in for heavy petting in the back seat of Jack's car. One time their lovemaking was interrupted by a state trooper who shone a flashlight into their car. Jack had Jackie's bra off at this embarrassing moment. The cop recognized Jack and apologized before speeding away on his motorcycle."

By March of 1952, Jackie broke off the engagement to Husted, writing him a letter in which she enclosed the engagement ring he'd presented to her.

That summer she was taken to Hyannis Port to meet the Kennedy clan. "I was not impressed," she later said.

She referred to Jean, Patricia, and Eunice Kennedy as the "Rah-Rah Girls." In retaliation, they mocked her as "The Debutante." Jackie tried to fit in, even joining them in a game of touch football. But a Harvard classmate of Teddy Kennedy's fell on her and broke her ankle.

In the beginning, she had little patience for Jack's many allergies. An accomplished equestrienne, she invited him to go horseback riding, but he began to sneeze uncontrollably. "Can you picture this?" she asked Janet. "Me, married to a man who can't even walk into a stable, much less ride a

Photofest

Three brothers, each a future sexual *roué*, line up in front of the Kennedy compound at Hyannis Port—**Teddy** (left), **Bobby** (center), and **Jack**.

After Joseph P. Kennedy, Jr. ("young Joe") was killed during World War II, Rose evaluated her remaining sons like this:

"Bobby is the best looking. Ted is a bit slow but trying to catch up with his brothers. And Jack is being reluctantly plotted a future in politics by my husband, much to Jack's discomfort. Except for Jack's bonding with Lem Billings, I believe that all my sons will grow up to be heterosexuals. If anything, I think they inherited too great an interest in women. Blame their father for that. I wanted all of them to settle down and be faithful to their wives. But dreams and wishes rarely come true. Life writes its own plot for us."

horse without going into convulsions."

She also told her mother, "The Kennedy clan is *so* Irish and *so* very bourgeois."

In spite of her reservations, she moved forward with her involvement with Jack, to some degree because she was in a race to the altar with her younger sister Lee.

Lee beat her to it, marrying the strikingly handsome Michael Canfield in April of 1953. "Lee got there first," Jackie complained to Jack as if to goad him along with that long-delayed proposal. She suspected that he was enjoying his life as a swinging bachelor too much to want to settle down with a wife. But Joe kept insisting on his son getting married—and to Jackie. She was the only woman Jack ever dated who had won Joe's stamp of approval.

Among Jack Kennedy's many sexual conquests, it was Judy Garland who later told her friend, Peter Lawford, "Jack was in bed with me at the Mayflower Hotel in Washington when a call came in from Jackie."

According to Judy, Jackie informed him that in her role as a reporter, she was flying to London to cover the May, 1953 coronation of Queen Elizabeth II.

"I couldn't believe it," Judy later told Peter. "Jack had fucked me twice the night before and was in the mood for a blow-job before he left for his office. With me only a foot away fondling his balls to get him in the mood, he asked Jacqueline Lee Bouvier for her hand in marriage. After all my experiences in Hollywood, I thought I'd seen it all. This was a first for me. When he put down the phone, I asked him if she'd accepted his

At the time of her Newport (Rhode Island) wedding to **John F. Kennedy**, **Jackie** had perfected what became known as "the American geisha technique." That was a reference to speaking in a gently modulated voice, which her critics called "a soft, whispering coo, somewhat like Jackie's rival, Marilyn Monroe, a master of the coo." The voice sounded like that of an unthreatening little girl.

Shirley Langhauser, Jackie's schoolmate, claimed, "She underwent a major voice transformation. Originally, her voice was quite normal, like any other gal's."

Jackie would carry the geisha syndrome through her White House years, her marriage to Onassis, and even into the offices at Doubleday, where she was an editor.

Richard de Combray, an author whose books she edited, said, "She always talked about you, which is part of the geisha syndrome, and it was enormously appealing to sit opposite this woman who, with all this baggage she carried, this fame and fortune, whatever, was totally absorbed by whatever it is you were saying to her, as if it was the most interesting thing in the world. Her trick was to talk about you, never herself."

proposal," Judy told Peter.

"Not really," Jack told Judy. "She said, I'll get back to you on that. But first, I've got a coronation to cover.'"

In reflection, Judy recalled to Peter, "I always wondered how Jackie knew that Jack was at the Mayflower Hotel—and even our room number. I suspected she must have been on to him long before her marriage to our boy politico with the roving eye and a perpetual hard-on."

When her old beau, Demi Gates, met Jackie in London just before Queen Elizabeth's coronation, he said he warned her not to get involved with Jack Kennedy. "He's a hopeless womanizer and has three or four gals a week, or so I hear," Gates said.

"All men are unfaithful," she told Gates. "At least Jack has money. I guess I could forgive him if he strayed from time to time."

On a quick side trip to Paris in the wake of the coronation, Jackie stayed at the apartment of her former flame, John P. Marquand Jr. They resumed their affair, which led to a marriage proposal from him.

Over morning coffee following a night of passion, she told him that she had made up her mind to marry Jack Kennedy.

He slammed down his cup. "You can't marry that…that mick!"

She countered, "He has money and you don't."

"Besides," he told her, "he's a sleazy politician with a crook for a father. You don't want to be the wife of some Irish politician spending the rest of your days meeting dull housewives at chicken *à la king* dinners."

It's true," she agreed. "I detest politics. Jack is also twelve years older than me. But he's fascinating, and I suspect there will never be a dull moment married to him. Besides, he has all that Kennedy money. Even if it's earned from crooked deals in Hollywood and bootlegging, it's still money."

Upon her return to New York, Jackie picked up a copy of the *Saturday Evening Post* which had published an article on Jack. It was entitled, "The Senate's Gay Young Bachelor." Of course, gay in those days had a different meaning. Nowhere within it was there even a sly suggestion that Jack occasionally maintained a sort of one-sided homosexual relationship with his eternal companion, Lem Billings.

Jack could get very vulgar in talking about Lem, at times putting him down. Once he told Senator George Smathers, "Sometimes you need a guy like Lem around to wash your dick thoroughly after you've fucked some whore."

Jackie's engagement to Jack was announced on June 23, 1953. Newspapers across America reported on the romance. Jack urged his bride-to-be to pose for pictures for a cover story in *Life* magazine. This article was the beginning of a massive publicity build-up on the long road to the White House. One journalist referred to them as "America's Most Romantic Couple."

In New York, Jack did not go to Van Cleef & Arpels to purchase the engagement ring. He sent Lem, who returned with a square-cut diamond and emerald ring, each stone 2.88 carats. Joe Kennedy had pre-ordered the ring and paid for it. All Lem had to do was pick it up. Joe also paid for the elaborate wedding.

Before her marriage, Joe told Jackie, "You've got to stop peppering your speech with girlish words like *golly, gee,* and *gosh*. Gloria Swanson would never be caught dead doing that. Also stop biting your nails and chain smoking. And whenever photographers are around, look up lovingly at Jack, like you're hanging on every word of wisdom he utters."

Right before his wedding, as he was getting dressed, JFK confided to Senator Smathers, "I don't really want to marry Jackie. But let's face. A man nearing forty who's in politics had better get married if he wants to stay in office. Otherwise, the public will think I'm queer."

Cardinal Richard Cushing, archbishop of Boston, traveled to Newport to perform the wedding on September 12, 1953. Jack was thirty-six, Jackie, only twenty-four. Tenor Luigi Vena performed "Ave Maria," although Jackie later told Jack, "I detest that song."

She would later be known for her chic apparel, but some reporters attacked her wedding dress as "atrocious." Janet had forced her to wear the dress. Jackie claimed she hated the work of Ann Lowe, denouncing her as a "colored dressmaker."

For their honeymoon, Jack and Jackie spent two days at the Waldorf-Astoria in New York.

On her wedding night, Jack finally told her a dark secret, claiming he had contracted a venereal disease in 1940 when he was only 23 years old, and that it had gone untreated for years. He said that this disease (*Chlamydia*) might have made him infertile.

Saddened at the news that she might never have children with her new husband, Jackie flew to Mexico with him to spend the rest of their honeymoon in a villa overlooking the Pacific.

When Jack saw the color of the villa, he called it "pussy pink." The villa was actually owned by Don Miguel Alemán, President of Mexico and a longtime friend of Joe Kennedy.

On his third night, Jack disappeared to visit the local bordello where he ordered teenage *señoritas*.

Evelyn Lincoln, who later became Jack's personal secretary said, "He carried on business on his honeymoon. The last thing on his mind was his honeymoon."

Back in Washington, before they had a home of their own, Jackie said she and her new husband "lived out of a suitcase."

She confided to her dear friend, Nancy Tuckerman, that Jack was very casual about

Caroline Kennedy looks bewildered as **John F. Kennedy**, the Democratic presidential nominee, holds her up for reporters to photograph on election day, November 8, 1960. Accompanied by a stylish **Jackie**, they're seen outside their home in Hyannis Port.

Peter Lawford recalled Jack's first day in office, at the conclusion of the inauguration balls. "I imported half a dozen starlets from Hollywood, each of whom wanted the newly elected president to seduce them. At the home of Joe Alsop, I arranged a line-up as it's done by a madame in a brothel. Jack chose two of the best-looking ones for a *ménage à trois*."

Jackie recalled waking up her first morning in the White House. "I was standing nude in the middle of the floor, wondering what to wear for the day. Without a knock, Jack barged into the room with the first official visitor. It was former president Harry S Truman. Other than his wife, Bess, I don't think he'd ever seen a naked woman before. In fact, I think Bess probably kept her clothes on the time they'd had sex—and that was to produce Margaret Truman, the pianist."

nudity. "Sometimes he walks into the living room naked to talk to his male friends about business. If a woman is present, he might wrap a towel around it. Also, did you know that married men sometimes don't come home at night and don't tell their wives where they have been?"

***

Long after passion's youthful fire had died down between Jackie and Marquand, they remained in touch for years to come, often writing a note or placing a call to each other whenever the mood struck.

John Marquand Jr. (alias John Phillips) died on April 30, 1995 at his home in Manhattan at the age of 71.

Shortly after Jackie died on May 19, 1994, an ailing John sent a bouquet of white roses. He signed his card, IN MEMORY OF WHAT MIGHT HAVE BEEN. FIRST LOVES ARE THE MOST PAINFUL.

Princess Grace and Jackie-O

Their Ongoing Competition
for Love, Sex, Power, & Prestige

Associated Press

On May 4, 1961, when President John F. Kennedy and **Jacqueline** entertained Prince Rainier and **Princess Grace** at a White House luncheon, the two combatants pictured above (Grace, of course, is the one in the silly hat), were later forced to have a cup of tea together when JFK excused himself to talk to Prince Rainier. Jackie at this point had heard about Grace's affair with her husband.

When they were seated, according to a White House staff member, Jackie provocatively asked, "Of the Seven Graces, which one are you?"

"I try to have the qualities of all of them," Grace shot back.

Continuing her provocation, Jackie asked, "Jack and I heard that when Prince Rainier was shopping for a bride, he first considered Marilyn Monroe. At least that was the plan that Aristotle Onassis said he proposed to your prince."

"Yes, I know," Grace shot back. "He found the idea disgusting. We're not promoting Monaco as a destination for Las Vegas style whorehouses."

Jackie wanted the last word, "Oh, I forgot to tell you how much I adore your hat. Did Oleg Cassini design it for you?"

MONACO'S PRINCESS CLASHES WITH AMERICA'S QUEEN

Princess Grace (aka Grace Kelly) detested Aristotle Onassis, who would in time become Jackie's second husband. She made her opinion of him widely known, although not on the record.

When Cary Grant visited her, she said she resented Onassis for trying to turn Monaco "into his own personal playground and regarding its prince as a mere puppet."

Grant and Grace had had an affair when they made *To Catch a Thief* together in 1955; it was set on the Riviera.

These two movie stars were very chummy and rather frank with each other, and Grace was well aware of Grant's bisexuality.

Reportedly she once asked him, "Did you ever have an affair with Black Jack Bouvier, Jackie's father?"

Grant's answer to her provocative question is not known.

In 1948 the handsome young prince of the Kennedy clan, JFK, met a beautiful blonde, Grace Kelly of Philadelphia. The introductions were arranged by their fathers, Joseph P. Kennedy and Jack Kelly. Both of them were sons of Irish immigrants, and both of them had made millions.

Joe was a big man in Boston, and Jack was a big man in the brick making and construction businesses of Philadelphia. Often, they compared notes and trophies, each man trying to outdo the other in tall tales.

These rich Irishmen had no compunctions against cheating on their wives. Perhaps it was Kelly who suggested that Joe should introduce Jack to his daughter, who was organizing an extended sojourn in New York and needed an escort to various social functions. There was even talk between the patriarchs about a possible union of their respective "dynasties" through marriage.

The exact circumstances of the eventual union of Jack with Grace are not known. What is known is that during the late 1940s, they were frequently spotted out on the town together in Manhattan. Jack was seen escorting Grace in and out of the Barbizon Hotel for Women.

"I knew Grace back then," said Ilona Berman, another aspiring actress. "The Barbizon had strict rules about men, but she wasn't going to adhere to them, at least not after she met Jack Kennedy. A pal of his from Harvard had a bachelor pad in Manhattan, and I know for a fact that Jack and Grace spent many an evening there. She told me that she was in love with Jack. She had such a pristine façade that no one in those days suspected her of all these indiscretions. From what I saw, Jack and Grace were hardly true to each other. They were going out with others but keeping it quiet. She even slipped men into the Barbizon and never got caught. Both Jack and Grace were hot to trot. I knew another aspiring young actress at the Barbizon. And when Grace wasn't available, Jack was shacking up with her, too."

It was later revealed in several biographies that Grace, still a teenager at the time, was having a torrid affair with drama instructor Don Richardson, a twenty-seven year old at the time.

This was either the first or among the first of many sexual affairs Grace would have with older men. On their first date, Don invited her back to his apartment. "I started a fire and within forty minutes we were in bed together," he recalled. "It was an amazing sight, seeing a girl as beautiful as Grace lying naked in my bed, bathed in light from the fireplace."

Jack was also warmed by "the fire under all that ice." He was at a party where Grace, in her late teens, literally let her hair down. As biographer James Spada revealed in *Grace: The Secret Lives of a Princess*, "The wild side of Grace, usually so well hidden beneath layers of propriety, sometimes surfaced even in public—when Grace had been drinking. Those who thought her chilly and decorous were stunned one night at a New York party when Grace suddenly jumped on top of a table, flipped off her shoes, and began to writhe sensuously to the guitar music being strummed by one of the other guests. Moving sinuously, she became more and more sexually provocative, undoing her topknot until her hair fell about her face and shoulders."

From all reports, Jack and Grace, who both came from intensely politicized families, talked a lot about politics on their dates. In 1934, Grace's father, Jack Kelly, had run for the office of mayor of Philadelphia. He'd been supported in his bid by then-president Franklin D. Roosevelt, who had publicly referred to him as "the handsomest man in America."

But even with Roosevelt's backing, he'd lost, partly because he was a hard-hitting Irish Catholic in a mostly Protestant town. "Even though that happened back in 1934, I think the prejudice against Catholics is still strong today." Grace said, "Religion will harm your chances if you ever run for higher office."

"I'll just take my chances," Jack assured her. "Someone one day will become the first Catholic president, the first Jewish president, even the first black president."

"Black?" she said astonished. "We certainly will never live to see that day!"

Jack was not always in New York, and certainly not always with Grace, but apparently they discussed the possibility of marriage. When Joe Kennedy heard of this, he was furious, because since his earlier discussions with Jack Kelly, he'd learned that Jack's daughter passionately wanted to be a big-screen Hollywood actress.

"Have you ever heard of a President of the United States bringing an actress to the White House as First Lady?"

At that time, of course, Ronald Reagan hadn't yet arrived in triumph at the White House with his wife, former B-actress Nancy Davis.

"The handsomest man in politics," or so Franklin D. Roosevelt maintained. **Jack Kelly** is seen here in 1920.

Grace's father, a bigwig in the Philadelphia construction business, had been an expert oarsman. George Kelly, Jack's brother and Grace's uncle, was rumored to have "serviced" his brother when they were growing up. Uncle George, a playwright, influenced Grace to become an actress.

Jack balked at the idea of paying a dowry to Prince Rainier, and fought with his Monaco lawyers for days before finally coughing up two million dollars to give Grace away.

Initially, he had opposed the wedding. "I don't want any god damn broken-down prince who's head of a country over there that nobody ever heard of marrying my daughter!"

Looking innocent and, in Grace's case, virginal, both **Jack Kennedy and Grace Kelly** were promiscuous youths. Jack lost his virginity when he was seventeen years old in a Harlem whorehouse to a black prostitute. Grace lost her virginity to an older, married man, the husband of a close girlfriend, one afternoon at his house when his wife was away.

Grace once told Cary Grant, "I fell in love with Jack, and never got over it. He's the man I should have married."

Before marrying Grace, Prince Rainier had a doctor check to see if she were still a virgin—remember this was 1955. The doctor's official report to Rainier stated that she was "intact." Perhaps Gary Cooper, Ray Milland, William Holden, JFK, Bing Crosby, and Clark Gable, et al, had not broken her hymen.

***

It took years for Grace to become fully aware of Jack's various illnesses.

After it was diagnosed, the Kennedy clan conspired to keep from the public news of Jack's Addison's disease. "There's no way Jack could ever have been elected president in 1960 if people knew he had an incurable disease that at least, potentially, was fatal," said his most intimate friend, Lem Billings.

Throughout 1954, Jack lived in almost constant agony, according to Lem. His ever-faithful friend accompanied him to the hospital, where he underwent surgery for a double fusion of his spine to correct a ruptured disk. Conveniently, during his tenure as Senator from Massachussets (1953-1960)), because of this operation and his recuperation, he would not be present on the Senate floor for the December 2, 1954 vote to censure Senator Joe McCarthy for his implacable and vindictive hunt for "commie pinkos." On that day, the U.S. Senate, in a vote of 67 to 22 in favor of censuring McCarthy, effectively ended one of the most controversial careers in American politics. Kennedy's abstention allowed him to sidestep confrontations from both liberals and conservatives after the fact.

As JFK later revealed to Charles (Chuck) Spalding, "Even though I detested some of the shit he pulled, how can I vote to censure Joe? Against my wishes, my own brother, Bobby, worked for Joe. How could I denounce the bastard when Bobby was one of his killer henchmen?"

Lem remembered meeting with Joe Kennedy before JFK's spine operation. "Usually he gave me wide berth, but this time he held me in his arms. He was sobbing. 'We're going to lose Jack,' he told me. 'I've called in Father Cavanaugh for last rites.'"

After that encounter, Lem cried all night, and then kept a vigil for Jack during his dangerous surgery, during which doctors gave him a bone graft and inserted a metal plate into his spine.

When Jack regained consciousness, Lem was at his bedside holding his hand. Two days later, Jack was told by his doctors that he might have to walk with crutches for the rest of his life.

Then in the days following the surgery, the doctors grew alarmed that the surgical wound was not healing. Lem visited Jack every day. One morning, Jack demanded to hear "the awful truth" about his wound.

He pulled the sheet off his nude body before slowing turning over. "Is it raw and oozing? Is the fucking wound still open? Is that green pus spewing out of it? How does it smell? Like a shithouse, huh?"

"The wound just wasn't healing," Lem later claimed. "It looked like a raw piece of meat. I came real close to fearing that I was going to lose Jack forever."

After that, doctors began to deal more aggressively with Jack's Addison's disease, inserting pellets of corticosteroid hormones into his thigh. It was estimated that this treatment would extend his life by between five and ten years. But Lem noticed the change in Jack's face, which had became more bloated. JFK also confided that "these fucking hormones have made my libido rage out of control."

Two months after the first operation on his back, JFK's doctors told him that he would need surgery for the second time. Jack's Addison's disease was preventing his back from healing properly.

Unknown to JFK, his doctors met with Joe. The head doctor warned him that Jack's surgery was risky but also very necessary. Joe heard the words he didn't want to hear, that the operation would be "potentially lethal." Joe gave them permission to go ahead, because the country's top medical specialists believed that his son's life would be jeopardized if nothing was done. Once again, Lem was there by his side when Jack regained consciousness the following morning. The entire Kennedy clan heard the good news: Jack's operation had been a success, and the prediction was that his back would heal properly this time.

Amazingly, even in his weakened state, Jack's mind was often on sex with women, much

Jack Kennedy and Jackie (above) were the handsomest, most dazzling couple ever to occupy the White House, but their detractors could be vicious.

As reported in David Heymann's 1990 book, *A Woman Named Jackie*, Mary Tierney, a reporter for the *Boston-Herald*, claimed, "Jackie had this inane smile that seemed to have been fixed in place by plasterer. I thought of her as an appendage to the Kennedy family. She was a little actress but without her lines she was lost. I mean she is one of those people who when you say 'hello' to and she's stuck for an answer. She certainly didn't care for the Irish Mafia that surrounded Jack. They weren't good enough for her. She was very snobbish. She was a nerd, a big zero. Her marriage was one of convenience."

to Lem's regret. During one of his hospital stays, he had a pinup of Marilyn Monroe pasted near his bed. But on this particular occasion, he talked a lot about what he'd like to do once again to Grace Kelly, according to Lem.

Jack had often told both Lem and Bobby about how desirable he'd found Grace a few years previously, but his plans to marry her had been foiled. When Bobby heard that Grace was in New York, he called her and told her how depressed Jack was. "He's feeling sort of lousy," he said. "Please come over. He'd love to see you."

She willingly agreed even when Bobby called back and told her he wanted her to dress up as a nurse and enter his room for "a rather invasive physical examination." At first she had objected, but she eventually relented. "What the hell. Anything to cheer Jack up."

Swedish aristocrat, **Gunilla von Post** *(photo above)* is noted for her affair in 1953 and 1955 with a young John F. Kennedy. He met her three weeks before marrying Jackie, and he claimed he fell wildly in love with her.

His letters to her, which observers cite as "seeping with regret on both sides," were auctioned off early in 2011.

Gunilla met JFK when he was 36, and she was 21. The setting was the romantic French Riviera. The attraction was immediate.

He told her, that if he had met her one week before, "I would have cancelled my wedding to Jackie."

In an American TV interview, Von Post told the audience, "I borrowed him for a week [in 1955, deep into his marriage with Jackie] in a Swedish castle—a beautiful week that no one can take away from me."

As a practical joke, Bobby got the hospital administrator to agree to allow Grace to dress in a nurse's uniform and pretend to want to take Jack's temperature "between the cheeks."

When she entered his room, he was still drugged and at first didn't seem to recognize her. Striding to his bedside, she ripped the sheet away, exposing a half erection as if he'd been playing with himself. "Turn over," she commanded. Reluctantly he did so, as she "inserted a thermometer where the sun don't shine," as she later told Bobby. After taking his temperature, she ordered him to turn back over. "Forgive me, but I've got to take a sample of your semen."

Although startled, Jack agreed. "Do you want me to masturbate into something?" he asked.

Grace had recently filmed *Mogambo* with Ava Gardner and Clark Gable. She remembered Ava telling her that when she'd visited aviator Howard Hughes in the hospital "the best cure for him was a blow-job." To Jack's surprise, Grace plunged down, just as she'd done on Gable himself, plus dozens of other Hollywood stars, including Gary Cooper.

Somehow, as Jack would later relate to Lem, "I suddenly realized that it was Grace Kelly giving me that blow-job."

"It's you, Grace," he said to her bobbing head. "Bobby sent you."

She raised her head, "Shut up and come!"

Some biographers have wrongly suggested that it was Jackie who had formulated and articulated the idea of Grace Kelly's impersonation of a nurse. That is not accurate. Instead, it was Bobby who wanted to cheer Jack up by having "the world's most beautiful night nurse" tend to his needs. As became obvious in the years to come, Jackie didn't want the glamorous blonde movie star anywhere near her husband.

In June of 1965, Grace collaborated in a cover-up when she provided an oral history for the Kennedy Library, wherein she asserted that she first met Jack when she paid that "night nurse" visit with him back in 1954, even though friends knew about how her romance with him dated from as early as 1949. Of course, in the details she related to the Kennedy Library, Her Serene Highness, the Princess, left out the sordid details of that hospital call.

After Jack's recovery, during the decades to come, he and Grace would meet on several more occasions during her visits to America. After he became president, she was especially pleased to have already added his name to the list of distinguished men she'd seduced. That list included Jean-Pierre Aumont, Oleg Cassini, Bing Crosby, William Holden, Frank Sinatra, Cary Grant, Prince Aly Khan, Ray Milland, David Niven, James Stewart, and Spencer Tracy, et al.

***

After her impersonation of a nurse, Bobby called Grace to thank her. For many years, Jack had bragged to Bobby about Grace's special charms, and he was anxious to visit with her. The depth and circumstances of Bobby's romantic link with Grace have never been fully revealed, but it is suspected that Bobby's affair with her began the night after that hospital visit. Their "sometimes" affair would be conducted over a period of many years, both before and after her marriage to Rainier, in New York, Washington, and Paris.

A beautiful blonde and aristocratic Swede, Gunilla von Post, born in 1932, also claimed she'd had an affair with JFK shortly before his marriage to Jackie. According to her, Jack asserted, "I fell in love with you tonight." He also admitted that he'd fallen in love only once before and that had been with Grace Kelly in 1948, "the first moment I laid eyes on her."

GUNILLA VON POST

Gunilla's hours were far too brief with Jack. But she wanted to set the record straight about his performance in bed. "He was not a slam-bam, thank you, ma'am kind of guy, like we've been led to believe. Rather, he was a sweet and tender lover—albeit one with a lot of back pain."

Joe Kennedy often managed to sample the sexual charms of a woman before his sons, but not in the case of Grace. The designer, Oleg Cassini, and Joseph P. Kennedy had long been friends, and Cassini had already designed expensive gowns for Rose, Eunice, and Patricia.

In 1955, Cassini lunched with Joe at Manhattan's exclusive La Côte Basque restaurant, during which he implored him to intercede on behalf of his desperately-in-love hope to marry Grace.

"I know her father," Joe said. "Introduce me to her, and I assure you the deal is done. I can sell anything to anybody, even a chump like you to the Kelly woman, although I always thought you'd want to settle down with your buddy, Victor

In her memoir, *Love, Jack,* Gunilla von Post related a dialogue she'd had with JFK:

"I love you, Gunilla. I adore you. I'm crazy about you, and I'll do anything to be with you."

To answer him, she blurted out: "you're married!" Very slowly and steadily, he said, "Gunilla, I've been married for two years. What's changed?"

She paused for a long moment. "Me," she finally said. "I've changed."

When he asked her exactly how she'd changed, she replied, "Maybe I'm in love with you now."

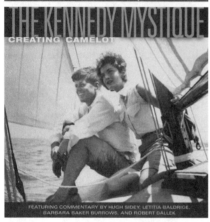

Letitia Baldrige *(top photo)* was an American etiquette expert and became famous when she was in the White House functioning as social secretary to Jackie Kennedy. She was responsible for details associated with those lovely state dinners during JFK's administration. She is also the author of nearly 20 books, most of them about manners and entertaining.

Along with Robert Dallek and Barbara Baker Burros, she wrote *The Kennedy Mystique: Creating Camelot*. The book lived up to its billing, doing more than most to create "the myth of Camelot," positioning Jack and Jackie as the perfect couple.

In one passage, Baldrige wrote: "The extremely attractive young couple in the White House had suddenly made all of the crowned heads of Europe look drab in comparison. The Kennedys received official invitations to visit almost every country in the world. There weren't enough days in the year to accommodate them all. The state visit competition was fierce!"

Mature, instead."

Cassini asked Grace to have lunch with Joe at the same La Côte Basque, and Grace agreed, no doubt thinking Joe might help her win a coveted film role.

Near the end of their very private luncheon, where Joe found Grace very flirtatious, he leaned over and took her hand, holding it tightly in his. "We Irish, both the Kelly and Kennedy families, have to stick together. We're part of the same clan. I've known Cassini for a long time—he overcharges for his gowns, by the way—and he's a pretty good boy if you like the effeminate type. But you'd make a terrible mistake to marry him."

Continuing to stroke Grace's hand, Joe pressed his case. "Of course, we'll have to discuss this thing in greater depth. I want you to come to my suite at the Plaza tonight around eight. We'll go into it then."

Although she smiled demurely and seemed to accept his invitation, she didn't show up at the Plaza that night even though he waited for her until 10:30pm. Back at the Barbizon, she told her actress friend, Ilona Berman, that she'd stood up a powerful man like Joe Kennedy.

Years later, in 1960, when Cassini became Jackie's couturier, he encountered Joe at a reception at the White House. "I did you a favor," Joe said. "Grace is better off with that prissy Rainier boy. The Kelly family would have been on you like octopuses. They would have driven you crazy."

The luncheon between Joe and Grace became one of JFK's favorite stories. Often, during parties at the White House, the president would approach Cassini in front of others. "Oleg, tell them how Dad screwed you up with Grace Kelly."

Instead of marrying Cassini, as he'd so clearly wanted, in April of 1956, Grace surprised her friends by marrying Prince Rainier of Monaco instead.

"I think Jackie's dislike of Grace began when she and Jack were looking at the press coverage of the wedding in Monaco," said author Gore Vidal, Jackie's kissin' kin. "Jack studied the pictures intently, then said, 'I could have married her.'"

Denouncing him, Jackie ran from the room in anger.

Their marriage seemed to go on hold after that, and for "sexual favors," Jack turned elsewhere.

Even though aide David Powers had tried to cover it up, Jackie learned that her husband, before Grace's marriage to Rainier, had spent the night in a Washington hotel with Grace. At Hyannis Port, Jackie confronted him with what she'd learned. Right in front of some members of the Kennedy clan, she told him that she was leaving him.

"Then get the fuck out of here!" he shouted at her. "I should never have married you in the first place. I really wanted to marry Grace Kelly. What a First Lady she would make, not some Bouvier trash like you."

It took three weeks and constant apologies for Jackie to forgive him for that. She left Hyannis Port that night and headed for New York. Somehow, with the passage of time, she managed to turn her hatred of Jack for what he'd said into anger at Grace.

Jackie's loathing of Princess Grace spilled over into the White House after Jack was elected president in 1960. JFK asked Jackie to plan an entertainment for Prince and Princess Rainier during the royal couple's visit to Washington.

Biographer Wendy Leigh quoted Letitia ("Tish") Baldrige, Jackie's social secretary, as to what happened next. "Grace had a relationship with the president before his marriage to Jackie, and Jackie knew about it. That, in my opinion, is why Jackie changed the White House meal in their honor from a four-hour black-tie dinner dance to a small luncheon. A bit of jealousy perhaps. Jackie never said anything, but you could tell. She didn't really want to talk about the arrangements and was very offhand about how they were made. A luncheon meant that Princess Grace wouldn't look as gorgeous as she usually did at night."

Tish later revealed that Grace "looked dowdy—exactly like an Esther Williams Aquacade in a flowered rubber bathing cap." The president sat on one side of the oval-shaped table with Grace, whereas Jackie occupied the other side with Prince Rainier. Nervous about facing Jack again, and with a jealous Jackie hawk-eyeing her every move, she'd quickly downed two double Bloody Marys before arriving by limousine at the White House. "She was bombed," Franklin D. Roosevelt Jr., another guest, claimed.

Roosevelt, Jr. had already been privy to many of Jack's secret affairs before his marriage to Jackie, and had once gone out on a double date with Jack and Grace before she abandoned New York for Hollywood.

Tish remembered that Grace "behaved like a schoolgirl around Jack," perhaps recalling that if she'd made the right moves she'd now be First

Associated Press

Designer **Oleg Cassini** was photographed standing next to movie star **Grace Kelly** at the world premiere of *Strategic Air Command* in New York City on April 22, 1955.

The designer wanted Grace to become Mrs. Oleg Cassini at this point, but she had more princely plans for marriage.

In reference to Cassini, Joe Kennedy had pointedly asked Grace, "Why would you want to marry a Russian Jew? Besides, he's a renowned womanizer and dallies occasionally in bed with men."

Grace's father, Jack Kelly, had said, "I don't want my daughter to marry some dress-designing queer—he probably wears some of the frocks himself."

Ironically, only a few weeks before the public appearance documented in this photo, Grace had been in bed with actor Ray Milland.

Lady of the ruling country of the Free World and not the princess of a small strip of land on the French Riviera. "She batted her eyelashes at Jack throughout the luncheon," Tish claimed.

She later told Roosevelt Jr. that Jack's rise in politics had been almost unbelievable, recalling that she'd warned him about how hard it would be for a Catholic to be elected. "But he was always such a handsome Irish boy, so full of life, so filled with charm, a real fighter just like his father."

Grace and Jackie were often compared in the press, and both women were considered valuable assets to their husbands. President Kennedy claimed he was the man who accompanied Jackie to Paris, and Prince Rainier called Grace "the best ambassador I have."

Actually it was Grace who had charmed Charles de Gaulle years before Jackie won his heart. Jackie enchanted the French in 1961, Grace having done so in a French/Monegasque state visit two years before, in 1959.

In the days following the 1963 assassination of her former lover in Dallas, Grace came in for an attack when a photograph of her cheerfully holding an air rifle was published around the world. John Cummings, writing in the *Philadelphia Inquirer*, accused Grace "of being selfish and imbued with a heartless insouciance at the time of JFK's assassination. While her native land was in deep mourning for the slain President, Princess Grace was on an outing in a Monaco park. A photograph shows her in a shooting gallery on that tragic weekend."

Always sensitive to criticism, and very thin-skinned, Grace shot back, claiming that the photograph was actually taken hours before the tragedy in Dallas.

She was right about that, of course, since Monaco is hours ahead of Dallas. The photo of Grace with the rifle was taken at least nine hours before JFK was assassinated.

As recompense for her trouble and embarrassment at the carnival shooting gallery, Princess Grace made off with a Kewpie doll.

Actually Prince Rainier and Princess Grace were preparing to attend the President's funeral. However, the day they were scheduled to depart, a confidential message came in. A French diplomat had heard Jackie quoted as saying, "I don't want that whoring bitch to show up at Jack's funeral." The Rainiers immediately cancelled their flight.

In spite of that rejection, Princess Grace, because of her

On an official visit to a White House luncheon in 1961, **the Kennedys** *(far left and far right)*, presiding over a large nation, receive royal visitors, **Prince Rainier and Princess Grace,** from a small principality in Europe. Except for Grace's lavish "bathing cap," both women dressed modestly, each perhaps deciding not to out dazzle the other.

In preparation for Grace's visit, Jackie in an impish mood drew up a list of lovers that the princess had shared with Marilyn Monroe.

At the top of the list in large bold letters she had written JACK KENNEDY. Others on her list included Frank Sinatra, Clark Gable, and Oleg Cassini.

Her distant relative, Gore Vidal, had warned Jackie, "Don't let Grace be alone for one minute with Jack. In Hollywood, she always laid her leading men—she was notorious for that."

love for Jack, flew to Washington about two weeks after the assassination, on December 3, 1963. She was spotted standing by the president's grave with tears streaming down her cheeks. Before leaving France, she'd purchased very special, unique toys for John-John and Caroline, each object meticulously crafted by French artisans.

When she called the White House to ask permission to visit with Jackie, who was still in residence, the former First Lady refused to see her.

In contrast, Her Royal Highness found Bobby only too willing to entertain her. It was the continuation of an affair that lasted on and off until the end of his life, but only during very rare occurrences when they could secretly come together. At one point, Grace was fantasizing that she might have a chance to become America's First Lady—"but only after Bobby was elected in 1968."

"Our joint divorces would screw his political future, and he'd be a one-time president unless we were so charismatic that the American public forgave us for deserting our spouses. By the time Bobby sought a second term, the public might adore us, even more than they did Jack and Jackie—strange things like that happen." She confided this to David Niven, her intimate friend and former lover.

Before Jackie married Ari in 1968, he'd told her that had she married him in 1966, "You and I would be the Prince and Princess of Monaco." He revealed that he'd owned fifty-two percent interest in Monte Carlo's *Société des Bains de Mer*, which controlled the casino, the Hotel de Paris, the Yacht Club, and about 34 percent of the principality itself. In a move to usurp his power and to thwart any takeover attempts, Prince Rainier had issued 600,000 shares of new nontransferable shares in the name of the principality.

That effectively reduced Ari's ownership to less than a third. "Beaten and defeated by the prissy Grimaldi faggot, I was forced to sell out, and I departed Monaco."

THE LOOK OF LOVE

Grace Kelly was still enamored with **Jack Kennedy**, her former lover, when this picture was snapped. Even though he rarely saw Grace after he became president, JFK was always eager to hear gossip about her. Truman Capote had told him that Grace had had an abortion right before her marriage to Rainier.

Later in the day of that now-infamous White House luncheon, Jackie was appalled when she heard Grace, in a self-mocking way, inform her end of the luncheon table about her "bosom problem."

She was discussing how, in 1954, on the set of *Rear Window*, her British director, Alfred Hitchcock, demanded that she wear falsies.

She protested, insisting that falsies would look artificial through the sheer fabric of her *negligée*. When the director insisted, she disappeared into her dressing room with her stylist. And although she refused to wear the falsies, they nonetheless made some "adjustments."

According to the story she told that day at the White House, when she returned to the set, Hitchcock praised her for her new look. Standing ramrod straight, with her shoulders back and jutting herself out, Grace didn't tell him those were her own breasts.

One of the most highly publicized trips that Jackie ever took was when the Duke and Duchess of Alba, along with Angier Biddle Duke, America's new ambassador to Spain, invited Jackie to Spain in 1966. After a night in Madrid, she flew to Seville where the Duke and Duchess installed her in the Palacio de Las Dueñas.

Also present were Prince Rainier and Princess Grace of Monaco. The stage was set for a catfight.

In the early 1960s the most written-about women in the world included Jackie and Grace, who shared honors with Marilyn Monroe, Brigitte Bardot, Elizabeth Taylor, Princess Margaret, and, of course, Queen Elizabeth II.

From the very beginning of *Feria de Abril*, the Spring Fair in Seville, held in April of 1966, the press viewed the reunion of Princess Grace and Jackie as a "duel." Their clothing was the first to be communally scrutinized.

Grace opened the festivities clad in a ruffled pink lace Andalusian dress presented to her by local flamenco dancers. In contrast, the president's widow was dark and svelte in a black-and-white Andalusian riding costume.

Jackie "completely stole Princess Grace's thunder," wrote a journalist "when America's former First Lady agreed to ride a horse in the *Feria*."

Looking spectacular, Jackie had dressed for the occasion in the traditional *traje corio*, a black trimmed red jacket, a black flat-brimmed hat, and flowing chaps. On the back of a white stallion, she looked spectacular.

Perhaps Grace never got to read a review in a Seville paper of Jackie's appearance. "America's former First Lady revealed to all the world that she should not only have been made a princess like Prince Rainier's wife, but Jacqueline should be anointed Queen of the World." Grace's name wasn't even mentioned, except for the reference to her as "wife."

As part of the festivities, Princess Grace and Jackie encountered each other at Seville's splendid bullring. At that time, the celebrated, handsome, and well-built *El Cordobés* (actually Manuel Benítez Pérez) was the leading matador of Spain.

The paparazzi stumbled over each other to photograph him in his "suit of lights," paying particular attention to the bulging crotch in his matador suit. There was even speculation that he padded himself, although his "dressers" throughout Spain claimed his endowment was real.

A child of poverty, *El Cordobés* had been reared in an orphanage and had once been a construction worker. At the low point of his career, he'd been a pickpocket.

Bypassing Grace, actually ignoring her completely, *El Cordobés* passed his matador hat to Jackie, who placed a Kennedy half-dollar into it before returning it. He then dedicated "the first bull" to Jackie.

Adding insult to injury, two other famous matadors were fighting bulls that day, Paco Camino and *El Viti*. Both of these bullfighters also bypassed Grace and extended their hats to Jackie for a Kennedy half-dollar. Each of them also dedicated their first bull to Jackie.

In front of Jackie, *El Cordobés* performed his most dangerous stunt, as she watched in horror. He broke his *banderillas* down to the size of a pencil, then stood with his back to the bull as it rampaged toward him. A moment before impact, he deftly moved his right leg out of the way of the bull's path. As the bull swerved, he thrust in the *banderillas* at a crippling point just behind its left horn. The audience went wild.

A "scoop artist" for a Madrid newspaper was in Seville just to record juicy tidbits about Jackie. When the results of his investigation appeared, it caused a sensation. He claimed, falsely or otherwise, that *El Cordobés* was seen entering the palace of the Duke and Duchess of Alba where Jackie awaited him. Ostensibly it was for drinks and dinner.

The reporter said he waited outside the palace until three o'clock that morning when *El Cordobés* was seen leaving the palace and getting into a limousine. In print, he claimed, "It is all but certain that *El Cordobés* and the widow of President John F. Kennedy had an affair that night. In seducing her matador, Mrs. Kennedy was blazing a trail originally taken by the movie star, Ava Gardner, who had a particular fascination for Spanish bullfighters, especially Luís Miguel Dominguin. What is it with this fascination celebrated American women have for Spanish bullfighters? I think it has something to do with the bull."

The highlight of the *Feria* was the International Red Cross Ball, a charity debutante party for 2,500 guests hosted by the Duke of Medinaceli.

As usual, Princess Grace expected to be the belle of the ball. She went all out and appeared wrapped in white mink. Her hair was upswept and she was wearing a prince's ransom in diamonds. But she was virtually ignored as the guests rushed to get a glimpse of Jackie when she entered the courtyard bare shouldered and wearing a blue gown designed by Oleg Cassini. Jackie had fashionably arrived an hour late.

Grace was also jealous that the designer, Cassini, her former lover who'd once passionately wanted to marry her, was now showering his attention on the creation of chic *couture* for Jackie.

After battling through the hordes of reporters and photographers, Jackie finally made it to the table of their host, the Duke de Medinaceli. Grace extended a limp handshake to Jackie, then turned her head to avoid her throughout the rest of the evening.

With the poor Duke sandwiched in between them, he tried to make conversation to no avail. The next morning the *New York Herald Tribune* captioned a picture of them, headlining, "Cool Conversation," and noting that Grace and Jackie had little to say to each other. In response, Grace wrote a letter to the newspaper, claiming "I have great respect and admiration for Mrs. Kennedy."

Prince Rainier seemed dazzled by Jackie, but Princess Grace remained frosty, and Jackie turned an Arctic shoulder to Her Serene Highness. Jackie had long ago learned the details of Grace's romantic involvement with Jack as well as her seduction of Bobby, who was Jackie's lover at the time. "Jackie

When **El Cordobés**, Spain's leading matador, spotted Jackie in the stands, he was mesmerized by her, dedicating his bullfight to her and her alone, ignoring Grace Kelly.

That night, friends translated for him, as he told Jackie that "to stand before the horns of a bull and risk one's life as a hungry man is one thing. I did that in Madrid. But to do what I did in the ring today with millions of dollars in the bank is pure madness."

He also told her that if the scars on his body were laid end to end, "they would stretch three times around my waist."

Jackie, who had a reputation for being flirtatious, was overheard telling him, "I prefer to do my own inspection instead of taking your word for it."

had reasons to detest Grace," Truman Capote later said, "especially when eagle-eyed Grace detected a gleam in the eyes of her prince."

In a huff, the Princess departed for an hour to the powder room. During her absence, Prince Rainier was seen in a secluded area of a patio smoking a cigarette with Jackie, away from the prying eyes of the paparazzi.

At the time of this flirtation between Jackie and Prince Rainier, international rumors were swirling that she was all but engaged to Antonio Garrigues, a widower with eight children. At the age of 62, he'd been appointed Spain's Ambassador to the Vatican. He and Jackie were later spotted together in Rome.

Unknown except to many of her friends, Jackie was a great mimic. After leaving Seville, she headed for some R&R at the swank Marbella Club on the Costa del Sol. Once there, she delivered a devastating satire of Grace as she'd appeared in *Rear Window* (1954) opposite James Stewart, another of Grace's sexual conquests.

"It should have been taped," said Antonio Cordova, a member of the chic clique who had gathered at the Marbella Club. "Jackie appeared with long white gloves and imitated Grace's speech pattern to perfection. Slowly those gloves were removed, and Jackie did the world's most amusing rendition of Grace Kelly imitating Rita Hayworth in her 'Put the Blame on Mame' number. What an evening!"

***

Photofest

Dressed for the part, **Jackie**, an expert horsewoman, awed the people of Seville at the April *Feria*, especially when she downed a glass of sherry from nearby Jerez de la Frontera.

"To visit Seville and not ride horseback is equal to not coming at all," she said.

Then she mounted a white stallion and made a leisurely *paseo* of the gaily decorated fair grounds, to the delight of 259 *paparazzi*.

After the *Feria* in Seville, Jackie and Grace virtually ended whatever meager relationship they had, but Grace continued to place calls to Bobby in Washington.

Whatever the nature of Grace's relationship with Bobby, the bond became so strong between them that, in an unprecedented move, Grace volunteered to return to America and campaign for him in his quest for the presidency in 1968. In volunteering, she defied the wishes of her husband, who did not want her to go.

RFK called Grace and thanked her, eagerly looking forward to her appearance in America. No doubt, he wanted to continue their affair. Even though he'd already opted to end a high-profile romance with Jackie as a condition of running for the presidency, "He suddenly had become as sexually insatiable as Jack had been," Langdon Marvin claimed. A former aide to JFK, Marvin had provided numerous women available for affairs with the president. "Almost no one refused," he recalled.

Suddenly, from the heat of the campaign trail, Marvin found himself procuring a "gaggle of women for Bobby—airline hostesses, starlets, secretaries, whomever. Bobby was sexually insatiable. He had a penchant for nymphettes."

Marvin admitted that one time at the Carlyle Hotel, he sent Bobby a trio of girls "no more than fifteen. They were attending a private high school in New York. Bobby later thanked me, claiming 'That was the best present I ever got from anybody,' admitting that he'd also enjoyed watching the schoolgirls engage in lesbian sex."

Bobby went out in a blaze of glory, moving ahead toward the presidency and adored by millions, with beautiful women making themselves available to him for the asking—and sometimes he didn't even have to ask.

And then an assassin's bullet hit its mark, and the party was over.

Apparently, Bobby's death affected Grace far more than Jack's assassination. She wasn't photographed with a rifle when Bobby was killed, but went into a period of deep mourning.

Jackie shunned any overture for future meetings with Princess Grace. In 1974, less than a year before Ari's death in March of 1975, she was invited to participate in Ari's last extended cruise through the Eastern Mediterranean, with its conclusion scheduled for Monaco.

Jackie had recently had a fight with Ari, ostensibly because he refused to buy her a luxurious villa in Acapulco. Christina, his daughter, agreed to accompany her father instead.

Jackie had told her husband, "You're a fucking ingrate—I don't want your money."

"So be it, my dear," he told her, "Then you won't be disappointed." The next day he drew up a new will.

When the *Christina* arrived in Monte Carlo, Ari called Jackie in Paris and asked her to fly to Nice where a limousine would be waiting for her. He wanted her to host a dinner for Prince Rainier and Princess Grace. She refused, which turned out to be a wise choice.

The dinner aboard the yacht evolved into a disaster, as Ari attacked the prince who had forced him to sell his shares in the *Société des Bains de Mer*.

After that dinner, Ari flew to Paris where Paul Mathias, a French journalist, saw Jackie and him dancing the night away in a Left Bank *boîte*. Jackie was demonstrating her new skill with castanets, which she'd learned from a flamenco dancer in Seville. She even lured a dying Onassis onto the dance floor where he loped about like a wounded antelope.

The last romantic link between the Kennedy family and the House of Grimaldi came when Ted Kennedy Jr. started to date Princess Stephanie. Before that, the Princess was rumored to have had an affair with John F. Kennedy Jr.

Edward (Ted) M. Kennedy Jr. was born in 1961 when his uncle was still president. The twelve-year-old earned international press when he was diagnosed with osteosarcoma in his right leg, a form of bone cancer. The leg was surgically amputated.

After the death of Princess Grace in 1982, *Ici Paris*, a popular French tabloid, suggested that Prince Rainier was considering marrying Jackie Onassis. Later, this rumor was dismissed, one reporter claiming that whatever attention Jackie was lavishing on Rainier was merely part of her attempt to persuade His Serene Highness to write his autobiography for Doubleday.

But there was far more to it than that. Jackie and the Prince were spotted together at certain discreet restaurants in Paris, and once cozily sharing drinks in a remote corner of a bar at

Paris' Ritz Hotel.

Aides to Rainier said he did seriously consider proposing to America's former First Lady after Grace died. "Marrying Jackie would be an even bigger coup for Monaco than marrying Grace," Rainier told his close friend, actor David Niven. "Princess Jacqueline could bring worldwide publicity to Monaco—new investments and first-class tourism. It would be a sensation far greater than marrying a mere movie star."

It is not known if the Prince actually proposed to Jackie. Surely with all this speculation, news reached her about the Prince's possible intentions.

Ted Sorensen, former JFK aide, said, "After marrying Jack Kennedy and Aristotle Onassis, Prince Rainier was about the only eligible male left in that class for her to marry. In passing, I once mentioned this prospect to Jackie. She hesitated and said nothing at first. Then she claimed, 'I would have to give such an offer serious consideration.'"

JFK: "I Do Not Have Addison's Disease"

But the president lied. Actually, he did.

JFK, at 43 the youngest ever to occupy the Oval Office, was viewed by his adoring fans as healthy and vigorous. Actually, he was anything but.

Amazingly, his advisers managed to keep from the public the extent of his illnesses—not only Addison's disease, but various other medical problems too, which he controlled with a daily regimen of steroids and other drugs, including "speed" injected directly into his veins by "Dr. Feelgood" (actually, Dr. Max Jacobson of New York), who flew frequently in and out of Washington.

JFK was history's most famous victim of Addison's disease, which is a rare, chronic endocrine disorder wherein the adrenal glands produce insufficient steroid hormones. He had all the symptons--low blood pressure, weight loss, muscle fatigue, stomach irritability, sharp back pains, and dehydration. Sufferers included the late Osama bin Laden.

The late Eunice Kennedy Shriver, JFK's sister, was believed to have suffered from Addison's disease as well. Historically, English novelists Charles Dickens and Jane Austen may also have been victims.

Treatment of JFK's Addison's disease gave him a jaundiced look, a peculiar yellow-orange coloring. His handlers explained it as a mild case of malaria originally contracted when he was a PT Boat commander during World War II.

At the time of his assassination, his adrenal glands, according to his doctors, had "virtually disintegrated." Although JFK planned to run for re-election in 1964, he was told, "It is highly doubtful that you will survive a second term."

Ironically, twenty years before, FDR had been told that he wouldn't survive a fourth term, but he ran, won in 1944, and then died in office, ceding the presidency to then VP Harry Truman.

Swapping Partners with the JFKs

Sex Games and Revenge in D.C. and Hollywood
Starring William Holden & Audrey Hepburn

Associated Press

(Left photo) When **Jackie** married **Senator John F. Kennedy** on September 12, 1953, at St. Mary's Catholic Church in Newport, Rhode Island, it seemed unlikely that the paths of this seemingly happy couple would ever cross with those of Audrey Hepburn and William Holden

(Right photo) **William Holden** gets amorous with the beautiful **Audrey Hepburn** in *Sabrina* (1954), a romantic comedy which also starred an alienated Humphrey Bogart, who did not particularly like either of them.

But both Jack and Jackie were products of an era when devoted movie-goers developed crushes on their favorite movie stars. Jackie told her sister, Lee Radziwill, that she'd become enchanted with William Holden ever since she saw him portray a beautiful, tormented boxer in the 1939 film version of the stage sensation *Golden Boy*. "He exudes masculinity," Jackie claimed.

Likewise, when JFK saw *Roman Holiday* (1953), he told his aide, David Powers, "All little boys jerk off at night dreaming of a fairy princess. When I saw Audrey, I knew at once that she was that fairy princess with whom I could live happily ever after. Unfortunately for me, somewhere along the way, reality set in, and I made the most politically acceptable marriage I could."

LOVE AND INFIDELITY
IN POLITICS AND THE
MOVIES

Even though she'd long ago lost touch with him, Jackie harbored a crush on William Holden throughout her years in the White House.

Through Truman Capote and other friends, she kept up with him and was horrified as he descended deeper and deeper into alcoholism. "If I had married Bill instead of Jack, I could have saved him," she told Capote From a friend in Rome, the author had learned that the actor had been charged with drunk driving and manslaughter in Italy.

His Ferrari had crashed into a small Fiat on the *autostrada*. The driver of the Fiat was killed instantly. Holden was pronounced guilty in an Italian court, but got off easy. The judge gave him an eight-month suspended jail sentence after he'd settled $80,000 on the victim's widow.

Months after JFK was assassinated, in one of Audrey's rare instances of immodesty, she spoke about the president to her closest friend, the French actress Capucine.

"I adored him. I think I made a big mistake in not marrying him. My greatest role should have been First Lady. Many members of the press claim that I have more grace, style, and flair than Jackie herself."

Audrey carried a picture of JFK around with her for years. She had cut Jackie out of the photograph and in its place, imposed a picture of herself instead.

Shortly after the April, 1953 wedding of her sister, Lee Bouvier Radziwill to Michael Canfield, Jackie, the roving reporter with a camera, interviewed Senator John F. Kennedy in Washington. Across the hall she also interviewed Richard Nixon, the Vice President of the United States.

Senator Kennedy told Jackie how much he admired the Veep and that he'd contributed $1,000 to Nixon's campaign in 1950 when he'd run a smear campaign against Democratic Senator Helen Gahagan Douglas ("she's as pink as her underwear"). The Nixon/JFK friendship, tenuous even at its best, wasn't going to endure for very much longer.

JFK called Jackie the next day and invited her out on a date for dancing at the Blue Room in the Washington, D.C.'s Shoreham Hotel. She bought a new gown for the occasion, but when he came to pick her up she was disappointed to see that he'd brought along his buddy, David Powers, as a kind of chaperone.

Powers, part of JFK's "Irish Mafia," helped the young naval veteran win his first election to Congress and then served as his personal aide and confidant throughout his short presidency,

After that night, JFK began to date Jackie, and she learned to get by without flowers, gifts, or love letters. He also had a strict rule, "No touching in public, there are photographers everywhere."

Meeting with David after work, JFK told him that he'd fallen in love with Jackie. He produced four pictures of Jackie and himself which had been snapped by an automatic camera in a photo booth in a penny arcade, "I could tell from the adoring look on each of their faces that they were in love."

Later in life, David said, "My friend Jack was full of surprises. Take the night he arrived late at my apartment in Boston."

JFK had come to him to talk over "a very pressing matter. I'm in real trouble."

David thought he'd been caught up in some scandal, no doubt having impregnated a married woman.

Sitting with a drink in David's living room, JFK said, "I'm in love with Jackie. But I'm also in love with Audrey Hepburn." He carried a picture of her which he pulled out of his wallet and showed to David.

The face had been world famous since her appearance with Gregory Peck in *Roman Holiday* (1952).

The knockout gamin looked and behaved like a Princess in the picture and also in real life.

"I'm having a very secret affair with her," JFK told David.

"I'll say this for you, you sure do have good taste in women," David told him.

"Pencil thin and doe eyed, that Hepburn was some dish," David said. "She was ravishingly beautiful. Throughout her life she would appear as the epitome of class but without the snobbery. She was real. Jackie, and I loved the gal dearly, was much more pretentious."

"Audrey dazzled us the first time she walked into Senator Kennedy's office," said secretary Mary Gallagher. "With her black-and-white dress, with a long stemmed scarlet red umbrella, she was impressive. She had the grace of a swan, the movement of a gazelle."

"Believe it or not, Jack's staff didn't know he was having a torrid affair with Audrey," David said. "Remember this was the Fifties. The image of a movie star and a handsome United States Senator, much less a future President, was not in everybody's mind back then. It would have sounded too far-fetched. Audrey escaped detection on the radar screen, even though she was seen leaving his Georgetown residence at three or four o'clock in the morning."

"All of us on Jack's staff knew that he was dating Jackie—not just dating her, but in love with her," Gallagher said. "Believe it or not, we didn't think anything was going on between Audrey and Jack. How naïve we were back in those days."

When Joseph Kennedy heard of Jack's "two loves," he called him to Hyannis Port for a father-son talk. "You want to be President one day, don't you?"

"You know that father," JFK said.

"Then it's got to be Jackie even though her father—that Black Jack faggot—is a complete shit. Hepburn is a cute little piece," his father continued. "But she's foreign born. She's not Catholic. She's about to make a movie with William Holden and Humphrey Bogart. At least one of them will end up fucking her. I'm putting my money on Holden. Take my advice. Audrey for fucking, Jackie for marriage."

Joe Senior was right. By the time "Jack & Jackie" announced their engagement, Audrey had returned to Hollywood to star in *Sabrina*. When the cameras weren't on her, she was indeed maintaining a torrid affair with Holden.

Jackie, who loved gossip, heard about the Holden/Hepburn affair. At one point Holden planned to leave his actress wife Brenda (Ardis) Marshall to marry Audrey. Audrey had even predicted, "I think we could have beautiful babies together."

But he was forced to tell her the truth. He'd had a vasectomy after the birth of the second of his two sons. He could have no more children. She was devastated, as she desperately wanted to have children. Finally, even though she was in love with Holden, she told him she couldn't marry him. Holden was devastated.

"After Audrey refused to marry me," Holden said, "I fucked my way around the world. My goal was to screw a girl in every country I visited. I'd had practice being a whore. When I was a young actor starting in Hollywood, I used to service actresses who were older than me." He was definitely referring to Barbara Stanwyck. "I'm a whore. All actors are whores. We sell our bodies to the highest bidders."

Audrey was very sad to learn about the marriage of Jack with Jackie. "It could have been me," she told Gregory Peck. "I know that Jack in his heart was in love with me and wanted me to be his wife. He was forced to choose Jackie for political reasons, for his career."

Two gay authors, both friends of Jackie's, weighed in with their views of the marriage.

"Jackie was always a *cash 'n carry* kinda gal," said Truman Capote.

"Jackie married Jack for the money," said Gore Vidal. "There weren't that many other openings for her. Actually, if she hadn't married Jack she would have married someone else with money, although it wasn't likely she would have gotten someone as exciting as Jack in the bargain. When given a choice of glory or money, most people choose glory. But not Jackie. She also wound up with plenty of the latter, of course, but she didn't need that like she needed to be rich."

Jackie was furious when JFK in 1956 did not appear at her bedside during the stillbirth of her daughter.

Later, she was informed that he had been "shacked up at the time with some bimbo."

She wanted revenge and would wait until the opportunity arose.

That came in January of 1957 when she went with her friend, William Walton, a gay artist and former journalist, on a ten-day trip to California. As President, JFK would later appoint Walton to head the White House Fine Arts Commission.

Producer Charles Feldman invited Jackie to a party at his home in Beverly Hills' Coldwater Canyon. It was here that she first met William Holden, who had long been her screen idol.

Holden became a household word in 1939 when he starred opposite Barbara Stanwyck in *Golden Boy*. During production of that movie, he also became bisexual Stanwyck's lover.

He'd already appeared in such classics as *Sunset Blvd.* (1950) and *Born Yesterday* (1950), and later, he'd win an Oscar for his role in *Stalag 17* (1953).

Although he suffered from alcoholism and clinical depression, he managed to conduct affairs with such luminaries as Grace Kelly.

Jackie was immediately captivated by him. He'd always been one of her screen idols. Up close and personal, he was even more charming, the archetypical macho American male with a strong open face and a disarming smile.

Regrettably, at least from Jackie's point of view, Holden was at the Feldman party with his wife, actress Brenda Marshall, whom he'd married in 1941 and with whom he had two sons. When Brenda went out on the terrace to talk with friends, Jackie seized the opportunity to speak privately with Holden.

Jackie told Holden that she was staying at a cottage on the grounds of the Beverly Hills Hotel and suggested that "it would be marvelous if we could go horseback riding in the morning. It's no one's business but our own."

As author C. David Heymann so accurately pointed out, "Jackie would regard Jack's wanderings as an inevitable feature of upper-class wedlock. Also, she would respond with several affairs of her own."

Holden not only showed up for horseback riding, but launched a week-long affair with Jackie. She did not want to be seen entering the Beverly Hills Hotel with such a famous actor, so Feldman agreed to give them the use of his house during the day.

After Jackie had flown out of Los Angeles, Holden on one drunken night with Feldman, said, "I had to teach Jackie how to suck cock. She told me that Jack had never insisted on that. At first she was very reluctant, but once she got the rhythm of it she couldn't get enough of it. If she goes back to Washington and works her magic with Kennedy, he will owe me one."

Jackie later told Capote, "I've gone to bed with men who have had a problem with hygiene. Not so Bill Holden. He was a compulsive bather before and after sex. He told me he took four showers a day."

Jackie later told Lee Radziwill, "William Holden reminds me of Black Jack. I don't mean in looks. They both love the bottle and adventure. And they're both reckless in love. Regrettably, they both were Republicans."

Jackie also revealed to both her sister and to Capote that she'd confessed her affair with Holden to her husband after her return to him in Washington. She revealed all to JFK, even saying, "Unlike some men I know, William Holden is not a selfish lover. He's very skilled under the sheets."

JFK's reaction is not known. From all reports, he clearly interpreted Jackie's behavior and its subsequent confession for what it was. Payback time.

Although the story may be apocryphal, JFK became so excited by his wife's confession that he seduced her on the carpet of their home.

All that love-making after Holden seemed to have paid off. Jackie announced to JFK in April of 1957 that she was pregnant again. This time she would see the child to term, giving birth to Caroline.

By then, JFK's attention had shifted. It was Frank Sinatra who introduced him to a leggy Las Vegas showgirl. Her name was Judith Campbell, and she would eventually evolve into one of the three most dangerous *femme fatales* of JFK's short life.

In 1959, when Holden took up residence in Switzerland as a means of avoiding US income taxes, he became the object of public vituperation. Even the future US Attorney General, Robert F. Kennedy, cited Holden as an example of "the rich who pervert our tax laws," and RFK's wife, Ethel, publicly referred to Holden as "a traitor."

Holden confessed how he eventually got even with RFK. "I had a brief fling with Jackie Kennedy," he claimed, "while she was married to Jack. She had long told friends that she thought I was the sexiest man in

Jackie's lover (**William Holden**) makes screen love to fading actress **Gloria Swanson** (Joseph P. Kennedy's former mistress). In the photo, they appear together in the 1950 film classic, *Sunset Blvd.*

Holden drew upon personal experience from his early days in Hollywood, when, in his struggle to get ahead, he seduced older mentors who included Barbara Stanwyck.

During the filming, Swanson told Holden about her final (disastrous) silent film project, *Queen Kelly,* on which Joseph P. Kennedy, her lover at the time, cut off funding, thereby sentencing the project to dustbin doom. As a result, the much-heralded movie was never completed.

Decades later, when Swanson, still furious and still bitter, got the news about Joe's crippling stroke, she said, "I hope he suffers."

Hollywood. Word got back to little Bobby, and he was seriously pissed off at me. Later, I learned the fucker was also getting into Jackie's pants."

The whole world seemingly remembers Marilyn Monroe singing "Happy Birthday, Mr. President" on May 29, 1962, only months before she was murdered.

Far fewer people know that it was Audrey, another movie queen and a former lover of JFK, who sang the final "Happy Birthday, Mr. President" on May 29, 1963.

Hepburn was invited to the White House to sing "Happy Birthday" on the occasion of JFK's forty-sixth year on Earth, which would be his final one. Her rendition resulted in thunderous applause.

Afterwards, she stood with singer Eddie Fisher in a receiving line to greet the president. "I knew they had been lovers, and the president seemed genuinely pleased to see her again," Fisher said. "Had Audrey pleased Joseph Kennedy as a prospect for marriage, she, not Jackie, would be the First Lady of the land."

"Kennedy's face lit up like a Christmas tree, when he came up close and personal with Audrey, who looked lovely," Fisher said. "He whispered something in her ear. I suspect it was an invitation for their final fuck—for old time's sake, you know."

Jackie had her own surprise planned for JFK's birthday that year. Even though it was raining, she had organized a cruise down the Potomac aboard the presidential yacht *Sequoia*. Bobby and Teddy Kennedy were obvious choices on the guest list, as was the ever-faithful Lem Billings. David Niven and Hjordis, his wife, were among the surprise guests. When he returned to Hollywood, Niven said, "I think that Lem Billings would eat Kennedy's shit if he asked him to."

Jackie may have been a bit impish in having invited the Nivens. She'd learned that Kennedy was having an affair with Hjordis. Audrey, however, was definitely not included on her guest list.

"If I'd invited all of Jack's lovers, the *Sequoia* would have sunk into the Potomac," Jackie said later.

Capote, a friend of both Jackie and Audrey, told the actress that "Jackie is very jealous of you. There are those who say that you out-Jackie Jackie herself."

Before JFK even boarded the *Sequoia* that afternoon, rumor had it that he had already deflowered Audrey in the Lincoln bedroom.

Even though her dignity might have been trampled upon during at least some of these events, Audrey retained an affectionate memory of the president, and always spoke with nostalgia of "what might have been."

On Friday, November 22, 1963, **Audrey** was on the verge of a nervous breakdown while filming *My Fair Lady* in Los Angeles, where daytime temperatures hovered between 110 and 118 degrees Fahrenheit. She'd been in bed for three days under a doctor's care, and had just returned to work. George Cukor, the film's director, was on the set discussing a scene with Audrey when a grip's portable radio brought news of the assassination of John F. Kennedy.

"I was too shaken to make the announcement or tell the crew," Cukor later said. "I asked Audrey if she'd do it. I knew how close she'd been to the president."

Putting up a brave front while holding back tears, she said, "I'll do it." She was trembling as she took the microphone and announced to the cast and crew, "The President is dead. Shall we have two minutes of silence to pray or do whatever you think is appropriate? May God have mercy on us all."

For Lana, The Postman

Did Indeed Ring Twice

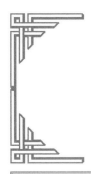

The 1946 *noir* drama, *The Postman Always Rings Twice*, was blonde **Lana Turner**'s most famous film. On screen she became the lover of John Garfield, and she also bedded him off screen.

But Lana never believed in confining herself to one man—just ask Desi Arnaz, Leonard Bernstein, Richard Burton, Sean Connery, Kirk Douglas, Clark Gable, John Hodiak, Howard Hughes, Peter Lawford, Dean Martin, Victor Mature, Tyrone Power, George Montgomery, Frank Sinatra, Robert Wagner, and Robert Stack.

She also found time to marry seven husbands, and even have an affair with a young naval lieutenant *(photo, left)* who was destined to become the president of the United States. Later, she'd repeat the experience with JFK during his tenure as a senator from Massachusetts.

Before he became a movie star, **Steve McQueen** *(photo, right)*, in a dinner jacket borrowed from Porfirio Rubirosa, escorted A-list beauties to parties in New York. Sometimes sex was involved. But not on this night with Lana. "I was Lana's beard," McQueen later claimed.

Lana's Greatest Role?
Her Own Soap Opera Life

Two legendary MGM beauties, **Lana Turner** *(above)* and **Joan Crawford** *(below)*, seduced U.S. presidents years before they ever set foot in the Oval Office. Lana racked up both Ronald Reagan and John F. Kennedy, Joan settling only for Kennedy. The two stars often got together on the MGM lot and compared notes on VIPs each of them had seduced.

Lana seduced young Reagan in 1937 at around the time he first arrived in Hollywood. It happened after they went horseback riding at the Warner's ranch.

Lana and Joan "doubled up" on the likes of Clark Gable, Hollywood lawyer Greg Bautzer, Kirk Douglas, John Garfield, Tony Martin, Tyrone Power, and Frank Sinatra. Bette Davis once claimed that Joan "slept with every male star at MGM except Lassie."

In the mid-1950s, during his years as a male escort, before breaking through into the national spotlight, Steve McQueen was asked to take Lana Turner to a private party being hosted by Frank Sinatra in a private dining room within New York's Plaza Hotel. Joan Crawford, who had previously configured Steve into her life for his services as an escort, had arranged for his services with Lana through Floyd Wilson, a high-class pimp and the owner of Steve's escort service. Joan had known Lana since their days together at MGM, when the younger and older actresses each took turns servicing Clark Gable.

Steve tended to prefer natural, down-to-earth women. But in some secret part of his heart he had a definite lust for the sexy, superficial glitz that Lana had represented during her reign in Hollywood in the studio era.

Picking her up at her suite within the Plaza, all he had to do was escort her to the party downstairs. In a form-fitting white gown with a ruby necklace, she looked as sexy to him as when he saw her in *The Postman Always Rings Twice*. The passing years had been kind to her; in addition, she was incredibly skillful at applying makeup.

"So you're a blond," she said, appraising Steve after he'd been ushered into the living room of her suite. "Usually I don't date blonds. [Hollywood agent] Henry Willson always told me I should date men with raven-black hair to offset my own blondness. That's why he fixed me up so often with Rory Calhoun."

"If I'd have known, I'd have dyed my hair black," he said. "That's what I did when I appeared in *A Hatful of Rain* on Broadway. I was playing an Italian, and I thought black hair would make me look more the part."

114

"Actually I like blond-haired men," she said. "You're adorable looking and you'll be just fine." She looked him up and down. "Of all my movies, which one did you like the best?"

"*The Merry Widow*," he said. "You were so beautiful. Incredible."

"It's true," she said. "I was. As for that Fernando Lamas, he can stick a dildo up his ass."

Over a pre-party drink, Lana told him she was furious about something that had recently appeared in a Hollywood column. "I wasn't named, but everyone in Hollywood knew it was me. Some jerk claimed that every time I saw a muscular stagehand in tight pants, I'd lure him into my dressing room. That is simply not true. It's gross, disgusting libel."

"All I can say is some stagehand must have been out of luck," he said.

"I will take that as a compliment," she said, rising like royalty from the sofa. "We'd better go downstairs. All the gang will be there. That means Frank, Dean Martin, Sammy Davis Jr., Judy Garland, Peter Lawford…"

Accompanying her downstairs to the party, where she made a grand entrance, Steve met each of these legends and a lot other big stars too. Months later, he'd tell Rod Steiger, "If someone told me I'd soon be co-starring in a big picture with Sinatra, I'd have thought they were out of their mind. And if someone told me that Sammy Davis Jr. would one day be teaching me how to fire a six-shooter in a Western, I'd have thought they were crazy. The same if they told me I'd get an invitation from Judy Garland to fuck her. And I hardly knew at the time that Peter Lawford would get off by sucking my dick."

Steve was particularly amused by Sammy Davis Jr. That evening marked the beginning of a beautiful friendship. A band had been hired for the night, and Sinatra sang four songs to his assembled friends. On the dance floor, Steve found himself holding Judy Garland in his arms. To his astonishment, she unzipped his pants and "felt her way up and down the family jewels," as Steve later reported to Steiger.

"She does that to all her dance partners, so don't think you were singled out as anything special," Steiger said.

At the end of the evening, Steve's only surprise came when Sammy, in saying good-bye, lip-locked him with a wet kiss. Steve later reported it to Lana with astonishment. "He does that to all his white friends. It's Sammy's way. It's so Hollywood. You'll get used

Associated Press

Ava Gardner *(left)* and **Lana Turner** *(center)* both shared the favors of that heartthrob from South America, **Fernando Lamas** *(right)*. Both Lana and Ava also bedded a young JFK before he became president.

Fernando later married the 1950s screen beauty, red-haired Arlene Dahl. Perhaps unknown to him, JFK got to her first. He dated Arlene when he was still a U.S. senator.

Fernando, who was always proud, justifiably so, of his endowment, swore that Ava told him he had "two and a half times as much as JFK."

When he wasn't chasing after Desi Arnaz, the gay actor Cesar Romero pursued Lamas, but to no avail. "Fernando was a beautiful man," Romero claimed. "Very much in love with himself. But instead of with me, he ended up in Esther Williams' swimming pool."

Here Ava, Lana, and Fernando are in a huddle at a lavish party tossed on October 2, 1952 in Beverly Hills by Marion Davies for gay singer Johnny Ray, who later gave Fernando a blow-job in the men's room.

to it."

"I hope he doesn't think I'm a fucking faggot," Steve said.

"Oh, darling, don't be so judgmental. Without so-called faggots, there would be no Hollywood, and I wouldn't have become a screen goddess."

He fully expected to escort her upstairs, where he hoped she'd invite him to spend the night. Instead she asked for her sable and headed for the exit. On the pavement outside the Plaza, a doorman hailed her a cab.

"Come with me," she said. "I have an errand to run. We're going to the Carlyle."

Once inside this other swanky Manhattan hotel, she directed him into the bar. "I have to see a special friend upstairs. He never takes very long, so I'll be back down here within the hour. I want you to wait for me."

Photo above: **Jayne Mansfield**

Based on confidential moments with Florida Senator George Smathers, JFK's aide, David Powers, revealed details about some of the "popcorn blonde" gossip attributed to JFK: "I'd rather have Marilyn Monroe or Lana Turner, but if they're not available, I'll happily switch from the A-list to the C-cup."

Of course, in Jayne's case that would be a D-cup, or even something more generous.

"She once told me that she tried to keep her sex appeal from becoming threatening by making it silly," Kennedy said to Smathers. "In that, I think she shared something in common with Mae West," a woman with whom she had a life-long feud."

"That reminds me. I'll have to ask Dad one day if he ever got around to Mae West during his Hollywood years."

About thirty minutes later, a waiter approached him. "You're wanted on the house phone." It was Lana calling from a suite upstairs.

"He says he knows you," Lana said.

"Who do you mean?" Steve asked.

"My friend," she said. "Come on up. He wants to have a drink with you."

To his astonishment, John F. Kennedy, clad only in his underwear, opened the door to the suite. Presumably Lana was in the bathroom, repairing her makeup.

"Come on in and have a drink," Kennedy said. "I'm still keeping our tally about seducing movie stars. I bet I got to Lana long before you did. We've been going at it on and off for years."

"I'm not opposed to sloppy seconds," Steve said, accepting a drink. "I'm sure you've got me beat, but I'm going to Hollywood, and I'm gonna catch up with you yet, you fucker."

"That's a good name for me," Kennedy said, smiling.

Standing beside him at the bar, Kennedy said, "I'll give you a tip about Lana. She claims she doesn't go in for the oral stuff. She wants her men to get right to the honey-pot."

"Thanks for the advice," he said.

He whispered something else. "Now I want you to get her out of here and quick. I've got something else lined up, and she's due here soon."

"Care to tell me her name?" Steve asked.

"Jayne Mansfield," Kennedy said.

"You partial to blondes?" Steve asked.

"Blondes for bedtime, brunettes for marriage," Kennedy said. "Remember that."

"All throughout my life, I'll follow your advice," said Steve.

And so he did.

116

JFK and the Cheesecake Hottie

How Bettie Page Entertained
the Senator from Massachusetts

Throughout his life, **John F. Kennedy** had "this thing" for pinup queens and strippers, including **Bettie Page**, who is seen posing for a bondage photograph, the collection wildly popular in the 1950s.

In WWII, during his stint as a naval lieutenant, JFK pinned a picture of Betty Grable to his locker door. By war's end, he'd switched to Rita Hayworth. The Marilyn Monroe calendar was his all-time favorite, but he pinned up other beauties in skimpy dress as well. He was especially fond of Jayne Mansfield (eventually, his mistress), who posed with her boobs practically spilling out.

For more class, he preferred the lavender blonde, Kim Novak. He also collected nudes of two of his stripper "shack-ups," Blaze Starr and Tempest Storm. He also got turned on looking at sexy shots of movie stars he had known, including Sophia Loren, Lana Turner, Gene Tierney, and sultry replicas of Hedy Lamarr.

Many of the paid prostitutes he hired later claimed that the future president liked "vanilla S&M," such as being tied up "while naughty girls do naughty things to me." Bettie Page's bondage photos were a particular favorite of his collection, and he was anxious to meet her for a "one-on-one."

CELEBRITY STRIPPER BETTIE PAGE

Photofest

"THE EMPRESS OF KINK" GETS DOWN AND DIRTY WITH HOWARD HUGHES, FRANK SINATRA, AND THE RAT PACK

Many of **Bettie Page**'s 1950s cheesecake photos, especially the bondage shots taken by Irving Klaw, outraged the puritans trying to "protect" innocent young America in the 1950s.

In Washington, Bettie's main critic was the coonskin-cap wearing senator from Tennessee, Estes Kefauver (1903-1963).

A political rival of John F. Kennedy, he had twice sought the Democratic Party's nomination for President of the United States. He made so many threats against Bettie that he drove her into hiding. At one point, Kefauver's committee uncovered a sexual liaison between Bettie and JFK.

Unlike roughly equivalent contexts during the Bill Clinton era, this revelation was interpreted by the press at the time as "too hot to handle."

At one point Kefauver told his aides, "Bettie Page is a pervert—no doubt a lesbian to judge from some of her pictures. Only a card-carrying lesbian would pose for some of those sordid pictures. I vomited just looking at them."

That's what he said in public. In secrecy, Kefauver was a *roué* and attended orgies.

Bettie Page, Queen of the Pinups in the 1950s, died on December 11, 2008. After a turbulent life, she managed to reach the age of 85.

She was one of the earliest "Playmates of the Month" for *Playboy* magazine. After aging in seclusion, no one would recognize Bettie Page in later life as the former "Empress of Kink."

She enjoyed a renaissance during the 1980s and 90s that continues to this day. "I'm more famous now than I was fifty years ago," she said in 1993.

Her bust was 36", her waist 23", and those measurements became known around the world. Her jet black hair—all bangs and bob 'do—became an iconic trademark during the rockabilly subculture of the Eisenhower years.

"I had all of them," Bettie Page later confessed. "All of them had big dicks, all except Peter Lawford. In Las Vegas they were cool cats but had a dark reputation. Pity their shamefully neglected wives and children. They discarded women like a used razor blade. They had talent; they brought joy to millions; and they were great in bed, except for Peter."

She was talking of course, about The Rat Pack.

At a lonely, desperate time in Bettie's life, a call came in from Johnny Meyer, who identified himself as a publicist for Howard Hughes. Throughout the entertainment industry, Meyer was known as Hughes' pimp.

Hughes regularly, even systematically, flipped through girlie magazines, selecting the model of his choice whom he then lured to Hollywood with the promise of an RKO contract. He had bought the studio in 1948, using it for the next decade or so as a vast casting couch. Hughes was a notoriously alienated and notoriously bisexual, seducing as many good-looking young actors as he did young actresses.

Thrilled at the prospect of a movie contract, Bettie accepted the offer. The next day a thousand dollars in spending money, plus an airline ticket on TWA, arrived at her hotel.

Wanting to leave the pinup world behind her and fearing that time was running out for her, she was eager to make it as a legitimate actress. After her arrival in Los Angeles, she was met by one of Hughes' chauffeurs, who drove her to a fairly luxurious house in Beverly Hills, where she was installed.

The next day Meyer called and warned her not to leave the house. "Mr. Hughes' schedule is never certain because the boss man is very busy," Meyer told her. "But he wants you there in case he drops in unexpectedly. Try to have yourself camera ready day and night because he keeps some strange hours."

Bettie later recalled that she remained a virtual prisoner in that house until one night Hughes arrived, unannounced, on her doorstep.

"He was a man of few words and had a hearing problem," she said. "He must have found me appealing. We retired to the bedroom where he pulled off his jacket but none of his other clothes. He performed oral sex on me and then left. I tried to ask him about the screen test, but he told me that Meyer would make those arrangements."

Meyer called the next day and said "the boss man has talked to Frank Sinatra in Las Vegas. Frankie is very interested in using you in his next picture. I'm arranging for you to be picked up in a limo and driven to Las Vegas to attend Frankie's opening night at The Sands."

"It all sounded so glamorous at the time," Bettie recalled. "I was thrilled. All the way across the desert to Vegas, I dreamed that stardom for me was just around the corner."

She not only attended Frank's star-studded opening night but accepted an invitation to dinner in his suite.

"It was the most thrilling night of my life. I adored Frankie. He was romantic and sensitive to my feelings. By morning I think I wanted to marry him."

"He made arrangements for me to stay at another suite at The Sands for a whole week, with all expenses paid," Bettie said. "But the next morning I realized that Frankie had other plans and other gals. I'm afraid he treated me like a whore."

"During that week, my suite was visited by Dean Martin, Peter Lawford, and, much to my horror, Sammy Davis Jr.," Bettie said. "All three of them treated me well. Although I was initially afraid of Sammy, he turned out to be the nicest of them all. I kept waiting for a call from the fifth member of The Rat Pack, Joey Bishop, but he never showed up."

"At the end of my stay, a bellhop delivered a note from Frankie," she said. "It contained two thousand dollars. He wrote, 'You showed me and my boys a great time. Let's do it again sometime.'"

Bettie Page was aptly named. She represented only a "page" in the notorious life of billionaire **Howard Hughes**, movie mogul and ace aviator, pictured above in 1954.

He was also one of the 20th Century's greatest Lotharios. He seduced an all-star cast of lovers—male and female—and even managed—for a while at least—to be identified as a genuine American hero.

In 1948, there was talk of running him as a candidate for President of the United States.

"He was an equal opportunity seducer," said Johnny Meyer, his pimp. "The gender of the victim didn't matter. He had just one requirement. Beauty. Bettie Page met that requirement."

"Except for Frankie, I never heard from the other Rat Packers again," Bettie said. "If I did, I guess I would have come running. After all, they were stars, weren't they?"

"There was a screen test at RKO and some still pictures, but nothing came of it. Hughes never showed up at the studio while I was there. Personally, I think he decided I was too old for him."

A month later, Sinatra called her again. She mistakenly thought that he was arranging another trip to Las Vegas, or at least another date, for her. He told her that he had a friend—"a very important friend"—who wanted to meet her, as he was one of her biggest fans. "He refused to divulge the name of his friend, however, but told me was charming, rich, and handsome. Trusting Frankie's judgment, I agreed to meet this mysterious stranger."

The meeting was to be conducted not in Las Vegas, but at a place Sinatra either owned or rented in Palm Springs. "I don't know which," Bettie said. "At the last minute, Frankie called again. The plans had been switched. Instead of having a limousine take me to Palm Springs, a chauffeur would drive me to a mansion in Beverly Hills. I still didn't know the name of this man, but I was mighty intrigued."

The rendezvous was set for four o'clock the following afternoon, Bettie claimed. "I must have changed clothes two or three times before deciding on the right outfit. I figured this was a man of culture who had taste, so I decided to go for the demure, girl-next-door look instead of arriving with whips and chains. I figured that if this guy was into S&M, Frankie would have warned me."

A manservant ushered Bettie through the living room and out toward the pool area where she saw a young man swimming. He called out to her. "Bettie, why not take off your clothes and jump in? It's a hot day."

"I told him I didn't have a bathing suit with me."

"You of all women aren't ashamed to show the human body, are you?"

"Not at all," I said. "Right before him, I pulled off all my clothes and jumped completely jaybird naked into the pool with him. I swam to him. He didn't swim to me. When I got close to him, he pulled me to him and gave me a long, lingering kiss. 'I've waited a long time for this,' he said, hugging me close. 'I collect your pictures.' It was all too obvious that he was naked and aroused. Our kissing continued until he wanted it

After Humphrey Bogart's death, **Frank Sinatra** *(left photo)* became the leader of the notorious Rat Pack.

In this group photo, **Sinatra** *(far right)* looks on skeptically at *(left to right)* **Peter Lawford, Dean Martin, and Sammy Davis Jr.**

Over pillow talk with each of them, Bettie learned some of their secrets. Dean Martin confessed that he had had a nose job. "Nature gave me two big things," he said. "I'm keeping one big gift but getting rid of the big nose."

Peter Lawford warned Bettie, "I'll go to bed with you but, don't fall in love with me." She responded, "Rest assured! I won't."

Sammy Davis Jr., according to Bettie, said, "Once a white chick has had a black dick, she can never go back to white meat again."

consummated under a cabana."

When pressed for details, she hesitated. "It was nothing out of the ordinary. He lay on his back. He wanted me on top. After he finished with me, he showered by the pool but didn't invite me to join him. He didn't kiss me goodbye but thanked me."

"By the way," he said, "I'm Jack Kennedy."

"I know it seems unbelievable, now that he became the most famous man on earth in the 1960s," Bettie said. "But you have to believe me. I only knew Ike in the White House. I had never heard of the Kennedy family. Millions of Americans in the 1950s didn't know who the Kennedys were, even though Jack had once sought the nomination for Vice President on the Democratic ticket. He didn't get it. I didn't even know that about him at the time. I never listened to those nominating conventions."

Bettie said that when she dressed and headed for the door and the waiting limousine, she expected to be handed a thousand dollar bill. "The man at the door offered me nothing," Bettie said. "I was a bit pissed off. Frankie had told me he was rich. However, the very next day, Frankie sent over ten one-hundred dollars bills and two dozen red roses. He also enclosed a note: 'JACK LIKED YOU A LOT AND WANTS TO SEE YOU AGAIN THE NEXT TIME HE'S IN LOS ANGELES.'"

"One night months later I was watching television, and I heard that Jack Kennedy had been nominated to run against Richard Nixon," Bettie said. "That night on the TV news I saw his beaming face. I couldn't believe it. It was the man who seduced me. He was running for president of the United States. Frankly, I didn't think he would beat Nixon. Everybody knew who Nixon was. But who was this Jack Kennedy with the funny accent? They would make fun of an accent like that in Tennessee where I grew up."

"He never called me again," Bettie said. "I would have gone to meet him in the White House when Jackie wasn't around. I regretted not seeing him again, although the sex was hardly special. But he was the president. I heard stories that he was seeing Marilyn Monroe, but I didn't know if they were true or not. I was real sad that day he was shot in Dallas. He was far too young to die."

After the death of Teddy Kennedy in 2009, F.B.I. reports cited "sex parties" that Marilyn Monroe and Frank Sinatra hosted for the senator on at least three of his visits to the Los Angeles area, ostensibly on official political business. Apparently, these "hot-and-heavy" entertainments were staged either in Hollywood or at Sinatra's villa in Palm Springs.

Jack Kennedy had told his younger brother, Teddy, about the delights of pinup queen Bettie Page and had showed him his extensive picture collection.

Sinatra paid Bettie to visit Teddy at his Palm Springs villa, but usually, the singer rounded up "the usual list of hookers."

Marilyn Monroe's best friend, Jeanne Carmen, could not pay her rent one month, and Marilyn suggested that Sinatra would handle it for her if she'd spend the night with Teddy.

Carmen readily agreed.

How Young Jack Kennedy Took It Up the Ass, and How He Described It Afterward

In 1934, when he was 17, some of the president's early (and graphic) attitudes about nurses, sex, and hospitals were revealed in letters he wrote to his gay pal, Lem Billings, when JFK was hospitalized and "facing medical torture" and a battery of tests at the famed Mayo Clinic in Rochester, Minnesota.

Years later, many of JFK's letters were published in books which included Nigel Hamilton's *JFK Reckless Youth,* and in *Jack and Lem* by David Pitts.

Here's a sampling of what the letters revealed:

"I've got something wrong with my intestines—in other words, I shit blood."

Still, in spite of his weakened condition, Jack was obsessed with sex. In his letters, he confessed to having masturbated only twice since he entered the hospital, complaining that his penis "looks as if it had been run through a wringer." Even so, he planned to seduce "some of the tantalizing blonde nurses who manhandle me--one nurse has promised to give me a workout as soon as lights out."

At one point, he suggested he might start to enjoy the sexual thrill of an enema. "I've had 18 enemas in 3 days!!! I'm clean as a whistle. They give me enemas till it comes out like drinking water which they all take a sip of."

"This doctor first stuck his finger up my ass. I just blushed because you know how it is to take it up the ass. He wiggled it suggestively, and I rolled the nurses in the aisles by saying, 'you have a good motion!!!' He then withdrew his finger. And then, the schmuck stuck an iron tube 12 inches long and one inch in diameter up my ass."

***

Although not known to the general public, the almost shocking extent of JFK's illnesses since his early days as a schoolboy were only documented long after his assassination, in such biographies as those by Richard Reeves (*President Kennedy: Profile in Power),* and Robert Dallek (*An Unfinished Life: John F. Kennedy, 1917-1963).*

It wasn't his mother, Rose, but Lem himself who stood by JFK through his many illnesses, beginning with those at Choate. Author Gore Vidal said he thought Lem's loyalty at times of illness was what formed a "bond-to-the-death" between the two young men.

"He needed a Lem to get around," Vidal said.

"Not only did Lem assist Jack physically, more importantly perhaps, he helped lift Jack's spirits during the many times when he could easily have sunk into despair," said Pitts. "Not only did Lem love Jack, he believed in him and was always ready to help him whenever he could, especially when he wasn't feeling good, which was often."

Lem recalled, "I seldom heard Jack complain, regardless of how serious the illness. I knew every one of his maladies, and there was a long list of them. He and I used to joke about the fact that if I ever wrote his biography, I would call it *Jack F. Kennedy, A Medical History.* At one time or another, he really did have almost every medical problem—take any illness, Jack Kennedy had it. Many of them were very, very painful."

How Blaze Starr Helped JFK

Win the Presidential Election of 1960

KENNEDY|NIXON

Like her rival Tempest Storm, stripper **Blaze Starr** (promoted by her managers as "the girl with the fabulous front") also found presidential candidate JFK "very penetrating," to borrow a line from another of his mistresses, Marilyn Monroe. Filled with wild adventures, Blaze's life became notorious. In Philadelphia a vice cop who wanted some action on the side got her thrown out of town when she turned down his demand for sex.

In New Orleans she attracted both Governor Earl Long and the visiting presidential candidate, young John F. Kennedy.

For thirty years Blaze "blazed" a trail in show business, becoming one of the most sought-after performers in the world. The line was a bit trite, but JFK told Florida Senator George Smathers, "There are two reasons for Blaze's success—actually a third one but she keeps that part of her flaming red hair a secret, but not from me. Just call me a trail-blazer."

"I envy you, you fucker," Smathers told him, threatening to take on his neglected wife, Jackie, one night. JFK wondered whether Smathers was making a threat or whether he was merely joking with him.

CHEERLEADING THE PRESIDENTIAL DEBATING TEAM

The affair that **Blaze Starr** sustained with Earl Long, the governor of Louisiana, almost cost her her life.

One night a "handsome, blond-haired man, with unusual blue-gray eyes," appeared in her darkened bedroom and attacked her. At first she feared rape, but instead he wanted the jewelry Long had given her, maybe $100,000 worth. Even before he assaulted her, he'd already stolen most of it, which she had carelessly left around the house.

When he could not remove a large diamond ring from her finger, he forced her to rise nude from her bed and go with him into her kitchen, where he took a butcher knife, supposedly to cut off her finger.

Impulsively she kicked him in the balls and ran back to her bedroom to retrieve her revolver. He knocked it from her hand and took a straight razor from his back pocket, slashing across her breasts. Falling on the floor, she played dead. Gathering up the jewelry, he fled into the night. It took two years of skin transplants to cover the three-inch gash across her "money-makers," her voluptuous breasts.

Blaze Starr, who became a notorious stripper beginning in 1950, was born in 1932 as Fannie Belle Fleming in a log cabin in remote West Virginia, fifty miles from the nearest school. She was one of eleven children, and she ran away from home at the age of fourteen. Discovered working in a doughnut shop, she was lured into stripping by Red Snyder, who became her first manager. "I'd never even shown my belly button before."

While a Senator in Washington, JFK patronized strip clubs and often had affairs with women who caught his eye. One night at a strip joint, he became entranced by Blaze with her red hair and voluptuous (38D-24-37) proportions.

That night, according to her memoirs, he invited her back to his apartment where they had sex. In spite of a bad back, she found him a voracious lover, who couldn't seem to get enough. Senator George Smathers of Florida, who often visited strip joints in Washington with Jack, claimed "the sight of a red-haired pussy used to drive Jack into rapture."

In an interview she gave in 1989, Blaze admitted that she visited Jack's apartment "several more times." Smathers was under the impression that Jack had sex with Blaze on eight different occasions, and had nothing but the highest praise for her as a lover. "She lives up to her name," Jack told Smathers. "The gal is on fire."

Jack would not be the only politician to bed Blaze. In 1959 she was appearing in a strip joint, Sho-Bar, on Bourbon Street in New Orleans. One night Earl Long, the long-time and spectacularly corrupt governor of Louisiana, escorted by two policemen, came into the club. The brother of the notorious Huey Long of Louisiana, Earl termed himself "the last of the red hot poppas" of politics. When he met Blaze, he was serving his third term as governor.

After the show, Earl came backstage and introduced himself. He stayed around for the second show. At the finale, he shouted to her, "Will you go to dinner with me tonight?"

"Can I trust you?" she shouted back.

"Hell, no!" he yelled at her.

Their affair, launched that night, became the scandal of Louisiana.

When JFK and Jackie arrived in Louisiana during JFK's campaign for president in 1960, Earl invited both of them to the joint where Blaze was stripping. Jack didn't want Jackie tagging along, but she insisted, claiming she'd never been to a strip club before.

After the show, Earl introduced Jack and Jackie to Blaze. Both of the Kennedys knew that Earl was having an affair with the stripper. Blaze later admitted in her 1974 autobiography, "In front of Jackie, I pretended I'd never met Jack before. We pulled it off."

Earl later invited all of them back to the Roosevelt Hotel for a late-night party. Jackie bowed out and returned to her own hotel, but Jack accepted.

"When Earl was elsewhere talking to some of his political cronies, Jack and I slipped away to have a quickie in the closet," Blaze claimed in her memoirs.

Kennedy aide Langdon Marvin estimated that "Jack spent at least twenty minutes in that closet with Blaze while I guarded the door." Later JFK told Marvin that he amused Blaze by telling her that in 1923, President Warren Harding had seduced Nan Britton, a 23-year-old fan whom some observers claimed had been obsessed with Harding since her middle teens, in a broom closet at the White House.

A short time after the Kennedys departed from New Orleans, Earl fell on bad days. Learning of her husband's affair with Ms. Starr, his wife, Blanche

Not knowing about the sexual trysts of JFK, American families watched in total innocence the presidential debates of JFK vs. Nixon. Most TV viewers agreed that JFK's good looks and charm gave him a big advantage over the badly shaved and sweaty Nixon.

When they were over, public opinion polls showed that TV viewers favored JFK, whereas radio listeners opted for the deep-voiced Nixon as the more commanding candidate.

Unlike Bill Clinton's presidential campaign, when his affair with Gennifer Flowers was widely exposed, not a word leaked out about Blaze Starr with JFK, or about JFK with a hundred other women. Ignorance was bliss, at least during this hard-fought campaign.

Revere Long, managed to have him committed to a mental institution. But since he was still governor, and because the hospital was a state-funded institution, he fired its administration and escaped. "Uncle Earl," as he was called, died in 1960 and never got to see JFK take over the White House.

JFK had become so stimulated during his previous seductions of Blaze that he proposed to his aides that immediately before each of the four upcoming television debates scheduled against Richard Nixon, he needed a stripper—a hired prostitute, that is—delivered to his room. C. David Heymann, the well-known Kennedy biographer, revealed the details of this in his biography, *RFK*.

The two candidates, Nixon and JFK, met on September 25 in Chicago for the first of their debates. Arrangements had already been made through Marvin and RFK for a young woman to be delivered to Jack's room at Chicago's Palmer House Hotel ninety minutes before airtime.

According to Heymann, Marvin stood guard in the corridor outside JFK's hotel room. "Jack evidently enjoyed himself," Marvin said, "because he emerged fifteen minutes later with an ear-to-ear grin on his face."

That night in front of TV cameras broadcasting to millions of viewers, Jack looked self-confident and assured, still basking in the lingering glow of hot sex back in his hotel room. Some TV critics found the nervous and tense Nixon, with his five o'clock shadow, looking more like an escaped convict who'd stolen somebody's suit.

Nixon, who had already served for two full terms as Dwight D. Eisenhower's vice president, campaigned on a slogan of peace and prosperity. JFK countered that America had become stagnant, the Republicans complacent, and that he wanted to get America moving again.

In that debate and in the three debates that followed, JFK projected youth, although he was only a few years younger than Tricky Dickie.

After glowing reviews of his televised performance, JFK ordered Marvin to provide him with a stripper before each of the next three debates—"preferably big busted and a genuine red-head down below, no dye job!"

A Louisiana newspaper columnist privately told his colleagues, "Do you think it is too far of a stretch to claim that Blaze Starr in some distant way propelled Kennedy into the White House?"

Governor **Earl Long**, the long-time lover of Blaze Starr, taught her a lot about Louisiana politics. In her memoir, she revealed some of his political wisdom.

Earl told her, "If it weren't for the niggers down here, the Longs wouldn't have a chance in politics. Of course, you know me and my brother, Huey, have always done more for the niggers than anybody else in the whole South. You know Blaze, it's a shame how the niggers have been treated anyway, and we're going to have to realize sooner than later that they're just like everybody else, that they've got a soul and they'll go to heaven. And sooner or later, we're going to have to live with them."

Sometimes Earl would accuse **Blaze** *(photo, left)* of not loving him because he was an old man. On one occasion he brought pictures of himself to show her what a handsome man he used to be.

"I told him that was not necessary. That I loved him for what he was now, not what he was then."

The governor's wife, "Miz Blanche" as she was called, eventually found out about her husband's affair. But as the governor told Blaze, "She'll die and go to hell before she'll say anything about it. It would be too much humiliation for her."

One night at the Sho-Bar, a New Orleans strip joint, Earl proposed marriage to Blaze, even though still wed to Miz Blanche. But before he could divorce his Southern belle, a steel magnolia, she arranged for him to be locked away in a mental institution.

P a u l   N e w m a n

PAUL NEWMAN AND JFK HAD A HISTORY OF SHARING SEXUAL FAVORS FROM THE SAME WOMEN

DO YOU KNOW THEIR NAMES?

(Turn this page upside down for the answers)

Marilyn Monroe
Audrey Hepburn
Judy Garland
Lana Turner
Susan Hayward
Ava Gardner
Grace Kelly
Elizabeth Taylor
Joan Crawford, and
Jackie Kennedy

Although he seemed an unlikely candidate to play a redneck Louisiana governor, an elegant Yankee, **Paul Newman**, wanted to portray Earl Long, a breast-fixated Southern politician, on the screen. He did, appearing in the romantic drama, *Blaze* (1989), with **Lolita Davidovich** as the stripper.

The director, Ron Shelton auditioned 600 actresses before Lolita met with both his approval and Paul's okay. Blaze herself appeared in a cameo as an elderly stripper. The box office returns were disappointing, but the director, Shelton, eventually married Lolita.

JFK Fiddles and Faddles in the White House

During a tour of the White House, Jackie Kennedy was personally directing a reporter for *Paris-Match*. She guided him past the office of Evelyn Lincoln, JFK's personal secretary. The First Lady noticed Priscilla Wear, a minor secretary, sitting at a typewriter. In French, Jackie said to the *Paris-Match* reporter, "This is the woman who supposedly is sleeping with my husband."

Unknown to Jackie at the time, Priscilla understood French.

Priscilla had been nicknamed "Fiddle" by the Secret Service.

There was another secretary in the orbit of the Oval Office nicknamed "Faddle." Collectively, they were referred to as "Fiddle and Faddle."

Faddle was actually Jill S. Cowen, who worked in the office of Pierre Salinger, JFK's press secretary.

Right after JFK moved into the White House, Secret Service agents learned that the president led a double life——charismatic leader of the Free World during the day, sexual *roué* at night, a cheating, reckless husband whose aides almost systematically sneaked women into the White House to appease what seemed like an insatiable sexual appetite.

(continued on next page)

The president didn't always have to import the consorts. He had some live-in women as well. One was Pamela Turnure, who had been his secretary when he was a senator representing the people of Massachusetts. The other two were Priscilla and Jill ("Fiddle and Faddle").

Larry Newman, a former Secret Service agent, claimed, "Neither Fiddle nor Faddle did much actual work unless you call having threesomes with the president work."

He recalled one afternoon when the president was cavorting in the nude with the secretaries when the Secret Service notified him that Jackie was returning to the White House a day earlier than previously announced and would, in fact, be arriving in just ten minutes.

JFK rose from the pool, reached for a large bath towel, and headed for the dressing room. "The president handed me his Bloody Mary, which had been placed at poolside for him," said agent Anthony Sherman. "Enjoy," JFK said. "It's quite good." He raced to his dressing room to change into a suit and tie and was at the entrance to greet Jackie, who was returning from Virginia.

By the time Jackie entered the White House, Fiddle and Faddle were back at their desks.

"It was a rule that when the president had lunch by the pool with Fiddle and Faddle, nobody was to go there. David Powers, a JFK aide, was assigned to job of rounding up Fiddle and Faddle. When this revelation first emerged, it was assumed that JFK was alone in the pool skinny-dipping with the two secretaries. But later, it was learned that a nude Bobby and Teddy joined their brother and the secretaries in the pool. The president was always delighted when Jackie and the kids headed for her family retreat at Glen Ora in Virginia's horse country.

The president later told Larry Newman that he "got headaches if I don't get laid at least once a day."

All of the agents liked and respected First Lady Jackie. One agent even fell in love with her. "She had our greatest sympathy for the way her husband treated her," another agent claimed.

Newman said that the men in the Secret Service were devoted to the president and wanted to protect him, even with their lives. "But we were sadly disappointed at the way he conducted his personal life," said one agent. "It not only made him vulnerable, it made America vulnerable as well."

Sherman was among the former White House agents who granted an interview to investigative reporter Seymour M. Hersh for his book, *The Dark Side of Camelot*.

Sherman revealed, "There were women everywhere in the White House when Mrs. Kennedy wasn't there. Very often, depending on what shift you were on, you'd see them going up, or you'd see them coming out in the morning from the president's private apartments."

Sherman protested that whereas his job involved protecting the president, he couldn't control the people going into JFK's private rooms. "I felt really spooky about it. Blackmail was a distinct possibility. I didn't know the names of these outsiders, or where they came from. A potential assassin could have been among them. There was no security clearance whatsoever."

It has since been learned that even the Secret Service agents were not immune from advances from the Kennedy clan, although they never came from JFK himself. "Three Kennedy women went after us," one agent, who refused to be named, claimed. "And Peter Lawford was alway trying to give us blow jobs. His wife, Patricia Lawford, was the most aggressive. We nicknamed her 'rancid ass.'"

Priscilla Wear
The President's office

Jill S. Cowen
Mr. Salinger's office

"Fiddle"

"Faddle"

JFK and Elvis

Shared Tastes, and a Tempest for The Queen of Burlesque

ELVIS & TEMPEST ARE DATING!

America's fabled stripper, **Tempest Storm**, was a friend of Marilyn Monroe. Tempest's springboard to stardom was her "Million Dollar Treasure Chest." The women became friends and shared their memories of bedding both John F. Kennedy and **Elvis Presley**.

Tempest said she developed large breasts while still in seventh grade, and "all the boys made fun of me." Like Marilyn, she was introduced to sex early in life at the age of twelve. "The sheriff's son grabbed me and threw me in a car when I was coming out of an ice cream parlor. They dragged me into the hills where they took turns raping me, five of them."

Elvis had to climb an eight-foot fence to get at Tempest, and according to her, "he tore his pants pretty badly." JFK seduced her in the comfort of his apartment. Tempest said, "All he had to do was take off his pants and drop his underwear. As far as Jack is concerned, I believed then, and I believe now, that when a man strays, there's something wrong at home, something he's not getting."

"THE GEORGIA PEACH"

FAMOUS FOR HER

44DD-25-35 FIGURE

*"A woman's greatest weapon
is a man's imagination"*
Burlesque Queen Anne Corio

Tempest Storm, so far as it is known, is the only known woman, except for Marilyn Monroe, who shared the bed of both JFK and Elvis. Reporters always asked her the same question: Which of these men was better in the haystack? Allegedly, the stripper said, "Both were quick on the trigger, but Jack had more stamina."

The American stripper, Tempest Storm, was born Annie Blanche Banks in Eastman, Georgia, on February 29, 1928. Her career in burlesque spanned half a century, one of the longest runs of all burlesque artists.

Like Blaze Starr (her rival), she became famous for her naturally red hair and her measurements (44DD-25-35). In the late 1950s, her breasts (she called them her "moneymakers") were insured by Lloyds of London for one million dollars. She was married four times, one time to Herb Jeffries, Duke Ellington's singer "and the first black singing cowboy."

In 1987 she shocked America by publishing *Tempest Storm: The Lady Is a Vamp*, in which she detailed her affairs with both JFK and Elvis.

She first met the young senator from Massachusetts in 1955 when she was performing at the Casino Royale, a cabaret-style strip club in Washington. After her show, one of JFK's aides came backstage to arrange a meeting, but the stripper wasn't interested. At the time she thought most senators were pot-bellied and bald. She asked the aide if Senator Kennedy was married, and he told her that he was "but it didn't matter."

She asserted that a wedding ring meant "mar-

In her memoirs, **Tempest** claimed that when JFK was angry, "He was even more handsome and appealing than when he was happy and flashing that famous smile. However he was, he melted me like butter over an open flame."

"That youthful side of him came through one evening after we'd finished dinner and his driver was taking us for a leisurely ride through Washington. We were passing a little park, down near the Potomac River. Suddenly he told the driver to stop. He said, 'I'll race you to the river.' I fell along the way, and he collapsed beside me, kissing me long and passionately. Then he picked me up and carried me to the car. He told his driver to take us to the Mayflower Hotel where I had a suite."

This must be the only time ever recorded that JFK's back was in working order.

ried" to her, and she wasn't going out with Senator Kennedy. Even though she turned down the offer to date him, she took a quick peek at him from behind the curtain, and was stunned by his good looks.

Not one to take no for an answer, Senator Kennedy and his pals appeared the following night to see her show a second time. The same aide appeared again backstage after her show with the same request.

This time, Tempest relented, joining JFK at his table, where she found him not only handsome, but charming and witty. They made a date for the following night when she had off from the club.

She wasn't overwhelmed by him on the first date, claiming she'd dated far more famous men in Washington than him. Even when he told her that one day he'd become President of the United States, she was very skeptical, ranking that in the category of every actor who announced in advance that one day he would win an Oscar.

Although it got off to a slow start, their relationship heated up, and he saw her every night he could during her extended engagement, even if their unions had to be scheduled at two o'clock in the morning. Their affair became "stormy" at times, especially when she was habitually late, like another of his mistresses, Marilyn Monroe. He demanded punctuality.

As he made love to her and indulged in pillow talk, she found him a contradiction—"both a little boy who wouldn't grow up and at times one of the most mature men" she'd ever bedded.

In a suite at Washington, D.C.'s Mayflower Hotel one night after making love, he confided in her that he was not happily married, "Jackie is very cold to me," he claimed.

"In my memory, Jack Kennedy's sex drive lives up to the legend that has developed around it since his death," Tempest wrote. "The man just never wore out."

Their affair went from being a "Tempest" to a slight breeze blowing across the Potomac, but it became one of his most memorable affairs. "I'd rather be screwing Tempest Storm than a dozen Marilyn Monroes," he told Senator George Smathers. "She's got better hygiene than Marilyn and doesn't let a man leave her bed until he's completely satisfied on all levels. And those tits can't be beat. She's amazing, and they're real, too."

Exit Senator Kennedy, enter Elvis Presley.

In 1957 in Las Vegas, Elvis developed a taste for strippers. At the time, Tempest was reaching the height of her fame, and Elvis went to see her perform as part of the Minsky's Follies

In 1951 when Jerry Lewis and Dean Martin were appearing in Vegas, they claimed that **Tempest** "has the two best props in show business."

There's no record of her having seduced Martin, but she did bed one of his fellow Rat Packers, Sammy Davis Jr.

ELVIS & TEMPEST ARE DATING! headlined a paper in Las Vegas.

In gold lamé, the stripper, **Tempest Storm**, was photographed with the pop star who was still a Hound Dog then and not "The King." Her right breast is seen practically stabbing him in the chest.

"We haven't done bad," she told him. "I went from a sharecropper's daughter to become the Queen of Burlesque, and you were a truck driver. Now all the gals in Vegas are trying to find out what's in your underwear. I hope it's not a disappointment."

When asked to appraise Tempest, Elvis later said, "I found her titillating."

Revue at the Dunes Hotel. Colonel Tom Parker, an expert on such matters, told Elvis that Tempest was the "real deal" when it came to burlesque.

Elvis got a seat down front and was immediately turned on when Tempest came out, her hair a flaming red, her bosom bursting out like spring. The Georgia sharecropper's daughter had Elvis murmuring under his breath, "Rock, Baby, Rock" as she heated up the room.

The next day, he telephoned her at her hotel, but she wasn't immediately turned on, admitting "at that time I could have my pick of celebrities, and Elvis wasn't that big a star at the time."

At first she didn't go out with him, but did agree to meet him at the Dunes Hotel. She wore a gold lamé, snugly fitting outfit and wanted to get some shots with him that she could use for publicity.

When he came face to face with Tempest, he licked every finger on her right hand.

"C'mon, Elvis," she said, "keep that up and I'll need a towel. What dime store clerk in Memphis taught you that trick?"

Obviously Elvis found Tempest's hand as "finger lickin' good" as Tennessee fried chicken. Throughout their encounter, he took note of her prominent breasts.

When a photographer arrived for their photo session, she instructed Elvis to think "naughty thoughts like we just got out of bed together."

In her steamy memoirs, *The Lady Is a Vamp*, the stripper claimed she and Elvis became almost inseparable after that posing session—"dining together, dancing together, laughing together. I enjoyed the feeling of power that came from having the idol of millions idolize me."

After the night he first seduced her, he claimed he was "as horny as a billy goat in a pepper patch."

After news of Elvis' affair with Tempest became widely gossiped about, Colonel Parker was furious. "If you keep hanging around that stripper woman, those screaming teenagers are going to quit screaming. And when they stop screaming, they'll stop buying your records, and then where the hell are you going to be? Back in Memphis driving a goddamn truck."

Even though she was genuinely attracted to Elvis, calling him the "most famous and desired man in the world," Tempest knew that their nights together were numbered. The colonel would see to that—"and that bastard called the shots for Elvis."

In the future, other singers lay in her boudoir, including Vic Damone and Frank Sinatra. "In some ways," Tempest told a girlfriend, "Vic and Frankie aren't as big as Elvis, but in other departments they are *so much bigger.*"

Other celebrity lovers included Mickey Rooney and Engelbert Humperdinck.

She could be reassuring to her boyfriends, as when Engelbert doubted his prowess as a lover, and once jokingly asking her if she thought he needed a transplant. She told him he had the right equipment but had to learn how to use it.

On November 10, 2010, the former Queen of Burlesque returned to the stage to shake her stuff and show her boobs. The queen's "flame hair," for which she was once famous, may have come from a bottle during recent years, but reviewers have nonetheless noted that her breasts are not altogether fallen.

She overcame personal adversity in her life, plus a changing entertainment scene, to remain "a force in show business," as she refers to herself. Even at her age, she claims she's still looking forward to forming "new relationships" to add to the notches on her belt.

She feels the great names of burlesque will endure, including Gypsy Rose Lee and Sally Rand, and "I'm proud that mine will be added to that list of enduring legends."

Hanging Out With the Kennedys

What Happened When Steve McQueen & Marlene Dietrich
Showed Up Together at Their Dinner-Dance

Marlene Dietrich, the femme fatale of the 20th Century, had a long history with the Kennedy family, especially Joe and his son Jack. She encountered Joe in Hollywood of the 1930s and Jack in Paris in 1939 at a party.

She seduced Joe to gain his help in financing a picture, but she seduced Jack when he was in his early 20s with no motive but lust. "I thought he was a very cute boy, and sometimes I grow tired of having sex with men past their prime."

When Jackie met Marlene, she was unaware that the German star had had sex with her husband, but Rose Kennedy knew all about Marlene and Joe. "I tolerate Gloria Swanson, Constance Bennett, and Nancy Carroll. Why not Dietrich? Rather she make pictures with Joe instead of doing propaganda films for Hitler and Josef Goebbels."

Marlene's husband, Rudolf ("Rudi") Sieber, warned her to stay away from Joe, but she never listened to his advice. "I can handle Mr. Joe Kennedy. He won't take advantage of me the way he did Swanson. You much realize that I've dealt with men far richer and far more powerful than this Irish bootlegger."

Pictured above is a group photograph of **Joe and Jack** (back row) standing in back of **Rose** (left) and **Jackie**. It was taken on November 9, 1960 at their home in Hyannis Port. *(Associated Press)*

Marlene Dietrich always said, "If you've got the figure, why keep it a secret?" She is seen here on October 25, 1957 when she was honored at Philadelphia's Crystal Ball as the woman having the greatest continuing impact on fashion through the years. She is depicted in a tailored evening dress of gold and white brocaded sari silk designed by Jean-Louis of Hollywood.

One night over drinks, Joe, Sr., asked Marlene if she could give some advice to Rose about how to dress better. "The other day in a Boston paper, Rose was called frumpy. I've known some of the greatest beauties of Hollywood, and I have to come home to Rose, and she's sitting in the living room in a housecoat from 1947 that didn't look good when she first bought it."

"I understand your plea for help, but I can't rescue Rose," Marlene said. "Who ever made a silk purse out of a sow's ear?"

With an utter lack of tact, Joe told Rose what Marlene had said. "Oh, Marlene," Rose responded. "She's all artifice. Just imagine what she looks like when she steps out of the shower without makeup. An old German hag, no doubt."

SEDUCING THE KENNEDYS

In a tuxedo borrowed from the playboy of the Dominican Republic, Porfirio Rubirosa, Steve McQueen (then known as Steven) hired himself out in the 1950s as a male escort, often to visiting Hollywood stars. He was young and handsome, and much in demand. Sometimes he was merely an escort, taking a star to a particular function. At other times, sex was involved.

One afternoon the director of Steve's escort agency, Floyd Wilson, called him. Over the phone, Wilson told him, "You did so well with Doris Duke, I've arranged the escort job of a lifetime for you—the date of dates."

"Another antique pussy," Steven said skeptically. "As you know, I'm not opposed to old pussy from time to time, providing it's not a steady diet of it."

"This is a genuine *grande dame*," Floyd told him. "*La Dietrich* herself."

"I can hardly believe that a woman like that needs to pay for a date," Steven said.

"You'd be surprised," Wilson said. "A friend of mine runs a similar escort agency in Hollywood. You can't believe the living legends sitting home at night waiting for a date. Most men assume, like you did, that they are fully booked or else they're too intimidated to call."

"I've always wanted to meet Dietrich, Mae West, Joan Crawford, and Bette Davis," Steven said. "I might as well start with the Kraut herself."

"I'll call later with the details," Floyd promised. "But for god's sake, don't call her a Kraut."

Later that evening a black maid ushered Steven into the living room of Marlene Dietrich in her suite at the Plaza. He was stunned to see photographs of her from movie stills lining the room. Dietrich came into the room and said, "Hello," in a voice that was instantly recognizable to him. Her shimmering gold gown was form fitting.

She sat across from him, revealing her world-famous gams when she crossed her legs. A strand of black pearls encased her throat, and she wore emeralds to set off her beauty and the dress.

Before her, she had some movie stills on a coffee table. She picked them up and began to examine them one by one. "Quite lovely, don't you think?" she said. "What am I saying? You haven't had a chance to enjoy them yet."

She hadn't even introduced herself or asked his name. He thumbed through the stills and looked over at her with a smirk. "God sure did know how to create some exceptional women. Trouble is, except for you and a few others, he didn't create enough of them."

With that remark, her carefully arranged face broke into a mild laughter. When she laughed, her wrinkles, in spite of the artful makeup, became more pronounced. Even so, as he was to tell his friends, "she was one gorgeous dame—nothing natural about her, though. It was all a carefully orchestrated creation."

Like General Dwight D. Eisenhower planning the D-Day landings, she outlined to him her plan for the night. They would be joining Joseph F. Kennedy and his wife, Rose, at a charity event in the Plaza ballroom. The former ambassador and his wife would also be joined by John F. Kennedy and his bride, Jacqueline.

"At some point in the evening, the ambassador will excuse himself," Dietrich said. "Your job will be to distract Rose Kennedy at this time. I will also excuse myself to repair my face. We'll be gone for no more than twenty minutes. Joe is quick on the draw. We will re-enter the ballroom at separate times. Again, make sure Rose Kennedy is distracted."

"When I entered the ballroom, I was quaking in my boots," Steven later confided to Shelley Winters. "I met the Kennedys, although I wasn't sure who they were until it was explained to me later. Jackie was beautiful, in spite of some bad skin which she'd tried to cover up with makeup. Rose was a bit dowdy. John was rather dashing, but old Joe was an asshole. Somehow I got through the evening—don't ask me how."

At the agreed-upon time, Marlene exited from the ballroom. In a few minutes, Joe Kennedy excused

After JFK had agreed to deliver a videotaped introduction to **Steve McQueen**'s film, *Hell Is for Heroes*, he met with him one final time for an extended drink. The president liked talking with McQueen about Hollywood stars each of them had seduced. JFK learned that McQueen had once escorted Joan Crawford to a function when he was a male escort before he broke into pictures.

McQueen startled the president by revealing that he liked "sloppy seconds. In Crawford's case, I got what I wanted, following Steve Cochran, Greg Bautzer, Yul Brynner, Kirk Douglas, Henry Fonda, Clark Gable, Barbara Stanwyck, Spencer Tracy, Tyrone Power, John Wayne, Rock Hudson AND John F. Kennedy."

"So, you found out about us?" JFK said. "It was 1946, I was out of the navy. Lana Turner introduced us. But I have a question to ask: Are her ninny pies still firm?"

Steve said, "She still calls her breasts ninny pies, and they aren't yet altogether fallen."

135

himself to go to the men's room.

"I sat in a plush chair talking to Rose, who immediately asked me what my religion was. I told her I didn't have one. Would you believe she tried to convert me to Catholicism right there in the ballroom?"

When the music started, Steven asked Rose to dance. She was short but skilled on the dance floor. Within minutes her son, John, cut in.

"I found myself dancing with his beautiful bride," Steven said. "She smelled wonderful, but not in any artificial way. It was a sort of natural smell, like dew on the grass at dawn. I thought Jacqueline was lovely in spite of the bad skin."

With Dietrich and Joe Kennedy still out of the room, Rose ordered drinks for the table. "Only Irish whiskey would do," Steven said.

Joe was the first to come back into the room. "I knew he'd visited the Garden of Delights, and I also felt that Rose knew where he'd been, but she didn't say a thing," Steven said.

"Joe asked Rose to dance, and I excused myself to go to the men's room," Steven said. "To my surprise John—he said I could call him Jack—decided to go with me. We stood side by side at the urinal, and I noticed he was checking me out. Christ, God, and Holy Mary, was he also a faggot?"

Steve McQueen, in a bit of an exaggeration, often compared himself to JFK—and not just when checking out cock sizes at the urinals, as they did one night in New York at the Plaza Hotel. "We both fucked blondes, but married brunettes," McQueen once told Paul Newman about JFK.

A bisexual, Steve was both attracted to Newman and also jealous of him. "Although we're different types, we were often up for the same roles," McQueen said."

One night when he was spending time with Newman, McQueen began discussing JFK, with whom both had had a passing acquaintance.

"I hear Jack likes orgies, and I think we should get him involved—perhaps you, me, the president, and five or six hot blondes. I think he'll go for it. I like having sex with more than one woman at a time, and I really like it when three or four of my buddies go first. You see, I like making love to a woman who is still warm."

"You're the first guy I know who ever liked sloppy seconds," Newman told him. "If Kennedy agrees to this, we have to let him go first. After all, he's the president."

"I see that you have more than I do," he said, "but I bet before it's all said and done, I will have fucked more movie stars than you."

"It's a bet," Steven said.

After shaking the urine from his penis, he shook Steven's hand at the urinal.

"We'll meet in a few years, compare notes, and see who's the best man," John said. "Size isn't everything, you know."

Back in the ballroom, Rose and Joe had departed for the evening. Dietrich sat talking with Jacqueline. When her husband returned, Jacqueline quickly excused herself, and she soon left with her husband.

Smoking a cigarette, Dietrich watched them go. "I'm sure she's already heard the story on the Riviera when Joe passed me along to his teenaged son, John," Dietrich said. "As a lover, I found him weak lemonade."

"You gotta give the kid a break," Steven said. "After all, he was pretty young."

"Yes, we have to go through life making excuses for the young."

Back in her hotel suite, she began to remove some of her jewelry and part of her wardrobe. "You men," she said, appraising him, "you always demand *numero segundo*. Why is it none of you will settle for *numero uno*?"

"I'll settle and happily," Steven said.

He'd later tell Shelley Winters that "Dietrich gave me the blow job of my life. That Kraut knows her business.

Such technique."

"No wonder," Shelley said, "she's sucked off everybody from George Bernard Shaw to Gary Cooper, even Howard Hughes."

"From all I know, even Hitler himself," Steven said.

***

Marlene's relationship with the Kennedys went back years.

Joe Kennedy first got involved with Marlene, who was "more notorious than famous," in the words of Louella Parsons, when they met in Hollywood in 1930. She was making *Morocco*, starring with and seducing Gary Cooper.

After his breakup with screen vamp Gloria Swanson Joe was looking "for the next big star." At first, Marlene rejected his amorous adventures, which seriously angered him. He told his cronies, "That German bitch and her lousy accent will never go over with American audiences."

Over the next few years, Joe and Marlene met casually and superficially from time to time, and she continued to refuse his overtures. In retaliation, he frequently attacked her behind her back, suggesting to the honchos at Paramount in 1936 that Marlene wasn't worth the high salary she was paid.

When she was named box office poison in 1938 by movie distributors, Joe told Paramount, "Didn't I already point that out?" Marlene had unexpectedly joined the ranks of Mae West, Katharine Hepburn, and Joan Crawford, among others, each of whom had also appeared on that poisonous list.

Jack Kennedy, Jr. was introduced to Marlene by Joe himself when Marlene and Noël Coward invited them to a cocktail party in Paris. It was a stopover before their vacation on the French Riviera. Jack was twenty-two years old at the time, having been born in 1917. Marlene had been born in 1901, maybe even earlier.

Jack later told Lem Billings, "She spent less time looking at my face and most of the time looking at my crotch. But she's not my type, and she's old enough to be my mother." He would later change his mind.

"For the first time, I think Joe began to see Jack as possible competition for himself in future romances," Lem Billings asserted years later in a dialogue with

Josef von Sternberg and Marlene Dietrich are seen as they appeared on the set of *Dishonored* (1931), wherein she played a Viennese streetwalker turned spy.

Joe Kennedy detested von Sternberg but didn't let the Austrian director know that. In fact, von Sternberg told the press that Joe "was a brilliant and charming man." To his face, Joe claimed, "the only objection I have with you is that in 1930 I arranged a date with Marlene, and she brought you along as chaperone."

One night in Cannes, Joe and von Sternberg sat drinking deep into the night. "I can't flaunt my affairs in front of Rose too much. But Marlene and her husband Rudi flaunt their lovers in front of each other. That's the kind of marriage I secretly want. Marlene even invites her busband to join her lovers for dinner. Not only that, but Rudi is told to bring Tami along."

He was referring to Rudolf Sieber and Tamara Matul. "Frankly if Rose were sophisticated like that, I wouldn't have all this Catholic guilt."

New York literary agent Jay Garon, to whom he was pitching the sale of a memoir he was writing about his years with the Kennedys. "Jack talked about it a lot. Joe at the time was getting a little long in the tooth. He used to be a fairly attractive man to judge from his photographs, but he was looking bloated and a bit jowly. Just as Jack entered his twenties, Joe was moving deeper into his fifties."

Joe had rented a villa for his family within the relentlessly posh resort of Cap d'Antibes on the French Riviera. Marlene and her entourage were also in residence.

Marlene was on the Riviera with her 13-year-old daughter, Maria Sieber (later Riva); her husband, Rudolf Sieber; and his girlfriend Tamara Matul.

At the age of thirty-eight, Marlene still looked sultry and gorgeous. She'd spend her vacation hopping from bed to bed. In addition to Joe and Jack Kennedy, three other lovers—one female—had also arrived on the scene.

The handsome, muscular German novelist, Erich Maria Remarque (1898-1970), showed up. Marlene had fallen in love with him when she saw his splendid nude body, with his heavy endowment, on a Venetian beach.

He'd become famous for writing his first novel, *Im westen Nichts neues*. It was filmed in Hollywood as the hugely successful *All Quiet on the Western Front* in 1930, starring Lew Ayres.

During dinners on the Riviera with Joe Kennedy and Remarque, both men urged Marlene to give up her German citizenship and return to America. Remarque told Marlene, "I'd rather die than live one day without you," a romantic but not a particularly realistic proclamation. She showed that note to numerous friends.

The very jealous film director Josef von Sternberg also turned up. His directorial and public relations efforts had transformed Marlene into a household name since the release of *The*

A fetishist and butch, too, **Marion ("Joe") Carstairs**, the Standard Oil heiress, is seen in both photos on this page with her constant companion, Lord Tod Wadley, a little doll who became her bosom companion. When she joined Marlene in her love nest on the French Riviera in 1939, Lord Wadley was always seated at table as a guest of honor, even when they visited the Kennedys at their compound in Cap d'Antibes.

Instead of being turned off by Carstairs' lesbianism, Joe Kennedy tried to lure her into backing Marlene's next picture. Even though Carstairs agreed to put up the money with Joe, the picture was never made.

On vacation, Erich Maria Remarque practically drank up all the Calvados in Antibes. He invited Carstairs and a young Jack Kennedy to go on a night drive along the Côte d'Azur. They got into his wire-wheeled two-seater with Jack, the skinny one, sitting on Carstairs' lap. Before this wild night was over, Remarque--Marlene called him "the world's most reckless driver"—ended up at a homosexual bar in Cannes, patronized mainly by transvestites.

Before that night ended, Jack allegedly got a blow-job in the men's room and Carstairs disappeared with one of the more alluring transvestites. Remarque was not found until the next day when Marlene conducted a search for him. She located his nude body upstairs over the bar in Cannes where the bar's owner, a male known as "Kiki," assured her that none of the patrons had taken advantage of her friend.

"Maybe a few men took pictures of that thing of his—but nothing else."

Blue Angel in 1930. Joe Kennedy didn't like him. An aggressive self-promoter who tended to misrepresent his middle-class origins, Von Sternberg was small, dark, and very intense, arriving on the Riviera in high-laced boots and jodhpurs with a drooping Oriental mustache crowning his small tight mouth. Perhaps it was his pretentious walking stick that turned off Joe.

To complicate matters, another of Marlene's lovers also happened to arrive during her complicated sojourn in the South of France. Marion ("Joe") Carstairs was a notorious and eccentric cross-dresser who favored women and smoked cheroots. She had inherited a Standard Oil fortune and knew how to spend her money—on fast boats, fast women, and wine.

In the 1920s she'd held the world record as the fastest speedboat racer, and eventually reigned as the virtual empress over her fiefdom on a Bahamian Out Island (Whale Cay) where she exerted all the powers of a feudal lord.

Her constant companion and obsessive fetish object was a little doll, Lord Tod Wadley, whom she maintained long dialogues with and carried close to her bosom all of her life. Marlene was her all-time favorite lover, although she'd long ago gotten used to sharing her with others.

The heiress made the summer's most dramatic entrance, sailing into a nearby harbor aboard a three-masted schooner with the full intention of resuming her lesbian affair with Marlene, which they'd left off the year before.

As the world moved toward war during that summer of 1939, Marlene enjoyed spending time with members of the Kennedy clan, often within their rented villa. She danced at the über-posh Hotel du Cap at Eden Rock with both Joe Kennedy and his young son, JFK.

With many of her past and present lovers, including young Jack, nearby, Marlene managed somehow to entertain the ambassador. Maria (Marlene's daughter) noticed that "he became a frequent visitor to my mother's cabaña." Rose was most gracious to Marlene, the way she had been with Gloria Swanson, when that actress was maintaining a much more prolonged affair with her husband.

Rose invited Marlene, her daughter, Maria, and Marlene's entourage for lunches on occasion, and acted as if nothing were going on between Marlene

Marlene Dietrich *(in both photos above)* appeared in a film called *Knight Without Armour,* made in London for Alexander Korda. She was paid $450,000 for the movie, which made her, at least in terms of earned income, the highest paid woman in the world for the year of 1936. When not filming, she was conducting torrid affairs in London, notably with Douglas Fairbanks, Jr.

Financially, *Knight Without Armour* came crashing in on Korda's head. Her other two pictures, made at around the same time, *The Garden of Allah* and *Angel,* were also financial disasters.

To escape her troubles she fled to the French Riviera with one of her lovers, the German novelist **Erich Maria Remarque**. She confided to Joe Carstairs, "Joe Kennedy would get me started but I had to escape to the suite of Erich to be finished off. The Kennedys have a lot to learn where sex is concerned."

Although he'd once been a cemetery stonemason and a German soldier during WWI, Remarque had become rich and famous after the publication of his first novel, *All Quiet on the Western Front*. That novel incited the German government at the time to withdraw his status as a citizen of Germany.

The Blue Angel, a German film (aka *Der blaue Engel*, 1930), brought international fame to **Marlene Dietrich**, cast as Lola-Lola. Her director, Josef von Sternberg, became her lover and mentor. When the director met Marlene, he claimed "my quest for the eternal woman is over."

When Marlene came to Hollywood to make *Morocco* with Gary Cooper, she caught Joe Kennedy's eye. He was shopping around for another beautiful movie star to add another notch to his belt. He eventually subdued Marlene, but only when she decided she could use him to help promote a stalled career.

JFK was so proud of his accomplishment of seducing **Marlene Dietrich** on the French Riviera when he was only in his 20s, that he was still bragging about it when he ran for president in 1960.

He told Claiborne Pell of his exploits. The son of Herman Pell, FDR's minister to Portugal, became the Democratic senator from Rhode Island in 1960, the same year JFK won the presidency.

Even though Marlene had been labeled as box office poison in 1938, producer Joe Pasternak arrived on the Riviera to offer her the comeback role of "Frenchy" in the 1939 release of *Destry Rides Again* for Universal. Joe Kennedy, whom Marlene called "Papa Joe," told her to take the part "but fuck Pasternak first to seal the deal."

and her husband. It is not known if Rose knew at the time that Marlene was also seducing her young son.

Jack would later recall that his affair with Marlene had begun one night at "hostess supreme" Elsa Maxwell's summer ball, also on the Riviera. "We were dancing to *Begin the Beguine*, and she held me real tight. I later found out why. She slipped her hand down my trousers and started masturbating me. I was already hard."

"I was intoxicated by her perfume," he claimed. "We agreed to meet the following day at a secluded inn up in the hills near St-Paul-de-Vence. After lunch we rented a room. I lost my cherry, at least to Marlene, on that hot, hot afternoon."

Lem Billings listened to all this with a profound jealousy he managed to suppress. Years later, Lem would transmit all of this and more to his literary agent, Jay Garon.

That summer of 1939, Marlene had two compelling reasons to want to hook up with Joe Kennedy and his entourage again. And although she hardly viewed him as a sex object, if it involved some action in the bedroom, she was willing to play. Her main purpose in meeting with him involved securing the financing for her projected French film.

Marlene wanted him to finance, *Dedée d'Anvers*, a film that would be directed by Pierre Chénal and co-starring Marlene with Jean Gabin ("the love of Marlene's life"), and Raimu. Orson Welles later referred to Raimu as "the greatest actor who ever lived."

Politically, Marlene also wanted to dissuade Kennedy, the ambassador, from his notorious appeasement policy with Hitler.

Since she had been labeled box office poison, she felt that Joe might jump start her career. She told him she'd flatly turned down Hitler's offer to "become the Queen of UFA" (the German film studio).

"Hitler said I could name my price," Marlene said. "Not only that, but I could select my own scripts and name my own director. But instead of taking him up on that offer, I applied for American citizenship."

Remarque warned her that Hitler might capture her in Europe and force her to return to Berlin.

While at Antibes, Marlene received an unexpected call from producer Joe Pasternak, offering her the starring role opposite James Stewart in a Western, *Destry Rides Again*. At first she denounced it as "a silly little Western," but both von Sternberg and Joe Kennedy urged her to take the part.

Later, she was glad she did. *Destry Rides Again* put her career back on the road. She also fell for her co-star, launching a torrid affair with Stewart, which eventually led to her having an abortion.

Joe really didn't want his son to ever see Marlene again, but when Jack came back to Hollywood in 1940 he called on Marlene at her studio, where she was making a picture called *Seven Sinners*, co-starring with John Wayne.

Jack went to the studio with his "pussy posse" buddy, the handsome actor Robert Stack. But Jack visited Marlene's dressing room by himself. He had turned twenty-three and, if anything, he was even better looking than before.

Having graduated from Harvard, he came to the set to give Marlene a copy of *Why England Slept*, a lavishly polished, with the help of a ghostwriter, elaboration of his senior thesis from Harvard.

Jack later told Robert, "Marlene gave me another of those fabulous blow-jobs. She is truly the Fellatio Queen of Hollywood."

***

In September of 1963, shortly before JFK's assassination, Marlene turned up in Washington for a one-woman show. Jack maintained fond memories of her from the Riviera in 1939, and Marlene had loyally campaigned for Kennedy in 1960. Hearing she was in town, he called her and invited her to the White House.

"Other than you," Jack told his friend, Lem Billings, "she gives the most seductive massages and best blow jobs I've ever had."

She later told friends, including Gore

Marlene Dietrich was **The Führer's** favorite movie star. Reportedly, he saw *Der blaue Engel* twelve times. He considered Marlene "the perfect embodiment of a Teutonic woman."

When Hitler rose to become chancellor of Germany in 1933, Marlene had long ago fled. She didn't see the book burnings, the anti-Jewish boycotts, or the establishment of Dachau.

In 1933, the National Socialists of Berlin banned *Dishonored* because of its criticism of imperial war politics. Although he didn't turn against Marlene, Hitler appraised the movie as "second-rate Remarque."

On opening night in Berlin, Josef Goebbels ordered the release of bushels of white mice, which sent the patrons screaming. Goebbels also launched a campaign to discredit Marlene, blaming her for abandoning Germany in pursuit of a career in Hollywood.

Marlene related all this to Joe Kennedy, Sr. when she vacationed with him on the French Riviera. When Marlene turned down the Führer's request to return to Berlin to make films for UFA, Goebbels banned Marlene, forbidding the showing of *Destry Rides Again*, a film not seen in Germany until 1960.

DID **BOBBY KENNEDY** EVER SEDUCE **MARLENE DIETRICH**?

The jury is still out on that one. Bobby's name often appears on the lists of men and women who are believed to have been intimate with Marlene. It is known that she seduced Joseph Kennedy, Sr. and a young Jack Kennedy.

Joseph Kennedy Jr. claimed he also seduced her in London in 1939, right before the war broke out. When asked, Marlene was always coy about whether her seduction chart included most of the Kennedy men. Teddy was never considered as a possibility.

It is known that in 1963, Bobby, then JFK's attorney general, sat next to Marlene at a luncheon in Washington. Surprisingly, he asked her a strange question.

"Who was the most attractive man you ever seduced?"

Without hesitation, she answered, "Jean Gabin." (Gabin was the French actor who had been her longtime lover.)

"What about me?" Bobby asked. "Chopped liver?"

"Not at all," she told him. "Actually you're the cutest of the Kennedys."

That night, Bobby was seen leaving Marlene's hotel suite at three o'clock in the morning.

Vidal, that JFK received her alone in an upstairs bedroom. She knew what to expect. He made a "clumsy pass" at her, and she reminded him, "Mr. President, I am not very young."

That didn't seem to bother the President, who really wanted only fellatio. During the act, she asked him not to muss her hair because she was soon due to perform.

She later claimed, "I gave him an ecstatic four minutes. But he wanted more. I didn't have time to take off my pink panties. He soiled them. After the dirty deed was done, he fell right asleep just like a little baby who's had his bottle."

While she rearranged herself in his bathroom, she noticed that she was running late. She woke him up. With a towel around his waist, he directed her to the elevator and rang for his valet. He asked for her car to be readied at once and a White House motorcycle security guard be assigned "to get Miss Dietrich on time to wherever in the hell she's going."

At the elevator, he asked her, "Did you ever go to bed with my old man?"

She paused, "He tried but I never did."

He flashed a smile. "I knew the son of a bitch was lying."

Actually it was Marlene who was telling a lie.

***

After the end of her Washington, D.C., engagement, arriving back at her New York apartment, Marlene greeted her son-in-law, William Riva, who was staying with her. She came into the living room waving a pair of pink panties under his nose. "Smell them! It is him! The President of the United States. He was *Wünderbar* and so quick on the draw."

Perhaps she was inspired to re-enact a scene from *The Blue Angel*, in which she, as the "harlot of harlots," threw her panties into the face of the lovesick old fool, the German actor Emil Jannings.

"In the 1930s," she proclaimed, "the *Führer* himself wanted me. Now in 1963, the president of the United States wants me." She appraised her still-slim figure in a full-length mirror. "I'm the timeless wonder."

Steve McQueen & JFK

Keeping Score

When **Steve McQueen** met with **JFK** in Los Angeles for a reunion, he had two requests. One involved having Kennedy appear in a brief prologue for his film *Hell Is for Heroes* (1962). He quickly won JFK's agreement on that.

But McQueen quickly learned that instead of his film, the president wanted to talk about the hot women of Los Angeles. McQueen did suggest that he might be ideal for the upcoming role of a naval hero (i.e., Kennedy himself) aboard PT109.

"He practically begged JFK to give him the key role," said actor Nick Adams, who also appeared in *Hell Is for Heroes.*

What JFK didn't tell McQueen at the time was that Frank Sinatra was the front runner for the role. Later, Sinatra bowed out, at least in part because Bobby Kennedy was convinced that Sinatra, with his many mob associations, was the wrong actor to cast into the role of "squeaky clean" JFK.

A POKE A DAY
KEEPS THE HEADACHES AWAY

Once, during the early 1960s, when John F. Kennedy flew into Los Angeles, Steve McQueen sent a request, via Frank Sinatra, to the president, hoping that JFK would remember who he was. Steve's most recent movie, *Hell Is for Heroes* had been based on a true incident of American heroism during World War II. It focused on the exploits of a squad of American soldiers who, during the autumn of 1944, managed to resist the advance of hundreds of heavily armed Nazi soldiers until Allied reinforcements arrived. Since the film had been based on a specific moment in America's wartime history, Steve thought the president might agree to appear in a brief prologue to introduce his film. Without seeing the film, and based on Steve's recommendation, JFK agreed to do it.

"Steve received an invitation, with the understanding that it would be strictly limited to ten minutes, to appear in Kennedy's hotel suite," actor Nick Adams later claimed. During the interview, "JFK talked about his favorite subject, Hollywood pussy."

According to biographer Christopher Sandford, JFK also asked Steve, "Don't you find you get a headache if you don't have at least a poke a day?"

Allegedly, the president and Steve tallied up their sexual scoreboards for the previous year, each of them estimating between 200 and 300 seductive conquests, an astonishing figure. Obviously, each of the men was exaggerating.

Actually Steve's real goal involved not having more seductions than Kennedy but "to have more pussy than Frank Sinatra."

Steve McQueen was bitterly disappointed when he lost his bid for the role of Jack Kennedy in *PT109*, the role eventually going, after many other actors were considered, to Cliff Robertson.

"Steve felt that JFK really let him down and Steve didn't have any trouble switching his political loyalties to Lyndon Johnson after Kennedy was killed," said actor Nick Adams. "I went with Steve to see Cliff in the film's final version. We both agreed that the movie sucked. Not that there's anything wrong with sucking."

At the White House, JFK reportedly screened *Hell Is for Heroes* a dozen times, but Jackie couldn't sit through "that boring thing" even once.

"In the pussy department, Sinatra was definitely McQueen's role model, not the president," Nick claimed.

According to Nick, during Steve's brief meeting with Kennedy, they agreed to continue to swap stories and "keep score" of their respective sexual conquests.

Even after the president of the United States, on film, recommended *Hell Is for Heroes* as an example of the heroism of American GIs, the "suits" at Paramount weren't that impressed with their own movie. Eventually, they released it as half of a double feature, pairing it with the lackluster *Escape from Zahrain*, a film about prisoners escaping from a Middle Eastern jail that starred Steve's nemesis, Yul Brynner, and his friend, Sal Mineo.

Both movies died a quick death and were eventually assigned to the graveyard of endless TV re-runs.

The Strange and Convoluted Saga of

Peter Lawford & the Kennedys

Part One

The Evolution of Brother-in-Lawford

Associated Press

On April 24, 1954, "I became a Kennedy," Peter claimed after his marriage to Patricia Kennedy, who had a rather, masculine chiseled face. He kept both Pat and Joe Kennedy waiting impatiently at the altar for him to arrive at St. Thomas More's Church in Manhattan. The ushers were Jack, Bobby, and Teddy, along with JFK's gay friend LeMoyne Billings. Lem had helped Pat pick out her Hattie Carnegie wedding gown in pearl-white satin. "Screaming women and uninhabited bobbysoxers" greeted Peter at his tardy arrival at church.

The marriage didn't live up to Pat's fantasies of wedding a movie star. On her honeymoon, Pat was shocked at Peter's preference for oral sex. He later told Frank Sinatra, "Pat crosses herself every time she goes to bed with me." Months later, he confessed, "I have liberated her sexually but wish I hadn't. She's turning into a whore."

Rescuing Peter from the Toilets and from "Hello, Smokey"

Late one night in California during the mid-1950s, long before he became very rich and very famous, Merv Griffin was awakened by the ringing of his telephone. In those days, he had only one phone, and it was in his living room. Arousing himself from bed, a nude Merv stumbled toward the phone.

Picking up the receiver, he heard a world-famous voice: "It's Judy. You've got to come over right away. I can't tell you over the phone. Promise me you'll come over NOW."

Reluctantly he agreed. He had hesitated because Judy Garland sounded drunk. He feared she might be making another suicide attempt. He dressed and drove over to Judy's house. If they were in the house at all that night, her husband, Sid Luft, and the children would probably be asleep upstairs.

At her door, Merv encountered Judy looking distraught and wearing no makeup. She'd been drinking and looked far older than her years.

Once he was inside, she spoke to him in a soft voice. "It's Peter Lawford. A member of the vice squad arrested him in the men's toilet of a state park. The charge is lascivious conduct. I just found out about it. He's supposed to be arraigned tomorrow. If the press finds out about this, you won't be seeing his name on any more marquees."

Hollywood actor **Peter Lawford** became the son-in-law that Joe Kennedy didn't want when he married the tycoon's daughter, Patricia.

One day on a fishing boat off the coast of Hyannis Port, Joe explained the Kennedy rules, which differed for his sons as opposed to his sons-in-law.

"I told my boys to get married and, for God's sake, to stay married. Have lots of kids. Of course, if they do that, they're free to sleep with any woman they so desire.

"Sons-in-laws are different. They're never to play around. They're expected to stay home attending to the wife and kids.

"In your case, Pat is the most adventurous of my daughters. If she strays a bit, you're to forgive her. If she's got a date, you can stay home and mind the kids. I hope you understand the rules."

Peter assured the family patriarch that he would abide by the rules, although a week later he was violating the Kennedy code in Hollywood.

"Oh, my God," Merv said. "I'm so sorry to hear this, but what can I do?"

"You know Howard Hughes, don't you?"

"Of course I do," he said. "We're playing tennis together later today."

"Howard will know what to do," she said. "He can get Peter out of jail and cover up this whole shitty mess. You'll go to Howard, won't you?"

"For Peter . . . anything," he promised.

Over badly made cups of coffee, Judy and Merv talked emotionally in her kitchen for about an hour, plotting what they could do to help Peter. Merv couldn't get Howard on the phone— no one ever could—but Merv told Judy that Howard always showed up faithfully on the tennis court exactly at nine-thirty every Sunday morning. Merv promised Judy he'd make the pitch to Howard then.

A few hours later, on the tennis court, Howard didn't want to talk business until he'd played a game. "I don't want to be distracted," Howard said.

After the match, which Merv deliberately let Howard win, Merv called Howard to the far end of the court and told him about Peter's dilemma.

"Shit like this happens in Hollywood all the time," Howard said. "I'm an expert in covering up for stars. You won't believe the jam I got Robert Mitchum out of one night. I'll help Peter. Not because I like the boy, but he's getting connected with the Kennedys. That family might be very useful to me one day."

Changing into his street clothes, Howard agreed "to take care of business."

As Merv had anticipated, Howard managed to quietly secure Peter's release from jail. No charges were ever filed against him, and the story of the men's room arrest was kept out of the press. Shortly thereafter, Merv tried to reach Peter by phone, but no one was picking up at his house. Merv placed a call to Judy to tell her the good news about Peter.

She immediately pleaded with him to join her on a drive to Palm Springs where Peter was hiding out after his ordeal. Merv agreed to drive her.

During the eastbound drive to Palm Springs, Judy was jittery and anxious, wanting the drive to be over. She drank from a flask she carried in her purse. "Don't be surprised when we get there," she said. "I mean, you'll meet Peter's new lover, and it may come as quite a shock to you."

"I read Hedda and Louella," he said. "I know about his fling with Patricia Kennedy, although I hear old Joe Kennedy is completely opposed to it. Apparently, Old Joe thinks all actors are faggots."

"He's probably right about that," she said. "The Ambassador is completely opposed to his Patricia seeing Peter, and he's persuaded that vicious drag queen, J. Edgar Hoover, to conduct a complete investigation. I hope Nelly Hoover doesn't discover Peter's fondness for tearooms."

"What do you mean tearooms?" Merv asked. "They seem harmless enough. It's his English upbringing."

"Oh, darling, you can be so naïve," she said, brushing his cheek lightly with her fingers.

As part of a publicity campaign for his first starring role, young actor **Merv Griffin** wows the fair damsels of Tennessee during a tour to promote the film he'd co-starred in with songbird Kathryn Grayson, *So This Is Love* (1953).

What these adoring young women didn't know was that Merv, later to become a famous TV talk show host, was a closeted and somewhat promiscuous homosexual. When Peter married Patricia Kennedy, Merv told his best pal, Roddy McDowall, "I got to Peter long before she did."

147

"A tearoom is homosexual slang for a men's toilet. It's called latrine sex. Some guys prefer that."

"Sex in a smelly toilet doesn't strike me as very romantic," he said.

"True, true," she said. "Incidentally, the lover you'll meet in Palm Springs isn't Pat. By the way, I'm having an affair with Pat's brother, and my philandering husband doesn't know about it. He's handsome and charming. Jack Kennedy, or John F. Kennedy if you want to get formal. I'll introduce you to him, but you can't have him. I saw him first. He calls me up sometimes late at night and asks me to sing 'Over the Rainbow' to him on the phone. Isn't that adorable?"

"You know I'm a bit of a voyeur, and I just have to ask," he said. "Is he great in bed? I heard that for years, his old man regularly fucked Gloria Swanson."

"Jack's no Frank Sinatra," she said, "but I adore him. He's got a bad back. Usually, I have to be on top doing most of the work."

Merv was absorbing all of this with the full intention of sharing every word, every sordid detail, with Roddy McDowall.

At the front door of a beautiful Spanish-style villa in Palm Springs, Peter in bathing trunks greeted Judy and Merv with wet kisses, inviting them in. Judy excused herself, rushing off to the nearest bathroom. While she was gone, Peter profusely thanked Merv for interceding with Howard Hughes. "It worked out OK this time, but you'd better clean up your act," Merv warned him.

"Oh, what the hell," Peter said. "I'm just a tearoom queen and that's all I'll ever be. There's nothing more sexually thrilling than giving blow jobs to strangers in a men's toilet."

When Judy returned, Peter kissed her lips gently again. "I've arranged for you guys to have the master bedroom." Judy led the way, asking Merv and Peter to bring her luggage.

Merv lingered behind, tugging at Peter's arm. "Judy and I are sharing a bedroom?" he asked.

"Yeah, she told me about the romance you guys are having," Peter said. "Nothing serious. Just fuck buddies."

"She told you *what*?" Judy was calling from the bedroom for Merv and Peter to hurry up with her luggage. Entering the room with suitcases, Merv spotted white sheets already turned down. A sense of panic overcame him. Peter gave Merv another quick kiss on the lips before departing toward the pool patio. "After you guys settle in, come and join Smokey and me on the patio."

"Smokey?" Merv was bewildered. He wanted to ask Peter who Smokey was.

Judy began undressing before him the way she'd done in front of dozens of people in the MGM wardrobe department. "C'mon," she urged him. "Shuck those duds." In Palm Springs all the stars go skinny dipping. Even Marlene Dietrich and Greta Garbo show off their pussies to each

Judy Garland and Peter Lawford often encountered each other, recalling their heydays at MGM.

One drunken night when the conversation shifted to Jack Kennedy, their mutual friend, Judy said, "I guess you and I, as a male and female, are the only couple in Hollywood who shares the joint distinction of having both of us give Jack a blow-job. Do you think if *The New York Times* found out, they'd run the story in a big headline on their frontpage?"

"I'm sure they would," he said. "After all, they print all the news that's fit to print.'

It was Peter who brought Judy into Humphrey Bogart's original Rat Pack, leadership of which was taken over by Frank Sinatra after Bogie died of lung cancer. Judy was elected "first vice president" of the Rat Pack. Without his knowledge, Jack Kennedy was made an honorary member.

148

other."

He stripped down but turned his back to her when he slipped into his bathing suit.

"Nice ass," she said before rushing out of the room. "Last one in is a rotten egg!"

Ignoring the invitation to go nude, Merv came onto the patio in his bathing suit. He immediately noticed that Peter had peeled off his trunks and was lying nude on the chaise longue. "Sammy, meet Merv," he called to a black man in the pool who was frolicking with Judy. She too had ripped off her bathing suit.

Merv had been promised an introduction to Sammy Davis Jr. but hadn't expected it to come like this. "Hi, kid, pull off your suit and come join us chitlin's," Sammy yelled to him.

"Yeah, Merv," Peter urged him. "After all, you're not Princess Tiny Meat."

"But to get naked with a black man" he whispered to Peter. "I'm not sure I can compete."

"It's not a competition," Peter said.

Hurriedly Merv pulled off his trunks and made a running leap into the pool.

Sammy swam over to him. "You can shake my hand or else grab King Kong," he said. "Whatever turns you on."

After that introduction, Merv soon overcame his shyness, finding Sammy enchanting and charming. They continued chatting even when the pool splashing ended. Peter and Judy donned robes and moved toward the bar to begin the heavy drinking of a fading afternoon. Dressed in a robe, Sammy lounged beside the pool with Merv.

"Peter used to be a part of our Rat Pack," Sammy said, glancing over at Peter and Judy at the bar. "I keep begging Frank to take him back, but he's too stubborn. Ever since Louella Parsons wrote that Peter was seen out on the town with Ava Gardner, Frank cut him off. The Rat Pack's not the same without him. Judy's only a sometimes member. Before Peter was banished, the Rat Pack consisted of two dago singers, a kike comic, a limey swell, a hot puta with red pussy hair, and a slightly off-color entertainer—the best in the business." He was, of course, referring to Frank Sinatra, Dean Martin, Joey Bishop, Peter Lawford, Shirley MacLaine, and himself.

Sammy looked over at Peter and blew him a kiss before asking for a drink. "Don't get the idea I'm gay," Sammy said. "I'm not! I've fucked more blonde showgals than Frankie himself. I've even fucked Ava Gardner. But don't tell Frankie that. He'd have some of the boys in the mob cut off King Kong if he knew that. But I like a little gay action on the side for variety. After all, you know yourself that Peter is the best cocksucker in Hollywood. That boy's got a very deep throat."

Drinks and more drinks preceded and followed a patio barbecue presided over by Sammy. "We niggers know our barbecue," he said. Shortly before midnight Sammy and Peter disappeared into the bedroom, leaving Merv alone with Judy.

She urged him to join her at the piano. "Let's sing

When Peter first propositioned **Sammy Davis Jr.** *(above)*, Davis turned him down.

But Sammy (known on Broadway as "Mr. Wonderful") soon became sucked up in the swinging, free-wheeling sexuality of the 1960s.

After he'd participated in all-night orgies in his Las Vegas hotel suite with Peter, bringing in prostitutes, it was Sammy who suggested that Peter and he lay off the girls for a night.

"I'd like a quickie. I want to see what homo action means." After their night together, Sammy told Peter, "Let's do it again...and again. You really know how to handle King Kong."

some songs together," she said. "You're the only person in Palm Springs who knows as many songs as I do." Merv sat and sang with her until around two o'clock that morning, as both of them were drawn to good lyrics and well-written melodies.

"You know," she said, finally rising to her feet, "we should take our act together on the road."

Reaching for his hand, she led him to the master bedroom, shutting the door behind them. Unfastening his robe, she also dropped hers at her feet. In bed she pressed her nude body against his. "There's always the first time," she said. "Didn't you tell me that as a little fat boy growing up in San Mateo, you told all your friends that you wanted to marry Judy Garland one day? Well, just imagine that this is our honeymoon night."

Late the following morning, Frank Sinatra called and invited Judy and Sammy as guests to his home in Palm Springs. Although he knew that Peter was within earshot, he pointedly didn't invite him. So after Judy and Sammy checked out, that left Merv alone with "the outcast," Peter. Merv agreed to drive Peter back to Malibu where he was scheduled to hook up with Patricia Kennedy.

En route to the coast, Merv learned that Peter's marriage to Patricia was imminent. Peter had little to say about his future bride, although he made it clear that he did not plan to give up sex on the side once he'd married "this Roman Catholic school girl who needs some breaking in about the way we do things here in Hollywood."

Until he actually met her, all that Merv knew about Patricia was that she was the sixth of nine children born to Joseph P. Kennedy and Rose Elizabeth Fitzgerald, and that her brother was a rising politician in Massachusetts. Peter claimed that Patricia was the most beautiful of all the Kennedy siblings, "although Jack is pretty cute—I'd like to fuck him too."

"I talked to Rose the other day," Peter confided. "She's not as opposed to the marriage as that monster she's married to. Once I assured her that our kids would be raised Roman Catholics, she became more at ease about her daughter's upcoming marriage. Pat is clearly not her favorite child. She told me that her daughter had a fine physique and a good mind, but then Rose complained that she puts neither of them to any particular use. 'She's not competitive like my other children,' *Mamma Mia* told me. 'Pat won't really succeed at anything,' she said. She told me that Pat's major accomplishment in life might involve marrying a movie star."

At Peter's house in Malibu, Merv was introduced to Patricia, discovering that, like her mother Rose, she had a certain regal bearing. Lithe and athletic, she seemed the epitome of grace and East Coast charm school breeding. Also in attendance that day was Lady May Lawford, Peter's mother. Rather formally dressed for a hot afternoon, Lady May sat under a large umbrella protecting her fair skin from the harsh rays of the California sun.

It was obvious that Lady May did not approve of her future daughter-in-law. She seemed to endure her presence. Peter and Patricia quickly excused themselves for a walk on the beach, leaving Merv alone with the stern and intensely judgmental Lady May.

Never in his life had Merv met a more outspoken woman. He didn't know if Lady May was sincere about what she said, or whether she merely uttered scathing observations as a means of shocking people.

No sooner was Patricia out of sight than Lady May launched into an attack on the Kennedys. "They're nothing but a bunch of barefoot Irish peasants," she claimed. "By marrying Peter, that bitch hopes to link herself with the British aristocracy. My God, the next thing I hear, old Joe Kennedy will be buying a title for her. There are a lot of them for sale these days. I told Peter he should have married Elizabeth Taylor. She's always been in love with him. Besides, Elizabeth is going to make a lot of money one day, and then Peter and I could live in the style to which we were once accustomed."

Lady May asked Merv if he'd get up "and fetch me another gin and tonic. I share my taste in drinks with the Queen Mother."

When Merv came back onto the patio, Lady May, by now a bit tipsy, wanted to continue with her tirade. Like the TV talk show host that he was to become, Merv was all ears.

"Peter told me that the Kennedy gal was a virgin when they met. Jack Kennedy introduced Peter to her in Palm Beach, and she fell madly in love with him right away . . . and started pursuing him that very day. Well, she might have been a virgin when she first met Peter, but she's not a virgin now. I found contraceptives in their bedroom. Old Joe gave the gal ten million dollars, but I've warned Peter he'll have to pay all the bills after they get married. That bitch holds onto every last red cent she's got."

Before she'd completely downed the gin and tonic Merv had brought her, and before she requested a refill, Lady May launched into an attack on The Rat Pack:

"I'm glad Peter is no longer fraternizing with that dried-up piece of spaghetti, Frank Sinatra. He hates me as much as I hate him. Even worse, Peter's still seeing that queer Van Johnson. He's the one who got Peter to wear those damn red socks. One night at a party I saw Peter and that Pat Kennedy kissing that darkie, Sammy Davis Jr. They call him 'Chicky.' I'd call him a nigger and tell him never to get within ten feet of me."

Merv sighed, wondering how Lady May would react if she knew what her son had been doing with Sammy recently. Certainly a bit more than kissing.

Just before sundown, after Peter and Lady May went upstairs to get ready for the evening, Patricia sat with Merv on the patio watching the sun go down. Still in her sports attire, she looked tan and lovely, and Merv was enchanted by her New England accent. "May must have filled you in on a lot of things—her version of things, that is. I find it rare that a so-called lady of breeding would be so uncouth. When Peter and I get married, we'll have to muzzle her, especially if Jack continues his career in politics. We definitely have to keep May away from the press. Her class prejudice went out of style with Queen Victoria."

Patricia would later express the same sentiments to dozens of her friends and, once, in an angry letter to Lady May herself.

Before she went upstairs to get dressed for dinner, Patricia turned to Merv. "Did Lady May tell you that she used to dress Peter as a girl until he was ten years old?" With that startling remark, she turned and left.

Merv felt the need to excuse himself from any further contact, including dinner that night, with this dysfunctional trio. He wanted to get home.

As Merv was leaving, Patricia rushed down the

Peter Lawford is seen here saddling up with starlet **Nancy Davis** before her wedding to a then-fading actor, Ronald Reagan.

Before marrying the future U.S. president, she was said to have a penchant for dating weak men. In this case, both Peter and Nancy were having sex with Robert Walker, who had been married to actress Jennifer Jones. Nancy began dating Walker after he'd been jailed for drunk driving in 1949.

Nancy's other crush was on Frank Sinatra, who became interested in her only after she became First Lady. Otherwise Sinatra claimed, "She's a dope with fat ankles." The Chairman of the Board then referred to Ronnie as "dumb and dangerous."

stairs and kissed him on the cheek. She even extended an invitation to him to visit the family compound at Hyannis Port. "You'll love my brothers, especially Jack. He's got more personal charm than any of the other Kennedys. Only Peter has more charm." As an afterthought, she said, "I hope you're athletic. The whole family is athletic, especially me. The only reason I was still a virgin when I met Peter was that I could outrun my brothers."

MOTHER BITCH

No memoir was more aptly titled than **Lady May Lawford**'s *Bitch!*. She was the suffocating mother of Peter Lawford. She informed homophobic Louis B. Mayer that Peter was a homosexual. She liked JFK, however, but loudly asserted to anyone within earshot that "he always had his mind down between his legs."

In her memoirs, Lady Lawford wrote this about her son: "Homosexual Peter tried hard to be thought one—by being persistently with Van Johnson."

Even though they lived together for a time, she continued to denounce her son, especially when he married Patricia Kennedy and he became "the First Brother-in-Law."

She referred to her son as "The White House pimp. What a bastard. Peter was such a big mistake! I guess I always knew he should have been born a girl. That's why I dressed him in girl's clothing for years."

"Jackie Kennedy put up with a lot," Lady Lawford continued. "When she saw a photo of JFK at a Beverly Hills whorehouse, she cried, 'I won't stay with him!' Old Joe Kennedy then quickly offered her a check for one million dollars if she'd remain married to Jack. Jackie was a clever girl—such a businesswoman. She told Joe Kennedy, 'Make it tax free and it's a deal.'"

Although Lady May derided her own son, and especially the Kennedys, she tried to cash in on their fame, hoping it would lead to a lucrative new career. Although he didn't want to, she forced Peter to get her a small part on his telecast of *The Thin Man* in 1957.

Casting agents told her, "Let's face it: There aren't many acting jobs for ladies a bit long in the tooth." She'd shout back at the agent, "Don't you realize it, you silly fool. My son, Peter Lawford, is the brother-in-law of President John F. Kennedy. He lives in the White House if you didn't know that, and is the single most powerful man in the world."

"In America, I'm known as Peter Lawford's mother," Lady May said. "But in England, Peter is known as my son."

When acting jobs didn't materialize, she blamed the Kennedys, citing some conspiracy on their part. "For all I know, Jack himself has told some little Jew in Hollywood not to hire me."

"Mother Bitch" never gave a believable reason as to why the Kennedys did not want her to find work. "They wanted to starve me to death, so I'll shut up and not tell dirty secrets about them. That cunt, Patricia Kennedy—I refuse to recognize her as a Lawford—won't even let me see my grandchildren."

The book that could not be published — not until after the death of her son Peter Lawford.

with an Introduction by Prince Franz Hohenlohe

As Told To Buddy Galon

The Strange and Convoluted Saga of

Peter Lawford & the Kennedys

Part Two

Hollywood Connection and White House Pimp

Clad in a sports shirt and slacks, **President Kennedy** *(left)* is photographed on the first tee of the Palm Beach Country Club on April 4, 1961. With him on the golf course is actor **Peter Lawford**, his brother-in-law and faithful companion.

After a drunken Peter fell asleep when Jack requested that he read the movie script for the upcoming film, *PT 109*, the president never asked him for advice such as that ever again. What he depended on Peter for was to supply him with an array of beauties on the West Coast. Peter Dye, of golfing fame, lived next door to Peter in Santa Monica. He revealed that when JFK came to visit, "It was nothing but *La Dolce Vita*, a goddamn whorehouse. Jack Kennedy even hustled my wife and wanted to fly her to Hawaii. It was the most disgusting thing I've ever seen."

MAR 2 5 1951

id to _____
(Date)

A MATINEE STAR'S
LIFE IN THE CLOSET

"Peter Lawford wants to be a woman.
He would like to be me."
—Marilyn Monroe

This photo ID snapped of **Peter Lawford** was taken when he was a household word in America, having made many high-profile films for Metro-Goldwyn-Mayer in the 1940s.

When he married Jack Kennedy's sister, Patricia, JFK often claimed, "I was once known as Peter Lawford's bother-in-law." Of course, as JFK became better known, the nomenclature was reversed.

In 1960, Peter told a reporter, "A strange thing has happened since Jack was elected. I seem to have lost my identity. There was a time when I'd be rushing through the airport and I'd hear someone say, 'There goes Peter Lawford.' Now, people don't remember my name. They say, 'There goes what's his name, the president's brother-in-law.'"

Before the 1954 wedding of his favorite daughter, Patricia Kennedy, to actor Peter Lawford, Joe Kennedy told her: "I hate actors. If there's anything I hate as a son-in-law, it's an actor. And if there's anything I think I'd hate more than an actor as a son-in law, it's an English actor. From Laurence Olivier to Noël Coward to John Gielgud—they're all fags."

Normally Pat listened closely to her dear old dad, but not in this case. She was in love with the handsome movie star, and she married him. She went on to have four children with him, including Christopher Kennedy Lawford (who also became an actor), plus daughters Sydney Maleia Kennedy Lawford, Victoria Francis Lawford, and Robin Elizabeth Lawford.

Through his Hollywood connections, Joe Kennedy had been the first in his family to learn about Peter's homosexuality. Although Peter had deliberately created an impression that he was "a stud" and "a womanizer," there was always a boy lurking in his background, claimed his sometimes lover, actor Sal Mineo. Even Peter's mother, Lady May Lawford, in an act of exquisite insensitivity, outed her son as a homosexual in front of his boss, studio chief Louis B. Mayer, a devout homophobe.

His mother claimed that "Peter had lived with a gay man to whom he gave a great deal of money," and she mentioned another affair Peter had "with a young man," a reference to actor Tom Drake, Judy Garland's "boy next door" in *Meet Me in St. Louis.*

The only serious biography of Peter ever written was James Spada's *Peter Lawford: The Man Who Kept the Secrets.* In this tell-all, he explored Peter's homosexuality, citing witnesses.

Peter Dye, the world-renowned golf course designer, lived next door to Peter in Santa Monica. "When I moved in, I heard that Peter was known as 'the screaming faggot of State

Beach,'" claimed Dye.

Wayne Parks, a young beach boy, often went to Will Rogers State Beach in the early 1950s. Spada interviewed him. The boy claimed, "I'd use the john on the beach, and I'd see Peter in there. He'd loiter for hours, sitting on the toilet playing with himself. It was a notorious john for that sort of thing. I'm sure Peter got picked up by guys in there."

Spada also interviewed Richard Fielden, a Lutheran Sunday school teacher. Fielden recalled walking along the beachfront of Santa Monica with his wife in the early 1950s, including the sands in front of Peter's beach house. "I guess we were trespassing on Lawford's property at one point, and I practically tripped over Peter Lawford and another young actor."

During Spada's dialogues with Fielden, he might have outed that actor, but Spada did not print who it was. "They were lying on the beach with their arms around each other," reported Fielden. "I recognized both of them instantly. They giggled and were very embarrassed that they were discovered."

It is believed that the actor who Fielden discovered in the arms of Peter was a very closeted gay, the blond male beauty, Troy Donahue. During his celebrity heyday in the late 1950s, whenever he was mistaken for another male blond beauty—Tab Hunter—Troy used to say, "I'm the straight one." He lied.

Actually, after Troy's career had peaked, he fell on hard times. One he was discovered sleeping on a bench in New York City's Central Park. Sometimes he hustled rich men who were still entranced with his former screen image. For a brief period, he lived with Merv Griffin, who had been one of Peter Lawford's lovers in the 50s.

Peter was also sexually involved with gay actors Van Johnson, Keenan Wynn, and Cary Grant, as well as with the unlucky Robert Walker, who was otherwise credited for making love to Nancy Davis (an actress later known as Nancy Reagan).

Spada also exposed a revelation made by Don Pack, a photographer for the *Santa Monica Evening Outlook*. Pack claimed that Peter made an "awkward, abortive pass at me," and that he also attended gay all-male parties in Hawaii two or three years after JFK's assassination.

Spada said that, "There can be no question that Peter Lawford was turned on by women. Still, there is enough evidence to conclude that he occasionally sought out homosexual liaisons, and it's surprising that he was able to keep them secret from his friends, just as he did his brothel visits. Surely he would have made every effort to keep his friends from finding out something that might have caused some of them to spurn his friendship."

He married four times. Patricia Kennedy knew of Peter's homosexuality before her marriage to him, because her father had told her so. Mary Rowan, his

"America's Sweethearts," **Peter Lawford and June Allyson**, appeared together in the light comedy, *Good News*, in 1947.

June "knew" both Peter and a young Jack Kennedy in the immediate post-war era. During the height of her affair with Peter, she was married to Dick Powell.

But she'd invite Peter to her parties, insisting that he bring a girl with him as a decoy.

"To go to June's house and not be able to hold her hand or talk to her was very painful for me," Peter said. "Yeah, I was crazy about her in those days."

Senator **John F. Kennedy** is seen here with his favorite sister **Patricia (Mrs. Peter Lawford)** during his presidential campaign of 1960. Jack once told his pal Lem Billings, "At one of our orgies, Pat is always at the bottom of the pile."

Peter was a whoremonger, but during the early months of his marriage he thought Pat was a faithful Catholic wife. But he became suspicious and hired a private detective, Fred Otash, a former LAPD vice cop, to have her followed.

He found out plenty. Later, he arranged for the installation of an eavesdropping device on Pat's phone.

As a result, Peter overheard a recording of a private conversation between Pat and Porfirio Rubirosa, "The Playboy of the Western World." Instead of Rubi telling Pat what he wanted to do to her, she told him what she was going to do to his monstrous penis the next time they met.

Pat Kennedy was not the prettiest girl in Hollywood; even so, she'd landed one of its handsomest and most sought-after movie stars as her husband.

During their honeymoon in Hawaii, Pat and Peter established the conditions of their "separate but equal lives."

Later, at a party in Santa Monica, Pat asked Marilyn Monroe, "Shouldn't a girl expect to get fucked at least once on her honeymoon?"

second wife, the daughter of comedian Dan Rowan, also heard about his homosexual affairs, as did Deborah Gould, his third wife.

Apparently, Peter tricked his fourth wife, the somewhat naïve Patricia Seaton, into believing that he was 100% straight. At least on two occasions, she has called newspapers touting his heterosexual credentials, protestations which provoked guffaws from Hollywood insiders coast to coast.

Fourth wives, or even first wives for that matter, are never considered reliable sources for their husband's peccadilloes which occurred before (in this case) Seaton was born.

The dean of Hollywood biographers, Lawrence J. Quirk, who knew Peter "from way back when," asserted that he went out with women "to help dispel rumors about his relationships with men—and there were a number of them. These relationships worried him; they were often a sexual release rather than a romance. When he fell in love with or entertained romantic feelings toward a man, Peter grew inescapably depressed. This side of his erotic life he found ominous, threatening, baleful, yet he needed it, too."

Seaton claimed that Peter was a great lover. Others have disagreed. Biographer Mart Martin wrote, "Lawford was regarded as a fairly lousy lover. Intercourse didn't interest him that much, due to his predilection for oral sex."

Director George Cukor agreed, claiming Peter "was not a good lover—not at all." However, gay actor Clifton Webb told friends that "Peter was enchanting in bed," a view not shared by actresses Anne Baxter or Rita Hayworth. Marilyn Monroe told friends that Peter was a homosexual.

Author Mart Martin claimed from his investigation that Peter patronized "male hustlers, young male extras, and studio messengers."

Peter was never made to feel fully included within the Kennedy clan. At the Los Angeles Sports Arena during the Democratic National Convention of 1960. Jack was designated as the party's presidential candidate, and he wanted to be flanked by his telegenic family members. Peter moved to join them but, Pat blocked his way. "You can't come on stage. You're not a Kennedy."

JFK overheard her and intervened. "God damn it, Pat, he's your fucking husband. I'd say that qualifies him. Besides, it doesn't hurt having a good-looking movie star to come out on stage to help me dazzle the audience."

After Jack won the nomination for president on the Democratic ticket in 1960, Peter and Patricia Lawford, as revealed by Kitty Kelley in *Jackie Oh!*, threw a raucous victory celebration at their Santa Monica home.

One guest claimed that the next President of the United States "got drunk and went skinny-dipping in the pool, splashing and howling until the wee hours of the morning," along with Bobby Kennedy, press secretary Pierre Salinger, and actress Angie Dickinson.

One neighbor called the cops, who hauled them off in the paddy wagon because in their nude state they had no identification. When the police realized that might have arrested America's future president, the "prisoners" were released with apologies. Power, after all, has its privileges, and Jack always knew that.

Bill Asher, hired to tape JFK's inaugural gala, recalled hearing Jack and Peter talk in front of Peter's beach house in Santa Monica. This dialogue was revealed in Spada's biography *Peter Lawford: The Man Who Kept the Secrets*.

Asher overheard JFK lamenting when checking out some shapely young women on the beach, each attired in a very brief bikini, "I'm gonna have to give all that up when I become president. I hope it's worth it."

Peter assured the newly elected president that he didn't have to. He claimed that he would keep JFK supplied with a whole string of beauties who would be available not only when he flew to California, but sent to the White House when Jackie wasn't in residence—and on a few occasions when she was. "You can frolic in the White House if we're discreet," Peter said.

"It's a deal," JFK assured Peter. "I'll count on you to be my poon man."

The evening of the day he was sworn in as president, Jack attended five inaugural balls. At the second ball, at the Mayflower Hotel, Jack excused himself from Jackie, Vice President Lyndon

Tom Drake, pictured here as **Judy Garland**'s "Boy Next Door" in the hit musical, *Meet Me in St. Louis* (1944), was a longtime lover of Peter's, even though the "love" was more on Tom's part than Peter's.

The sweet, soft-spoken Tom was in direct contrast to the charismatic Peter. Tom often complained to his pal Merv Griffin that Peter spent far more nights with either Nancy Davis (later Reagan) or fellow actor Robert Walker than he did with him.

Merv gave Tom some good advice—"Peter is the kind of guy you have an affair with, not a man you fall in love with."

Blond, blue-eyed **Troy Donahue** was a closeted bisexual. He became known in the late 1950s and early 60s more for his pinup image than for his acting skills.

The New York-born actor met Peter during the period when both of their careers were beginning to decline.

When Peter propostitioned Troy at a mostly gay party in Hollywood, Troy was at first hesitant. "If you're a size queen, you'd better call Rock Hudson.

"I'm not a size queen," Peter said. "I'm equally adept at handling four inches as I am ten."

After that interchange, their romance blossomed. One morning at the Santa Monica house Peter shared with Pat, Troy spent the night when Pat was out of town. Peter left early for the studio leaving Troy to catch up on his sleep.

Pat returned unexpectedly that morning. When she found Troy in her bed, she seduced him too, and bragged about it to Peter that evening when he came home from the studio.

Johnson, and Lady Bird to go upstairs. He dashed upstairs where he allegedly had a "meeting" with actress Angie Dickinson. Appearing thirty minutes later, he was breathless but carried a copy of *The Washington Post* under his arm. "Anything interesting going on in the world tonight?" Jackie asked with an icy stare.

Just before midnight, Jackie announced that she was retiring, and that Jack could continue celebrating without her. At the home of the syndicated news columnist Joe Alsop, Peter had arranged for Jack to meet six starlets, each of whom wanted to be with the president.

"I arranged a line-up as they would at Madame Claude's brothel in Paris," Lawford later said. "Jack chose two of them. The *ménage à trois* brought his first day in office to a resounding close."

JFK liked Peter but also mocked him, the way he did with his gay pal Lem Billings. After a newspaper published a photograph of JFK listening to Peter, the president made fun of it, laughing derisively, "Who would ever that believe I was listening to *you*?"

As C. David Heymann revealed in his biography *A Woman Named Jackie*, Peter provided

Both JFK and Peter Lawford seduced Hollywood's "ultimate movie star," **Lana Turner**.

JFK met Lana in 1946, but Peter had beaten him to her, falling in love with her in 1944.

Of course, JFK faced some serious competition: Frank Sinatra, Victor Mature, Robert Stack, Howard Hughes, Buddy Rich, and Tony Martin. Likewise, she had competition for JFK's favors, notably from Betty Grable, Rhonda Fleming, Anne Baxter, Judy Garland, Marilyn Monroe, and Ava Gardner.

Peter said that Lana was the kind of girl whom you could call up and say, "Come and help me bury Dad—I just shot him" and that without any questions, Lana would be on her way to the rescue.

JFK with "every imaginable amenity from dates with actresses and showgirls to a California safehouse where Kennedy could carry out his West Coast assignations. Lawford often acted as a beard for Jack, distracting the press and providing a convenient front for Jackie's benefit."

Jeanne Martin, wife of Dean Martin, was a frequent guest of Pat and Peter. She told Marilyn Monroe biographer Anthony Summers (*Goddess, The Secret Life of Marilyn Monroe*), "I saw Peter in the role of pimp for Jack Kennedy. It was a nasty business—they were just too gleeful about it, not discreet at all. Of course, there was nothing discreet about either of the Kennedys, Bobby or Jack. It was like high school time, very sophomoric. The things that went on in that beach house were just mind-boggling. Ethel could be in one room and Bobby could be in another with this or that woman."

Summers also revealed that both Pat Kennedy and her husband Peter were heavy drinkers. "Peter liked to drink until dawn in his own private bar, and he was an indiscriminate user of prohibited drugs."

The author also claimed that Lawford "liked bizarre sex." He cites an intimate who claimed that "he wanted me to bite his nipples until they bled."

George Jacobs, the right-hand assistant for Frank Sinatra from 1953 to 1968, often overheard "pussy talk" between Peter and JFK. "To Jack's delight, Peter had actually *been* with some of the stars he described, hence, tales of Lana Turner's perfect breasts, Judy Garland's perfect blow-jobs, Judy Holliday's perfect ass. For all his stars, however, Peter said flat-out that he preferred whores. I can see how he and JFK bonded over pussy. Peter had a special thing for black girls, not mulattos like Lena Horne, but jet-black pure African types not readily available through Hollywood madams. It was often back to Watts for this sex safari and again, I was Peter's guide to the jungle."

On occasion, JFK also expressed a preference for "black pussy," but only after Peter had tried out a prostitute and personally recommended her. Sometimes, the president wanted to be serviced by two of these women at the same time in the same bed.

Throughout the short years remaining for Jack, Peter related outrageous stories about his comings and goings as the White House pimp.

At one point, Jack ordered Peter to get women who would perform oral sex while he read through presidential papers. "I'm too busy on many occasions to go through with the whole enchilada. The staff at the White House has me so busy that I've got to conduct affairs of state even when having sex."

Sometimes JFK complained to Peter that he was getting bored and wanted "a novelty act." At a party hosted by singer Vic Damone in a New York hotel, Peter introduced JFK to a teenaged "blonde and bubbly" striptease artist. The president wandered off to one of the bedrooms with her and had "normal sex," or so he informed Peter.

But on another occasion at a Manhattan apartment building—The Towers on West 55th Street—Peter hired two prostitutes to dress up as doctor and nurse. JFK requested that he be the patient.

One weekend in the White House, JFK launched a contest among his brothers and brothers-in-law. The winner would be the first one to seduce a woman other than his wife within the Lincoln bedroom. Peter won but he cheated. The beautiful woman he maneuvered into the bedroom turned out to be, to his dismay, a lesbian.

JFK wasn't fair in staging the contest. Even before launching it, he had already won the contest by seducing a woman there right after he moved in. So both Peter and JFK were deceiving each other.

At New York's Hotel Carlyle, Peter arranged a sexual liaison between his brother-in-law, Jack, and a high-priced call girl, Leslie Devereux. She found the president "mechanized and cold with hard glazed eyes and a high-powered smile." Later she revealed to author Heymann, "We did some mild S&M. I tied his hands and feet to the bedposts, blindfolded him and teased him first with a feather and then with my fingernails. He seemed to enjoy it." On a subsequent visit to the White House, he seduced her in Abraham Lincoln's bedroom. The rendezvous had been arranged by Peter.

Peter met **Judy Holliday** in the spring of 1953 when director George Cukor cast them to appear together in his new picture, *It Should Happen to You.*

Peter was kept busy on the set, bedding his gay director, Cukor, who found him "disappointing" in bed. Peter fared better with his seduction of the bisexual Holliday.

Judy fell madly in love with Peter, and they traveled from Los Angeles to New York together by train.

After their picture was finished, Peter grew tired of Judy and stopped taking her phone calls. His break from her was so uncompromising that later, when he encountered her in the lobby of the Latin Quarter, a nightclub in New York, he wouldn't even speak to her.

His press agent, Milton Ebbings, claimed that "Peter was a gentleman but not when it came to breaking up with a gal. Then Dr. Jekyll turned into Mr. Hyde."

In early 1963, Peter and Pat decided that their marriage was unsalvageable. She informed her father and many others in her circle that she had to give up on Peter because of his womanizing and heavy drinking. "Drugs are also a problem," she claimed.

This would be the first time there had ever been a divorce in the Catholic Kennedy family.

Peter flew to Washington to break the news to Jack personally, informing him within the Cabinet Room of the White House, where he, Peter, broke down and cried. At first Jack thought it was no big deal and assured Peter that he wasn't going to lose him as a friend. But after thinking it over, he decided that Pat and Peter should delay their divorce until after the 1964 presidential election.

From then on, it was just pretend. Peter and Pat even presided over dinner parties and called each other sweetheart or darling. But when the guests left, their violent arguments resumed. On several occasions Pat tossed Peter out of her house.

The questions about the embarrassments associated with a divorce in the months leading up to an election no longer mattered in November of 1963 after Jack was assassinated.

On November 20 of that year, a Wednesday, JFK called Peter to tell him that Jackie had agreed to go with him on a political "fence-mending" trip to Dallas. "Isn't that great?" he asked Peter. "We leave in the morning."

JFK had contacted Peter, who was staying in Lake Tahoe, by telephone. The night before Peter had had sex with a good-looking, well-built waiter at Harrah's.

The following day, Chuck Pick, a friend of Peter's who was rooming with him, had to wake him out of a stupor to tell him that his brother-in-law had been shot in Dallas. He'd been rushed to the nearest hospital, but his condition was not known.

Peter was in the kitchen making Bloody Marys when Walter Cronkite on CBS made the announcement: "President Kennedy died at one p.m., Central Time in Dallas."

Peter fell on the floor, sobbing and vomiting. "I never saw a man break down like he broke down," Pick claimed.

Peter said he was never in love with **Judy Garland,** but they often ended their shared evenings together with sex. Both Peter and Judy were acclaimed as "oral artists."

In later life Peter fell on bad days. With no money to buy groceries, he even sold an exposé about Judy Garland to *The National Enquirer* for $62.50.

Once, years later, the situation was reversed when the government demanded Judy's first installment of $3,000 on back taxes. That night Sid got on the phone and called all her friends, begging for contributions.

Peter Lawford came up with half the payment, sending Sid and Judy $1,500.

***

In the summer of 1966, Peter knew he might be making a mistake when he called Jackie and asked her to join him for a vacation in Hawaii. His divorce from Pat had not negatively affected their relationship. Jackie not only accepted his invitation to Hawaii, she even suggested that they fly there together.

Peter asked his best friend and business manager, Milton Ebbins, if the trip would be all right, fearing that it might generate bad publicity. "Why not?" Ebbins asked. "Mrs. Kennedy will be traveling with her children, Caroline and John-John, and you'll be with Christopher and Sydney. Just call it a family affair."

"Yeah," Peter said, "but I was afraid that the press might view it as an affair, forgetting about the kids. I already rejected Jackie's sister, but I don't think I could turn down the lady herself if she came on to me."

"Don't flatter yourself," Ebbins said. "Take the trip. It'll be fun."

Peter always claimed that Lee Radziwill had made a play for him in the early 60s when they were taking a stroll through Hyde Park in London. He said that he had turned her down "because I had too much respect for her husband."

From gossip, Lana Turner, Peter's former lover, heard that he would soon fly to Honolulu with Jackie. Lana took a dim view. "If Lee Radziwill wanted him, Mrs. Kennedy might also want Peter. After all, sisters sometimes go for the same guy. I hear Jackie has a high libido. I can personally vouch for the libido of John Kennedy. I, of all the stars in Hollywood, knew what a strong sex drive he had."

Flying out of New York on June 6, Jackie arrived in San Francisco with her children, where she rendezvoused with Peter, his son Christopher, and his daughter Sydney for the ongoing flight to Hawaii.

A *paparazzo* snapped the arrival of this Kennedy/Lawford party departing from their plane in Honolulu. Pat had given permission for Peter to take their sons to Hawaii, but Ebbins hadn't informed her that Jackie would be along.

When Pat found out, Ebbins claimed she wasn't just boiling mad, she was livid. She'd told friends that she'd long suspected that Peter "had this thing for Jackie." Rather sarcastically, Pat added, "And you know Jackie. She's the girl who can't say no."

The so-called Hawaiian honeymoon of Jackie and Peter lasted for seven weeks. To keep up appearances, Jackie technically lived in an oceanfront house near the base of Diamond Head, which she rented for $3,000 a month. Peter's hideaway cottage on the grounds of the Hilton was just down the beach.

In Hawaii, Peter perfected the famous cigarette routine that Bette Davis and Paul Henreid did so well in *Now, Voyager* (1942). Over cocktails in the Hilton bar, he was seen placing two cigarettes in his mouth, lighting each of them, and then handing one to Jackie.

The only time Jackie and Peter were separated was when she took the children, with architect John Carl Warnecke, on an overnight camping trip. John-John fell into the fire and severely burned his but-

"It was the greatest twenty seconds of my life," actress **Angie Dickinson** *(pictured above in 1962)* allegedly said about her first sexual encounter with JFK in 1960. Even so, rumor has it that Dickinson owns a photograph inscribed by JFK: "Angie, the only woman I've ever loved."

According to unconfirmed reports, the president-elect seduced Angie in the White House's Lincoln Bedroom as Lyndon B. Johnson, Lady Bird, and Jackie waited for him downstairs at an Inaugural Ball.

Except for a provocative statement or two, Angie has remained close-mouthed about her relationship with JFK. She was either introduced to him by Frank Sinatra or Peter Lawford--sources differ. What is known is that the beautiful North Dakota-born woman met JFK in 1960 when she was 29 and he was 43.

Her former husband, composer Burt Bacharach, is often asked, "Did your wife really have an affair with President Kennedy?"

tocks, arms, and hands. A Secret Service agent, John Walsh, rushed him to a local hospital.

Writing for a local paper, reporter Gwen Holson tracked every public move she could of Peter and Jackie. She was hoping to sell a piece to a national magazine. "Throughout their vacation," Holson said, "Peter acted like Jackie's gallant husband. He took her everywhere, and he behaved like a father to her children. Lawford was very familiar with Hawaii, and he became Mrs. Kennedy's tour guide. He introduced her to all his friends, and they were great as a couple, dazzling everyone."

"Lawford even threw this big garden party for Mrs. Kennedy at the Kahala Hilton. *Tout* Honolulu turned out to greet her. Everybody wore their finest clothing, and we expected Mrs. Kennedy to turn up in an Oleg Cassini original. She arrived in a light beach shift with sandals."

"In front of everybody, Lawford hovered over Mrs. Kennedy, even taking her hand to guide her over to the next group of friends to show her off. Unlike that whispery Marilyn Monroe voice she used on camera, Mrs. Kennedy spoke in a normal voice.

"I know that Jackie spent a lot of time at the beachfront house Lawford had rented on Oahu. I paid a servant one hundred dollars for the lowdown. She virtually confirmed on the Bible that Mrs. Kennedy and Lawford slept together. Today, it would be front page tabloid news, but back then no respectable paper wanted to touch it."

"But rumors were flying over Honolulu, and I think many mainland newspapers made veiled references to reports of an affair between Lawford and Mrs. Kennedy. We now know that Jackie slept with Bobby. Why not Lawford? If you sleep with one brother-in-law, why not another?"

Peter, at this point in his life, was deeply troubled, and reportedly Jackie rallied to his side. He was worried now that he was cut off from the Kennedy clan, he would not be offered any more film roles, at least good ones. He admitted to Jackie and to others that he had been too imperial when he was the president's brother-in-law and had made a lot of enemies, including Frank Sinatra. He also feared that he could not provide for his children the way the Kennedys could their brood, and that his kids would lose respect for him.

"I'm going to find a life after the Kennedys, and I'm sure you will too." Jackie said that in front of other guests, as if she wanted other people to believe it. Few did. After the Kennedy connection, it was all downhill for Peter.

In Hawaii, Peter got to know Jackie as never before. Such prolonged intimacy between the two of them would never be repeated. In the future, Jackie would withdraw more and more from Peter upon hearing news of his alcoholism and drug taking.

"Jackie wasn't completely honest about herself," Peter said. "She doctored up her family background. She told social fibs to avoid having to make appearances. She

Peter Lawford and Jacqueline Kennedy are seen disembarking with their children on a plane that landed in Honolulu for a "family vacation," that became the source of international rumors.

Was Jackie actually having an affair with her former brother-in-law, the White House pimp for her late husband?

Peter and Jackie shared many experiences together, including visits to Dr. Max Jacobson ("Dr. Feelgood"). He had injected both President Kennedy and Jackie with Speed. As Peter soon learned, these injections, with prolonged use, were addictive, and associated with both mental and physical deterioration.

162

would tell the press practically anything to get them off her back. She obviously had known about Jack's affairs. She told me she knew. She said she once caught him in the act."

When author Truman Capote heard about a possible Peter/Jackie affair, he said, "I'm not at all surprised. Jackie, dear heart that she is, believed in the revenge fuck. She'd always known that Peter supplied Hollywood actresses to Jack. By fucking Peter, she was probably getting even with Jack, even though his bullet-riddled body was in the grave."

Years later, when funds were running so low he could hardly pay his rent, Peter sold the story of his role as his brother-in-law's pimp to a tabloid. In the article, he claimed that JFK would examine women "like he was admiring some fine China."

Commenting on his marriage to Pat, he said, "I always felt that her love for her father took precedence in a funny way over her love for me. She worshipped him."

The wildest rumor spread about Peter, other than the Jackie affair, was that in the late 70s he encountered the increasingly handsome hunk John F. Kennedy Jr. one evening at a night club and fellated him in a toilet stall of the men's room, with the door securely locked. At the time Peter was encouraging JFK Jr. to become an actor, but Jackie was dead set against it.

Since his heyday during Camelot, Peter, according to biographer Larry Quirk, has frequently been vilified as a "playboy, opportunist, bisexual, nymphomaniac, drug addict, alcoholic, and pernicious sycophant to both Frank Sinatra and the Kennedys." But despite those extremes, Quirk nonetheless, from personal encounters, remembered him as a kind and gentle man.

"The banner of male beauty has passed to John-John," said **Peter Lawford** (left) about **John F. Kennedy Jr.**, who had grown up to become known as "The Handsome Hunk."

As the characters in their family drama aged, Jackie began to feel that JFK Jr., and Peter were becoming too close, and she didn't like his encouraging her son to become an actor. Peter was delighted when he saw John Jr. play the lead in a stage rendition of Ken Kesey's *One Flew Over the Cuckoo's Nest* when he was a senior in college.

"You've got what it takes to become a movie star," Peter told JFK Jr. To Jackie and others he said "Acting gives John-John a chance to step out of his skin and become someone other than John J. Kennedy's son. On stage he can be acclaimed for both his male beauty and his talent, and he is very talented indeed, a natural for the movie camera."

Jackie was not convinced.

JFK AND PETER LAWFORD: "WITH ANYBODY BUT OUR WIVES"

There was much that John F. Kennedy admired about his new brother-in-law, Peter Lawford. He liked the smooth way he talked, his *savoir faire,* his Continental manners, even the way he dressed.

Soon, in their relationship, he learned that Peter had a flair for attracting women, and was more than willing to pass on many of his conquests to Jack. Peter was also an "expediter" in the arrangement of various sexual trysts with Marilyn Monroe, among others.

It was Peter who told JFK that Marilyn was "up for grabs," during the course of her 1954 marriage to Joe DiMaggio. "The marriage was already on the rocks, I think, by the time they went on their honeymoon," Peter claimed to Senator Kennedy.

A few months after Marilyn slipped JFK her phone number at a party given by producer Charles Feldman, Jack had to go to the hospital to alleviate his chronic and painful back problems.

It was Peter who brought a big color poster of Marilyn to his bedside. "I want you to have a reason to get well," Peter told the ailing politician.

Peter hung the poster, a sexually provocative shot of MM in tight-fitting blue shorts, on the hospital room's wall. "No, no!" Jack objected. "Turn it upside down. That's the way I'm going to take her when I get out of this damn bed."

In the wake of his surgery, JFK nearly died, with a condition so grave that he was administered the last rites (Extreme Unction) of the Catholic Church. "I rose from the dead," he told Peter. "And something else is rising. You'd better get me a hot tamale to take care of this hard-on, or you'll have to come over here for one of those fabled Peter Lawford blow-jobs."

"That wouldn't be a bad idea," Peter said, and he wasn't joking.

"Shut up, pervert, and bring me a movie star—any movie star—if Marilyn isn't available."

During 1961 and 1962, JFK defined the Santa Monica beach house owned by Peter and Pat as the Western White House. For appearances sake, JFK usually stayed at a suite at the Beverly Hilton Hotel. His promiscuous sister, Pat, was familiar with her brother's sexual trysts, and he openly flaunted girls in front of her. He never wanted Jackie to accompany him to California, however.

Jeanne Carmen, Marilyn's best friend, recalled a night she was invited to the Lawford house in Santa Monica: "I couldn't believe my eyes. There were at least twenty people there, men and women, cavorting in the nude. Even the president of the United States was naked. It was the prelude to an orgy. I couldn't believe that Jack would take such chances. He was as reckless as Marilyn."

"I didn't join in the orgy, but made it with a handsome twenty-nine year old Secret Service agent in the Lawford garage," Carmen claimed. "The guy was really hung and knew how to drill his tool."

Living next door, golfer Peter Dye referred to the Lawford home as "the biggest bordello in the West, rivaling anything Las Vegas has to offer—and no one charged. Everybody was giving it away."

One night, Peter Lawford confessed a sexual problem he was having with Patricia. "I go to bed with her, and she's into it, but I can't get it up for her. I'm not impotent, because I did fine with two call girls the night before."

"I have that same problem with Jackie," JFK confessed. "Alas, the curse of married life. Why does society make us take wives?"

Owned by Louis B. Mayer in the 1930s, and later bought by Peter and Patricia (Kennedy) Lawford, the sprawling beachfront estate at 625 Palisades Beach Road, Santa Monica, functioned as JFK's "Western White House" and f*** pad.

JFK's Kinky Affair with
Jayne Mansfield

Hollywood's most buxom blonde, Jayne Mansfield, let it all hang out on the cover of Kenneth Anger's second edition of *Hollywood Babylon*, published in 1975. Jayne led a short, tragic, and ultimately pathetic life. Tony Randall, her co-star, said, "She wasn't really beautiful, and she couldn't sing, dance, or act. But she had two things going for her—call it double dynamite."

"Jayne presented all of her body to the nation to observe, and one of the horny young men who responded was a senator from Massachusetts. It didn't matter that he was already married to a beautiful woman without the mammoth bosom. JFK told Peter Lawford that "Jayne's ass is better if not a lot better than Marilyn Monroe's."

Jayne wasn't that impressed with Jack as a lover. "He lies on his back and makes me do all the work. After he blasts off, you don't even exist for him."   *(Photofest)*

165

Associated Press

THE MASSACHUSETTS SENATOR AND THE *FAUX* MARILYN

"Jayne Mansfield's brains are in her boobs."
Jackie Kennedy

A self-made star, the blonde bombshell, busty Jayne Mansfield, led a short, tragic, and ultimately pathetic life. She competed with her rival, Marilyn Monroe, to become the sex symbol of the 1950s, the only decade that could have produced both of them.

"Jayne caught fifties sex like a malignant fever, and it burned her out with sixties complications," said writer Martha Saxton. "She bought a picture of herself as a sexy, dumb broad in return for the thrill of turning men on. But, as they used to say in junior high school, they didn't respect her. She tried to ride the tiger of sexism and failed."

"I wore brassieres until I was fourteen and then I abandoned them forever to be free," she said. "I like to feel my body free as though I am floating in air. I hate underthings. I love to sleep nude. This shocked my mother, who insisted I wear a nightgown. But none of my lovers ever complained. Incidentally, my measurements are 46-18-36."

From 1948 to 1965, Jayne was famously married to bodybuilder Mickey Hargitay, who had become Mr. Universe in 1955. Columnist Walter Winchell once said "What President Eisenhower did for golf, Mickey Hargitay did for bodybuilding, because he brought it to the forefront."

When it came to sex among Hollywood stars, Jack Kennedy was a voyeuristic listener. When he asked Jayne Mansfield about movie stars she'd seduced, he expected her to tell tall tales about the likes of Errol Flynn or Tyrone Power. What he got instead was a shocking revelation.

She claimed that she'd been seduced one night by Anton LaVey, the founder of the Church of Satan, of which Sammy Davis Jr. was a member.

She said that about a month after that, she was initiated into the hierarchy of that church as a high priestess. Her initiation involved her being spreadeagled on a marble slab while six male members of the church, each a high priest, appeared before her nude except for "movie studio horns" and a red cape.

"Each of the priests deflowered me that night," she said, giggling. "I was thrilled.

Peter Lawford was a show-biz friend of Jayne's, and he introduced her to a handsome, young senator, Jack Kennedy, who was visiting Hollywood from Massachusetts. He seemed mesmerized by her, and she invited him to visit her on the set of what turned out to be her most successful movie, *Will Success Spoil Rock Hunter?* released in 1957. The film starred Tony Randall and Betsy Drake, with Joan Blondell in the third lead.

"I remember when Senator Kennedy turned up on the set one day," Blondell said.

"Everyone knew he was there to visit Jayne. All of us in Hollywood knew of his old man, Joe Kennedy. But Jack himself wasn't all that well known on the West Coast at the time. I knew he'd tried to be nominated for Vice President on the Adlai Stevenson ticket in 1956, but he lost."

She said the senator seemed rather shy, but he soon disappeared into Jayne's dressing room. "They were in there for about two hours. We knew what was going on. Later I saw a picture in the paper of Kennedy with his wife, Jackie. I couldn't figure out what he was doing hanging out with Jayne with a wife like that waiting for him at home."

Jayne later claimed that she told Senator Kennedy that she believed "that sex is the most important human factor between two people. I believe that in physical relationships everything goes. The wildest form of love is beautiful. It should be tender. It should be brutal, sadistic. It should, at times, even be masochistic."

According to Jayne, JFK favored the missionary position, and "I had to teach him some tricks. I begged him to bite my nipples and he finally did. He got into it, and I screamed in pain. Before me, he told me that he'd never paddled a woman. He had a hard time getting started. I screamed, 'harder, harder.' Finally, he got the message. I walked around with a blistered butt for a week."

"Jack liked to go in through the front door, but he much preferred anal sex," Jayne said. "He didn't have a long thick penis like my husband, Mickey. Jack said he experienced a much tighter fuck by entering from the rear."

Her next encounter with Jack occurred in Washington, where she arrived for a nightclub engagement, after having appeared in several seedy joints in the South, including New Orleans. Once checked into a suite in a Washington hotel, she called the senator's phone number, using a secret code he'd given her. JFK himself picked up the phone.

He told her he would not be free until after midnight, but that he'd visit her at her hotel after she'd finished her ten o'clock show at the club. She invited him to the club, but he said he was "too well known in Washington," and preferred to meet with her privately.

"He was in a pretty raunchy mood that night," she said, "and he wanted me to do something to him his girlfriends, and presumably his wife, wouldn't do. He wanted an around the world. I started with his big toe

Mickey Hargitay (Mr. Universe) and Jayne Mansfield took their nightclub act on the road during the late 1950s.

Jayne stole this Hungarian muscleman from the clutches of the aging screen vamp, Mae West.

Jayne spotted the gorgeous hunk of male flesh during a presentation of Mae's stage act. Standing six feet two inches tall with a forty-eight-inch chest and a thirty-inch waist, he weighted 230 pounds.

He also had a hidden talent that he claimed "just rose and rose..and then rose some more." Jayne proclaimed to a friend, "This powerhouse of a man is for me, and I'm gonna get him."

And so she did.

Mae was furious when Jayne announced to the press, "Why shouldn't he prefer a beautiful twenty-year-old like me to a post-seventy-year-old woman who was a big name way back in 1928."

167

and worked myself up to his nose. My tongue explored every crevice. He practically screamed when my beautiful, succulent pink tongue hit the bull's eye, the rosebud itself." Regardless of their raunchy nature, Jayne seemed rather proud in relaying the specific details of her sexual experiences with JFK to both Randall and Blondell.

After a night of hot sex with JFK in Jayne's hotel suite, he got up and showered with her the next morning. She didn't have to go to the club until six o'clock that evening. He told her that he wanted to have his younger brother, Bobby, come over to meet her. At the time she didn't know anything about the Kennedy brothers and sisters.

"If he's as handsome as you, I'd like to meet him," she said.

She later told her friends that when Bobby showed up at her hotel suite, he looked more like a boy than a man. "He was a very different type of lover than Jack. He was tender and much more affectionate. In sex, Jack seemed to just want to get his jollies and the woman didn't seem to matter. But Bobby was far more interested in getting the woman off too. I liked him for that. I couldn't believe it when I heard on TV months later that Jack had made such a kid Attorney General of the United States. Of course, by then my handsome senator had become the President of the United States."

The Queen of England, **Elizabeth II** *(left)* meets the Queen of the Bosoms, **Jayne Mansfield** *(right)*. The November 4, 1957 meeting took place at London's Odeon Theatre as part of the annual Royal Film Festival.

In anticipation of the meeting, Buckingham Palace's etiquette brigade had sent a message to Jayne that a low-cut gown would not be acceptable for presentation to Her Majesty.

In acquiescing to their wishes, Jayne covered her bosom with a custom-made brassiere that had been designed specifically with her in mind. "I want my tits to stand up like Mont Blanc itself," she told her designer. "And I also want my succulent nipples to be more than obvious."

She got what she wanted.

She confided some of the details of her affair with JFK to Hollywood publicist Raymond Strait, who functioned as her press secretary for ten years. At the time, Jayne was one of the few women in Hollywood who employed a press secretary. He later described his experiences with Jayne in a memoir entitled *The Tragic Life of Jayne Mansfield.*

After Kennedy became president, and he flew in from Washington to Los Angeles, Lawford arranged for a rendezvous between Jayne and JFK at a luxurious home in Malibu which was owned by a rich gay friend of Peter's.

At first Jayne was very secretive with Strait about the liaison, as he related in his memoirs. At the time of the notorious weekend in Malibu, Jayne was going through another one of her trial separations from her muscleman husband, Mickey. Jayne had instructed Strait that if a "Mr. J" leaves a message for her on her answering service, she was to be contacted right away.

Two hours later, the phone rang. It was the mysterious "Mr. J." Strait vaguely recognized the voice but claimed "I couldn't place it." Mr. J. told him that his car would pick Jayne up at two o'clock that afternoon. When Jayne called Strait to pick up her message, she became very agitated when she learned that Mr. J. was coming by. She hurried home and began to prepare herself, putting on an elegant black silk dress with a mink collar. She made up her face as if getting ready to face a movie camera.

Almost exactly at two o'clock, according to Strait, a shiny black Cadillac pulled up in front of the apartment building where she was living at the time. Strait was in her apartment and remained behind, waiting for her to return.

It was around ten that evening when Jayne came back to her apartment and thanked Strait for everything. She had a cup of coffee and a cigarette with him before kissing him goodbye and heading off into the night again. When he was cleaning up, he noticed that she'd left a book of matches. When he examined it, he saw that it contained the presidential seal on the back of its cover. Suddenly, Strait knew who Mr. J. was.

It was President John F. Kennedy.

What Jayne apparently didn't tell Strait was that she visited JFK once again a few days later before he flew back East. This time it was within a hotel suite in Los Angeles.

As Jayne revealed months later to her friend, Blondell, JFK showed up at her suite accompanied by the playboy, Porfirio Rubirosa of the Dominican Republic, who had notoriously been married to each of the two richest women in the world, Doris Duke of the tobacco fortune, and Barbara Hutton, the Woolworth heiress.

Jayne was momentarily surprised. She later told friends, "I've had three ways before. Besides, Jack was President of the United States, and isn't a good citizen supposed to do what the president asks her?"

Rubirosa was a well-known name in Hollywood, having bedded such actresses as Marilyn Monroe, Joan Crawford, Zsa Zsa Gabor, Ava Gardner, and Veronica Lake.

At the time of Rubi's visit with Jayne, he swung the most famous and talked-about penis in the world. The society photographer, Jerome Zerbe, claimed, "It looks like Yul Brynner in a black turtleneck sweater." That assertion appeared in Mart Martin's *Did He or Didn't He? The Intimate Sex Lives of 201 Famous Men.*

Jayne later claimed that it was at "least a foot long and as thick around as a Budweiser can." The fame of Rubi's penis was so great that diners in restaurants often referred to "a Rubirosa," when asking a waiter for a pepper mill.

She said that Jack insisted on screwing her first. "If Rubi goes first," Jack told her, "he'll ruin it for me."

To Blondell, she later compared getting screwed by Rubi as "the equivalent of giving birth to a baby. Jack got down real close to oversee the action. He'd heard so many stories about Rubi being the world's greatest lover, and he wanted to see everything for himself."

"I had three orgasms." She may not have exaggerated. Rubirosa was known for sustaining an erection for hours. Many of his lovers reported having multiple orgasms with him.

"Jack had some fun that night, but I think he got off more by being a voyeur than a stud."

JFK's last sexual liaison with Jayne, according to Raymond Strait, occurred at a villa in Palm Springs. "It was about a year later after the Malibu incident," Strait claimed. "Mr. J. called one more time and wanted to send a limousine for Jayne and have her delivered to Palm Springs. At the time Jayne was pregnant with her fourth child, Maria."

Strait expected that once the President learned about Jayne's pregnancy, he would have thanked her, told her good-bye, and arranged for another of his actress friends to spend the weekend with him instead.

But that was not the case. JFK wanted to see Jayne, whether she was pregnant or not.

169

After her weekend in the desert, Jayne virtually dined out on having had sex, as a pregnant woman, with JFK.

Allegedly, when she once encountered her rival, Marilyn Monroe, at a night club, the two blonde bombshells once indulged in "girl talk" with each other, comparing their very different experiences with JFK.

Hollywood publicist Bradford Denham was with Jayne and Marilyn on that particular night, and he tried to hawk a story about what he heard to the tabloids. Although in its entirety it was too hot for a national publication in those days, excerpts appeared in the short-lived hippie paper, *Revolution.*

Reportedly, Jayne said, "Jack was more fascinated with my pregnant belly than he was with Suzi." As all her lovers, dressers, friends, and publicists knew, Suzi was the nickname she frequently associated with her vagina. Mart Martin picked up on this nickname in another book of his, *Did She or Didn't She? Behind the Bedroom Doors of 201 Famous Women.*

In his underground interview, reporting the alleged conversation between MM and Jayne, Denham revealed Jayne's revelations to Marilyn. "Jack rubbed my belly and kissed it, and even wanted to masturbate on it," she was quoted as saying. "When I told him we thought the baby was going to be a girl, that really excited him. Before I left that weekend, Jack bent me over on the bed and entered me from behind, all the time while feeling my belly. I'd never seen him so excited."

Shortly before his assassination, Jack called her one final time. She received the call in the Polo Lounge of the swank Beverly Hills Hotel. Strait did not hear what was being said on the other end. It was later believed that the president was suggesting a three-way among singer Eartha Kitt, Jayne, and himself.

Finally, despite much urging, she refused the president.

Before hanging up the phone, Strait heard her tell Mr. J., "Look, you'll be president for only eight years at the very most. But I'll be a movie star forever!" Then she hung up the phone.

Even though they ended their relationship on a harsh note, Jayne cried all day when she learned that the president had been assassinated.

Like the president himself, Jayne would die young. Death occurred on the night of June 28, 1967, after an engagement in Biloxi, Mississippi, at Gus Stevens' Supper Club. At 2:30 in the morning on U.S. Highway 90, Jayne's driver, Ronnie Harrison, crashed into the rear of a tractor trailer that had slowed down because of a truck in front of it spraying mosquito fogger.

Riding in the front seat, Jayne was killed instantly. Rumors that she was decapitated are untrue, though she did suffer severe head trauma. Her three children—Miklos, Zoltan, and Mariska riding in the back seat of the 1966 Buick Electra 225—survived, suffering only minor injuries.

After JFK died, Jayne often complained that "Everybody talks about President Kennedy and Marilyn Monroe. No one talks about Jayne Mansfield and President Kennedy. I called Peter Lawford and really gave him hell when he selected Marilyn to sing 'Happy Birthday, Mr. President.' I could have pulled that off far better than Marilyn. My tits are far bigger than hers, too. It seemed that all my life I had to be compared to Marilyn. I lost choice roles that went to her. I would have been so much better than Marilyn in *Some Like It Hot.* Also Jack himself told me I was far better in bed than Marilyn ever was. It seems I just don't get credit for my accomplishments."

Lee Remick & Bobby Kennedy

Pulchritude Meets Power

The brother-in-law of the Kennedys, Peter Lawford, later claimed, "Bobby caught the 'adultery infection' from Jack." In 1961, Bobby was married and Lee was married when they first met at a Washington party.

Bobby, at age 36, was devoted to his wife, Ethel, at least as a baby factory, but he had the same wandering eye as his brother.

Lee was a gorgeous 26-year-old when she bounced into Washington on the arm of her husband, Bill Colleran (married 1957 to 1968).

Bobby, according to reports, "couldn't take his eyes off Lee," who responded with some very come-hither smiles when her husband wasn't looking. Close friends of both Bobby and Lee claimed, "They were destined to hit the sack together."

Lee fell for Bobby more than he fell for her. Frankly, he wanted sex, and she wanted to make something more permanent out of their relationship. "I'm bored with my marriage and seducing married men is a big turn-on for me," she preclaimed.

LEE & BOBBY
DAYS OF WINE AND ROSES

Lee Remick stunned audiences when she made her film debut in Elia Kazan's *A Face in the Crowd*, co-starring with Andy Griffith in the 1957 release. She lived with a family in Arkansas, where the movie was shot, and practiced baton twirling in her role as a teenage cheerleader who wins the heart of "Lonesome Rhodes" (Griffin).

Her career bagan to rise when she appeared as the hot-blooded daughter-in-law of Orson Welles in *The Long, Hot Summer* (1958). More fame came when she starred as the rape victim whose husband is tried for killing her attacker in Otto Preminger's *Anatomy of a Murder* (1959). Her greatest success came when she played the alcoholic wife of Jack Lemmon in *Days of Wine and Roses*, which brought her an Academy Award as Best Actress for 1962.

That was another award winning year for her, as she seduced both Bobby and Jack.

No survey of the private lives of the Kennedys is possible without presenting actress Lee Remick as a footnote. The star (1935-1991) was born in Quincy, Massachusetts, and in time would share much in common with her two fellow New Englanders, RFK and JFK, including their beds.

Lee was a natural-born beauty and a consummate actress. She attracted America's attention in her film debut in Elia Kazan's 1957 *A Face in the Crowd*, cast as a baton-twirling teenager who wins the heart of Lonesome Rhodes (played by Andy Griffith and based loosely on radio jock Arthur Godfrey).

She also gained attention when she starred in *Anatomy of a Murder* (1959), a role intended for Lana Turner, who was fired when she insisted that her off-the-rack costumes, suitable for the part of an Army wife, be replaced with original *haute couture* designed by Jean-Louis.

When Marilyn Monroe was fired from *Something's Got to Give* (1962), Fox assigned Lee to replace her. But co-star Dean Martin refused to work with Lee and demanded that the studio reinstate MM.

Lee was a spokesperson for the Democratic Party and a strong advocate for JFK during the 1960 presidential race. It was only inevitable that she would be invited to the White House after his inauguration in 1961. She arrived on the arm of her husband, the American director and television producer Bill Colleran, with whom she was married from 1957 to 1968.

When he was introduced to her, Bobby Kennedy seemed mesmerized, although he tried to conceal his feelings in front of Colleran.

Before flying to Los Angeles on his next visit, Bobby called Peter Lawford and asked him if he could arrange a meeting with Lee. To his astonishment, Peter claimed that he was having an affair with her. But since the Kennedy brother-in-law believed in "sharing the wealth," a rendezvous was scheduled in California between Lee and Bobby.

Peter discreetly arranged for a friend to turn over his secluded home in Malibu to Lee and Bobby. That friend was on a trip to France.

Lee later told Peter, "I fell for him after the first night. He was boyish and charming in bed. After the third fuck, I was madly in love with him. Bobby has more drive and energy than ten other young men. But I really upset him when I suggested I should divorce Bill, and he should divorce Ethel so we could get married."

"Isn't that sort of rushing things after only one night in the hay?" Peter asked.

But like Marilyn Monroe chasing after JFK even after he'd discarded her, Lee continued to pursue Bobby, even making unscheduled trips to Washington where she told her husband she was fund-raising for the Democratic Party.

In 1962, Lee and Bobby were seen staying together at a villa in Palm Beach that belonged to an associate of Joseph Kennedy.

At the age of thirty-six, and newly installed as his brother's attorney general, Bobby was on the dawn of his greatest political power. Lee was just beginning to launch a fabulous career, which in 1962 would see her nominated for an Oscar as Best Actress for her stunning performance as the alcoholic wife of Jack Lemmon in *Days of Wine and Roses*.

Lee told Peter that Bobby was "the best sex I've ever had, and as you know I've had Sinatra."

Lee told her dear friend, Merv Griffin, about her bizarre relationship with Frank Sinatra. "When my husband, Bill Colleran, had a car accident, I flew to Los Angeles and stayed at the Beverly Hills Hotel for a week. Bill had directed Sinatra in a TV special, but I didn't know him. That's why I was shocked when he paid my hotel bill."

"When Mia Farrow, his wife, could not finish *Rosemary's Baby* in time to star in *The Detective,* he cast me instead. I thought we were just going to have a mere fling on location, but he fell for me big time. He said he was going to divorce Mia to marry me, but I didn't want that. I was scared to turn him down. After I left the set, I wrote him a 'good-bye Frank' note and pasted it on his dressing room door. He exploded. I didn't take his calls, but he left a dozen phone messages for me, calling me every vulgar name you could ever call a woman—'whore' being the kindest word."

She could barely tolerate mention of Ethel Kennedy, and she threw temper fits whenever she heard rumors about RFK with other women. She became furious when she learned that her suitor had developed a crush on Claudine Longet, who was at one time married to singer Andy Williams. Columnist Hedda Hopper got wind of the Peter Lawford/Lee Remick affair and ran a blind item in her syndicated column. "The big news in Hollywood is a romance that can't be out in print. I guarantee that if this one hits the papers it will curl hair from Washington to Santa Monica."

Imagine what Hedda would have written if she'd known Bobby himself was part of this

As her two lovers, Lee found JFK and RFK very different personalities.

Both Jack and his younger brother Teddy were often reckless in their pursuit of women, taking outlandish chances of getting caught. In contrast, Bobby was more discreet. As Lem Billings put it, "Jack and Teddy could be found nude with several beauties in the swimming pool. But Bobby was doing the dirty deed in the bushes."

When Lee became too aggressive in her love affair with Bobby, he backed away from her, fearing exposure. Most of RFK's lovers found him more sensitive to a woman's needs than Jack, who did not linger for pillow talk. Once the deed was done, "he (JFK) put back on his shorts and called the Kremlin," in the words of Lem.

Lee herself more or less agreed with this evaluation. She later told Jack Lemmon, "I fucked Bobby for love; I fucked Jack because he was the President of the United States."

173

three-way romance.

Bobby, according to reports, wanted to keep Lee on the string for occasional romps in the hay. He had no permanent plan for her, and became alarmed to see her becoming obsessive about him. She tried to read every word written about him and defended him loudly at Hollywood parties.

Elements conspired to break up their relationship.

From both Bobby and Peter, JFK heard what a "great gal" Lee was in the sack. The president became intrigued and asked Peter to set up a rendezvous between Lee and himself when he flew to the coast.

Normally, he and Bobby shared women on occasion and freely exchanged details about them with each other. But JFK seemed to sense that Bobby held Lee in a special regard, so he chose not to tell him of his plan to seduce her.

There may have been another reason: JFK was growing alarmed at Lee's slavish devotion to Bobby, and JFK knew that Bobby would never leave Ethel. Perhaps he wanted to seduce Lee to demonstrate to Bobby that she would sleep around. There were rumors that Lee was also having an affair with Gregory Peck while professing undying love for Bobby.

Peter Lawford, the Kennedy brother-in-law, began his affair with Lee Remick before the Kennedys and Frank Sinatra got her.

Lee and Peter really fell for each other. It became so serious that he considered divorcing his wife, Patricia Kennedy, to marry Lee.

At that time Peter had a very open dialogue with Jack, and Peter told him that he and Pat (Jack's sister) were drifting apart. He also revealed that he wanted to divorce her.

The president urged him to stay in the marriage, at least until his re-election in 1964. "You could damage my chances," he warned Peter, who agreed to hold off.

Peter and Lee remained friends after Peter's reconciliation with Patricia. And in its wake, Peter stepped back "and let Bobby have her," in the words of Frank Sinatra.

Peter delivered Lee to JFK's hotel suite in Los Angeles, where she spent most of the night. She later told Peter, "He wasn't the lover Bobby is. He just sort of lies down on his back and expects the woman to do all the work."

Bobby eventually heard about his brother's seduction of Lee. He never confronted the president about this indiscretion, but from that time on he never accepted any of Lee's calls to his office. He told Peter, "Tell her to stop calling me. It's over. I've moved on."

On April 29, 1991, Lee made her final public appearance, at a ceremony that marked the appearance of a star with her name on the Hollywood Walk of Fame. When she arrived, her loyal fans loudly gasped in horror. The once-beautiful star was unrecognizable. Her face was blotched and bloated by the chemo treatments she was undergoing during the final stages of kidney and liver cancer.

On hand that day to lend support was Jack Lemmon, her favorite co-star. He later said, "Dear, dear Lee suffered from a lack of self-esteem. By seducing some of the biggest names in America—the Kennedy brothers, Gregory Peck, Peter Lawford, even Frank Sinatra—she felt wanted and desired. But in the end, all of these men dropped her. She was used. When she came to realize that, she felt even worse about herself."

After her final appearance, Lee had only weeks to live. She died in Los Angeles on July 2, 1991. Her last words to Lemmon were, "If Bobby had married me, like I wanted, I wouldn't be dying today."

Marilyn Monroe
vs. The Kennedys

Some Like It Hotter

Marilyn Monroe made the rounds, going through all the Kennedy men, beginning with Jack Kennedy *(upper left)* in 1946. When she met Senator Kennedy years later at a Hollywood party, he didn't remember deflowering Norma Jean Baker. But, in fairness to the senator, in 1946 she didn't look like the woman who had turned herself into Marilyn Monroe. She was also accompanied by her husband, Joe DiMaggio. "Joe and Jack were like roosters when they came together," Marilyn later recalled.

Sometimes Sammy Davis Jr. served as "the black beard," escorting Marilyn to a party at the home of Peter Lawford, though she later disappeared with Jack. When Joe Kennedy *(lower left photo)* first seduced Marilyn, she was so little known she was referred to as "a minor starlet." When his son was running for president, Marilyn told Joe, "It would be nice to have a president who looks so young and good looking."

John Miner, an associate clinical professor at the University of Southern California Medical School, heard the tapes recorded for Marilyn's psychiatrist, Dr. Ralph Greenson. Miner later claimed, "Marilyn was very explicit about the sexual relationship she had with both Jack and Robert." It wasn't until 2010 that her relationship with Teddy Kennedy *(lower right)* was revealed in F.B.I. reports.

The Sad Saga of MM
& the Kennedy Menfolk

"Happy Birthday...Mr. Pres...i...dent,
Happy Birthday...to you."

Marilyn Monroe, May 19, 1962
at Madison Square Garden in New York City

The Kennedy brothers *(left to right)* Bobby, Teddy, and JFK—often passed women around, including Marilyn Monroe. Many of these same women were also enjoyed by Joe Kennedy *(center photo)*.

As president of the United States and attorney general, both Jack and Bobby were vulnerable to scandal, and each of them became duly alarmed when an out-of-control Marilyn threatened to destroy their political dynasty.

To remove her from the scene, both men urged her to remarry Joe DiMaggio. But Marilyn told the Kennedys that she could never do that. "As a husband he is too possessive. He is capable of physical violence."

Marilyn entertained fantasies of marrying either Jack or Bobby, but not Teddy. "He's just a plaything for me," she told Jeanne Carmen. "I call him my overgrown Teddy Bear." Joe feared scandal and was planning to buy Marilyn off. But before he could do so, he suffered a devastating stroke.

According to dozens of biographies, Marilyn Monroe met Senator John F. Kennedy at a party in 1954 at the home of agent and producer Charles Feldman. She was there with her husband, Joe DiMaggio.

"Don't we know each other?" Marilyn asked JFK in front of DiMaggio.

JFK said, "Surely not. If I ever met you before, you'd be unforgettable."

By then, DiMaggio was fuming. After he'd had a few drinks and had to go to Feldman's ground floor bathroom, Marilyn slipped JFK her private phone number. She whispered in his ear, "It was at Robert Stack's place." Suddenly he remembered her. "But you were so different then."

"Norma Jean Baker has become Marilyn Monroe."

Stack had guided a pre-war Jack Kennedy through a galaxy of Hollywood stars in 1940. When JFK returned from the Navy, Stack also arranged a number of introductions to young starlets. Stack had never liked Marilyn; his animosity began on their first date. He'd arrived to take her to a dinner party, and she kept him waiting one and a half hours while she decided what gown to wear from her meager selection. When they finally arrived at the party, the other guests had already eaten.

Ultimately, Stack remembered his sexual tryst with Marilyn as unsatisfactory, claiming "there was just no chemistry between us." But when Jack spotted her picture in a portfolio of photographs, he wanted to have a chance at her. Stack warned him about her shortcomings, but Jack was persistent, and eventually, an evening rendezvous was arranged between Jack and Marilyn.

That night in Stack's apartment, Jack seduced Marilyn for the first time. He apparently told no one, not even Stack, his reaction to the experience. Marilyn later claimed she gave him her phone number back then, but he never called. When he met up with her again, in 1954, he could hardly imagine that she'd be the biggest star in Hollywood.

Of course, even at that point, Jack had had sexual experiences with so many women, often for such brief periods, that he could hardly be expected to remember all of them, even Marilyn. In fairness, Marilyn in 1946 hardly resembled the Marilyn he encountered in 1954, during his stint as one of the senators from Massachusetts, at Feldman's party.

She tried to explain to him. "When you met me after the war, I wasn't Marilyn Monroe yet."

At Feldman's party, he told her that he'd call her as soon as he had a "little work done on my back—an old sports injury." That made him sound more athletic than he really was.

The day after her reunion with Jack, Marilyn informed her best friend, Jeanne Carmen, "That Jack Kennedy couldn't take his eyes off me." Before he returned to the East Coast and the hospital, he was eager to see Marilyn and impetuously telephoned her at the home she was sharing with then-husband, Joe DiMaggio.

The first time he called, DiMaggio picked up the phone. Hearing a man's voice he did not recognize, DiMaggio asked, "Who's this?"

"A friend," JFK said.

DiMaggio slammed down the phone.

After his return to the East, during Jack's post-surgical stint in the hospital, several visitors noted a pinup poster of Marilyn wearing tight-fitting blue shorts, with her legs spread apart. JFK had hung the poster upside down, thereby making it more suggestive.

Arthur James, who had known Marilyn during the early 1950s, was a witness to the blossoming of the Monroe/Kennedy affair. He told all to biographer Anthony Summers, author of *Goddess, The Secret Life of Marilyn Monroe*.

James associated the JFK/MM sexual liaison with the final months of her crumbling marriage to DiMaggio. According to James, their favorite watering hole was the raunchy Malibu Cottage; a battered bar and grill with fewer than a dozen stools, sawdust on the floor, and a handful of rentable bedrooms. "Kennedy wasn't known on the West Coast then, and he and Marilyn were very open. They also used rooms at the Holiday House Motel in Malibu." The two lovers were also seen coming and going from the Chateau Marmont on Sunset Boulevard.

Marilyn once told the columnist, James Bacon, with whom she'd had a brief fling, that "Jack won't indulge in foreplay because he's on the run all the time."

Henry Rosenfeld, MM's New York confidant, said Marilyn not only saw JFK at an apartment of a friend on 53rd Street near Third Avenue in New York, but also visited him at the Mayflower Hotel near the White House in Washington, DC. Rosenfeld was almost certain that she was never smuggled into the White House in disguise.

When Robert Kennedy was Attorney General in the 1960s, Marilyn and JFK used the bedroom above his office at the Justice Department for their sexual trysts. Often, when working late, Bobby himself slept there, too tired to drive back to his home in Virginia, Hickory Hill.

During the course of the MM/JFK affair, the lovers rendezvoused every time Jack flew to Los Angeles. The affair was usually conducted at the beachfront home of Patricia Kennedy and Peter Lawford.

"Pat knew all about what was going on," said Frank Sinatra. "She knows her brother wasn't a saint. Neither was Pat. I even made it with her when she was married to Peter." He told that to Joey Bishop, Judy Garland, and Sammy Davis Jr.

Peter Summers, a senior Kennedy aide, said that once, he had to locate Jack because of some sort of emergency, and he saw Marilyn and him emerging dripping wet from the shower together. "They didn't seem in the least embarrassed."

Dean Martin and "some floozie" [his words] had reported seeing Jack and Marilyn walking hand in hand on the beach in the early evening.

Jeanne Carmen told a red-hot story to the tabloid newspaper, the *Globe*, which ran a four-part series called *True Confessions of a Hollywood Party Girl*.

In the series, Carmen recalled a wild pool party at Peter Lawford's house to celebrate JFK's nomination in 1960. Both Carmen and Marilyn were invited to the party.

Carmen claimed that after a swim, she retreated to a back bedroom within the Lawford home to take a shower. MM, she said, knocked on her door and told her that the Democratic presidential nominee wanted a three-way.

At first Carmen turned down the offer, telling MM, "I don't do that."

But Monroe pleaded with her, claiming "We can think of it as doing something for our country." Finally she told Carmen that she'd have to reject JFK herself, up close and personal. Accordingly, Carmen went into another of the house's bedrooms, finding Jack in his underwear.

A master seducer, he began to massage her shoulders. He whispered that MM and herself should think of themselves "as pioneers on The New Frontier of the 1960s."

Carmen admitted that finally she gave in—"overwhelmed by Jack's extraordinary charms, good looks, and a buzz from the alcohol I'd consumed at Peter's party."

As she looked up after JFK had tongue kissed her, she saw Marilyn dropping her towel and moving toward the bed.

***

After Marilyn's divorce from DiMaggio early in 1955, she took a small apartment in New York. Once installed in Manhattan, she had a rendezvous with JFK in his duplex penthouse suite at the swanky Hotel Carlyle.

Her friend, Henry Rosenfeld, said that Marilyn was as excited as a teenager to be having an affair with the handsome senator. "He told me he's going to become President of the United States on day," Marilyn said, breathlessly.

After a session with JFK at the Carlyle, Marilyn confided to columnist Earl Wilson, "I think I made his back feel better—but don't print that."

Before leaving that night, she said, "Earl, you're a dear. Take a good look at me. You're looking at the future First Lady of the United States."

"But what about Jackie?" Wilson asked.

"He'll divorce that old bag," she said. "I heard it from Jack himself that she won't do all of the things I'll do. She's too much of a lady, I guess."

Because of his bad back, JFK liked to have sex with a woman on top of him. Lem Billings told biographer Lawrence J. Quirk that "Jack had claimed that Marilyn gave great head—hers was a true labor of love."

Marilyn confided to her friend, Helen Ferguson, that Joe DiMaggio didn't think of me "as another notch on his belt like Jack Kennedy. But he is a square—strictly missionary position, macho Italian athlete." The star confessed to Ferguson that fellatio was her favorite sexual position. But she claimed that "Joe didn't like to be fellated." She admitted, however, that JFK "loved me to do that to him."

Launched into an affair with Marilyn, then the hottest thing on celluloid, Jack placed a call to his father, Joseph P. Kennedy, in Palm Beach to tell him the latest news.

Joe had constantly bragged to his son that he had "bagged" Marilyn around 1950. He claimed he'd seduced her one night at the Chateau Marmont, and that later she'd accepted an off-the-record weekend invitation to go with him to Palm Springs, where they stayed in a private villa.

Marilyn was desperately looking for a father figure, and after a weekend with Joe Sr. she referred to him as "Daddy."

"You didn't get to her first," Jack told his father, according to Jack's closest friend, Lem Billings. "I got to her first. While I was staying with Robert Stack, she was one of the girls I fucked." Joe reportedly was furious, because he often played a one-upmanship game with his

Hollywood actress and pinup queen, **Jeanne Carmen**, a Marilyn Monroe clone, was also her best friend and confidante. She recalled the night she drove with Marilyn to meet JFK.

She saw Marilyn gushing over the presidential candidate. "I just know he's going to be the next president," Marilyn told Carmen. "Wouldn't it be funny if we got married and I became the First Lady?"

Carmen warned MM that Jack was already married. "So what?" Marilyn asked. "So was Arthur Miller. But that didn't stop me. If they want you bad enough, they'll do whatever it takes to get you."

son as to which of the Kennedys could seduce a woman first. Seductions that followed were graphically referred to as "sloppy seconds."

Director John Huston had introduced Joe to Marilyn on the set of *The Asphalt Jungle*, a film in which the budding starlet had a minor role.

Huston later capitalized off his friendship with Joe Kennedy. In Richard Condon's *Winter Kills*, a thinly disguised story about the Kennedy assassination, Huston played the role of the patriarch, who is the villain who orders his son's assassination.

Jeff Bridges played Nick Kegan, a Bobby Kennedy-like character, brother of an assassinated U.S. President. John Huston, cast as "Pa Kegan," admitted to co-star Anthony Perkins that he based his characterization on Joe Kennedy himself—"a friend from yesterday, but not that much of a friend."

The part was originally offered to Frank Sinatra, but he rejected it because he didn't want to appear in any film that libeled the Kennedy family, even though his own relationships with many of them had been strained.

Huston also directed Marilyn in her last picture, *The Misfits*, in which she co-starred with her childhood idol, Clark Gable, and her emotionally disturbed friend, Montgomery Clift. The director prophesized that within two years, "Marilyn, bless her, will be either stark bonkers or else at Forest Lawn."

Several people have suggested that during his pursuit of Marilyn, Jack was, in essence, following in the footsteps of his father. Joe Sr. had conquered Gloria Swanson when she was the reigning screen vamp of the silent screen, although she was about to lose her crown at the time. In contrast, Jack pursued Marilyn at the time when she was the most talked about movie star in the world.

In 1938, when Jack was twenty-one years old, he had entered the hospital to be circumcised because of a tight foreskin. Lem was away but writing letters to him. Jack later chastised him for taking undue interest in his circumcision. Years later, Lem told Quirk that "When you're circumcised at a much later age like that, you think of it as a kind of castration, a threat to

In this 1955 photo, fashion photographer **Milton Green** works his magic on Marilyn, becoming her Svengali. Marilyn was told that Milton was a warm and sensitive guy, but, if crossed, his enemies claimed he would become a killer. "Nobody takes me seriously as an actress," MM told Green.

"I do," he said, reassuring her. "Hang in with me and I'll see to it that you become more acclaimed than Garbo. You are the hottest talent in Hollywood, far better than the dumb blonde parts they give you. Fox is only paying you $1,500 a week. You should be getting a million dollars per picture. What about launching Marilyn Monroe Productions?"

manhood, so you have to keep on proving 'it' is okay by any means possible."

"Jack kept proving that 'it' was okay with Marilyn time and time again," Lem claimed.

When JFK became president, Marilyn was thrilled, telling Jeanne Carmen that he was going to divorce Jackie and marry her.

"That would be political suicide," Carmen cautioned her. "Surely by now, you know a line when you hear one."

"You're awful," Marilyn said. "I know Jack. He's sincere. He'll carry through on his promise."

Carmen told her friends, "Marilyn is heading for heartbreak. The president will dump her one day sooner or later. I heard he does that with all his women."

Marilyn told her sometimes lover Robert F. Slatzer, "the next time I see the president I want to be wearing my Somalian leopard coat. That way, he will think of me as a predatory animal."

According to reports, Peter Lawford used to dress Marilyn up like an ugly secretary with a stringy black wig and slip her into the Carlyle for a sexual tryst upstairs in JFK's suite. Once, the blonde bombshell was even slipped aboard Air Force One wearing this dowdy disguise.

Marilyn was given Jack's private phone number in the White House, but he warned her that if Jackie answered, she was to hang up because her voice was too well known.

When Jayne Mansfield learned that Marilyn had replaced her as one of Jack's mistresses, she sneered, "Marilyn is just a dumb broad. One of Jack's fucks handed down by me when I was finished with him."

Joe desperately wanted Jack to run for a presidential second term in 1964, and he viewed Marilyn as a "walking time bomb." He feared if news about her having sex with Jack was revealed, it would destroy his son's political career.

Joe called Marilyn and offered a huge financial statement; some sources place it as much as a million dollars. "The price of silence," he told Jack. Marilyn, or so it is said, agreed to make the deal.

But as negotiations lingered into the Christmas season of 1961, and before the deal was consummated, Joe suffered a stroke. He was left sitting in a wheelchair, helpless, mute, and drooling. Marilyn would soon go to her own death, with very little money left in her checking account and her mortgage not yet paid off.

JFK, as noted in numerous biographies, was fond of having himself photographed naked with various beautiful women, sometimes pictured during fornication with him or else when one of these women was fellating him.

It was rumored that Peter Lawford was called in to photograph some of these vignettes in Santa Monica. During one of her reunions with Shelley Winters, her former roommate, in the late 1940s. Marilyn confided that Peter had taken nude pictures of President Kennedy and herself within a large bathtub at Peter's house. She also claimed that after one of the photo shoots, Peter joined JFK and herself in bed for a three-way. "Peter has quite a gay streak in him and welcomed the chance to get at Jack," Marilyn claimed to Carmen. "Just for a thrill, Jack allowed himself to be serviced. All of us had a gay old time, especially the president. He didn't do much for us that night. But both Peter and I serviced him."

The existence of the notorious photograph of Marilyn performing fellatio on JFK while lounging in that large marble bathtub was first exposed in C. David Heymann's *A Woman Named Jackie*. The whereabouts of that photograph is not known today; it may have been destroyed, but then again…

***

Bobby, or so it is believed, met Marilyn in early February of 1962 during a trip to Los Angeles at the home of his sister, Patricia Kennedy Lawford, and her actor husband, Peter.

Another blonde beauty, Kim Novak, was also present. Bobby already knew "Hollywood's lavender blonde" (there had been rumors).

When Peter had asked RFK what star he most wanted to meet in Hollywood, his first choice had been MM.

In a letter to Arthur Miller's teenage son, MM praised Bobby's sense of humor and also claimed, "He's not a bad dancer either."

Peter later warned Bobby, "When Ethel's in the room, you shouldn't hold Marilyn so close when you dance with her. Her bosom was pressing into your chest, not to mention something else."

Joan Braden, a family friend of the Lawfords, recalled Marilyn's arrival at their home in Santa Monica. The blonde star was dressed in black lace, wearing no brassière. Throughout the night, Bobby devoted all his attention to her, finishing off a bottle of champagne with her. She even taught him how to do the twist. Right in front of Pat and Peter, Marilyn asked Bobby, "As Attorney General, have you ever arrested a woman in bed?"

"No, but I've done other things to them," he said.

After that night, Bobby made frequent trips to Los Angeles, promoting his book on organized crime. *The Enemy Within*, which he wanted developed as a film project.

Bobby's sister, Jean Kennedy Smith, wrote from Palm Beach, "Dear Bobby, I hear you and Marilyn Monroe are the new, hot item among Hollywood gossips."

After he finished a fourteen-country goodwill tour with Ethel, Bobby immediately called Marilyn for a rendezvous. Their affair was about to begin. At the time, Marilyn was also sending handwritten love poems to JFK at the White House.

One of Marilyn's closest friends, Carmen, who lived nearby, remembered opening the door to Marilyn's house to discover Bobby Kennedy on the doorstep. When she heard who it was, Marilyn came rushing out of the bathroom. "She jumped into his arms," Carmen said, "and they started kissing madly. We had a glass of wine together before Marilyn reminded me that I had important business to take care of."

After that, Marilyn logged many calls to Bobby at the Justice Department. "She called him almost daily during that summer of 1962, her last on Earth," claimed Ed Guthman, a Kennedy press aide. Then he added a tantalizing note, one that hasn't yet been fully documented within the Kennedy scandals. "Judy Garland placed almost as many calls to Bobby as Marilyn. What was going on between Dorothy and Bobby? I never found out."

"When Bobby wasn't on the West Coast, they talked for hours on the phone," claimed Hazel Washington, Marilyn's maid at the time. "I think they invented phone sex. Marilyn actually made love to Bobby on the phone. I heard everything."

"Jack was the first to sample the honeypot," Marilyn told Slatzer. "Bobby had his turn. I wasn't in love with Jack, but I fell in love with Bobby."

Carmen also claimed that she went with Marilyn and Bobby to a nude beach near the present Pepperdine University north of Santa Monica. Marilyn, according to the report, wore a black wig, and Bobby had on sunglasses and a fake beard. Each of them went unrecognized. "Could you imagine what a sensation it would have been if a nude Marilyn Monroe and a nude Attorney General had been snapped on the beach by some photographer?" Carmen asked.

Bobby bragged about bedding Marilyn to Kennedy aide David Powers. Powers at first didn't believe him, calling him "the biggest bullshitter in the world." He later claimed, "Bobby wouldn't have the balls to play like that in the big league."

But Bobby claimed it was true. "Not only have I had Marilyn's pussy but I think she's in love with me."

***

Nearly every person in America has heard about President Kennedy's affair with Marilyn. And at least a million have heard about her affair with Bobby. But only a few thousands know that she also had an affair with Teddy.

That revelation came to light in 2010, thanks to disclosures within formerly confidential files from the F.B.I. In June of 2010, in the wake of Teddy Kennedy's death from cancer in August of 2009, the bureau released some 2,352 pages of formerly secret documents.

According to the files, there were several orgies staged at JFK's suite at the

In spite of the fact that she'd just had gynecological surgery, **Marilyn Monroe** with her husband, playwright **Arthur Miller**, face the cameras during their departure from Lenox Hill Hospital in New York City on June 26, 1959, heading back to her New York apartment.

Marilyn told best friend Jeanne Carmen, "I'm still married to Arthur but he makes me unhappy. My marriage to him has only months to go."

Her friend, Henry Rosenfeld, said, "Marilyn lived in her own dream world. Her fantasy was to marry Jack Kennedy after his divorce from Jackie. She contemplated calling Jackie and urging her to divorce her husband."

Carlyle. At least three included Marilyn Monroe as "guest of honor." Rat packers Frank Sinatra, Sammy Davis Jr., Peter Lawford, and even Patricia Kennedy attended at least one of the orgies.

The F.B.I. named Mrs. Jacqueline Hammond as a source of much of this information. Hammond was the divorced wife of a former ambassador to Spain.

Marilyn's eight-month affair with Teddy, which began at an orgy within the Carlyle attended by all three of the Kennedy brothers, extended until right before her murder.

Jack's younger brother, Teddy, had been very competitive about Judith Campbell Exner when she was the mistress of the president. He pursued her, and one night, he openly propositioned her in Las Vegas. But she turned him down, finding him "childishly temperamental."

After that orgy at the Carlyle, Teddy pursued Marilyn. One night in New York, she agreed to let him come to her apartment, where he found candlelight, roses, champagne, and Marilyn in a see-through nightgown.

"Teddy was all too eager," said Peter Lawford when he learned about their coupling. "The night Teddy met Marilyn at the Carlyle, he had to wait his turn, taking sloppy thirds after Jack and Bobby had finished with her. But I was glad to hear that Teddy got to have Marilyn all by himself for a night and didn't have to wait in line."

Teddy's seduction of Marilyn, although known by many Kennedy aides, never surfaced in any public way during the star's lifetime.

The F.B.I. documents were so explosive that Teddy's widow, Victoria, fought to have them squelched forever. She was ultimately defeated by a law court which upheld the Freedom of Information Act.

Teddy told Senator George Smathers, "I'm now screwing the woman whose poster Jack used to jack-off to when he was in the hospital. MARILYN MONROE HERSELF. She told me I make better love than either of my two brothers." Unknown to Teddy, she'd also told Bobby that he was a "far better lover than Jack."

Author Christopher Anderson claims, "Teddy, like the rest of his family, was engaged in an almost frantic pursuit of power, money, and sex."

In a particularly bizarre revelation, Carmen remembered drinking wine one late afternoon with Marilyn in her living room. The star was dressed in a stunning gown, but wouldn't tell her friend where she was going. "I have a date tonight."

The doorbell rang and Marilyn hurried to the bathroom to check her make-up. "Be a doll, Jeanne, and get the door," she called out. Carmen was stunned to open the door to discover both John and Robert Kennedy, with two men standing behind them, presumably Secret Service agents. She ushered them into the living room. JFK claimed "We don't have much time."

"Marilyn rushed out of the bathroom and gave each of them what looked like a prolonged tongue kiss," Carmen claimed. "Neither the President nor the Attorney General seemed embarrassed. Of course, Bobby and I had been intimate, so I didn't expect him to turn red faced. I guess Jack Kennedy, considering his lifestyle, was beyond mere embarrassment at that point in his life."

She claimed that the brothers didn't stay long, and that both of them left very soon afterwards, with Marilyn in the car's back seat. She apparently never confided to Carmen any of the details about where she was taken that night. Charles (Chuck) Spalding later revealed that JFK had told him that Marilyn was taken to the private villa of a friend of his in Bel Air. Teddy Kennedy arrived later. "Marilyn got to sample not only Jack's charms but Teddy's and Bobby's that night. Of course, as president, JFK was first in line." At least that is what Spalding claimed that JFK had revealed to him.

If this testimony is true, it means that Marilyn and the Kennedy brothers were repeating the theme of their orgy at the Carlyle Hotel in New York, details of which were revealed in those F.B.I. files.

Rumors still persist that Marilyn checked into Southern California's Cedars of Lebanon Hospital under an assumed name to have President Kennedy's child aborted. Others insist that it was Bobby's child. It has never been explained how Marilyn persuaded a doctor to perform an illegal abortion within a major U.S. hospital, when other movie stars were crossing the border into Mexico.

Never revealing the identity of the father, Marilyn claimed she had had a miscarriage. She told that to her publicist, Rupert Allen; her hairdresser Agnes Flanagan, and to a Laguna Beach realtor, Arthur James. She was considering at the time buying a house in Laguna Beach.

Marilyn's gynecologist, Dr. Leon ("Red") Korhn, denied any abortion stories, although he did say that Marilyn had become pregnant three times, losing each fetus in a miscarriage because of the massive amounts of drugs and liquor she shared with the unborn.

Considering the timing, chances are that if any of the Kennedy brothers had been the father, it would be Bobby and not JFK. Marilyn made a crude joke to Saltzer about "Bobby Baby-maker's big dick."

When Jackie learned the details of JFK's affair with Marilyn, she threatened to divorce him, which would have cost him the 1964 election, had he been alive to run for office.

According to Senator Smathers, the president told Jackie, "Look, it really is over. It was nothing anyway."

Jack told Smathers that his affair hadn't been worth it. "Jackie more or less gives me free rein around here, and I don't want to fuck this up. Let's face it; Marilyn's day has peaked in Hollywood. For these 36-year-old glamour gals, it's all downhill from there. I can live without Marilyn. In fact, she's become a god damn nuisance calling up all day. It's time for an *adios*."

There would be one more grand event incorporating the lives of Marilyn, Bobby, and JFK. It would eventually capture the imagination of the world and become part of the JFK/MM legend.

When Jackie learned that Marilyn had been invited to his birthday celebration, she said, "Screw Jack" and left the room. Then she packed to leave town, heading for Virginia.

On May 19, 1962 Marilyn ran away from the set of her film, *Something's Got to Give,* to sing for the president in New York City at a fund-raising birthday party at

Madison Square Garden. Peter Lawford was the Master of Ceremonies.

After Marilyn missed her first cue, Peter introduced her as "the late Marilyn Monroe," a word usage which would prove eerily prophetic.

She dazzled the world that night in her tight, glittering, almost transparent $12,000 Jean-Louis dress of "skin and beads." The flesh-colored dress had to be sewn on her. She didn't wear underwear, of course.

The president stared in fascination at Marilyn. "What an ass! Gene. What an ass!" That was JFK's comment to his writer Gene Schoor, who sat in the presidential box with him.

When JFK came onto stage, he joked with the audience, "Now I can retire from politics after having Happy Birthday sung to me in such a sweet, wholesome way."

After her appearance before the entire world, Marilyn retreated to her dressing room where she had to be cut out of her designer dress. After a bath, she headed for a party given by Arthur Krim, the theater magnate, president of United Artists.

Statesman/politico Adlai Stevenson was there. He later claimed, "I never got to dance with her. Bobby Kennedy put up strong defenses around her. He was dodging around her like a moth around the flame."

Dorothy Kilgallen reported in her column that Bobby danced with Marilyn five times. What she didn't report was that Ethel, in a far corner of the room, stood glaring at them with a bubbling fury about to spill over.

Before dawn of the next day, Marilyn was slipped into the Carlyle where she later told Peter, "I had sex in one bedroom with Jack, then I came to the other bedroom and took care of Bobby." This was the last time the president, as far as it is known, ever saw Marilyn again. Bobby still lay in her future, his exact role the subject of ferocious debate today.

JFK was seen leaving the Carlyle at around 6am the following morning. It would be the last time he ever saw the blonde goddess. Bobby left at ten o'clock that morning.

In a stern chastisement of her son, Rose Kennedy urged Bobby to drop Marilyn "and spare your family another disgrace."

Although the lid had been kept on them for years, by 1963, stories about JFK and Marilyn were about to break wide open in the press. JFK told Senator Smathers, "It's all become too public. I can't see her any more."

JFK even sent William Haddad, a former *New York Post* reporter working at the time for the Peace Corps, to the top editors at *Time* and *Newsweek*, cautioning them not to print news about his alleged affair with Marilyn. "It simply isn't true," Haddad claimed.

Peter Lawford later claimed that "Marilyn couldn't get it through her head that the party was over. I kept telling her that she didn't know Bobby and Jack like I did. When they're through with a woman, they're toast. She really knew that, but somehow couldn't bring herself to admit it. She wrote constant letters to Jack at the White House, begging him to take her back. At one point, she was so bitter she told me that Jack made love like a thirteen-year-old boy. When she wouldn't let up, Jack sent Bobby out here to cool her down."

Like Jack, Bobby believed that his romance with Marilyn was becoming high profile, and he, too, retreated from her. He also claimed that she was consistently reckless because of her high consumption of alcohol and drugs. "Bobby is moving on from me the way Jack did," Marilyn told Peter. "The Kennedy brothers…they treat women like that. They use you, then they dispose of you like so much rubbish."

She also confided to Jeanne Carmen that she exempted Teddy from that charge. "He truly loves me, and wants to be with me anytime I'm willing. I let him do it because he loves it so much, but I'm not in love with Teddy. What I really want is for Jack and Bobby to make love to me at the same time. At the Carlyle one night, they both made love to me but not in the same bed at the same time."

In California, Bobby delivered the news to Marilyn in person. She was not to see Jack or him again. Nor was she to place any more calls to the White House or the Justice Department.

In hysterics, she began to scream after hearing this ultimatum from Bobby himself. He tried to comfort her. When a man went to comfort Marilyn, that meant only one thing, sex. At least for a moment, he was overcome by her seductive charms.

But by the following morning, a clearer head would emerge on Bobby. Holding onto power, both for himself and his brother, was far more important to Bobby than bedding an aging sex symbol.

Marilyn refused to obey Bobby's ultimatum and continued to call both Jack and Bobby in Washington.

"Jack was the first to refuse my calls to the White House," Marilyn told Jeanne Carmen. "And now Bobby won't speak to me at the Justice Department either. But Teddy is in touch with me. He still loves me and we're going to get together soon. I don't love Teddy, but I'm in love with the idea that one of the Kennedy brothers still worships me, unlike those older meanies."

"I've already sent word to both Jack and Bobby that I'm going to call a press conference and reveal everything about our relationships," Marilyn said. "But because of Teddy I will probably not do that. Peter Lawford is dead set against it too."

"Monroe could not accept that her affair with Bobby was over," said author Lucy Freeman, who interviewed Monroe's psychiatrist on several occasions. "Bobby's rejection reawakened her father's complete abandonment of her. Because of her father's early desertion, she created the sex goddess, the one that no man could possibly abandon."

RFK called Peter Lawford. The two men had never liked each other. The Attorney General ordered Peter to "cut Marilyn off from all contact with the First Family—see to that." Then he abruptly hung up the phone, offending Peter.

Not only had JFK and RFK abandoned her, but on June 2, 1962, her studio fired her. Fox press agents were instructed to launch a negative publicity blitz, defining their former star as mentally ill.

Bobby would be forced to make one final visit to Marilyn's home in an effort to contain her and keep her from going public about her affairs with the Kennedy men. Of course, as the world knows, Marilyn never activated that threat. She was found dead on August 5, 1962, before she could make good on her promise.

Langdon Marvin, a Kennedy aide, remembered being called to RFK's Hickory Hill estate in Virginia during January of 1964. There his boss handed him a dozen or so letters, ordering him to "get rid of them—burn them."

Marvin did as he was told, and shredded each of the letters. Later he learned from RFK they were "love missives" to both JFK and RFK from Marilyn herself. "I should have saved them. If genuine, they would be worth a fortune if sold today to collectors."

Director George Cukor later said, "Marilyn was not a lady who would have taken aging well. Her forties would have been a horror for her. She didn't have the integrity of a true actress—she would not have welcomed the richness of character interpretations, as a true actress would have. She was a star trading on certain gimmicks, and in her heart she knew that."

WHO MURDERED MARILYN MONROE?

On the day she died, author and journalist Darwin Porter began gathering evidence, focusing on tantalizing details about her mysterious demise.

Over the decades, at least 650 "people of interest" were interviewed. There was a massive cover-up, and an extraordinary number of people seemed to have been included in its deceit.

Hopefully, the results, available in time for the 50th anniversary of Marilyn's death, will help to have solved a half-century of speculation.

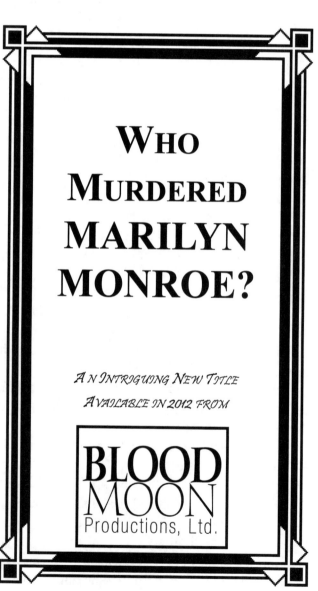

WHO MURDERED MARILYN MONROE?

AN INTRIGUING NEW TITLE
AVAILABLE IN 2012 FROM

BLOOD MOON
Productions, Ltd.

MM and Shelley Winters

Sexual Politics from Roommates Who Swing

Two blonde bombshells, **Shelley Winters and Marilyn Monroe**, roomed together early in Marilyn's career. Shelley admitted that Marilyn was "great in the boudoir but lousy in the kitchen. I asked her to wash the lettuce for a salad, and she scrubbed each lettuce leaf with a Brillo pad."

Unlike Marilyn, Shelley took a keen interest in the civil rights movement. She supported the marches of Dr. Martin Luther King Jr., and campaigned for both Adlai Stevenson in 1956 and John F. Kennedy in 1960.

"Marilyn was fucking Kennedy, and I was trying to get him elected president," she said. She later claimed that Stevenson dated her just to neutralize all those rumors in 1956 that he was a homosexual when he ran the second time against Dwight D. Eisenhower.

The two-time presidential loser also dated Joan Fontaine, but decided that neither Shelley nor Joan "would be suitable as a First Lady."

MARILYN & SHELLEY: IN PURSUIT OF PRESIDENTS

Shelley Winters might have been opting for the gun owner's vote when she posed for this picture in the film *Bloody Mama* (1970). She played Ma Barker who robs a bank with her four beloved sons.

When Adlai Stevenson campaigned for the presidency in 1956, she was not only sleeping with him but giving him advice.

"Adlai," she said. "Remember that not all of your audience went to Harvard,"

"Shelley," he responded. "Not all of these ladies went to the Actors Studio."

In the late 1940s, when she was still a struggling young actress, Shelley Winters shared lodgings in Los Angeles with Marilyn Monroe. Rumors still persist that on the rare nights they didn't find a date, they took care of each other's needs. A two-time Oscar winner, Winters is as famous for her movie roles as she is for the men she bedded, including such heavily hung guys as John Ireland, Howard Hughes, Errol Flynn, and Sterling Hayden, as well as the more modestly endowed—Burt Lancaster, Clark Gable, and Marlon Brando.

Sean Connery was one of her all-time favorite lays. "He makes a woman feel sexual chemistry," she said of him. "To be his leading lady today, I'd lose 50 pounds and get my face lifted. As a matter of fact, I'd get everything lifted." Winters became known for being outspoken and occasionally abrasive. "I desperately needed to get fucked," she once told her director when she flew cross country one weekend while she was on location for a film. Why she couldn't get laid on the West Coast remains a mystery. Where was her lover, Anthony Quinn?

Frank Sinatra called her a "bowlegged bitch of a Brooklyn blonde," and women have had other, sometimes even pithier, comments. Marlene Dietrich, referring to Winters' weight gain in later life, said, "It is surprising what some people will let happen to themselves. Shelley Winters is a prime example."

Winters and Monroe remained "best gal pals" for life. In 1955, Winters told Monroe, "I'm fucking Adlai Stevenson, and he's going to become President of the United States, beating the hell out of Ike."

A few months later Monroe told Winters, "I'm fucking Senator John F. Kennedy, and he told me that by no later than 1960 he was going to become the president of the United States, not your friend Adlai. He's also prettier than Adlai."

"Bullshit!" Winters replied. "If Kennedy ever becomes president, I'll spend three hours a day eating out your asshole."

It is not known if Monroe ever held Winters to that promise.

Marilyn Monroe's Topless Negotiations
For an RFK Film That Was Never Made

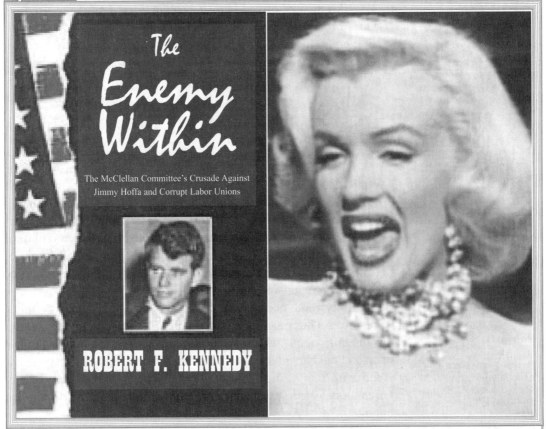

The McClellan Committee's Crusade Against Jimmy Hoffa and Corrupt Labor Unions

ROBERT F. KENNEDY

It is highly doubtful that Attorney General Robert F. Kennedy ever intended a movie role for Marilyn in the screen version of the political exposé he wrote entitled *The Enemy Within*. It may have been merely a seductive tool he used to manipulate her.

Bobby's book, originally published in 1960, offered an insider's peek into his efforts to regulate corrupt labor unions. As such, Bobby found himself in a well-publicized feud with labor boss Jimmy Hoffa. Bobby's exposé also provided a detailed account of the workings of the McClellan Committee, whose self-defined mission involved the cleanup of the country's labor unions.

According to Marilyn, Bobby described Hoffa's reaction to news that JFK had been assassinated. "That's great!" Hoffa said. "Now we have the biggest crook in America in the White House." He was referring, of course, to Lyndon B. Johnson.

Previously, Paul Newman had been considered as the star who would portray JFK in the screen version of *PT 109*, but that didn't work out. Subsequently, Bobby wanted Newman to play himself in the screen version of *The Enemy Within*.

Later, Newman quipped, "I think Marilyn and I should have done *Bus Stop*--not this labor union shit."

Above (right photo) is Marilyn as she appeared in *Gentlemen Prefer Blondes (1953)*, proclaiming that, indeed, "Diamonds Are a Girl's Best Friend."

DEFINING THE ENEMY WITHIN

"Marilyn was obsessed with becoming First Lady. She used to dance around the house like a belly dancer, singing, 'First Lady, First Lady.' Maybe First Lady with Jack or First Lady with Bobby. It didn't matter. She craved power she could not get just being a movie star."

—Jeanne Carmen

About three weeks before her death on August 5, 1962, Paul Newman, as he appeared in his movie *Hud* (released in 1963, the year of JFK's death) received an urgent call from Marilyn Monroe, who wanted to meet with him privately at the Chateau Marmont in Hollywood.

Rushing to her side, he encountered an unkempt Marilyn wearing no makeup and looking her worst after a sleepless night. He'd never known her to show such self-pity. She was lashing out at Hollywood and all the people who'd used her, especially the Kennedy brothers.

"They won't return my calls," she told him. "I guess I turned out to be just another piece of ass to them. What a fool I was. At one point in my relationship with each of them, I actually believed their promises about leaving their wives for me. First, the bullshit from Jack, then the same bullshit from Bobby. Jack will have to stay married to Jackie for the rest of his life. Bobby will go back to Ethel and have even more brats."

Published early in 1960, shortly after the election of JFK to the White House, *The Enemy Within,* authored by the president's brother, attorney general Robert F. Kennedy, rose almost immediately to the ranks of the New York Times bestseller list. The attorney general donated the royalties it generated to retarded children.

The volume's title was meant to place the internal threat of crime and corruption on par with the ongoing and eternal menace of world communism.

Hollywood became interested in acquiring the film rights. There was a buzz as to who would play RFK on the screen, similar to the buzz about who would play JFK in *PT 109.* About the last person Paul Newman expected to hear from in any capacity associated with this grim political film was Marilyn Monroe. But her breathless voice was instantly recognizable as it came over the phone.

Paul Newman hadn't heard from her since he'd seen her in Las Vegas, although Hollywood was buzzing with rumors of her involvements with Kennedy brothers, Jack and Robert. There was the hint of secrecy in her voice. She claimed that she was calling from a "secure" phone, as her own residence had been bugged.

"Paulie," she said, "I've missed you. Have you also missed your baby?"

"Of course, I have," he said. "Anyone who has been with you will miss you forever."

"You're so sweet, the sweetest lover I've ever had. Joe is so brutal and Arthur so cold."

She was, of course, referring to husbands Joe DiMaggio and Arthur Miller. He didn't dare ask her about the Kennedys.

She told him that she couldn't talk long on the phone, but that she wanted to meet him the following afternoon at a mansion in Beverly Hills. She claimed she was hiding out there, running from the mob. He was completely baffled as to her link with the mob. But he agreed to meet her at the appointed time.

"Tell no one about our getting together," she said, "especially your wife. I've learned the less wives know about their husband's affairs, the better."

Arriving at a mansion owned by God knows who, Newman was ushered in by a black maid and out onto a patio where Marilyn in a white bikini awaited him. She jumped up and ran toward him, giving him a sloppy wet kiss.

Over lunch, where she nibbled and Newman ate lustily, she delivered a highly edited version of what was going on in her life.

"Bobby wants you to play him in a movie based on his book, *The Enemy Within*."

Newman just assumed that Bobby referred to Robert Kennedy, the Attorney General of the United States.

"It's about Jimmy Hoffa and the mob," she said. "Bobby wanted me to contact you because he wants you to star in it."

"I'd be honored," Newman said. "I'd like to meet with him to discuss it."

"That's not possible right now," she said. "We have to be careful. People are spying on us, watching our every move. Jerry Wald [a well-known Hollywood film producer] is negotiating with Bobby for the screen rights. I want to co-star in the movie with you."

"I haven't read the book yet," he said. "Is there a strong woman's role? Sounds like a man's picture to me."

"There isn't a strong woman's part as of yet, but Jerry has promised to write in a role for me. Bobby has agreed. I want to play a tough prosecutor in a business suit who, arm in arm, works with Bobby to bring Hoffa to justice. With me in the picture and with you as Bobby, we can virtually guarantee box office. Besides, I'm tired of those dumb blonde movies. I want to sink my beautiful teeth into a strong, hard political drama like Frankie did." She was no doubt referring to Frank Sinatra's appearance in *The Manchurian Candidate*, an upcoming release she'd seen at a special screening in Las Vegas.

At one point, Marilyn ordered the maid to bring her guest a bikini. "Make it as revealing as possible," she instructed her maid right in front of Newman.

Before the afternoon ended, Jerry Wald arrived on the scene and was ushered into the pool area. "I spotted Marilyn, topless, at the far end of the pool," he later said. "She was making out with a man in a white bathing suit. I thought at first that it was Bobby Kennedy. After all, we were here to discuss *The Enemy Within*. I cleared my throat and moved closer. The man rose to his feet. I was stunned. It was Paul Newman. I'd wanted to meet with him to discuss his starring in the picture."

Marilyn hardly needed to introduce Wald to Newman, as he was already well known to both the Newmans. Newman only hoped that Wald would be discreet about his obvious intimacy with Marilyn the next time he encountered Joanne Woodward.

Wald had already produced *No Down Payment* and *The Sound and the Fury,* both of which had featured Woodward, as well as *The Long, Hot Summer*, which had featured her husband, Paul Newman. And in a touch of irony, he was about to produce *Hemingway's Adventures of a Young Man*, in which he'd cast Newman, and also *The Stripper*, a film in which he'd cast Woodward.

Wald had been long familiar with Marilyn as well, having produced her *Clash by Night* (1952) with Barbara Stanwyck and *Let's Make Love* (1960).

Wald later claimed that throughout the duration of their dialogue, Marilyn remained almost defiantly topless, in spite of his presence. "It was very distracting trying to talk to Paul with

Jeanne Carmen, Marilyn's closest friend and confidante, always said that "To Jack, Marilyn was just another fuck. One night, when Marilyn wasn't up to it, she sent me to Jack's suite and I serviced him."

"He wasn't very good in bed," Carmen continued. "He was a two-minute man. I had Bobby, too, and he was better in bed, with a much larger penis. I think Bobby fell in love with Marilyn. That was too bad. No good would come out of that affair. Look what happened."

According to Carmen, "The biggest explosion came when Bobby discovered that Marilyn was keeping a diary of her involvement with both of them. 'Get rid of the god damn thing,' he shouted at her. 'You could bring down a government.'"

Marilyn's breasts exposed," Wald later recalled. "When she got up to go upstairs to get dressed, I quizzed Paul about everything that had happened before I got there. He'd confided in me before. He gave me a complete account, but was puzzled about how I was going to create a strong role for Marilyn in a movie devoted to Bobby and the mob. 'Who is Marilyn going to play?' Paul asked me. 'Jimmy Hoffa?'"

"Scriptwriters can work wonders," Wald assured him. "Besides, Bobby demands that we create a role in the movie for Marilyn. He owes her a favor or two."

"I can well imagine," Newman said.

Wald later discussed privately with friends why *The Enemy Within* was never made. The studio, 20th Century Fox, began to receive death threats, no doubt from some shady members of the Teamsters' Union. Wald claimed that he was warned that if the movie were made, "It'll be your last picture." The producer also asserted that he was told that movie houses showing the film would be bombed.

"Marilyn and Paul also received death threats," Wald said. "Marilyn had many reasons to fear the mob—but that's a story for another day—and *The Enemy Within* loomed as another nail in her coffin."

"That role for Marilyn never got written," Wald said. "It was just as well. With her in the picture in a totally made-up part, it would have thrown off the focus of the film anyway. Her relationship with Bobby was deteriorating rapidly. Also, Paul pulled the plug. He was very concerned with those death threats, and was very anxious that no harm come to his family. The final blow came when he read the first draft of the film script and rejected it. He called it a piece of shit. I don't know why he was so violent in his objection. He'd made shit before."

Pierre Salinger, the press secretary at JFK's White House, privately told friends that "Bobby was furious when Newman rejected the role to play him in *The Enemy Within*. And Bobby was a guy to hold a grudge. He even sent Paul a note under the letterhead of the Attorney General. It was short, but not sweet. FUCK OFF!!!"

Wald said that after Newman walked off the picture, he turned to a rising young actor, Jack Nicholson. "With makeup, Jack could be made into a more convincing version of Bobby Kennedy than Paul ever could."

But like so many other projects in Hollywood, the film died a slow death. It just drifted into oblivion. Everybody—Newman, Marilyn, Bobby—was caught up in different agendas. And each of their lives was changing, quickly and dramatically.

Wald's own life was also about to change for all time. He died in the summer of 1962.

JFK's Affair with Janet Leigh

Extending His Campaign Trail
into Her Bedroom

Associated Press

One of JFK's most effective campaigners, and one of his favorite bedmates, was actress Janet Leigh, wife of film star Tony Curits. They reigned in the early 1950s as "America's Sweethearts."

Eventually, Tony discovered that his wife was sleeping with the presidential frontrunner. Tony couldn't afford to point fingers, since he was sleeping with practically every attractive female and/or male on the block. He was a famous womanizer and a closeted homosexual. Allegedly, Tony told Janet, "Tell Jack he can fuck me any night he wants—just give him my number."

Janet can be seen in the larger of the two photos above on the far left at the East Angeles Junior College Football Stadium on November 1, 1960, at a rally for the presidential candidate. From left to right are **Janet herself, singer Jo Stafford, Louis Prima, Milton Berle, and Stan Froberg.** The 22,000-seat stadium was packed, with the police holding off some 15,000 fans outside the gates.

In the inset photo, Janet appears in her most memorable screen role, as the victim in Alfred Hitchcock's 1960 suspense thriller, *Psycho.*

"NO ONE WAS SAFE FROM JFK— NOT YOUR WIFE, YOUR SISTER, OR YOUR MOTHER"

Senator George Smathers

Tony Curtis and Janet Leigh had a more or less open marriage, meaning that each of them played around during their joint reign as "America's Sweethearts." Gossip maven Louella Parsons claimed, "They were fearfully ambitious kids, so determined to make it, they were tiresome."

Janet is still remembered, even among younger fans, for the bit part she played in that shower scene in Alfred Hitchcock's *Psycho* (1960).

Janet was pursued by Howard Hughes and tried to keep him at bay. But when she got that call from Senator Kennedy, she came running.

"I always wanted to bed a president of the United States," she told Tony. "Eisenhower and Truman weren't my type, although I would have liked to have gone to bed with Marlon Brando and Cary Grant. But you stole them for yourself, you dirty, stingy dog."

Actor Robert Stack had become a close friend of John F. Kennedy right before America's entry into World War II. The actor also became intimately involved with Paul Newman. Both men were bisexuals and had spent a number of weekends together at Stack's house in Palm Springs. When Stack and Newman got together, they often talked about politics.

Stack predicted that JFK would be president one day. "Would you like to meet him?" Stack asked Newman. "He flies into town every now and then. I arrange dates for him with beautiful actresses. All he has to do is look at a gal, and she tumbles into his bed."

"Sounds like my kind of guy," Newman said. "Mainly I'd like to screw his wife. That is one hot woman. I'd marry her if she'd propose to me, or else let me be her lover. With her husband screwing around so much, she's probably lonely on many a night."

"I saw Jackie before you did," Stack said. "I'm first in line."

Newman got his chance to meet JFK when he was running for president in 1960. Invited again to Palm Springs by Stack, Newman was going to stay in his villa there.

When Newman arrived, Stack was very excited. "He's here! He's in the back room entertaining a visitor."

"Exactly who is here?" Newman asked.

"My buddy Jack Kennedy," Stack said. "He's in the guest room with one of my favorite gals. She's married. He's married. You're married. What does a wedding ring mean in Hollywood anyway?"

"A wedding ring is just a license to screw around and make a hasty retreat, claiming you're a married man," Newman said.

"You've got that right, baby," Stack said. "Now gimme a kiss before my guests emerge from the den."

In bathing suits, Newman and Stack were having a beer when JFK emerged from the back bedroom. He was fully dressed in a suit and tie. All smiles, he shook Newman's hand firmly, as he was introduced. He glanced nervously at his watch. "I'd like to sit and chat," Kennedy said, "but I'm very late as it is. "Great meeting you. Give me a rain check. I'd like to get together with you sometime."

Newman assured JFK he'd be eager for that to happen, and told him he'd been rooting for him since 1956 when he'd sought the vice presidential nomination, losing to Estes Kefauver, a liberal Democrat from Tennessee.

"My Boston accent worked against me," JFK said. "America preferred a redneck in a coonskin cap."

An aide arrived to tell Kennedy that he had to leave at once for the airport. He thanked Stack for his hospitality, and seemed to disappear almost as quickly as he'd entered the pool area.

"So who's the babe he shacked up with?" Newman asked. It was an hour later before the question was answered. Emerging from the bedroom was Janet Leigh (Mrs. Tony Curtis) dressed in a conservative business suit.

She seemed in a bit of a rush, but she was warm and gracious to Newman. "Maybe we'll make a movie together one day, sweetie," she said, leaning over to give him an air brush kiss on the cheek." Their co-starring roles in *Harper*—a movie representing the full flower of Newman's anti-hero hero phase and released in 1966—still lay in their futures.

During her brief poolside chat with Stack and Newman, Leigh made it clear that she was in Palm Springs drumming up grassroots support for JFK. She claimed that she'd fallen in love with him when he'd appeared at the 1956 Democratic Party Convention in Chicago. "I was so disappointed when he lost to Kefauver. But all of us, including Pat and Peter, swear that it will be the last election he ever loses." She was referring to her friends, Patricia Kennedy, JFK's sister, and her husband at the time, Peter Lawford.

Then Leigh announced that she had to leave, but before her departure, she secured promises from both Stack and Newman that she could count on them for generous contributions when Kennedy actually announced his bid for the presidency.

After she'd gone, Stack asked Newman, "Do

Starlet **Janet Leigh** first attracted JFK's attention in 1948 when she was voted "No. 1 Glamour Girl of Hollywood."

Tinseltown weaves a tangled sexual web:

Janet, above, had already seduced gangster Johnny Stompanato and Lex ("Tarzan") Barker. She had also seduced JFK and the president's brother-in-law, Peter Lawford, who one night managed to fellate JFK. Peter had already been intimate with Marilyn—"bad hygiene."

Included within yet another sexual link, Janet seduced Frank Sinatra during the time they spent together making *The Manchurian Candidate* (1962).

Sinatra seduced Marilyn Monroe and Judith Campbell Exner, who, in turn, seduced the president.

Janet also seduced Stewart Granger when they shot *Scaramouche* (1952). He in turn seduced Deborah Kerr who seduced Joseph P. Kennedy Jr.

With the Kennedys, we could play this game all night.

you think he has a chance?"

"No," Newman said. "He's too sophisticated, too young, and too urbane. And, from what I hear, too prone to scandal. Besides, his old man carries too much baggage. Not only that, he's a Catholic. America hasn't grown up enough to elect a Catholic president. But I liked him. I'll support him if he makes the run. Mostly I'd like to meet Jacqueline Kennedy. If I had a woman like that at home, I wouldn't be leaving her while I chased Janet Leigh. Even Joan Crawford and Lana Turner have told me they've had affairs with him. What's his game plan? To seduce every major star in Hollywood?"

"He could if he wanted to," Robert said. "I've pimped for him. There's not an actress yet who's turned him down."

"What's he got that we don't have?"

"It's not dick size, I can assure you," Stack said. "It's personal charm and magnetism. The ladies lap it up.

In her memoirs, *There Really Was a Hollywood,* Janet wrote that when she first met JFK, "I had found my sun. I believed in that man. Once I was committed, I didn't do things by halves—it was gung ho!" She recalled that she, along with Sinatra, Peter Lawford, and her husband, Tony, spoke for Senator Kenneday at a 1960 rally in "Frank's stamping ground," New Jersey.

When JFK later invited her to his suite for a political huddle, she thought it was to talk about the campaign. As she later told Lana Turner and Ava Gardner, "He seduced me that night, and I was raring to go. Ava and Lana told me that they'd already had Jack, and I didn't want to be left out."

Both **Robert Stack and Paul Newman** were seduced by **Judy Garland**. Robert had met her when he first came to Hollywood. Newman met Judy when she was hoping to appear opposite him in *The Helen Morgan Story* (1957). The deal fell through, and eventually, the role of the girl singer in that film went to Ann Blyth.

When his pal, JFK, arrived in Hollywood for a visit in 1940, Robert invited him along with Judy to the Cocoanut Grove Night Club in Los Angeles, which at the time was the hottest spot to be after dark. Robert later said, "I should have warned Jack about Judy's habit on the dance floor." She had a peculiarity that was described within the memoirs of more than one male star.

On the dance floor, Judy pressed her body tightly into JFK's. He suddenly was aware that she was unzipping his pants. Later, he told Robert, "I got an erection right away. She really checked out the Kennedy family jewels."

Robert cautioned JFK, "Don't be too flattered. She's done that to many a good-looking guy, especially me."

Jack told him, "Not that I'm bragging, but Marlene Dietrich on the French Riviera once did the same thing to me."

Jackie Vs. Screw Magazine

Al Goldstein, the Prince of Porn, and the Flash from the Flashing of

JACKIE'S BUSH

Associated Press

Al Goldstein, publisher of the notorious *Screw* magazine, displays his favorite reading material, *How to Talk Dirty and Influence People*, by Lenny Bruce. He displayed the book upon leaving the federal courthouse in Kansas City on October 25, 1977. He was being tried for distributing alleged obscene materials in the mail.

Goldstein launched *Screw* during the sexual revolution of the late 1960s. He became the first editor to review porn films and to "test drive" sex aides. He was also the first to interview porn stars, and once received a blow-job from Linda Lovelace, star of *Deep Throat*, the highest grossing porn film of all time.

What would have become the obscenity legal battle of the century, *Jacqueline Onassis vs. Goldstein*, never happened. When *Screw* published those nude photographs of Jackie, she wanted to sue, but Ari Onassis talked her out of it. Years later, the real reason he didn't want such a law suit to go forward was discovered.

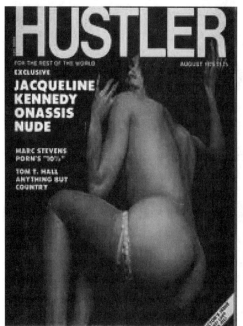

Thanks to Larry Flynt's *Hustler* magazine and Al Goldstein's *Screw*, nude pictures of Jackie, taken illegally on the Greek island of Skorpios, became the most celebrated nude photographs of all time, rivaled only by those of Marilyn Monroe.

MM and Jackie had something in common: They were both lovers of John F. Kennedy.

Admittedly, Jackie's rail-thin body didn't stack up favorably when compared to the voluptuousness of the film goddess.

But nonetheless, much of the world wanted to see Jackie in revealing close-up, perhaps to learn what turned on such men as the Kennedy brothers, Marlon Brando, Frank Sinatra, and even the gay ballet dancer, Rudolf Nureyev.

THE BILLION-DOLLAR BUSH

Al Goldstein, the founder of the notorious *Screw* magazine in the 1960s, became a legend on the streets of New York. Once he enjoyed a great fortune but, in a self-admission, he "cannibalized" it and ended up a full year living homeless on the streets.

During his 34-year tenure as publisher of *Screw*, he faced a constant barrage of legal attacks. In the meantime, he went through four marriages, endured two dozen arrests, and survived death threats and Mafia hit contracts. Today he is living quietly on Staten Island, surviving on his memories and very little money.

Back during his heyday, in March of 1962, he accompanied First Lady Jacqueline Kennedy as a photographer during her Goodwill Tour of Pakistan.

He admitted that "she never had diarrhea like the rest of us. That's because she only drank water flown in from the United States. At the Khyber Pass, I wanted to patriotically quaff her bush, but these feelings remained deep down and far removed from my professional demeanor."

He didn't get Jackie, but the Pakistani government was generous enough to supply hookers to all male members of the press corp. He found the girls beautiful "but very conservative. They didn't like having their Islamic pussies eaten."

As for Jackie, Goldstein settled for "jacking off" over a picture he'd taken of her.

In 1973, Goldstein forked over $10,000 to an Italian magazine called *Playmen* for full frontal nudes of Jackie. They had been snapped through an extra-long telephoto lens on the island of Skorpios. He ran them under the headline JACKIE KENNEDY'S BILLION DOLLAR BUSH.

Selling for 75 cents each, *Screw* sold 530,000 copies, a record for the underground paper. The pictures also were published in *Screw*'s calendar for that year. Six months later, Jackie graced the pages of *Hustler*.

Jackie, as reported by Broadway columnist Leonard Lyons, writing for the *New York Post*, wanted to sue Goldstein, but Aristotle Onassis urged her not to. "You don't get in a pissing contest with a skunk. Don't do a thing."

Dean Latimer, a satirist for *Screw*, wrote a fantasy piece in 1977 entitled "If Jackie Worked for Screw."

Subsequent to its publication, Goldstein wrote, "If only it were true. Jackie followed me to editorial meetings, took dictation, and when she farted I levitated in rapturous ecstasy, the aroma wafting into my nostrils."

On their private island of Skorpios, Aristotle Onassis and his bride, Jackie Kennedy, were not shy about sunning themselves in the nude. Neither had been Jackie's first husband, the President of the United States.

During the late 1960s, in Paris, Ari was interviewed by a reporter-photographer at the Crazy Horse Saloon, the city's most famous strip joint.

The reporter asked him to name some of the most famous women he'd ever seduced. Ari rattled off references to Doris Duke, Paulette Goddard, Veronica Lake, and Lee Radziwill.

"I missed out on Greta Garbo, although I came on to her," Ari said. "The sexy Swede told me, 'Go to sleep, Ari.'"

"I also missed out on Marilyn Monroe, but I almost got her," Ari claimed. "One afternoon I spent at the palace with Prince Rainier of Monaco. He was looking for a wife who would bring great publicity to Monaco to increase tourism and development. I suggested Marilyn Monroe. I even offered to bring Marilyn over from the States on my yacht. I figured during the sail, I'd get the bitch. But my plan fell through. Grace Kelly, of course, got him instead."

The reporter then asked him to define the secret of his success. Ari invited him to the men's room. Once there, he dropped his trousers and lowered his underwear. In front of the reporter, he hoisted a big set of testicles and an ample penis. "Here's my secret," he said, "as you can plainly see, I've got balls."

Al Goldstein's notorious autobiography, *I, Goldstein*, written with Josh Alan Friedman, captures the tumultuous life of the publisher who in the late 60s blazed a path to sexual freedom.

Through it all he survived constant arrests, four ex-wives who were drawn to his seven inches, Mafia hit contracts, thousands of death threats, and even Jackie Kennedy herself.

The ribald book even reveals what Goldstein would have done with the hot air emanating from Jackie.

Ari was an exhibitionist, as was President Kennedy, who didn't mind flashing the family jewels at those nude swimming parties at the White House. Even JFK Jr. became an exhibitionist, often showing "a larger endowment than that of Brown University," said a male classmate.

Jackie did not believe in disrobing in front of a camera. "Don't confuse me with Madonna," she once said.

The story of how those nude pictures of her became a worldwide sensation took years to be revealed.

Ari had begun to tire of Jackie's profligate spending and her constant complaints about the paparazzi, and he decided to teach her a lesson. He plotted with a group of paparazzi to take pictures of Jackie one afternoon when she was sunbathing nude on Skorpios. The photographers had to fit themselves with diving outfits and use waterproof cameras and telephoto lenses.

The end result was a twenty-page feature called "The Billion Dollar Bush," appearing in *Playmen* magazine in Rome.

It was these photographs that *Screw* magazine purchased to run in New York.

SMASH HIS CAMERA

MAGNOLIA PICTURES and GOT THE SHOT PRODUCTIONS present "SMASH HIS CAMERA"
original music by CRAIG HAZEN and DAVID WULFERT cinematography by DON LENZER creative consultant ROGER ROSENBLATT edited by DOUG ABEL
executive producers JEFFREY TARRANT WILLIAM ACKMAN DANIEL STERN produced by ADAM SCHLESINGER and LINDA SAFFIRE directed by LEON GAST
magnolia

On July 30, 2010, HBO officially released its documentary, *Smash His Camera,* the story of Ron Galella, the infamous photographer. The poster *(see above)* for the film featured perhaps the best-known shot the photographer ever took of Jackie, snapped on a Manhattan sidewalk.

Smash His Camera was the creation of Leon Gast, the Oscar-winning director known for his film *When We Were Kings.*

Galella, of course, is called "the Godfather of U.S. paparazzi culture" and "Paparazzo Extraordinaire." He is without a doubt the most controversial celebrity photographer in the world, best known for his obsessive pursuit of Jackie Kennedy and his subsequent legal battles with her. In a 1972 "free-speech" trial, *Galella vs. Onassis,* she obtained a restraining order to keep Galella 150 feet away from her and her children.

He also has had run-ins with dozens of other celebrities. The reclusive actor Marlon Brando, Jackie's former lover, punched Galella without warning outside a restaurant in New York City's Chinatown, breaking his jaw and knocking out five of his teeth.

Galella was always known for taking risks and for eventually getting "the perfect shot."

Later, Larry Flynt of *Hustler* also bought them. It is estimated that before the feature ran its course, nude photographs of Jackie appeared in 210 tabloids around the world from Canada to Japan, from the Soviet Union to Brazil.

Jackie wanted to sue "every single tabloid who ran the picture," but there were far too many of them.

Rose Kennedy called her from Hyannis Port. "I thought you told me that Onassis was going to provide security for you. Some security!" Jackie's own mother, Janet Auchincloss also phoned with a point of view. "What is happening to the world? Now we have the dirty paparazzi going under water to spy on you. The dirty sneaks. Onassis should have all of them thrown in jail."

When Jackie returned to New York, she encountered the most widely read economist in the United States, the always-pithy John Kenneth Galbraith, at a cocktail party. "I didn't recognize you with your clothes on," he quipped.

Although in this instance, Ari had cooperated with paparazzi who wanted to photograph his wife in the nude, he was not always so cooperative with photographers.

One of his more complicated relationships was with Athens-based Nikos Koulouris, the most aggressive of the *paparazzi* who had spent time and trouble scoping out the photo-ops on Skorpios.

Perhaps as a means of showing solidary with Jackie's complaints about privacy invasions, Ari had listened and eventually reacted to her many complaints about Koularis, and one day decided that he had gone too far. Once, during her crew's attempt to

Paparazzo Ron Galella, then and now

maneuver her boat to a safe dockage on Skorpios, Koulouris had roared his motorboat dangerously close to Jackie's landing route and yelled violent insults at her, hoping to provoke a hostile (and photographable) reaction.

"I am scared of this man. He is dangerous. He could have killed my son and myself," she later raged.

Using his influence with the Greek judicial system, Ari arranged to have Koulouris brought to trial in Athens, where the photographer was found guilty of endangering Jackie and sentenced to six months in prison for taking the resultant photographs of JFK Jr. and herself. During the trial, it was revealed that Koulouris had pelted John-John with stones, hoping that he could get pictures of the boy hurling stones back at him.

During Koularis' trial, lawyers for Ari claimed (perhaps falsely) that their clients, Mr. and Mrs. Onassis, were thinking of abandoning Skorpios forever because Koulouris would not let them live there in peace. Ari's attorney also stated, in court, that Koulouris "has made the life of Mrs. Onassis unlivable."

***

Jackie, one of the most photographed women of her era, had always complained about the paparazzi snapping pictures of her. The real villain in her life was one photographer, Ron Galella, who seemed to wait for her every time she walked out her door. Although Onassis advised her not to, she pursued an aggressive legal vendetta against him.

Long after the assassination of JFK, **Jackie** (left) is seen with her mother-in-law, **Rose Kennedy**. Rose was very upset when nude pictures of Jackie were published and distributed around the world.

"You will look vindictive, very mean-spirited to your adoring public. After all, he's only trying to make a living."

Galella countersued Jackie, but Judge Irving Ben Cooper of the U.S. District Court agreed with the former First Lady that Galella was an annoying pest. The judge imposed a permanent injunction against the photographer, forbidding him from coming within 150 feet of Jackie, and within 225 feet of her children.

Gallela won an appeal to that decision, wherein a second judge from a higher court allowed him to come within, but not less than, 25 feet from Jackie and within no less than 30 feet from her children.

After the end of her legal battle, Jackie presented Ari with half a million dollars in legal fees. Through Roy Cohn, widely known in political circles as "the scariest lawyer in America" at the time, Ari negotiated the settlement done to $235,000.

Rose was no stranger to nudity: Once, when author Truman Capote was staying as the guest of a neighbor, in a house adjacent to the Kennedy compound in Palm Beach, Rose asked to use the pool, because her own pool was under repair.

According to Capote, "Here I was with four gay men enjoying a libation or two, and we look up and there is Rose Kennedy, jaybird naked, walking across the lawn toward the pool. We pretended not to notice, although she gave us a weak 'hi.'"

Rose and Jackie may have had their differences, but the First Lady respected the matriarch of the Kennedy clan.

"I lived with her through The Agony and the Ecstasy," Jackie recalled. "She was intensely ambitious for her family, and she gave birth to nine children. In most of them she instilled a vision of the American Dream."

Of course, dreams often become nightmares.

Galella didn't take defeat lying down. He published a best-selling book of Jackie photographs and also went on highly attended lecture tours throughout the country, lamenting Jackie's fall from grace. Ironically, Galella took credit, through his long term photographic obsession with her, for making Jackie the style icon that she eventually became. The *New York Post* once referred to it as "the most co-dependent celeb-paparazzi relationship ever."

Kitty Kelley, in her biography, *Jackie Oh!,* wrote, "All of Galella's 4,000 photographs of Jackie showed her looking exquisitely beautiful. Not one was unflattering. He never photographed her smoking or drinking, and always took his pictures in a bright light to camouflage her grey teeth and soften the wrinkles around her eyes. In one year, he made $15,000 selling Jackie photographs to national publications. These pictures he took by vaulting over hedges, leaping from behind coatracks, and following her to Capri, Naples, Skorpios, Peapack, Jersey, and Brooklyn Heights. Each picture showed an undisguised love of his subject."

Ari had no problem with nudity. One afternoon he ordered the *Christina* to the Italian island of Sardinia. He noticed a *paparazzo* who had positioned himself on a nearby beach, taking secret pictures of his passengers. Ari ordered a member of his crew to row him to the beach.

Once ashore, he dropped his bathing trunks and shouted to the photographer. "Now it's my turn!"

The photographer snapped Ari fully nude, and the picture appeared on the pages of a French-language tabloid, *France-Dimanche*. However, that publication's photo editor didn't fully expose a view of the aging tycoon's crotch. It was airbrushed to appear hidden within the shadow of a nearby tree.

Ari wasn't always so forgiving and cooperative with photographers. Once in 1972, while dining with Elizabeth Taylor in Rome, he tossed a glass of champagne in the face of a paparazzo who got too familiar.

In 2008, long after Jackie and Ari were dead, and simultaneous with the campaign of Barack Obama, Al Goldstein had the final word when he ran for President of the United States, hoping for the seat in the Oval Office once occupied by Jackie's husband. His platform was one of "pro-tit, pro-clit, pro-pot, pro-books, pro-thinking, anti-war."

As part of his campaign, he also expressed "a desire to eat scream queen Linnea Quigley's ass."

Elizabeth Taylor, pictured above at the Lido nightclub in Paris with Ari Onassis in December of 1964, nine months after the first of her two marriages to Richard Burton. Years later, Ari told her, "You're the woman I should have married instead of Jackie."

He was amused that Richard Burton, her husband, was trying to live like the richest man in the world, almost like a potentate.

"Throughout most of his life, Richard has been so very poor," Elizabeth told Ari. "That's why he's living so extravagantly and buying me diamonds the size of golf balls."

Later, aboard Ari's luxurious yacht, the *Christina,* Richard confided to Ari that he had recently spent $192,000 on his own yacht, *Kalimza.*

As a means of trivializing both Burton and his yacht, Ari said, "In my crowd, we'd call that a boat."   *(Associated Press)*

Jackie Goes Hollywood

With Warren Beatty

In some quarters, **Jacqueline Kennedy** was considered "The Most Desirable Woman in the World," and actor Warren Beatty was hailed as "The Sexiest Man Alive." Ironically, that same title would later be bestowed on her son, JFK Jr. Jackie, pictured above with a Connie Francis hairdo, seemed gleeful at encountering her favorite screen actor, Warren himself, even though their relationship got off to a rough start. According to rumors, Warren was a bit hard to get.

Of course, at the time, he had virtually every woman at his feet, with hordes of gay men left to dream about what might have been. The picture on the right has been hailed by some Warren aficionados as the sexiest he'd ever posed for, discounting a stray nude or two on the Internet. When Jackie saw *Bonnie and Clyde*, (1967), she was a bit dumbfounded. "There's no way in hell that Warren can be impotent," she told the gossipy Truman Capote and Lee Radziwill. "Some day I'll have to conduct my own personal investigation. Hopefully, neither of you will have beaten me to him."

Jackie's Crush On "The Sexiest Man Alive"

"Warren is a pussy, a wimp, but it's a perfectly wonderful size."

—Madonna

"Sex is his hobby, you could say,"
—Warren's sister, Shirley MacLaine

"He [Warren] is a masculine dumb blond"
—Actress Anouk Aimée

"God! I must be the only woman in Los Angeles or New York that Warren hasn't tried to schtup."

—Sue Mengers, Hollywood agent

"Three, four, five times a day, every day, was not unusual for him, and he was able to accept phone calls at the same time."

—Joan Collins

After her stunning, Oscar-winning performance in the Tennessee Williams drama, *A Streetcar Named Desire* (1951), Vivien Leigh decided once again to interpret one of the playwright's *grandes dames* on the screen. She agreed to star in *The Roman Spring of Mrs. Stone* (1961) cast (or was it miscast?) opposite Warren Beatty as the Italian gigolo. Vivien told her lover, Jack Merivale, "I think he's had some casting couch sessions with Tennessee."

The German actress and *chanteuse*, Lotte Lenya, befriended Vivien during the shoot, and became her *confidante*. "At first she disliked Beatty intensely, really didn't care for him at all, but he exerted a powerful charm and ended up seducing her."

Rumor had it that when then-First Lady Jackie saw Warren Beatty emote in *Splendor in the Grass* (1961), with Natalie Wood, she fell in love with him. *PT 109*, chronicling JFK's alleged WWII exploits, had not been cast, and Jackie suggested Warren. "He'd be perfect in the role—and, oh, so handsome."

JFK told her he'd already promised the role to Frank Sinatra. "Thank God I'm not in the movie," she said. "Sinatra would probably get that dreary Angie Dickinson to play me."

Even so, JFK was flattered to have the latest male sex symbol in the nation play him, so he sent his press secretary, Pierre Salinger, to Hollywood "to feel Beatty out."

Peter Lawford brought Salinger and Beatty together at his home. Salinger had heard reports that Beatty was "all mixed up."

"Quite the contrary," Salinger claimed. "I found him intelligent, very personable, and thought he'd photograph very handsomely as a young Navy lieutenant."

Near the conclusion of his talk with Beatty in Hollywood, Salinger thought it was a "done deal," that Beatty would definitely take the role of JFK in the movie. "Then he delivered a bombshell."

"I loathe Bryan Foy and under no circumstances can I work with him," Beatty claimed.

Salinger's heart sank. Foy happened to be the producer of *PT 109*.

Salinger brought the bad news back to Washington. Beatty wouldn't do the picture. Finally, JFK and Salinger suggested Cliff Robertson, who was then thirty-six years old.

Jackie was furious when she heard of this. "I don't know who in hell Robertson is, and I don't want to know. Invite Warren for dinner at the White House. I'll sit next to him. Before the evening is over, he'll definitely agree to play Jack. I can be very persuasive."

Amazingly, Warren refused to take any more calls from the White House.

Jack Warner, head of the studio set to release *PT 109*, wanted to cater to the wishes of the White House. He called Beatty and told him that JFK wanted him to fly to Washington "to soak up some atmosphere." Arrogantly, Beatty sent word back to the president. "Come to Los Angeles and soak up some atmosphere. We have a lot of hot babes here. I'll introduce you around."

Salinger couldn't reach Beatty, so Jackie said, "I'll have my social secretary put through a call to him. He'll definitely talk to me."

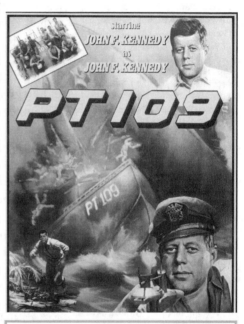

Beatty did not accept her call, which infuriated her. "The better looking they are, the more arrogant they are," she told her secretary. Even a personal handwritten note from Jackie on White House stationery went unanswered.

After *PT 109* starring Robertson opened and flopped, JFK encountered Beatty at a social gathering. "You sure made the right decision on that one," the president told the actor.

The aging Lothario didn't enter Jackie's life until the late 1970s when Beatty was no longer celebrating "The Sweet Bird of Youth."

At the time, the former First Lady had gone through two husbands and was working as an editor at Doubleday. She lived in a luxurious apartment on Fifth Avenue.

It was in this apartment, on December 20, 1978 that Jackie decided to invite a list of celebrities who included Andy Warhol and Bob Colacello of *Interview* magazine.

Warhol later claimed that "Jackie was mad as hell when Warren showed up with Diane Keaton on his arm. I suspect Jackie planned to seduce him that night, and Keaton was needed like a third arm."

When Warren called Jackie the next day for a date, she accepted. The dates were casual, but confidants of Jackie claimed they usually ended "with a roll in the hay."

"Jackie was not serious about Warren," Truman Capote claimed. "She was using him like a plaything. She was attracted to him just for his looks, not

Using all of her seductive powers, Jackie Kennedy as First Lady was not successful in luring Warren Beatty to star in *PT 109*, an action-adventure/documentary film about the heroic naval exploits of her husband, the president.

Although JFK considered many actors for the role, Senator Teddy Kennedy claimed, "My brother saw *Splendor in the Grass* while in the White House and thought Warren would be fabulous in the part."

Within a period of a year, Beatty was offered seventy-five scripts, including *PT 109*. When he rejected it, it caused a minor scandal. The actor allegedly told the press, "If the president wants me to play him, tell him to come to Hollywood and soak up some of my atmosphere." Later, that remark was cited as an example of Beatty's "narcissistic behavior."

Pierre Salinger, press secretary of JFK, was sent to Hollywood to conclude the film deal with Warren Beatty. Salinger thought "he'd jump at the opportunity to play a sitting president in a heroic moment," and was stunned when Beatty rejected the role. "It's one of the worst scripts I've been offered this year," Beatty said. "Very poorly written. I don't want to disgrace myself by appearing in this crap."

Later, Beatty recalled, "Jack Warner kicked me off the lot when I told him that I had spoken to Kennedy, telling him he should not allow the movie to be made. I know what makes a good movie," said the star of the ill-fated *Ishtar* (1987). "But no one, and certainly not the president, listened to my warning, and *PT 109* was one big, fat disaster."

Once, Beatty encountered Robert Kennedy in an elevator. All the attorney general said to him, was "You're the guy that turned down my brother in *PT 109*." No further words were exchanged. Beatty later issued a statement, denying the quotation attributed to him. "Even as a joke, I never said it, never thought it. Actually, I don't believe there is any actor who wouldn't be pleased at being considered for the role of President Kennedy as a young man. I turned down the script for the simple reason I did not feel I was right for the part."

his brain. In fact, she told me he can't even formulate a complete sentence at one time."

When Beatty was interviewed on *Entertainment Tonight* in 1997, the host asked him if he were sleeping with Jackie. Beatty denied it, but was not convincing in his denial.

The relationship ended one night after an intimate party at Jackie's apartment. Warren was in the corner talking to about four or five male guests. One of Jackie's woman friends overheard his conversation. She went to Jackie and told her that "Warren is bragging about having gone to bed with you."

Jackie walked over to Warren and asked to see him alone. As she started to confront him, she noticed Colacello nearby. She quickly shut up and walked away. She didn't want her private conversation with Warren reported in *Interview* magazine.

She liked to think she was the most discreet person on earth, and she couldn't tolerate Warren gossiping about their sexual trysts.

After that, Jackie was no longer in to receive Warren's calls. "Let him go back to Joan Collins, whoever in the hell that is," she told Capote.

One afternoon at Doubleday, Jackie's secretary presented her with a just-published list of the rumored sexual liaisons of Warren. It included the usual suspects such as Jane Fonda, Vanessa Redgrave, Barbra Streisand, and Natalie Wood. But what horrified Jackie was her own name on the list, followed by Lee Radziwill and Christina Onassis.

"I don't like sharing men with my former daughter-in-law and my sister. Of course, it's not incest, but . . . ."

She never finished her sentence.

(Photo, right): The homosexual playwright and sentimental sudser William Inge fell madly in love with **Warren Beatty** and fashioned two screen properties for him, *Splendor in the Grass* (1961) and *All Fall Down* (1962) and Beatty is pictured above with actress **Natalie Wood**, who fell in love with him during the filming of *Splendor*.

Both the young stars came together on the rebound. "He was depressed because his sweetheart was in England," Natalie said, "and I was devastated over the end of our marriage." The references were to Joan Collins and Robert Wagner. She also claimed that "Warren and I spent hours ruminating and analyzing each other's problems." "Yeah, right," said the jealous Inge. "I'm sure they did when they took time off from fucking."

JFK, The Mob, & Judith Exner

ENTERTAINING A MOBSTER'S GUN MOLL
BETWEEN THE SHEETS AT THE WHITE HOUSE

John F. Kennedy, Judith Exner *(lower left)*, and Mob boss **Sam Giancana** became involved in a strange "love triangle" in the early months of JFK's presidency.

After the 1960 presidential elections, when JFK was firmly ensconced in the White House, Giancana told Exner, "Listen, honey, if it wasn't for me, your boyfriend wouldn't even be in the White House." He is credited with "throwing" the election in Chicago.

After meeting Jack, Exner recalled lying in bed fantasizing about him. "Something wonderful was happening to me," she claimed. "I was almost giddy. It was a feeling that I had when I was young and had a crush on someone—that first meeting when you realize that he's someone special. It's all anticipation, hoping and wondering and feeling good. Then doubt creeps in: I wonder if I'll ever see him again. There was not much doubt after that first time I met him. I slept well and woke up feeling like Scarlett O'Hara the morning after Rhett Butler had carried her up the stairs."

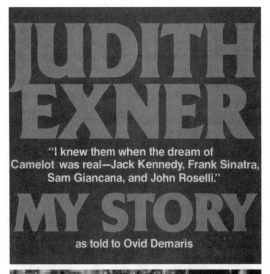

JUDITH EXNER

"I knew them when the dream of Camelot was real—Jack Kennedy, Frank Sinatra, Sam Giancana, and John Roselli."

MY STORY

as told to Ovid Demaris

As a guest of **Frank Sinatra, JFK** was asked by the singer's butler and valet, George Jacobs, what he wanted on the West Coast.

The President was blunt: "I want to fuck every woman in Hollywood." When Frank Sinatra entered the room, he also asked JFK what he wanted. "I want to have a Naked Lunch," taking the title from the hip heroin novel by William Burroughs. Sinatra didn't get it.

"Okay," JFK said, "I'll explain it: Shaved pussy sprinkled with cocaine." Frank got that. He looked startled for a minute. "I can arrange that, I'm sure."

When Dean Martin found out that Sinatra was catering to JFK's every whim, he called it "brown nosing." Sinatra got that. He didn't mind the women (who was he going to condemn?), but he worried about JFK taking cocaine. "He's the leader of the Free World. One word from him and the world explodes. Should he have a straw up his nose at the same time?"

MM, JFK, Marlene, and Sinatra...Judith Dated from the A-List

"Judith Campbell Exner was a user, a manipulator—common as dirt!"
—Jackie Kennedy

On February 7, 1960, when Frank Sinatra introduced "girl-about-town" Judith Campbell to JFK at the Sands Hotel in Las Vegas, she had never heard of him. She didn't know that JFK was the U.S. Senator from Massachusetts, and she had no idea that he was running for President. "I didn't even know he was married," she later said. "All I knew was that he was gorgeous. After one night of lovemaking, I fell for him, little knowing it would ruin the rest of my life."

"Jack was the world's greatest listener," she recalled. "I was a nobody and the first day we spent together, we talked for three hours before the bed, and he seemed fascinated with everything I said."

Ironically, Judith's meeting with JFK did not represent her first link with the Kennedy clan. Frank Sinatra's valet, George Jacobs, in the memoir (*Mr. S: My Life With Frank Sinatra*) he wrote chronicling his years working close-up and personal within the singer's entourage, stated that Joseph Kennedy, Sr., JFK's father, had visited Frank Sinatra during the late 1950s in Palm Springs, where he expected his host to pick up the tab for sexual services arranged by Sinatra and provided by local prostitutes. In

Palm Springs, according to Jacobs, Sinatra introduced Joe, Sr., to the sexual services of Judith Campbell.

As described by Jacobs in his memoir, Judith Campbell "was the perfect Eisenhower era pinup of the girl next door. That she charged for her wholesomeness was beside the point. Judy would go on to infamy as the fourth corner of a quadrangle that included Sinatra, Sam Giancana, and JFK. But before his son took a bite off the poison apple, the father was there first. Talk about chips off the old block!"

***

Judith was born in New York City into a wealthy family in 1934. When she was a child, her father, a German-born architect, moved his family to a 24-room Mediterranean-style villa in Pacific Palisades, a suburb of Los Angeles, Their home was later bought by movie star Joseph Cotten of *Citizen Kane* fame.

As a child she remembered her family associating with Hollywood celebrities, including Jack Warner, Cary Grant, and Robert Stack.

Shortly before Judith's death in 1999, she confessed that as a teenager, she lost her virginity to Bob Hope, who, while posing as a family friend, forced sex onto her at a beach cottage. "Hope hurt me, and I bled, but I didn't tell my father," Judith claimed. "I was brought up a strict Catholic. I feared that he'd kick me out of the house, even though it wasn't my fault. Bob Hope made me do it."

Based on her belief that she had been "ruined" by the comedian, she claimed "I had to get married." She met actor William Campbell, marrying him in 1952 over her parents' objections.

"I divorced him in 1958 when I became intimately involved with Sinatra," Judith said.

In later life, she claimed that Sinatra "used me like a prostitute for the Rat Pack. It all began one night in Las Vegas when he demanded in his hotel suite that I 'deep throat' Sammy Davis Jr., Dean Martin, and Peter Lawford. Sinatra was such a voyeur. He wanted to see me blow his friends. First I objected, but then I gave in. I actually ended up enjoying it and liking the guys, especially Dean Martin. He was my favorite. I had affairs with all of them."

Not at first, but in later revelations she claimed that Sinatra liked three-ways with two women in the bed. Originally, she had said, "When he brought another woman to join us in bed, I absolutely froze.

Judith, age six, holds her pet on Sunday, December 7, 1941, a day that would "live in infamy," when the Japanese attacked Pearl Harbor, plunging the United States into World War II. She was too young to understand the war, but she grew up quickly. When she was an early teenager, **Bob Hope** *(inset photo)* was a frequent visitor to her parents and their home.

Once, he dropped in and gave her a large pink teddy bear. When he found out her parents were away, he invited her out to the pool. In the beach cottage, he stripped down and urged her to take her clothes off too. She'd never seen a naked man before. Afraid, she tried to run back to the house, but he held her down and raped her. She kept that "dirty secret" until later in her life when she became more confessional.

211

I went rigid. No one could have moved my arms or legs."

But as the years passed, she altered her story, ultimately asserting that she did join Sinatra in three-ways with other women, most memorably in Las Vegas with the legendary Marlene Dietrich. For years, Sinatra had conducted an on-again, off-again affair with Marlene. Judith felt they had "some sexual arrangement between them."

"Frank wanted to watch Marlene make love to me," Judith claimed in one of her later interviews. "She was an oral artist with both men and women. Fortunately, I didn't have to do anything but lie there. She brought me to a climax which so excited Sinatra he immediately penetrated me. He was real kinky at times."

Judith said she first met Sam Giancana in late March of 1960. Sinatra made the introduction on Miami Beach, but referred to him as "Sam Flood."

A short, dour, and rather ugly Sicilian, Giancana, or so it is estimated, had directly organized, arranged, or been personally responsible for some 200 murders up to 1960 when Kennedy became president. He was a leading member of La Cosa Nostra, the international crime syndicate.

As Chicago's Mafia boss, he was the successor to the notorious Al Capone. Amazingly, he'd been arrested 70 times, including three times on a charge of murder. His close friend and associate in crime was John (Johnny) Roselli, who represented the Chicago mob on the West Coast.

As part of an ironic coincidence, the Mafia boss and the President of the United States ended up sharing the same girlfriend—Judith Campbell Exner.

"What tangled lives we lead," JFK later told Bobby Kennedy as their ties with Giancana became more linked. Giancana was enlisted to help win the 1960 presidential election for Kennedy against his Republican opponent, Richard M. Nixon. Giancana provided both union support and money for the campaign.

It was Sinatra who had originally arranged the link between the mob (as represented by Giancana) and the Kennedys. It was perceived as vital by JFK's advisors that he carry the "swing state" of Illinois. The plurality was narrow, but JFK was pronounced the ultimate winner, though even today there is a claim that the 1960 presidential election, thanks partly to the collusion of then-mayor of Chicago, Richard J. Daley, was stolen from Nixon.

"I wouldn't have gotten involved with Sam if Jack didn't tell me to," Judith later claimed. "After all, I was being ordered to by the President of the United States. I did what he wanted me to do."

She claimed that in 1960, she had personally organized a meeting between Giancana and JFK at the Fontainebleau Hotel on Miami Beach. Although she did not attend the meeting, she said that the President (then a Senator) later came to her suite and gave her $2,000 in cash

As Judith matured, admirers defined her as "a little bit of Jackie Kennedy, a little bit of Elizabeth Taylor."

Actor **William Campbell** (above, left) would become the first of a string of men who seduced the mature Judith. She married him.

"Love to him was sex, and sex was just something you did at every opportunity to prove your manhood. It was strictly a biological function. He got an itch and he scratched it. Instantly! He could have cared less how I felt. He was such a dull, selfish human being. That was in the days before we knew about chauvinistic pigs. I was nothing more than a possession."

after making love to her.

Apparently, the gangster and JFK had discussed the upcoming West Virginia primary, where JFK's Catholicism had emerged as something of a problem—a definite factor to consider.

Judith said she was amazed when JFK sent her a plane ticket and money to fly to Washington. She had thought he'd meet her in some out-of-the-way hotel, but he invited her to dinner on April 6, 1960 at his home in Georgetown. "I learned Jackie was away. We did it that night in the same bed where he slept with her."

"He told me that Jackie was no good at the oral stuff, and that he had to turn elsewhere for that," Judith claimed. "He wanted to know all the details about how I'd become such an accomplished deep throat artist. I told him I was broken in by Sinatra and The Rat Pack. He told me his greatest sexual fantasy would be to go to bed with both Shirley MacLaine and me at the same time. That never happened."

On July 11, 1960, the opening day of the Democratic National Convention in Los Angeles, JFK summoned Judith to his hotel suite. "He told me he was highly nervous about the convention and needed to relax. On our previous encounter when we'd kissed passionately, and with his lips on mine, he'd asked me, 'Do you think you could love me?'"

"Yes, yes, yes, I said into his open mouth. 'I love you.' When I said that, he plunged his tongue into my mouth and ordered me to drink all his saliva until his mouth was completely dry. At that point, I was under his spell."

After such passion and such a declaration of love, Judith later said she was shocked when he told her there was another woman who would be arriving soon. "I just couldn't believe it," she said. "I thought he was satisfied with me, but he seemed insatiable."

"We were sitting in robes in the living room when this other woman was ushered in. To my shock, it was Marilyn Monroe. I'd heard stories that Jack was having an affair with her. I knew that another three-way was in the offing. I'm about the last woman on earth who could be called a lesbian, but I found Marilyn attractive. She kissed each of my cheeks before turning her attention to JFK."

"She pointed a finger at Jack like he was a naughty boy," Judith said. "'You brought along this lovely girl,' MM told Jack. 'She looks like Elizabeth Taylor. What fantasy are we having tonight, Mr. President?'"

"He wasn't president yet, but she had already started calling him that," Judith said. "Right in front of me, she went over to the sofa where Jack was sitting. She unzipped his

Judith Exner (above) and **Marlene Dietrich** *(below)* came from such different worlds that it seemed unlikely that they would ever meet. The man who introduced them was Frank Sinatra, who knew both of them as David knew Bathsheba. In time he would invite both of them to share his bed at the same time.

Marlene and Frank went way back to 1942. When the blonde goddess first showed up in public with Frank, it was at ringside to watch a title fight at Madison Square Garden. Her other date that night was Joe DiMaggio. Rumors still persist that they had a three-way that night. Frank found Marlene versatile. He could bring another man to her bed—in this case DiMaggio—or a woman, in one case Judith Exner. Marlene considered Frank and Joltin' Joe as two more trophies to add to her collection of seductions. They had already included Joseph P. Kennedy Sr., his son, Jack, John Wayne, and the French singer, Edith Piaf.

trousers, took out his penis, and began to give him a blow-job. She took her mouth off him and looked back at me. 'This is just to get the party going,' she said. 'Come over here and give it a try so I can rest my mouth for a minute.'"

"Nothing could have surprised me more when Jack was elected president," Judith said. "Even Frankie had his doubts. 'Too much scandal, too much sexual baggage,' Sinatra said."

"I didn't vote for him," she later claimed. "I voted for Nixon. I did that to protect myself. I feared that if Jack became president, I would be exposed and featured in all the tabloids. Talk about a fear coming true."

Judith felt that "once Jack became president, he'd clean up his act. He was being watched by too many people, and he had a lot of political enemies who were working to destroy him. But he was completely reckless. Once in the Oval Office, he had power. With that power, he became more reckless than ever. It was like he felt he was above being harmed by a scandal, especially a sexual scandal."

"Like Sinatra, Jack liked his three-ways," Judith claimed. "He was known for bringing

Mob boss **Sam Giancana** *(above)* is pictured handcuffed to a chair during one of his many arrests in Chicago. The son of Sicilian immigrants went to work in the 1920s for the ultimate *Mafioso*, Al Capone. Giancana rose to the pinnacle of the Chicago mob, implicated in beatings, kidnappings, and murder.

During WWII, the Selective Service rejected him, finding him a "constitutional psychopath showing strong eremitic *[editor's note: not concerned with the temporal world or swayed by mundane considerations]* trends."

Frank Sinatra became a crony of his. This led to a connection with Joseph P. Kennedy. Giancana later claimed he helped run a vote-stealing fraud in Cook County, a district that helped push JFK to victory during the presidential elections of 1960. During his tenure as president, JFK shared the same girlfriend with Giancana—Judith Campbell Exner.

Al Capone sent gangster **Johnny Roselli** *(four photos above, each snapped at different times in his life)* to Hollywood in the 1930s to rule as its Mafia lord. He moved between Capone's Chicago, Harry Cohn's Hollywood, Howard Hughes' Las Vegas and ultimately within John F. Kennedy's Washington.

A ladies' man with surface charm, he seduced everyone from Judith Campbell Exner to Marilyn Monroe. Frank Sinatra became a close friend of his and was often seen coming and going from his address at 1333 South Beverly Glen in Los Angeles.

Johnny ended up knowing too much about too many major American figures and suffered a grisly murder in Miami.

whores to the White House for nude swims. Once he invited me to the White House for a nude swim. I found him in the pool with another woman. I would have preferred to keep him to myself, but at that point I was giving in to all his wishes."

"After we swam," Judith said in an interview shortly before her death, "we went to his suite in White House bathrobes," Judith said. "He wanted to watch this whore go down on me. He became so excited that when I climaxed he penetrated me at once. He was so worked up at that point that it took him only twenty seconds to reach his own climax."

Although JFK seduced dozens of women during his tenure in the White House, Judith was the first to admit to having had an affair with the sitting president. "I realized that it was a blow to his image. It virtually destroyed the public image of Camelot, and it led to scandalous stories to come, including his sexual trysts with Marilyn Monroe. I came to realize that Jack's affair with me exposed him to blackmail from the mob."

In her most startling claim, Judith said that when he became president, JFK often used her as a courier between the White House and Giancana. Her role as an intermediary became even more important after the bungled Bay of Pigs invasion of Cuba in April of 1961.

She remembered bringing JFK and Giancana together on April 28, 1961 in a suite at Chicago's Ambassador East Hotel.

JFK was scheduled that night to address a Democratic Party dinner, but not before he talked over a possible assassination of Fidel Castro with the Mafia don. Judith was not privy to the details of that plot.

During a period of eighteen months between 1960 and 1961, Judith was the president's link to the mob. In that capacity, she crisscrossed the nation, carrying messages from Washington to Florida, Chicago, and Los Angeles.

In her later recollections, Judith went on to assert that she had arranged a total of ten meetings between JFK and Giancana, two of which were within the White House. Kenneth O'Donnell, JFK's aide, had Giancana slipped in *incognito*, of course.

Judith said that she was once asked by JFK to carry $250,000 from Washington to Giancana. On this trip, O'Donnell, part of JFK's Irish Mafia, shadowed her, sitting on the train in the same compartment with Judith, even though she was unaware of his role as a watchdog and spy. In Chicago he watched her get off the train and hand a satchel to Giancana, who was waiting for her. Before heading back to Washington, O'Donnell watched Judith and the Mafia boss leave the railway station together in a black limousine.

As she later admitted, she also delivered "gobs of money" from California businessmen to the Kennedys, presumably to help finance JFK's re-election campaign of 1964. Later, after JFK's death, charges were leveled that some of this money went to the president's personal use, including

As time went by and JFK's sexual tastes became more decadent, he began to prefer three-ways. For the most part he had no trouble luring two women into the same bed with him.

His fantasy, as he revealed to Florida Senator George Smathers, involved bringing Judith Campbell Exner and **Marilyn Monroe** together, an event his aides arranged on the eve of his nomination for president at the Democratic Convention at Los Angeles in 1960,

Before Marilyn's meeting with Exner, JFK's makeup man had made Exner look as much like Elizabeth Taylor as possible. "Marilyn detests Elizabeth Taylor, so I know I'll never get those two into bed at the same time," Jack told Smathers. "Marilyn will be real, of course, but instead of Elizabeth I'll have to settle merely for the mock."

215

bills to madams who imported working girls into the White House for orgies when Jackie was away.

Judith also revealed that she carried payoffs, in cash, into the White House from California defense contractors wanting government business.

One night during dinner at the White House—Jackie was away, of course—JFK introduced Judith to Bobby. As she told columnist Liz Smith, "He squeezed my shoulder solicitously and asked me if I was OK carrying these messages from Jack and him to Chicago. 'Do you feel comfortable doing it?' Bobby asked me. I told him I did."

Her most memorable moments in the White House came that night after dinner when she retired with the president to his suite. "Jack stripped down and got into bed, while I went to the bathroom to freshen up a bit. When I came back into the room, all the lights were turned off. I crawled into bed with Jack. To my surprise and shock I found it was Bobby in the bed with me. He was completely naked."

"I always thought Bobby was the cuter Kennedy, and I was only too glad to have sex with him too," she said. "As we were going at it, Jack, also nude, crawled into bed with us. After Bobby shifted my body to accommodate Jack, the president entered me from the rear. I became the meat in a Kennedy sandwich."

The death of Marilyn Monroe on August 5, 1963 had a profound effect on Judith. She feared that Marilyn had been wiped out by either the mob or by friends of the Kennedys, eager to see that they remained in power. "I became afraid for my life. I knew too much. I wanted out."

"When the president called me to come to the White House for another roll in the hay, I didn't let him know that I was leaving him," she said. "I arrived at the White House in the usual way. I don't think Jack suspected a thing."

"When we came together, I told him, 'I can't see you anymore—it's too painful, too dangerous.' Even when I told him that, he still wanted to be intimate with me for one final time. I was still in love with him, as much as that was possible, and it broke my heart to tell him goodbye. I never saw him again after that cold day in Washington."

After that final sexual encounter with JFK, she discovered she'd become pregnant. "Since I knew it was Jack's child, I called him at the White House, not knowing if he'd speak to me. He came to the phone right away."

"When I told Jack I was pregnant and wanted to have his child, he went ballistic," she said. "First he claimed our kid might belong to Sinatra—'Let Ol' Blue Eyes pay for it.' He also claimed that the child might belong to either Sam or Roselli. But the timing wasn't right. I knew he was the father. During sex together, he refused to wear a condom, claiming it deadened the sensation for him."

"I pleaded with him to let me have the child, but he insisted that I have an abortion," she said. "Both of us were devout

Historians are still debating the role that gangsters Sam Giancana and Johnny Roselli played in plotting the unsuccessful assassination of Cuban dictator **Fidel Castro**.

Working with the CIA in Miami, Giancana came up with a rather inventive plot that involved reaching Castro's mistress and settling a few million dollars on her to "drop a poison pill in Castro's food or drink." Even before JFK became president, the CIA Office of Medical Services in Miami had been given a box of Castro's favorite cigars with orders to treat them with a lethal dose of poison.

The mob hated Castro because when he had taken over Cuba, he had ruined their profitable gambling and prostitution businesses.

Through Bobby, President Kennedy was alleged to have sent word to the mob that "assassination of a foreign leader is a dirty word. Don't use that word on paper."

Catholics, but he demanded I abort our baby. As I always did, I gave in to him."

Finally, JFK said, "Do you think Sam would help us?"

"I realized then I wasn't going to get help from him, and I called Sam. Unlike the president, he was very loving and caring and arranged for me to have the abortion at Chicago's Grant Hospital on January 28, 1963, even though such an operation was illegal. The president's kid was not to be."

She stayed in Chicago and, when she recovered, had sex with Giancana one final time. "In spite of his awful reputation, he was rather gentle in bed. I much preferred him over Johnny Roselli, his friend. Johnny treated women brutally and wanted to cause them pain. He once told me he wasn't satisfied until he made a woman scream in agony."

The public did not know of the JFK/Judith Campbell link until a decade after the president was assassinated.

The goal of the Senate's Church Committee was to investigate the CIA's involvement with organized crime in its effort to have Fidel Castro assassinated.

To her shame and regret, Judith was called upon to testify. Word of her links with JFK and Sam Giancana had become widely known throughout Capitol Hill.

Even though her testimony before the Church Committee was almost squeaky clean considering the breadth of the true story, Kennedy aides attacked her veracity.

David Powers, who had functioned as appointments secretary to the president, publicly claimed, "The only Campbell I know is a can of chunky vegetable soup." He lied, of course. He had actually been the aide who had arranged each of the president's trysts with Judith.

Another JFK aide, Kenneth O'Donnell, also lied, claiming he had never met Judith Campbell. He knew everybody who had access to the president, including all of his girlfriends. It was O'Donnell who had cleared JFK's prostitutes for entrance into the White House.

O'Donnell achieved a certain infamy when it was learned that he was the aide who had organized JFK's trip to Dallas in November of 1963. With David Powers, O'Donnell was riding in the car behind the president.

Lightning struck again for O'Donnell, who had later in his career managed RFK's campaign for president. After Bobby was assassinated on June 5, 1968, O'Donnell never really recovered, even though he subsequently functioned as campaign manager for Hubert Humphrey during his ill-fated attempt in 1968 to win the presidency.

Evelyn Lincoln was the private secretary to President Kennedy. As JFK talks on the phone in the Oval Office, she keeps John-John amused. He kept Lincoln up to date about which of his mistresses he would talk to and which ones were to receive a "Sorry, he's in a meeting" brush off.

During the course of her career, she frequently put through calls to him from both Marilyn Monroe and Judith Campbell Exner until he told her to tell them he was no longer available.

In the two memoirs she wrote about her years in the White House, *My 12 Years with John F. Kennedy* and *Kennedy and Johnson*, Evelyn never revealed details about JFK's extramarital affairs, but she did reveal a political shocker: She claimed that JFK once told her that he was dropping Lyndon B. Johnson as his running mate in 1964.

"Who is your choice as a running mate?" she asked.

"I am thinking about Governor Terry Sanford of North Carolina. But it will not be Lyndon."

O'Donnell made an unsuccessful attempt to get elected as governor of Massachusetts in 1970, but failed miserably. It all became too much for him. He died in September of 1977, having long ago succumbed to alcoholism.

Evelyn Lincoln, JFK's secretary, also lied, claiming that Judith was only a campaign volunteer. However, the dates in the White House log annotating Judith's visitations more or less coincided with what Judith had claimed.

. White House logs indicate that Judith had telephoned called Lincoln at least 80 times. To validate her charges, Judith published fifteen phone numbers she had used to communicate with both Lincoln and Kennedy in the period between 1960 and 1962.

In 1950, during the height of the "Red Menace" scare, the California politician **Richard Nixon** won his seat in the U.S. Senate by asserting that his liberal opponent, Helen Gahagan Douglas, was "as pink as her underwear."

But during the presidential elections of 1960, and in his encounters with JFK, Nixon met his match. The public applauded JFK for his style, charm, and smile. But Nixon knew a darker side.

He told aides, "Jumping into bed with him would be like falling into a pit of vipers. I've been through rough campaigns, but in Kennedy I went from the minor to the major leagues. The Kennedy clan is the most ruthless gang of political bandits ever mobilized for an election in the history of the Republic. They know every dirty trick invented. After them, I vowed I'd become the master of the dirty trick."

Nixon was right. Shortly after his election to the White House, JFK began plotting the assassination of arch enemy Fidel Castro.

Judith remained formally identified as Judith Campbell throughout most of her life, until she married golf pro Dan Exner in April of 1975. They divorced in 1988. Firmly entrenched today as an indelible part of the Kennedy legend, her story has been portrayed in books and films. Natasha Henstridge portrayed her in the 2002 movie *Power and Beauty*. Norman Mailer modeled his character Modene Murphy after her in his novel *Harlot's Ghost*.

"I wrote my autobiography in 1977 with Ovid Demaris," she said. "All the major publishing houses turned it down as being too controversial. Called *My Story*, it was published by Grove Press. Even though Jack, Johnny, and Sam were dead, I was still afraid of the mob, even the Kennedy family. I have to admit it, I left out a lot of the more scandalous details."

That fear was well founded. Before Senate investigators could call Giancana to testify, he was shot seven times in the head in the kitchen of his Oak Park (Illinois) residence on June 19, 1975.

Roselli was also called before the committee to testify about the CIA's attempts to kill Castro, including the role of Giancana in this planned assassination. One year later, his dead body was found in a 55-gallon oil drum weighed down with heavy chains and floating in Dumfoundling Bay near Miami.

A review in *The New York Times* interpreted Judith's evidence within her autobiography as overwhelming. "It makes the defensive protestations of the keepers of the Kennedy flame somewhat dubious."

Near the end of her life, Judith admitted that she had not told the truth to the probing Church Committee looking into her relationship with the president. "I was afraid I was next on the hit list," she confessed. "I didn't tell the true story to the committee or in my memoir. I knew the mob. They could wipe out a person in a minute."

As time went on, Judith became more and more explicit in her interviews. In an article in *People* magazine by Kitty Kelley, the notorious biographer of both Sinatra and

Jackie, Judith said, "I lied when I said I was not a conduit between President Kennedy and the Mafia. Jack knew everything about my dealings with Sam and Johnny Roselli because I was seeing them for him."

As she became less and less afraid as the years went by, Judith added to her story and changed details significantly.

She was interviewed, for example, by columnist Liz Smith for an article in *Vanity Fair*, and also by Seymour Hersh for his book, *The Dark Side of Camelot*. It soon became apparent that she had given what Nixon called "a limited hangout" in her earlier testimonies.

As her shadows deepened and cancer continued to eat away at her body, Judith in her final years provided more and more details to what few friends she still had. To the percolating brew, she added increasing numbers of florid tidbits about her sexual intimacies with JFK, Sinatra, and The Rat Pack.

Weeks before her death, she was deeply wounded by her critics, many of whom still denied her role in JFK's life. She particularly resented being portrayed as a vapid party girl, the mistress of both a president and a Mafia don.

"I was not a tramp! I was not a slut!" she said. "I was never anybody's kept woman."

Each night for the final ten years of her life, she'd fallen asleep with a gun under her pillow, a gift from Giancana, who warned that the Kennedys "might have you wiped out one night."

Suffering from breast cancer, Judith Exner died at the age of 65 on September 24, 1999.

(Illustration, above)

JFK hated the Broadway musical *Camelot*, but Jackie loved it. JFK accused her of having a crush on singer Robert Goulet, who had eighth billing in the Broadway show.

After her husband was assassinated on November 22, 1963, Jackie summoned author/journalist Theodore White to Hyannis Port for an interview for *Life* magazine.

During the course of the interview, she likened JFK's presidency to an American Camelot. White used the imagery of King Arthur's Court and the Knights of the Round Table to fuel his writing. He wrote about how Camelot represented "a magic moment in American history." Jackie was defined as a modern-day Lady Guinevere. A legend was born.

The photo above appears on the back cover of a book, *Johnny, We Hardly Knew Ye*, that **Kenneth O'Donnell** *(far right)* and **David Powers** *(center)* wrote about their years as top aides to JFK. But they left out all the juicy stuff, including their slipping hookers in and out of the White House for nude pool parties and orgies.

During their White House days, the dynamic duo was known as "Butch and Sundance." O'Donnell and Powers were key members of the "Irish Mafia" in the early 60s.

Except for anything associated with sex, their book is filled with behind-the-scenes stories of one of the most compelling figures ever to occupy the Oval Office.

DID MICKEY COHEN ORCHESTRATE
JFK, RFK, & MM IN A PORN FILM?

Mickey Cohen (1913-1976) was one of the most colorful gangsters in Hollywood. He functioned as a boxer, a bodyguard for Las Vegas mobster Bugsy Siegel, a pimp for movie stars, a crooked gambler, a sleazy haberdasher, a notorious racketeer, a grand scale thief, and a confidant of both Frank Sinatra and Jack Ruby, who fatally shot JFK's assassin Lee Harvey Oswald a few days after the assassination of JFK himself.

In his exposé, *Celebrity Gangster*, investigative reporter Brad Lewis revealed yet another dubious career achievement of Cohen: Blackmailer of the stars and potential blackmailer of the Kennedy brothers. Lewis wrote: "Misogynist Mickey Cohen regularly set up famous actresses, including Marilyn Monroe and Lana Turner, with many of the young men who worked for him. He secretly filmed them having sex, so that he could sell their movies on the black market. If he wanted to influence the activities of an actress, he would threaten to make the film public."

Cohen usually hired handsome, well-built henchmen, many of them in their twenties. He wasn't a homosexual, but he insisted that his men be well hung. Before hiring them, he ordered them to "drop your pants—I want to see how it's hanging." It was clearly understood that their duties included stud duties to the stars.

In Lewis' book, he revealed that a former police investigator, Gary Wean, discovered that Marilyn was dating two of Cohen's "most gorgeous guys," George Piscitelle and Sam LoCigno. They were seen around Los Angeles at such joints as Barney Ruditsky's Plymouth House, often retiring for the night to a motel where Cohen had already installed hidden cameras.

When Cohen showed Marilyn the "blue movies" of her having separate episodes of "raunchy sex" with both Sam and George, she wept. "My career survived the nude calendar, but it won't survive this."

Cohen then blackmailed Marilyn into agreeing to have tapes made of RFK seducing her, with the intention of extending her cooperation into a taping of sex play with JFK as well. Tight security around the president made the latter plan less feasible, but Cohen told his longtime girlfriend, MM clone Liz Renay, "When Bobby becomes president in 1968, and then gets re-elected in 1972, I'll be set for eight good years, free of government interference in any of my activities."

Of course, Marilyn's death in 1962, followed by Bobby's assassination in 1968, prevented that plan from being carried out. But if the MM/RFK sex tape exists today, it was either destroyed or rests in some collector's vault, perhaps to be screened around the world at some future date, at which time it might top the all-time porno grosser, *Deep Throat*.

Three isn't necessarily a crowd, unless it's being filmed for blackmail.

The Widowed Jackie

Contemplated Suicide

Associated Press

Two grieving widows, **Jacqueline Kennedy** (veiled, on the left) in 1963 and the mentally unstable **Mary Todd Lincoln** around the time of her husband's assassination in April of 1865.

To prepare for her slain husband's funeral, Jackie asked Angier Biddle Duke, Chief of Protocol for the U.S. State Department, for the details associated with the funeral rites of an earlier slain president, Abraham Lincoln.

Within twenty-four hours, Rutherford Rogers, Acting Librarian of Congress, forwarded information about Lincoln's funeral, along with rites observed at the burials of George Washington, Woodrow Wilson, and Ulysses S. Grant. For reasons not fully understood, Rogers also sent details of the funeral of Edward VII, son of Queen Victoria.

During her organization of JFK's funeral rites, the most bizarre communication Jackie received came from the Soviet Embassy. Soviet leader Nikita Khrushchev reassured her that neither he, nor anyone else in his government, had anything to do with the assassination of her husband. Khrushchev claimed that he suffered "deep personal regrets and shock" at the death. "I had great admiration and respect for your husband."

Nevertheless, Khrushchev responded aggressively to a rumor that the new president, Lyndon B. Johnson, was preparing to launch a nuclear attack on the Soviet Union. The Kremlin ordered an immediate state of national alert.

Friend of the Kennedy family, **Father Richard McSorley**, holds a young John-John. McSorley was a Jesuit priest, theologian, author, activist, teacher, and a legendary figure in the Catholic peace movement.

During his time with Jackie, she revealed many secrets to him. Although he never recorded it in his diary, he did reveal to several Jesuit colleagues that Jackie claimed that President Johnson, protected by the Secret Service, once arrived at her Georgetown residence a few weeks after JFK's assassination. "He wanted to have a few drinks," Jackie allegedly told McSorley.

Before an hour had passed, or so she said, LBJ made his intentions clear: "I know that a young woman like you needs a man in her life, and, with the greatest of secrecy, I am prepared to fulfill Jack's duties. I know you have needs, and so do I, needs that Lady Bird no longer fulfills for me. We can satisfy each other's needs, and no one will ever suspect, much less catch us with a smoking gun."

Although he was by now the officially sworn-in President of the United States, she ushered him out of her house.

"Wouldn't God Understand if I Wanted To Be With Him?"

In the wake of President Kennedy's death, Jackie Kennedy entered a long period of pain and despair. This was all too evident when Richard McSorley, a Jesuit theology teacher at Georgetown University, visited her at Bobby Kennedy's Hickory Hill estate. Confronting McSorley, she said, "I don't know how God could take him away."

She'd provided a brave front for the nation, but privately McSorley encountered a woman who was beginning to unravel. He recorded details about each of his meetings with Jackie in a personal diary, for which he would later be severely criticized.

McSorley bonded with Jackie that day on Bobby's tennis courts, and soon became her confessor and confidant.

The most detailed account of her relationship with the priest appears in Thomas Maier's biography, *The Kennedys: America's Emerald Kings*.

Jackie feared that her mental condition might deteriorate the way Mary Todd Lincoln's did after her husband was assassinated.

McSorley knew a lot about survival, having once eaten worms to stay alive when he was imprisoned in a Japanese concentration camp for three years after the Japanese bombing of Pearl Harbor.

Eventually, when she came to trust McSorley enough, Jackie asked him the all-important question on her mind. "Do you think God would separate me from my husband if I killed myself? Wouldn't God understand that I just want to be with him?"

This contemplation of suicide was revealed to McSorley by Jacqueline in 1964, but not made public until after the priest died in 2002 and donated his private papers to Georgetown University.

"During the daytime, she tended to her children and worked on initial plans for a Kennedy presidential library," McSorley wrote. "At night she was like a lost soul."

"I am a living wound," she said to Ethel.

Bobby told Jackie that "sorrow is a form of self-pity," and urged her to go on. He urged McSorley to provide guidance to the grief-stricken widow, under the guise of giving her tennis lessons.

"I was melancholy after the death of our baby," Jackie told the priest, referring to the passing of their infant son Patrick. "I stayed away from Jack longer than I needed to."

That was a reference, of course, to her extended cruise of the Mediterranean with Aristotle Onassis.

"I could have made his life so much happier," she said, "especially those last few weeks in October and early November. I could have tried harder to get over my melancholy."

McSorley told her that she had to live for the sake of her two children. "Don't mourn the dead but get on with the living." He also reminded her of the Catholic faith's belief in resurrection of the body, and he promised her that one day she'd be reunited with the slain president.

Jackie was also consumed with guilt that she didn't try to save her husband's life as their limousine made its way through Dallas. "I would have been able to pull him down, or throw myself in front of him, or do something if I had only known," she told McSorley.

She was not easy to console, and even asked the Jesuit if he would pray to God to take her life.

"Yes, if you want that," he said. "It's not wrong to pray to die."

In May of 1964, around the time of the late president's birthday, Jackie revealed to the priest once again that she was contemplating suicide. Then she made a statement that absolutely astonished him. "I hope my suicide will set off a wave of suicides. I'd like that because I want to see people leave their misery behind. I was happy when Marilyn Monroe died. She is out of her misery now."

In her final phone call to McSorley, Jackie told him she was "much better now because love has entered my life in a way I never expected."

He started to congratulate her, but she interrupted. "It is not a love of which the Catholic Church would approve. In fact, the love I'm experiencing now would be called ungodly in the eyes of the church. I wouldn't even dare to confess it to you."

"Then God save your eternal soul," McSorley said before putting down the phone.

She never called him again.

Hickory Hill: John F. Kennedy and his bride, Jacqueline, once owned this stately 19th-century residence, which sits on six prime acres, a short drive from Washington, D.C., with majestic trees, a pool, stables, tennis court, and a movie theater. JFK and Jackie sold it to Robert F. Kennedy for his family home.

"Bobby turned it into a breeding factory," Jackie told Jack and others. "When will those two stop having kids?"

As a house-warming gift, Jackie painted a whimsical and semi-satirical picture of the new tenants, her in-laws, occupying the house. It depicted the RFK brood running wild around the property. They are seen hanging off the roof, sliding down the bannisters, and generally destroying the place. A cook is depicted fleeing out the back door as a new, more naïve, cook enters throught the front.

JFK's Botched Autopsy

Back in 1963, Texas law demanded that the body of any person murdered within the borders of the state have an autopsy on Texas soil. But on November 22, 1963, when Dr. Earl Rose, the Dallas county medical examiner, tried to enforce this law, he encountered the Secret Service removing the slain president's body from Parkland Memorial Hospital for its immediate return to Washington. He tried to prevent the move. After a brief scuffle, the president's mutilated body was hauled aboard the presidential plane and whisked far away.

Jackie had refused to have the autopsy performed "by some Texas butchers," and wanted the autopsy performed at the Bethesda Naval Hospital near Washington. She claimed that her choice was appropriate since her husband had once been a naval officer. Actually, she'd have preferred to have no autopsy performed at all, but she relented to demands.

The autopsy, both its procedures and its results, are still controversial. Amazingly, no forensic pathologist was present. An unidentified pathologist later studied the evidence, and said, "The JFK medical evidence is so confused and contaminated with false and deceptive information that the only way to truly know the truth about JFK's death would be to exhume the body for a proper autopsy by objective pathologists not under government control and filmed in a public setting, with neutral witnesses."

Perhaps on orders from Robert F. Kennedy, a number of body materials removed from JFK's body and examined at the initial autopsy later disappeared. These include the president's damaged brain, blood smears, organ samples, and certain tissue sections. Allegedly, RFK didn't want this body tissue preserved for display in some museum exhibit. But if, indeed, RFK did order the destruction of this material, he almost had to have the approval of Jackie herself.

When Ramsey Clark became Attorney General, Jackie called him, requesting that he suppress all autopsy X-rays and photographs of "my husband on that marble slab." Although he at least appeared to respect her wishes, JFK's autopsy photos are available today to anyone who knows how to surf the Internet.

Even so, there is something seriously wrong with the photographs of the body of the murdered president. The facial images are definitely those of JFK. But the images showing damage to the president's head are not of JFK. These faceless photographs do not show the pattern of damage observed by the medical professionals at Parkland in Dallas. But what cadaver was used as the subject of these fake photographs--and why?

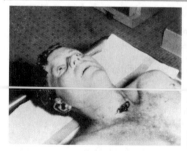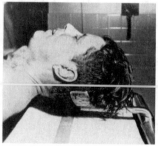

ALL THREE OF THESE PHOTOS WERE DESIGNATED AS OFFICIAL AUTOPSY PHOTOS OF JFK,
BUT WHO IS ASSOCIATED WITH THE CADAVER ON THE RIGHT?

Is It True, Blondes Have More Fun?

Jackie, as Choreographed by Capote, Confronts Marilyn

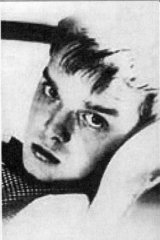

Starring the Notoriously Provocative

Truman Capote

Jackie Kennedy and **Truman Capote** had long, drawn-out discussions about the affairs of the Kennedy men, including the founding papa, Joseph Kennedy, Sr. and his relationships with actresses such as Gloria Swanson. "I don't think Jackie realized what she was walking into when she married Jack," Capote said. "He was in constant competition with his old man to see who could nail the most women. Jackie wasn't prepared for quite such blatant womanizing. She hadn't expected to find herself stranded at parties while her husband went off with somebody new."

In her anger one night, Jackie told Capote, "Jack has a miniscule body and a huge head." Capote was far more direct. "All those Kennedy men are the same. They're like dogs, having to stop and pee on every fire hydrant."

In another startling conversation, Capote listened to a drugged and slightly demented **Marilyn Monroe**, shown above in her depiction of Cheri in *Bus Stop* who shared her dream with him. "Jack told me only last week that he plans to divorce Jackie and marry me. No later than 1964, I will be by his side when he seeks re-election. Imagine me, *First Lady of the land*. I had ambitions when I was struggling in the early days. With Jack, I will preside over America from 1964 to 1968 as his First Lady. I'll be a very different First Lady from Jackie. I'll be more human, more down to earth. I was the most dreamy starlet to ever arrive in Hollywood. I dreamed of becoming the biggest movie star of all time, bigger than Betty Grable, Lana Turner, and Ava Gardner. That dream came true for me. But in my wildest imagination, I never dreamed I'd become First Lady of the United States."

Truman Capote wanted **Marilyn Monroe** to play Holly Golightly in the film version of his novella *Breakfast at Tiffany's*.

But the studio had other plans, and cast Audrey Hepburn in the role instead.

Capote later said, "Marilyn would have been absolutely marvelous in the role. She wanted to play Holly and even worked up two whole scenes all by herself and did them for me. She was terrifically good, but Paramount double-crossed me in every conceivable way and cast Audrey instead."

"Audrey is an old friend and one of my favorite people, but she was just wrong for the part."

THE WORLD KNEW THEM
BY THEIR NICKNAMES:
JACKIE OH! AND MM

In the great tradition of Southern storytellers, author Truman Capote was clearly the master. Regrettably, he dined out on more stories than he recorded on paper. There is no doubt that he was privy to many of the secrets of the rich and famous, some of whom he betrayed by writing thinly disguised portraits of them when he published excerpts from his unfinished novel, *Answered Prayers*.

One night in Key West in 1969, Truman told an astonishing story that he claimed was going to appear as an entire chapter in his upcoming novel. Listening with eager ears were Truman's hosts, Tennessee Williams and his longtime companion, Frank Merlo, along with James Leo Herlihy (author of *Midnight Cowboy*) and the co-author of this book, Darwin Porter.

All biographers assume that Marilyn Monroe and Jacqueline Kennedy never met face to face, although they occasionally shared the bed of the same man—namely President John F. Kennedy.

Jackie had first met the handsome young politician in May of 1951. But a half-decade before that, way back in 1946, Jack had already seduced Marilyn, although he didn't remember her. As Norma Jean Baker, she hardly resembled the shimmering creature later known worldwide as Marilyn Monroe.

By the time the Kennedys moved into the White House, the new First Lady was aware of her husband's affairs with other women, including Marilyn. Jackie called it, "the curse of being married to a Kennedy man."

According to Truman, Jackie tried to ignore the affair but plotted revenge. That would come on the night of May 19, 1962. On learning that Peter Lawford had asked Marilyn to fly in from the West Coast and sing "Happy Birthday, Mr. President" to JFK in Washington, Jackie placed a secret call to Marilyn one week before the event. She advised Marilyn to make the song "as sexy as possible because Jack will adore it." Marilyn told her that she thought that was a "great idea," and that designer Jean-Louis was putting the finishing touches on a dress that Marilyn was describing as "just flesh and diamonds."

Appearing late at the televised event, Marilyn walked onto the stage to sing her song. As columnist Dorothy Kilgallen later so aptly put it: "It was like Marilyn Monroe was making love to the President in direct view of 40 million Americans." Jackie wisely had skipped the event to go horseback riding in Virginia.

Although officially, the President had thanked Marilyn for singing "in such a sweet and wholesome way," backstage he was furious, blaming Peter Lawford for the disaster. Meeting privately with Marilyn, JFK whispered to her that their affair was over, even though he invited her back to his suite at the Hotel Carlyle for "a farewell fuck." He warned her never to call the White House again. Belatedly, Marilyn realized that Jackie had tricked her.

Back on the West Coast, Marilyn was fuming and "full of fury," in Peter's words. She phoned him one night to inform him that she was going to call a press conference next week and reveal her long-running affair with the President. She also said that after her press conference, "Mr. President can kiss a second term good-bye."

Peter beseeched her not to, but fully believed she'd do it. He placed an urgent call to Bobby Kennedy, urging him to warn the President. Peter also claimed that Marilyn was growing more and more dependent on drugs and sounded "unhinged."

It is not known how Jackie learned about Marilyn's threat, but apparently she did. Through Peter's help, she placed another call to Marilyn and asked to meet secretly with her at the apartment of Truman Capote, in Manhattan, the following week. The author had agreed to play host at this secret rendezvous.

Marilyn flew in from the West Coast to New York, where she checked into the Hotel Carlyle, earlier site of several secret trysts with the President.

Years later, in Key West in 1969, Truman either was being deliberately vague or did not want his audience to know the exact date of this rendezvous. Obviously it had to have occurred some weekend during June or July of 1962. He did reveal the time of the meeting in his apartment, placing it at around ten o'clock in the evening. He claimed that Marilyn arrived first, looking "camera ready" in a white satin gown with a white sable, even though it was summer. Jackie, according to Truman, arrived twenty minutes later and wore a plain black and severely tailored business suit.

Marilyn sat on a sofa opposite Jackie, who preferred Truman's favorite armchair. "Marilyn oozed charm, but Jackie was distant," Truman

Two months before her death in 1962, Capote dined with **Marilyn**. "In spite of all the pain she was suffering from both Jack and Bobby Kennedy, she had lost a lot of weight for the film *Something's Got to Give*," Capote said. "George Cukor had been set to direct her. There was a new maturity about her. She wasn't so giggly anymore."

"I told her, 'Marilyn, why cry over Jack or Bobby? Between the two of them, they can't raise a decent hard-on.' 'Truman,' she chastised me, 'You've always been such a size queen.' If she'd lived and held onto her figure, I think she would have looked gorgeous and glamorous for years. Bobby and Jack didn't really kill her, at least in the literal sense. She committed suicide."

"But they did pay one of her best friends to keep quiet about their affairs with her," Capote claimed. "The friend knew where all the skeletons were. After Marilyn died, Peter Lawford gave this friend a year-long cruise around the world. For that entire year, no one, not even the police, knew where she was. A cover-up, for sure."

recalled.

After social pleasantries were exchanged, Jackie asked Truman to excuse himself while they conducted private business. He said that he retreated to his bedroom with a drink, and before the evening ended he had a few more. Eventually he drifted off to sleep.

A loud pounding on his door woke him up around one-thirty a.m. Opening it, he encountered a hysterical Marilyn, her makeup smeared. She too, or so it appeared, had been drinking heavily. The First Lady had left the apartment.

"It's all over!" Marilyn sobbed to Truman. As best as he could ascertain, Marilyn had agreed to call off the press conference. She also said that Jackie had forgiven her for her affair with her husband, saying that "only a cadaver can resist Jack when he turns on the charm." Jackie's icy facade had "melted" at some point in the night as she begged Marilyn "not to publicly humiliate me in front of the world." She also pleaded with Marilyn not to make her children victims of a divorce. According to Marilyn, Jackie even spoke of how John-John's face "lights up when his daddy walks into the room."

True to her word, Marilyn, who had only weeks to live, never held that press conference. But through the rest of June and July, Peter reported to Jackie that Marilyn was continuing to make threats against the Kennedys. When Jackie learned that Bobby Kennedy was flying to Los Angeles, she asked him to call on Marilyn to see what kind of trouble she might make for the Kennedys.

Long after Marilyn's death, and long after the assassination of her husband, Jackie told Truman: "Sending Bobby to comfort Marilyn was like sending the most succulent lamb into the wolf's lair. Bobby didn't have a chance. He'd already had an affair, and was still in love with Marilyn. If Marilyn had lived, she would probably have gotten around to Teddy too."

Marilyn Monroe was found dead in her bed early on the morning of August 5, 1962. Murder? Suicide? The debate will go on as long as the public still remembers the star's brief and incandescent, but tragic life.

One of Capote's biographers (who doesn't want his name revealed) tried to track down this story by hiring a private detective. He later refused to answer questions about the date of the alleged

Capote learned that **Jacqueline Kennedy** *(above)* was so upset over her husband's affair with Marilyn Monroe that she went to Valleyhead, a private psychiatric clinic in Carlisle, Massachusetts, for electro-shock therapy.

Capote had met Jackie when she was a college student working for *Vogue* magazine in New York. He'd been in on her early days of romance with the senator from Massachusetts.

"From the beginning," Capote said, "Jackie knew that her husband was dating other women. She even knew that he had begun his affair when Marilyn was the most famous movie star in the world and Jack a relatively unknown senator. At times when I saw her, Jackie was coming unglued. I never knew what was wrong with her. She's way out in orbit somewhere most of the time. I don't think she can stand the pressure of being a politician's wife. I think she'll snap."

Her friend, Paul Mathias, the New York correspondent for the France-based *Paris-Match* said, "Jackie was hurt very young in connection with both her father and mother. She never came out of the shock of growing up. I don't think she was born happy. She fills her days as best as she can, but she suffers a lot. I have great compassion for her. It sinks into me more and more just how irreversibly unhappy she is."

meeting between Marilyn and Jackie, even though he was not going to write about it in his biography. He had a policy of not running stories unless he was able to confirm them with some other source, but wanted to keep the detective's report secret in case he wished to write about it in the future.

All that he would confirm was that Marilyn, on a summer night unspecified, left the Hotel Carlyle around 9:30 and was helped into a private limousine, not the hotel's usual car service. Jackie was also in New York that night to attend some charity event, but called and cancelled at the last minute, citing flu-like symptoms.

There were no paparazzi to record where the two most famous female icons of the 20th century went on that historic night, which adds veracity to Truman's account, although the Secret Service had to be aware of Jackie's whereabouts. The detective, according to the biographer, concluded that "in all possibility" Truman was telling the truth.

After Truman left that 1969

Robert Kennedy and Jackie wait to go on the air at Hyannis Port on May 29, 1964, less than a year after his brother and her husband was assassinated in Dallas. The program, discussing the late President's spiritual legacy, was broadcast from the home of Joseph P. Kennedy via CBS news to England, Ireland, and Germany.

Behind Jackie's back, Capote betrayed her friendship. Unknown to Jackie–at least at the time– Capote spread the rumor that, "Jackie is having an affair with Bobby."

"Even though those rumors appear to have been true, it was a dastardly thing to do," said Tennessee Williams. He severely chastised Capote for gossiping about Jackie. "The poor woman has suffered enough. Give her a rest. If she is finding some comfort, even some love with her brother-in-law, she should be left alone to do so. The human heart, and its needs, sometimes follows unorthodox patterns. Of all people on this earth, you and I, as artists, should know and respect that."

social gathering in Key West, Tennessee Williams virtually echoed the detective's report. He told his remaining guests that, "I think we have to entertain the possibility that Truman indeed is spilling the beans. But even if he's lying to us, it still makes a hell of a good yarn."

JACKIE VS. ELIZABETH TAYLOR

At the peak of his popularity, in developments that surprised almost everyone, Michael Jackson forged friendships with the two most publicized women on Earth—Jackie Kennedy and Elizabeth Taylor, America's two Queens. For the first time ever, movie magazines treated the former First Lady like a film star, chosing her to grace the covers of *Motion Picture, Photoplay, Movie Mirror, Screen Stories,* and *Modern Life.* Only Dame Elizabeth appeared on the covers of more fan magazines than Jackie, whose reign as a "movie goddess" lasted for the most part between 1961 and 1973. Tabloids screamed from the checkout displays at supermarkets: JACKIE WILL MARRY! LIZ WILL DIVORCE!!

Author Wayne Koestenbaum (*Jackie Under My Skin*) put it this way: "Liz was the swinging vixen, greedy for love and jewels; Jackie was the princess, tasteful and decorous. Liz was trash, Jackie was royalty."

HOW MARILYN TRIED TO KILL BOBBY KENNEDY
AND WHAT JACKIE SAID ABOUT IT AFTERWARD

As First Lady, Jackie immediately became suspicious of David Powers, who had been Jack's longtime aide and intimate friend. She believed that Powers was covering up the fact that Jack had to have his "daily dose of sex."

After JFK was assassinated, Powers wrote a book, *Johnny, We Hardly Knew Ye,* in which he claimed that every time Jackie left Washington, he and the president dined together. Then the president, according to Powers, said his prayers like a good Catholic and went to bed alone. When Jackie read this, she said, "What a piece of fiction!"

Infuriated over Jack's sexual conquests, Jackie often left the White House in a huff. But she had a spy (or spies), who told her what went on during her absence.

She was especially concerned whether Marilyn ever visited the White House in disguise. Her friends at the Hotel Carlyle in New York said that on occasion, Marilyn had arrived disguised in a brunette wig, hiding behind large sunglasses, the kind that Jackie herself was often photographed wearing.

When Jackie read a play, *The Best Man,* written by her distant relative, Gore Vidal, she knew at once that the character of William Russell had been based on her husband. In the play, the womanizing character wonders how, after he becomes president, he'll be able to sneak women into the White House.

In an impudent mood, Vidal gave copies of the play to both Jack and Jackie. Each of them read it in bed. Jackie asked her husband if the character of William Russell reminded him of anyone in politics. "Not at all," Jack said. "It's pure fiction."

At one point before the election of 1960, Jackie confronted Bobby, warning him that her husband's affair with Marilyn might jeopardize his chance of ever occupying the Oval Office. "I think if the American public knew that their future president was cheating on his wife and humiliating his family, those same people would not vote for Jack."

Jackie was aware that Bobby knew the details of Jack's affair with Monroe, but he never revealed any of them to Jackie.

But in 1965, in the midst of his own affair with Jackie, Bobby did tell her that on the last day he saw Marilyn, only hours before her death, she had become a candidate for a padded cell. He confessed that in the midst of a violent argument, she'd taken a butcher knife and tried to stab him in the chest. He overpowered her, knocking her to the floor and wrestling the knife from her hand.

"Marilyn may have died at a convenient time," Jackie said. "She could have brought down the Kennedy House of Cards."

Marilyn was studying acting with the brilliant "theatrical dragon," British-born **Constance Collier (1878-1955;** *below, right).* Noël Coward once branded Collier as "The Great Dyke of the Western World." Never a great beauty, Collier personified theatrical glamour to Katharine Hepburn, who was rumored to have been her lover. Collier had intuitive good taste, a wicked sense of humor, and "more talent than any actress deserves," Hepburn once said.

As regards Marilyn, the legendary British actress told Capote: "Oh yes, there is something there—a beautiful child, really. I don't think she's an actress at all—certainly not in a traditional sense. What she has is this presence, a certain luminosity, a flickering intelligence. These marvelous traits could not be captured on stage because they are too subtle, too fragile. Her wonder can only be captured by the camera. It's like a hummingbird in flight. Only a camera can freeze the poetry of it. But anyone who thinks this girl is simply another Harlow or harlot or whatever, is mad. I hope, I really pray, that she survives long enough to free the strange lovely talent that's wandering through her like a jailed spirit."

JFK's Mysterious Saga of Another Mistress with the Initials "MM," and Another Unsolved Murder

> "Mary Meyer offered to fellate the president for keeping abortion legal."
>
> THE WASHINGTON POST

Marilyn Monroe's murder, erroneously reported as a suicide, is still unsolved. So is the murder of another JFK mistress, Mary Pinchot Meyer. At the age of forty-four, she was mysteriously shot while taking a walk along the towpath near her Georgetown studio. The date was October 12, 1964.

A young man, Raymond Crump, was arrested, charged with first degree murder, and went on trial on July 19, 1965. The evidence was circumstantial, and the jury took less than a day before its members came back with a verdict of not guilty. The Mary Meyer murder remains the subject of lurid speculation within the Kennedy saga.

Mary's sister was Toni Bradlee, the ex-wife of Ben Bradlee, publisher of *The Washington Post* and one of JFK's closest friends. Toni said, "Mary and Jack...it was just another of Jack's flings."

As a young, handsome, and swinging bachelor, JFK had met Mary while she attended Vassar. She had married Cord Meyer, Jr., a military aide to Commander Harold E. Stassen. Apparently, Jack paid too much attention to this talented and lovely new bride, and he and Cord had a falling out.

"Jack was so young, so boyish, so attractive, and he looked straight into your eyes, making you think you were the only woman in the world," Mary said. "He had a way with women, who fell all over him."

According to Evelyn Lincoln, Mary visited the White House thirty times between January of 1962 and November of 1963, paying a visit only days before Jack and Jackie flew to Dallas. Around the White House, Jackie called Mary, "The Secret Jezebel of Camelot."

One night, after Jackie returned to the White House, she discovered a pair of woman's panties tucked under her pillow. She held them up between thumb and forefinger. "Would you please shop around and see who these belong to?" she asked Jack. "They're not my size."

James Truitt, a close friend of Mary's, was the former vice president of *The Washington Post*. Mary confided in him that while visiting Jack at the White House, she often "snorted coke and smoked pot with him"

"One night, he jokingly informed me that there was going to be a White House Conference on Narcotics in just two weeks." Mary told Truitt. She also admitted that on one occasion, "Hashish and acid were on the White House menu. Imagine that! What if the Soviet Union had chosen that moment to attack America?"

Near the final weeks of his administration, JFK told his aide, David Powers, that "Marilyn and Judy are out...Mary is now the court favorite."

The president, of course, was referring to Marilyn Monroe, Judith Campbell Exner, and Mary Meyer, respectively.

Mary kept a red leather diary, similar to the one kept by Marilyn Monroe. This tell-all diary devoted many pages to JFK. Mary had informed her friend, Truitt, of the existence of this diary, and instructed him, in the event of her untimely death, to turn it over to James Jesus Angleton, chief of counterintelligence for the CIA.

Angleton accepted the diary at the end of October, 1964, but in the immediate wake of Mary's death, he claimed that he did not. However, after the passage of many years, he ultimately admitted that he was responsible for its destruction.

It was Truitt himself who in 1976 turned the details of the MM/JFK affair over to the *National Enquirer,* which exposed the liaison. Truitt later said that his action was a response to his anger over Ben Bradlee's lack of candor in his autobiography, *Conversations with Kennedy.*

"Here is this great crusading Watergate editor who claimed to tell everything in his Kennedy book, but really told nothing," Truitt charged.

After Truitt's attack on Bradlee, a story appeared in *The Washington Post,* asserting that Truitt suffered from mental illness, which impaired his judgment and "caused him to act irresponsibly."

The murder of Mary Pinchot Meyer, former mistress of John F. Kennedy, is still listed as unsolved.

Mary Pinchot Meyer
1920-1964
REST IN PEACE

TRUMAN GETS GRAPHIC   (DISHING THE KENNEDYS WITH CAPOTE)

Truman Capote not only saw **Jack Kennedy** *sans* bathing suit, but also attended dinner parties with "Jackie and Jack" in the 1950s during the early years of their marriage. At one such party on Park Avenue, Capote showed up with Babe Paley, the wife of William Paley, then chairman of the board of CBS.

After dinner, Jackie and Babe left for a brandy in one part of the apartment while the men retired for brandy and cigars in the library.

"Some high roller from Texas was recounting his experiences with a $1,500-a-night call girl in Las Vegas," Capote claimed. "He knew their telephone numbers and their specialty – sucking cock, rim jobs, around the world. He knew how well they did it, how long, how deep, how big a cock they could take, and what they could do with it that nobody else had ever done. That's how he talked. It was nauseating, a real stomach-turner."

"Jack was lapping it up," Capote continued, "practically taking notes. He did write some names and numbers on a scrap of paper for future use. Later when he and Jackie were leaving, she asked him what the men had talked about. 'Plain old politics,' he lied to her. But Jackie knew the score. She knew everything!"

A QUESTION OF SIZE. "What I don't understand is why everybody said the Kennedys were so sexy," said Capote. "I know a lot about cocks – I've seen an awful lot of them – and if you put all the Kennedys together, you wouldn't have a good one."

"I used to see Jack when I was staying with Loel and Gloria Guinness in Palm Beach," Capote continued. "I had a little guest cottage with its own private beach, and he would come down so he could swim in the nude. He had absolutely nuthin'!"

"Bobby was the same way; I don't know how he had all those children. As for Teddy – forget it! I liked Jack, and I liked many things about Bobby. But I wouldn't have wanted him to be president. He was too vindictive. Teddy is crazy. He's a menace. He's a wild Irish drunk who goes into terrible rages. I'd want anybody to be president before Teddy!"

Biographers who include Mart Martin compile lists of which celebrities have seduced which other celebrities. There are a lot of surprises on most lists.

Take John F. Kennedy, for example. On the list of his former lovers, you expect to encounter Lana Turner, June Allyson, Judith (the gun moll) Campbell, Joan Crawford, Marlene Dietrich--even his lifelong best pal, LeMoyne Billings. Billings was a homosexual who had been in love with Kennedy since 1933. Robert Kennedy often referred to "Lem" as "Jack's second wife."

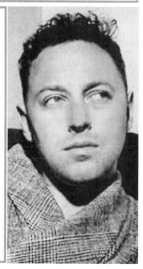

But what is the playwright **Tennessee Williams** *(right)* doing on a list of JFK's lovers?

Gore Vidal, a former friend of Williams, provided a tantalizing clue. When he introduced Tennessee to JFK in Palm Beach and when JFK went away for a moment to get a drink, the playwright told Vidal, "He's got a nice ass on him." Vidal chastised Tennessee, claiming, "You're talking about the President of the United States, Tenn."

In Key West years later, Williams said to dozens of his friends and acolytes, "About as far as I got with the President was his allowing me to give him a tantalizing blow-job in the beach house that afternoon. That was the extent of our grand affair."

Marlon Brando (Part 1)

Pimping for JFK in Hollywood

When **John F. Kennedy** first met **Marlon Brando**, the President of the United States perhaps had no idea that wild boy Marlon would one day seduce his widow. Although he had only weeks to live, JFK was continuing to lead the life of a high roller, at least where women were concerned.

Since he was no longer calling on Frank Sinatra or Peter Lawford to pimp for him, it occurred to the president that Marlon, with all his contacts, might be the ideal candidate to arrange sexual trysts with the most fabled beauties of Hollywood. "I've had all the second rate ones," JFK confessed. "Now that I'm getting older, I want only choice sirloin, not hamburger."

Both agreed that Hedy Lamarr, whom they'd both already seduced, was one of the world's most beautiful women—"even more so than Jackie," Marlon claimed.

The slight put-down didn't put JFK on the defensive at all. "Hedy was great," Marlon said, "but while doing it I had the uncomfortable feeling I was plunging in after the Führer."

MARLON AND JFK
UNZIPPED

Marlon claimed to his best pal Carlo Fiore that he first met Marilyn at a bar on Eighth Avenue in New York City way back in 1946. According to Fiore, he offered her fifteen dollars to come back to his rented room, where he claimed they made love all night.

When **Marilyn and Marlon** went to Hollywood, their occasional lovefests continued until just before her untimely death. Throughout the rest of his life, Marlon insisted that she'd been murdered and had not committed suicide.

He also maintained that just hours before her death, Marilyn confided to him "a story so shocking that it would blow the lid off this town and lead to a rewriting of all those Marilyn and Kennedy biographies."

As a liberal and a Democrat, Marlon Brando had supported John F. Kennedy in his run for the presidency against Richard Nixon in 1960. But as JFK's campaign evolved, Marlon concluded that the Senator from Massachusetts was far too conservative and "much too moderate" for Marlon's left-wing politics. "But given the choice of Kennedy or Nixon, what else can we do?" Marlon asked director Elia Kazan.

Marlon had other reasons for being skeptical of the newly elected President Kennedy. For years, Marlon had conducted an on-again, off-again affair with Marilyn Monroe.

As her friend, Marlon had heard all the stories of the alleged abuse she'd suffered at the hands of Kennedy during their affair.

Before Frank Sinatra and Kennedy went their separate ways, Marlon had resented the crooner's close associations with the President.

"I positively loathe Sinatra," Marlon told anyone who wanted to listen. Most of their animosity stemmed from their ill-fated co-starring roles in *Guys and Dolls* (1955).

In contrast, the president had always been fascinated by Marlon, considering him "the greatest womanizer who ever set foot in Hollywood." JFK loved sexual gossip, and was amazed at the scope, range, and magnitude of Marlon's sexual adventures, concluding that the actor had seduced more women than Sinatra himself.

Despite his self-identity as a Catholic, and ostensibly opposed to abortion, the president on occasion had had to use the services of an abortionist himself. Through the grapevine, he'd heard that Marlon kept two abortionists on retainer to cope with his women who got pregnant, because the star did not want to wear a condom.

In Los Angeles, Marlon was surprised when he received a call from a presidential assistant inviting him to join JFK for a drink in his hotel suite. The meeting between these two icons occurred just months before the president's assassination in 1963.

Eager to see what the president had on his mind, Marlon rushed over. He planned to pitch to the president the plight of Native Americans and perhaps enlist JFK's aid in helping with the various tribes.

But when he was ushered in to meet the president, he found him sitting in an armchair in his underwear, taking a phone call.

Once the call ended, JFK turned his attention to Marlon. After only two minutes of listening politely to Marlon's political agenda, the president immediately changed the subject.

As Marlon was later to tell his pal Carlo Fiore, "In a second, I came to realize that Kennedy didn't want to talk politics with me. He wanted some serious pussy talk. Now that Sinatra and he had broken up their friendship, I think he wanted me as his Hollywood pimp, perhaps introduce him to the beauties like Sinatra and Peter Lawford used to do. The first question he asked me was, 'Is Shirley MacLaine's pussy really red?' I hated to disappoint him. It was embarrassing, but I told him I'd never muff dived on Shirley, much less let her enjoy my noble tool."

Marlon later claimed that he and the president talked for two hours as part of a dialogue devoted mostly to "our mutual list of A-list conquests in Hollywood."

Before that talk ended, Brando came to believe that Kennedy was "the master of the Folodex when it came to women."

Ultimately, Marlon seemed to resent the president's womanizing and overt masculinity, feeling somehow it threatened his own. Fiore reported that when Marlon felt threatened by a man, he often tried to seduce their wives, as if to prove his superior manhood.

"You'd better watch her," Marlon warned the president. "Even Jackie is not safe from me."

As if to burst the swelling bubble of Marlon's ego, JFK countered, "I think William Holden and Warren Beatty would be higher on her list than you."

"From that point on, we became two roosters," Marlon said.

It became apparent that the president was jealous of Marlon's sex appeal. As if he hoped for a kind of short-term revenge, JFK quipped, "I think you'd be too fat to play Stanley Kowalski today."

"Have you looked in the mirror lately?" Marlon asked him. "Those jowls. If you and Nixon had that debate today, you'd be more jowly than him. On TV, you look like the moon. I can hardly see all of your face in a close-up."

"I weigh a hell of a lot less than you," JFK asserted. "I've got a scale in the bathroom. Let's see."

Marlon weighed in first. When the president stepped on the scales, Marlon surreptitiously hooked his toe on the corner of the scales. JFK was shocked to see that he'd gained an unexpected twenty-five pounds.

"You lose, Fatso," Marlon said. Before leaving the bathroom, Marlon suggested that he and the president share a "mutual leak" around the porcelain toilet bowl. "That way, we can judge who's got the bigger tool." JFK rejected the idea.

"After that little show and tell in the bathroom, we came back into the living room, where he made his sales pitch to me," Marlon told Fiore. "He wanted me to arrange sexual trysts with Elizabeth Taylor and Ava Gardner. He said both women were his type and he 'just had to have them. Blondes are not really my thing, with an exception here and there. I'm one of those gentlemen who prefer brunettes.'"

Frank Sinatra had served the president well, providing him with sexual access to some of the big names in Hollywood, but because of a falling out they had, he was no longer JFK's White House pimp.

But before **Brando** could get started as Sinatra's replacement, the president was assassinated in Dallas.

Brando had hated Sinatra ever since they'd made *Guys and Dolls* (1955) together. In a scene from that picture, Marlon looks like he wants to choke Sinatra. He wanted to carry through on that choking off screen as well.

"Sinatra is pissed at me," Marlon claimed, "because I fucked Ava Gardner. That means he's pissed at everybody, because everybody has fucked Ava Gardner. Ol' Blue Eyes has got to learn to live with that reality."

Before leaving, Marlon promised he'd set something up. "I've already had Ava," he bragged to the president. "She's terrific in bed, but I fucked her primarily to get back at that son of a bitch Sinatra."

JFK stood up to shake Marlon's hand. "It's been great talking to a fellow pussy hound. Keep your promise. I'll have one of my assistants get in touch with you. Ava Gardner, first, since you've already broken her in for me, and then Taylor. Sinatra has already broken both of them in."

"Considering his endowment, he's a touch act to follow," Marlon said. Unknown to Marlon, JFK had already seduced Ava when he had come to Hollywood as a young naval officer in 1946. Her agent, Charlie Feldman, had arranged the sexual liaison. JFK wanted a repeat performance from Ava.

That night Marlon asked Fiore, "I'm charismatic, I'm brutishly handsome, and much more athletic than the president with his bad back. Now, tell me, if a beautiful movie star like Elizabeth Taylor was given a choice, who would it be? Brando or Kennedy? Give me an honest answer."

"You, Marlon, by a country mile," Fiore said.

"Glad to hear that," Marlon said. "Get me a drink and then give me a foot massage. After that, I want you to try to get Elizabeth Taylor and Ava Gardner on the phone. I've got something to ask them to do for their country."

JFK HAD HIS "ASSASSINATION" FILMED

It was one of JFK's more bizarre ideas, but he had long been obsessed with his possible assassination. "Any time some psycho wants to trade his life for mine, he can—it's possible, you know."

During the Labor Day weekend of September, 1963, JFK was at Hammersmith Farm in Rhode Island with family and friends, who decided to go sailing on the presidential yacht, *Honey Fitz,* which was docked nearby.

During the sail, JFK rehearsed his actors for their parts in an amateur film he wanted shot by his Navy photographer. Jackie also agreed to perform in the movie. The photographer got off the boat when it docked and trained his camera on JFK emerging from the yacht, walking down the gangplank onto the dock, and then walking along the pier towards dry land.

Suddenly, the president clutched his chest as if hit by a bullet. He fell to the ground.

The first passenger, Countess Consuelo Crespi, stepped over the body of the "slain" president, followed by Jackie who also stepped over the body. JFK's friend, Red Fay, who stumbled over the body, was next. At that moment of impact, red liquid, simulating blood, spurted from the president's mouth.

A reporter, Merriman Smith, was aboard the yacht that day and later wrote a description of this macabre home video. After it appeared, the President denounced him for his lack of taste in publishing the story.

"But what about the taste of a president who wanted to film his own assassination?" Smith asked, in his defense.

When Jackie saw the home movie at a White House screening, she had only one objection: "I should have worn makeup had I known I'd be in a film."

JFK: "Let's Make a Movie!!"

Marlon Brando (Part 2)

America's Prima Donna & Her Contender

"I could have been a contender," **Marlon Brando** might have said had he followed up on his 1964 fling with **Jackie Kennedy.**

"She's the most famous woman in the world, and I'm the most famous—and the best—actor, so we would have made the perfect couple."

Jackie had long admired Brando, especially his "sexy performance" in Tennessee Williams' *A Streetcar Named Desire*, and she was eager to meet him. That happened during the period when Marlon's best friend, George Englund, the writer, producer, and director (he'd helmed Marlon in *The Ugly American*), was dating Jackie's sister, Lee Radziwill.

A double date was arranged, as revealed in Englund's memoir about Marlon, *The Way It's Never Been Done Before*. "There were Secret Service inside and outside the Harriman House," Englund wrote. "We felt like college boys calling on our dates. We were shown into the living room and there were two of America's prettiest people. Jackie and Lee rose to greet us."

At Washington's upmarket restaurant, Jockey, Jackie's favorite, her appearance, especially with Marlon, became a feeding frenzy, and they were forced to flee.

After Marlon departed from her home the following morning, she told him, "It was good to know that I have not forgotten how to laugh and be happy."

Songs His Mother Never Taught Him

"As far as I am concerned, he can drop dead. He has the manners of a chimpanzee, the gall of a Kinsey researcher, and a swelled head the size of a Navy blimp."
—Louella Parsons, gossip columnist

"Should sex and desire die in me, it would be the end. It doesn't matter if I have almost never been happy with a woman."
—Marlon Brando

Jackie Kennedy was an exceptional choice for Marlon Brando, who usually preferred more exotic women. Here he is seen with the beautiful Polynesian actress, **Tarita Terriipaia,** as they appeared on the set of *Mutiny on the Bounty (1962).* She would become his common law wife.

A bisexual, Brando's choice of partners covered a vast field, ranging from the delicately pretty Pier Angeli to the rather ugly author, James Baldwin, even to grand dames such as Tallulah Bankhead and tobacco heiress Doris Duke. Marilyn Monroe was a particular favorite, as were Rita Moreno and French actor Christian Marquand.

About three months after the assassination of JFK, George Englund, a close friend and partner of Marlon Brando, was separated from his wife, Cloris Leachman, and spending a lot of time with Jackie's sister, Lee Radziwill.

Lee invited Englund to visit her and Jackie in Washington, and she asked him to bring Marlon along for the visit. The two sisters were staying at the home of the former U.S. Ambassador to both Great Britain and the Soviet Union, Averill Harriman, who had lent Jackie his home as a refuge following the assassination of her husband in Dallas.

At the house, guarded by the Secret Service, Englund introduced "the two best known people in America," Mrs. Kennedy and Marlon Brando. Fueled by martinis, Marlon told them about his travels in the South Pacific during the filming of *Mutiny on the Bounty* (1962) and discussed his work on behalf of Native Americans.

In turn, Jackie demonstrated how Jawaharlal Nehru (prime minister of India, 1947-1964) taught her how to stand on her head to meditate. Although a bit tipsy, Marlon followed suit. He would continue the practice throughout the next three weeks. Finally, complaining of headaches, he gave up head stands.

Jackie suggested that all four of them go to her favorite French restaurant in Washington, the Jockey Club. It was the evening of January 29, 1964. At the restaurant, the party was ushered to the most private table. But nonetheless, someone spotted the quartet and tipped off the press. Within half an hour, paparazzi and reporters descended in record numbers to cover Jackie's first social appearance since the funeral of JFK.

Abandoning hope of having dinner in privacy, the quartet fled through the restaurant's kitchen door.

Back at Jackie's temporary home, and still hungry because they had to skip dinner, Marlon went into the kitchen and prepared some omelettes for them. Jackie, Lee, and Englund sat in her living room, going over the recent, traumatic events in Dallas.

Once the omelettes had been consumed, Jackie turned down the lights in the living room and put on Wayne Newton's rendition of "*Danke Schoen*." Englund and Lee began to dance and neck, and they were soon joined by Marlon and Jackie.

To the sound of the soft music, Jackie danced close to Marlon "pressing her thighs against me." As Lee and Englund wandered off, Marlon—as described in the first draft of his memoirs, joined Jackie on the sofa, where, they began to make out passionately.

"From all I'd read and heard about her, Jacqueline Kennedy seemed coquettish and sensual but not particularly sexual," Marlon wrote in the first draft of his 1999 autobiography, *Songs My Mother Taught Me.*

Joe Fox, a friend of Jackie's and an editor at Random House, prevailed upon Marlon to cut that sequence.

"If anything, I pictured Jackie as more voyeur than player," Marlon wrote. "She kept waiting for me to try to get her into bed. When I failed to make a move, she took matters into her own hands and popped the magic question, 'Would you like to spend the night?' And I said, 'I thought you'd never ask.'"

"Some people thought Jackie was more of a voyeur than a practitioner—that she liked to watch," claimed Gore Vidal in his memoirs. "I'm not at all convinced of that. She and Jack both loved gossip and could go on talking endlessly about other people's sex lives, but I always got the distinct impression that she was very interested in sex the same way that Jack was very interested in sex. It was a game for them, and they *both* played it."

Some published accounts have asserted that Marlon had had too much to drink that night and turned down Jackie's invitation for sex. Because of his drunken state, according to these claims, he feared he'd be impotent and would damage his reputation as one of the world's greatest lovers.

He denied these reports to his best pal Carlo Fiore. "I have never been circumcised, and my noble tool has performed its duties through thick and thin and without fail. Jackie was the recipient of my skill in the boudoir. Proof of that was when she called me three weeks later and invited me for a repeat performance."

Jackie's friend, Franklin D. Roosevelt Jr., claimed that Jackie was "enchanted" by Marlon and found him "extremely attractive." Chuck Spalding, another close observer of the Jackie scene, said, "Like half the other women on the planet, Jackie found Marlon Brando completely irresistible."

She followed up her seduction with a thank you letter to Marlon, claiming that "I found the omelettes wonderful and the conversation even more wonderful." She asked him not to tell anyone, but invited him to join her for a secret weekend in New York away from the prying eyes of the press. In Manhattan she had checked into the Hotel Carlyle, where JFK had enjoyed trysts with Marilyn Monroe among others.

The second seduction took place at a small apartment on swanky Sutton Place, which belonged to some unknown friend of Jackie's.

In that section of his memoirs never published, Marlon wrote of her "boyish hips and her muscular frame. I'm not sure she knew what she was doing sexually, but she did it well."

He later told Fiore, "In some ways it was like fucking a very beautiful boy, and you know how I like to do that."

In his infamous 1956 interview with Truman Capote, Marlon had admitted that he had "gone to bed with lots of men. I'm not gay. These men are attracted to me, and I was doing them a favor."

After his two brief flings with Jackie, Marlon back in Hollywood wrote her a letter in which he proposed marriage. He claimed that his own marriage to Movita Castenada, the Mexican actress, survived in name only. "I can easily get a divorce," he wrote her. In the letter he promised that he could provide privacy from the press and comfort for Jackie and her children on an island in the South Pacific.

Jackie found his proposal "amusing" and filed it with some 2,000 other offers she'd received, including one from a Greek shipping magnate that looked the most promising, at least in terms of financial gain.

In 1974, after Jackie had become Mrs. Aristotle Onassis, Marlon had a violent run-in with Ron Galella, America's most notorious *paparazzo*. He was known to all tabloid readers for his constant harassment of Jackie. After his release from the hospital, Galella sued Marlon for half-a-million dollars. The lawsuit was settled out of court for $40,000.

Jackie reportedly was "thrilled that Marlon was still out there, looking out for me."

It was said that James Dean, after watching Marlon Brando perform in *The Wild One* (1954), fell in love with him.

Marlon later concluded that Dean needed someone to change his diapers more than he needed a male lover. "He could also use a psychiatrist," Marlon claimed.

Jackie was believed to have become mesmerized by Marlon when she saw him perform as Stanley Kowalski in *A Streetcar Named Desire*. (see above).

He once invited Jackie to "come on down. We'll be married on a South Pacific island, away from the prying eyes of Ron Galella and his camera."

"I'll give it my most serious consideration," Jackie said diplomatically.

Marlon Brando wasn't **Jackie**'s only celebrity lover. There was William Holden. There was dancer Rudolf Nureyev, although he much preferred Bobby Kennedy to Jackie. There was Warren Beatty, also Peter Lawford.

Other lovers were less widely known, including writer Peter Hamill, John G. W. Husted Jr. (an early *fiancé* whom she discarded), and government official Roswell Gilpatric.

Jackie told her sister Lee that author John P. Marquand Jr. took her virginity.

Allegedly, she asked, "Oh! Is that all there is to it?"

Living In Her Sister's Shadow (the title of **Lee Radziwill**'s autobiography), Jackie's younger sister often received acclaim all on her own.

That was the case when she appeared on the cover of *Life* magazine. Lee also reappeared perennially on the list of the World's Ten Best Dressed Women.

In her memoir, there was no mention of an affair with George Englund. She didn't mention Marlon Brando either. Originally it appeared that Lee was going to become Onassis' next bride until Jackie boarded the *Christina*.

Jack Kennedy liked the younger sister a lot—maybe too much so. At one point he told his pal, Lem Billings, "At times I think I should have married Lee, not Jackie."

Bobby Kennedy

"The One Person Jackie Ever Loved."
(Gore Vidal)

"The family that fucks together stays together," said Truman Capote mockingly, referring to the post-assassination affair that began between Bobby and Jackie. The author was kept abreast of the affair by his close friend, Jackie's sister, Lee Radziwill.

Before Jackie in the early months of 1964, there was Lee herself. As author Christopher Andersen claimed, "A decade before the assassination, Lee's first husband, Michael Canfield, had listened in one room while his wife made love to Jack Kennedy in the next. In the early months of 1964, she threw two parties for the Attorney General in London and to those present it was apparent that Lee had more than passing interest in her guest of honor."

As Capote recalled, "Lee also wanted to sleep with Bobby, and Bobby, like all those Kennedy men, was not one to pass up the opportunity."

By the winter of '64, Jackie and Bobby had become lovers. As revealed in Secret Service files, he was almost her constant companion, either dining in New York at the Four Seasons; tongue kissing at a private club, *L'Interdit* in Manhattan, or spending long nights at the 950 Fifth Avenue apartment of Steven and Jean Kennedy Smith.

BOBBIE KENNEDY: THE LANCELOT IN JACKIE'S CAMELOT

"If the Kennedy dynasty is restored, it will be Ethel Kennedy (with whom she has little affinity) and not Jackie who will occupy the center of the stage. There cannot be two First Ladies in the White House. Yet the fact that she is doomed to be discarded by her brother-in-law should he become president has not deterred Jackie from doing all she can to further Bobby's political fortunes. And because they frequently holidayed together, often without Ethel, there have been rumors that something untoward was going on."

—Victor Lasky

In one of the most famous pictures ever taken in Washington, Bobby Kennedy was on hand to comfort Jackie when she arrived at the airport with the coffin containing the body of her assassinated husband in 1963. She was still wearing her blood-stained pink Chanel suit, wanting to show the world what "they" had done to Jack.

In the days and weeks ahead, no brother-in-law in Washington political life ever stood by his sister-in-law with such devotion. Along the way, Bobby fell in love with Jackie.

At the time she was also addicted to speed, as was her husband. Earlier in 1963, Bobby ordered the Food and Drug Administration to test a vial of substance that Dr. Max Jacobson of New York was injecting into both Jack and Jackie. He was called "Dr. Feelgood," or a "strange man, a mad scientist type," as JFK's close friend, Charles ("Chuck") Spalding once said. "And I was the fucker who introduced this quack to Jack." The drug agency concluded that the Jacobson substance contained not only speed, but a massive dosage of steroids. Jack once claimed to Spalding that it increased his libido—"one night in the White House I had to order three prostitutes brought to my room before I got satisfaction, unlike Mick Jagger."

Even in her black mourning dress, Jackie rolled up her sleeve to receive an injection from Dr. Jacobson.

A photograph of Jackie and Bobby walking hand in hand at the president's funeral was flashed around the world.

Jackie's relative through marriage, Gore Vidal, later said, "Bobby was the one person Jackie ever loved."

"I suspect Bobby would have liked to dump Ethel and marry Jackie, but, of course, that wasn't possible," said the late Franklin D. Roosevelt, Jr. "The reason being the Kennedys were staunch Catholics."

Truman Capote, who at the time was a close "pal" of Lee Radziwill, later claimed he received almost daily updates on the Bobby/Jackie romance. He taped a series of interviews in 1976 for film producer Lester Perksy. He called the Bobby/Jackie liaison "the most normal relationship either one ever had. There was nothing morbid about it. It was the coming together of a man and a woman as a result of bereavement and her mental suffering at the hands of her late, lecherous husband. In retrospect, it seems hard to believe that it happened, but it did."

British journalist Peter Evans claimed in his book, *Nemesis*, that both Eunice Shriver and Ethel were aware of Bobby's affair with what Ethel called "the widder."

"Ethel may have been naïve, but she wasn't *that* naïve," Evans maintained. "In fact, Ethel had reached the same conclusions as Capote about her marriage. Thanks to their children, her husband's Catholicism, and his concern with the Kennedy legacy, she realized that their marriage was largely intact."

Allegedly, Jackie reported the affair to her suitor, Aristotle Onassis. He later told his cohort, Johnny Meyer, "By going public with the details of the senator's affair, I could bury the sucker. But I'd lose Jackie in the process. But can't you just see those headlines?"

Edward Klein, author of *Just Jackie*, said, "There were many who thought that Jackie secretly wanted to replace Jack with Bobby. And it was true that if Bobby could have been divided in two, Jackie might have considered marrying the half that was devoted to her."

When news of Bobby and Jackie first became public, Kennedy defenders wanted to sweep the scandal under the carpet or bury it forever in some deep closet. But FBI and Secret Service reports, released in 2007, more or less confirmed the affair. The Bobby/Jackie liaison was reportedly active between the years 1964 and 1968.

Amazingly, for years RFK had previously enjoyed a reputation somewhat akin to that of a choirboy. But from all reports, Bobby was as much of a sex addict as his brothers,

It was the beginning of a love affair, and it was captured on film by a paparazzo. Just two weeks after Dallas, Jackie, along with Caroline and John-John, moved into the Georgetown home of Averell Harriman, using it as a temporary shelter. Bobby and Ethel came to call.

Only the night before, Jackie had wept for hours, unable to sleep. To Bobby's parting glance, Jackie smiled demurely, a promise of more to come in their relationship. Newsman Ben Bradlee, a close friend, recalled, "Bobby was almost catatonic for several days. It was like he was glued to Jackie. If he left her for a moment, he became jittery, unable to focus on business."

Spalding added to the post-assassination memory bank. He accompanied Bobby and Jackie to a private hour of mourning alone with the president's coffin the night before the burial. "They were actually conversing with his corpse, both of them...I mean, carrying on a long conversation. They later told me that they could actually hear Jack's voice speaking to them. It was eerie. Both of them had become unglued."

only he was much more discreet and in general he preferred that his women be smarter than Jack or Teddy did. He once told aide David Powers, "Unlike Jack and Teddy, I don't get off on bimbos."

When Bobby began his affair with Jackie, he had previously enjoyed the beds of everyone from singer Rosemary Clooney to Princess Grace Kelly. He'd also seduced two of the same blonde bombshells that his brother had, notably Marilyn Monroe and Jayne Mansfield.

Author C. David Heymann alleged that Jackie's affair with Onassis drove Bobby into the arms of actress Candice Bergen, whom he met in 1965 when she was nineteen. Both Shirley MacLaine and Catherine Deneuve recalled seeing Candice and Bobby together at a party in Paris. Their affair even made the society pages of *Paris-Presse*. Capote alleged that Ethel found out about her husband's sexual tryst with Candice. "They weren't being furtive, they were being rather obvious."

With Ethel and the children left behind at Hickory Hill, RFK's Virginia estate, Jackie and Bobby intensified their love affair during the latter part of 1964. "Bobby and his brother's widow did little to hide their affection for each other," wrote biographer Christopher Andersen. "They continued embracing, kissing, and holding hands."

Classified Secret Service files revealed that the romantic pair were in each other's company several times a week.

Still married to Patricia Kennedy at the time, Peter Lawford told his wife that Bobby was filling in for Jack "in all departments."

Clare Boothe Luce, long-time friend of Joe Kennedy, later exclaimed, "Well, of course, *everybody* knew Jackie and Bobby were involved, if that's the right word for it. At least everyone who knew them was aware of what was going on between them."

Charles ("Chuck") Spalding was one of the most intimate members of Bobby Kennedy's entourage, and a compelling witness to the Jackie/Bobby affair. "Bobby's love for Jackie helped restore her emotional health after that horrible assassination. I really believe that Bobby was happier from 1965 until early 1968 than he ever was in his life. He still loved Ethel and his kids, but he really wanted to marry Jackie, but didn't dare. After all, he planned to run for president. I often went on vacations with Jackie and Bobby. I didn't stand over their bed watching them make love, but I know they often went into a single bedroom around eleven o'clock at night and didn't emerge until noon of the next day."

In the months ahead, communal sightings of Bobby and Jackie became frequent. Dozens of persons close to both of them reported evidence of their affair. These included socialite Audrey Zauderer (later Audrey de Rosario) who lived at ultra-exclusive Round Hill, a villa compound and resort in Montego Bay, Jamaica. She claimed they were having an affair—"absolutely!"

Maud Shaw, also a client and guest at Round Hill, claimed that Jackie and Bobby had separate bedrooms, but they "kept dodging in and out of each other's boudoir, making no secret of their dalliance."

The German screenwriter, Bernard Hayworth, also on vacation at Round Hill, reported seeing Jackie and Bobby swimming and sunbathing at a secluded cove. "He began massaging her back and kissing her neck," Hayworth claimed. To grant them their privacy, Hayworth turned and left before the action heated up.

In the wake of the assassination of John Fitzgerald Kennedy on November 22, 1963, the eldest remaining son of patriarch Joseph P. Kennedy became more or less "the man" of the Kennedy household.

Bobby was not present in Dallas, of course, that fateful day, but he was at Andrews Air Force Base, just south of Washington, D.C., for the arrival of the presidential jet carrying Jackie and her husband's corpse. Bobby was the first to embrace the grief-stricken widow who at the age of thirty-four was reportedly "completely out of it." The previous morning she had been First Lady of America. Now this.

On the jet, Bobby rushed past Lyndon B. Johnson, the new President of the United States, without acknowledging either him or Lady Bird. He headed at once to his sister-in-law. "Hi, Jackie. I'm here."

"Oh, Bobby." She fell into his arms, sobbing.

In the days following his brother's assassination, RFK spent every waking hour he could comforting Jackie and holding her in his arms.

On the day of the funeral, RFK accompanied Jackie and her children. They shared the limousine ride with President Johnson and his Lady Bird, heading from the White House to the Capitol Rotunda, where JFK rested in his coffin.

When RFK decided to run for President in 1968, he told Jackie he had to end their love affair "because too many eyes would be watching." She understood that the intensity of their love could not continue under these new circumstances. It had been dangerous enough before. "Our love will endure," she told him.

He told her that if he did not win the presidency, "I will come back to you. In the meantime don't run off with Onassis." That was a warning she would not heed.

Throughout Bobby's race to the White House, Jackie had nightmares that he too would be assassinated. Then "On that dreadful pre-dawn," in June of 1968, as Jackie remembered it, a call came in from Charles ("Chuck") Spalding with news about the shooting of RFK.

Jackie demanded that she be flown to Los Angeles at once. En route, she kept repeating, "It can't have happened. It can't have happened."

Spalding met her at the Los Angeles airport. Getting off the plane, Jackie demanded, "Give it to me straight. No bullshit."

"He's dying," Spalding told her.

Jackie let out a scream like a trapped animal.

In the hospital room, Ethel sat by her husband's side, whispering her love to him in his ear. Getting up when Jackie entered, she embraced her. "I'm so glad you're here." Then she very graciously surrendered the room so that Jackie could spend some time alone with her dying husband.

At 12:45am on a Thursday morning on June 6, 1968, RFK's doctors approached Jackie and Ethel to tell the widows the grim facts. "There is no brain activity," Dr. Henry Cuneo said. "He's only being kept alive by artificial means. There is no chance ever of recovery."

Ethel ran screaming down the corridor. "I won't do it! I won't kill Bobby!"

With nerves of steel, Jackie confronted the doctor. Very calmly she told Dr. Cuneo, "I am speaking for the family. We want you to disconnect the respirator. I'll sign the consent form."

After the respirator was disconnected, Jackie came into the room. She stood there as RFK breathed on his own for

Three bathing beauties on the beach at Cape Cod, with the very skinny one (**Bobby**) on the left, the skinny one (**Jack**) in the center, and the chunkier **Teddy** on the right.

"And at various times Jackie seduced all three of them," claimed Truman Capote in the presence of William and Barbara Cushing (Babe) Paley. The story was just too fascinating for them to keep to themselves, and soon *tout* Washington heard about it, but only in hushed whispers.

Whether it was true or not, Capote amplified his story, claiming that on one drunken night at his apartment, Jackie even rated the sexual performances of the three brothers. On her scale of 1 to 10, Bobby got a 9, Jack a 6, and Teddy a 3.

"With Teddy," Jackie allegedly confided, "it was like going to bed with a college freshman. Bobby was the one with the power and the drive. He seduced a woman like he was going after Jimmy Hoffa."

When Capote asked her to describe Jack's performance, she refused. "Just go to any party in New York Washington, or Hollywood and ask around. You'll get your answer."

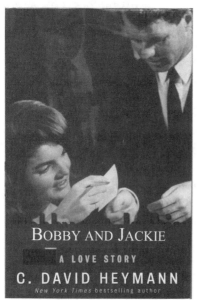

BOBBY AND JACKIE
A LOVE STORY
C. DAVID HEYMANN
New York Times bestselling author

The New York Times bestselling author, C. David Heymann, has almost made a career out of investigating the private lives of the Kennedys, publishing intimate biographies of Jackie, RFK, and even John F. Kennedy Jr. and Caroline.

More than any other investigative reporter, he introduced the secret love affair between Jackie and Bobby to the world, even though it was an open secret in Washington in 1964.

The book, *Bobby and Jackie,* is loaded with revelations about their affair, and of Jackie's attempts to learn as much as possible about what Bobby had been up to before their affair was launched.

Jackie even found out about the sex act between Bobby and Marilyn Monroe that had been secretly videotaped in the blonde bombshell's bedroom.

J. Edgar Hoover had called Clark Clifford, former counsel to the president during JFK's administration, to his office to show him the film and discuss possible fallout from it. No one knew how many copies had been printed.

At a dinner party in New York hosted by Vogue editor Diana Vreeland, Jackie confronted Clifford for more details, but he denied any knowledge of the explosive film.

five minutes. Then he stopped. He was dead. It was 1:44am. Within minutes, bulletins went out around the world.

Robert Francis Kennedy was dead at forty-two years of age.

Most of the world, except for his enemies, went into mourning. Not so Aristotle Onassis. "At last Jackie is free of the Kennedys," he said in a call to his friend, Costa Gratsos. "The last link just broke."

In another call to his henchman, Johnny Meyer, he said, "Somebody was going to fix the little bastard sooner or later."

At the White House, Johnson, was awakened with the news. I couldn't stand the shit," he said. "But send Air Force One to Los Angeles to bring the body back to New York."

En route East, Teddy sat alone with the casket. Ethel and Jackie were seated next to each other up front, but really had nothing to say.

Once in New York, Jackie placed a call to her trusted friend and former lover Roswell Gilpatric, the Under Secretary of Defense during JFK's administration, "Oh, dear God, please tell me. This is just a bad dream. The dawn will come. I will wake up. Please, please tell me that. When will my nightmare end?"

The burden of another assassination—this time of Bobby—became almost too much for Jackie. After the funeral on June 8 at St. Patrick's Cathedral in New York, Lady Bird Johnson encountered Jackie. "I found myself in front of her and called her name, putting out my hand. She looked at me as if from a great distance, as though I were an apparition. I murmured some words of sorrow and walked on. . . ."

After that funeral, Jackie's anger turned to bitterness. As Heymann wrote, "If she had felt any doubt or obligation to consider the impact of her actions on the political prospects of the remaining Kennedys, they were resolved by the shots that ended Bobby's life. Once again it did not matter who had pulled the trigger, or for what twisted reason."

Jackie and the Aviator

Flying High With Howard Hughes

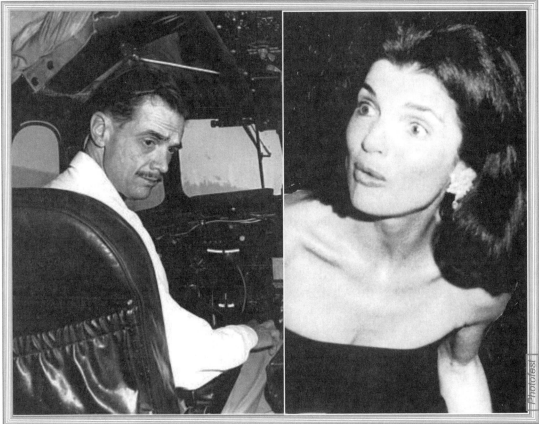

The aviator, **Howard Hughes** *(above, left)*, along with other powerful men, knew that after the assassination of her husband in Dallas in November of 1963, Jackie Kennedy, JFK's widow, had become the most desirable woman in the world on the marriage market. By Christmas of 1963, her staff estimated she'd received at least 2,000 proposals of marriage, often from men of influence.

Even though she was carrying on an illicit affair with her brother-in-law, Bobby Kennedy, it is believed that Jackie gave serious attention to some of these offers, especially one that originated with Howard Hughes and was personally delivered to her by Johnny Meyer, Hughes's so-called publicist (i.e., pimp).

Hughes had made millions on a drill bit whose patent was inherited from his father. Jackie knew he possessed America's most mammoth fortune. But before she'd accept his proposal of marriage, she made her highest-ever demands on his bank account.

Johnny Meyer:
Pimping for Howard Hughes
and Aristotle Onassis

A blaze of gunfire on November 22, 1963 in Dallas, Texas, Howard Hughes' home state, ended the reign of Camelot. Howard was sitting with his pimp, Johnny Meyer, discussing plans when news came over his television set that President John F. Kennedy had been shot in a motorcade in that city. The extent of his wounds was not immediately known.

Before his own death, Meyer had shopped a tell-all book about his former employer. As part of its sales proposal, he claimed that in the immediate wake of the assassination, Howard dropped all of his plans and stayed glued to the television for the next eighteen hours without sleep.

"I knew that bossman had known young Jack Kennedy years before," Meyer claimed in his book proposal. "I also knew that Howard hated old man Kennedy and wasn't a particular admirer of the 'left wing' politics of his son. Yet he stayed glued to that set like he'd lost his best friend. I just didn't get it. It was weeks before I learned the full extent of bossman's scheme. He wasn't mourning the slain president. He was planning to replace him!"

In the year of Kennedy's death, Howard refused to face business emergencies. He either postponed decisions or ignored them completely. "There were more than brush fires to put out," Meyer said. "There were bonfires. Everybody on the planet was suing Howard, sometimes successfully."

Johnny Meyer claimed that there was a certain irony in his boss man (**Howard Hughes**, *above*) pursuing Jackie Kennedy in 1964.

In 1940, the bisexual aviator and mogul had ardently pursued her husband to no avail.

According to Meyer, "I think Howard's fantasy would have been to get a young Jack Kennedy and a young Jacqueline Bouvier into his bed at the same time," Meyer claimed. "When both of them became powerful and celebrated people, he was not only attracted to them but jealous of them. He knew he had all the money he'd ever need. What he didn't have was power."

One morning at 3am when he couldn't sleep, Hughes placed a call to Meyer. "The world doesn't seem to talk or even care about me any more," Hughes told Meyer. "But I've come up with an idea to change all that. Get your ass over here, now!"

The spring of 1963 had gone badly for Howard. On February 11, 1963, he had refused to appear for deposition in a TWA lawsuit. On May 13 of that same year, a Federal judge in New York had awarded TWA a default judgment for Howard's refusal to show up. He was ordered to pay his own airline $135,000,000 in damages and sell his own stock. "That was a bitter pill for Howard to swallow," Meyer said.

"I think Howard was lusting for other worlds to conquer, but he hadn't made up his mind what those worlds would be," Meyer said. "By 1967, he would channel his fading energy into acquiring the Desert Inn Hotel and Casino in Las Vegas, the first step on the road to building an empire in Las Vegas and becoming King of the Desert."

In the aftermath of Kennedy's assassination, Howard began to develop a dream that was far greater than Las Vegas. In September of 1960, he'd turned fifty-five, and with his gray hair and declining health had begun to refer to himself as middle aged, even though he hated the term. "Who in the fuck decided that a man in his fifties is middle aged?" he once asked Meyer. "How many men do you know who are a hundred years old?"

As November faded into a bleak Christmas of 1963, Howard began to take stock of himself. He'd conquered many fields—more or less sucessfully—including aviation and motion pictures. Satellites his company manufactured were orbiting the planet, bringing *I Love Lucy* into homes in Bombay and Sydney. TWA was flying passengers across the globe. But three years before Kennedy's assassination, Howard had lost control of TWA.

"One time he turned to me and I'd never seen such a pathetic look on his face," Meyer said. "Normally when I looked into his eyes, I saw a feudal baron of immense power staring back at me. Even though we'd been asshole buddies for years, and I knew all his secrets, those blazing eyes of his sent shivers through me. Howard scared the shit out of me, he was so vindictive. I never wanted to cross him. I like eating too well, as one look at me will quickly reveal. He'd already turned on Noah Dietrich and made him the enemy. I knew he could do that to me as well."

"He seemed obsessed with Kennedy's assassination and couldn't wipe it from his mind," Meyer claimed. "I don't know how he got it, but he'd obtained a copy of the Zapruder film, which he watched endlessly. He must have seen it a thousand times. He wasn't just watching a home movie, but studying it with the eyes of a cobra."

A Dallas-based manufacturer of women's garments, Abraham Zapruder just happened to be shooting a home video recording of Kennedy's Dallas motorcade at the precise moment of the assassination. Had he not done so, the actual assassination would not have been captured on film. Zapruder sold this historic film to *Time Life* for $50,000, although Howard thought that it was worth at least two million—"maybe more"—he confided to Meyer.

It was rumored, with much justification, that **Johnny Meyer** (above), aide to Howard Hughes, possessed some of the most dangerous secrets in America. "I knew stuff that would bring down a government," he'd once boasted.

"He was watching it for some clue, although I didn't know what at the time," Meyer said. "At first I thought he was seeking some clue as to who shot Kennedy. But he had something else on his mind."

"Mrs. Kennedy is being portrayed in the press as the grieving widow," Howard told Meyer one day after viewing the Zapruder film for at least three playbacks in a row. "But I see something else there. This woman is a me-first type gal. She's a survivor."

The Zapruder film did, in fact, contradict Mrs. Kennedy's future testimony in front of the Warren

Biographer Peter Evans wrote, "Sometimes mistaken for a well-groomed gangster, the kind of New York hood who did business between the wars, Meyer liked to think of himself as a super troubleshooter, the ultimate fixer. 'I don't know where all the bodies are buried," Meyer once said, "but I do know where most of them are sleeping—and that's even better.'"

Hughes chose Meyer as his "agent" to contact Jacqueline Kennedy with a most unusual proposal.

249

Commission. As all the world now knows, the Texas governor, John Connally and his wife, Nellie, were riding in the motorcade with the Kennedys. At the first sound of gunfire, Nellie pulled her wounded husband into her lap and out of the line of fire. She even bent over him with her own body. Before the Warren Commission, Mrs. Kennedy testified, "If only I had been looking to the right, I would have seen the first shot that hit him," she said, referring to her own husband. "Then I could have pulled him down, and then the second shot would not have hit him."

But thanks to his obsessive reviews of the Zapruder film, Howard came up with another conclusion. Mrs. Kennedy *was* looking to the right. After the first bullet hit, she was riveted to her seat. It appeared that she stared for at least seven seconds at her husband after he'd taken the first bullet. But unlike Nellie Connally, she didn't reach to aid him.

In the film, she appeared shocked and stunned. Instead of coming to the aid of her husband, she jumped up and scrambled out of her seat and onto the trunk of the moving convertible. As she did, the heel of her shoe accidentally kicked her husband in the head. Howard felt that she was probably trying to reach a mounted rubber handgrip at the rear of the trunk. This handgrip could be a way of egress from the limousine, which at that point had begun to accelerate.

Later, Mrs. Kennedy had tried to put a better spin on her attempt to flee the vehicle, claiming that she was trying to retrieve a piece of her husband's skull.

"That's one bitch who had survival on the brain," Howard told Meyer. "My kind of woman! I admire that. She probably concluded that Jack was dead and there was nothing she could do for him at that point. She didn't want to be the next victim of a bullet. But in her panic she was also stupid. She should have buried herself on the floorboard of the car and pulled Jack's body down on top of her to serve as her human shield. By trying to crawl across the trunk in that very visible pink dress, she made herself more vulnerable to a potential assassin's bullet."

Jackie was in Mexico when she heard that Bobby was announcing his intention of seeking the nomination for President of the United States, running, of course on the Democratic ticket.

Johnny Meyer broke the news to her, and he later claimed that Jackie became hysterical.

"They'll kill him just like they gunned down Jack," she shouted at Meyer. When he calmed her down, he drafted a statement for her to read to the press. "I will always be with him with all my heart. I shall always back him."

In the weeks to come, Howard ordered Meyer to gather up all the information he could about those HUGHES FOR PRESIDENT clubs that had sprung up across the country in the wake of his August, 1947 testimony in front of Senator Ralph Owen Brewster's Senate committee. Although they had virtually disappeared, Howard instructed Meyer to "reactivate them—money is no object."

In the weeks ahead, Howard's plan began to reveal itself to Meyer more fully. Howard had more or less assumed that Lyndon B. Johnson, a fellow Texan, would seek and win the presidency in 1964. "Howard announced to me that he was going to run for president in 1968 on the Democratic ticket even though he was an arch-conservative," Meyer said. "He wasn't a Democrat. Neither was he a Republican. Politically, Howard lived in limbo land."

The way Howard saw it, his chief competitors for the 1968 Democratic Presidential nomination would include Lyndon B. Johnson and Robert Kennedy. Richard Nixon, he surmised, would seek the nomination on the Republican ticket.

"Howard felt he could eliminate Nixon by offering him bribes," Meyer said. "He believed that Nixon was such a crook that he'd accept any bribe. Once Howard had him where he wanted him, he'd release news of Nixon's dirty deeds to the press, which would destroy his political career and cost him the election."

"But how do you plan to knock out Bobby Kennedy and LBJ?" Meyer asked Howard.

"Howard looked at me for an astonishing moment, then said, 'I plan to marry Mrs. Kennedy!' You could have knocked me over with a feather. At first I thought he was joking, but when I saw that steely look in his eyes, I knew he was determined."

"My surprise wasn't over," Meyer claimed. "Later that day, he told me that I was to be the go-between in negotiating a marriage between Mrs. Kennedy and himself. It was to be a marriage of convenience. I was to contact Mrs. Kennedy and offer her ten million dollars if she'd marry Howard and campaign for him in the 1968 election. For her cooperation, he would also set up separate trust funds for her children, John F. Kennedy Jr. and Caroline Kennedy."

"Tell Mrs. Kennedy that I'll reinstate her in the White House," Howard said. "She can return in triumph, and I'll promise to give her unlimited power for a First Lady. I understand that dame loves power."

"I'll pay for the next goddamn redecoration of the White House—if that's what it takes to please her," Howard told Meyer. "That's not all. I'll even call that shithead Oleg Cassini, whom I hate, and tell him that Mrs. Kennedy will have *carte blanche* to order clothes from him, as many outfits as she wants even if it's three gowns a day. Tell her I'll also open charge accounts—the ceiling's the limit—at both Tiffany's and Cartier. I'll also provide 24-hour-a-day security guards for her and her kids."

Meyer said that he made at least eight attempts to get in touch with Mrs. Kennedy, both via hand-delivered courier and by telephone, as he'd easily obtained her private number. "She would not answer my letters, nor take my calls," Meyer said. "Someone else always answered the phone at her house. Sometimes it was a man, but more often a woman. One time the voice on the other end sounded like Bobby Kennedy."

"It must have been three o'clock in the morning in Washington, D.C., when Mrs. Kennedy finally returned my call," Meyer said. "I was in bed with, of all people, Ann Miller. I had lured Ann to my bed with three pieces of incredibly expensive jewelry that Howard had originally given Ava Gardner and that she'd thrown back at me, telling me to return the jewelry to Howard. I never did. I presented the gems to Ann, who seemed willing to give me a night of pleasure for the stones. I don't mean to imply that Ann was a hooker. But, unlike Ava, she respected the value of Howard's baubles."

"Mrs. Kennedy's voice came over the phone

During the final months of Bobby Kennedy's life in 1968, a drama unknown to the public was occurring behind the scenes.

Bobby was battling his rivals in the race to the White House, but he was also trying to put out brush fires in the "triangle" that existed between Jackie, Onassis, and himself.

He'd cut off his sexual relationship with Jackie when he decided to make a run for president, but he'd warned her, "If you marry Onassis before the election, I will have lost the White House. You're still an integral part of the Kennedys, and the public will not buy this marriage."

He left her baffled and confused.

wires," Meyer said. "I would have recognized that little girl voice anywhere. 'Mr. Meyer,' she said. 'This is Jacqueline Kennedy. I've received your latest letter and would like for you to fly to Washington Tuesday night to meet with me. I'm at least willing to hear what Mr. Hughes has to say.' She proceeded to give me instructions on how to reach her. After doing that, she gently put down the phone."

"I could swear she was drunk," Meyer told Ann. The next morning, he informed Howard of the news, and "bossman seemed elated. His plan to take over the White House, and ultimately the nation—maybe the world—was about to be launched. I'm not exaggerating when I say world. Howard believed that the man who controlled the White House in 1968 could ultimately control the world. He even had a plan to wipe out the Soviet Union in a sudden, unexpected missile attack. 'With Russia out of the way, no one will stop me,' he told me."

Meyer flew to Washington and at the pre-designated hour appeared at Mrs. Kennedy's Georgetown dwelling, finding her alone in her house. "She even answered the door herself," Meyer said. "She asked me if I wanted tea but I requested a drink instead. I was trembling all over. I mean, here I was in the presence of the most famous woman on the planet. In terms of fame, she ranked up there with Helen of Troy, Catherine the Great, and Cleopatra."

Meyer recalled that he sat on a sofa facing Mrs. Kennedy, who occupied a winged armchair, positioning her legs in a typical "debutante pose—all prim and proper."

Aristotle Onassis detested Bobby Kennedy, and the antagonistic feeling was mutual.

"When Bobby becomes president, he will still be the same sonofabitch Jackie said she'd put her hand in the fire for," Ari said to Meyer.

In Washington, Bobby told aide David Powers, "Onassis is a rich prick moving in on my brother's widow—what a shithead!"

Ari ordered Meyer to cast doubt in Jackie's mind about Bobby. "By November he'll hold all the cards. You'll be shuffled out of the deck once he's sitting in the Oval Office. All the news photos will be of Bobby and Ethel and his one thousand brats."

Ari took delight when Bobby learned of Jackie's intention to marry him. "I have turned the cat loose among the pigeons of Hickory Hill," Ari told Meyer, referring to RFK's country estate in Virginia.

"I tossed out Howard's offer to her even though I knew I was treating her like a hooker," Meyer said. "She didn't seem shocked—nor even surprised."

"In that little girl voice, almost a whisper, she finally said, 'I thought it was something like that.' I remember her leaning back in her chair and saying, 'You go back to your Mr. Hughes and tell him I'll accept his proposal of marriage, but not for ten million. I put a higher price tag on myself than that. Tell him my price tag is fifty million. Also my attorneys will set up trust funds for each of my children. Enough money to give each of them a lavish lifestyle, if that's what they want, for the rest of their lives. I like the offer of 24-hour security protection. But the Hughes Tool Company will have to agree in contract to offer that protection not only for the rest of my life but for the rest of the lives of both John and Caroline."

"Of course, Mrs. Kennedy," Meyer said, "I'll take that counter-offer back to Mr. Hughes."

He then remembered Mrs. Kennedy leaning forward in her chair. In almost a whisper she said, "There is one final thing, Mr. Meyer. A delicate issue. Mr. Hughes will have to agree, and put it in contract form, that

252

marriage to me will not entail conjugal visits."

"That hit me like a lead balloon," Meyer claimed. "But I told her I'd also convey that request to Howard. Frankly, I think Howard would have accepted the offer. He wanted to marry Mrs. Kennedy to gain political power unlike anything he'd ever known. He wasn't marrying her to get some pussy, although with her brunette hair and good looks, I think she could have gotten a rise out of bossman. But his libido was pretty much shut down by 1964."

Meyer flew back to the West Coast, conveying the astonishing news to Howard. "The financial terms didn't bother him at all," Meyer claimed. "Bossman knew he'd have to pay many more millions to get into the White House, and he seemed prepared to do that. He said he was going to delay for three weeks a formal response to Mrs. Kennedy, which he was going to deliver in person, meeting her at a secluded cottage on Martha's Vineyard, which I was to rent out and secure for him. I went ahead with plans for the Martha's Vineyard rendezvous, but it never came off."

At this point, Meyer hesitated in his remembrance, claiming that what he was about to reveal was so shocking that "it defies believability."

"Howard delivered his answer to me in about three weeks, more or less, but it wasn't the message that Mrs. Kennedy was waiting to hear," Meyer said.

"He had concluded that he could not run for president because of one thing: He'd have to shake the hands of half the male and female population of America, if not the world."

"In the years to come, I'll have to shake all those slimy paws," he said. "Some of whom will have just emerged from the toilet after wiping their ass and not washing their hands. The germs will surely kill me. I can't make the run. I have to thank Mrs. Kennedy for her acceptance, but withdraw the offer. I can't go through with it!"

"Frankly," Meyer said, "even though bossman instructed me to, I didn't have the balls to write or call Mrs. Kennedy with the turndown. It was too goddamn embarrassing. But perhaps my visit to Mrs. Kennedy jarred her into a new reality. I'd heard that she'd been drinking heavily, was in a deep depression, and was carrying on an affair with her brother-in-law after her husband's assassination. At least, I got her thinking in the right direction. Another rich man, but not Howard Hughes, lay in that gal's future."

***

Meyer did not appear again in Jackie Kennedy's life until after she married Aristotle Onassis. When Hughes was finished with Meyer, he hired himself out to Ari as a "spy, cover-up, flunky, procurer, asshole-wiper, whatever

One evening, in the weeks following her second marriage, Jackie Kennedy Onassis was sitting with Johnny Meyer as part of a strategy session in Ari's deluxe apartment on the Avenue Foch in Paris. They were watching a tape made of a show **Joan Rivers** *(above)* had performed in Las Vegas.

"Come on, be honest," Rivers asked her audience. "Would you sleep with Onassis? Do you believe she does? Well, she has to do something. I mean, you can't stay in Bergdorf's shopping all day."

Jackie jumped up and turned off the video. "It seems in America I have gone from being the beloved widow to a caricature."

When Ari learned of the incident, he told Meyer, "Jackie's got to reconcile herself to being Mrs. Aristotle Onassis because the only place she'll find sympathy from now on is in the dictionary between shit and syphilis."

253

you want," Meyer said. "I'd do everything but rim jobs, although in spirit I do those too."

To Meyer's surprise, one of his jobs involved spying on Jackie after her marriage to "The Greek."

Years after their initial encounter, when Meyer came face to face with Jackie again, no mention was made of their earlier negotiations. At first she was cold and distant with him until he learned how to break through to her. He soon found out that she loved indiscreet gossip, and since Meyer was more informed about the secrets of the nation's personalities than Walter Winchell, Hedda Hopper, and Louella Parsons, she slowly began to let down her guard.

One day he relayed to her the latest gossip about two of her dearest friends, Truman Capote and Bobby Kennedy, who lived in the same New York City apartment complex near the United Nations.

One night a drunken Capote had encountered Bobby in the elevator and propositioned him, asking him if he could give him a blow-job. At first Meyer thought Jackie would respond coldly. But she smiled, lit a cigarette, leaned back and said, "If I knew Bobby, he accepted. I hear Capote has mastered the art. I was never good at that."

From that moment on, Jackie accepted Meyer into her good graces, often inviting him for a private luncheon. Sometimes she had special requests: "Tell me all you know about Lyndon Johnson's mistress."

One afternoon after Jackie's second marriage, Ari sent Meyer with her on a shopping expedition to Athens. They lunched together in a little out-of-the-way Turkish restaurant.

"I know Ari has hired you to spy on me," she said. "But since we've become *confidants*, why don't you tell me the most hideous secret you've ever learned about Ari."

At first reluctant to do so, Meyer was eventually won over by her charm.

"Ever since he was a boy and raped by a Turkish lieutenant in his native land, he discovered he has a gay streak in him," Meyer claimed. "But with a very perverted twist. He has a boy stashed in an apartment in Paris, another one in Athens. They are only kids. I've met both of them. They're each in their late teens. Ari likes to beat them severely before sodomizing them."

She looked startled. "Sometimes," she said, "It's better not to know everything."

GLORIA SWANSON TO JACKIE: *"I HAD ARI FIRST, DEARIE!"*

Jackie encountered silent screen vamp **Gloria Swanson** *(photo, right)* at a party, decades after her heyday. For years, Jackie had been hearing stories about Swanson's long-running affair in Hollywood during the late 1920s with her deceased father-in-law, Joseph P. Kennedy. Virtually unknown to the world, Swanson had also had an affair with Aristotle Onassis.

At the party, Swanson provocatively told Jackie, "I got to Ari first, dearie. In fact, Ari sent Johnny Meyer to meet with me recently. He's heard talk that I might write my memoirs, and he doesn't want me to mention our affair."

"I told Meyer that I was surprised Ari thought I would want to rake up our long-ago friendship at this point. I also told him to tell Ari that his 'injunction' is a compliment to my memory but an insult to my integrity."

What Swanson didn't tell Jackie was that Meyer had arrived at her swank apartment in New York with $250,000 in cash to offer her for the removal of Ari's name from her upcoming memoirs. She refused the money. "Great stars have great pride," she said, using the famous line of Norma Desmond in *Sunset Blvd.*

"I got her to agree not to mention you, and I saved you a quarter million," Meyer later told Ari. "Sounds like bonus time to me."

Rosemary Clooney & Bobby Kennedy

Come On-a My House

Ever since **Rosemary Clooney** met Patricia Kennedy and her husband, Peter Lawford, at a Democratic Party rally at Janet Leigh's house, the singer became a Kennedy devotee. Word of her support led to an invitation to Hickory Hill, where she was "charmed by **Bobby Kennedy**'s Irish wit." All Ethel wanted to know was the name of any star in Hollywood upon whom Rosemary had developed a crush. Her crush wasn't in Hollywood, but sitting at the table at Hickory Hill.

Rosemary later got to meet President Kennedy, who had his shoes off, wearing red socks, a trademark of Peter Lawford's. Believe it or not, in an upstairs kitchen at the White House, the president scrambled eggs for her. "I adore him, but my heart at that point belonged to Bobby, and always would," Rosemary claimed.

In the Oak Bar of the Plaza Hotel in New York City, on November 22, 1963, Rosemary got drunk after hearing the news from Dallas. That was hard enough to deal with, but she managed. What she never really recovered from was Bobby's assassination in 1968.

"When Bobby died, my heart died with him."

—Rosemary Clooney

Bobby always claimed that Rosemary's *Red Garters* (1954) was his favorite of her films. The movie was a pointed spoof, but it wasn't Rosemary's favorite. Her dearest friend, Marlene Dietrich (there were rumors), came by the set to teach her how to roll a cigarette.

"Did you have an affair with your leading man?" Bobby asked her one night. "I hear all you gals out in Hollywood do that."

"Hell, no!" she said. "Gene Barry hated me. One day he was supposed to carry me, but the bastard deliberately dropped me. He constantly upstaged me because he wanted first billing, which went to me."

In Camelot, the songbird Rosemary Clooney fell in love with Robert Kennedy, even though he was a married man. Merv Griffin was one of her best friends. It was imperative that Rosemary and RFK not be seen in public. When the singer asked Merv if they could use his New York apartment for their secret trysts, Merv readily agreed.

"I'd like to get to know the Kennedys better," Merv said. "But I agreed to stay out of their way when the apartment was in use for an off-the-record weekend. I found it rather thrilling that they were shacking up at my place. I encountered Robert on several occasions, but he seemed embarrassed. We mostly exchanged pleasantries. I think he didn't really want me to know he was banging my best gal pal Rosemary. Who am I to judge? I'm not exactly a candidate for sainthood myself."

RFK was assassinated in the early hours of June 5, 1968, at the Ambassador Hotel in Los Angeles. Rosemary had spent months campaigning across the country for the man she wanted to be president and the lover she could never have just to herself. She'd been forced to share him not only with his wife, Ethel, but with Marilyn Monroe, Lee Remick, and surprise surprise, Rudolf Nureyev, who had also enjoyed the charms of Jacqueline Kennedy.

The days had long passed when Robert and Rosemary conducted their sexual trysts in Merv's hideaway. Even though Robert had moved on to other lovers, Rosemary was still madly in love with him.

"Bobby was the passion of Rosie's life," Merv confided. "He never really loved her—he was still in love with Ethel—but he wanted her friendship and support. He abandoned her bed, but he never abandoned the friendship."

With two of her five children in tow, Rosemary arrived at the second floor Embassy

Room of the Ambassador. The crowds were overflowing that night, and at one point Rosemary went to the floor below and entertained the burgeoning crowd with her rousing renditions of "When Irish Eyes Are Smiling" and "This Land Is Your Land."

"I was in the VIP section," Rosemary later said, "and I never got to say a final goodbye to Bobby. After his victory speech, he was supposed to come into the roped-off VIP area to greet us and thank us. Instead some aide led him toward the adjoining banquet room, where he was directed to take a short-cut through the kitchen." Tears welled in her eyes. "Even now, I can't stand to think of what happened next."

Other than Ethel Kennedy, perhaps no woman in America suffered the death of Robert Kennedy more than Rosemary. "She literally went into exile," Merv said. "Reports reached me that she had begun dangerously mixing excessive booze with drugs. The pain in her heart was just too great. She had to dull it. She literally became a basket case. I knew she'd always loved Bobby and had for years, but until I went to see Rosie at the hospital, where she'd collapsed into a nervous breakdown, I never realized the full extent of that obsessive love.

Rosemary *(left)* and **Betty Clooney** *(right)*, those singing sisters from Maysville, Kentucky, had never heard of the Kennedys when they launched their first act.

Flat broke and clean out of the soda bottles they'd been collecting and cashing in for their deposits, Betty and Rosemary Clooney began their career on Radio Station WLW singing "Hawaiian War Chant." They didn't know all the lyrics so they made up lines.

The station manager liked them and hired them in April of 1945, paying them $20 each per week. Rosemary was sixteen, Betty only thirteen.

After Bobby's death, he was all she could think about. I'd never seen anything like it. She was behaving like the grieved widow, as if she were the mother of all of Bobby's children."

After his visit that day to the hospital, Rosemary cut Merv out of her life and wouldn't answer his urgent phone calls. Years went by before he finally reached her by showing up, unannounced, on her doorstep. "A nanny or somebody let me in," Merv said, "and I marched immediately to her bedroom and confronted her. 'For God's sake,' I told her, 'get the hell out of that God damn bed and get on with your life. Bobby's dead. He's not coming back.'"

At least this is the story that Merv told his friends in Los Angeles. In his second autobiography, he claimed he reached her on the telephone.

After that painful reunion and confrontation, Merv admitted that he nagged the singer day after day. Even so, it took weeks before she agreed to come onto his show.

Merv had predicted to Rosemary that she'd be a big hit if she appeared in public again—and she was. The fans in the studio responded with massive applause after her beautiful rendition of "What Are You Doing the Rest of Your Life?" Even Merv admitted that he teared up at the end of that song.

For the rest of her life, Merv stayed in touch with her, even though the remainder of their friendship was mostly conducted over the phone. He called frequently and offered his moral support during Rosemary's eventual bout with lung cancer. Then a call he'd dreaded came in on June 29, 2002. Rosemary had died in Beverly Hills.

As Merv later told the press, "Those lungs that gave us some of the most beautiful music of the 20th century will breathe no more. I was hoping until the very end that she'd pull through. I called her as often as I could. She was one of my closest friends. The spot she occupied in my heart will never be filled by anyone else."

"And the spot Bobby occupied in her heart could never be replaced," Merv continued. "In some sense, she died of a long, lingering heartbreak. There's no doubt about it: Bobby was her lifelong obsession."

A very young and handsome **George Clooney** appeared opposite his rather dowdy aunt, **Rosemary Clooney**, in an episode of NBC's hit hospital-based television series, *ER* (1984-1985).

The young actor first found his niche in that series portraying Dr. Doug Ross.

"We never sat down and talked about it," Rosemary claimed, "but George says he's been helped by watching how I did it, how I learned the things I had to learn first hand, often painfully."

Rosemary was delighted with the success of her nephew, labeling him, "the New Cary Grant."

When the Emmys rolled around, George was nominated as Outstanding Actor in a Drama Series. Rosemary was also nominated for an Emmy as Outstanding Guest Actress. He was grateful to Rosemary for letting him crash at her guesthouse.

To return the favor, he secured a part for her in *ER* as a patient suffering with Alzheimer's.

TV talk show host **Merv Griffin** was one of Rosemary Clooney's closest friends and confidants. He revealed to her all his gay affairs, and he lived through all her romantic trysts. He turned over his New York apartment to Rosemary and Robert Kennedy during their affair.

He had a pang of guilt, however, because he concealed details from Rosemary about Bobby's affair with another friend of his, actress Lee Remick.

Griffin, in fact, had been designated as the godfather to Kate, the daughter of Lee and her husband Bill Colleran.

"I felt like Mata Hari. I knew too much and I couldn't speak with loose lips," Merv said.

Paul Newman's Rendezvous

With "The Most Desirable Woman on Earth"

Photofest

Before he'd even met **Jackie Kennedy, Paul Newman** had campaigned vigorously for JFK, contributing both his money and his time.

In the wake of JFK's assassination, during the 1964 presidential campaign, Paul decided to throw his political support behind Lyndon B. Johnson. He later told Lem Billings, "I am sadly disappinted. I thought Johnson would de-escalate the war in Vietnam. From this day on, I've become leary of politicians."

After their one night together at the Hotel Carlyle in New York, there is no evidence that Jackie and the actor ever connected sexually again. Billings asked Jackie why not. "He was always on your fantasy list of actors to seduce."

She startled him with her confession. "It was the most amazing thing," she said. "Paul and Jack have an identical penis. It was like getting seduced by my husband all over again. It was eerie."

259

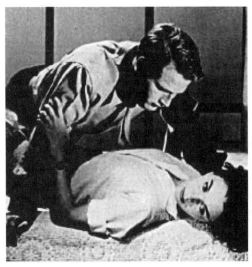

Paul Newman and Elizabeth Taylor are depicted together in a tense scene from Tennessee Williams' *Cat on a Hot Tin Roof.* "In your darkest hour," James Dean once told singer Eartha Kitt, "Paul could always offer you comfort."

Newman did just that during the filming of *Cat on a Hot Tin Roof,* when he "comforted" Elizabeth Taylor when she heard the tragic news that her husband, showman Michael Todd, had died in a plane crash.

In 1968, Paul was among the first to get through to Jackie to express his condolences when Robert F. Kennedy was assassinated in Los Angeles. "I want to come to you and hold you, and tell you it'll be okay. You'll go on."

Jackie later told Lem Billings, "I think Paul wanted to come and live with me. For how long, I don't know. I got the feeling he wanted to replace Bobby in my life."

"THEIR PENISES WERE IDENTICAL"

Every straight or bisexual male has his fantasy woman. For Paul Newman, he still considered Elizabeth Taylor one of the most enchanting women of her time. But, as he'd once told intimate friends, "Jacqueline Kennedy is the most desirable woman on the planet. Our Helen of Troy."

In 1968, after her brother-in-law, Robert F. Kennedy, announced that he was going to run against Eugene McCarthy for the Democratic nomination for president, she placed a discreet call to Newman, who was backing McCarthy.

He was thrilled to be speaking to her and hearing that famous voice that in some way reminded him of Marilyn Monroe. He agreed to meet her in the bar of the Hotel Carlyle in Manhattan—the same hotel where John F. Kennedy had had sexual trysts with Monroe.

The sale of her home in Georgetown in Washington, DC, had allowed her to purchase a Fifth Avenue apartment, but despite that, she chose to meet him at the Carlyle Hotel, perhaps as some kind of symbolic assertion of her independence.

Of his many involvements with famous personalities, Newman's short-lived link with Jackie is clouded in the most mystery and the subject of the most speculation. A doorman reported that he arrived at the pre-designated time of eight o'clock in the evening, and was seen leaving the following morning around 8:30, hailing a taxi and quickly disappearing. He wore dark sunglasses and a hat. The sunglasses were familiar; the hat was not. Even so, the staff at the Carlyle recognized him and spread the word. The story was too good, too hot to keep to one's self.

Susan Strasberg claimed that within days, the rumor was making the rounds at Downey's Restaurant, sometimes known among hipster New Yorkers as "the poor man's Sardi's," where it quickly spread through the grapevine to Washington and on to Hollywood.

The only recognizable name who spoke openly about the night Newman spent with Jackie in her hotel suite was Truman Capote, her treacherous friend. In Tennessee Williams' New York apartment, Capote claimed that Jackie had confessed to him "only some of the details of that night."

Capote asserted to a many of his friends that one night he and Jackie, drunk on champagne, named the three movie stars they'd most like to seduce. For Capote, the size of their appendages seemed to dominate his selection of John Ireland, Steve Cochran, and Rock Hudson.

As her most-desirable sexual candidates of choice, Jackie named Marlon Brando, William Holden, and Paul Newman, claiming, "I've already attained two-thirds of my goal." At that time, she was referring to Brando and Holden, not Newman, whom she was yet to meet.

From what Capote claimed, a sketchy report has emerged. He said that over drinks he'd discussed Newman with Jackie.

In a secluded corner of the bar at the Carlyle, Jackie in dark sunglasses greeted Newman. He kissed her on both cheeks. She casually pointed to a man in a dark business suit sitting a few tables away. She told him that he was a member of the Secret Service assigned to guard her. "He's also my lover," she allegedly told Newman. If he were shocked, he masked it effectively. He even assumed that she might be joking because it was unbelievable that she'd be this frank with him.

Upon his arrival, he'd presented her with a porcelain rose, which was investment enough for him, even though he'd heard she would spend as much as $100,000 on an antique snuff box.

That night he met Jackie, he encountered a very different woman from the brave but beleaguered widow he'd read about in the press. Sitting opposite him was a flirtatious and attractive woman, with a mischievous gleam in her eyes, not the grieving widow of a slain American president.

When she'd had enough champagne, Jackie could become outrageous, not the "steel butterfly" so often depicted on camera.

One night at a White House gala, when she'd had more than her share of the bubbly, Jackie took off her shoes and danced and flirted with every handsome man in attendance, much to the annoyance of her husband, who hawkeyed her every move. Perhaps she was paying him back for his own sexual trysts with his women *du jour*.

A minor friend of Jackie's, Paul Mathias, the New York correspondent for France's *Paris-Match* Magazine, summed her up. His assessment later appeared in *A Woman Named Jackie* by C. David Heymann. In Mathias' words, the former First Lady "was the tease, the temptress of her age. She perfected the art, she invented it. She was Miss Narcissist, perpetually searching mirrors for worry wrinkles and strands of prematurely gray hair. She didn't worry about growing old, she worried about looking old. Within 18 months of JFK's assassination she had two dozen of the world's most brilliant and important men dangling like marionettes, dancing at her fingertips, most of them very married, very old, or very queer."

In Paris, Aristotle Onassis told a reporter, "Jackie is too young and too vibrant a woman to spend her life maintaining the Camelot legend. It is time for her to come down from that pedestal and do something very, very indiscreet, like marrying Truman Capote."

Even John Kennedy told associates that "Jackie is known for developing crushes, like on Warren Beatty. But she's very fickle. They don't last long. She becomes bored quickly."

From what Capote learned, Newman spent a good part of the evening hearing about the Kennedys. Although Jackie was very supportive of Bobby, and urged Newman to switch his allegiance, she was highly critical of Rose Kennedy. "She'll eat a juicy steak for lunch and serve the rest of the table hamburgers, even hot dogs. To save money, she orders the chef not to make desserts, even bread pudding from stale bread."

One speculation she may have shared with Newman that night was her belief that her husband would not have been re-elected. "His indiscretions had become so plentiful, so well known, that they would have made headlines during the campaign and would have destroyed him."

According to Capote, during the course of the evening, she revealed to Newman that former Democratic presidential candidate Adlai Stevenson had pursued her after the death of her husband in Dallas.

Alone in the hotel suite with Newman, Jackie is alleged to have repeated her standard selling points with Newman, as she did to anybody she was hoping to "win over to our side." She spent at least an hour extolling the virtues of Bobby Kennedy. Allegedly, she asserted that she personally knew Eugene McCarthy but that she believed that he was a one-issue candidate, and that his political obsession revolved solely around "the war," she reportedly said, "that God damn Vietnam War."

She went on to warn Newman that there were other issues associated with the upcoming race, including the war on poverty. "Bobby can offer hope to the downtrodden that McCarthy can't. Bobby is a candidate whose stand on the issues, not just the war, is all-encompassing. He can save this nation from itself. That is, if he can save himself from an assassin's bullet. They've already killed one Kennedy in this country. They might strike again." Supposedly, she never revealed who "they" were.

The most provocative shared indiscretion of the evening, if Capote is to be believed, is that Jackie confided to Newman that she'd never been able to satisfy her husband sexually. "Perhaps I can change that state of affairs with you tonight," she may have told him.

At least for one night, Jackie may have convinced Newman to switch his political alliance. But in the sober light of morning, after he left Carlyle, he remained in McCarthy's camp. He later told Tony Perkins, "I faced more temptation that night than Antony when he met Cleopatra."

Of course, when Bobby Kennedy was assassinated in June of 1968—allegedly by Sirhan Sirhan, although rampant speculation about the assassination remains—Newman's support of Jackie's brother-in-law became a moot issue.

Howl!, a scandal sheet emanating from New York City's East Village that flourished for only two months during hippiedom's "Dawning of the Age of Aquarius," was the only newspaper, if that's what it could be called, that carried the rumor. The headline, as were all that short-lived paper's headlines, was blunt and to the point: PAUL NEWMAN FUCKS JACKIE O.

PAUL & JACKIE: GOSSIPING ABOUT SEX

Jackie and Paul Newman may not have always agreed on politics, but both of them found each other compatible as friends. Jackie was one of the first to call and express her sympathy to Paul when his son, Scott Newman, was found dead.

During dinner one night, Jackie told Newman, "I read a quote about you from Janet Leigh. She said, 'Paul makes you respond to him. That is the basis of his sexual appeal.' Is that true?"

"You'll have to answer that yourself," he told her, raising an eyebrow. "After all, you're qualified to do so."

"Touchée," she murmured.

"When Janet and I made *Harper* (1966) together, I stole a gimmick from Bobby Kennedy. For my character of Lew Harper, I borrowed Bobby's technique of listening to people without actually facing them."

"Bobby always referred to that as 'The Sideways Approach,'" she said.

Rather flirtatious with her, he said, "I hope he didn't do everything sideways."

"Not at all," she said. "During sex, he was on top, with his eyes boring into mine."

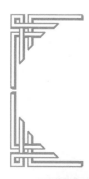
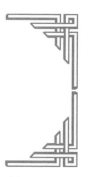

Teddy & Jackie

Coveting His Brother's Wife

In a cozy *tête-à-tête*, **Jackie Kennedy and Teddy Kennedy** share an intimate moment. In Washington, Hyannis Port, New York, a Greek island, and in Palm Beach, they would share many intimate moments away from the prying eyes of the paparazzi. When Teddy and Jackie came together, they made "the Devil's pact," in a charge attributed, falsely or otherwise, to author Gore Vidal.

According to insiders, that pact involved the promotion of the legend of Camelot, not the real man. JFK actually never went too far to the left of public opinion, but Teddy and Jackie plotted to make him a stalking horse for a Kennedy-style liberalism.

While all this plotting was going on, they fell in love. As Jackie told another author Truman Capote, "I'm in love with two men at the same time, both Bobby and Teddy. What to do?"

TEDDY ABOUT JACKIE:
"I WILL LOVE HER FOREVER"

A member of Kennedy's "Irish Mafia," JFK's legal aide David Powers, saw the affair in the making. "Let's face it," he told his cronies, "Teddy has had the hots for Jackie ever since he laid eyes on her. He's one determined brother. He'll get her yet. The moment will come—maybe not today, but tomorrow. If Jackie went for two of the brothers, why not a third? Women are like that. I've known cases in Boston where a woman lost her husband and then turned around and married his brother. You figure."

In August of 2009, Edward (Teddy) Kennedy, the long-standing senator from Massachusetts, died at the age of 77 of brain cancer, greatly mourned by his devotees. But despite their adulation, he was an object of scorn from his conservative enemies, who objected to, among other things, his scandalous past.

But very few of his enemies knew of one scandal so horrendous that if it had been more widely known, would have doomed his political life, which had somehow managed to survive in spite of the drowning of Mary Jo Kopechne in that black Oldsmobile accident at Chappaquiddick back in July of 1969.

Teddy recorded both his good and bad deeds in a personal diary he kept. These diaries contained his most intimate thoughts. He left specific instructions on his deathbed that they not be made public until 2034.

A magazine voted this the "sexiest picture ever taken of **Teddy Kennedy**." There are those who disagree, but Jackie kept this picture on a night table beside her bed except when Bobby came. With Bobby in her boudoir, she displayed a picture of him. There was always a picture of JFK on public display in her living room, and that was acceptable.

Some biographers have dismissed Teddy's affair with Jackie as "another one of those newspaper romances." But his diaries and his close personal friends claim it was "an affair of the heart."

Kennedy aide David Powers, who once went sailing with Teddy and Jackie, later told friends, "I went below. I guess they didn't hear me. I saw something I wish to this day that I had never seen. All three of us were beyond embarrassed."

The existence of these very private diaries was revealed in the summer of 2010 when the FBI released heretofore sealed files.

Although family members are protecting the contents of the diaries, in honor of Teddy's final wish, some of the major revelations came to light when the senator left one of his diaries on a plane after taking a trip to Mexico and Central America.

The airline turned over the diary to the FBI, and it was eventually returned to Teddy, but not until it was read. Some of the most salacious contents were leaked, and became cocktail party chatter in Washington and Georgetown.

This Beltway crowd was already familiar with the affair of Jackie and Bobby in the wake of the president's death, but news of her sexual liaison with the family's youngest brother, Teddy, resonated like a bombshell.

Journalist Leon Wagener was the first to break the story. He quoted a source close to Teddy who claimed, "When Ted finally made love to Jackie, he fulfilled the dream he'd had to possess his brother's beautiful wife. Obviously he knew it was a grievous sin and an insult to his late brother, but he couldn't control himself."

Wagener quoted another family insider who asserted, "Ted in his diaries wrote about his romance with Jackie in great detail and didn't want his family, especially his wife, Vicki, and his son, Congressman Patrick J. Kennedy, to read it now when it could cause great hurt."

Before he died, Teddy confessed his "sin" to a priest and asked for forgiveness.

Powers revealed to Kennedy insiders, who included Ted Sorensen, that "the Kennedy family has long known that Teddy was more than a brother-in-law to Jackie. But it's a subject that dare not speak its name. No one wants to talk about it. The revelations about Bobby and Jackie were already too much for this overburdened family. The thing between Jackie and Teddy was just too much to handle."

One night in Boston, Teddy told Powers, "I've always been in love with Jackie, right from the beginning, although I was barely 21 when I met her. She's always been special to me. When Jack died, I knew she was seeing Bobby, too, but that didn't stop me. Bobby couldn't always be with her."

Teddy revealed that he continued his affair with Jackie long after she and Bobby had ended their sexual liaisons.

"She was trapped in a miserable marriage with Onassis," Teddy said. "After Bobby died, she turned more and more to me as her confidant. We once took a romantic trip to Greece together. It was the happiest moment of my life."

Jackie's friendship with Teddy began when he was still an undergraduate at Harvard, and she agreed to help him with his term paper on art history, a subject he didn't know much about and she did.

Neither Teddy nor Bobby wanted Jackie to marry Onassis. But when Teddy saw that she was determined to go through with it, he agreed to fly with her to Greece and handle financial matters with her new groom. He didn't welcome the task "but for you, Jackie, I'll do it. Someone has to see that your interests are protected."

Of the many powerful men she knew, Jackie wanted Teddy to negotiate the details of a prenuptial agreement with Onassis. During the most intense of the negotiations, Jackie flew to Athens on a shopping expedition, leaving her husband-to-be with her brother-in-law and lover.

Onassis was known as a hard bargainer, but Teddy found him willing to relent to his

Talk about body language. Jackie was often alienated from her husband, Ari Onassis. But John-John seems to be getting along just fine with Ari. The president's son was telling his friends at school that, "One day, I'll inherit all of his millions. He really likes me."

Like his brother, Bobby, Teddy did not approve of Jackie's relationship with Ari but, since she was involved in it already, he promised her that he'd protect her interests at all costs. Ari knew of Jackie's affair with Teddy. When his aide, Johnny Meyer, asked him what he was going to do about it, Ari said, "She knows about my affair with Maria Callas. In Arizona, isn't that called a Mexican standoff?"

demands. The senator revealed that Jackie's income from the Kennedy Trust was only $175,000 a year, which shocked Onassis. "So little money for such a rich family," he told Teddy, who quickly explained that Bobby was supplementing that with a check for $50,000 a year. Teddy also pointed out that by marrying again, Jackie would lose her $10,000 annual widow's pension from the government as well as the protection of the Secret Service.

Onassis assured him that he would replace the pension and also ensure that she was protected. He invited Teddy to inspect his kennel of well-trained German shepherd police dogs which would patrol Skorpios.

When Jackie returned from Athens, Teddy reported that the negotiations had gone splendidly, and that Onassis had agreed to everything—and more. To celebrate, Onassis invited both of them for a party aboard the *Christina*. Knowing Teddy's fondness for beautiful young women, he arranged for eight of them to be flown in from Athens.

As a means of concealing his affair with Jackie, Teddy deliberately made a play for one of the blonde bimbos. For whatever reason, Onassis invited Nico Mastorakis, a professional journalist and photographer aboard as well.

When Mastorakis snapped a photo of Teddy, soaked in ouzo and holding a blonde in his arms, the senator became furious. He grabbed the camera from Mastorakis and tossed it overboard. "If you report any of this," Teddy shouted at him, "I'll have your ass."

The next day Jackie and Teddy told Onassis they had to discuss private Kennedy business, and he turned over the *Christina* and its crew to them to sail to an uninhabited offshore island. He assigned two of his security guards to accompany them. Suspicious of their motivations, Onassis ordered one of his guards to discreetly spy on Jackie and Teddy.

Once they arrived at the island, Teddy asked one of the guards to direct them to its most secluded cove. The guard found a beauty spot for them with warm water and white sands. Teddy instructed the guard to stand at a lookout point and signal if anyone was coming, and he also asked the guard to turn his eyes away to allow them some privacy.

Of course, the guard didn't do as instructed and spied relentlessly on his two charges. He later reported to Onassis that he'd seen them nude and lying together on a blanket, kissing each other passionately. And whereas the Greek tycoon had long ago learned about Jackie's affair with Bobby, it was the first time that Onassis learned that Teddy was also sexually involved with his sister-in-law

Although Onassis decided not to confront Jackie with this indiscretion, he vowed to get "revenge" on Teddy. He did not specify what that

The burial of Aristotle Onassis became the most notorious tabloid funeral of the year. **Christina Onassis**, leading the mourners, is not only grieving over her dead father, but furious at **Jackie**, who's walking behind her.

After Ari's death, Jackie had issued a statement to the press. "Aristotle Onassis rescued me at a moment when my life was engulfed in shadows. He meant a lot to me. He brought me into a world where one could find both happiness and love. We lived through many beautiful experiences together which cannot be forgotten, and for which I will be eternally grateful."

When Christina heard that, she told her aunts: "It's all bullshit! Jackie is at the funeral with her lover boy, Teddy, to try to bleed every cent from the estate. I've got to pay the whore off."

revenge would be.

Somehow, Teddy learned that Onassis had uncovered details of his affair with Jackie. "Onassis is powerful and he's ruthless," Teddy told Powers. "He could easily put out a contract on me. He's killed others, maybe Bobby himself."

The Massachusetts senator had long been suspicious that Onassis had been behind the assassination of his beloved brother, Bobby. Reportedly, his diaries revealed that Teddy lived in "constant terror" that Onassis might have him murdered. "I'd wake up in a cold sweat, fearing a killer was in the house."

The romance of Jackie and Teddy didn't entirely escape the radar screen. Word spread in the London tabloids about a possible romance between them when in January of 1985 they each attended the funeral of Lord Harlech, formerly known as David Ormsby-Gore, in North Wales.

Teddy was seen on several occasions entering Jackie's quarters after eleven at night and not departing until dawn.

On the occasion of Onassis' funeral in 1975, Jackie called upon Teddy once again to fly to Skorpios to negotiate her share of the estate, this time with Ari's daughter, Christina.

Having flown in from Paris, Teddy showed a lack of sensitivity the moment he sat in the limousine with Jackie and Christina en route to the funeral.

After the limousine pulled away from the curbside, Teddy immediately turned to Christina, telling her, "Now it's time to take care of Jackie."

Christina burst into tears and escaped from the limousine, joining her bereaved aunts in the limousine behind. She later spoke of that moment to friends and business associates. Some of her comments reached the press and were published in biographies.

Apparently, she said, "I was in a limousine with a pair of hungry vultures waiting to feed off the corpse of my dead father. Ted Kennedy was absolutely ruthless trying to protect his mistress. But it was her smile that drove me from the vehicle. Have you ever seen a carnivorous hyena come to feed as a scavenger? That was Jackie Kennedy. I never called her Jackie Onassis, because she was not a real wife to my father."

Almost deranged out of her mind, Christina arrived on Skorpios to bury her father. She didn't want "The Professional Widow," as she called Jackie, to even attend. "The gold digger has arrived for more gold," Christina told her aunts.

Time had run out for Ari on March 15, 1975. After the funeral, Christina told the people of Skorpios, "Both my father and my mother know how short life can be and how terribly death can strike. This island is mine. You are my people now."

Onassis left an estate of $1 billion, the major share going to Christina. After his funeral, Jackie and Christina engaged in an 18-month legal battle over Jackie's share.

Jackie's attorneys threatened to have a court invalidate Ari's will. Greek law required that a precondition of a will's validity demanded that it had to be composed "in a single sitting in a single location." Ari's final will had been composed during a flight with Jackie from Acapulco to New York. During its composition, in a fit of anger, Ari had interrupted the process for lunch in a Florida coffee shop while his plane was being refueled.

Technically, therefore, the will had not been prepared in one sitting, but at various times in various countries. Jackie's main attorney, Simon Rifkind, argued that if the will was invalidated, Jackie, as Ari's wife and according to the estate laws of Greece, would receive 12.5 percent of Ari's estimated billion-dollar estate. In U.S. dollars, that would total $125 million.

Abandoning a protracted battle in the courts, Jackie agreed to accept Christina's offer of a flat sum of $20 million. Jackie would agree to abandon all future claims to the estate, including her share of the yacht *Christina,* and her one-quarter share of the island of Skorpios.

Rufkind successfully negotiated for another $6 million, which would cover estate taxes. Jackie insisted that all of her personal letters to Ari be returned. Both she and Christina agreed not to publicly discuss the terms of the final settlement.

It is estimated that during the time Jackie was married to Ari, her allowances, jewelry, clothes, and living expenses, including travel, came to some $42 million. That averaged about $7 million annually for every year they were married.

Jackie later regretted the amount of the settlement, telling Teddy and others, "I came away with peanuts. Ari's will was not properly drawn up and, according to Greek law, as his widow I should have received $125 million of his billion dollar estate."

After her fight with Jackie, Christina's life would take many disastrous turns before its tragic conclusion.

On November 19, 1988, a bulletin was announced from Buenos Aires, claiming that Christina Onassis, after multiple episodes of drug and alcohol abuse, had suffered a pulmonary edema and was DOA at a local hospital. Her remains would be laid to rest on the island of Skorpios beside the bodies of her father and brother.

The press hounded Jackie for a statement. None was forthcoming. Finally, a spokesperson for Jackie said, "Mrs. Onassis will not be attending the funeral."

Jackie herself took her last walk through Central Park on Sunday, May 15, 1994, on the arm of her long-time companion and financial advisor, Maurice Tempelsman. Wearing a brown wig and a large scarf, she held onto his arm. She looked at the winding paths, the mowed grass, and the trees that she'd known since she was a toddler, trying to implant their images on her dying mind.

Only three days before she'd called Teddy. "I don't think I can take it anymore," she told him. "The pain is unbearable."

In the remaining hours of her life, John Jr. read her two poems by Colette and kissed her goodbye for a final time.

Teddy flew to New York to be at her deathbed. He spent thirty minutes alone with her in her bedroom with the door shut. He never discussed those final minutes with her.

At 10:15pm, on May 19, 1994, Jackie's heart stopped beating in the presence of John Jr., Caroline, and Maurice Tempelsman. The following morning, her son made an announcement in front of the photographers and reporters who had gathered outside her apartment building.

"Last night, at around 10:15pm, my mother passed on," he said. "She was surrounded by her friends and family and her books and the people and things that she loved. And she did it in her own way, and we felt lucky for that, and now she's in God's hands."

At her funeral a few days later, and after kissing Lady Bird Johnson and Hillary Rodham Clinton on the cheeks, Teddy delivered the eulogy:

"No one else looked like her, spoke like her, wrote like her, or was so original in the way she did things. No one we knew ever had a better sense of self. During those four endless days in 1963, she held us together as a family and as a country. In large part because of her, we could grieve and then go on. She lifted us up, and in the doubt and darkness, she gave her fellow citizens back their pride as Americans. She was then thirty-four years old. Jackie was too young to be a widow in 1963, and too young to die now."

In the limousine after the funeral, Teddy broke down and cried. He sobbed, "I will love her forever."

Months later, he said, "Jackie would have preferred to be herself. But the world insisted that she be a legend, too."

Rudolf Nureyev

Seducing His Way Through the Kennedy Clan

LOVE TRIANGLE In November of 1968, deep in the English countryside, **Lee Radziwill** *(left)*, **Jackie Kennedy** *(center)*, and **Rudolph Nureyev** enjoy the great outdoors.

Even in the presence of these world-class dressers, Rudi managed to appear as the most fashionably attired.

Rudi captivated the hearts of both Jackie and Lee, as well as the hearts of two male members of the Kennedy clan. "When it came to seducing, it was hard to say no to Rudi," said ballerina Margot Fonteyn. "He usually got what he wanted. Even otherwise straight men, or at least some of them, couldn't resist this bundle of Slavic charm." Rudi never kept his affairs with the Kennedys a secret, and often relayed boastful tales about his conquests.

The love of his life was Erik Bruhn, the Danish-born *danseur noble*. "A totally reciprocal deep passion existed between the two men," said Rudi's biographer, Julie Kavanaugh. Rudi was never faithful to Bruhn.

One night at Maxim's in Paris, he told Bruhn: "I was just in New York. I fuck Jackie Kennedy. Now I take you back to hotel, and I fuck you--all night!"

FROM RUSSIA WITH LOVE
(TALES OF TARTAR TAIL)

*"I know what it is like to make love as both
a man and a woman."*
—Rudolf Nureyev

*"When you've known Nijinski,
you don't want to see Nureyev."*
—Coco Chanel

*"Rudolf had a street life that was probably as wide
ranging as anyone's in this century."*
—Film Director James Toback

"I don't care what the magazines say," said ballet star **Rudolf Nureyev**. "I am the sexiest man alive. Just ask Lee Radziwill. Just ask Jackie Kennedy. And if you still don't believe me, ask Bobby and John-John. Nobody in the world can resist me. Everyone who has ever gone to bed with me has fallen madly in love with me."

Rudolf Nureyev was the greatest male ballet dancer of his generation. Along with Nijinski, he was one of the most spectacular ballet dancers of all time.

He had a stunning Slavic physical beauty, an extraordinarily athletic and sexual persona, a prodigious endowment that he liked to exhibit, and oodles of Russian charm.

As a stellar member of the glitterati, he attracted the attention of international café society—specifically Lee Radziwill, Jackie Kennedy, Bobby Kennedy, and John F. Kennedy Jr. In time, he would seduce all four of them.

In 1961, during the darkest days of the Cold War, Rudi was touring Western Europe with the Kirov Ballet Troupe. At Paris's Le Bourget airport, he had been scheduled to board a flight for London. But shortly before takeoff, KGB officials ordered him to board the next plane to Moscow because his mother was dying.

Sensing a trap, the 23-year-old dancer fled into the arms of two French policemen. "Save me! I want to stay."

Later he told friends that he was carrying a pair of scissors with him. "Had anything gone wrong," he said, "I was prepared to plunge the scissors into my heart."

Rudi knew that if he returned to Moscow, he'd never dance again. The KGB had accumulated an extensive file on him, detailing his homosexual encounters.

He was "born wild" in 1938 on a train chugging beside Lake Baikaal in Siberia. In 1945, at the age of seven, he fell in love with the world of dance when he saw his first ballet. He would dance for the rest of his life.

His father nicknamed him "Ballerina." He despised his son and the world of ballet and frequently beat Rudi.

In spite of his father, Rudi stubbornly insisted on taking ballet lessons. He was an amazing pupil and by 1958, he'd evolved into a sensation within the Soviet dance world. His performances, so the critics claimed, were "erotically charged."

Two weeks after his defection, Rudi was performing at the Thêátre des Champs-Elysées in Paris, to shouts of "traitor" coming from Russians or their sympathizers.

A call from the English ballet diva, Margot Fonteyn, changed his life. She was the aging *prima ballerina* of Britain's Royal Ballet. At a charity event, the offstage and onstage liaison of the 42-year-old ballerina and the young Russian exile began.

Prince and Princess Stanislas Radziwill saw Rudi perform in London's Covent Garden and were mesmerized by him. While he was trying to find some permanent residence, the Polish aristocrat, married at the time to Jackie's sister, Lee, invited the ballet dancer to stay with them at what was called "the two prettiest houses in England," their townhouse in London and their country home.

In either house, Lee led a privileged life. Her friend, the French actress/dancer Leslie Caron, claimed that Lee was "overprotected, a child-wife evocative of Nora in Ibsen's *A Doll's House*."

At first, Rudi was suspicious of the Prince and Princess. He told Fonteyn that he thought he was being set up for a "three-way."

"We even have those arrangements in Moscow," he said. As it turned out, Rudi's sexual suspicion was only half founded. Lee was powerfully attracted to him. He would be their guest for seven months, as "Rudimania" swept across London. Arguably Rudi became the first pop icon of the 1960s.

Fonteyn and Rudi were the hottest cultural ticket in the west, creating a sensation in the United States when they performed there in 1960s.

His first American review called Rudi "a cheetah behind bars."

Truman Capote said, "Everybody, man or woman, wanted to fuck with Rudi, and most of them did, even the Kennedys. Whether he was dancing *Swan Lake* or *Romeo and Juliet*, all eyes were glued to Rudi's ample crotch. I sampled it myself. All nine and a half inches of thick Slavic meat."

Lee called Rudi "my eternal flame," and photographers liked to capture them in intimate situations as they danced together. She was caught on film clinging suggestively to him.

Friends reported that Lee was deeply in love with Rudi and "continued her campaign to

Succumbing to Rudi's charms were **Jackie Kennedy** *(upper left)* and her younger sister, **Lee Radziwill** *(upper right)*. In the lower left is **Robert (Bobby) Kennedy**, smiling, but not, at least then, at Rudi.

Bolstered and supported by Peter Lawford, Rudi urged **John F. Kennedy, Jr**. *(lower right)* to become a Hollywood movie star. "You already look like one," Rudi told JFK's impressionable young son. "Why not be one?"

One night, Rudi persuaded JFK Jr. to wear a pair of his purple ballet tights. When he saw how JFK looked, Rudi said, "The way you wear those tights, you'd be a sensation, if you could only dance."

make him straight." But as Capote warned her, "It was a hopeless undertaking. Once you've enjoyed the taste of cock, you can't keep them down on the farm."

A free-lance journalist, Diana DuBois, claimed: "Lee was put off by Rudi's homosexuality. That was always a bone of contention. He would tell her that he wanted a 'big cock,' and she would react with disgust."

In the early days, Lee was so taken with this ballet dancer that she purchased for him a Russian double-headed eagle of solid gold studded with diamonds and rubies.

Lee allegedly admitted to Capote (at least he claimed so) that she did have sex with Rudi one time. "It was the most athletic experience I've ever known in bed," Capote quoted her as telling him.

Lee visited Rudi on the French Riviera where he'd rented a villa, "Arcadie," in La Turbie, high in the hills above Monte Carlo. In the guest bedroom, she came across pictures of men engaged in sex.

She came to realize that her sexual pursuit of the young dancer was a losing proposition.

Associated Press

Prince and Princess Stanislaw Albrecht Radziwill (aka, "Stash" and Jackie's younger sister, as she was widely known) enjoy balmy weather at the Half Moon Resort in Montego Bay, Jamaica, during a holiday in March of 1961. JFK had only recently become president of the United States, and Lee was beginning to enjoy worldwide attention as the sister of Jackie and as the sister-in-law of the U.S. president.

Although she was smart, talented, and charming in her own right, Lee often suffered unfavorable comparisons with her more formidable sibling. The press constantly compared them: Which of the sisters was better-looking? Which could more easily attract men? Which was the better-dressed?

Yet their friendship survived, and would stretch over some three decades. It began on a note of intense animal passion and developed into an enduring friendship.

When Rudi arrived in America and was introduced to Jackie, Lee found herself competing against her own sister for Rudi's affection. It would not be the first time the two sisters pursued the same man.

Lee was still in love with Rudi, and maybe the problem was that he was much more in love with Jackie than he was with Lee. He thought Jackie had the more alluring personality.

Capote claimed that Jackie fell in love with Rudi on the day she invited him and his dance partner, Margot Fonteyn, to the White House for tea.

Unlike her husband, "Rudi," as Jackie came to call him, admired her passion for the arts and even her choice of antiques. Sitting in the president's old North Carolina porch rocker in the Cabinet Room, he ordered his favorite drink, port with ginger ale, from a White House waiter.

Lee had warned Jackie that Rudi was "ninety-nine and a half percent homosexual," but Jackie wasn't so sure. Rudi was flirting outrageously with her, and she was a notorious flirt herself.

When the room emptied, he impulsively rose from the rocker, grabbed her, and passionately kissed her. "Unlike your beautiful husband, I do not have a bad back," he said. "A strong Russian back made for leaping through the air."

From that point on, according to Capote, Jackie was mesmerized.

After her husband's death, Rudi, on many a

night, "warmed the sheets" [his words] of the former First Lady's bed.

Capote claimed that Jackie "stole" Rudi from her sister, Lee, with whom the dancer was temporarily feuding. "She destroyed my baby," he charged to Jackie. "Had it cut in little pieces from her body. But with you, I will make nine beautiful children—five boys, four girls."

"I'm not a breeding factory," she warned him. "Better call Ethel for that."

"But I've already told my friends about the babies we're going to make."

"Don't you dare!" she shouted at him. "Stop this talk about our private relationship! It'll be fodder for the tabloids. Those friends of yours are malicious gossips!"

"But every part of your life has been in print already, although that is not good for the soul," he said.

Rudi not only admired Jackie for her beauty, but for her financial advice. "The first real money Rudi made was under Jackie's influence," said one of his associates. "She's the one who got him to buy gold just before gold shot up to the sky."

Jackie was hesitant to introduce Rudi to either her son or to Bobby Kennedy. At times Rudi could be flamboyantly homosexual. She feared Bobby might be put off by his exhibitionism. Even so, she arranged a dinner between Bobby and Rudi. "I've never seen two men bond in such a way," she told Lee when their relationship resumed. "Bobby seemed fascinated by Rudi." Jackie later admitted that she had no idea at first that Bobby and Rudi were seeing each other outside her home.

She became aware of that when the phone by her bedside rang one night. She was in bed with Rudi at the time. She picked up the phone. "Bobby," she said, her face lighting up.

A sudden look of distress crossed her brow. She muffled the phone. "He wants to speak to you. I must warn you, he's dangerously jealous of any man who gets near me. He must have had you trailed here."

Rudi eagerly took the phone from her. "Bobby, Bobby, you are the greatest American of them all. Fonteyn has taught me a new word for us—*peccadillo*."

As she made her way to the bathroom, she heard Rudi giggling into the phone like a young teenage girl with her first crush on the star football captain.

Two weeks later, over cocktails with Capote, Jackie said, "I think Rudi systematically plans to seduce every member of my family, even my son when he grows up. Or before he grows up. He's already talking about teaching John ballet at an early age."

Photographed here on the French Riviera, the blond beauty with the bulging basket (**Tab Hunter,** *left*) was enthralled with **Rudolf Nureyev,** whom he described in his autobiography as a "bone white body with blue veins clad only in a sliver lamé swimsuit. Rudi looked like a finely chiseled corpse freshly risen from an ancient crypt, and he walked as if the world was far beneath him."

Eventually, shacked up within Nureyev's exquisitely styled home at 6 Fife Road in the Richmond Park district of London, "Tab & Rudi" abandoned their posturings and got down to some primal intra-male bonding.

Nureyev in those days was known for "fucking like a rabbit." Another of his lovers, Monique Van Vooren, the actress, claimed that Rudolf liked "street boys, toughs, the lowest of the low." Obviously Tab, the ultimate example of a handsome blond beach boy of the 50s, was an exception to the dancer's usual conquests.

"Watch out for that Cossack," the author warned her. "Rudi has enough charm to seduce Richard Nixon. Forgive me for prying—how unlike me—but I must ask. Is it true what they say about Rudi in bed?"

"Afraid so," she said. "On stage, his movements are the most graceful of any man on earth. But in bed I have a nickname for him: *Mr. Jack Rabbit*."

There were many sightings of Bobby and Rudi at New York night spots, especially Arthur's. The celebrity-haunted joint was the most exclusive disco in New York; it was operated by Sybil Burton, the Welsh actress who'd lost her husband, Richard Burton, to Elizabeth Taylor, that "Serpent of the Nile."

Janet Villeha, a prima ballerina with the New York City Ballet in the 1960s, spotted an arrival one night. "I saw Bobby come in with both Jackie and Rudi. Later on, as I went to make a phone call, I saw Bobby and Rudi in a telephone booth. They were kissing passionately."

All of his lovers knew that Rudi was a devotee of "deep throat" kissing. As one of his boys put it, "He went for your tonsils."

In his famous memoir, *Palimpsest*, Gore Vidal wrote of a revelation Rudi made to him:

AUTHOR CELEBRITY PSYCHIC JOHN COHAN

CATCH 'A FALLING STAR
The untold story of celebrity secrets

Celebrity psychic **John Cohan** wrote a tell-all book in 2008, revealing relatively unknown secrets of the stars. No revelation was more shocking than the romantic link between John F. Kennedy Jr. and Rudolph Nureyev.

As a psychic, Cohan warned JFK Jr. about his possible early death by advising him to avoid racecars, airplanes, and scuba diving.

John patted him on the back. "I'll start calling you my brother, an older brother, who worries a bit too much about me."

Once, when Cohan suffered from a sore shoulder, JFK Jr. offered to massage it. To JFK Jr. Cohan said, "I'm glad I'm straight, because this kind of feely stuff from an attractive, sexy man could certainly tempt the best of them."

JFK Jr. replied with a knowing smile. "I take the fifth."

"Between Bobby's primitive religion and his family's ardent struggle ever upward from the Irish bog, he was more than usually skewed, not least by his own homosexual impulses, which, Nureyev once told me, were very much in the air on at least one occasion when they were together.. 'Nothing happen,' said Rudi. 'But we did share young soldier once. American soldier. Boy not lie . . . maybe.' Rudi gave his Tartar grin, very much aware, firsthand, of the swirls of gossip that envelop the conspicuous. Yet anyone who has eleven children must be trying to prove-disprove? Something other than the ability to surpass his father as incontinent breeder."

No one encouraged JFK Jr. to pursue a theatrical career more than Rudi. "John-John" shared his dreams with the Russian ballet dancer, who was falling in love with him.

A bit of a mama's boy, JFK Jr. told Rudi that Jackie was "dead set" against his going into the theater.

"Have some balls," Rudi said. "I know you've got a pair on you. We can't always do what mommy says."

John Cohan, who has been a celebrity psychic to the stars for more than three decades, delivered several bombshells when he wrote: *Catch a Falling Star: The Untold Story of Celebrity Secrets*.

One night at New York's infamous Studio 54, he encountered John F. Kennedy Jr. in the company of family friend, Rudi, and New York's "hottest" male prostitute who advertised his services for $1,000 a night.

"This was a threesome I saw with my own eyes," Cohan wrote. "I think John wanted a new experience. He had confessed to me that he became bored with people and things quickly."

"He always talked about an acting career, which his mother adamantly refused to permit," Cohan said. "I used to caution him on many occasions—no race cars, no airplanes, and no scuba diving. I didn't feel good about these adrenaline rushes he got."

At the club, Cohan also warned Rudi, "Leave John-John alone, because this scene isn't his first preference."

"I love the challenge of seducing a straight man," Rudi told Cohan. "That night he did just that."

The male prostitute later tried to sell an exposé article about that night with Rudi and John Jr. But there were no takers—the allegation at the time was too controversial.

In his accusation, the male hustler claimed, "John fucked me, really hard, but when I tried to return the favor, he told me that part of him was 'off limits.' Rudi went down on him later in the evening. John-John was strictly rough trade, but what an evening."

Although Rudi could have seduced some of the most famous men and women on the planet, and did on occasion, he much preferred anonymous encounters in public toilets, New York bathhouses, and other gay cruising venues.

In his dressing room, he often received celebrities in the nude. One night Arnold Schwarzenegger came backstage to congratulate him. Rudi sucked on the muscleman's index finger. "I want to know how you taste," he allegedly said. "I've seen pictures of you nude. I want you to put your cock in my mouth."

"You're the sixth person today who has requested that," Arnold reportedly said, retrieving his finger before it was devoured.

Monique Van Vooren, who wrote about Rudi in her 1981 book, *Night Sanctuary*, claimed he "was tortured, and tormented by his sexuality. He was ashamed of being homosexual. And I think he wanted to be degraded." In Diane Solway's *Nureyev: His Life* (1998), she wrote that he preferred "rough-trade, pickups, sailors, lorry drivers, and the like."

One night at one of Rudi's openings (the exact per-

Associated Press

JFK, Jr.'s straight life, frat boy style, was best chronicled by his former roommate Robert T. Littell in 2005 in his memoir, *The Men We Became*. They first met as freshmen during orientation week at Brown University.

"Going out with John at night was like having a key to the city," Littel asserted. "Doormen bowed and velvet ropes fell when he stepped out of a cab. Sometimes, I felt as though I was with Moses at the parting of the Red Sea."

Littell claimed that their shared apartment was the venue for some strange sexual adventures. One night, one of their friends returned with a female flight attendant and took her to the spare bedroom. Later, Littell and JFK Jr. peeked in on their friend. The door was open a crack.

Inside, they saw their lusty friend rubbing the sheepskin collar of President Kennedy's official commander-in-chief leather jacket across the woman's bare breasts.

Her seducer was getting her excited by informing her that it was "The First Coat" actually worn many times by the assassinated president.

formance unknown), Jackie was in the audience and the stage manager urgently summoned her to come backstage to Rudi's dressing room.

There she found him completely nude. He told her that he was tired of his fans shouting, "We want Rudi in the Nudi," and that he was going to dance one ballet completely naked.

Using the force of her personality, she urged him to put on some purple tights. After holding the curtain fifteen minutes, Rudi agreed to go on, but his tights were so thin they were almost see-through. Jackie later told friends, "His fans got to see him almost naked, but he was covered enough so that the policemen weren't called."

She later became miffed at Rudi. In her working capacity as an editor at Doubleday, she went to him in 1986 and asked him to write his memoirs.

He turned her down. "Jackie darling," he said, "you know I can't write story of life. Story of life must tell what happened . . . I mean, really happened, not pack of lies. It should not be a cover-up, no truth in it. My not writing book will protect you and Bobby. Even your son."

Jackie's face flashed anger. "And what about my son? What did you do to John?"

"Nothing, not so excited. I encouraged him to be an actor. That's all. Nothing else. I swear it!"

Her upset with Rudi didn't last long. He charmed his way back into her good graces.

Valentino portrayed a scene from its namesake's life wherein **Nureyev** (playing Valentino) is arrested because his second marriage license was processed before his divorce was finalized.

In this enactment of an L.A. prison, female prostitutes attempt to undress him, and male inmates taunt him and threaten him with rape. A warden mixes a diuretic drug into a mug of coffee, which Valentino unsuspectingly drinks. In the film, he tries not to wet his pants, but his bladder eventually, and very visibly, gives up.

During the shoot, Nureyev fought bitterly with the film's director, Ken Russell, about the size of his penis, since the scene portrayed him pissing his pants. To suggest the long length of his penis, Nureyev kept demanding that the hose (a prop) in his pants be pushed farther and farther down the leg of his pants.

Finally, an exasperated Russell told his cameraman: "It looks like Rudy is wrestling with a snake halfway down his pants. No one, not even John C. Holmes, is hung like that!"

She was greatly concerned in 1987 when Rudi announced he was returning to Russia to see his ailing mother. She asked Ted Kennedy as a senator to write to the Soviet ambassador in Washington, requesting protection for Rudi.

For twelve years Rudi carried the AIDS virus. His final artistic statement involved the choreography of a production of *La Bayadère*, which opened in February of 1992 at the Palais Garnier in Paris. During the ten-minute ovation that followed, he needed help to walk across the stage. He is quoted as saying, "The main thing is dancing. Before it withers away from my body, I will keep dancing till the last moment, the last drop."

Rudi died on January 6, 1993 at the age of 54. He was buried at a Russian cemetery in Sainte-Geneviève-des-Bois near Paris, a pilgrimage site even today for his still loyal fans.

Jackie's List

Merv Griffin's Attempt to Bring Her Onto His Show, & His Spin on the Celebrities She Wanted to Seduce

Naughty Truman, Spreading Naughty Stories About Naughty Celebrities

When **Merv Griffin** told **Truman Capote** that **Jackie** had confided in him the names of the ten men she most wanted to seduce, the gossipy author later quizzed her about the list. Jackie, with a few drinks in her, was impish in her answers as to why these particular men appealed to her:

* * *

Dr. Christiaan Barnard: *"A man after my own heart."*

Robert McNamara: *"He's so commanding in public, and I bet in the boudoir as well."*

John Glenn: *"As the first American to orbit the Earth, he would be celestial, I'm sure."*

André Malraux: *"When I stood with him at the unveiling of the Mona Lisa at the National Gallery in Washington, he told me my smile, like the Mona Lisa's, would enchant future ages."*

Prince Philip: *"His girlfriends speak of a very large endowment."*

Henry Kissinger: *"I'm always drawn to men who are experts in foreign affairs."*

Franklin D. Roosevelt Jr.:
"I have this thing for World War II naval heroes."

Eugene R. Black, Sr.: *"As head of 'Black's Bank' [a reference to the World Bank] he could take a million from me and turn it into twenty million."*

Gianni Agnelli: *"One of the five best dressed men in the world—we'd make a lovely couple."*

Alistair Cooke: *"After the screwing's over, you need someone to talk to."*

Cary Grant: *"Maybe he's not so great in bed with a woman, but he called for gun control after Bobby was shot."*

Maxwell D. Taylor: *"Jack and Bobby adored him. I'm sure I would be singing his praises after...you know."*

Jackie:
Negotiating an Interview
with the King of Daytime TV

The A-list celebrity that television talk show host Merv Griffin desperately wanted to introduce to his weekday audience of 20 million viewers was Jacqueline Bouvier Kennedy, whom he described as "the most fascinating woman of the 20th century."

Jackie seemed flattered by his attention, and asked him to meet her at a pre-arranged time in the elegant bar of Manhattan's Carlyle Hotel, where their privacy would be more or less protected.

She was ten minutes late, rushing in wearing an Oleg Cassini aqua-blue dress, and kissing him on the cheek. When he appeared hesitant to embrace her, she assured him, "You can touch me. After all, I'm not the queen of England!"

Throughout their rendezvous that afternoon, he wanted to look into her eyes, but she kept them hidden behind large dark glasses.

Although she never agreed to appear on his TV talk show—"I'm not a showgirl"—Jackie and **Merv Griffin** had several confidential talks. She called him when she read the novel *Dolores* by the best-selling author Jacqueline Susann in 1974. The author died before it was completed, and movie critic Rex Reed finished the tale.

Jackie complained to Merv that "the bitch based it on me." "Don't worry about her," Merv told her. "Nobody with a brain reads her. She's the Joan Crawford of novelists—and part dyke, too."

Jackie knew that Merv was gay, and once, after a drink or two, she impishly asked him, "Have you and I ever shared a lover in common—and you'd better not say Jack or Bobby."

"No," he said, "but I know of two, Marlon Brando and Frank Sinatra."

"Marlon, I can believe," she said, "but surely not Frank. But on the other hand, he is a womanizer, and I always believe womanizers will occasionally try a boy for a change."

Unlike the serene princess she evoked in front of TV cameras, in person, she was warm and rather earthy. She obviously had a love of gossip, and she pumped Merv for scandalous revelations in the movie industry. She was particularly interested in who was sleeping with whom. Merv filled her in on some shocking details, carefully avoiding speaking of his friend Marilyn Monroe. Actually, he'd wanted to ask her about her own affairs with various movie stars, notably Marlon Brando and William Holden, but he didn't dare.

Jackie spoke candidly about their mutual friends, especially Truman Capote and Peter Lawford. "I know that Truman befriends me to my face," she said, "then spreads the vilest gossip about me behind my back. But I still adore him. He tells me more about what's really going on the world of celebrities than any other person. As for Peter . . ." She hesitated, putting down her glass. "I don't know how to say this. He's confided to me about your own involvement with him, so we can speak frankly. Peter's in love with me, and I don't know how to handle it." She didn't say anything for a long moment, perhaps realizing she'd revealed too much.

To rescue her from her embarrassment, he immediately changed the subject. He urged her to come onto his show. "Talk about ratings. We'd blow everybody else off the air."

He could only imagine the mischief reflected in her eyes when she came up with an idea for one of his shows. "I could list all the men in the world I'd like to seduce—that is, if I haven't gotten around to some of them already."

"Name names," he said. "I'm all ears."

"Henry Kissinger."

"But he's so ugly," he said.

"Beautiful women down through the ages have not always sought out equally beautiful men," she said. "Perhaps just the opposite. A woman can be attracted to a man's brain. Or his power. Look at all those silly German housewives throwing themselves in the path of Hitler."

"I think beautiful women should bed ugly men, and only for their money," he said.

Later in her life, after Jackie married Aristotle Onassis, Merv told friends, "I think I planted the idea in her head."

Back at the Carlyle, Jackie seemed to be enjoying their game. She continued to name names. "Prince Philip, of course. He's so handsome, so stately. John Glenn, most definitely. André Malraux. Dr. Christiaan Barnard. Robert McNamara. General Maxwell Taylor. If he wasn't gay, I'd add Cary Grant to the list. I could go on and on. Alistair Cooke. Franklin Roosevelt Jr., Gianni Agnelli. And out of deference to your opinion, Eugene R. Black. If you want money, who better than the president of the World Bank?"

Months later, shocked and horrified at the assassination of John F. Kennedy in Dallas, Merv sent his condolences to Jackie. A few weeks later he received a warm reply, thanking him.

At the beginning of her marriage to Aristotle Onassis, Merv received another call from Jackie. She was seriously tempted to go on nationwide television to counterattack headlines around the world calling her a gold-digger. Such rumors had existed since she was first seen with Onassis. But these rumors exploded when a steward on the shipping tycoon's yacht wrote a tell-all book.

In it, he claimed that he had personally witnessed Jackie sign a 170-clause marriage contract that stipulated, among other agreements, that man and wife would occupy separate bedrooms throughout the marriage. According to the steward, the contract also called for Jackie's receipt, every year, of an allowance of $585,000 a year. In case of a divorce, she was to be given $20 million in cash.

"Such lies!" Jackie said to Merv. "The day I married Ari, my annuity from the Kennedy Estate was cut off. I also lost my widow's pension from the government, which I'd been drawing since Jack died. There was no prenuptial agreement with Ari. Right now I have less than five thousand dollars in my bank account. To manage, I have to charge everything to Olympic Airlines."

Merv, as he told colleagues at his studio, was elated at the prospect of such an appearance on his show by Jackie, knowing it would be one of the most watched interviews in the history of television. But two weeks later she phoned him again. "You must forgive me," she said. "I called you in a fit of madness. I can't go on your show and make a public spectacle of myself."

"But you are a spectacle, Jackie," he said. "Through no fault of your own, of course."

"Such an appearance would be too personal," she said. "It would only generate more unwelcome headlines." She seemed near tears as she put down the phone.

BRAINS OVER BEAUTY
The Sexual Appeal of Successful Men,
as Appraised by Jackie-O and Remembered by Merv Griffin

Henry Kissinger
US Secretary of State

Prince Philip
The Duke of Edinburgh

John Glenn
Astronaut and U.S.Senator

André Malraux
Culture Minister of France

Christiaan Barnard
Heart Surgeon

Robert McNamara
U.S. Secretary of Defense

General Maxwell Taylor

Cary Grant
Movie Star

Alistair Cooke
Television and Cultural Critic

Eugene Black
Finance Mogul and Banker

Gianni Agnelli
Principal owner of FIAT

FDR Jr.
Diplomat & Statesman

The Ballad of Teddy & Mary Jo

What Really Happened at Chappaquiddick?

Dr. Donald R. Mills of Edgartown, Massachusetts, the officiating medical examiner of the corpse of **Mary Jo Kopechne**, reported his grim findings to the world press: "The body was rigid as a statue. The teeth were gritted; there was froth around the nose, and the hands were in a claw-like position."

After it was learned that Senator **Edward (Teddy) Kennedy** had allowed the blonde beauty to drown as he fled to safety, the first reports surmised that he was finished as a politician. Even at this low point in his fortunes, Kennedy, with a certain savvy, appealed to the court of public opinion, at least among the voters of Massachusetts.

Their decision prevailed overwhelmingly in his favor, and indeed, when he sought re-election to the Senate in 1970, he retained his seat.

The case, of course, has never been solved. There are too many unanswered questions. The incident at Chappaquiddick generated an entire body of literature—both accurate and false.

The prolific novelist, Joyce Carol Oates, who seems to turn out a book every week, wrote a chilling fictionalized article in Lear's magazine, re-creating the incident from the point of view of Mary Jo Kopechne, arguably with a deadly accuracy.

A Scandal More Newsworthy than the Nation's First Walk on the Moon

"Just because you're getting married doesn't mean you have to be faithful.

—JFK to Teddy Kennedy

Astronauts were setting foot on the surface of the moon at 11:15pm on that fateful evening of July 18, 1969. Viewers around the world were absorbed with the implications of that event until something occurred that evening that knocked stories about the moon landing off the front pages.

Kennedy associates Joe Gargan and Paul Markham had arranged a weekend party for the "Boiler Room Girls" on Chappaquiddick, a tiny islet off the coast of Martha's Vineyard. These secretaries had previously worked as aides to Robert F. Kennedy, who had been assassinated about 13 months previous to the night in question.

"She was nothing but a whore," or so claimed one of the Boiler Room Girls who worked in the secretarial pool with Mary Jo Kopechne. "She'd go to bed with any man who had Kennedy written on his zipper." The secretary refused to be quoted in print.

When one of the secretaries working with her heard the Boiler Girl make that claim, she said, "She's just jealous that Bobby or Teddy didn't pick her up. If either or both of them had, the bitch would be running off to the nearest seedy motel."

World opinion is still mixed about pert little Mary Jo, who went to a watery grave with Kennedy stars dancing in her eyes.

Based on events that transpired on that long ago July evening, one of the secretaries, a blonde, blue-eyed beauty from Pennsylvania, Mary Jo Kopechne, would have her picture plastered during the week that followed on the front page of virtually every newspaper in the world.

Early in 1968, Bobby Kennedy had been forced to abandon his love affair with Jackie to make a run for the U.S. presidency, and at that point he had more or less "surrendered" Jackie to Aristotle Onassis. But he still needed a sexual tryst here and there, as he flew from city to city across the vast American continent.

Bobby's eyes fell on a campaign worker, Mary Jo Kopechne, who was pert and pretty. She'd taught school in Alabama before migrating to Washington in 1963, where she got a job as a secretary to the hard-partying Senator George Smathers of Florida, one of John Kennedy's best friends.

At a staff party in Washington, Smathers introduced Mary Jo to both Bobby and Teddy Kennedy. It was rumored—never proven—that Bobby flipped a coin with Teddy to determine who got to her first. "You know the rules, Teddy," Bobby is alleged to have said. "One of your older brothers always gets there first, if Dad hasn't already beaten us to her."

Mary Jo had already sustained a brief fling with Smathers, who was a known and notorious womanizer specializing in blondes. But when Smathers moved on to another woman, Kopechne switched jobs and began working for attorney Joe Dolan, one of Bobby's legal advisors.

What she'd really wanted involved working for Bobby himself, and consequently, when a position opened up, she was hired to join RFK's secretarial pool. As such, she shared a townhouse in Georgetown with four other young women. All of these secretaries were members of Bobby's staff. It

If Teddy had reported Mary Jo's accident immediately, it might have appeared like two young people rushing off to have sex on a beach on a moonlit night.

But his post-accident behavior, in his own words, was "irrational, and indefensible and inexcusable and inexplicable," especially when he made an appearance within an Edgartown hotel lobby at 2:30 that morning, trying to create a false alibi for himself.

was rumored that Bobby had already seduced two of the secretaries. Mary Jo blatantly told the other women, "I just know I'm next. I can tell from the way Bobby looks at me when he walks in."

Even after Mary Jo left her job within his office, she still stayed in touch with Smathers, who had gone from being her lover to someone she could turn to for advice. Perhaps he was still jealous, but the senator advised her not to go and work as a secretary for Bobby on his presidential campaign plane.

Smathers knew what would probably happen to her, and he was right. Soon Mary Jo and Bobby were engaged in a torrid affair. They booked separate hotel rooms in whatever city they were visiting, but Bobby slipped into her bedroom when the hotel hallways cleared. According to an aide, even when Ethel, Bobby's wife, was campaigning with him, Bobby still managed to work in a quick session with Mary Jo.

Mary Jo and Bobby launched an affair that was still going on at the time of his assassination in 1968. After Bobby's death, Mary Jo mourned him for a while, but not for long. Soon she was secretly dating another married Kennedy brother: Teddy.

Smathers later asserted that "The call from Mary Jo that I had been anticipating finally came in. She told me she was pregnant with Teddy's child. If word of her condition ever leaked out, the Republicans would take the White House."

Eventually, Teddy's most trusted advisors learned that on the night of Mary Jo's last automobile ride, he had planned to discuss the delicate subject involving her having an abortion. For Teddy it was the only way, although apparently she did not believe in abortions and actually wanted to have Teddy's baby.

At the party, he announced to the guests that he was driving Mary Jo to the departure point for the ferry departing for Edgartown, the last boat scheduled to leave that evening.

One Boiler Room secretary didn't believe it. Not wanting to be identified, she later said, "We thought she and Teddy were running off to have sex. He had the use of a private villa on the island. Of course, there were a number of deserted beaches, and it was a balmy night." She also reported that Mary Jo left her purse and keys behind, suggesting that she was planning to eventually return to the party.

What happened next is still disputed today. Mary Jo got into Teddy's "scraped up knockaround," as he called it, a 1967 Oldsmobile 88. She would never be seen alive again.

At 12:40am on that fatal night, Christopher Look, Martha's Vineyard's part-time deputy sheriff, spotted a parked car near Dike Road. This was more than an hour after the Senator asserted that the accident had occurred. Teddy stated that he had returned to the cottage, site of the party, on foot.

When Look saw the couple, a man and a woman, parked in the car, he approached the vehicle, assuming that the driver might be lost. But before he reached the Oldsmobile, the vehicle suddenly accelerated, heading for Dike Road and toward the bridge. The deputy sheriff opted not to follow the car, but noticed the license plate, noting only that it began with the letter L. Teddy's license plate was L78207.

Robert Kennedy was assassinated more than thirteen months prior to the involvement of his younger brother, Teddy, in "the scandal of the year," the drowning of Mary Jo on Martha's Vineyard.

"In many ways, Bobby sowed the seeds of that tragedy when he more or less passed Mary Jo on to Teddy," said Senator George Smathers.

"I always got the hand-me-downs." Teddy once told Kennedy aide David Powers. "The used clothing--Rose was very frugal--the used cars, the worst bedroom, and the women who had passed through the beds of Jack and Bobby, and sometimes the old man himself."

Traveling at about twenty miles an hour, Teddy's car headed toward Dike Bridge, a wood-timbered span angled obliquely to the road. It was unlit, with no guardrail. Even though he applied the brakes, to his horror, he drove over the side of the bridge, plunging into tide-swept Poucha Pond. After crashing into the murky waters, the vehicle came to rest upside down.

Battling great odds, he managed to free himself from the car and swim to the surface. He later claimed that he tried to swim down and free Mary Jo, but failed—"maybe seven or eight times." He then stated that he rested for fifteen minutes on the bank of the pond before returning to Lawrence Cottage, site of the Boiler Room Girls' party.

He denied seeing any house with a light on during his walk back. En route, he passed four houses, two of which were lit, according to the owners. Each of these homes had a phone, and each would surely have accommodated a request for aid to a famous figure like Senator Kennedy.

"Dike House," one of the homes, was only 150 yards from the bridge. Sylvia Malm, its owner, said her light was on and she had a phone. If a call had been made from her house, Mary Jo might have been saved, since she was surviving in an air pocket, her time of survival later estimated at between one and four hours.

In later testimony, Teddy claimed that Gargan and Markham, the hosts of the party, returned to the pond and made several attempts to rescue Mary Jo. This heroic act has been disputed. One deputy in the sheriff's office, speaking off the record, claimed "it never happened."

Even if it did happen, no one at Lawrence Cottage called the police even though there was a phone there.

According to more testimony, Teddy, Gargan, and Markham returned to the cottage after their failed rescue attempt. Teddy claimed he would notify the authorities and asked his friends not to tell the secretaries inside, as he did not want to unduly alarm them.

One of the many amazing stories that never surfaced for public consumption that night was that an FBI agent telephoned J. Edgar Hoover at his home in Washington, which he shared with his lover, Clyde Tolson.

Around 1:45am, Hoover was informed that Teddy's car had sunk into the pond and that the senator had escaped with his life but "a female passenger had drowned." Obviously Hoover was having Teddy trailed that night, and perhaps on many other nights, hoping to accumulate blackmail evidence on him in the way he had on his brothers. That was, in case Teddy ever became president. Above all else, Hoover wanted to have enough evidence on Teddy to blackmail him into not firing him should he ever be in a position to do so.

It was never explained why this mysterious FBI agent didn't attempt to rescue Mary Jo after Teddy fled from the scene. He'd been spying on Teddy and had obviously seen him leaving the party with the young blonde, and had then proceeded to tail them. He could have saved her, but perhaps he was more concerned with protecting his anonymity, no doubt on orders from the FBI chief himself, and as such, he never came to the rescue. The FBI agent was apparently instructed not to report the accident and not to let anyone know that Teddy had been the driver. Hoover seemingly wanted Teddy to hang himself with the consequences of this tragedy.

After leaving Lawrence Cottage, Teddy walked to the departure point for the Edgartown ferry, which had long ago shut down for the night. Amazingly, in his weakened condition, he swam the 500-foot channel, although he later claimed he almost drowned.

Back in his room, he took off his clothes and collapsed, but still made no calls. He later said, "I had not given up hope all night long that, by some miracle, Mary Jo would have escaped from the car."

At 8am the following, Gargan and Markham joined Teddy at his hotel. The banter between them was heated. Apparently both men were "shocked" that Teddy had not notified the authorities.

Still, Teddy did not report the accident in spite of repeated urgings. He began to call friends for advice. Surprisingly, his first call was to Jackie in New York City. They were engaged in an affair at the time, even though she was married to Aristotle Onassis.

Jackie, according to unconfirmed reports, advised Teddy to

Associated Press

After staying awake all night after the accident, Teddy told Gargan and Markham the following morning how he "willed that Mary Jo still lived. Somehow I thought you guys would arrive in the morning and tell me that she was still alive. I just couldn't gain the strength within me, the moral strength to call Mrs. Kopechne at two in the morning and tell her that her daughter was dead."

Mary Jo's grieving parents, **Joseph and Gwen Kopechne**, are seen attending their daughter's funeral. Accompanied by his pregnant wife, Joan, Ted also attended the funeral, along with Ethel Kennedy and Lem Billings, JFK's longtime homosexual friend.

Days after the funeral, Joan suffered a miscarriage. She later said, "The funeral was a terrible experience, one of the worst of my life. It was the beginning of the end for Ted and me."

call the police at once and to assert that when he left the scene of the accident, he was in a state of shock and did not realize a passenger was left inside the submerged car. "Plead temporary amnesia," she advised, but he did not heed her warning.

Before he finally turned himself over to the police later that morning, he phoned at least two dozen Kennedy advisors. Long before the crime was officially reported to local authorities, the cover-up had begun.

Teddy's second call was to Joe Gargan, his cousin. Joe had arranged the party. In later testimony, Gargan claimed that Teddy had asked him to say that he was driving the car. Gargan absolutely refused to take the blame.

Two early-rising fishermen noticed the submerged vehicle and called the police at 8:20am that morning. Their discovery prompted a local diver, John Farrar, to don his SCUBA gear. In the aftermath, he discovered Mary Jo's body within the submerged car at 8:45am. Later, the Oldsmobile was towed out of the pond. Farrar later testified that the body of Mary Jo was pressed up in the car where an air bubble had formed. Examiners asserted that she'd "lived for at least two hours down there."

Only when Teddy learned that the police had discovered Mary Jo's body did he cross back and head for the station in Edgartown.

He showed up in person at police headquarters to report the accident. It was widely assumed at the time that he had been drunk and needed time to sober up. If it had been proven that he was driving while drunk, the charges would have been far more serious.

***

A week later, on July 25, Teddy pleaded guilty to a charge of leaving the scene of an accident and causing injury. Judge James Boyle sentenced him to two months in jail but suspended the sentence because of the Senator's "unblemished record." Teddy strenuously denied press speculation that he and Mary Jo had "any romantic relationship whatsoever."

No autopsy was ordered which, of course, would have produced the devastating news that Mary Jo had been pregnant. Dr. Donald Mills, the medical examiner, signed the death certificate, claiming that the cause of death was accidental drowning.

In theory, at least, the District Attorney's office in Massachusetts did investigate the fatal accident, but their data was never made public. A year later when there was a call for retrieval of the file on the accident, the entire dossier had mysteriously disappeared. It has never been recovered.

Facing the hostile eyes of Mary Jo's family, Teddy attended the funeral with his wife Joan. Joan was pregnant at the time, but suffered a miscarriage one week after the funeral.

For some reason, Ethel Kennedy also turned up. Apparently, at the time she did not know that Mary Jo had been the mistress of her husband.

By September 18, too much speculation was reaching the office of District Attorney Edmund Dinis, who tried to have Mary Jo's body exhumed for a belated autopsy. Her parents opposed this, and consequently, the body was not exhumed.

At the inquest in January of 1970, it was determined that there was "probable cause" that Teddy had committed a crime. However, no warrant was ever issued for his arrest, and Dinis chose not to pursue the Senator on a charge of manslaughter.

Teddy sat out the presidential race of 1972, refusing to run as George McGovern's vice presidential running mate. Four years later, because of renewed interest by the media in Chappaquiddick, he also chose not to run again in 1976.

In 1980, in his pursuit of an impossible dream, Teddy foolishly sought the Democratic nomination for president against Jimmy Carter. He would lose the nomination and Carter himself, as the Democratic Party candidate, of course, then lost the election to Ronald Reagan.

Jackie called Ted and bluntly told him, "Even if you had won the presidency, you'd be the fourth Kennedy brother to be killed. Let's face it: you get dozens of death threats every week, and all you need is for one of them to be valid."

In his biography, *The Deeds of My Fathers*, author Paul David Pope wrote about how his grandfather and father founded the *National Enquirer* and then expanded it into the best-selling tabloid in America. Maxine Cheshire, a gossip columnist for *The Washington Post,* had stumbled across the facts associated with Mary Jo's pregnancy. In 1980, on the eve of the election, she was willing to sell her information when Teddy was challenging Carter.

"Once people read it, there'd be no way that Ted Kennedy could ever run for president, maybe not even for dog catcher in Massachusetts," Pope wrote.

Pope said, "the story named names, none of them lacking attribution, and included no anonymous quotes. There were dates, times, places, and supporting documents."

Peggy Dattilo, an *Enquirer* reporter, found the details associated with the assertions that Mary Jo had been pregnant by Teddy were "airtight—good, solid reporting." She told her editors that when the story hit, it would "be huge, bigger than anything since Watergate." In all likelihood, she believed, Teddy would have to resign from the Senate.

But against everyone's expectations, the paper's founder, Generoso Pope Sr., never ran the story. He bought the story simply as a means to kill it, in effect suppressing this scandalous revelation by trading it in a murky back-room deal for an innocuous vanilla-flavored feature article dictated directly by Ted himself.

For Pope and his *Enquirer*, for reasons never fully understood, the benefits involved a personal behind-the-scenes interview about how Teddy had become a father figure to his late brother's children. Pope ran the story under the headline: THE HEARTACHES & HAPPINESS OF RAISING 16 KENNEDY CHILDREN.

A fair trade? Nearly all newspeople today think not.

"What people cared about was Jackie Kennedy and her two teenagers, Caroline and John Jr.," Pope maintained. "They cared about them a whole lot. JFK's three direct survivors were the Holy Grail of the tabloid world."

As his grandson surmised, "Gene figured Teddy might someday help clear the way for him to get to them. He was willing to bank that chit, even though he might never have a chance to collect on it."

As Arthur Schlesinger would say some time in 1970, "With Chappaquiddick, the iron went into Teddy's soul."

Burton Hersh, author of *The Education of Edward Kennedy*, claimed: "It is no psychodramatization to insist that, in the midst of that weeks-long nightmare, a great deal died for Edward Kennedy: the deteriorated leaving of Camelot, the dependencies Bobby was able, somehow, to impose still, the deep confusions every time Edward met the unblinking eyes of his paralyzed old father, for whom all this was about to prove the ultimate shock too many."

Death threats continued to mar Teddy's life until the very end, most of them claiming that an assassination awaited him the way it had his two brothers.

A typical one read: GET YOUR PINE BOX READY. BULLET IN YOUR NECK.

One particularly vicious letter was sent to Joe Kennedy. "Your suffering has hardly begun. Teddy is next on the Kennedy 'hit parade.' And we won't rest until he gets his. We are sick of your family and all the damn Kennedy crap. Jack had to die. Bobby had to die. Teddy has to die. We hope you live long enough to see total destruction of your family and to suffer again and after before you die and go to Hell for eternity."

One of the strangest hate mail letters sent to the Senator's Washington office contained a used condom with something that "looked like green slime inside."

In Teddy's memoirs, published posthumously after his death on August 25, 2009 of brain cancer, he claimed that his behavior that night on Chappaquiddick Island was "inexcusable." He also said, "That night has remained with me and haunted me for the rest of my life

The wooden **Dike Bridge**, one of America's most obscure, noticeable at the time for its lack of guard rails, overnight became one of the most famous in the world when Teddy's Oldsmobile (seen above) plunged over the side and into the fast-moving water. Without really remembering how, he managed to free himself, and although he claimed he made attempts to rescue her, Mary Jo stayed behind to drown.

Teddy's claim that he was taking Mary Jo back to Edgartown to catch the midnight ferry was shattered when an eyewitness, Christopher Look, spotted the couple at 12:45am.

On a visit to the Philippines, **Teddy Kennedy** was snapped in an embarrassing position with his bunny, **Claudia Cummings**, with whom he was having an affair. Teddy's *fiancée*, Victoria Reggie, was not so happy when tabloids ran this picture on newsstands in both the United States and Europe. His affair survived this candid photograph, and Victoria eventually became Teddy's second wife.

A recently divorced mother of two, Victoria ("Vicki") was an attractive Louisiana-born brunette and a corporate lawyer in Washington, D.C. She married Teddy in a civil ceremony on July 3, 1992 in McClean, Virginia. When Claudia heard of the marriage, she crumpled to the floor, had to be given tranquilizers, and was in shock for four days.

Two years later, the Catholic Church granted Teddy an annulment of his long-standing first marriage to his first wife, Joan Bennett Kennedy, with whom he had produced three children and whose divorce by civil authorities had been granted in 1982.

TEDDY KENNEDY
THE FOURTH WOMANIZER
IN THE KENNEDY CLAN

Like his father, Joe, Sr., and like his brothers, Jack and Bobby, Teddy Kennedy also chased young women until he got too old for the chase. Richard Tuck, longtime confidant of the family, said, "From the moment he married Joan, and long before, Teddy was philandering. It was in his blood stream. Not everything was a one-night stand. Sometimes, his affairs stretched on for years."

Such was the case with a 36-22-35 Miss Alabama runner-up, Claudia Cummings, who sang with Jimmy Buffet's band. She claimed, "He's as cuddly as a big ol' teddy bear!"

From Cape Cod, to New York, from Las Vegas to Hollywood, Teddy was even less discreet than Jack or Bobby had been. Many of his wildest exploits were fueled by alcohol. One night in Vegas, the local sheriff assigned eight deputies to "watch Ted Kennedy day and night. If he gets into trouble, cover it up."

Teddy once told actress Gene Tierney, Jack's former mistress, "All Kennedy men are irresistible and having a mistress, or mistresses, is the norm for us."

Former Kennedy aide Richard Burke caught the senator having intercourse with a Greek (female) singer while Joan slept in a bedroom upstairs. Burke later said, "All the Kennedy brothers had an aura of moral invincibility. My job became juggling the senator's personal life. As the years went by, his philandering increased, with a marked preference for three-ways, although some of his girl friends objected to that. In time, he became known as 'Hot Tub Teddy.' He taught his ladies the joys of poppers and coke."

Porno star Jack Wrangler, the husband of songbird Margaret Whiting, said that one night at Studio 54, he saw "a drunken Senator Ted Kennedy getting a blow-job in the bowels of the club from none other than Andy Warhol. I also heard that in Hollywood, he indulged in some kinky stuff at the home of Jack Nicholson."

The Reinvention, Remarriage, and Death of Aristotle Onassis

Photofest

At New York's El Morocco Night Club in 1971, a rail-thin **Jackie** looks like a giggling school girl. **Aristotle Onassis** appears as if he's pondering, "What in hell have I gotten myself into?"

The Greek tycoon had once compared Jackie to a diamond—"cool and sharp at the edges, fiery and hot beneath the surface." His opinion of her had long ago changed to "coldhearted and shallow." At this point in his marriage, Ari was turning to his mistress, Maria Callas, "for the pleasure of her company," and not to Jackie.

The night Jackie and Ari drank and dined at El Morocco, she told him she had no room for him at her 1040 Fifth Avenue apartment. "The decorators have everything torn up," she falsely claimed. "You'll have to check into a hotel."

Ari actually maintained a permanent suite at New York's Pierre Hotel. He rightly suspected that Jackie was privately having intercourse with Teddy Kennedy. His plan involved entrapping the lovers by wiring her phone. That way he could sue her for divorce, charging adultery.

But Jackie's Secret Service agents kept too close a watch on her Fifth Avenue apartment for him to have men successfully bug her phones.

WHERE LOVE HAS GONE?

Sailing aboard the *Christina*, Aristotle Onassis heard a bulletin on his radio. It was out of Dallas. John F. Kennedy, President of the United States, had been assassinated.

Without alerting anyone, even his closest aides and especially Maria Callas, Ari launched into what he'd later call "my change of plans. My new strategy."

Ari joined Maria in Paris and spent his days watching the coverage of the President's death on television. Noting how brave and courageous Jackie was, Ari told Maria: "There's something Greek about Jackie." The diva was not impressed. "She's just putting on a grand show for the media."

Even when members of the press learned that Ari had been seen with Jackie, they did not immediately connect a romance between "The Beauty and the Beast." Over the years, Ari had been seen with some of the most famous and beautiful women in the world, paying homage to the likes of Greta Garbo and Elizabeth Taylor.

Months went by before Maria learned that Ari had been secretly seeing Jackie at her Fifth Avenue duplex apartment in New York throughout 1966 and into 1967. Even as late as January of 1968, Maria and most of the American public did not know how serious the relationship between Jackie and Ari had become. Jackie, it was learned later, had been entertained by Ari on the island of Skorpios and at his plush apartment on the Avenue Foch in Paris.

As Bobby started to run for the presidency in 1968, Ari and Jackie popped up everywhere. They were seen in New York at the exclusive "21" or at El Morocco, even Ari's two favorite Greek restaurants in New York, Mykonos and Dionysus. Both of them were photographed entering Maxim's in Paris.

Jackie began to confide in him, complaining bitterly

Aristotle Onassis *(1906-1975)* at age 26 and *(lower photo)* near the end of his life.

As the 70s deepened, and even long before, Onassis wanted to dump Jackie. He took her aboard the *Christina* to Haiti where he urged her to get a quickie divorce. "I will marry you the very next day. That way you will show the world that you trust me. By marrying you the next day, I will show the world I love you."

"No way!" Jackie said. "You think I'd fall for that?"

Their marriage in the early 70s was in name only. They were dating others, including Teddy for Jackie and Maria for Ari.

On a shopping expedition to Athens, a handsome young Greek architect shared Jackie's suite. On Skorpios a beautiful young Greek girl from another island was seen each morning rising from Ari's bed.

that she was "emotionally shackled" by the Kennedys, who held tight purse strings.

Ari had to face Maria and break the news. He was blunt. "I'm going to marry Jackie. I still love you, but I need Jackie in my life. It will not be a marriage of love. I need Bobby to win the presidency and look favorably upon my using U.S. docks. Jackie needs me to buy privacy that she can't find in America. If Bobby loses, I'll back Teddy in the next election. Jackie fears she'll be murdered in the States or that her children will be kidnapped. She needs me and the armed security guards I can provide. Those Secret Service agents assigned to her are a pack of faggots."

Their lives changed quickly after the assassination of Robert F. Kennedy at the Ambassador Hotel in Los Angeles on June 5, 1968. Jackie called Ari at once. "If they're killing Kennedys, my kids are number one targets. I want to get out of the country."

Before flying to Greece to marry Jackie, Ari paid a farewell visit to Maria.

"I could never influence you to do anything," Maria said. "Go, then, to your woman who sounds like Marilyn Monroe playing Ophelia."

At the door, Ari told her, "You know I will always love you."

"My pain is too deep to speak anymore," she told him. "Please leave. You will not be the first man to marry a woman you do not love, and Jackie will not be the first woman to marry a man she does not love."

On the wedding day of Aristotle Onassis to Jacqueline Bouvier Kennedy on October 20, 1968, Maria went into seclusion in her apartment in Paris. To protect herself from the paparazzi, she ordered her heavy draperies to be drawn.

When she finally faced the press in Paris, Maria said, "Mrs. Kennedy did well to give a grandfather to her children. Onassis is as beautiful as Croesus," a reference, of course, to the ancient King of Lydia (ruled 560 BC-546 BC), famed for his wealth.

At least in public, Maria seemed to interpret the announcement of Ari's marriage with a stoic but painful calm. But Lee Radziwill became hysterical in a call to Truman Capote. He later reported, "She was screaming and crying and carrying on."

Fashion designer **Coco Chanel** (inset photo) wanted Jackie to dress exclusively in her *haute couture*, and the imperial Parisian resented that the First Lady sometimes used other designers, including Valentino and Oleg Cassini.

"She's the worst dresser on the continent," Chanel pontificated, years after JFK's assassination. "I design for mature women, not teenagers in mini skirts. I hate 'old' little girls like Mrs. Kennedy in a miniskirt. She is responsible for spreading her bad taste all over America. That white Courrèges dress she wore to the dedication of the monument to President Kennedy in Runnymede, England, was shocking."

At that point a reporter reminded Chanel that Jackie had been wearing Chanel's strawberry pink wool suit and matching pillbox hat that day in Dallas. That blood-stained suit that Jackie insisted on wearing all the way back to Washington—"Let them see what they did to Jack"—became the most famous outfit in the world. When Chanel was confronted with this, she rose to her feet and dismissed the reporters.

When **Lyndon B. Johnson** was sworn in as President aboard Air Force One en route from Dallas back to Washington, D.C., on November 22, 1963, —"a nightmare come true"—Jackie was wearing the now-famous pink Chanel, which still contained some particles of JFK's brain.

"How could she do this to me?" Lee sobbed into the phone to Capote. "How could this happen?"

Capote later said, "Lee really thought she had Onassis nailed down. She wasn't in love with him, but she loved all those tankers."

There was a great irony in Jackie's marrying Ari. Years previously, Jackie had warned her that Lee would damage JFK's presidency if she married the Greek tycoon. "Obviously Jackie could give advice, but not take her own advice," Capote said.

After the wedding, Jackie faced Christina. "I hate you," Christina told Jackie.

Later she said, "Christina is a spoiled monster with fat legs and chunky ankles, who dresses like a Greek peasant."

Ari told his daughter Christina, "Jackie has no illusions about the Camelot myth she helped perpetuate."

His daughter's response was, "I don't like the bitch. Don't trust her. She'll bring you only grief."

In Paris, when Coco Chanel heard about the upcoming marriage, she said, "Everyone knew she was not cut out for dignity. You mustn't ask a woman with a touch of vulgarity to spend the rest of her life over a corpse."

Chanel was just one of thousands, even millions of opinions heard around the world. Comedian Joan Rivers mocked the marriage. "Come on, tell the truth. Would you sleep with Onassis? Do you believe she does? Well, she has to do something—you can't stay at Bergdorf's shopping all day."

Headlines around the world denounced Jackie for marrying Ari. One tabloid in London claimed "JACKIE WEDS BLANK CHECK." *Bild-Zeitung* in Germany claimed JACK KENNEDY DIES TODAY FOR A SECOND TIME. Even the staid *New York Times* claimed AMERICA HAS LOST A SAINT.

In her defense, Cardinal Richard Cushing came forward, asking, "Why can't she marry whomever she wants to marry?"

Dorothy Schiff was the long-time publisher of the *New York Post*. During the course of 1968, she sometimes dined with Jackie.

In her autobiography, *Men, Money, and Magic*, she wrote: "Jackie wanted to marry Onassis more than Onassis wanted to marry Jackie." Johnny Meyer later confirmed that that was true.

When Jackie did marry Ari, the Greek mogul boasted of his sexual prowess to Pierre Salinger, who had been JFK's press secretary,

"Five times a night," Ari claimed. "She surpasses any woman I've ever known. She really goes for my Greek pole."

Salinger later asserted, "Onassis could get very graphic in describing his physical relations with Jackie. Poor Jack must be turning over in his grave."

In the weeks to follow, Cardinal Cushing's defense of Jackie brought an avalanche of hate mail, "some of which is in the language of the gutter." He decided to retire as archbishop on August 24, 1970, two years before what he'd announced previously. "I could no longer stand being the victim of such hatred and such violent attacks for expressing an honest and true opinion."

In fewer than five months, Ari was calling Maria, wanting her to take him back, including letting him sleep in her bed again.

His marriage, as he reported, had been a disaster. Jackie had spent millions, nearly $8 million to redecorate the *Christina*. "She spends her $30,000 monthly allowance in ten days," Ari claimed. "She runs up astronomical bills. She charges every piece of designer clothing in Paris and New York. She makes sure she is somewhere else when I fly into town. Instead of letting me stay in her New York apartment, she tells me to rent a hotel suite."

He told Maria that Jackie was "cold hearted and shallow, a gold digger, the biggest international whore on the planet."

He confided to Maria that he no longer had sex with Jackie.

Eventually, Ari was drawn back to the bed of the women he really loved, Maria herself. Their affair began anew at her 36 Avenue Georges Mandel apartment in Paris. And as the weeks went by, she was seen with Ari at nightclubs and high-profile restaurants such as Maxim's.

Even though Maria had agreed to become "the other woman," her renewed relationship with Ari was just as turbulent as before. There were good weeks and then violent explosions between these two temperamental lovers.

Even though involved with two of the most famous women on the planet, Ari began to wind down, losing his stamina. As the months went by, he was frequently dizzy and he tired easily.

Tabloid headlines on May 26, 1969 blared: CALLAS ATTEMPTS SUICIDE OVER ONASSIS.

A sick and dying Aristotle Onassis arrived at Orly Airport in Paris for his final visit. En route to France his mind had been consumed, after years of "incompatibility," with his looming divorce from Jackie and with the painful loss of Olympic Airlines to the Greek government.

In a final display of his macho persona, he insisted on walking off the airplane unaided. After clearing Customs, he walked weakly but steadily to a waiting limousine to take him back to his apartment at 88 Avenue Foch.

Once there and in bed, he called Maria at her apartment, telling her that "The Widow," as he called Jackie, was in Paris. He promised her he'd arrange to slip her into the American Hospital where he planned to check in the following morning. He admitted that both Christina and Jackie were opposed to her visiting him in the hospital.

Before going to sleep that night, he told his aide, Johnny Meyer, "You know, I'll soon be joining Alexander on Skorpios."

In the hospital, Ari was operated on to have his gall bladder removed. Every forty-eight hours, doctors replaced his blood. He faded in and out of consciousness.

His daughter checked out of the Avenue Foch apartment and into the Plaza Athenée Hotel so as not to have to share lodgings with Jackie, whom she loathed even more than she had on the day she had married her father.

Miraculously his condition improved, and Jackie returned to New York. She later was spotted skiing in New Hampshire.

But back in Paris, Ari took a turn for the worse and entered a rapid decline. The Onassis staff could not reach Jackie. Maria was called secretly by a member of the Onassis staff, who told her she could come to the hospital for a final goodbye.

Wearing a blonde wig, Maria arrived at the back entrance of the hospital and was directed to the service elevator, which still contained a cart of smelly waste products. She crossed her heart before entering Ari's darkened bedroom. He was under an oxygen tent and appeared unconscious, barely alive.

At one point he opened an eye and seemed to recognize her. "It's Maria, your canary," she called out to him. "I will love you forever." Those were her farewell words to her longtime lover.

After that, she flew at once to Palm Beach to hide out and avoid "the attack of the paparazzi."

Christina was in the hospital room with her father one hour before he died. Although he was unconscious at the time, she bent over his body and, in a soft voice, whispered to him, "God is punishing you for your sins."

On March 15, 1975, Ari, under a morphine-induced sleep, with tubes attached to every part of his body, departed from the world. It had rained all day and night in Paris.

Jackie was in bed in New York and asleep when a call came in for her, telling her that her husband was dead. On hearing the news, she called the airlines and began packing at once to go to the funeral.

For her arrival in Paris the day after Ari died, Jackie was greeted with a sea of reporters and paparazzi.

In a black Valentino dress and a black leather coat, she read a statement:

"Aristotle Onassis rescued me at a moment when my life was engulfed in shadows. He meant a lot to me. He brought me into a world where one could find both happiness and love. We lived through many beautiful experiences together which cannot be forgotten, and for which I will be eternally grateful."

Maria was still awake in her rented Palm Beach villa. She'd been unable to sleep that night. A bulletin came over the radio that Aristotle Onassis had died in Paris. On hearing that news, she went into seclusion, although reporters and the paparazzi began to converge around her villa, hoping for a statement.

Maria opted not to attend Ari's funeral, figuring that her appearance would make the solemn ceremony "a battle to the death for paparazzi, hoping to catch Mrs. Kennedy and me in a catfight, or Christina pulling the hair of Mrs. Kennedy."

"Let Christina and Jackie fight it out over Aristo's estate," Maria said. When the Onassis will was read, his attorney called her in Paris. "I am so sorry," he said, "Mr. Onassis left you nothing. If you wish, I can return the letters you wrote him."

After the death of Ari, and after the loss of her once golden voice, Maria told friends in Paris, "I have now entered the Norma Desmond period of my life." She was referring, of course, to the tragic heroine of the movie, *Sunset Blvd.*, which had starred Gloria Swanson, former mistress of Joseph Kennedy.

Maria Callas died of a broken heart on September 16, 1977. She'd told a friend, "Life is no longer worth living after Aristos is gone."

Thousands of letters from fans around the world poured in. One ardent admirer in Milan wrote: "Maria Callas will live forever." An opera fan in New York sent a card, "Maria Callas, *prime donna assoluta* forever."

Author Nicholas Cage wrote the most romantic epitaph to Maria and Ari:

"In the end, happiness evaded Onassis and Callas. But it is not impossible to imagine that after Maria's remains were consigned to the sea, the tides of the Aegean carried those ashes in a southerly direction, around Cape Sounion, below the cliff crowned by the temple to Poseidon, through the Corinth Canal, where the yacht *Christina* passed so often, to the Gulf of Corinth and into the Ionian Sea. In a world where the winds and tides brought Odysseus home to Ithaca after ten years of wandering, it's not hard to envision the last relics of Maria Callas finally coming to rest on the green shores of Skorpios, still flowering with the oleander and jasmine that she and Aristo brought there from the Caribbean."

Associated Press

In August of 1968, Doris Lilly, a columnist for The New York Post, went on *The Merv Griffin Show* and proclaimed that Jackie Kennedy was preparing to marry Aristotle Onassis. The shocked audience vigorously booed her for such an outlandish suggestion. As she left the studio, a hostle crowd had gathered to denounce her. She made her way to a taxi, and en route, she was spat upon. But the gossip columnist was right.

Jackie, seen above with her children, **John-John and Caroline**, leaves the chapel with her new husband, **Onassis**, after their October 20, 1968 Greek Orthodox wedding on the island of Skorpios.

In Rome, the magazine *L'Espresso*, reflected a world viewpoint, writing that Jackie's marriage to "this grizzled satrap, with his liver-colored skin, thick hair, fleshy nose, and wide horsey grin, who buys an island and then has it removed from all the maps to prevent the landing of castaways; and, on the other hand, an ethereal-looking beauty of 39, renowned for her sophistication and her interest in the fine arts, and a former First Lady at that."

The marriage found two supporters, Elizabeth Taylor, who had been frequently entertained by Onassis, and distant relative Gore Vidal. "He is charming, kind, and considerate," said Taylor. "Jackie made an excellent choice."

Vidal noted that the match was "highly suitable. They have something in common. Both are heavy smokers."

Rose Kennedy said, "Jackie is one of the world's most expensive women to maintain, and Onassis has one of the world's greatest fortunes."

WHAT EVER HAPPENED TO MARIA CALLAS?

"I want to be burned," she said hours before she died. "I don't want to become a worm."

Her friend Peter Andry remembered visiting her in her bedroom in Paris where she was dressed in a gray gown. A Greek cross and one long-stemmed red rose had been placed on her bosom. "She looked so beautiful, so peaceful. Her long auburn hair was so rich, so full of life. I shuddered at the thought that in a few hours it would all be ashes. I felt a strong urge to touch her, to cut a lock to preserve it forever. I wish I had."

Her funeral was held on September 20, 1977 at the Greek Orthodox Church on rue Georges Bizet in Paris. But it wasn't until June 3, 1979 that her final wishes were fulfilled.

Greek Air Force officers carried an urn wrapped in a Greek flag containing her ashes. The Greek minister of culture scattered her ashes over the Aegean sea.

JFK and the Nazi Spy: "Honeysuckle and Inga-Binga"

JFKs scandals with women predated his 1953 marriage to Jackie. And whereas Aristotle Onassis maintained mistresses, and in some cases, boys, using them for adultery during his marriage to Jackie, Ari's philandering was mild compared to what she had experienced during her marriage to Jack Kennedy throughout the 1950s and during his short term in the White House.

In November of 1941, JFK served as an ensign in the U.S. Navy's Office of Naval Intelligence in Washington, D.C. One night at a party, he met **Inga Arvad**, who later claimed "He took me to bed that very night—three times before dawn broke...I called him 'Honeysuckle.' He nicknamed me 'Inga-Binga.'"

At the age of 15, she'd won the Miss Denmark contest, thanks partly to her thirty-six inch bust and her eighteen-inch waist. Born in 1913, she was four years older than Jack.

In 1936, at the voluptuous age of 23, Inga, by then a journalist focusing on celebrity gossip, had been Adolf Hitler's widely publicized companion at the 1936 Summer Olympics. But between 1941 and 1942, during the darkest years of World War II, she evolved into the "hot-to-trot" mistress of John F. Kennedy.

Before Jack, she had been mesmerized by the Führer, writing, for publication, "You immediately like him. He seems lonely. The eyes, showing a kind heart, stare right at you. They sparkle with force." Adolf told her, "You are the perfect example of Nordic beauty." Her youthful liaison with the Reich and its chief mass murderer would follow and plague her until her death from cancer in 1973 in Nogales, Arizona. Inga also maintained an affair with Hitler's *Reichsmarschall,* Hermann Göring, whom she described as "very kind, very charming, and insatiable in bed."

She also functioned for a time as the mistress of the notoriously controversial Axel Wenner-Gren, the fabulously wealthy but oft-disgraced Swedish industrialist rumored to have promoted the interests of the Third Reich to, among others, the Duke of Windsor and his scandalous Duchess. Wenner-Gren's mammoth yacht supplied fuel to Nazi U-boats in the North Atlantic.

From the beds of Berlin, the brilliantly multilingual Inga had migrated to the mattresses of Washington, where she got a job as a writer/reporter on the *Washington Times-Herald.* There, she wrote a gossip column documenting the exploits of the movers and shaker in America's capital. Powerful men fell in love with her, including America's best-known financier, Bernard Baruch, who was 71 at the time. A friendship with Kathleen (Kick) Kennedy led to an eventual meeting with JFK.

Her torrid affair with Jack Kennedy captured the attention of Kennedy-hater J. Edgar Hoover at the F.B.I. He told his lover and chief assistant, Clyde Tolson, "The bitch is the Mata Hari of Washington, and that upstart Kennedy brat is fucking her and giving away naval secrets which she's reporting back to Hitler himself."

Hoover called Captain Seymour A.D. Hunter, JFK's superior officer. "Jack Kennedy is revealing naval secrets to some Nazi bitch," Hoover charged.

It was agreed that JFK could not be dismissed or disgraced because of the powerful position of his father. "I'll tell this Kennedy boy that he's going to be transferred to a naval unit at sea. He'll learn no secrets that way to share with the Nazis. In the meantime, I'll give him a desk job in Charleston, out of harm's way."

Consequently, JFK was assigned to a station in South Carolina in January of 1942 in the frenzied aftermath of the Japanese attack (December 7, 1941) on Pearl Harbor. "Inga came down a few times and I fucked her, but right now I've rounded up three Scarlett O'Haras to fuck," he wrote Lem Billings, "So I told Inga to go back to Hitler."

JFK had seemed to know that Hoover's G-men were following him and bugging his rooms. One night in bed with Inga, he addressed the hidden microphones: "Whoever is listening, the next sound you hear will be of me fucking her." He also said, to witnesses, "Hoover's on the take from the Mafia, which pays his heavy gambling debts. With the high cost of dresses and wigs these days, he needs financial assistance from the Mob."

Hoover later claimed, "This Nazi spy scandal was my attempt to end the Kennedy political dynasty even before it began."

When JFK commanded his PT 109, Hoover abandoned his surveillance activities of him for the duration of the war, and Inga went to Hollywood to try to snare a husband, as she correctly perceived that her youth was fading. She eventually married the then-55-year-old cowboy star Tim McCoy in February of 1947. Seven months later, she gave birth to a son, Ronald McCoy. Years later, Inga told her boy, "I don't know who your father was for sure. It was either Tim or John F. Kennedy. And you look more like a Kennedy."

Danish Journalist
Inga Arvad (1913-1973)
Rest in Peace

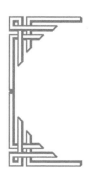

Jackie-OH vs. Jacko

Walking On the Moon

When **Jackie Onassis** was hired as a $45,000-a-year editor at Doubleday, management wanted to pitch a high-tone art book as a project she'd begin working on. Someone on the editorial board suggested a lavishly illustrated biography of Leonardo da Vinci. But she showed little enthusiasm for the project.

Elevated to the rank of a full time editor in 1982, she commissioned New York City ballet star Gelsey Kirkland and her husband, Greg Lawrence, to pen *Dancing on My Grave*. This confessional memoir revealed the ballerina's sexual escapades and her personal experiences with drugs, including her stint as an addict.

But what Jackie really wanted to do, she told her bosses, was to convince Michael Jackson to pen his memoirs. At first the editorial board did not take her seriously but she was determined.

Jackie was very persistent in pursuing Michael, who at first didn't want the contract. She finally got his name on the dotted line, and her colleagues in New York threw a party for her, celebrating the deal, which turned out to be the biggest publishing coup of the season.

She found the manuscript disappointing, but she'd anticipated that. After the financial success of *Moonwalk*, she called Michael again. In her most persuasive voice, she beseeched him to "do one tiny, tiny little favor for me. Get your friend Elizabeth Taylor to agree to do a complete and honest tell-all book about her life, not that crap that's been published before."

Knowing that Elizabeth would never agree to do that, Michael told Jackie, "I'll get back to you on that one."

JACKIE:
Jacko's Role Model

JFK Jr.: The Voyeur's Hunk

Jackie and Jacko were an unlikely combination to form any sort of relationship, much less a friendship, but such strange occurrences happen in the world of celebrities.

One night at the Rainbow Grill, Michael Jackson was introduced to Jacqueline Kennedy Onassis, who would play an important role in his future. "All memories of his goddess, Diana Ross, were forgotten when he encountered Jackie O," said the gossipy Truman Capote to Lee Radziwill. "He developed a fixation on her. All he could talk about was her voice, which sounded a bit like Michael's own whispers. Her clothing. Her hair styling. Her manner. Her polite manners. Her sophistication. Until that meeting at the Rainbow Grill, I think Michael had wanted to transform himself into Miss Diana. But after meeting Jackie, I think then and there that Michael raised the bar on his transgendered dreams. Instead of a black diva like Ross, he apparently decided that he wanted to transform himself into a white woman like Jackie. After all, she was the most famous and most admired woman in the world at the time. Who wouldn't want to walk, act, talk, and look like Jackie? Even *moi*. Actually, to tell the truth, if I could become a woman, I would want to be Marilyn Monroe. As Marilyn, I would fuck Warren Beatty, Robert Redford, Steve McQueen, Paul Newman, Burt Reynolds, Nick Nolte, Tom Jones—big dick that one—Robert Goulet, Rock Hudson, you name it. But I was more realistic than Michael. I knew I was trapped with my own voice and physicality and could never escape it. Michael, however, felt no such limitation. He truly believed the American Dream—in his case, that you could be born a poor black ghetto boy and grow up to become a rich white woman."

Michael's interest in Jackie was first piqued weeks before he actually met her. Bob Weiner, a reporter for the *New York Daily News*, invited Michael to his apartment for an interview and a home-cooked meal. While Weiner was in his kitchen preparing a chicken and rice dish,

Jackie was frankly bored with the details of Michael's life, even though she'd commissioned his so-called autobiography.

She spent much of her time with him seeking juicy details about Elizabeth Taylor. Her interest in Taylor began at the time of her affair with Richard Burton. The Taylor/Burton scandal during JFK's administration competed with the public's hunger for news about Nikita Khrushchev and the Cuban missile crisis.

Michael did share some tidbits with Jackie. "Elizabeth complains to me about her stumpy legs and double chin," Michael said to Jackie. "She considers you one of the three most beautiful women in America, right up there with Ava Gardner and Lena Horne. Elizabeth told me that you are exquisite, your dignity enhancing your beauty."

"She also told me that she and Burton consoled Maria Callas when Onassis tossed her under the bus to marry you."

Michael amused himself by "grazing" through the wealth of books and photographs that were scattered across the apartment.

At one point, Weiner heard Michael let out a yelp. Rushing in from the kitchen, he spotted Michael staring at a celebrity nude calendar. One of the snapshots was of a nude Jackie. "I can't believe what I'm seeing!" Michael said. "Why would a woman like Mrs. Kennedy pose nude for the paparazzi?"

Weiner patiently explained that the picture had been taken on Skorpios with a hidden camera. Jackie had no idea that she was being photographed and that her privacy had been invaded.

Later, the former First Lady found out that her husband, Aristotle Onassis, had hired a Greek photographer to take the picture. Apparently, her husband felt Jackie was getting "too grand," and he hoped to embarrass her—"bring her back down to earth," as he allegedly said at the time.

Weiner later expressed surprise that he had "encountered an eighteen-year-old millionaire with his innocence intact."

After their first meeting, Michael virtually "stalked" Jackie, if the not always reliable Capote can be believed. "He showered her with invitations. If she had agreed, Michael would have taken her out every night. I don't know what she saw in this inexperienced black boy from somewhere in the Middle West, but Jackie told me that she was intrigued with Michael and his sheer audacity."

"Of course, Jackie was a pro at gracefully turning down invitations and keeping ardent pursuers at arm's length," Capote claimed. "Everybody tried to fuck her after John Kennedy died—some succeeded. Marlon Brando, William Holden, Frank Sinatra, and, of course, such 'family' as Robert Kennedy and Peter Lawford. She was far too hip to suspect that Michael's motives were sexual. That would have been laughable to her. But she was aware that she'd become his new role model."

"As of yet, I have no opinion of Michael Jackson," Jackie allegedly told Capote. "I am just formulating one. I can't figure him out. It seems he's stalled on the bridge between boyhood and manhood. He also seems strangely asexual. I honestly believe that even though Michael is an adult, he hasn't completely figured out for himself yet if he wants

In Jackie's talks with Michael, she quizzed him extensively about his former mentor, **Diana Ross**. She had allowed him to produce a single for her second RCA album, *Silk Electric*. Except for the Jackson single, most music critics came down hard on her "dreary" album.

In contrast, Jacko went on to record *Off the Wall* after filming was complete on *The Wiz*. It sold 7,000,000 copies in 1979, while Ross more or less scored a failure with *Silk Electric*.

By the following year, Michael had become such a recluse that he was no longer receiving Jackie's calls. She wanted to capture some of the dynamic tension that had existed between Michael and Ross in his bio, but Michael said, "I don't want to hurt her feelings. It's always difficult when a new star rises to replace an old star—take Betty Grable getting replaced by Marilyn Monroe."

to be gay or straight. I, naturally, have my own ideas about where he's going, which road he'll take. I think his future sex life—that is, if he has a future sex life—is going to be very difficult for him. Fraught with hazards."

If Jackie did say that, and Capote maintained to Lee Radziwill that she did, it was a perceptive observation.

Jackie invited Michael to accompany her to the Robert Kennedy Tennis Tournament where she introduced him to her children, John Jr. and Caroline. Later, Michael would invite his new friend, Capote, to escort him to another tennis match to watch young John play.

Originally, before (in the words of his critics) he wanted to become a white woman, **Michael** often used **Diana Ross** as a role model. He once lived with her and tried on her gowns when she was away. At Neverland, he wanted to be addressed by his staff as "Miss Ross."

He later dumped Diana and replaced her as his role model with Jackie. Although they came together for this 1984 photograph, Jacko and Ross saw less and less of each other over the years.

After "Thriller" became a mega-hit in 1984, Michael preferred to spend his spare time with Jackie and with such other legends as Elizabeth Taylor, Sophia Loren, Liza Minnelli, Jane Fonda, and even Katharine Hepburn.

Diana extended invitations to Michael, but usually, they were not accepted. She told friends, "I think he's getting stranger and stranger. God knows what really goes on at Neverland."

The son of the slain American president was just a teenager at the time, and had not come into his full male beauty with a chiseled physique that would contribute to his being referred to as "the hunk" in American media.

"Even though John-John was quite young at the time," Capote later recalled, "he was still a Prince Charming, even with all that long hair. It was obvious that afternoon that Michael was smitten with John-John. I was only becoming aware of Michael's interest in teenage boys. I'd met John-John once or twice through Jackie, but had not paid much attention to him until that afternoon."

Capote told his friend, C.Z. Guest, that after the game, John had invited both of them to join him at some grill along Ninth Avenue because he said he was ravenously hungry. "But, first, we were also invited to join him in the locker room where he had to shower and get dressed. At the time, I didn't know that John-John was an exhibitionist. The world learned that much later. Before both Michael and me, John-John peeled off. He might have been just a boy at the time, but that was a man's cock he was flaunting at us. The kid was hung . . . and hung big. Michael appeared fascinated. Jack Kennedy often took nude swims at the family's estate on Palm Beach. Anyone who was interested knew that the president wasn't hung at all. So where did John-John get this octoroon dick? I think I know. From Jackie's daddy, Jack Bouvier—called 'Black Jack.' His many girlfriends claimed Black Jack was hung like a horse."

Capote admitted to Andy Warhol that he did not know the outcome of Michael's attempt to forge a relationship with the handsome young teenager. "I understand that Michael pursued John-John, and they were seen together on a few occasions. As everybody knows, President Kennedy's closest friend, Lem Billings, was a homosexual and was madly in love with John Kennedy all his life— a one-way affair, I might add. But John-John didn't seem ready, willing, or able to use his father's relationship with Lem as a role for Michael and himself."

"Exhibiting himself in front of Michael was one

thing—he did that in front of any number of gay guys—but carrying it farther than that was out of the question," Capote claimed to Warhol, "Jackie always had homosexual panic fears about her son, especially when he wanted to become an actor. She may have intervened and nipped Michael's friendship with John-John in the bud. Somebody told her that Michael was collecting pictures of 'the hunk,' all shirtless, and decorating his bedroom walls with them. I don't know for a fact if that were true or not. But it was enough of a rumor to cause concern in Jackie's head. In the future, she would continue to pursue her own relationship with Michael, at least on a professional level. But at a point not known to me, John-John faded from Michael's life. Unlike Madonna, Michael never really got a piece of John-John. In that kid's case, the line formed on the right and the left."

Although Jackie wanted Michael to stay away from her kid, she did want to grab him for an autobiography.

***

At the family compound in Encino, California, Michael Jackson was leaving for the afternoon. He was accompanied by an unknown blond-haired boy of great beauty, a Tadzio, perhaps no more than twelve. Michael was going on a shopping expedition to buy the child as many toys as he wanted.

La Toya ran after him. She had an urgent message. "The First Lady of the World is on the phone, and she wants to speak to you," La Toya said.

"You mean, Nancy? I've already been to the White House, accepted that award."

"More famous than Nancy," La Toya said.

"That could be only one person," Michael replied.

Racing back into the house, he nervously picked up the receiver. In a whispery voice, he said, "Hi, this is Michael."

On the other end of the phone, an even more famous whispery voice greeted him. "Michael, you dear. It's been far too long. As they say in the Garment District, have I got a deal for you. This is Jackie Onassis!"

When Michael accepted the call from Jackie, she was working for Doubleday in New York and was at the time the most celebrated editor in publishing. Her boss had given her a budget of $300,000 to offer Michael for his memoirs, although in his mid-twenties he was still a bit young to be penning an autobiography. One editor at Doubleday told Jackie, "If Michael agrees to this, we should call his memoirs *An Unfinished Life*."

After exchanging pleasantries about their few previous meetings, Jackie got down to business and pitched the offer of a memoir.

"My life has only begun," he protested.

Truman Capote and Michael often discussed Jackie with each other.

"Jackie once told me her husband was somebody with a minuscule body and a huge head," Capote said. "Early in her marriage, she came to realize that Jack was in competition with Joe as to who could bed the most women."

"Because of her father, Black Jack, Jackie was prepared to have a husband who indulged in blatant womanizing, even though she never really accepted it. She did think that Jack would be more discreet and not leave her stranded at parties while he ran off with some floozie."

"She suffered a lot with him until she developed the theory of the revenge fuck."

"There's such a great interest in you—millions of fans around the world—that we at Doubleday wanted to hear your story as you saw your life. The early years. The struggles. The incredible success. What it's done to you."

"If memoirs are such a great idea, then why haven't you written one?" he asked provocatively.

"Doubleday has a standing offer with me of $5 million for my autobiography, but I have too many secrets. A memoir from me couldn't be honest, and therefore I'll never write one."

"I know you must have many secrets—not only your own but the intimate details of so many other famous lives. But what secrets do I have? I'm still a virgin. Never been kissed. At least not on the mouth."

Jackson knew another First Lady. She was **Nancy Davis Reagan**.

Ronald Reagan had invited Michael to the White House to present him with an award. Nancy asked her aide, "Doesn't he know to remove his sunglasses when the president is honoring him?"

Greeting Michael, Reagan said, "Well, isn't this a thriller?" Michael was startled to learn from Nancy that the president had been married before (to Oscar-winning actress Jane Wyman).

When Michael saw that there weren't enough children to greet him in the White House, he locked himself in the bathroom and wouldn't come out until Nancy rounded up more kids.

"That's a unique story in itself," she said with a slight sense of mischief. "Imagine a man living for a quarter of a century and still a virgin. You and my late husband, Jack, had a lot in common."

"Now you're pulling my leg," he said. "I'm told that when you let your hair down, you have a wicked sense of humor."

"If you only knew," she said. "One time at the White House, I was doing this really horrendous impersonation of Lady Bird Johnson. Guess what? In flies Lady Bird herself."

"I'm also told you like gossip."

"I don't deny that."

"Then I think you'd be very disappointed in any memoir I wrote," he said. "I have no gossip to share."

"Perhaps I would be disappointed," she admitted candidly. "But I don't really expect you to tell *everything*. But because you're the biggest star in the world, we at Doubleday want your story."

"I don't know . . ."

She'd later recall that he seemed so hesitant, yet wavering. "Let me fly to the coast and pitch this idea to you in person. As you know from having met me, I'm very persuasive."

"That you are." He hesitated again, leading her to conclude that he was one of the least articulate men she'd ever encountered.

"I'm not going to debase myself in any book," he warned. "The tabloids already do that for me. Do you know a good libel lawyer?"

"I never sue for libel," she said. "Let the jackals write what they wish. Just tell your story from your heart. Just be Peter Pan. That's all you have to do."

"I'd like that!" He agreed to a meeting in Los Angeles.

"I'm packing my bags," she promised.

After putting down the phone, he was eager to tell family and friends of this remarkable offer he'd just had from Jackie. "I remember every word of the dialogue," he claimed.

Privately he confessed that he had little or no interest in writing a memoir. "As for that $300,000 advance, that's peanuts in the music business," he said. "We count in the millions." He confided to his family that if he agreed to do the memoir, he would have a chance to solidify his friendship with Jackie. "Imagine me, Michael Jackson, born in a bungalow in Gary, and growing up one day to be friends with Jackie Kennedy Onassis. She gave me her private phone number in New York. Imagine that!"

Jackie, along with her assistant, Shaye Areheart, flew to Los Angeles in the autumn of 1983 to convince Michael to write his autobiography. Their initial meeting had been pre-arranged as a luncheon at Chasen's, a posh Los Angeles restaurant. Jackie and Areheart arrived on time and were kept busy as well-wishers came to their table. In a city known for famous movie stars, Jackie outdazzled all of them—all except Michael. Their meeting had been scheduled at one o'clock. By two-thirty, Michael still hadn't shown up, and Jackie and Areheart went ahead and ordered lunch.

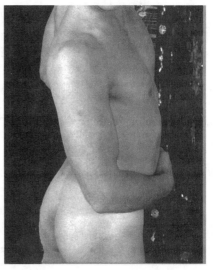

Jackie Onassis, hailed as the world's most desirable woman, wasn't used to being stood up. Initially embarrassed, she decided to forgive Michael. "He's very shy," she told her colleagues. Privately she was enraged.

The woman who'd charmed Charles de Gaulle and Nikita Khrushchev didn't give up that easily. She called Michael the following morning, using her most seductive voice. At first, he seemed intimidated and didn't want to take her call. Finally, he relented. He came to the phone and pleaded for her to forgive him for his rudeness. "The idea of writing an actual book devoted to my personal life paralyzed me," he said. "I changed costumes three times that morning and was ready to go. Then at the last minute I got cold feet."

President Obama always demanded that photographers not take pictures of him shirtless. After all, he's all skin and bones.

If John F. Kennedy Jr. had gotten elected president in 2008, as was his plan, the problem would have been different. The Secret Service would be trying to get him to keep his clothes on.

Before the end of their conversation, he invited her to tea that afternoon at Hayvenhurst. When a chicly dressed Jackie arrived at Encino, she found only two staff members. Michael had ordered the rest of the household to leave, including photographer Steve Howell, who wanted to capture the historic union of this famous pair on film. "He kicked us out. We didn't get to see her. All of us were horribly disappointed and mad at Michael for his insensitivity."

JFK, Jr. was proud of his body and the family jewels. As one classmate said after a semester at Brown, "John John walked around campus in shorts so tight it revealed an endowment larger than the university's."

Even at the age of seventeen, caption writers were posting copy on the shirtless John, calling him, "Portrait of the Stud as a Young Man."

Michael was awed by Jackie, considering her the epitome of grace, style, and charm. Once he'd held Diana Ross in such awe, but seemingly had graduated from that, moving on to bigger game. "And what bigger game could there have been than Jackie Onassis?" Howell asked. "My God, she was the most famous person on Earth meeting the second most famous person on Earth."

"It was a lovefest," said a staff member who was

His storied good looks and physique got only "studlier" as he matured in his 20s and brought that wild youthful coiffure of his into line.

Pop artist **Andy Warhol** once encountered John F. Kennedy Jr. at the chic night club Régine's on Park Avenue in New York. At the time, it was, arguably, the most upscale, sophisticated, and exclusive nightclub in New York.

Dubbed *La reine de la nuit Parisienne*, Régine, its owner and namesake, seemed enchanted to have such a "big name" within her club, and she greeted him warmly.

He was with a female date, "some minor actress of no importance," Régine recalled. Régine, as everyone in France knew at the time, did not believe in wasting her time on "nobodies."

She introduced John Jr. to Warhol.

In the course of the evening, Warhol approached John Jr. with a proposition. "Michael [a reference to Michael Jackson] told me you want to be an actor," Warhol said.

Warhol then informed John, Jr. of a movie he wanted to make. "It's called Blow-Job. I will photograph only your face while someone—male or female, your choice—is giving you a blow-job. The frame will show only your face, including your climax. No genitalia will be depicted—just the face."

"No thanks," JFK Jr. said. "My mamma told me never to make porn."

allowed to remain behind to serve tea. "Jackie and Michael were practically cooing at each other. I couldn't tell where Jackie's whispery voice ended and Michael's whispery voice began."

As Jackie would later reveal, "I didn't end up interviewing Michael. He ended up interviewing me."

"How do you live with the dread that every time you walk out your door, fans or the paparazzi are waiting to take your picture?" he asked her.

"I consider the alternative," she said. "Life as a recluse. A Georgetown widow peering out through the draperies at throngs gathered on the street in front of my house. That wasn't an option for me, so I moved to New York. Of course, I can't take the rush of people at times. Perhaps that's why I married Ari. He could almost guarantee my privacy when he wasn't invading it himself." She was referring, of course, to her second husband, Aristotle Onassis.

"How do you handle being a celebrity?" he asked.

"I don't know anything else," she said. "It comes easy for me. I couldn't imagine being unknown. Almost from the beginning of my life, I was on stage or being exhibited somewhere. Of course, not the kind of notoriety that came later. Actually, I've often pondered your question myself. Maybe I would miss the fame. At first anonymity sounds wonderful, at least the freedom it would give you. Imagine going shopping on Fifth Avenue without the gawkers and the paparazzi. I've asked a few movie stars what it was like to have known world adulation, then neglect. Gloria Swanson once told me, 'It's like the parade has passed me by.' She said she missed the adoring fans and the hysteria they once generated for her."

At the end of the afternoon, Michael still hadn't agreed to write his memoirs. Instead, he proposed *The Michael Jackson Scrapbook*. "You know, a picture of my boa constrictor, Muscles. My first report card. The first song the Jackson 5 ever recorded. Stuff like that."

"I once compiled a book devoted to memorabilia of an early trip to Europe with Lee," she said, referring to Lee Radziwill, her sister, and obviously turned off by the idea of a Jackson scrapbook.

The next day, Michael invited Jackie on a tour of Disneyland, with him as her personal guide. "He knew all the hidden corners, the names of all the animals, the thrill of every attraction," she said. "I found it boring, but he was mesmerized. I think he has the heart of an eight-year-old."

After that day at Disneyland, Jackie seemed fascinated by the topic of Michael's sexual orientation. For such a worldly woman, this was out of character. Among others, she discussed it with J.C. Suares, who would become the book designer for *Moonwalk*. According to Suares, "She repeatedly asked me if I thought Michael liked girls."

She even discussed it with Peter Lawford, thinking that as a Hollywood insider he might know something. "I have never known Jackie to be so intrigued with someone's sexual orientation," Lawford later said. "She was one of the most sophisticated women in the world. Both she and Lee included many homosexuals, especially those in the arts, among their best friends. Truman Capote, Rudolf Nureyev. Jackie even had a distant kinship with gay author Gore Vidal."

She confided to Lawford, who was to die the following year, that, "When I first met Michael in New York in the late 70s, I just assumed he was gay, but hadn't admitted that to himself yet. After seeing him so many years later on his home turf in Encino, I think he's figured out he's gay. But his gayness, I suspect, has a strange twist to it."

"What do you mean exactly?" Lawford asked her.

"I mean, it's not gay like two handsome men who look like Paul Newman and Rock Hudson getting together. I have great intuition about these matters. Michael is gay, but his gayness is different. There's something fishy going on here. Something he's hiding from the world, something that will never be revealed in *Moonwalk*. The book will hardly be a candid confession, but a glossy, glitzy thing. Michael's mythology of himself. But in spite of what I've said, I predict it'll be a bestseller."

The staff at Doubleday was eager to hear Jackie's impressions of Michael even before she eventually landed the deal to publish a memoir, not a scrapbook.

"He seems to have no perspective on his life" she claimed. "That's understandable. He's only twenty-five. Of course, I've met men his age who ruled kingdoms. I think he's more interested in projecting an image of himself than he is in telling any truth. Maybe his truth would completely destroy his image."

It took Michael two weeks to make up his mind to accept Jackie's offer. "Of course, I'll need a ghostwriter," he told her.

"I can arrange that," she promised. She confessed that she'd been less successful in pursuing other celebrities. "I even went to your rival, Prince, and tried to get him to write a memoir. He turned me down. There have been other rejections. Katharine Hepburn, Bette Davis, Greta Garbo, Ted Turner, Brigitte Bardot, Barbra Streisand, Barbara Walters, Rudolf Nureyev."

"I've heard of some of these people, but some of those celebs are too obscure," he said. "Their biographies won't sell."

She concealed her astonishment.

Jackie amused friends with her description of

La Toya Jackson

As Michael Jackson's editor, Jackie was disappointed in the editorial content of *Moonwalk*. But she was delighted that it sold half a million copies in 14 countries.

La Toya Jackson didn't like the book, finding it "cold and impersonal. What did he leave out? The beginning. The middle. And the end."

Michael's brother, Marlon, said that "three-fourths of the book is a lie."

Jackie had urged Michael to include many incidents he'd related to her, including the disastrous filming of *The Wiz* with Diana Ross.

But he refused, insisting, "I don't want to embarrass anyone."

Hayvenhurst. "It's La La Land," she claimed, "with a damn chimpanzee running amuck. Jack would have hated it, and Ari would have called in moving vans to cart off every tasteless stick. I haven't seen such kitsch since I saw photographs of Mrs. Khrushchev's home. Animals in cages. Tacky awards and trophies. Jackson family pictures. Furniture that only a demented queen could have purchased. It wasn't even *nouveau riche*, not even 'Jewish Renaissance,' but artifacts from the Land of Oz. Let me put it this way: Michael decorates like he selects his wardrobe."

In the months ahead, Jackie, from her publishing base in New York City, listened to Michael's endless demands and insecurities about the project. She also read one disappointing chapter after another. Finally, in despair, she told her staff, "Dealing with the mercurial Mr. Jackson is like being in a train wreck—worse, an airplane crash."

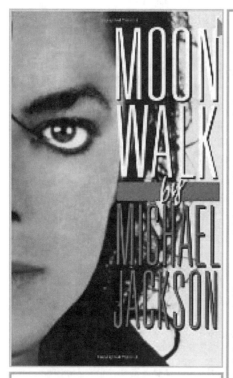

In her role as the book's editor, the usually articulate Jacqueline Kennedy Onassis penned the forward to *Moonwalk*. It was one of her less than elegant public statements:

"What can one say about Michael Jackson? To many people, Michael Jackson seems an elusive personality, but to those who work with him he is not. This talented artist is a sensitive man, warm, funny, and full of insight. Michael's book *Moonwalk* provides a startling glimpse of the artist at work and the artist in reflection."

She later told members of her staff at Doubleday, "I didn't believe a word I wrote."

ROSWELL GILPATRIC: JACKIE'S LOVER BETWEEN MARRIAGES

In addition to Bobby and Teddy, Jackie was pursued by many men in the wake of the assassination of her husband in November of 1963.

Surprisingly, one of the men who pursued her was Adlai Stevenson, who had run for president unsuccessfully against Dwight D. Eisenhower in 1952 and 1956. He also had backing to run again in 1960, although he lost the nomination, of course, to John F. Kennedy.

After JFK's death, Adlai seemed to want to replace the slain president in more ways than one. While Jackie was living in Georgetown in 1964, he began writing intimate notes to her, including one in which he beseeched her to "be merciful and indulge an old man."

When Jackie moved to New York, he stepped up his campaign to woo her. He wanted to be her escort and even invited her on trips with him, including to Spain.

Jackie went out with Adlai, but there was no serious romance. "When Adlai ran for president, the Republicans tried to smear him and said he was a latent homosexual," she told Truman Capote. "I believe that for once in their lives, the Republicans are correct."

The very distinguished Roswell Gilpatric, long-time advisor to JFK, was luckier. He'd known Jackie back in her debutante days, but their romance took a long time to blossom.

When Jackie first moved into the White House, she began to see Gilpatric at least two or three times a week, most often at social functions. Their friendship developed as JFK referred to him as "an indispensable figure in the White House."

Along with then Defense Secretary Robert McNamara, Gilpatric proposed a blockade of Cuba, discouraging an all-out military bombardment. He was pivotally involved in the development of "Operation Mongoose," a dirty tricks campaign aimed at destabilizing the Communist government of Fidel Castro.

Gilpatric (1906-1996) functioned as Deputy Secretary of Defense from 1961 to 1964. From 1972 to 1975, he served as Chairman of the Federal Reserve Bank of New York. Previously, between 1951 and 1953, he had served as Under-Secretary of the

(continued from previous page)

Air Force. Between political appointments, he functioned as a high-powered corporate attorney for Cravath, Swain, & Moore, on Wall Street.

Gilpatric had three children, was married five times, and lived on Sutton Place, Manhattan, and Desert Island, Maine, where he was buried after his death in 1996.

Even during the tenure of her husband in the White House, Jackie visited Gilpatric at another of his homes on the eastern shore of Maryland. Even though there was speculation, Gilpatric said, "We're just close friends." Jackie said nothing.

Friends and employees of the couple disagreed, one servant claiming "The First Lady and Mr. Gilpatric spent the night together following a clambake on Chesapeake Bay."

After JFK's assassination, Jackie's relationship with Gilpatric intensified, even though she spent most of her evenings with Bobby. She also traveled with Gilpatric, appearing often with him in Palm Beach where "they shared the same bedroom," a servant claimed.

The trip that brought their romance into the public light was when both of them flew to the Yucatán peninsulat in 1968 to visit Mayan ruins.

Writing in *Women's Wear Daily,* Agnes Ash claimed that Jackie and her new lover did "a lot of smooching and hand-holding in Mexico. They weren't shy. They were carrying on in full view of the press."

Ash claimed that at one point, she was threatened by John Walsh, one of the Secret Service agents assigned to Jackie's ongoing protection, who told her that if she continued pursuing her story, "You might end up in a Mexican jail." In the embarrassing aftermath, Rose Kennedy herself intervened with *Women's Wear Daily* and got "some embarrassing photos" killed.

Shortly after Gilpatric returned from the not-so-secret Yucatán trip with Jackie, his wife at the time served him with divorce papers.

Over a period of five years that extended into the time she was married to Aristotle Onassis, Jackie exchanged very personal, rather intimate letters with Gilpatric. Later, a fellow Wall Street attorney put up for sale several personal letters exchanged between Gilpatric and Jackie. Gilpatric filed a protest, trying to prevent the auction of these personal lettters, maintaining that they were stolen property, having been removed from his law office at Cravath in New York.

In the aftermath, during her procurement of a legal separation from him, the third Mrs. Roswell Gilpatric subpoenaed the letters for introduction in court.

Although Gilpatric had dreams about marrying Jackie, he knew he could not support her and maintain her in the lavish style that Onassis could. "I entertained no such illusion," he told friends. "I was one among many men who wanted to marry Jackie. She didn't love Onassis, but he could protect her and her children. I lost her as my lover, but never lost her love."

When Jackie decided to marry Onassis, she wrote Gilpatric: "I hope you know all you were and are and will ever be to me. With my love, J."

Before his death on March 15, 1996, Gilpatrick admitted, "Jackie was extremely fond of me, and she maintained a certain loyalty to Jack. But one night she told me that after Jack was re-elected president in 1964, she planned to divorce him to marry me. I knew that was just pillow talk. The one man she really loved, she couldn't have, and that was Bobby Kennedy."

In June of 1968, when Jackie heard news that Bobby had been shot in Los Angeles, Gilpatric was the first person she called. "Come over at once," she asked him. Sloppily dressed, he arrived by taxi at 1040 Fifth Avenue.

"Jackie wanted to fly at once to Los Angeles," Gilpatric said. "I called Tom Watson, chairman of IBM, and he agreed to lend her his private jet and crew."

All the way to the airport, Jackie kept saying: "It can't be happening again. It can't. It can't. If there's a god in Heaven, it can't. I can't be expected to go through this nightmare twice."

"I was with Jackie at Bobby's funeral," Gilpatric said. When he was being buried, she looked into my eyes. She didn't say a thing. We both knew that the only man she'd ever loved was going into the ground."

Jackie with Roswell Gilpatric in 1968

Jackie, as Editor, Got an OK from Jacko for the Publication of His Memoirs

But as for Publication of THEIR Memoirs,
K.O.'s Came From These Other Legends:

| Katharine Hepburn | Editor Jackie | Greta Garbo |

| Ted Turner | Bette Davis | Barbra Streisand |

| Barbara Walters | Brigitte Bardot | Rudolf Nureyev |

Callas Vs. Jackie

How *La Divinissima*, Maria Callas, Suffered a Spectacular Emotional and Fiscal Loss to JACKIE, the Beltway Bombshell

Associated Press

The greatest opera diva of the 20th century, **Maria Callas**, and **Aristotle Onassis**, the promethean tycoon who revolutionized the international shipping industry, began a tumultuous courtship in 1959 that scandalized and fascinated the world. Although storm clouds were looming on the horizon, the star soprano and the Greek mogul appear in a happy moment aboard his yacht, the *Christina,* when it sailed into Nassau, The Bahamas, in 1967.

"Maria Callas was the greatest artist we in Greece have produced since the age of Pericles," said Manuel Kulukundis, a spokesman for the Greek shipping industry.

Both Ari and Maria were Greeks, although the soprano was raised above a drugstore in Brooklyn. In later life, she sang only when she wanted to—one night she walked out on a performance for the president of Italy.

Other than Jackie Kennedy, her most hated enemy was her operatic rival, Renata Tebaldi.

WHEN TITANS CLASH

Three men shaped the life of the great diva, **Maria Callas**: Luchino Visconti, the homosexual genius of a director whom she loved in vain; Giovanni Battista Meneghini, her Italian husband who was 30 years older and who used her for his own ambitions; and Aristotle Onassis, who loved her but shamelessly discarded her for bigger "game."

In the summer of 1958, the operatic superstar Maria Callas was introduced to a handsome young senator from Massachusetts, John F. Kennedy. Aboard Aristotle Onassis' yacht, the *Christina*, she was sailing with Sir Winston Churchill and Dame Margot Fonteyn in The Bahamas.

Churchill had known Joseph Kennedy when he was ambassador to Britain and had wanted to meet his son because he'd heard that he might run for president one day.

Jack and Jackie were vacationing in The Bahamas and came aboard to meet Ari, Maria, Fonteyn, and Sir Winston.

Ari virtually ignored JFK but seemed mesmerized by his twenty-nine-year-old wife who came aboard in a white St. Laurent dress in a trapeze style. Later he would claim, "She's got a carnal soul."

Maria, Ari's lover, took note of the Greek shipping tycoon's fascination with the senator's wife. That night, as the soothing Bahamian breezes wafted across the deck of the yacht, a life-long feud between Maria and Jackie would be launched, although Jackie didn't know it at the time.

Years would go by before Jackie and the great opera star would meet again. By then Jackie's role as First Lady of America had tragically come and gone.

In February of 1965, Maria flew to New York to present *Tosca* at the Metropolitan Opera. Jackie, in mink and diamonds, attended the performance and came backstage to congratulate Maria. In a white satin Dior gown, Jackie looked stunning, "Madame Callas, this was one of the most thrilling nights I have ever had at the opera," Jackie said. "You were magnificent."

The prima donna replied, "You are magnificent."

Never again would the two divas meet, even though each would become a central figure in each other's turbulent lives.

Jackie was not the first of the Bouvier sisters to be seduced by Ari. Maria and Ari, "illicit lovers," often entertained Prince and Princess Stanislas Radziwill. The Polish aristocrat, claiming some long-forgotten title, had married Jackie's sister, Lee, but their relationship was heading for rocky shores.

Somewhere during the friendship of this quartet of international jet-setters, Lee and Ari became secret lovers. Their affair was conducted almost in front of Maria and Prince Stanislas, but for months neither of the cuckolded lovers knew what Ari and Lee were up to.

When Lee made a play for Ari, he had reasons other than her charm and beauty to become involved with her.

After all, her brother-in-law was President of the United States, and Ari had suffered through many unresolved problems with his shipping interests in the United States.

When Dwight D. Eisenhower was president in the 1950s, Ari had been hit with criminal charges, claiming he had conspired to defraud the U.S. government by his use of surplus American ships on which he failed to pay taxes. Instead of going to court, he settled for $7 million.

Maria followed Ari around the world, usually on his yacht. For a decade or so, they conducted an international, flamboyant, and tempestuous relationship. Maria referred to themselves as "the two most famous Greeks on earth."

Maria's suicide attempt came not over Ari's later marriage to Jackie, but when she learned that her lover was having an affair with Lee Radziwill. Maria had discovered an empty Cartier box with a love note to Lee.

Maria's close companion, Mary Carter, claimed, "When Maria found out in 1963 that Onassis was having an affair with Princess Radziwill, she was so upset she overdosed. It was Onassis who discovered her on the floor of her apartment in Paris. He walked her around, fed her black coffee, and, of course, called a doctor. Onassis saved her life."

The world first learned of Ari's romance with Lee when Drew Pearson in his *Washington Post* column wrote, "Does the ambitious Greek tycoon hope to become the brother-in-law of the American President?"

Once free of their spouses, Maria always begged Ari to marry her, but he kept postponing it. He told confidants, "Marriage is not on my mind. The reason I won't marry Maria is because I can't stand the thought of sitting through an entire opera and staying awake."

Collapsing in pain on August 7, 1963, Jackie was rushed to a hospital. A four-pound son was born six weeks early. She selected the name of Patrick Bouvier Kennedy, and insisted he be baptized.

The infant experienced difficulty breathing, and doctors told JFK that Patrick could not live. After struggling for life for forty hours, he lost the battle on August 9.

When Lee told Ari that her sister had been depressed after little Patrick's death, he invited her for an R&R cruise aboard the *Christina*. He turned over the yacht to her "without my presence."

Unknown to Lee, Ari had always been far more entranced by the image of Jackie than he was by her younger sister.

Worried about the cruise adversely affecting his 1964 presidential election campaign, JFK told her, "Christ, Jackie, Onassis is an international pirate." But he finally relented and let her go on the cruise.

Jackie wanted to get away from her husband. She'd had a difficult birth with John Jr., and now little Patrick had died. Dr. Janet

Maria Callas changed opera forever, and her recordings became legendary.

All her life she fought "The Battle of the Bulge." After seeing sylphlike Audrey Hepburn in *Roman Holiday* in 1953, she went on a rigid diet—no liquor, no pasta, no bread, only one lean meal a day. Transforming herself, she took off nearly 70 pounds. She showed off her new look in landmark performances of *Tosca* (*top photo*), and *Medea* (*below*).

The world's *couturiers*, especially Dior and Givenchy, made her a symbol of Parisian and Milanese high chic. But in spite of all that, she faced an adversary more glamorous than she could ever be.

"How can I compete against this international prostitute and gold-digger?" she asked.

Ari liked to invite the rich and/or famous for cruises aboard the *Christina*. Here his "concubine" (as Ari referred to **Maria**) interacts with an aging **Sir Winston Churchill** in the Monaco Harbor on August 15, 1959. Later, in discussions about her, he said, "If I were twenty years younger, Aristotle would have some serious competition."

Although friendly and intimate in this photograph, she insulted him that night when she rejected his request to "sing something for me." She astounded Ari, cast, and crew when she said, "I'm not the ship's canary who takes requests from the audience."
(Associated Press)

Ari Onassis met Maria Callas at a gala party hosted by Elsa Maxwell in Venice.

From that night onward, he pursued her across Europe. Their favorite watering hole was Maxim's in Paris. The date was April 2, 1965, and Ari & Maria were about to attend the French premier of the film, *Zorba the Greek*.

When Callas finally gave in to Ari, he said, "How could I help but be flattered if a woman with the class of Maria Callas fell in love with a lowly peasant like me?"

She claimed "When I met Aristo, so full of life, I became a different woman." *(Associated Press)*

Travell, JFK's doctor, had warned Jackie that her husband suffered from the chronic venereal disease, Chlamydia (*nongonococcal urethritis*). "The disease terrified Jackie, and certainly made her husband a less-than-desirable sexual partner," said one of Dr. Travell's aides.

Jackie had become convinced that Jack's venereal disease, picked up by all his philandering, was the cause of Patrick's death. Dr. Travell told her that pregnancies could be affected by Chlamydia, including not only miscarriages but stillbirths or premature deaths.

At one time, Jackie in the White House was heard screaming at her husband, "Your whoring killed Patrick!"

The President was relieved to learn that Ari was turning over the yacht to Jackie and her friends, but she went behind his back and insisted on Ari's presence for the cruise aboard the *Christina*.

Knowing how well publicized the cruise would be, Jack wanted to shape the guest list. Lee Radziwill and her husband were totally acceptable, even though Prince Stanislas often referred to Ari as "a moral leper." JFK also asked Franklin D. Roosevelt Jr. and his wife, Suzanne, to go on the cruise as chaperones. The son of FDR didn't really want to go, but gave in to his president's request.

Maria wanted to go on the cruise, but Ari told her no. "Aristo kicked me out. He told me he couldn't have his concubine on board with the First Lady of America."

Sometime during the cruise, even with Lee aboard, Jackie began her affair with Ari. The source for that was Franklin D. Roosevelt Jr., who saw Ari leaving Jackie's suite at three o'clock one morning.

When he returned to Washington, he told both Senator George Smathers and even Lyndon B. Johnson.

Hoping to discredit a president he loathed, LBJ, who liked gossip, spread the news.

No doubt, the Secret Service agent who had been assigned to Jackie during the cruise also transmitted the news to JFK. The president was devastated to hear that, even though during Jackie's absence he was conducting perhaps at least five or six illicit sexual trysts a week, usually from within the White House.

JFK called Jackie aboard the *Christina,* demanding that she leave the cruise and return to Washington at once. She refused and slammed down the phone on him.

She had another motivation for defying her husband: During the course of the cruise, she was confronted with the most damaging rumor she'd ever faced in her marriage. Somehow, Ari had heard the accusation that JFK had slept with Jackie's sister, Lee, once back in 1957, when Jackie was in the hospital giving birth to Caroline.

Author January Jones printed this accusation as fact in her biography, *Jackie, Ari & Jack: The Tragic Love Triangle.* She wrote: "Another reason for Jackie's erratic moods was the fact that her husband, Jack, had slept with her sister, Lee, while she was in the hospital having Caroline. This was revealed by her step-sibling Nina Auchincloss. Now who wouldn't be depressed? Can you blame her? As you can see, none of this could ever be revealed without doing irrevocable damage to the Kennedy image."

The rumor that Jack slept with Lee is just that, one of the most notorious alleged scandals of the Kennedy era. Such a sexual tryst may not have happened. Another source of the rumor was the gossipy Truman Capote, a confidant of both Jackie and Lee. He was often loose with his facts, but never let that stop him from telling a good yarn.

Jackie apparently believed him. Capote later claimed that Jackie slept with Ari aboard that cruise shortly before the president's death "as an act of revenge."

This romantic triangle may be too murky ever to be straightened out, but the Lee/JFK alleged liaison remains one of the most painful rumors Jackie had to confront, and it may not even have been true, although it was widely publicized. Because of the Internet, the rumor spread around the world.

At the end of the cruise, Ari presented Jackie with a stunning

Associated Press

Jackie Kennedy, First Lady of America (*center figure, seated*), talks with **Onassis** (*standing*) and **Franklin D. Roosevelt, Jr**. (*seated, far right*), as they sail aboard the luxury yacht the *Christina,* to major ports in the Mediterranean during the autumn of 1963. It became the most notorious cruise of the Kennedy years.

Roosevelt, the oldest son of former U.S. president, FDR, was personally sent by JFK as a sort of chaperone. But Roosevelt couldn't stop the blossoming romance between Jackie and Ari, who wooed her with diamonds and rubies.

He even took her to his dream island of Skorpios, which he had purchased six months previously for $100,000. It was shaped like a scorpion. "Lovely, lovely," Jackie said, little knowing it would become her home in her very near future. He falsely told her that he was going to build a copy of the Cretan Palace of Knossos on a hilltop with 180 rooms. He never did. It went the way of so many of his promises of yesterday.

diamond-and-ruby necklace worth about $50,000 in 1963 dollars.

It is believed that Lee wrote the President, informing him of this lavish gift to his wife. She may also have claimed that Ari had been showering Jackie with gifts throughout the cruise. "All I got from our Greek tycoon was three little bracelets that even Caroline wouldn't wear," Lee claimed.

Publicly, FDR Jr. denied that there was anything romantic between Ari and Jackie during the cruise. JFK's personal secretary, Evelyn Lincoln, later challenged that statement. "I felt they did have an affair. I think so, yes. Jackie loved money. Onassis had money."

That debate of a possible JFK/Lee affair continues to this day. What is known is that the cruise marked the end of Ari's affair with Lee. "He fell in love with Jackie on that cruise," said Ari's aide, Johnny Meyer.

Christina was one of the first to learn of Ari's new attachment to Jackie, referring to it as "my father's unfortunate obsession."

Jackie, in the words of one of the Secret Service agents, returned to the White House "with stars in her eyes—Greek stars."

The White House staff noted a stronger and more independent woman after the cruise. She had successfully beguiled one of the richest and most powerful men in the world, and she was married to the leader of the Free World.

Back in Washington, Jackie was willing to give in to her husband's latest demands. He wanted her to help him counter the negative publicity of her Onassis cruise. With a sense of guilt she finally was persuaded to accompany him on a political trip.

"Where are we going?" she asked. "What God-forsaken place in the American wastelands?"

"Dallas," he said.

Jackie Kennedy was startled when JFK asked her to go on a goodwill visit to India and Pakistan in March of 1962 without him. She agreed, but with the stipulation that her sister, **Lee Radziwill** (*seated, left*) went with her. The crowds in both countries became hysterical, crying out, "*Jackie Ki Jai! Ameriki Rani!*" ("*Hail Jackie, Queen of America!*")

Jackie drew bigger crowds than Queen Elizabeth during her visit as head of the British Commonwealth. "Nothing else happened in India whle Mrs. Kennedy was here," asserted the *Times of India*. "Her presence completely dominated the Indian scene."

She picked up a small fortune in gifts, including necklaces studded with diamonds, rubies, and pearls. Of course, there were the invariable protests, some critics attacking Jackie for wearing high fashion in a poverty-stricken country. Jackie told the press, "I only buy second hand, and everything at the Ritz Thrift Shop."

Her itinerary was planned for her, but she did insist on viewing the erotic carvings of the Black Pagoda of Konarac, especially one of a woman making love "to two violently tumescent men at the same time."

Back in New York, she told Truman Capote, "I'll have to try that position some time."

Associated Press

Cross-Dressing with Ari

Male Hustlers, Roy Cohn, and Getting Paid for Sex with the Richest Man in Greece

"Mad Twins" photo courtesy Justino Esteves (www.justinoesteves.com)

Aristotle Onassis spun an orbit of dizzying riches, twisted intrigue, and questionable mores. Yet with all the revelations about him, during his lifetime, much of the world never learned some of his darker secrets. His true story revealed a deeply complicated man who was much more complex in his desires than the public ever realized.

As Ari once confessed to Richard Burton in the presence of others, "I've been known to walk on the wild side. And I just know that you have, too. We are larger-than-life figures with passions no single woman can satisfy, not even a series of women. For the ultimate satisfaction, and I may be speaking just for myself, I have to go outside the boundaries of usual morality. I visit clubs, particularly in Paris, where unspeakable acts are performed and strange trysts are arranged. I know what it is to be raped—that is, being on the receiving end—and I know what it is to rape others. Sex is one thing and can quickly become routine. But when you're raping a virgin ass and causing great pain, you feel like the ruler of the universe."

Hustling His Way Through the Wartime Ravages of Smyrna

"When he hated, nobody was spared. It destroyed us all in the end."
Christina Onassis

When Johnny Meyer worked for the aviator and mogul, Howard Hughes, he was defined as Hughes's "public relations consultant"—read that "pimp"—catering to Hughes' bisexual proclivities, arranging dates for him with the likes of Errol Flynn.

Later, when Meyer was employed by **Ari Onassis**, he was referred to as "an *aide-de-camp*," an elegant name for a cover-up man. And just as he had done for Hughes, he also arranged sexual trysts for Ari.

Meyer wasn't at all surprised when Ari requested for him to arrange rendezvous, often aboard his yacht, with some of the most beautiful boys in Europe.

"He had a thing for Swedish or Danish boys," Meyer later confessed. "He was real rough on them. At some point they were left bleeding. I think Ari didn't consider it really good sex unless he drew blood from somewhere on the boy."

"It's sick, I know, but I got well paid. And I never lost one night's sleep over the morality—or lack thereof—of my clients."

Named after the two most famous philosophers of ancient Greece, Aristotle Socrates Onassis (1906-1975), the second husband of Jackie Lee Bouvier, was broke at twenty-one and a millionaire at twenty-three. In later life his ever-present sunglasses evoked memories of Al Capone, the Chicago gangster. Critics claimed that Ari's business practices also evoked Capone's.

By the age of eleven, when growing up as a member of the prosperous Greek minority in Smyrna (A Turkish city known today as Izmir), Ari showed a lusty interest in women, but was forbidden to date. His sexual induction came in the basement of the Onassis home in Smyrna's suburb of Karatass with the family laundress, who was only about twelve years old herself. His stepmother, Helen, came home unexpectedly and caught her stepson seducing the young girl on a pile of dirty laundry. It was *coitus interruptus*.

Socrates, his father, found out about it. He was rather proud that his son had discovered sex at such an early age, but he advised him, "Never do it with some peasant girl. *Sleep up*."

Throughout his life, Ari would follow that advice. As his future mistress, opera diva Maria Callas, recalled, "Aristo was obsessed with famous women. He was obsessed with me because I was famous."

As a newly impoverished young man fleeing from the Turkish/Greek conflicts of the early 20th century, he migrated to Buenos Aires in 1923. In time, he managed to seduce Evita Peron, who made him an omelet after their night of lovemaking.

As he traveled the globe, he seduced everybody from silent screen vamp Gloria Swanson to tobacco heiress Doris Duke.

Like other Greeks living in Smyrna at the turn of the 20th century, the Onassis family had survived under Turkish rule, their lives controlled by the sultan.

In 1919, at the conclusion of World War I, Greek troops, backed up by Allied war ships, occupied Smyrna. But after three politically inconclusive years, during the summer of 1922, the Turks mounted a massive and particularly brutal invasion as a means of reconquering Smyrna. Seeking revenge on the Greeks, the Turkish soldiers slaughtered Greeks by the hundreds. Greeks were hung from lampposts and trees. The smell of burning flesh filled the air.

When the subsequent Turkish occupation of the city, Ari's father, Socrates Onassis,

Ari Onassis never quite recovered from the trauma of the Turkish rape of his native city of Smyrna in 1922. Three of his uncles were executed. His aunt, Maria, and her husband, Chrysostomos Konialidis, and their daughter perished when the Turks set fire to a church in Thyatire in which hundreds of Christians had sought refuge.

When Ari was allowed to visit his father, Socrates, in prison, he found him sharing a cage with twenty other prisoners. Unshaven and unwashed, he was suffering from dysentery and wracked with nightmares.

Ari told Socrates, "I will do anything—and I mean anything—to obtain your release." After saying that, he returned to their former home where a Turkish general and a lieutenant were waiting for him

was arrested and tossed into a Turkish prison. His wife, Helen, along with his three daughters, fled to an evacuation center, waiting transportation to Greece.

Only sixteen years old at the time, Ari remained in Smyrna with his doughty grandmother. A Turkish general, accompanied by a very handsome lieutenant, requisitioned the Onassis house, kicking out the old grandmother who went to live with relatives.

But the general and his lieutenant ordered Ari to stay, especially when they learned that he spoke perfect Turkish. He was a reasonably attractive boy back then, not the man who married Jackie and was frequently ridiculed as "the toad."

The general and the lieutenant needed a servant boy, someone to cook for them and bathe them at night after heating the water. Before the dawn of the next morning, Ari had been introduced to sodomy.

One would have to see a picture of young Ari to understand why two Turkish officers were interested in his sexual favors. In 1922 George Sevdayan was selling newspapers on the street when he first met Ari, who was hawking cigarettes. "I saw a very handsome young boy peddling those newspapers. Though not very tall, he had particularly penetrating eyes. In spite of his shabby clothes, he was totally different from the other poor kids in the streets. He already had an outstanding personality, and I knew he was going far and didn't give a fuck how he got there, just so long as it was on the way to the top."

In the 1960s, British journalist Peter Evans was summoned to Paris for an interview with Ari about the possibility of writing his autobiography. During their discourse, Ari talked about his homosexual relationship with the Turkish lieutenant, apparently not mentioning the general. But he claimed that he cooperated as a means of securing his father's freedom, since he was in a Turkish prison at the time.

He was smart enough not to resist the sexual advances of the older Turkish officers, who brought food home for him to cook. In time he managed to find bootleg liquor for them. According to reports, Ari became very fond of the general and especially that young lieutenant. Even when they didn't want to have sex with him, he nonetheless made himself available.

His first heartbreak came when he heard that his benefactors had been reassigned and were leaving Smyrna.

Abandoned by his newly acquired friends, Ari made a clever move. He distracted some Turkish border guards and fled to the safety of the U.S. Marine compound. He was a very persuasive teenager and within a day was allowed to board an American destroyer steaming for Lesbos, relative safety, and freedom.

The first chapter of Ari's life had ended. Fame and fortune, and far more adventures than his young mind could have conjured up at the time, awaited him.

After reuniting with his relatives, he decided that Greece could not contain his ambitions. He felt that the New World offered far greater opportunities, and in 1923, he sailed to Argentina, landing in Buenos Aires.

Ari Onassis had the walls of his bathroom on his private island of Skorpios decorated with Grecian homoerotic art printed on specially commissioned wall paper he had made in Athens.

Ari regaled his guests with stories of Alexander's great love for his companion, Hephaestion. When the youth died in 326 BC, Alexander had the attending doctor arrested and crucified. As an homage to their male-male love affair—the most famous in the ancient world—he also ordered the tails and manes of "all the king's horses" be clipped. He also erected a memorial to his lover—the Lion of Hamadan, which stands in northern Iran to this day, awarding Hephaestion the status of a minor deity.

"The rest of my story," as Ari so often recalled, "is history."

Or, as his enemies put it, he was a "poor boy who became a rich boy, smuggler, thief, liar, lover, family man, international playboy, and the most glamorous tycoon of the 20th century, wallowing in fabulous wealth and fabled extravagance." He combined famous mistresses and kept boys with infamous, often corrupt deals and unholy alliances.

Throughout his life, Ari, according to friends and enemies, always seemed to have a handsome boy or young man stashed somewhere—Athens, Monaco, New York, Paris.

The best reporting on this subject was done by Christopher Andersen, a *New York Times* bestselling author, known for works which include *Jack and Jackie* and *Jackie After Jack*.

When Ari sailed with famous friends (they included Sir Winston Churchill) aboard his luxurious yacht, the *Christina*, he often amused them with stories of ancient Greece and spoke openly about homosexuality. One night he told Franklin D. Roosevelt Jr., that "every Greek man worth his salt has a wife, a mistress, and a beautiful young boy on the side. It is our custom."

He had read everything he could about Alexander the Great (356-323 B.C.), the King of Macedonia who overthrew the Persian Empire and went on to conquer the known world. He could talk endlessly about Alexander's love for his boyhood friend, Hephaestion. Both boys had been tutored by Aristotle, Ari's namesake.

Aboard his yacht, Ari would explain that homosexuality, like hunting, was thought to foster masculine, especially martial, bravery.

"Alexander sacked cities, tortured his captors, killed his rivals, and even sold hordes of people into slavery," Ari claimed. "But he was really a great guy, and that's why I named my son after him."

For years, Ari had kept two boys, one in an apartment near his residence on the Avenue Foch in Paris and another in Athens. His bodyguards claimed that when he first met these boys they were either twelve or thirteen years old.

He also kept two Italian boys in Rome. In Andersen's biography, he quotes Frank Monte, Ari's bodyguard, as saying, "One lived in Ari's apartment and the other was always on call when Ari wanted him. One was dark, the other was blond haired but deeply tan. They were handsome in their early twenties. Ari would play around with them, making lewd jokes in front of me and other bodyguards. He mistreated them, even beat them for pleasure."

"Onassis would talk quite openly about his two regular boys and other occasional boys," according to Monte. "He'd say, 'There's nothing wrong with it, I just like to do it with boys.' He'd often take one or the other to his bedroom and after a while there would be the sounds of punches and screams. Then we'd get a call from Ari to fetch the poor kid and throw him out. Sometimes a boy would be yelling, 'No, no, I love you.'"

In New York in the 1960s and 1970s, Ari befriended Roy Cohn, the lawyer who became notorious in the 1950s as the chief honcho for Senator Joseph McCarthy in their witch hunt for "pinko commies."

Much of the early animosity between Bobby and Ari stemmed from Cohn's friendship with Onassis, which Bobby resented. Long before Arti became intimately involved with Jackie, Bobby had intensely disliked the Greek shipping tycoon.

The tension between Cohn and Bobby grew so viperish that Bobby left the Subcommittee in July of 1953 after only five months of service.

It is a little known fact, and one that the Kennedy clan in later years didn't want publicized. But Bobby and Ethel announced that their first choice for their firstborn's godfather was none other than Red-baiting Senator Joseph McCarthy. (**McCarthy** is pictured in the left photograph with his legal aide, **Roy Cohn**).

Bobby *(center photo)* was involved with McCarthy's search for Communists during one of the most extraordinary episodes of political theater in the history of the Republic. That involved the dispute between the U.S. Army and McCarthy over the draft status of G. David Schine, the boyfriend of **Roy Cohn** *(right photo)*. J. Edgar Hoover watched the hearings in fascination.

Meanwhile, F.B.I. director J. Edgar Hoover also began to cool on McCarthy, fearing that the Senator was overplaying his hand.

Joe Kennedy stayed in touch with the FBI director and, at one point in the 1950s, urged him to resign from the F.B.I. to become his own personal director of security, but Hoover was determined to stay on.

Both Bobby and Hoover learned that Cohn was supplying beautiful young hustlers to Ari every time he visited New York.

"Ari worshipped physical beauty in men, the Grecian ideal," Cohn told his best pal, New York literary agent Jay Garon and others one night at a gay bar in Manhattan called Country Cousin. "Ari wanted only the best and was willing to pay for it."

"He often preferred blonde boys, but occasionally made special requests," Cohn confided to Garon, who himself had been Hollywood director George Cukor's kept boy when he was young.

"One time he requested a hustler who looked like Sal Mineo, and I came up with a dead ringer," Cohn said. "Ari paid very well, at least five-hundred dollars back in the days he could have gotten the boy for fifty bucks. He did like to manhandle guys, though. In the old days, he paddled their butts until they were scarlet red, then sodomized them. In later life, he mauled them viciously, and word got out to the hustler community. It got so bad that at one point only masochists would do his bidding."

A young French-Canadian, who danced professionally at a male strip joint, The Gaiety Theater in midtown Manhattan under the name of "Spike Jones," recalled a weekend he spent with Ari in the late 1960s at an estate in Greenwich, Connecticut, which Cohn rented.

"I was taken there in a Rolls Royce painted money green. The chauffeur's uniform matched the color of the car. Once there, I was ushered into Cohn's private bedroom. The room was dimly lit but I knew at once it was Onassis waiting for me. He was lying completely nude on the bed. He had a large, thick, uncut prick, and I feared he'd cause me some damage."

"The room itself was a bit bizarre," Jones claimed. "A big oak four-poster bed, like something from *Gone With the Wind*, dominated the room, with a mirror overhead so the client could see the action. The walls contained dozens of toy soldiers and a lot of stuffed animals, including Teddy Bears in all colors. There were a lot of statues of oversize devils, showing very large cocks painted pink with scarlet red tips. When I went into the bathroom, it was covered in tiles depicting pink and chartreuse frogs fucking. It was really weird."

"I knew that Onassis would want to screw me," Jones said. "And he did. He turned me over on my stomach. He wasn't interested in the front part of my anatomy. Before penetration, he paddled my ass until it blistered . . . I mean really hard. Then with no preparation, he entered me forcefully, and I screamed. That turned him on. He piled on top of me and pounded me without mercy. He was an older man, and it took him a long time to get off. All the while he was fucking me, he bit into my neck like a vampire. I was bleeding. I think he actually got off drinking my blood. I was told later that he was a Satanist, just like Sammy Davis Jr., who was also one of my clients one dark night. But that's another story."

"Onassis gave me a thousand dollars that night and told me to keep my mouth shut," Jones claimed. "I usually had to take on ten clients for that kind of money. I couldn't believe that Jacqueline Kennedy was married to that sicko. I bet he didn't pull that shit on her. For the money he paid, I was willing to take him on again, but he never requested me after that one night. He did use other guys from our agency but they were sent to the townhouse where Cohn lived in Manhattan. Cohn was definitely the pimp for Onassis."

"Two weeks later, Cohn called me back to the same estate," Jones said. "My neck had healed somewhat. He thanked me for taking care of his friend Onassis, but warned me he could pay only one hundred dollars. He wanted me to penetrate him but when I took a look, I just couldn't. His entire anus was covered with venereal warts. My hard-on became a softie, and Cohn kicked me out of the house."

In the late 1950s, Ari became a frequent visitor at Le Carrousel, a club that featured a stage with female impersonators, in Paris. Partly thanks to regular injections of female hormones, many of the young men were "incredibly beautiful, feminine, and sexy," as critics claimed.

A "Doctor Burou" performed sex-change surgery on many of them. After the genital surgery, some of them returned to Le Carrousel. In the words of Ari, "they were more beautiful than ever."

The club owner once told the underground press that Ari and "some other very wealthy men" often sponsored the sex-change surgeries so that these "newly liberated bodies could be turned into women."

According to the mistress of ceremonies, "Onassis paid for more surgeries and took more girls as his mistress than any other patron."

***

Ari's fun-loving personality, according to friends and staff, underwent a significant change when he faced what he called "the greatest tragedy of my life."

Although he had been critical and demanding of his son, he also loved him "more than life itself." But on January 27, 1973 Alexander, then aged twenty-four, crashed in a two-engine Piazzo lightcraft as it was about to become airborne outside Athens.

At the hospital, doctors told Ari that his son could be kept alive by artificial means, and then for a maximum of only three or four days. "I had to pull the plug," Ari later told his daughter Christina. "There was nothing else to do." Alexander lived for only three hours after going off life support.

Friends and servants reported that Ari never recovered from the loss of his son. He didn't want to see anybody, even though Jackie tried to console him.

Ari became obsessed with the belief that Alexander had been murdered, his plane sabotaged. He offered a half million dollar reward to any person who had evidence to prove his charge.

"When Alexander died," claimed author Nicholas Cage, "Onassis' *raison d'etre* may have died with him."

Usually a man of charm and wit, Ari grew testy and even cruel to his staff. He cut off most of his friends and would not take their calls. His close friend, Peter Duchin, the bandleader, claimed that Ari "became morose, snapping, nitpicking, critical—just extremely difficult to even be in the same room with. All the spark he had was gone. Jackie got the worst of it."

Finally, tired of his denunciations, Jackie fought back. He punched her in the face, blacking her eye, which she concealed

Ari Onassis was anxious for his son, Alexander, to lose his virginity. He took him to a bordello in Athens, but not one staffed with women, but with beautiful young boys from all over Europe.

Allegedly he told his son, "A rich, handsome boy like you can have any girl he wants. But, first, I want you to have sex by subduing a male. Exerting your power and manhood over another male will show that you're dominant. Women will be only too eager to do your bidding, but men are objects to conquer and subjugate."

the next day by wearing large dark sunglasses, even at night. He would hit her again on several occasions. When questioned about this, he said, "All Greek husbands, I tell you, all Greek men without exception beat their wives. It's good for them."

As if the homosexual link wasn't shocking enough for some of his friends, over the years there have been revelations from his staff that Ari was also cross-dresser, a trait he shared with J. Edgar Hoover of the F.B.I.

"When he didn't have important guests—or when Jackie wasn't aboard the *Christina*—he often liked to dress up in women's clothing late in the evening," claimed party planner Stratis Kopoulos, who once catered all-male parties for Ari aboard the *Christina*. "When Mrs. Kennedy was aboard, he never wore women's clothing. But he used to with Maria Callas. She was much more tolerant and understanding of such things. In fact, I think he dressed in her gowns. It was bizarre. But during my employment with Onassis, before he fired me for some silly reason, I saw plenty. I could write a book, but he'd probably have me murdered."

His penchant for wearing women's gowns dates back to the 1930s.

Ari liked to dress up in the gowns of his mistresses, including those of Ingebord Dedichen, a socialite whose toes he liked to lick between. He'd met this woman—a tall, blonde Norwegian—in the summer of 1934. "He found my feet as smooth as a baby's bottom," Ingebord claimed.

She also noted that he enjoyed anal humor, which she did not. One night he complained that he was suffering from piles and wanted her to investigate before he was scheduled to visit a doctor the following morning. He asked her to check that part of his anatomy. When she did, she was rewarded with a fart in the face.

This tawdry incident was revealed in an incendiary biography, *Aristotle Onassis*, compiled by the *London Sunday Times* team.

In his bitterness and in his suffering over the loss of his son, the sadistic side of Ari surfaced as never before. Jackie found him insufferable and tried to keep an ocean between herself and her husband. If anybody suffered, according to Ari's bodyguards, it was his kept boys.

Photofest

"He seemed to take out all his frustrations on them," claimed former bodyguard Tony Harvey. "He beat them with violence. One kid I had to take to a hospital in Athens. Legal action was threatened, and Onassis paid him off handsomely, at least enough to set him up for life."

Harvey claimed that one afternoon Ari told him, "I'm now going to deal with Mrs. Kennedy before she becomes a widow once again."

Ari's last call to Roy Cohn was not to arrange a hustler, but on a far costlier matter. According to Johnny Meyer, Ari's confidential aide, he asked Cohn, who specialized in high-level divorces, to draw up papers to serve on Jackie. No action was ever taken.

Ari was still planning to divorce Jackie at the time of his death.

Although she was one of the most glamorous women in the world, **Jackie** with that kerchief looks like she's en route to cleaning out her garage. Who would really believe that she was spending more money on clothing than any other woman on the globe?

After getting hit with a $9,000 bill for gowns from the Roman couturier Valentino, Ari slashed Jackie's $30,000 monthly allowance by a third.

Jackie-OH NO!!

Jackie's Half-Brother Pleads Guilty to Possession of Child Porn

James (Jamie) Auchincloss, the half brother of Jackie Kennedy, was born to a life of luxury and privilege. Sadly, he was convicted in 2010 of possessing porn, including pornograpy of boys 16 and under engaged in sexual acts.

Auchincloss's porn collection was reported to the police by Edward McManus, a 44-year-old Ashland, Oregon, artist and university student, who had previously been employed as Auchincloss's assistant. Auchincloss charged that McManus had an ulterior motive in going to the police, accusing him of stealing $18,000 from him, McManus denied that and claimed he told the police about the porno "because it was the ethical thing to do."

In refuting the charges against him, Auchincloss asserted, "I don't think I have done something that harmed anybody and that would harm anyone. I don't think I'm that type of person." He claimed he was prosecuted because he is a member of a prominent family. "I have been singled out unfairly."

Auchincloss and Jackie shared the same mother, Janet Lee Bouvier Auchincloss. Caroline Kennedy Schlossberg is the half-niece of James Auchincloss.

323

A Disturbing Cache of Child Porn Goes Public

Pictured here in happier times, **James Auchincloss, Jackie, and John-John** listen to a musical performance.

Early on, Jackie became painfully aware of her stepbrother's interest in young JFK Jr. She told her husband that she feared that "James is fondling the boy."

JFK ordered Jackie to cut off all contact with her kin at once, in essence ostracizing him from the clan because of his fascination with her son.

It was never proven that Auchincloss was the source of the rumor, but word reached Jackie that someone had spread the word that JFK Jr. had an "exceptionally large penis for a boy of nine." Unfairly or not, Jackie blamed Auchincloss for that rumor and disowned him because of what she called "a kinky lifestyle."

He was just a boy himself when James Auchincloss carried the wedding train of his half-sister, Jacqueline Lee Bouvier, up the aisle as she married John F. Kennedy in 1953.

Fast forward to 2010. James Auchincloss is now 63. No longer a boy himself, he has had a life-long interest in other boys, especially naked ones.

In Oregon in August of 2010, he pleaded guilty to possessing child porn and for having computer images of naked boys. It was rumored that for years he liked to see pictures of young boys "with undeveloped penises."

Allegedly, he once told a devotee, "There is nothing more sensual than the emerging penis of a young boy. It's like a flower right before it bursts into bloom."

After a cache of child porn was found in his home, Auchincloss resigned from the board of a local theater, Oregon Stage Works, a group that boasts a highly regarded kids' theater program.

After the police were tipped off, they raided Auchincloss's Oregon home, retrieving thousands of photographs and videos of young boys, some of which had been taken by Auchincloss within his home. The slides and videos were of naked 7- to 16-year-old boys in various sexual poses, often indulging in sex acts with one another.

None of the indictments charged Auchincloss with actually having sexual contact with young boys. Auchincloss was said to have used the pictures for "his own sexual pleasure," suggesting that he masturbated while looking at the images.

He shared these images with Dennis Lee Vickoren, a local school bus driver, who received an equivalent sentence as his friend.

In 2009, Jackie's relative was indicted on 25 counts related to child porn. Within the courtroom of Jackson County (Oregon) circuit judge Mark Shiveley, Auchincloss pleaded guilty to two felony counts for encouraging child sexual abuse. The judge sentenced him to serve thirty days in jail on each count, concurrently, as part of three years of supervised probation. The judge also ordered that Auchincloss be formally registered as a convicted sex offender and that he agree to undergo psychiatric treatment for his affliction. In addition, he was ordered not to have any "unauthorized contact" with minors.

McManus denounced the sentencing of his former employer. "I am disappointed," he told reporters. "The sentence was not enough."

Auchincloss and Jackie shared the same mother, Janet Lee Bouvier. James's father was Bouvier's second husband, Standard Oil heir Hugh Auchincloss Jr.

Heir to a banking and oil fortune, Auchincloss, in addition to being a child porn aficionado, is also a patron of the arts. When Jackie disowned him—"He'll never get near John-John again"—James got even. He dished the dirt with poison pen biographer Kitty Kelley for her controversial biography of the former First Lady, *Jackie Oh!*

Both the Auchincloss and the Kennedy families were saddened that one of their relatives would fall so low. His life had started out with such promise.

Janet Auchincloss gave birth to her only son on March 4, 1947. She named him after her father, James Thomas Lee. Janet's second husband, Hugh (Hughdie) Auchincloss was nervous about his thirty-nine year-old wife giving birth "so late in life." At the time of her son's birth, Janet was angry at the Catholic Church for defining her marriage to Hughdie as invalid. By implication, at least in the eyes of the Catholic heirarchy, that made Jamie "illegitimate."

The most exciting moment in young Jamie's life came in 1953, when he, along with other pages, carried Jackie's train into the church at the time of her wedding to John F. Kennedy. Only six years old at the time, Jamie was the youngest of twenty-seven attendants. He'd balked when he entered the church and had seen the large crowd. It scared him. But he was prodded to go forward.

JFK later revealed to Jamie that "all the kneeling killed my back. I needed help to stand up at the end of the service. So much for these High Masses that involve all that god damn kneeling."

It was a very breezy day, and during the reception, Janet controlled her nervousness by constantly fixing Jamie's lace jabot and straightening his black velvet shorts.

The other great moment of young Jamie's life occurred when Jamie accompanied his parents to the inauguration of President Kennedy. "I'm thrilled that my son-in-law has become president," Janet told her son. "It seems I'm wandering in a dream. In just a few hours, Jackie will become First Lady."

During one of her stays at her mother's estate, Hammersmith Farm, near Newport, Rhode Island, in 1962, the president had criticized Jackie's casual dress during one of her sessions in church. He ordered Jamie to spy on her and call the White House. Stationed outside, Jamie saw

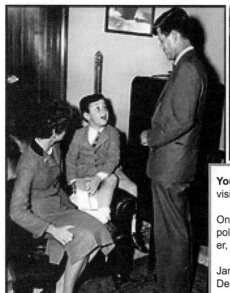

Young Jamie Auchincloss, age 6 *(left photo),* was invited by JFK to visit Jackie and the president at the White House.

On the *right*, he sits on JFK's desk in the Oval Office. He liked to talk politics with the president. "He hero-worshipped Jack," said his mother, Janet. "He was so proud of his charismatic brother-in-law."

Jamie later said, "It's because of Jack that I've become the first Democrat in the history of the Auchincloss family."

Jackie emerge from church in what appeared to be a scarf and gloves. On closer inspection, he realized that she'd covered her head with a decorated dish towel. The gloves were those Janet used for gardening.

Later, when the president visited Hammersmith, Jamie told him that he'd used JFK's advice and political connections to win the presidency of the local young Democrats Chapter.

As Hughdie Auchincloss's financial problems intensified, Janet often took out her frustrations on Jamie, treating him unfairly. He was not allowed to know that his father was having money problems.

Relationships between Janet and Jamie were often troubled. He once drove virtually nonstop from Washington to Newport, covering the distance in a then-record eight hours, only to have her attack his sloppy dress. After their confrontation, Jamie immediately got back into the car and drove another eight hours back to Washington.

On that dreadful day in November of 1963, Janet heard the TV blaring with news about the assassination of JFK. She called Jamie at the Brooks School. It was Jamie who spoke first. "Mummy, I think he's dead."

In the emotional days that followed JFK's assassination, Jamie was forced to attend a final funeral that he considered "ghoulish." In the immediate aftermath of her husband's death, Jackie had became obsessed with returning her dead children to their father's grave. They included Arabella Kennedy, born a still birth, and Patrick Bouvier Kennedy, who had lived for such a short time.

Jackie insisted that her mother supervise the exhumation of Arabella's coffin. At Newport's St. Columba's Cemetery, Janet witnessed the excavation of Arabella's grave. Janet took the coffin and its rotting contents for temporary storage to her farm at Hammersmith.

Jackie called Cardinal Richard Cushing and asked him to oversee Patrick's disinterment from the Kennedy grave site at Brookline, Massachusetts, the following day.

Subsequently, flying together on the same plane, Caroline, Janet, and Ted Kennedy brought the coffins of Patrick and Arabella to Washington.

Jamie was invited to the funeral, but he was haunted by the coffins of the dead babies. At Arlington National Cemetery, in a December 5, 1963 ceremony scheduled during the dead of night as a means of avoiding the press and photographers, Jamie, along with Jackie, Bobby, and Ted, watched the reburials. Jamie later said, "Jackie needed to do this and she did—at night, in the dark, by the Eternal Flame."

Jamie became interested in photography during his second year at New York City's Columbia University. He didn't know that this relatively harmless hobby would one day lead to his downfall when he was found guilty of taking pictures of nude or semi-nude young boys.

Ironically, Jamie formed a bond with JFK that he didn't really have with Jackie. After the president's death, he usually restricted visits with his half sisters, Jackie and Lee Radziwill, to the Christmas holidays.

Jamie was in Janet's will, a testament which had been compiled five years before her death in July of 1989. She divided her estate equally among her six living children and stepchildren, with a small percentage going to three of her grandchildren—those born to her daughter, Janet Jennings Auchincloss Rutherford.

More or less exiled in Oregon, Jamie later protested that Jackie and Princess Radziwill should not have been cut into Janet's estate. "After all, they are not Auchinclosses, and I am. Lee and Jackie have money of their own."

John-John & The Material Girl
Plugging Madonna

The romance of **Madonna with John F. Kennedy Jr**. was as unlikely a mating as the sexual link between President John F. Kennedy and Marilyn Monroe.

Madonna and John came from such different worlds. He was born the son of the President-elect of the United States, becoming the most famous baby in the world. He followed in his father's footsteps, seducing some of the most famous and exciting women anywhere, notably Madonna and Princess Di. As a seducer, he was called "His father's son in more ways than one."

Madonna in the 1980s became the planet's top female pop star, a self-made icon who rose from obscurity to shock the world.

The son of the late president was just one in a long string of conquests that reportedly included Warren Beatty (her *Dick Tracy* co-star), Mick Jagger, Jack Nicholson, and Prince, plus lots of Latin men and light-skinned black males.

A former friend claimed, "It's no joke, size counts to her. She's not interested in somebody who's not above average." The men she seduced, from all reports, met her measurement standards.

BLONDE AMBITION ENCOUNTERS THE HANDSOME HUNK

Pictured above *(left)* **Marilyn Monroe** performed her most celebrated dance number, singing "Diamonds Are a Girl's Best Friend" in the film *Gentlemen Prefer Blondes* (1953), in which she co-starred with another busty star, Jane Russell.

Above *(right)*, **Madonna** imitates Monroe, wearing an equivalent gown in the same shocking pink. Madonna always wanted to be a comedienne in the movies like MM.

In her video, Madonna, in the words of Christopher Andersen, was "Gowned and coiffed like Monroe, dripping with diamond bracelets. She prances over a platoon of panting tuxedo-clad suits while she sings her unrepentant paean to greed."

"I will be a symbol of something," Madonna predicted. "Like Marilyn Monroe stands for something. It's not always something you can put a name on, but she became an adjective."

Madonna's role model, a virtual icon for her, was Marilyn Monroe. Marilyn had had an affair with John F. Kennedy, Sr. It seemed almost logical that Madonna should follow in her footsteps. The president wasn't around to seduce any more, but his son, John F. Kennedy Jr., was around—and in her words, "hot."

The unlikely pair met when JFK Jr. launched his glossy political lifestyle magazine, *George*, named after the nation's first president.

As a novel idea, he contacted Madonna, asking if she would write an essay for the inaugural issue, to be entitled, "If I Were President."

She sent him the draft of an essay which more or less outlined her case of why she did not want to become President of the United States. As if to back up her point, she enclosed a picture of herself (for publication) in a sexy blue bikini straddling a diving board.

"I like the idea of being an inspiration to the downtrodden, of educating the masses. I like the idea of fighting for equal rights for women and gays and all minorities. I like the idea of embracing other countries and other cultures and promoting world peace. Fighting the good fight, as it were. But I think I'd rather do it as an artist. Because artists are allowed to make mistakes and artists are allowed to have unconventional ideas and artists are allowed to be overweight and dress badly and have an opinion. Artists are allowed to have a past. In short, artists are allowed to be human. And presidents are not. So the question is: How can someone be a good leader if he or she isn't allowed to be human? I'd rather eat glass."

When she did meet with JFK Jr., she told him what she'd do as president: "Send Rush Limbaugh, Bob Dole, and Jesse Helms to a hard-labor camp; welcome Roman Polanski back into the country; deport Howard Stern; and invite the entire armed forces of America to come out of the closet."

When the magazine was first published, it had the largest circulation of any political magazine in the nation because of the celebrity status of JFK Jr. But it soon began to lose money in both advertising and circulation.

JFK Jr. went backstage to greet Madonna after her "Who's That Girl?" performance in Madison Square Garden. Don Johnson, then at the peak of his *Miami Vice* fame on TV, was also there with flowers, but Madonna rejected him before walking away with the prize hunk of the night, JFK Jr. himself.

The JFK Jr./Madonna sightings began in New York during the weeks leading up to Christmas of 1987. "Could it really be true?" the public asked, "that Madonna was actually dating the son of Marilyn Monroe's former lover, his father, President John F. Kennedy?"

The symbolism that MM, the blonde bombshell of the 50s had been replaced by another bombshell in the 80s, Madonna, wasn't lost on the tabloids.

JFK Jr.'s biographer, Wendy Leigh, claimed, "In her own mind, Madonna wasn't just Marilyn emulated but Marilyn reincarnated, sent here to fulfill her psychic destiny. At every step, Madonna continued her consumption of the Marilyn mystique, but she craved something more. John F. Kennedy Jr. was just the dish to finish off the meal—the ultimate Monroesque experience."

Associated Press

Sean Penn and his then-wife, Madonna, were captured on film together on April 17, 1986 attending the screening of his new movie, *At Close Range*, in Los Angeles.

During their years of marriage, the press labeled them the "Poison Penns," as, fueled by jealousy, alcohol, and even violence, they veered from one tabloid scandal to the next. At one point, Penn was said to have tied the Material Girl up to a chair and "abused" her for several hours.

Their marriage on August 16, 1985 got off to a rocky start. A bevy of press helicopters churned overhead, as Penn ran down to the beach and scrawled FUCK OFF in twenty-foot-high letters in the sand,

He also loaded a semi-automatic pistol and crept into the bushes commando style. Over Madonna's screams, he shouted obscenities at her when she tried to stop him, but he emptied the guns in the direction of the helicopters. No one was killed.

Thus, the Penn/Madonna marriage was launched. It was later called a "miracle" that one of the helicopters didn't crash.

At a newsstand, John purchased the latest edition of *Vanity Fair* with a provocatively posed Madonna on the cover. Inside she had posed for two nude pictures as part of an "Homage to Norma Jean" pinup layout.

JFK Jr. and Madonna were seen working out together at a private gym, Plus One, in Manhattan's Soho district, after which they were also spotted jogging together in Central Park. Here was America's Prince Charming, its most eligible bachelor, dating the world's "most glamorous and exciting woman."

Madonna, a woman who doesn't shock easily, was surprised when she saw the latest issue of *George*. It featured Drew Barrymore on the cover, and she was dressed as Marilyn in a replica of the gown MM had arranged to have sewn on her before singing "Happy Birthday, Mr. President" to a startled President Kennedy at Madison Square Garden in 1962.

"I just couldn't believe that John would pay homage to such a woman," said Ted Sorensen, "especially considering all the pain MM had caused Jackie."

Christopher Andersen's book, *Madonna: Unauthorized* had a certain shock value in 1992 when it more or less predicted that Madonna "was almost bound to die an untimely death."

Actually, he had associated that idea with the wrong party in the Madonna/JFK Jr. love affair. It was the son of the former president who would die an untimely death several years later in an airplane crash.

The book maintains that Madonna had read every Monroe biography ever written and felt she "was the undisputed heiress to the Monroe *Persona*." She confided that she "felt fated to consummate a sexual relationship with JFK's only son." When Jackie heard of her son's new main squeeze, she asked friends, "What designs does this volatile creature have on my son.?"

Ever since the 1940s, Jackie had read *Life* magazine. One issue shocked her, the one featuring Madonna imitating the physicality of Marilyn Monroe. Sorensen said, "It was like Marilyn coming back from the grave to haunt Jackie. Marilyn stole her husband. Now Madonna was trying to take her son away."

During her son's affair with Madonna, Jackie could be seen purchasing the tabloids in the lobby of Doubleday's offices on Fifth Avenue where she was employed as an editor. John didn't keep her abreast of developments, so she had to read about her son in the papers.

"Madonna realized that adding John F. Kennedy Jr.'s scalp to her sexual belt would be another publicity coup," said author Leigh.

In his biography of Madonna, Andrew Morton wrote: "Although JFK Jr. and Madonna were lovers for a brief period, the affair was not a success. John Junior was intimidated by Madonna's reputation as he was by his mother (he was a mother's boy). For all her outward aggression, explained one of her former lovers, Madonna is a woman who expects her man to take control, more of a kitten than a tigress in the bedroom. Rather ruefully, she explained to friends after the end of her affair with Kennedy that he was just too nervous for them to click sexually. The chemistry certainly wasn't there. 'Some guys can handle the fame, others can't,' said a former lover. "He couldn't.'"

Madonna's boudoir escapades were described differently by Stephen Spignesi in his slim volume *J.F.K. Jr.*: "As anyone who has seen Madonna's photo book, *Sex*, can attest, the Material Girl is a sexual virtuoso. If sex were a high school, she'd be in the advanced class. She apparently is familiar with S and M, lesbianism, interracial sex, and multiple partners; and she is also an uninhibited exhibitionist who reportedly prefers sex partners as wild and experienced as herself."

Madonna has been quoted as saying, "I don't like to give blow-jobs, but I do like getting head—for a day and a half."

Even though JFK Jr. may not have been the greatest lay of Madonna's life, their intimacy continued for a few weeks. He gave her the keys to his apartment. One afternoon when he came in from the office, he found her lying on his couch clad in nothing but sheets of transparent plastic wrap. "Dinner's ready, John," she allegedly called out to him.

Stories began to run in the tabloids that as part of his lovemaking John would apply creamy peanut butter to her legs and would then lick it off like a puppy. Madonna denied such rumors. "What the fuck! Do you know how many calories there are in peanut butter? Yes, to low fat whipped cream. No, to that fucking peanut butter story."

She told a friend, "I'm dating someone respectable, not some rent boy picked up on a street corner. For all we know, John might even become President of the United States one day."

Even if mad-dog passion wasn't there, Madonna knew a hunk when she bedded one. She became particularly intrigued by a color photograph of John without his shirt. "His body is chiseled, raw-boned, lean, and muscular," she told a gay pal. "He is extraordinarily handsome, and when he's on top of you and looks down at you with those bedroom eyes, you melt."

If Madonna began to collect male beauty photographs of him, he returned the compliment by plastering provocative posters of her on the walls of his bachelor apartment.

Even his clothing style changed. Madonna lured him into a more punk look, and he was photographed in leather jackets and ripped jeans. He even grew a goatee resting under his mop of spiked hair. According to Andrew Morton, Thomas Lift, a friend from college, claimed that John told him, "It's like she put a spell over me. I'm obsessed with her."

According to reports, Madonna wanted to hurry up and divorce Sean Penn so she could marry John and "become part of the Kennedy clan. I want to have a little boy with John. He, too, I predict will grow up to be a president some time in the 21st century."

Author J. Randy Taraborrelli quotes a friend of Madonna who claimed, "I heard from good sources that Madonna did what she could to interest John in having a baby, but he didn't take the bait and wanted to wear protection."

In his biography of Madonna, Morton quoted a good friend of John's, Steven Styles, who had gone to Brown University with John.

According to Styles:

"He telephoned me one day and sounded uncharacteristically depressed. He eventually confessed that he had fallen in love with a married woman who was a very celebrated personality. Conflicted, he said he didn't know what to do. He was torn by his desire for this woman and his need to conform to societal pressure that he find the so-called 'right girl,' someone whom his mother and the other Kennedys would approve. And he said, 'Believe me when I tell you that this is not the right girl.' I asked him who she was. When he told me, you could have knocked me over with a feather. It was Madonna."

At one point after their lovemaking, Madonna told John that he should let a gay man make love to him. "That way you'll understand more what a woman feels from a man."

"Been there, done that," John reportedly said.

During her affair with John, Madonna was still married to Penn, an estranged husband prone to jealousy.

Penn had an arsenal of rifles and handguns in the basement of his Malibu villa. He would go down there on

Sex, Madonna's coffee table book, became notorious, as it featured strong adult content and softcore pornographic photos depicting simulations of sexual acts which included sadomasochism and analingus. Featured in the book were Isabella Rossellini, Vanilla Ice, Naomi Campbell, and gay porn star Joey Stefano.

Rumors still persist that Madonna was sent a nude picture of JFK Jr. when he was caught urinating off the side of his boat by a passing craft. There was speculation that the editors would include this picture of JFK Jr. letting it all hang out, golden stream and all, but obviously someone somewhere along the line decided all this was "too much."

Everyone who saw the picture agreed that JFK Jr. was "very well hung."

occasion to practice his marksmanship. At one point he put up a poster of John and fired with bullets from his .357 magnum. He got John right between the eyes.

John attended a party that was a tribute to Robert De Niro sponsored by New York's Museum of the Moving Image. Penn showed up with Liza Minnelli, Jeremy Irons, and Matt Dillon.

After about fifteen minutes John walked up to Penn and extended his hand.

The handshake was not intercepted. "I know who you are," Penn said in a voice cold as an Arctic night. "You owe me a god damn apology." Fearing a scene, John turned and walked away.

The next morning a funeral wreath of white roses with a black-and-gold ribbon was sent to John. The inscription read, "My Deepest Sympathy," and a personal card read, "Johnny, I heard about last night. M."

Of course, all of Madonna's plans to snare John could be dashed if she did not win favor with "The Queen of America," the formidable Jackie herself. Madonna realized early in her dating with John that he was very much influenced by his mother. "Jackie ultimately was the decider," Madonna said.

Madonna not only wanted to screw around with John, but meet his mother. To her, Jackie Onassis was a far greater American icon than Marilyn. "Her style, her grace, her beauty, there's no one like Jackie O," Madonna told a friend.

It took a lot of persuading on John's part to get Jackie to agree to entertain Madonna at her elegant Fifth Avenue apartment.

Reportedly, the meeting was stilted. Jackie was stiff and formal with Madonna and made it clear that she did not welcome intimacy. It was doubly clear that the former First Lady also didn't want her son dating a "notorious" figure like Madonna. As if to remind Jackie that she was a married woman at the time, Madonna provocatively signed her name in Jackie's guest book as "Mrs. Sean Penn."

After Madonna left the apartment, Jackie angrily called John from her office at Doubleday the next morning. "What in hell's name are you doing dating such a tramp?" she demanded to know. "You know she's just using the Kennedy name for publicity. She's just a social climber. At least you don't have to worry about her being after your money. She can buy and sell you any day."

Steven Styles, John's friend from Brown, claimed that John told him, "My mother wants the best for me. But sometimes, that means I have to keep secrets from her. Otherwise, I'd never be able to date. Let's face facts: No woman will ever be good enough for her. Unless she's royalty....but even then."

Madonna was a Roman Catholic, at least technically, but she was hardly as devout as Jackie. In fact, Jackie's priest called her when he heard that John was dating Madonna. "She's a heretic and should be excommunicated from the church," the priest said. "She uses crucifixes and other of our sacred images in her music videos. To mock us. She's immoral and sacrilegious. Nothing good will come out of John's involvement with a woman like that."

At Jackie's powerful urging, John eventually withdrew from Madonna. Both of them moved on to other partners. But they parted with that famous line, "Let's be friends."

When Cher heard of the JFK Jr./Madonna affair, she summed up her feelings on the subject: "Madonna could afford to be a little more magnanimous and a little less of a cunt."

Christina and John-John

Offering JFK Jr. "All the Ships at Sea"

The heiress, **Christina Onassis**, had nothing but contempt for her stepmother, Jackie Kennedy. "She thinks, talks, and dreams of nothing but money," Christina charged. She didn't harbor such ill will toward JFK Jr. Although in the 1960s, she regarded him as a mere kid, she was astonished when she met up with him again in the Manhattan of the 1980s. She told friends, "That is one hunk and a half."

During her time with the fully grown JFK Jr., Christina laughed at how grim she and her brother, Alexander, had appearing during the wedding of Ari and Jackie. "I kept looking over at you and Caroline. Your sister looked so dazed she could be in a trance, and you kept your head down all during the ceremony as if the wedding wasn't happening."

"The world didn't like it either," he told her. "Within a week after the wedding, three postal bags of hate mail were delivered to my mother." Christina took his hand. "That was that and this is now. You and I are adults. We can choose for ourselves. Perhaps the House of Kennedy and the House of Onassis should be reunited."

"The Richest Woman on Earth" Re-Unites with "The Next President of the United States"

When Christina Onassis met her future brother-in-law, JFK Jr., as preface for the 1968 wedding of their respective parents, she was eighteen and he was only eight. But little boys grow up.

Even after her father's death Christina still maintained some contact with John, if nothing more than a birthday card and a Christmas card.

But one sultry summer night in 1982 at Studio 54 in New York, she ran into JFK Jr., who was dancing with (of all people) Andy Warhol.

She was startled at the physical changes in JFK Jr., whom she remembered as a boy. Without her knowing it, he'd become a man. She later told friends, "John is a hunk and a half, a perfect ten and maybe a lot more."

At Studio 54, he listened politely to her compliments about his good looks. Very modestly, he said, "I'm just a low Irishman."

"Oh, so much more than that," she countered.

JFK Jr. quickly dumped his dancing partner, Warhol, and spent the evening talking to Christina. She confided in him that "Ari forced me to become an adult when I was only nine years old."

"It was the opposite for me," he told her. "Jackie is still running my life."

Christina Onassis had everything that money can buy—everything except love. After their initial "week of seduction," JFK Jr., on orders of his mother, Jackie, bolted from the relationship and a potential marriage. He became just one of a long line of failed love affairs and husbands for Christina.

Her fling with Yvon Coty, the perfume heir, was typical. As the most famous heiress in the world, she could always attract men to her, even JFK Jr. But with Coty, she complained to friends, "All he likes from me is a blow-job. He can go screw himself! I want to reinvent myself, remake my life. John can help me do that."

Alas, her chosen was not willing.

Both of them shared memories of a privileged life, JFK Jr. growing up protected by the Secret Service and adored by most of America as the son of two of the most celebrated parents in the world. Although relatively neglected by her father, Christina enjoyed a girlhood of luxury. Even the clothes for her dolls were designed by Christian Dior.

From bits and pieces, often snippets of hearsay, what transpired between Christina and JFK Jr. during their brief fling can be re-created.

JFK Jr. reportedly claimed to Christina that, "I got along very well with your father but Caroline did not. She was very distant from him and remained so during my mother's marriage to your dad. Caroline worshipped her father, and she was also very close to her Uncle Bobby. No one, especially Ari, could replace those towering figures in her life."

Later Warhol and his party spotted JFK Jr. and Christina dancing the *syrtaki* in the center of Studio 54. Ari himself had taught JFK Jr. the dance.

Before the night ended, Christina invited JFK Jr. back to her hotel suite. He spent the night with her and presumably made love to her. He was seen leaving her suite shortly before noon of the following day. He'd agreed to spend the upcoming weekend alone with her so they could talk privately and get to know each other better.

She invited him to some mansion on Long Island that was owned by a former friend of her father's. The owners, unknown to JFK Jr., were gone, leaving three servants behind. Nicolas Stravinni, one of the servants, later told a reporter that he saw JFK Jr. and Christina walking hand in hand along the ocean. She always said, "The ocean is life to a Greek."

"The ocean can give life, but it can also take it away," JFK Jr. said. Was he predicting his own watery grave?

It was a weekend wherein they'd review their collective past and rediscover one another as adults. In the weeks that followed, both Christina and JFK Jr. talked at length with their friends about what had transpired between them that memorable weekend.

"I warmed to almost any kind of affection," Christina told him. "I didn't get any from my father. Your mother seemed to hold me in disdain. But I'll always remember that day on the island of Ithaca. We'd sailed over from Skorpios. Ari and your mother were there on our outing, also Caroline. I was surprised that you guys also invited Martin Luther King III. He was only ten years old. Until that date, I didn't even know there *was* a Martin Luther King III. You went for a walk with me and held my hand. Right before we got back to the party, you hugged me and kissed me gently on the lips. That was one of the most loving, one of the kindest things anyone had ever done to me. After that day, I decided you were all right in my book."

Even as teenagers, JFK Jr. and Christina reached some kind of mutual understanding about the turbulent marriage of their parents. Once in the presence of others, John, Jr., claimed, "My mother once told me that Ari was about the only man on the planet she could marry who wouldn't be called Mr. Jacqueline Kennedy." She once told Truman Capote, 'I can't marry a dentist from New Jersey, and I sure as hell can't marry Eddie Fisher.'"

Bunny Melon, intensely private and immensely rich, was a friend of Jackie's. Melon warned her that if she married Ari, she'd fall off the pedestal the American public had put her on. Jackie told

John F. Kennedy Jr. was often called the perfect specimen of young American manhood.

But was he really? In some respects, his mother, Jackie, was his harshest critic, and to some extent his sister Caroline echoed Jackie's sentiments. She called him "an underachiever."

He defended himself by claiming "I'm dyslexic." He was often overly medicated, taking pain medication for a broken ankle on the day he crashed into the sea. He also was taking Ritalin for Attention Deficit Disorder. Not only that, but he suffered from the thyroid condition know as Graves' Disease, which left him completely devoid of energy for long periods of time.

Bunny, "I'd rather fall off than get frozen there forever."

"Ari was far too old to take on the burden of being a father to you and Caroline," Christina claimed. "Alexander and I confronted Ari and let him know that's how we both felt. He wouldn't listen to us. In fairness to your mother, both Alexander and I were also dead-set against his affair with Maria Callas. We blamed her for breaking up my father and my mother, Tina." (i.e., Athena Livanos Onassis Blandford Niarchos, aka "Tina.")

"I didn't want mother to marry Ari either," John, Jr., said. "Even though I was just a kid, I accused her of arranging a business deal instead of a marriage. I felt she was dishonoring my father's memory. I told her that marriage wasn't a great idea."

"It was great for Mrs. Kennedy financially at least," Christina said. "I can vouch for that."

"Ari even tried to select my husband for me," Christina claimed. "He wanted me to marry Peter Goulandris, the Greek shipping heir."

Tina Livanos Onassis, the formidably chic mother of Christina, referred to her daughter as, "the ugliest little girl in the world—a troll really. There must have been a mix-up at the hospital. I can't believe such a creature came from my womb. After all, I am one of the world's most celebrated beauties."

Both she and her brother, Alexander, were looked after by private tutors and nannies. At the age of five, Christina lapsed into silence, a condition known as mercurial mutism. When she did speak again, for a period that lasted a full six months, it was only to her brother.

Unlike his sister, Alexander was attractive and charismatic. Sir Winston Churchill even invited him to sit on his knee. Ari often bathed the boy until he was nine years old. Maids reported that Ari often kissed the boy's genitals when towel drying him, claiming it was an old custom where he grew up. "Men kissed the genitals of their boys so they would grow big and produce many children for their papa."

"Some marriages are made in heaven; others on Skorpios," Ari said. She bolted and refused to marry the darkly handsome and very rich Goulandris, whose family controlled four shipping lines, with ownership of more than 135 vessels.

"Loving is a quest, not a business deal," she lectured her father.

JFK Jr. spoke about how he bonded with Alexander. "He was a very skilled aviator, and he was the one who first made me want to become a pilot. He often flew Mom, Caroline and me from Skorpios to Athens. I got to sit next to him at the control panel. In fact, in some ways Alexander and I were closer in that Kennedy/Onassis family bonding than anyone. It was a sort of Big Brother/Little Brother relationship."

"Ari always loved Alexander more than he loved me, because his attention was focused on a male heir, and I was a mere girl," Christina said. "I worshipped my father, but in time we grew apart, beginning with his marriage to your mother. Even my brother Alexander hated me. He called me a spoiled brat and constantly complained that I was spending $200,000 a year, and he was getting only $12,000 a year from Olympic Airlines, because father wanted to make a man of him and teach him how to handle money."

Christina made a shocking revelation to JFK Jr., about what her father told her after Alexander died in a plane crash.

"With the death of my son, the Greek father's hope of immortality has been taken with him," Ari told her. "Why couldn't it have been you who died in that plane crash—and not my beloved son?"

"Perhaps both my brother and I were unkind to your mother," Christina told him. "We called her 'The Black Widow.'"

In his book *Jacqueline Bouvier Kennedy Onassis*, author Stephen Birmingham wrote: "Some superstitious strain out of her Smyrna peasant past suggested to Christina that some sinister force had to be connected with all these deaths—first her aunt, then her brother, now her mother. It must be Jackie who was bringing all this bad luck to her family, 'undermining everything' as her brother had predicted. To Christina it seemed as though Jackie killed everything she touched. She was the Angel of Death. This terrible conviction was all the more powerful because, by then, Christina could see that her father was also dying."

A long-standing friend of the Onassis family, Costa Gratsos, asserted that "Christina felt Jackie was somehow to blame for all these deaths. Death was never far from the 'Black Widow,' as Christina called her. Jackie was the world's most inveterate bystander to tragedy. Witness John and Robert Kennedy. Christina feared Jackie. She felt she had magical powers. Everybody around her had perished."

Christina had lost her mother on September 10, 1974. Tina was found dead in the Paris townhouse of the Niarchos family. A doctor cited edema of the lungs as the cause of death.

Christina had wept at her mother's gravesite. "Surely fate can't be that cruel," she had lamented. Back in Athens, the locals began to refer to her family as "The House of Atreus," in reference to a multigenerational family of ancient Greece whose vengeful and arrogant descendents were repeatedly punished for their transgressions by the gods.

Stravinni, who functioned as a waiter and butler at the Long Island estate during a candlelit dinner for JFK Jr. and Christina, said that at one point he overheard the heiress proposing marriage to her former brother-in-law. "Right now Mrs. Kennedy has you under her thumb," the heiress allegedly told him. "Only death freed me of Ari. Your mother is in fabulous health and, except for smoking, takes great care of her body. She'll live to be a hundred. You can become the CEO of all my business interests. You can be a powerful man in your own right, not like I was, waiting for my father to die before I could really take charge of my own life."

Stravinni had left the dining room and wasn't there to hear JFK Jr.'s response.

Meeting **Ari Onassis** on the island of Skorpios, **John-John** *(above, right)* was won over when the Greek tycoon showered him with love and affection. He often sat on his stepfather's knee as Ari spun stories of Greek myths. He routinely gave the boy a hundred dollars at a time in Greek currency. "Buy what you want," he told John, "even a woman if the need arises." John was only eight years old when Ari said that.

Whereas Ari complained about the outrageous clothing bills Jackie submitted every month, he never objected to the seasonal wardrobes she purchased for her son. Ari vied with Senator Teddy Kennedy to become the "surrogate father" to John.

"I'm not sure I want either of these men with their tarnished reputations to be a role model for John," Jackie said.

She told him, "I still have fifty tankers, and I know their routes by heart." That was not true. By 1982 she no longer had that many tankers.

This was the second time that the wealth of Onassis had been dangled in front of JFK Jr. When he was much younger and rather cocky, he'd told the Kennedy clan, "I'm going to be filthy rich when Ari dies. He's going to leave me a $15 million trust fund." When the Onassis will was published on June 6, 1975, Ari had left JFK Jr. only $25,000.

John surprised some of his friends by talking about Christina's proposal, although usually he was more tight-lipped about family secrets.

"I was tempted," he admitted. "I was Adam in the Garden of Eden. She was Eve tempting me to take a bite out of the apple. She also told me I was the best sex she'd ever had. But life with her wasn't my dream. Mother marrying one Onassis was enough for me. I didn't need to repeat her mistake. There's another reason. Christina has a lot of unnecessary hair on her body, a bit monkey-like for me. I hear that that didn't turn off Warren Beatty, Jack Nicholson, or Jean-Paul Belmondo."

Christina's grandest dream, according to her friends, was her belief that John would one day run successfully to become the next President of the United States. "Wouldn't that freak Mrs. Kennedy out?" she asked friends. "Imagine, me, First Lady of America."

A friend of Athena ("Tina") Livanos, the shipping heiress and first wife of Ari, spoke off the record in Monte Carlo. "I think young John was still impressionable enough that he might have fallen for Christina's deal. After all, she had it in her power to offer him the world. But I think what sabotaged the deal for Christina was the 'Black Widow' thing."

A very superstitious person, Christina confessed to JFK Jr. that she determined the course of her life by listening to a psychic who had been born on the island of Lesbos. "He even predicted your father's death in 1963." Two years prior to JFK's assassination, the psychic had claimed that the president would be shot by a gunman in Texas.

That revelation shocked and horrified JFK Jr., but he was nonetheless fascinated. "Do you think he can predict my own future? Whether I will be president? If I do become president, can he see into the future and warn me of a possible assassination on my own life?"

Christina arranged for a secret meeting between the psychic and JFK Jr., which she attended.

From all reports, young John was completely freaked out by his encounter with Christina's psychic. Christina paid the visionary the equivalent of $5,000 in U.S. dollars.

John became almost panic stricken when the psychic predicted that he would not live to see the centu-

There was one fan who would have overlooked all of JFK Jr.'s flaws, and that was pop artist **Andy Warhol**. At Studio 54, author Truman Capote watched the "hopeless infatuation play out between the two of them."

"John-John was a prick teaser." Capote claimed. "He would let Andy feel him up, and one time they even went to the urinals together so Andy could get a peek. But, as far as is known, that was about it. Perhaps a few dances on the floor, but men often danced with other guys at Studio 54, and no one thought a thing about it."

Also according to Truman, "Andy told me 'John is the man of my dreams.' I chided him, 'Come on, Andy, the boy is the man of everybody's dreams. Even straight men would go to bed with him if he asked them.'"

ry's end and that he would never hold any elected office.

Back in New York, JFK Jr. was deeply depressed. Somehow Jackie had found out about his involvement with Christina, and she was furious, threatening to disinherit him. "You'll ultimately get the Onassis money but through my will and only when I die. Christina will just use you and betray you." She forced her son to write Christina a farewell letter.

It was short: "Dear Christina, it cannot be. Love, John."

When she received this brief farewell note, Christina was devastated. She went into hibernation for two weeks before receiving anyone. When she emerged, she told friends, "Dreams die hard. I've had so much pain in my life I appear to be a walking Greek drama."

Two years after their brief fling in 1982, Christina sent JFK Jr. an invitation to her wedding to a French businessman and her fourth husband, Thierry Roussel. John, Jr. pleaded another engagement, but sent the couple a wedding present.

He was saddened to hear that the sad life of the heiress ended on November 19, 1988 when she had a heart attack in Buenos Aires.

He sent a wreath of white roses, which was placed on her grave at the family plot at Skorpios where she was reunited with her brother, Alexander, and her father, Aristotle Onassis.

MARILYN MONROE'S FINAL MESSAGE TO JFK

Norma Jean Loves Jack

Mimi Beardsley (see following page) was the least publicized of JFK's mistresses. His most publicized squeeze was Marilyn Monroe, as the world knows. But a detail associated with the MM/JFK affair is little known. For years, it's been a time bomb waiting to explode.

Ten days after singing "Happy Birthday Mr. President" to JFK in Madison Square Garden, Marilyn sent him an expensive Rolex watch, along with a love poem, to the White House.

Inscribed on the watch were the words: "Jack, with love as always, Marilyn. May 29, 1962." Her handwritten poem, transcribed below, was entitled, "A Heartfelt Plea on Your Birthday."

> *Let lovers breathe their sighs*
> *And roses bloom and music sound*
> *Let passion born on lips and eyes*
> *And pleasure's merry world go around*
> *Let golden sunshine flood the sky*
> *AND LET ME LOVE, OR LET ME DIE!*

Interpreting the poem and the watch as incriminating, JFK turned to his chief aide, Kenneth O'Donnell, who was with him in the Oval Office at the time. "Get rid of it! Now!" he ordered O'Donnell.

JFK's aide, however, could not stand the idea of destroying such a "valuable piece of American history" and consequently, he opted to keep it, preserving it among his personal heirlooms.

Four decades later, O'Donnell's family sold the watch at Connecticut's Alexander Autographs Auction House to an unnamed collector. The Rolex sold for $120,000.

JFK Had an Intern Too

Monica Lewinski wasn't the only intern who got seduced in the White House. Early in 1962, reporters heard about a beautiful nineteen-year-old who had shared the sheets with the president.

Back in those days, reporters went "wink wink" at such allegations and wrote about something else—perhaps Jackie's new wardrobe. After all, *The New York Times* printed only the news fit to print.

As an intern at the White House, **Mimi Beardsley** wandered the corridors looking for a desk and for something to do. Of course, that secretarial job had to preclude shorthand or typing or any other known secretarial skills. When anybody asked, the person was told, "Mimi has a special relationship with the president."

At long last, and not until the 21st century, did revelations emerge that the mysterious "Mimi" is actually Marion Fahnestock, mother of two and grandmother of four. Not only that—Marion, now in her 60s, works as an administrator for the tony Fifth Avenue Presbyterian Church in Manhattan.

Marion has come forward and admitted to her relationship with JFK.

Oldtime reporters recalled seeing her on Air Force One or in JFK's 1962 motorcade in Bermuda for the summit meeting with Harold Macmillan, then the Prime Minister of Britain.

Mimi (aka Marion) was one of the "harem of young girls hired by the press office principally to be at the president's disposal," in the words of one of the U.K.'s most prominent newspapers *The Guardian*.

As a coincidence, Mimi had attended the same exclusive college as Jackie. Originally, in her role as editor of her college's newspaper, Mimi came to the White House as part of an attempt to write a profile of the First Lady, but Jackie was too busy that day to see her. The president, however, accidentally encountered her in a hallway and asked her to become a secretary in the White House. "But sir, I can't type," she protested.

"I'm sure you have hidden talents," JFK responded, and hired her on the spot.

Mimi might have opted to remain discreetly silent about her White House years, but her life changed in 2003 after she was "outed" by historian Robert Dallek, whose discovery was picked up by reporters who included the staff at *The New York Daily News*. Subsequently, Mimi (aka Mrs. Fahnestock) issued a curt statement: "From June, 1962 to November, 1963, I was involved in a sexual relationship with President Kennedy. For the last 41 years, it is a subject that I have not discussed. In view of the recent media coverage, I have now discussed the relationship with my children and my family, and they are completely supportive. I will have no further comment on this subject, period. I would request that the media respect my privacy and the privacy of my family in this matter."

How different Mimi is from blabbermouth Monica Lewinski, who revealed graphically explicit details about "that cigar," and the stains on her dress.

In Washington circles, even back in the early 60s, the most savvy member of the press suspected that JFK's political career was surviving on borrowed time. More and more members of the press were learning of his adulterous affairs with such young women as Mimi.

In *Time* Magazine, Hugh Sidey wrote: "The media were beginning to change; their fascination with the young president and his family was intensifying daily. Had he lived into a second term, there was a good chance that one of the numberless and heedless stories of sexual indulgence would have broken over his head, embarrassing him and his family, perhaps crippling his presidency. In that case, Mimi might have gotten into the history books a lot sooner."

Marion "Mimi" Beardsley in 1963

A Royal Tempest over John-John

Princess Di and Fergie Catfight for JFK Jr.

In happier days, in 1987, **Sarah Ferguson** *(left)*, the Duchess of York, and the Princess of Wales, **Diana**, hold onto their hats at the Derby at Epson Racecourse in England.

Both the Duchess and the Princess shared the same titillation over "the absolutely gorgeous" JFK Jr., a Prince Charming of another nationality and another stripe. Allegedly, the daughters of Buckingham Palace speculated what a honeymoon would be like with JFK Jr. "I bet I'd never be allowed out of bed, at least for the first six weeks," Di jokingly suggested to Fergie.

The Princess confided that her sixteen-day cruise with Prince Charles didn't turn out to be the romantic idyll she had envisioned. Charles brought along a collection of books by Sir Laurens van der Post, a South African philosopher. At breakfast, he discussed his night's reading in detail. At one point Van der Post came aboard to discuss philosophy with both Charles and Diana. "This Princess of Wales stuff isn't what I thought it was going to be," she said.

After Jackie's latest lecture on how unsuitable Madonna or Daryl Hannah were as girlfriends, JFK Jr. finally yelled at his overprotective mother. "Just what woman on the planet do you think is worthy of getting plugged by me?"

Perhaps impulsively, or so he later claimed to friends, Jackie blurted out: "Princess Di. After she divorces Charles, of course, which I know she will."

The way his mother saw it, Princess Diana, unlike many of her son's other conquests, would fit comfortably into the fishbowl world in which her son lived. "She, too, is used to being followed by photographers every time she steps out the door. She knows how to remain cool even under the most trying of circumstances. She might even overlook the fact that you have a tendency to stray once in a while, though nothing like your dearly departed father."

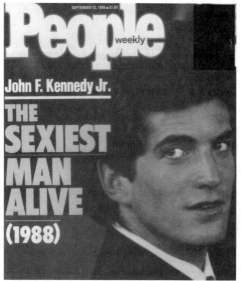

John F. Kennedy, Jr., was featured on the cover of *People* Magazine as the sexiest man alive. The 6'1" hunk was also cited as the sexiest magazine editor in America. Chery Eastwood, a trainer at Cape Cod's Hyannis Athletic Club, said JFK Jr. "Looks terrific and is really healthy."

His visit to a gym caused near riots when female staffers and curious males, especially gay ones, wanted to get a peek at the scion of America's most illustrious family of Democrats.

His celebrity stylist haircutter, Frédéric Fekkai, said, "He fits my definition of a man's man. And he's more than handsome. I think he's just going to look better and better."

Most political insiders claimed that "When he runs for president, he'll be the best looking man who ever pursued that office in America, far better looking than his father."

BUT IF JUNIOR'S THE PRINCE, WHO GETS TO BE THE SHOWGIRL?

Like his father and his two uncles, JFK Jr. also had a fascination with Marilyn Monroe. He once told some college pals in a Boston tavern, "Of all the women I would have liked to fuck, Marilyn Monroe is at the top of my list."

"Anybody alive today interest you?" asked one of his buddies.

"There is one: Princess Di herself. I hear Prince Charles neglects her, and I'm the man for the job."

Diana's own fascination with the handsome young hunk had been widely reported long before they actually met. *People* magazine once wrote, "Princess Diana was crestfallen when John F. Kennedy Jr. was a no-show at a Manhattan luncheon she attended."

Dozens of other newspapers and tabloid gossip column items have written of the Princess's determination not only to meet but to have a relationship with JFK Jr.

The poison pen biographer, Kitty Kelley, claimed, "I know for a fact that Princess Diana would very much like to meet JFK Jr. When you think about it, it's a beautiful coupling."

JFK Jr. may have been intrigued by Princess Di because of the constant comparisons with his mother. As author Jay Mulvaney wrote in *Diana & Jackie*, "Both were the daughters of acrimonious divorce. Both wed men twelve years their senior, men who needed 'trophy brides' to advance their careers. Both married into powerful and domineering families who tried, unsuccessfully, to take their willful independence. Both inherited power through marriage and both rebelled within their official roles, forever crushing the archetype. And both revolutionized dynasties."

The battle for JFK Jr. may have inspired a catfight between Princess Di and Sarah Ferguson, Duchess of York. Rumors began surfacing in March of 1995 that "Fergie," as she was called, got "agitated" looking at pictures of the handsome hunk, especially those without his shirt.

The tabloids of London broke the story that Fergie—allegedly at least—was so enraptured by young John that she was losing weight and undergoing a "makeover" in hopes of snaring the American prince. "When he meets me, he may fall for me all in one flash," she reportedly said.

According to "friends" of the Duchess, Fergie had nicknamed JFK Jr. "Ken." She told friends that "Everything will be all right when Ken and I get married."

The Duchess was said to have rated her men on a scale of one to ten. Her former husband, Prince Andrew, came in only at a 2; her toe sucker friend, Johnny Bryan, was given a 3, with another lover, Steve Wyatt, the Texas oilman, ranking only a 1. However, according to the report, she gave JFK Jr. a 9 without ever going to bed with him.

A psychic was said to have told Fergie that her marriage to JFK Jr. was "inevitable."

One tabloid printed revelations from Madame Vasso Kortesis, who claimed that she'd been advising the Duchess for years and had even tape-recorded some of Fergie's most intimate revelations. Kortesis claimed that Fergie had not only fantasized about marrying JFK Jr., but dreamed of becoming First Lady in the White House, assuming that he one day would become President of the United States.

Stephen Spignesi, author of *J.F.K. Jr.*, wrote: "Fergie, who was married to England's Prince Andrew before their divorce in 1996, is reportedly a sex, money, and fame junkie. Tabloids around the world have published photos of her in extremely bawdy (and embarrassing to the British monarchy) situations. Fergie has been photographed topless on a beach and, in what was her most notoriously infamous series of photos, seen getting her toes sucked erotically on a beach by American businessman Johnny Bryan. Apparently, John-John would have to cultivate a foot fetish to satisfy the Duchess if they ever do get together."

John died in that plane crash with his wife, Carolyn Bessette, and her sister, Lauren, before Fergie got her chance to seduce him. But Princess Di was far luckier, according to Simone Simmons in her tell-all, *Diana: The Last Word*. Simmons, a natural healer and clairvoyant, became an intimate fixture in the life of the troubled Princess.

Simmons claimed that she formed a unique bond with Diana, and they met almost every day or spent hours on the phone. "No subject was taboo between us," she said. "We discussed everything and anything, sharing laughter and tears over cups of chamomile tea."

It was during one of their confessional periods together, that Diana reported on her one-time fling

Associated Press

The author, Dominick Dunne said, "Fifty years from now, they're not going to be writing musicals about Princess Margaret and Princess Anne. They're going to be writing about Diana. She upstaged the British royal family. The aristos hate her. The crowds love her. She's a great character. The same is true about Jackie. Nobody is writing about Mamie Eisenhower or Bess Truman." When Sarah Ferguson *(left)* married Prince Andrew and became the Duchess of York, she, too, was compared to Diana, but always unfavorably.

In the beginning, **Fergie and Di** *(left and right in photo, above)* were allies. Both had an independent streak and were unwilling to toe the royal line issued from Buckingham Palace. But in time Di turned on Fergie. The Duchess claimed, "The knives are out for me at the palace."

In several calls Di placed to JFK Jr., she told him she wanted to break free and also urged him to escape from Jackie's hovering presence. He refused to budge. "Financially speaking, I can't do that. If you break from Charles, you will get alimony. If I break from my mother, I would no longer be able to support myself in the style to which I have become accustomed."

with JFK Jr. at the swanky Hotel Carlyle in New York.

Diana claimed she met JFK Jr. in New York in 1995, telling Simmons she found him "very good looking." The young man tried to persuade her to grant an interview for his magazine, *George*. She turned him down but invited him to her suite at the Carlyle on New York City's Upper East Side, for which she was paying $3,200 a night.

"We started talking, one thing led to another—and we ended up in bed together," Diana said. "It was pure chemistry."

"John made me feel desirable, wanton, and very womanly," Diana said. "It was a moment of pure lust, the only time in my life that I succumbed in that way."

Unlike Fergie's nine, Diana rated JFK Jr. "a ten—the tops!"

She also rated her other lovers as well, including the heavy-hung James Hewitt, who got a nine. Rumors have it that Hewitt is actually the father of Prince Harry. The two men bear an amazing resemblance to each other. Diana gave Oliver Hoare a six. Out of politeness, her husband, Prince Charles, didn't get a rating.

Simmons claimed that seducing JFK Jr. put a notch on Diana's belt. "She was tickled pink. He was one of the best looking and most sought after men in America, with a real body beautiful that came from endless workouts in the gym. He was a year older than her and three inches taller, which counted for a lot because Diana didn't like short men. What gave their brief liaison an extra dimension was that she admired him and the way he had dealt with pressures which came with being the son of America's best loved president. Looking at her eldest son and the responsibilities he was born to inherit, she said, 'I'm hoping that William grows up to be as smart as John Kennedy Jr. I want William to be able to handle things as well as John does.'"

There was speculation that Diana in her wildest fantasies, dreamed and talked about "what a powerful team we'd make if he ever reaches the White House. We could become America's royal family. I can just imagine me First Lady of the United States. I knew I'd never become the Queen of England."

For some two decades, Simone Simmons, a natural healer and clairvoyant, has been writing about the Royal Family since her appointment as editor of *Majesty Magazine*.

Her 2005 publication of *Diana: The Last Word* made tabloid headlines with her allegations of a brief fling between Princess Di and JFK Jr. Diana told her friend, "Simone, if anything happens to me, write a book and tell it like it is."

Di also befriended her butler, Paul Burrell. He said, "Simone and her Majesty could often spend up to eight hours a day chatting on the phone. She was the Princess's friend and *confidante* who was entrusted with her personal documentation."

Diana had to face the reality that to win JFK Jr. she'd have to pursue him. After she left New York, they talked over the phone across the Atlantic. But she heard that he was moving on with his life. The following year when she learned he was marrying Carolyn Bessette, she wrote to wish him well in his marriage.

"I hope your marriage works out better than mine did," she added as a postscript. By then, she'd moved on to the Pakistan-born heart and lung surgeon Hasnat Khan, who consistently kept refusing to go to bed with her until her divorce came through.

Simmons in her book speculates what would have happened had John and Diana mated. "They might be alive today."

Torn Between Two Lovers

The Tragic Saga of Carolyn Bessette

Associated Press

Carolyn Bessette, a six-foot tall, blue-eyed beauty, was voted "The Ultimate Beautiful Person" by her classmates at St. Mary's High School in tony Greenwich, Connecticut. **John F. Kennedy Jr**., of course, was America's Prince Charming and *People* magazine's "Sexiest Man Alive."

She became his live-in girlfriend in March of 1995 and his wife on September 27, 1996. To the world it appeared that it was a fairytale marriage, although it wasn't. Adultery and early death lay in each of their immediate futures.

The picture above is grim and their body language indicates a strain in the marriage. Admittedly, it was taken at the funeral of JFK's cousin, Michael Kennedy at Our Lady of Victory Church in Centerville, Mass. The funeral on January 3, 1998 followed Michael's fatal skiing accident on December 31, 1997 in Aspen, Colorado.

Carolyn was hardly John-John's first beauty. Over his years, he'd been linked to a bevy of belles: Apollonia, Audra Avizienis, Meg Azozi, Julie Baker, Paula Barbieri (O.J. Simpson's ex), Jenny Christian, Cindy Crawford, Princess Diana, Janice Dickinson, Christina Goodman, Melanie Griffith, Christina Haag, Tony Kottie, Elle MacPherson, Madonna, Sally Munro, Sinead O'Connor, Catherine Oxenberg, Sarah Jessica Parker, Ashley Richardson, Molly Ringwald, Julia Roberts, Stephanie Schmid, Claudia Schiffer, Princess Stéphanie of Monaco, Sharon Stone, Brooke Shields, and Xuxa.

THE HUNK THEY CHOSE
TO FILL MARKY MARK'S BRIEFS

Although he is supposedly straight, supermodel **Michael Bergin**, the ex-lover of Carolyn Bessette, is wildly popular with gays. He's not afraid to take on a gay role or to interact with the homo press. He also works for AIDS charities.

Over the years these roles have earned him a devoted fan base in the gay community. Of course, another reason for this is that he is one gorgeous hunk of male flesh.

In choosing both JFK Jr. and Michael as her lovers, Carolyn showed the world she had supremely good taste in men.

He was just a small-town kid, growing up in the blue collar town of Naugatuck, Connecticut. Michael Bergin was born on March 18, 1969, the son of a state policeman and a mother who was a hairstylist. His early years were relatively uneventful: Little League baseball team, teen hood breaking streetlights or lobbing snowballs at passing cars.

He was a sort of ugly kid with pimples and a big gap between his two front teeth. To judge from his high school yearbook, he was just an average Joe.

But, almost overnight, his dick started to grow and grow some more, and he blossomed into one of the most stunning male beauties of the Northeast.

In April of 1994 he made his Time Square debut as a Calvin Klein Underwear model. Passers-by stopped and stared. Was that package for real? It was. As Michael put it, "You could see my crotch in New Jersey."

Two years before this, he'd picked up a beautiful blonde, Carolyn Bessette, in a bar. He later claimed, "She was unlike any woman I'd ever known—sophisticated, successful, with bewitching charm and grace." It was a case of The Beauty meets The Beauty. A passionate affair was launched.

In both his private and public life, he was in white heat.

After posing almost naked on that billboard in New York, the modeling jobs flowed in from Valentino, Gucci, Perry Ellis, and Karan. He'd also spend four years as a star of *Baywatch* and appeared in many other TV and movie roles.

In his memoirs, *The Other Man,* he recalled that when he was together with Carolyn, an ice cold blonde, all he needed was a red futon to warm her up. "We were perfect together," he claimed. "It went beyond chemistry, beyond the way our bodies fitted together, and beyond the way we responded to each other's touch. It was as if we were built for making love to each other."

Early in his relationship, he discovered that she knew JFK Jr.

While Michael was working as a doorman at a Manhattan hotel, they had a tiff. She abruptly dropped him and wouldn't return his calls.

Weeks went by, and the next time he saw her was when he had a gig for Calvin Klein at a swanky rooftop swimming pool on a terrace associated with a Manhattan penthouse. He was hired, along with three other male models, to walk around the pool in very revealing underwear. "We were just hunks of beef," he said, "ornaments—just there to look pretty and scrumptious. It was humiliating."

Carolyn herself showed up for the party. Not only that, but JFK Jr. made a spectacular appearance to the delight of the paparazzi. When Michael saw them kiss, he realized that his competition for Carolyn's love was Prince Charming, the most eligible bachelor in the world.

After JFK Jr. departed, Carolyn remained behind. He asked her, "So how's your buddy John Jr.?" He admitted it was "a shitty thing to say, but I was hurting. I was a fucking cabana boy; he was a goddamn prince."

She claimed that JFK Jr. wasn't her type, and she wasn't interested "in him or the life he leads."

That night—"hungry for each other"—they shacked up. And then nothing. No calls, just nothing. He must have decided she was a love 'em, leave 'em type of woman.

Candace Bushnell, the *Sex and the City* author, may have had a fling with Michael. The character in her novel, dubbed "the Bone," bears a resemblance to the real-life Michael. In the book, the character is described as "well-ripped, pseudo gay, and a wannabe actor cum underwear model."

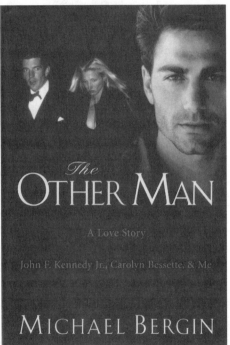

In addition to being used as the inspiration for a fictional character in *Sex and the City,* the real-life Michael often appears on gay websites so his admiring fans can appreciate his charms. In one picture, only his hand covers his crotch. Unforunately, Michael has a big hand, so his gay fans never got a view of the family jewels.

Michael's affair with Carolyn eventually resumed, but it was a casual relationship, with few questions asked. Under her sink one morning he found a five-year-old copy, dated 1988, of *People* magazine, naming John Jr. as "The Sexiest Man Alive."

"How can I compete with that?" Michael wondered. Even so, he took her to meet his parents in Naugatuck.

One weekend rolled into another and suddenly Carolyn announced, "I'm pregnant." She told him that "I can't even consider having a child." He took her to have an abortion. Both of them felt guilty, but she recovered quickly. "Life throws some shit at you," he said, "and you deal with it."

As time drifted by, Carolyn and their relationship evolved into an on-and-off-again affair. One night she announced once again, "I'm pregnant."

He asked the wrong question. "Is it mine?" She still didn't want children. Another trip to an abortionist was in order.

It could have been one of her other boyfriends,

In his 2005 tell-all confessional, **Michael Bergin** revealed the details of his on-again, off-again affair with Carolyn Bessette. Their sexual link continued even after her marriage to JFK Jr.

The book was rightly promoted as romantic tale of love gone wrong. *The Other Man* "is a testament to the enduring power of love and a story about the painful choices we make with our all too human hearts."

On the fifth anniversary of Carolyn's death, Michael was arrested on a DWI charge. Love's memory lingers on.

and there was speculation that the kid belonged to JFK Jr., because she was having sex with what she sometimes called "The President's Kid."

Soon pictures of JFK Jr. and Carolyn began appearing in newspapers and on TV. Michael asked one of his close friends. "How do I compete with that? I'm a fucking underwear model. He's American Royalty."

Finally the inevitable happened. The news flashed around the world on September 21, 1996. JFK Jr. had married Carolyn on a remote island in Georgia.

Time went by. Then one night he received an urgent message from Carolyn asking him to call her.

She was arriving in Los Angeles with a gay pal and asked if she and her friend could room with them. By the third night, Michael seduced her. She wanted it as much as he did.

In bed with him, she told him that she suspected "John is having an affair." She was right about that. After their West Coast shack-up, he immediately claimed, "I was in love with her once again."

Carolyn left Michael and flew back to New York to a deteriorating marriage. JFK Jr. had already told his mistress that he planned to divorce Carolyn, whom he referred to as "a slut."

Someone had tipped him off about Michael. "I know," he snapped at a friend. "The guy who's always flashing his meat on billboards. I don't have to show my dick in public. My reputation is all I need to seduce a woman."

When Michael flew back East, another call came in from Carolyn, who wanted a rendezvous. To ensure that they wouldn't be recognized, they checked into a seedy motel in New England. "It was a case of the married woman and the amoral cad. After she left the hotel I still loved her. I was in love with John F. Kennedy Jr.'s wife."

There would be more secret trysts

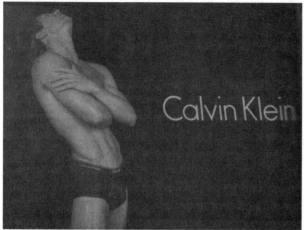

Michael Bergin was Mark Wahlberg's (Marky Mark's) successor in Calvin Klein's racy series of black-and-white billboard ads.

Carolyn Bessette's lover stands 6'1" and boasts washboard abs cited as his professional signature—that and a bulging crotch, which excited women and gay men across the country. His billboard in New York's Times Square *(photos above)* created a sensation and became a tourist attraction, launching Michael on the road to model stardom.

From Paris to Milan, the telephone rang—Gianfranco Ferré, Sonia Rykiel, Valentino, Giorgio Armani, Donna Karan, Yves Saint Laurent. In time he became the exclusive model for Claiborne for Men, a division of Liz Claiborne. Also lusting for Michael was Perry Ellis.

Michael became so popular he launched his own brand of man's underwear, advertising the undies in provocative poses. Fitness photographer John Falocco shot revealing pictures as well as nudes of Michael in his MBs (the name of his underwear line).

before their final one. Michael had learned that JFK Jr. wanted a divorce.

The last tearful time Michael saw Carolyn, she begged him to let her come and live with him. "To hell with scandal," she said.

As he rode away that morning in a taxi, he saw her in tears standing on the sidewalk. His final word to her was, "No!"

One morning he turned on the news. JFK's private plane carrying his wife Carolyn and her sister Lauren was reported missing.

In the days that followed, he said, "Everyone was writing about the American Prince and his Beautiful Princess," depicting their love as a fairy tale. At the time only he knew the real truth.

Even now Michael wonders what would have happened if he'd accepted Carolyn's offer to run away with her. "Would she still be alive today?"

Then-president **Bill Clinton** meets a possible future president and confronts him eye to eye, following a viewing of "From the Earth to the Moon" in the East Room of the White House on March 5, 1998. Privately in a secluded room of the White House, Clinton talked to **JFK Jr.** about his future plans to run for President of the United States.

"You would get 75% of the women's vote, all the gay vote, 90% of the black vote, and 30% of the male vote. The other 70% of men would be too jealous to vote for you."

Jackie had warned her son that if he wanted to be president, "You've got to stop dating all those floozies. America likes its First Ladies respectable. Posing nude for *Playboy* is not the way to go if you want to sit in the Oval Office one day."

He did not remind his mother that nude pictures of her were in circulation around the world. Jackie Kennedy, in fact, was the first First Lady ever featured in a nude centerfold, an "honor" that never happened to Eleanor Roosevelt, Mamie Eisenhower, or Bess Truman.

SPORTS ★ ★ ★ FINAL

DAILY NEWS

NEW YORK'S HOMETOWN NEWSPAPER

Sunday, July 18, 1999

LOST

JFK Jr., wife presumed dead in plane crash off Vineyard

This front page stunned New Yorkers, as did similar headlines around the world. LOST was soon replaced with another headline: AGAIN. On July 17, 1999, **JFK Jr**. followed his father to an early death.

The night before, piloting his own plane, JFK Jr. had taken off from Essex County Airport in Fairfield, New Jersey, with passengers **Carolyn** and her sister, Lauren Bessette. The craft was a Piper Saratoga II HP. The plan involved dropping Lauren off in Martha's Vineyard, with John and Carolyn planning to fly on to Hyannis Port for the wedding of Rory Kennedy, youngest son of Robert Kennedy. Of course, as the world knows, the plane never made it to Martha's Vineyard, but met an ocean grave instead.

As a relatively inexperienced pilot, John began his descent toward the airport on Martha's Vineyard at 9:40pm on Friday, July 16. His descent was ten times faster than normal. Aviation experts claimed he may have experienced "black hole vertigo," a pilot's failure to distinguish up from down.

On July 20 the wreckage of the plane was found. The bodies of the three air crash victims were discovered a day later. The bodies were taken to the local state medical examiner's office where they were autopsied. Remembering those post-autopsy pictures of his brother, Teddy Kennedy requested that no pictures be taken. JFK Jr.'s body was cremated, his ashes buried at sea.

In this day when seemingly everybody has a camera, a nude picture of John's body was taken and was secretly distributed. It's amazing that this ghoulish photograph has not made its way onto the web yet. It invariably will.

Rushing past reporters and the paparazzi, **John F. Kennedy Jr**. and blonde-haired actress **Daryl Hannah** swiftly head into St. Andrew's Church in New Shoreham on Block Island, Rhode Island. They were attending the wedding of Ted Kennedy Jr. on October 10, 1993.

The press had speculated for years that JFK Jr. and Daryl would soon be having their own wedding. But within a year they had broken up their relationship, which had begun in September of 1988, at the wedding of John's aunt, Lee Radziwill, to film director Herb Ross, who had helmed Daryl in the movie *Steel Magnolias*.

At the time, she was sharing a $2.5 million home with singer Jackson Browne, and JFK, Jr. was dating such belles as Sarah Jessica Parker or Christina Haag.

During the summer of 1989, Daryl left JFK Jr. and resumed her relationship with Browne. When Brown was alleged to have severely beaten her in 1992, John rushed to her side and nursed her back to health, and, in doing so, resumed their rocky relationship.

Sugar Rautbord, a novelist friend of Daryl's, claimed, "Daryl was desperate to marry John," but he suddenly dropped her for reasons not fully explained.

JFK Jr. was often a frequent escort of his mother, **Jackie Onassis**, especially at charity events in New York. Jackie was always overly protective of her son, and became almost hysterical on the subject after the assassinations of both JFK and RFK. She feared her family would also be targeted for assassination.

She had cause for alarm, as John's life had already been endangered on several occasions, as on July 15, 1972 when Greek authorities announced the arrest of two gangs who had plotted to kidnap him. One of the gang members, Panayotis Kabanis, claimed, "We could have blackmailed Mrs. Onassis for as much money as we wanted."

Jackie had other worries. She opposed John's ambitions as an actor, and she feared he might grow up to be a homosexual. She tried as long as she could to suppress stories about his father's womanizing. Whenever Marilyn Monroe came on TV, and JFK Jr. was listening, she switched channels.

In the background, coming through the revolving glass door, is the much-respected Maurice Tempelsman, sometimes referred to as "the poor man's Aristotle Onassis." In her final years, he became Jackie's companion, beau, financial advisor, and lover.

Born into an Orthodox Jewish family in Belgium, he had known Jackie since the late 1950s. Maurice and his since-then estranged wife, Lily Bucholz, were frequent visitors at the White House during the Kennedy era. He is short, portly, and older looking, though born the same year as Jackie. He took the millions Jackie got from Christina Onassis and invested them, creating a vast fortune, especially in the gold and silver markets.

"You can be sure that this diamond merchant gives Jackie lots of rocks that don't lose their shape." said Truman Capote.

Neither JFK Jr. or Jackie lived to see the publication of **Daryl Hannah's** notorious centerfold for the November, 2003 edition of *Playboy*. To Jackie, the *Rolling Stone* cover story in April of 1984 was publicity enough. From the beginning of her son's relationship, Jackie did not approve of Daryl.

It began when JFK Jr. threw a party at his mother's Martha's Vineyard home one Memorial Day weekend when she was away. Daryl was among the guests. Upon Jackie's return, she discovered marijuana and banished John to the silo section of the detached guest cottage on her estate.

When her son was entertaining Daryl at her home, Jackie often asked her maid to bring a dinner tray to her bedroom so she wouldn't have to share meals with the romantic pair in her dining room. Some of Jackie's most explosive fights with her son were over Daryl. "She will blacken the family name," Jackie warned JFK Jr.

Psychiatrist Dr. Carole Lieberman said, "Because of the constant comparison with President Kennedy and Marilyn Monroe while Daryl and John were dating, Daryl probably saw herself as a modern day MM."

Associated Press

Nineteen-year-old **John F. Kennedy Jr**. was photographed on a warm day on September 19, 1979 off the shore of Hyannis Port. This would be one of the first of the countless shirtless pictures that were taken of him during his short life. An hour after this candid shot was taken, "John-John" was photographed with his trunks down urinating off the side of the boat. A young woman on a passing boat took the picture of the JFK Jr. waterworks. The photograph is now a collectors' item.

In 1990, Rudolf Nureyev, who was alleged to have always "carried a torch" for John, Jr., invited him to the fashionable French island of St. Barts, where the ballet dancer maintained a luxurious home.

One day, John went swimming in the nude on the public Governor's Beach, taking time off from being an assistant Manhattan district attorney. A New York travel agent spotted him dangling his jewels as he walked along the beach and snapped his picture. So far, the agent has turned down exceedingly generous offers from the tabloids who want to run the picture.

352

Sybil Hill

The Secret Mistress of Camelot's Prince

Courtesy of Sybil Hill

Had fate acted differently, **Sybil Hill,** a beautiful and talented blonde artist from the golden west, might have become the second Mrs. John F. Kennedy Jr. JFK Jr. shared many memories with her, and she states today that the true complexities of their relationship "will never be revealed."

Here, Ms. Hill poses against the backdrop of one of her paintings, a metaphor for the free-flowing spirit of the American West. "I love the horse's spirit, the clairvoyant energy that envelops them; their eyes evoking an unseen aura of awareness – ancient, timeless. I try to paint that." Ms. Hill has sold well over 300 paintings in the last six years. Her work hangs in prominent art collections throughout the world.

Sybil cried on July 22, 1999 when the *USS Briscoe* carried the ashes of her former lover for burial at sea off Martha's Vineyard. During happier days, he shared his dreams about his magazine *George* with her, and his belief that politicians could be just as fascinating as movie stars if given the glossy magazine treatment. He also said that George might be a platform to launch himself into political life. "Who knows?" he said. "Tomorrow the White House. My dad, against all odds, did it."

Marital Infidelity and Sexual Healing in the Kennedy Clan

John had trouble expressing his feelings for her. The lower photo shows a love note he wrote her.

Sybil often called John at his office, and he took her calls. Recalling a previous conjugal visit, he said, "I'm glad I rose to the occasion."

Sybil Hill met John F. Kennedy Jr. at the Moondance Diner on Sixth Avenue in New York on January 6, 1991.

She walked into the dining area with her *boyfriend du jour* when she spotted "a gorgeous looking man wearing a baseball cap. She remarked to her boyfriend that he looked like John Kennedy Jr.

"No way!" the boyfriend said.

At table and without alerting her boyfriend, she stole glances at JFK Jr. whenever she could. After a few lagers, her boyfriend excused himself to go to the bathroom.

Seizing the moment, she walked over to JFK Jr., still not certain if he were the man himself. After a few hurried exchanges, he scribbled "John" and his phone number on a piece of paper. As she remembered it, "that piece of paper was burning a hole in my pocket until the next day when I could call him."

That call led to her first date with America's Prince Charming and the beginning of an affair. Over dinner that first night, she said, "I'm from Dallas. Does that bother you?"

He said it did not. Although neither of them was married at the time, he still took her to out-of-the-way places because he didn't want to be chased by the paparazzi like Jackie was.

One night, in a surprise move, he invited her to a club in Harlem where most of the patrons wanted to buy JFK Jr. a drink and have their picture taken with him.

"We didn't make love all the time," she said. "He liked to relax and enjoyed painting. "I still have one of his paintings," she said.

During their sex together, he never used a condom. "I hate condoms. It destroys the sensation."

"That was fine with me," she said. "I would love to have had his baby. But it didn't happen."

"Sex with him was absolutely fabulous," she said. "He told me I was so uninhibited, so adventurous…"

At a dinner for JFK Jr.'s cousin, Bobby Shriver, Sybil came face to face with Caroline Kennedy. "She gave me a very cold look," Sybil said. "It was obvious to me she was wondering if this girl was good for her little brother."

The affair of JFK Jr. and Sybil grew hotter throughout the summer of 1991. But then came the devastating news. In September of that year, he planned to marry Carolyn Bessette on Cumberland Island off the coast of Georgia. When Sybil saw Carolyn's picture, she told friends, "The new Mrs. John F. Kennedy Jr. and I look amazingly alike."

As John-John's marriage deepended during the 1990s, Sybil occasionally received a phone call from the man she still loved. But it wasn't until February of 1998 that she came face to face with him again.

By then, she was running a ritzy boutique in Aspen, Colorado. JFK Jr. flew into Aspen for a gathering at the pricey and private, members-only, Caribou Club.

He called Sybil and agreed to meet her in the parking lot of the

Associated Press

John liked sharing memories of his adventures with Sybil, including details about a youthful trip to Europe with Robert T. Littell, who had attended Brown University with him.

Waiting for cash from Jackie, they crashed in sleeping bags pitched in London's Hyde Park. Later, they stayed at a youth hostel in the red light district of Amsterdam where JFK Jr. sampled "some reasonably priced talent that had sat preening herself in a ruby-lit storefront window."

John confessed, "The girl didn't know who I was. What if she'd known she was getting royally screwed by the president's kid?"

At the Ritz Hotel in London, Littell and John almost got busted for smoking pot.

club. They embraced and kissed before she drove him to the rustic, two-story house where she lived.

"We began making love on a sofa, then on a Persian rug in the living room, before finally moving into the bedroom," she recalled.

After sex, he poured out problems he was having in his marriage to Carolyn. "I'm miserable," he told her. "The marriage is a sham. She's taking a lot of cocaine and Ecstasy." He'd also found out that she was having a torrid affair with super hunk Michael Bergin, an old flame of hers. "She also has Jekyll and Hyde mood swings," John said.

At the time, he also discussed a possible divorce.

His fear was that if he ran for President of the United States, the divorce might be used against him. Several of his friends had reminded him about how "that barrier has already been broken."

"Ronald Reagan divorced Jane Wyman—actually it was the other way around," David Kindle, a close friend of JFK Jr., had told him.

"John felt guilty about resuming our affair," Sybil claimed. "We both knew it was wrong,

This rustic home in Aspen, Colorado, became the final love nest in 1998 for John and Sybil. It actually belonged to her boyfriend who was away at the time. During their time together, she never realized that this was the last time she'd ever see him.

He had left her once previously to marry Carolyn Bessette, who was working as a publicist for Calvin Klein. Sybil painfully recalls what she interpreted back then as her final goodbye to JFK Jr. "I put my hand over John's heart and told him, 'You have to follow your heart.'"

He dropped his head, filled with sorrow. "I'm so sorry," he told her.

but we couldn't help ourselves."

He asked her, "Where will you be two years from now?" The suggestion was that he might be free of Carolyn and might marry her.

She responded, "I'll never stop loving you, and I will love you forever."

"At three o'clock in the morning, I drove him back to the Caribou Club where he'd parked his rental car," Sybil said. "After a farewell kiss, he gave me the peace sign and walked away. It was the last time I saw him."

When the first bulletin came on television, Sybil stayed glued to her set. JFK Jr.'s plane was missing, carrying not only himself but Carolyn and her sister Lauren.

"At first I couldn't accept the news of his death," Sybil said. "To me, John was immortal. I fully expected to see him walking out of the water. But when they found his body, my fantasy was shattered."

"I was heartbroken," said Sybil. "I'll never know if John would have come back to me. But I treasure the thought that he would have."

After his death, Sybil recalled, "He had a premonition of his upcoming death. He told me, 'I don't think I'll make it to 40.' He didn't explain why. But *he knew*."

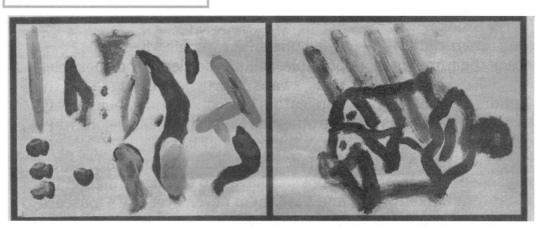

John liked to paint, and painting sessions with Sybil were sometimes tinged with sex. She claims that these finger paintings were done by John during one of their many trysts. He created them as part of their "Art Therapy and Sexual Healing" sessions.

She guided him through artistic endeavors combined with passion. "I think my love-making and John's finger painting helped him ease some of the tensions caused by his troubled marriage to Bessette," said Sybil.

"Carolyn and I are not communicating," he told Sybil. "Often we live in two different worlds. The worst example of that came in 1996 when Carolyn had a miscarriage of my baby—at least I assume it was my baby—and didn't even tell me until months later."

JFK & The Honey Trap

How Profumo Whores, Soviet Spies, Congressional Mendacity, and an Awakening Media Signaled the Beginning of the End for Camelot

Associated Press

FBI Director **J. Edgar Hoover** (*center figure*) captures the attention of two intent listeners during his scandalous revelations: President **John F. Kennedy** *(left)* and **Bobby Kennedy,** JFK's brother and U.S. attorney general (*right*). Bobby loathed the FBI director: In the photo, he's turning away from him as Hoover reveals that the women the brothers have been cavorting with are KGB spies.

Evoking a warning that would be made to a future president, Richard Nixon, less than a decade later, the chief G-man told JFK, "There is a cancer growing on the presidency." This point of view was bluntly relayed during a tense White House meeting on February 23, 1961.

Looming as an inset photo over the president's right shoulder is the notorious **Ellen Rometsch**, rumored to be an East German spy, She was another of those Elizabeth Taylor lookalikes that lured JFK into her "honey trap." She had a penchant for heavy makeup, including blood-red lipstick on her "Deep Throat" mouth, and "glossy upswept ebony hair that looked more like a big pink Teutonic *houri* bred for the trade," in the words of author Burton Hersh. He noted that Ellen was known for her "sloe-eyed, come-hither manner."

A TASTE OF BELLADONNA
SWEET, STICKY, AND DEADLY

Two birds of a feather, **Bobby Baker** (*left*) and then Vice-President **Lyndon B. Johnson** (*right*) use smiles to camouflage their next devious move, aimed at taking down enemies who included President Kennedy. "He has an Achilles heel—and that's all his womanizing," said LBJ, even though he was a womanizer himself, but without the impressive celebrity-studded track record of JFK.

In LBJ, Baker found a powerful mentor, a wheeler-dealer to match his own achievements in that field. "He [Baker] is the first person I talk to in the morning, and the last one at night," LBJ said. Often, those candid conversations confronted the same thorny but ongoing issue: "What can we do to contain Jack Kennedy and that vile rattlesnake of a brother?"

As LBJ's power increased within the DC infrastructure, so did Baker's, until no door in Washington was closed to him.

"The American government is democratic but corruptible," Baker said. "Power is something to be used by those who understand it." And Baker's sponsor, LBJ himself, wasn't above blackmail when it served his purpose.

"Lyndon Johnson was much more close-mouthed about his extramarital affairs than John F. Kennedy. Kennedy seemed to relish sharing the details of his conquests; though he was not without charm or wit in relating the clinical complexities, he came off as something of a boyish braggart. Those who have frequented beer hall or locker room sessions will know what I mean. Once in the Senate restaurant, he introduced me to one of the prettiest women I had ever seen...from Paris. 'Bobby, look at this fine chick. She gives the best head in the United States.'"

Bobby Baker

At the height of the Cold War in 1963, President John F. Kennedy and, to a lesser extent, Robert F. Kennedy, became victims of a self-styled "Honey Trap" plotted by the KGB from its bases in London and Washington. The purpose of the plot was to use beautiful girls to seduce prominent politicians and extract secrets from them to send behind the Iron Curtain.

In England, an equivalent plot had already been widely exposed and publicized by the British press as "The Profumo Affair," after John Profumo, the Secretary of State for War in the cabinet of Harold Macmillan's conservative government. Profumo's sexual involvement with Christine Keeler, the alleged mistress of a Soviet spy, and Profumo's subsequent "misstatements" when he was questioned about it in the House of Commons, forced his resignation and irreparably damaged the credibility of Prime Minister Harold Macmillan's government. Macmillan himself, blaming it on poor health, resigned a few months later.

Ironically, in 1962 and 1963, top government officials in Washington became embroiled in an equivalent scandal, but JFK was assassinated before his sexual involvements with "Soviet spies and Profumo whores" became public knowledge.

Secret members of the KGB had already infiltrated Bobby Baker's Quorum Club (aka "The Q Club"). Senators, lobbyists, businessmen with government contracts converged on his establishment for the food, drink, and the good times with strikingly attractive women. Decorated "with sports prints and paintings of women with imposing facades," and billing itself as a place for the pursuit of "literary purposes and promotion of social intercourse," it was located in a three-room suite within the Carroll Arms, a railroad hotel lying near Washington, D.C.'s Union Station. On its upper floors, rooms were rented for ten dollars a night.

Born in Pickens, South Carolina in 1929, and designated as a Senate page boy at fourteen, Bobby Gene Baker became Lyndon B. Johnson's right-hand man in the Senate.

"If I had a son, this would be the boy," Johnson said about Baker.

Baker became Washington, D.C.'s leading pimp, providing "entertainment facilities" for persons doing business with the government. Entertainment facilities was another term for party girls. Articulate and ingratiating, Baker became one of the capital's leading practitioners of the "get-a-contract-with-a-girl" form of doing business.

Former aides to the ultra right-wing and always-terrifying Joseph McCarthy, attorney Roy Cohn and his lover and *protégé* David Schine, once lived together in a hotel room within the orbit of the Q Club, where they were rumored to have carried on a torrid homosexual affair. This more or less was revealed at the McCarthy hearings involving the U.S. Army. It was these hearings that exposed the Cohn/Schine connection, marking the beginning of the end of the career of the controversial McCarthy's "reign of terror."

Unknown to KGB agents, LBJ was operating his own sting operation, having Baker gather secrets of the senators which he could use to blackmail them into following his legislative agenda.

At the club, Baker employed several prostitutes from Communist countries, most notably Ellen Rometsch and Mariella Novotny. Although born in London, Suzy Chang was also suspected of being a foreign agent.

The Honey Trap operation in London was run by Dr. Stephen Ward, a fashionable osteopathic surgeon, who supplied call girls to everyone from Profumo himself to Prince Philip, Duke of Edinburgh.

Some conspiracy theorists make much of the fact that Baker's secretary, Nancy Carole Tyler, shared an

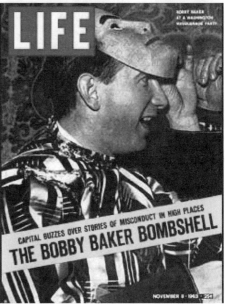

A small-town, good ol' Southern boy, the ambitious 15-year-old *(top photo)* **Bobby Baker** was still in long-handled underwear when he arrived in wartime Washington in 1943. In no time at all, he became the 'bag-man' for Senator Robert S. Kerr, an oil-industry entrepreneur from Oklahoma who had turned to politics and who was frequently mired in a swamp of bribery and corruption.

Kerr was referred to as "the uncrowned king of the Senate." Baker recalled that Kerr was so powerful that "Mr. Kennedy asked, Mr. Kerr decided."

When the "Bobby Baker Bombshell" burst into the media in November of 1963, LBJ knew he'd have to disconnect himself from his once-trusted assistant. But implications of wrong-doing on the part of both LBJ and, by implication, JFK, were hastily and conveniently forgotten in the hysteria associated with JFK's assassination a few weeks later.

Mandy Rice-Davies *(left)* and **Christine Keeler** *(right)* became "as famous as the Queen of England," in the words of one tabloid reporter when they appeared as the principal witnesses in the vice charges against Dr. Stephen Ward. (Ward, in the aftermath of the scandal, committed suicide.) Seen arriving at court in London on July 22, 1963, they were photographed on the first day of Ward's trial.

Both were rumored at the time to have also been sexually intimate with President Kennedy, although these charges were never proven.

JFK feared a Profumo-style scandal exploding around him the way they had around the British Minister of War in London. JFK, too, was sexually involved with prostitutes, including some rumored to have been transmitting information back to the KGB.

Profumo met Keeler, a London call girl and the mistress of a Russian with murky ties to the Soviets, at a house party at Cliveden, one of the most opulent country houses in Britain, a Buckinghamshire estate owned at the time by Lord Astor. Profumo's relationship with Keeler lasted only a few weeks, but it was associated with enough dynamite to destroy his reputation and his political career. The associated scandal is almost always cited as the main reason for the collapse of the conservative prime minister Harold Macmillan's government.

The British press trumpeted unfolding details about "The Profumo Affair" week after week as the story unfolded. Keeler, in her ghost-written memoir, *The Truth at Last,* published in 2001, said, "I believe the Americans were convinced that a worldwide sex-for-information network, an elaborate blackmail operation, was going on. And that the most powerful man in the world, their president [a reference, of course, to JFK] had sampled the pleasures of these female sex spies."

Actually, Keeler described the situation accurately. As Bobby Kennedy later confided to members of JFK's "Irish Mafia," Kenneth O'Donnell and David Powers, "Jack and I have been fucking the wrong broads. In the future, we'll fuck only Stars & Stripes women, not Hammer & Sickle whores."

apartment with Mary Jo Kopechne of Chappaquiddick notoriety. Tyler, after evidence of an dysfunctional affair with Baker, died mysteriously in an airplane crash in 1965, and Mary Jo drowned while trapped in Teddy Kennedy's car in 1969. But other than coincidence, there seems little meat on the bone of this so-called conspiracy.

In 1963, a beautiful, German-born prostitute, Ellen Rometsch, was hired by Baker as a waitress at the Quorum Club. As one of the members put it, "She was clad in a scanty black and skin-tight uniform, with black mesh hose. There was a voluptuous nude painting in the bar. Despite her constant use of heavy makeup, Ellen compared favorably with that painting."

It was Baker who introduced JFK to the devastatingly attractive Ellen, a liaison so dangerous it could have led to the president's impeachment.

After a night with the East German, JFK called Baker, proclaiming, "This was the best time I've ever had in my whole life. Send her over again on an as-need basis."

Ellen reciprocated, giving JFK a equally glowing review. "Jack was as good as it got with oral sex—made me happy."

Like another JFK mistress, Judith Campbell Exner, Ellen was also referred to as an Elizabeth Taylor look-alike.

Her affair with JFK continued, and Ellen became one of the regulars at the naked pool parties the president staged at The White House. Ellen's charms were praised so highly by JFK to Bobby, that the attorney general also wanted to give her a try.

On occasion, she was sent to the Justice Department. Bobby got to sample her charms in his secret bedroom over his attorney general's office.

He, too, praised her skill as a seductress. As news of Ellen's talents spread, she became the most talked-about "Deep Throat" in Washington, sarcastically referred to as "The Fellatio Queen of the Potomac."

Ellen's seductive powers were not confined just to JFK and RFK. Baker allegedly estimated that she was "passed around" to a staggering fifty senators and congressmen during 1963, and all of them agreed on what an exciting choice she was.

Throughout the duration of her affair with JFK, Ellen was married to Rolf Rometsch, a sergeant in the West German air force, who had been assigned to his country's embassy in Washington. Rometsch was an indulgent and understanding husband—at least at first.

Although Ellen rented a $200-a-month brick house in North Arlington, Virginia, she spent little time at home, even though she was the mother of a four-year-old son.

Unknown to the Kennedy brothers, Ellen was born in 1936 in Kleinitz, Germany, which in the aftermath of World War II, became part of the DDR: Communist East Germany.

As a young woman growing up amid the rubble of Communist East Germany she had been a member of the party, with strong evidence that during the peak of the Cold War, she functioned as a Communist spy.

Ellen was not the most powerful spy in Washington, of course. That designation was reserved for J. Edgar Hoover, director of the FBI. Within days of Ellen's involvement with the Kennedy brothers, Hoover had her investigated, and the agency would continue its probe long after Hoover's death in 1972. By 1987, the bureau had accumulated 478 pages of files on her.

After Hoover compiled the bulk of these files, he went to the attorney general's office and warned RFK that he and his brother were sexually involved with a Communist spy from East German, working for that country's leader, Walter Ulbricht.

When he learned of this, RFK ordered that Ellen be deported. Under the auspices of the State Department, she was deported to West Germany, where supposedly, that country, as an ally of the U.S., would keep an eye on her, on August 21, 1963.

LaVern Duffy, one of RFK's aides when he served on the Senate Rackets Committee, escorted her out of the country, flying with her to Europe on a U.S. Air Force plane.

Her husband finally got the message, divorcing her on grounds of "conduct contrary to matrimonial rules."

Ironically, Duffy, a lifelong bachelor who was rumored to sleep with as many handsome young men as beautiful girls, was also having an affair with Ellen. Perhaps that's why Bobby asked him to return with her to Germany. Privately, and somewhat sharply, Bobby reminded Duffy, "With you escorting Ellen, you might try a girl for a change."

Ellen may have been in love with Duffy, as passionate love letters between them later revealed. Although there is no smoking gun, Duffy is the prime suspect in the payoff money that went to Ellen in Germany. Once of her letters specifically stated, "The bank is telling me that it would be more easy for them and the money would be fast in my hands if you should make up a check payable to me." [English, of course, was not Ellen's first language.]

When news of the JFK/Ellen affair reached a Senate investigating committee, Duffy was dispatched once again to Germany to meet with Ellen. He carried a bundle of money and got her to sign a statement denying "intimacies with VIPs in the White House." Decades would go by before the source of that payoff money would be revealed.

The president knew that blackmail money had to be raised to pay off Ellen. He ordered Grant Stockdale, the business partner of Bobby Baker, "to raise the loot wherever you can get it."

Stockdale was a real-estate broker in Miami, and had known JFK since he was a young congressman. In 1960, Stockdale was Democratic National Committee's fund-raising chairman for the southern states. JFK later appointed him ambassador to Ireland, but in eighteen months, he had spent his own money so lavishly, he wrote JFK that he had to resign and return to his lucrative real estate business in Florida.

JFK was so close to Stockdale that he even invited him to attend his orgies at the Hotel Carlyle in New York City. Stockdale attended once, later asserting, "I encountered the most beautiful women in the world there, but that scene is not for me."

Back in Florida, Stockdale began raising as much money as possible, ostensibly for the Democratic National Committee. But there was a problem. His friends already knew that he was broke, and many refused to give him any funds, fearing he would use their money to pay off his debts. Under the circumstances, he could not have their names listed as contributors to JFK's upcoming (1964) election, which made his friends doubt Stockdale even more. This embarrassment filled him with great regret, and caused many a sleepless night.

On November 26, 1963, four days after JKF's assassination, Stockdale flew into Washington for private talks with Teddy and Bobby Kennedy. Reportedly he told them, "The world is closing in on me." If he explained what he meant by that, it is not known.

His attorney, William Frates, later recalled, "He wasn't making much sense. He kept talking about 'these guys out to get me.' He didn't really identify them. At one point, he made a chilling assertion. 'They got Jack in Dallas. I'm next.'"

On December 2, 1963, only a few days later, Stockdale was pushed from his office window on the thirteenth floor of the Dupont Building in Miami. His secrets went hurdling to earth with him, and the person who murdered him was never revealed.

A few weeks earlier, in Washington during October of 1963, a month or so before JFK's assassination, the noose had already begun tightening around the throat of Bobby Baker. On October 7, 1963 he had been forced to resign as secretary to the Senate. Lyndon Johnson was also trying to limit his connection with Baker and had cut him off. There was a suspicion that LBJ was involved in political corruption, an example of which was the awarding of a $7 billion contract for a fighter plane to Texas-based General Dynamics.

Unlike Johnson, JFK was not connected with Baker through any financial misdeeds, but through sexual liaisons.

"There's only one man in Washington who can suppress this investigation of Baker, or at least contain it," JFK told Bobby in front of his aide, Kenneth O'Donnell. "That's J. Edgar, the old queen himself. Of course, in spite of past favors—financially in Lyndon's case, sexually in mine—both of us might have to toss Baker under the bus. I can just see the headlines: KGB PROSTITUTES SERVICE THE WHITE HOUSE."

The president deliberately made the word "prostitutes" plural. As the scenario unfolded, it seemed that Baker had also introduced JFK to two more prostitutes—Mariella Novotny and Suzy Chang—who may have been Soviet spies. Mariella was a bleached blonde Czech and Suzy was a Chinese beauty.

To make matters worse, and glaringly obvious to anyone searching for bait, these two beautiful hookers had been key players in the Profumo scandal that was already rocking the Macmillan government in London.

Had JFK lived, thanks to this particularly incendiary situation, his womanizing would probably have reached the press in spite of any attempted cover-up.

JFK did little to conceal his illicit involvements. As a senator in the 1950s, he had invited Suzy to dinner at "21", one of the most highly visible dining spots on the celebrity circuit in New York City. Gossip columnist Walter Winchell, a frequent visitor to "21," spotted the handsome young senator and the prostitute, but chose not to write about it in his influential column.

In London, Mariella, an on-again, off-again striptease dancer, became a notorious prostitute. She traveled to the United States in 1960 in the company of Suzy. Both women were eventually hired by Bobby Baker at the Quorum Club.

In time, both Suzy and Mariella were introduced to the two Kennedy brothers, with whom they each had affairs. Baker arranged the introductions.

The daughter of two Chinese immigrants, Suzy had been born in New York City in 1934. During the late 1950s in London, she became involved with osteopath and pimp Stephen Ward, who rounded up prostitutes such as Christine Keeler and Mandy Rice-Davies for sex parties with key members of Her Majesty's government, including John Profumo. Ward turned out to be a prophet. He told party girl Keeler, "I believe Kennedy will be assassinated. He will not be allowed to stay in such an important position of power in the world. I can assure you of that." Ward never explained what led him to that conclusion.

One of Ward's friends was Prince Philip, Duke of Edinburgh, who sat for a portrait painted by Ward. "He's a snob," Ward later said, "not the man he used to be at my parties. I knew him before he married…what's her face, Elizabeth."

Although both of the Kennedy brothers had managed to keep news about their adulterous affairs out of the papers, there were various printed hints of what was going on. The *New York Journal-American,* in a blind item, wrote that "a man who holds a very high elective office in the Kennedy administration is linked to a Chinese prostitute."

Both Mariella and Suzy were not only named as members of the same spy ring that had trapped Profumo a few months earlier, but both woman had "connections" to antagonistic communist adversaries of the U.S.

Mariella moved to New York, where she opened an international brothel. After her return to London, she was questioned by Scotland Yard and admitted that she had had sex with JFK in 1960 "at a New York hotel." She also claimed that her second encounter with the president was simultaneously with two other prostitutes on West 55th Street in Manhattan.

In New York, her partner was Harry Allen Towers, a Soviet agent, who had previously fled from England and was last seen in what was then known as Czechoslovakia.

Mariella's testimony could have been particularly damaging to JFK. Reportedly, she tied up the leader of the Free World for a "mild beating." S&M was a specialty.

Novotny was described by Christine Keeler, the famous prostitute at the center of the Profumo scandal: "She had a tiny waist that exaggerated her ample figure. She was a siren, a sexual athlete of Olympian proportions—she could do it all. I know. I saw her in action. She knew all the strange pleasures that were wanted and could deliver them."

Later, Jack reportedly told his brother, "I couldn't keep up with her. I hope you could."

"Nobody ever said I had a bad back," Bobby answered.

In an unpublished memoir written right before her death in the 1970s, Novotny maintained that she had been "recruited" by Peter Lawford to have group sex with JFK right before his inauguration.

In addition to Profumo, Keeler was also having sex with Eugene Ivanov, a naval *attaché* at the Soviet Embassy in London. There was a fear that she was transferring to him government secrets learned during pillow talk with Profumo.

Keeler was known to have visited New York, with Mandy Rice-Davies. Robert Kennedy asked Hoover to see if FBI agents could find out if the president had slept with either girl, especially Keeler. Of course, Bobby could have simply asked his brother, but since JFK slept with so many prostitutes, he simply could not remember.

This revelation appeared in a book called *An Affair of State: The Profumo Case and the Framing of Stephen Ward* by Phillip Knightley and Caroline Kennedy (no, not that one).

The book said that "Robert Kennedy had a right to be concerned. On July 23, 1963, according to an FBI internal memorandum, the tape recording which Christine Keeler had made with her new manager, Robin Drury, mentioned President Kennedy as one of Keeler's lovers. All that needs to be said about this allegation is that if Keeler had indeed slept with Kennedy, then it would have been completely out of character for her to have kept it quiet on her return to London. She would have told everyone. The fact that she never mentioned it until she was recounting her memoirs for sale to Fleet Street strongly suggests that she invented it to make them a more valuable property."

Apparently, Keeler had wanted to have sex with JFK, but he died before she could orchestrate it. However, because of her notoriety, she received many offers for sex. She claimed that movie stars Warren Beatty, Maximilian Schell, and George Peppard "banged" her.

In February of 1983, Mariella Novotny was found dead in London. Police reported an overdose of drugs as the cause, but Keeler didn't believe that. "I think she was murdered. She knew too much."

As the investigation of Baker continued in Washington, more and more roads were leading directly to the Oval Office. The press became aware of the unfolding scandal.

Wesley Pruden, editor of *The Washington Times,* claimed, "A few brave Republicans were screwing up the courage to make something out of it, on the grounds that a president shouldn't be taking off his clothes with a *femme fatale* from the 'Evil Empire.'"

When word leaked out about this impending GOP assault, Bobby Kennedy, in his role as Attorney General, asked J. Edgar Hoover of the FBI to threaten and intimidate inquisitive Republicans in Congress.

Seeking to gain favor with Bobby, whom the FBI director despised, Hoover came through. He warned Republicans on Capitol Hill not to investigate the JFK/Ellen Rometsch affair. "If you do, I'm going to open all of your closets, and believe me, there are skeletons in there that will get you impeached."

Hoover reminded the senators—"bitter opponents of civil rights"—that many of them had used "Negro prostitutes for sleepovers. Surely, you gentlemen wouldn't want this shocking fact exposed to your lily white voters back home, especially when many of you are coming up for re-election this year."

RFK then forced Hoover to meet with Mike Mansfield, the Democratic leader of the Senate, and Everett Dirksen, the Republican counterpart. Details about that meeting have been suppressed. Hoover obviously had "blackmail on everybody in Washington," as he privately proclaimed to the Senate leaders. In the aftermath of this meeting, the Senate Rules Committee decided not to investigate the Rometsch scandal.

In exchange for this favor, Bobby told Hoover that his job at the FBI was secure and allowed him to proceed with his wiretaps on Martin Luther King, Jr.

Betraying RFK, Hoover, behind his back, ostensibly worked to suppress the scandal, but also wanted it leaked. Information was supplied by Hoover at various points to investigative reporters Courtney Evans and Clark Mollenhoff. Mollenhoff wrote an article incorporating a highly veiled version of the information in a story for the *Des Moines Register.*

In it, he claimed that the FBI had established "that a beautiful brunette had been attending parties with congressional leaders and some prominent new Frontiersmen from the executive branch of government. The possibility exists that her activity might be connected with espionage is of some concern, because of the high rank of her male companions."

Mollenhoff later claimed, "Had JFK lived to run for president in 1964, his House of Cards would have come tumbling down. Perhaps I would have seen to that. I had the goods on that fucker. Sex scandals crippled Macmillan's government. I would have done the same for

Camelot."

During the closing months of JFK's presidency, the attorney general was kept busy "putting out brush fires," as he characterized it. Some of those fires were threatening to become major conflagrations.

Fearing that he would become the central figure in U.S. version of the Profumo scandal, JFK as president ordered David Kirkpatrick Bruce, U.S. ambassador to the Court of St. James's, to provide him with a daily behind-the-scenes report on the Profumo case then unfolding in London.

"To quote Ike, I want to be as clean as a hound's tooth when I run for president in 1964," JFK told Ben Bradlee of *The Washington Post*. "I plan to dump Lyndon. I considered a Democratic governor here and there, but I've come up with an unbeatable choice to offer the Democratic National Convention. A Kennedy/Kennedy ticket. I'll serve out my terms, then Bobby takes over for two terms, and by then we will have groomed Teddy to fill in for two terms. At some point, son John-John will be old enough to run. We could carry this a little further. Caroline might become the first woman president of the United States. Perhaps we could have her run for senator from New York to get her launched into politics."

That was JFK's political fantasy. The more realistic Lyndon Johnson had a different take: "Not that I'm one to throw stones," LBJ told Bobby Baker, "but I think Jack's womanizing is about to be exposed as a national security risk. You're looking at the next president of the United States. After Jack steps down, I'm the obvious choice to get the nomination. And even win the election. Who are the Republican shitheads to run against me? Barry Goldwater? Ronald Reagan? Get serious."

In 1967, after JFK's assassination and before the 1968 assassination of Bobby Kennedy, Bobby Baker was convicted on seven of the nine counts of fraud on which he was charged. "I vomited breakfast in the men's room," he later recalled. He had to serve eighteen months in a federal penitentiary.

His case was called "The most bizarre Washington scandal of the 1960s."

Back in Washington during that fateful November of 1963, the case against the president was about to explode.

Upon his return from Dallas, JFK was scheduled to be questioned by a Senate committee about his "relationship with KGB prostitutes."

Journalist John Simkin wrote, "I think it possible that John Kennedy's relationship with Ellen Rometsch played a role in the cover-up of his assassination. LBJ and Hoover both knew that JFK had a sexual relationship with a KGB spy. Did this influence Bobby Kennedy's decision not to publicize his own doubts about the assassination of his brother?"

Some of the most tantalizing "what if's" associated with this case raise some questions:

WHAT IF J. EDGAR HOOVER HAD NOT GOTTEN INVOLVED AND DIDN'T THREATEN ALL THOSE SENATORS WITH THE INFORMATION HE WAS HOARDING?

WOULD THE INVESTIGATION OF THE PRESIDENT HAVE GONE FORWARD?
WOULD KENNEDY HAVE BEEN IMPEACHED?

AND WOULD KENNEDY, IN THAT CASE, HAVE BEEN IN DALLAS ON NOVEMBER 22, 1963?

BUT WHO WAS THAT NUDE MAN
WITH BRUISES AND A MASK?

As increasingly lurid testimony came out of London during the Profumo trial, stories began to be leaked to the press in Washington and New York about JFK's nude orgies around the swimming pool in the White House.

The president read each account, wondering when he would be implicated with some of Stephen Ward's prostitutes.

Columnist Dorothy Kilgallen would later interview Jack Ruby, who shot Kennedy's alleged assassin, Lee Harvey Oswald. Additionally, she also covered the Profumo case, and printed several hints that that scandal might extend "across the pond to Washington."

She once wrote: "Authorities in Britain are searching the apartment of one of the principals in the Profumo case. They came upon a photograph showing a key figure disporting with a bevy of ladies. All were nude except for the gentleman in the picture, who was wearing an apron. And this is a man who is on extremely friendly terms with the very proper Queen Elizabeth amd members of the Royal Family."

Her reference was to Anthony Asquith, a leading English film director and the son of H.H. Asquith, who had functioned as the prime minister of the U.K. during the First World War. Charming, despite his status as an alchoholic and a closeted homosexual. Anthony was well-liked and articulate, Never married, he had a penchant for being beaten by his male conquests.

After Dr. Stephen Ward's trial, the London tabloids reported on the notorious sex parties attended by two of Britain's most famous prostitutes, Christine Keeler and Mandy Rice-Davies. The *Washington Star* quoted Mandy as saying "There was a dinner party where a naked man wearing a mask waited on table like a slave," imploring the guests to whip him if the service wasn't good.

In her autobiography, *Mandy* (1980), she was more candid, describing a party hosted by Mariella Novotny, JFK's paramour, in London's Bayswater district. "The door was opened by Stephen Ward, naked except for his socks. All the men were naked, the women naked except for wisps of clothing like suspender belts and stockings. I recognized the host and hostess, Mariella Novotny and her husband, Horace Dibben, and, unfortunately, I recognized too a fair number of other faces as belonging to people so famous you could not fail to recognize them, including several politicians, especially a cabinet minister. Stephen told us with great glee that a dinner of roast peacock had been served by a man in a mask and bowtie instead of a fig leaf."

The hostess of that party had been born in wartime London in 1942 and would go on to conduct a torrid affair with the leader of the Free World, John F. Kennedy. Originally known as Stella Capes, she later changed her name to Mariella Novotny "because it had a more whiplash ring to it."

To support her mother, she became a striptease dancer and a prostitute in London. But in 1960s, she was on her way to the States, where, via a link with Bobby Baker, she was "fucking the God Damn President.of the United States," as she described, colorfully, in her unpublished memoirs.

The FBI arrested Mariella on March 3, 1961 and charged her with soliciting. Before her trial, on May 31, 1961, she slipped away aboard the Cunard liner *Queen Mary,* traveling under the name "Mrs. R. Tyson." Upon the ship's arrival in Southampton, she was intercepted by British immigration services, who had received word from the FBI that she was wanted in the United States

British film director
Anthony Asquith

(continued from previous page)

in a "sex-for-sale" scandal that involved men in "high elective office in the United States.

As J. Edgar Hoover himself said, "You don't get much higher in an elective office in America than that one man, the Irish son of a bootlegger."

Two years earlier, Mariella had announced that she had started to work on her own autobiography, and that it would include details of her work for MI-5. That, of course, suggested that she was a double agent, working for both the British and the Soviets.

She went on to inform the press that in her upcoming tell-all, she was going to write about "the plot to discredit Jack Kennedy. I kept a diary of all my appointments with various men, including the president. Believe me, it's dynamite. The diary is now in the hands of the CIA."

Mariella never lived to dish the dirt. In February of 1983, she was found dead in her London apartment. The Westminster Coroner blamed it on a drug overdose. Her friends called it murder. One friend in London suggested that, "We always knew that Mariella would be killed by American or British agents, probably the CIA, since they'd read the secrets in her diary. There was no way that either that diary or that memoir would ever be published."

According to Stephen Dorrel, a reporter, "Shortly after Mariella's death, her house was burgled and all her files and large day-to-day diaries from the early sixties to the seventies were stolen."

Mariella had shared some of the pages of her diaries with friends. At the United Nations in New York City, she'd met foreign dignitaries, even visiting kings. When asked who were some of the biggest names mentioned in her unpublished material, a friend, who preferred to remain anonymous, said, "Would you believe, Averell Harriman and billionaire J. Paul Getty?"

In the White House, as JFK watched the downfall of British War Minister **John Profumo** *(right figure in photo above)*, he told staff members "I could just imagine what revelations about me fucking Soviet whores would do to my presidency. It would make the scandals of the Macmillan government read like a children's book of verses."

Profumo was caught lying to the House of Commons when he was questioned about his sexual trysts. After his resignation, he worked as a volunteer cleaning toilets at Toynbee Hall, a charity based in the East End of London.

His wife, British film star **Valerie Hobson** *(left figure in photo above),* who stood by him throughout his disgrace, later in life turned to charity work too, focusing on mentally retarded children and lepers.

By 1976, Profumo's reputation was redeemed, and he was honored at Buckingham Palace for his charity work. In 1995, at the 70th birthday of then Prime Minister Margaret Thatcher, Profumo was seated immediately adjacent to Queen Elizabeth II herself.

Mariella Novotny being taken into custody by an FBI agent

Jackie: "I Hate Elizabeth Taylor."
Elizabeth Taylor on Jackie:
"A Gold-Digging Bitch."

When her husband was running for president of the United States, Jackie Kennedy had not only to face the competition of blonde bombshell Marilyn Monroe, she also learned that her philandering husband was engaged in a torrid affair with Elizabeth Taylor.

Revelations about the affair came to light after the death of Dame Elizabeth in 2011. Details were leaked to the press from her private diaries which may, in time, be edited and published.

But long before the world found out about the ET/JFK affair, Jackie knew about it. Her informant in such matters was Peter Lawford himself, who often functioned as a "double agent," feeding Jack information about Jackie and vice versa.

Reportedly, Elizbeth was mesmerized by JFK, whom she was supporting in his presidential bid. During his 1960 campaign, she had several private evenings within his bungalow at the Beverly Hills Hotel. Her marriage to Eddie Fisher (her fourth husband) didn't stop her from sleeping with America's future president.

Being married to Jackie never prevented JFK, of course, from having affairs on the side. Except for Marilyn Monroe, none of his paramours was quite as famous as Elizabeth.

"Kennedy did more than fund raising when he came to California," Eddie Fisher later said when he learned about the affair his then-wife was conducting with the president. "Kennedy was widely known for fucking Elizabeth Taylor lookalikes like Judith Campbell Exner. I guess he decided he wanted the real thing."

"Elizabeth swore to me that her relationship with Kennedy never went beyond friendship," Fisher said. "But I never believed her. I'm sure she never believed me when I told her that I was 'just friends' with some of the women I was bedding. When Jackie heard of the affair, she said some really vicious things about Elizabeth. And you should have heard my potty mouthed Elizabeth talk about Jackie. It was a real catfight."

The tabloids eventually picked up on the Elizabeth/Jackie rivalry, and sometimes the "two Queens of America" made the front page of magazines, appearing in separate photographs blended together.

As Elizabeth was being condemned in the press for "stealing" Eddie Fisher from America's sweetheart, Debbie Reynolds, Jackie was being presented as a saint. As she said at the time, "I'm so beloved as the grieving widow that anyone who is against me will look like a rat. Unless I run off with Eddie Fisher."

Jackie's rivalry with Elizabeth broke out again in 1968, when the former First Lady married Aristotle Onassis. Word leaked out of Greece that the shipping tycoon had originally wanted to marry Elizabeth when he heard that she was breaking up with Richard Burton. "I can give you even bigger diamonds that Burton, because I have more money," Ari told her.

But when he realized that Jackie might be available, he told his pimp, Johnny Meyer, "I think I'll marry her instead. After all, she's a bigger prize than even Elizabeth Taylor."

When she heard about the marriage, Elizabeth told a reporter for *Modern Screen*, "It will be the strangest marriage of the century. Mrs. Kennedy is now reduced to taking my rejects." The comment was never printed.

Jackie turned down an invitation to accompany them, but Elizabeth accepted an invitation to sail aboard Ari's yacht, the *Christina*. Word reached Jackie that Liz had flirted with Ari throughout the entire trip.

When Jackie confronted Ari about this, she told him, "It's either the Taylor bitch or me. Your friendship with that international tramp has to end—NOW!"

Movie Mirror picked up on this feud, running headlines that included "What Really Happened the Night Liz Tried to Cut Jackie Out! and The Night Onassis Turned to Liz.

After the death of Ari in 1975 and Elizabeth's divorce from Burton in 1974, *Motion Picture* magazine began labeling Elizabeth and Jackie as AMERICA'S TWO FALLEN QUEENS.

And by the time *Photoplay* published its November, 1976 issue, the world had changed. Instead of cheesecake, there was beefcake on the cover, and coverage of the exploits of Elizabeth and Jackie had been reduced to the last words on the cover, without even a headline or a picture. And they ran beneath the (larger) headline THE SALLY STRUTHERS NOBODY KNOWS.

Ironically, with her marriage to Jack Warner of Virginia, Elizabeth had assumed the same official role that Jackie had once held—that of a U.S. senator's spouse.

Their only face-to-face meeting came on June 20, 1976, when both Elizabeth and Jackie attended New York's Uris Theater to see a performance by the legendary British ballerina Margot Fonteyn.

Backstage, they encountered one another on the way to Fonteyn's dressing room.

Each woman smiled politely.

What did the two world-fabled women have to say to each other? Someone who stood behind them revealed all:

"They said absolutely nothing," he claimed. "Not a word."

JFK and Lee Harvey Oswald

The Final Days

Associated Press

Associated Press

Left photo: The sun was bright and the skies over Dallas were blue, but it was twilight time for the President of the United States, **John F. Kennedy**, as he rode into history on November 22, 1963.

Jackie, seated on his left, seemed at first to be more concerned with her hair blowing in the wind of this open-air limousine than she was for any potential danger that lurked along the trail.

Earlier, she'd told Nellie Connally, wife of the governor of Texas, John Connally, who was riding in the limo with them: "Lyndon has invited us to his ranch for barbecue. I'm not big on ribs. I'm more a champagne-and-caviar type of woman."

Right photo: Suspected assassin of JFK, **Lee Harvey Oswald,** a former U.S. marine who had briefly defected to the Soviet Union, holds up his manacled hands at police headquarters in Dallas, where he has been arrested for questioning about the death of both a Dallas police officer and the U.S. president. At that very hour, Oswald was becoming one of the most famous names, with one of the most recognizable faces, in the world.

Earlier, he'd told police, "I'm being framed. I didn't shoot Kennedy, although millions of his enemies will make a hero of the man who did it. But it wasn't me."

New testimony of the type of ammunition used in the assassination raises questions about whether Oswald acted alone, according to a study by researchers at Texas A&M University.

"Don't Go to Dallas, Mr. President."

"God dammit, I hate flying to Texas. I had to practically wring Jackie's neck to get her to go with me. I just hate to go. I have a terrible feeling about going."
> —**Jack Kennedy** to Senator George Smathers

"I didn't want him to go to Texas. I was afraid for him. A lot of people in the south and a hell of a lot of people in Texas hated Jack. They'd like to see him dead, and there are a lot of guns in Texas. Up to the last minute, I begged him not to go. I claimed he could plead illness with his back. He appeared almost fatalistic on our final night together. He told me, 'If God wants me to end my life on Texas soil, then so be it.'"
> —**LeMoyne Billings**

"Both Bobby and Adali Stevenson warned Jack it was dangerous landing in Texas. But Johnson practically begged him to go to save his own political neck."
> —**Jackie Kennedy**

"If anyone wants to kill Jack or me, it won't be difficult."
> —**Robert F. Kennedy**

"I woke up this morning with the strangest feeling. You know how I always feel something in my gut before anyone else has a clue. Well, this morning I felt I was going to become President of the United States before nightfall."
> —**Lyndon B. Johnson** to Lady Bird

"There can be little doubt that the Warren Commission came to the unvoiced conclusion that it might be all for the best if Oswald turned out to be homosexual. That would have the advantage of explaining much even if it explained nothing at all. In 1964 homosexuality was still seen as one of those omnibus infections of the spirit that could lead to God knows what further aberration."
> —**Norman Mailer**

CAMELOT

Associated Press

President Kennedy had only moments to live when a bystander snapped this shot of JFK (right-hand figure in the rear passenger seat) with First Lady **Jacqueline Kennedy** on his left. The pink hat so clearly visible in this photograph was about to become the most famous fashion accessory in the world. The whereabouts of that hat is unknown today, although there's a rumor that it was acquired by a drag queen who lives in Connecticut. Although elderly, he is said to bring it out of storage to wear on special occasions.

Following the ill-fated limousine is another limousine filled with Secret Service agents, some of them standing on the running boards. JFK might have had a chance if the second bullet hadn't struck him.

In *The Dark Side of Camelot,* Seymour Hersh wrote: "In September, 1963, while frolicking poolside with one of his sexual partners, JFK tore a groin muscle. He had to wear a stiff shoulder-to-groin brace that locked his body in a rigid upright position. It was far more constraining than his usual back brace, which [in addition] he [also] continued to wear. [Collectively,] the two braces made it impossible for JFK to bend in reflex when he was struck in the neck by a bullet fired by Lee Harvey Oswald. The president remained erect for the fatal shot from Oswald."

A Life Ends, a Legend Begins

Associated Press

Veiled, and wearing a black mourning suit, Jacqueline Kennedy is seen leaving St. Matthew's Cathedral in Washington, D.C., before the funeral procession of her late husband, President John F. Kennedy. The date was November 25, 1963.

Waking up that morning, Jackie had asked her staff, "Where am I going to live with my children?" All morning, she'd been receiving calls and telegrams for her to launch an investigation into her husband's death. But she told Bobby Kennedy, "Will it bring Jack back? I don't think so."

That day, the dignitaries of the world would come to pay homage to her, Charles de Gaulle requesting a private meeting. Eight chiefs of states and eleven heads of government waited to greet her. Queen Elizabeth II sent Prince Philip.

In Washington, D.C., before boarding Air Force One with Jackie, President John F. Kennedy was handed an urgent telegram. It was from evangelist Billy Graham. "Last night God spoke to me, warning me to tell you not to get on that plane. Don't go to Texas today!"

"Hell with that!" JFK said. "Graham is a preacher, not a prophet. C'mon, Jackie."

Before the plane touched down in Texas, Jackie could not control her nervousness. She feared what might happen on this tour, which called for them to visit the major cities in Texas, coming to a farewell stop at the LBJ Ranch where the Vice President and Lady Bird had planned a mammoth barbecue—"downhome Texas style"—and a horseback ride for Jackie.

On the plane, Jackie worked on a speech with Pamela Turnure, her press secretary. The young woman was a Jackie look-alike. The First Lady was well aware that her press secretary had been involved with her husband since her days as a Georgetown debutante. Before becoming press secretary to Jackie, back in the 1950s, Pamela had worked in JFK's senatorial office.

In Georgetown, Pamela's landlord, a strict and uncompromising Catholic, Florence Kater, had become aware of Jack's late night visits to Pamela. The moral crusader became so outraged at this adulterous affair that she tried to derail JFK's presidential campaign.

A one-woman crusader, Kater was the first major source of exposure for the young politician's womanizing. She even took a photograph of Jack leaving Pamela's apartment at three o'clock in the morning.

That photograph taken on July 11, 1958 when Jack was a highly visible celebrity in the U.S. Senate, was sent to all the major newspapers, magazines, and TV stations in the country. But except for a veiled reference in the

Washington Star, media ignored this assault. Kater even sent information she'd gathered on the Kennedy/Turnure affair to J. Edgar Hoover at the FBI. The director merely filed it in his ever-growing dossier on JFK.

Kater even placed a tape recorder in an air vent funneling into Pamela's bedroom so she could record sounds of her lovemaking with JFK.

When he staged political rallies in his run for president in 1960, Kater showed up with signs denouncing him as an adulterer. She even flew to Independence, Missouri, to picket the home of former president Harry S Truman, when JFK came to call. She also appealed to Joseph P. Kennedy, who ignored her as a Kook, and she even called on Cardinal Richard Cushing, who advised her to devote all this time, energy, and money to more worthy causes. Finally, in desperation bordering on fanaticism, she picketed the White House.

Kater didn't need to inform Jackie of her husband's affair with Pamela. The First Lady had long been aware of it. She agreed to accept Pamela as her press secretary mainly as a means of "keeping an eye on her."

At one point aboard the flight to Texas, JFK called Pamela to the back of Air Force One to take an important letter. She was gone for nearly forty-five minutes. Jackie later recalled to Kennedy aide, David Powers, "I was sure a mile-high fuck was going on, but I decided not to make a scene. After all, there was press aboard."

The flight from Andrews Air Force Base to San Antonio took three-and-one-half-hours, followed by forty-five minute flights to Houston and then Fort Worth. At all three airports, Jack and Jackie had greeted hundreds of fans and supporters, along with the idly curious. Only a few minor right-wing protesters showed up.

So far, the whole Texas trip had passed like a blur before Jackie's eyes. It had gone reasonably well, although she'd told Pamela, "I think my smile has become ingrained on my face, like it was captured in stone."

The following morning aboard the brief flight to Dallas, in a seat beside her husband, Jackie sat rigidly on the final lap of the journey, the flight to Love Field in Dallas. Once again, LBJ and Lady Bird would be waiting to greet them as they had so many times before.

That previous night in their three-room suite

Associated Press

Jackie Kennedy (*center*) shows **Empress Farah of Iran** (aka Farah Pahlavi, aka Farah Diba) the White House grounds on April 12, 1962. In the background is **Pamela Turnure,** Jackie's press secretary—or "The White House Concubine" as Jackie referred to her behind her back. Jackie is seen restraining Caroline's pony, Macaroni, which had been nuzzling the daffodils held by Farah.

During her reign (beginning with her marriage to the Shah of Iran in 1959 until her exile from Iran in 1979), Farah was referred to as "Tehran's Jackie O." Reporters pointed out the similarities between the Empress of Iran and the Empress of America—both of them symbols of fashion and glamour. Both women lost a powerful husband at an early age, and both endured numerous triumphs and tragedies. Both were left widows to rear their children alone. Like Jackie, Farah was also beautiful, charismatic, and a patron of the arts.

at the Hotel Texas in Fort Worth, she had not been able to sleep. When she'd pulled back the draperies in her own bedroom, she was greeted with a pink neon sign proclaiming BEST RIBS IN TEXAS. The sign would advertise its outrageous claim throughout her final night with JFK.

He'd injured his back once again—she did not want to speculate as to how—but she decided to enter into his adjoining bedroom. Nude except for a back brace, he had not even turned down the bed covers, but lay on top of them, reading a newspaper.

She'd become sexually aroused and made her intentions obvious. Even in physical pain, he always managed to make love on demand.

"Jackie," he protested. 'It's too soon after Patrick's birth." He was referring to their lost child. "I might hurt you."

She was far too gone at that point, and she straddled him, moving her body up and down over him, arousing him. As he had so many times before, he gave her the orgasm she wanted before he collapsed underneath her, exhausted after three days on the campaign trail. She put a blanket over him before turning out the light on his nightstand.

***

Aboard the flight to Dallas, he saw something in the paper that attracted his attention, causing consternation. It was a black-bordered announcement in a Dallas newspaper calling him a "50 times fool" for signing the nuclear test ban treaty with the Soviet Union.

He handed the paper to her. "You know, last night would have been a hell of a night to assassinate a president. I mean it. There was the rain and the night, and we were getting jostled. Suppose a man had a pistol in a briefcase." He mocked pulling the trigger of a gun. "Then he could have dropped the gun and the briefcase and melted away in the crowd."

She paid no attention to the paper, but complained and worried about how her hair would survive in a open-air limousine instead of a bubble top. She had wanted a bubble top but he'd overruled her. "The people will want to see me."

Looking at another early morning newspaper from Dallas, he'd read accusations that he was soft on communism while he allowed his brother, the attorney general, to prosecute loyal Americans. That ad was paid for by the right-wing John Birch Society, who had labeled him a "Communist sympathizer."

"We're heading into nut country today," he told her.

Before disembarking at Love Field, JFK said, "Show those Texas broads a lady with style."

The time was exactly 11:30AM, as Air Force One winged in for a smooth landing. JFK and Jackie walked down the ramp to a boisterous crowd of supporters and enemies. He managed to read only one sign: HELP KENNEDY STAMP OUT DEMOCRACY!

Lyndon and Lady Bird Johnson waited at the bottom of the ramp to welcome them.

Getting into the back of a big blue Lincoln limousine, Jackie felt she was melting in her pink Chanel wool suit. She squinted her eyes to protect herself from the sun, and reached into her purse for her sunglasses and put them on. He ordered her to take them off. "It's important that the people along the motorcade route see you."

Ten minutes after the airplane came to a stop, the Presidential motorcade pulled out of the airport. The Secret Service estimated that it would take forty-five minutes to reach downtown Dallas.

She'd resented getting into the open-air limousine with Texas governor John Connally and his wife Nellie. Before disembarking from the plane, she'd told Jack that, "I hate that smug Connally with his petulant, self-indulgent mouth. I just can't bear sitting with him in that limousine listening to him praise himself."

"Let's be friendly," he said. "I hear he may be planning to challenge me for the nomination next year." His right hand touched his stomach. "I've got these awful cramps."

"Then maybe you'll keep it zipped up in Dallas," she scolded him.

***

As Franklin D. Roosevelt might have said, November 22, 1963 would be a day that would live in infamy in American history. Almost everyone in the world heard of that day, and would remember it.

Not only that, but thousands came forth with "eyewitness" accounts even though many of them were nowhere near the motorcade.

Robert Morton, an avid Kennedy fan, even though his wife was a staunch Republican, was also a bird watcher. He'd arrived at Dealey Plaza before anyone else. The route of the motorcade had been published in the newspaper. He decided that the best vantage point to see Jack and Jackie was from a grassy knoll whose summit rose a few feet higher than the pavement of Elm Street.

As he looked around him, no one else had appeared on the knoll. He glanced at his watch. It was 7AM.

In the air, high above the looming bulk of the Texas School Book Depository, he saw a flight of birds winging in, eventually landing on the roof of the building. He prided himself in knowing all the bird species, but didn't recognize this type of bird. They were black but they weren't crows.

He was amazed he couldn't identify the species. The birds didn't stay long. Something must have frightened them. Maybe someone had come onto the roof. In the distance he saw a young man with a rifle pointing down at Elm Street where the motorcade would pass by. He aimed his rifle at the street.

But he didn't seem to like this stake-out and quickly disappeared inside the building. Morton wondered of this could be a possible assassin. He thought at first he might report it to the police, but decided against it. He didn't want to appear to be a fool.

As the sun rose higher in the sky, more and more people appeared on the grassy knoll. After seeing that man with a rifle, he'd become suspicious of anyone. He felt the knoll would be an ideal perch in which to assassinate a president. Three men who stood together looked suspicious. They were obviously from out of town, and were wearing

375

overcoats although the weather hardly called for that. Did one of the overcoats conceal a rifle? It seemed to him that a lot of people in Dallas would like to see Jack Kennedy end his presidency on this particular day.

In the distance he saw the motorcade approaching. He was relieved because he'd grown tired of waiting for it and he was hungry. The three men were still there and hadn't removed their overcoats even in the noon-day sun. Morton moved as far away from them as he could.

The next few minutes would become a blur, although until the end of his life he would attempt to describe what he saw that day to anyone willing to listen to him.

He heard the sound of gunfire but wasn't sure where the shots were coming from. Everything happened so suddenly. Eventually, all he could remember was the sight of those three men in overcoats running from the grassy knoll.

Morton later told his wife, "I think those strange black birds landing on the roof of the Depository was a very bad omen. A very bad omen indeed."

***

In the home of Lee Harvey Oswald on the morning of November 22, the clock alarm went off exactly at seven o'clock. Oswald's wife, Marina, had risen at 6:30 and was in the kitchen preparing a light breakfast. When she heard the alarm, she assumed he would be getting up to go to work at the Texas School Book Depository, a job he hated. "I'd much rather read books than sell them," he'd told her.

After ten minutes, when he hadn't come into the kitchen, she went to see what was happening, finding him still asleep. He'd been up for most of the night, pacing the floor. She wondered if he were planning to leave her for another woman. He hadn't been very attentive lately.

She shook him awake. He bolted up in bed, looking alarmed. He checked the clock. "Fuck!" he shouted to her. "I overslept. I'll miss my ride to work."

She returned to the kitchen and asked him if he could grab something for breakfast.

"Don't have time," he shouted back at her, racing out the door. Through her kitchen window, she watched him go. He was carrying "a package of some sort…in a heavy brown bag. What was it and why would he be taking it to work?"

As it was later discovered, the package contained a mail-order Italian rifle he'd purchased shortly before JFK's arrival in Dallas.

A neighbor, Linnie Mae Randle, was also standing at her kitchen sink and looking out the window as she saw Oswald approach her carport carrying a package. She'd later describe it as "something in a heavy brown bag."

He opened the rear door of her brother's car and put the package in the backseat.

She told her brother, Buell Wesley Frazier, who also worked at the Book Depository, that Oswald had arrived and was waiting for him in the car. Taking a final sip of black coffee, Frazier glanced at his watch and got up. He kissed his sister goodbye and hurried outside to the carport. Oswald was already in the passenger's seat.

Getting into the driver's seat, Frazier noticed the brown package resting on the seat in the rear. "What's that?" he asked.

"Just some curtain rods," Oswald said.

Fearing they would be late for work, Frazier didn't ask any more questions, but would later wonder why Oswald was taking curtain rods to work. Shouldn't he have left them at home?

Breaking the speed limit, Frazier parked his car about two blocks north of the depository, the only available space nearby.

Oswald seemed nervous and in a big hurry as he quickly removed the package from the rear seat. Without thanking Frazier for the ride or saying goodbye, he walked rapidly ahead.

All the way to the employee entrance to the Depository, Oswald stayed at least 50 yards ahead of Frazier and never once looked back. Frazier thought that was strange, but then, he had always considered Oswald an oddball.

The last time Frazier ever saw Oswald was the sight of him entering the Depository with that mysterious package.

***

On November 22, when JFK was in that Dallas motorcade, elsewhere in the world, including Washington and Paris, the business of government was grinding on in a potentially deadly, ruinous way.

Burkett Van Kirk, the minority counsel of the Senate Rules Committee, was hearing damaging evidence from Donald Reynolds, a Washington insurance broker, that Lyndon Johnson and Bobby Baker had accepted *payola*. Also, reputation-destroying evidence was being provided that the president at the White House had engaged in an extended sexual liaison with a communist spy, who may have been employed by the KGB to learn and then transmit vital U.S. government secrets.

Even Lady Bird Johnson was implicated in accepting gifts she'd selected from a sales catalogue.

The hearing was interrupted when a hysterical secretary burst into the chamber with breaking news out of Dallas. "A Secret Service agent just called from Texas," she shouted. "An assassin blew off Kennedy's head."

The committee members looked at each other in stunned disbelief. It seemed pointless to be investigating the misdeeds of a dead president. Political bases had to be attended to, as the power structure in Washington had just become radically unhinged. What did it matter anymore that Lady Bird got a free deluxe stereo and some advertising money for one of her radio stations, and that Lyndon had done some arm twisting to encourage people to come forth with gifts?

The sexual misdeeds of JFK and his communist prostitutes were hardly worth investigating anymore. In fact, to air such charges would probably invoke the condemnation of the American people, who would no doubt go into a prolonged state of mourning.

From this moment forth, each of the committee members would be facing the press with only praise for America's slain leader.

**

At the precise moment that JFK was shot in Dallas, an undercover CIA agent in a Paris hotel was presenting former Cuban student radical, Rolando Cubela, with a "poison pen," an actual fountain pen designed for the assassination of Fidel Castro.

Although this sounded like something out of a James Bond movie, the pen, with its syringe full of poison, was to be presented to the Cuban leader and somehow it could lead to his death when he used it. Cubela was still trusted in Castro's inner circle and was still allowed to meet with him privately.

Since the details of such a mission have never been made public, it remains a mystery how the poison in the pen could enter Castro's blood stream. Somehow the pen, filled with Black Flag 40, a commercially sold insecticide, was to be used like a hypodermic needle. Was Cubela instructed to jab the point of the pen into Castro's arm or hand? If he had done so, it would surely have been a suicide mission.

**

U.S. flags were flapping in the wind as William Greer, the driver of the presidential limousine, turned onto Elm Street heading for Dealey Plaza, which was about to become the most talked about square in the world. It was a three-acre, triangular shaped park with grass and concrete pergolas.

The motorcade was on the way to the Trade Mart where the president was to address a luncheon. As the limousine neared the Texas School Book Depository, Nellie Connally said to JFK in one of the most ironic statements made on that fateful day: "Mr. President, you can't say Dallas doesn't love you."

"No, you can't," the president said, waving at the crowds. A rumor spread that Nellie Connally claimed that she heard Jack's promise to his wife. "After last night, there will be no more women—only you. That's one promise I'll keep for the rest of my life."

Jackie is alleged to have responded, "Oh, Jack, if only you meant that."

A sudden sound of gunfire, thought at first to be the backfiring of a police motorcycle, startled the passengers in the limousines, including Lyndon and Lady Bird Johnson in the rear of the motorcade, as well as the sightseers along Dealey Plaza, including those on the grassy knoll.

JFK cried out, "My God, I'm hit."

Those were the last words he'd ever utter.

The mysterious first shot missed, the second shot—the infamous "magic bullet"—hit both the president and the governor, who was riding with his wife on the jump seat just in front of the president and Jackie. The bullet entered JFK's back and exited through his throat.

Still on a deadly course, the bullet was said to have then struck Governor Connally in the shoulder, exiting from his chest and continuing through to then pierce his right wrist, which he was holding at the time in front of his body. Finally exiting, the incredible bullet, if reports are to be believed, came to a stop in the Texan's left thigh.

Until the moment it was deflected by the governor's rib, the bullet, according to expert testimony, didn't make any detours in its deadly direction.

Connally's wife, Nellie, jerked her wounded husband into her lab and out of the line of fire, using her own body as a shield from further shots.

JFK's last view on Earth was of a Hertz-Rent-a Car sign atop the Texas School Book Depository. Its clock signaled 12:30 in the afternoon, his last minute alive.

A back brace held JFK erect to receive the third and fatal shot to the back of his head. A Secret Service agent compared the sound of the third bullet to "that of a melon shattering on the sidewalk."

Amazingly, Jackie, looking to her right, was staring into the face of the president when the third bullet struck, splattering his brains in every direction, including onto her dress.

When Secret Service Agent Clint Hill saw the president's head, he compared the wound to a "bloody, gaping, fist-sized hole clearly visible in the back of his head."

The third shot blew away the right rear quadrant of his skull, which splattered brain tissue and a cloud of blood onto Jackie's pink suit. She looked in horror at the part of Jack's skull that was missing, taking in the gushing, cavernous wound. "They've killed Jack!" she screamed. "They've killed my husband! Jack, Jack!"

Her last words were "Jack! Jack! I love you!"

Before the Warren Commission, she gave false testimony. "I was looking this way to the left," she told the commissioners. "I used to think if only I had been looking to the right I would have seen the first shot that hit him, then I could have pulled him down, and then the second shot would not have hit him."

A film shot by Abraham Zapruder, a Dallas manufacturer of woman's lingerie, proved that her testimony was incorrect. She actually was looking to the right, almost in stunned disbelief, at her husband for seven seconds without pulling him down.

When she swung into action, it was to save herself. She'd heard the governor's anguished cry of pain, "God, they're going to kill all of us!"

In a moment of panic, she climbed onto the trunk of the limousine, ostensibly to reach a large rubber handgrip at the rear of the trunk. If she could manage that, she would have had a means of egress from the fatal vehicle. At this point, however, the Secret Service agent driving the car accelerated, rushing to the nearest hospital to try to save the life of the dying president.

Agent Hill jumped onto the rear of the limousine and shoved Jackie back into her blood-soaked seat where she made the historic ride with a husband who was merely breathing at this point.

On the way to the hospital, six miles away, Jackie held her husband in her arms, shielding him from view. Hill begged her to let him go until he figured out why she was doing that. She didn't want the public to see her husband with his splattered brains. He ripped off his coat and covered the president's head.

Her cowardice was downplayed by the press. Jackie testified that she had attempted to crawl out onto the trunk to retrieve a piece of her husband's brain. Actually, in trying to escape from her seat, she accidentally kicked what was left of JFK's gun-blasted, bullet-ridden head.

In a Lincoln convertible two vehicles behind the Kennedy limousine, Lyndon B. Johnson became the thirty-sixth president of the United States. He assumed leadership of the Free World while crouched down on the floor of the speeding limousine, his body shielded by Secret Service agent Rufus Youngblood.

On March 9, 1964, in front of the Warren Commission, Secret Service agent Roy Kellerman claimed, "A flurry of shells came into the car." He was the man closest to the shots.

Of the 178 witnesses at the scene on that fateful day, 61 claimed the shots came from a grassy knoll in front of the presidential motorcade. Some believed the shots came from the Book Depository itself. Others stated that they were not certain where the shots originated—"perhaps from several directions."

The official conclusion was that three bullets were fired in six seconds from a window of the book depository, and that the lone assassin was Lee Harvey Oswald.

The number of rounds of gunfire and the identity of the assassins will no doubt be debated a hundred years from now.

As in the assassination of Abraham Lincoln, conspiracy theories abound.

***

When he got to the Parkland Hospital with Lady Bird, Johnson demanded a full report from a Secret Service agent. Under his breath, he muttered, "The torch has passed." It was almost as if he were talking to himself, and not to Lady Bird.

A shell-shocked Jackie confronted Dr. M.T. ("Pepper") Jenkins in the corridor at the Parkland Hospital where her slain husband had been wheeled into the trauma room, his clothing cut from his body. According to the doctor's later testimony, "I noticed that Mrs. Kennedy's hands were cupped in front of her, as she circled around. She was cradling something. As she passed by me, she handed it to me. I took it. It was slimy. I determined it was a big chunk of the president's brain tissue. Long before TV programs were interrupted around the world with a bulletin, I knew that John F. Kennedy had gone to meet his maker."

At this point, Jackie rushed past two Secret Service agents into the trauma room.

Just as she entered the door, she saw a priest giving her husband the last rites of the Catholic Church. She dropped down on the floor in a pool of blood, and she heard the final words spoken over the body. "Eternal rest grant unto him, O Lord." The priest blessed the president's head with oil.

In a barely understood murmur, Jackie said, "Let perpetual light shine upon him."

Then, according to a doctor, Jackie did a strange thing. She pulled back the white sheet that had covered her husband's body. She'd perhaps never seen him so naked, so exposed before. She slipped her hand under his penis for one final caress before a

Secret Service agent gently pulled her away and covered up, once again, the nude body of the slain president.

Before JFK was laid in a bronze casket to fly to Washington, she kissed JFK's lips lightly. "Goodbye, forever, my darling."

On Air Force One, after Johnson had been sworn in as the new president, Jackie sat in the back of the plane, as David Powers held her hand. She told him, "This is the first day of the rest of my life, a life without Jack. I still have my children. I must protect them."

HISTORY'S MOST FAMOUS FAREWELL SALUTE FROM A THREE-YEAR-OLD

***

At his home, Hickory Hill, Robert F. Kennedy had just had a swim in his backyard pool. Ethel had prepared him a tunafish sandwich for lunch.

The phone rang in the hallway. Ethel picked up the receiver. "This is J. Edgar Hoover. I must speak to your husband at once. Get him at once. *At once!*"

On the phone, the FBI director was blunt. "The president has been shot in Dallas. I'm told he's either dead or has only moments to live. His brain was splattered everywhere. Lyndon thinks he's next. He suspects a nuclear attack any minute on the United States."

***

Two days after the assassination of President John F. Kennedy, a veteran who'd served with Oswald in the Marine Corps spoke to a reporter: "One night in a bar he [Oswald] told me that he was going to become the second most famous man in America and would go down in history books."

The former marine claimed, "I chided him. Oh, sure you will. What's your ambition? To become president of the United States? With your record, you can forget that. What a pipe dream."

JACK, WE HARDLY KNEW YOU!

Associated Press

IN MEMORIAM / REST IN PEACE
JOHN FITZGERALD KENNEDY
MAY 29, 1917 - NOVEMBER 22, 1963

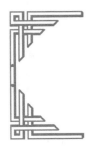

About the Authors

Darwin Porter

One of the world's leading celebrity biographers, **Darwin Porter**, as an intense and precocious nine-year-old, began meeting movie stars, TV personalities, politicians, and singers through his vivacious and attractive mother, Hazel, a somewhat eccentric Southern girl who had lost her husband in World War II. Migrating from the depression-ravaged valleys of western North Carolina to Miami Beach during its most ebullient heyday, Hazel became a stylist, wardrobe mistress, and personal assistant to the vaudeville comedienne Sophie Tucker, the bawdy and irrepressible "Last of the Red Hot Mamas."

Virtually every show-biz celebrity who visited Miami Beach paid a call on "Miss Sophie," and Darwin as a pre-teen loosely and indulgently supervised by his mother, was regularly dazzled by the likes of Judy Garland, Dinah Shore, Veronica Lake, Linda Darnell, Martha Raye, and Ronald Reagan, who arrived to pay his respects to Miss Sophie with a young blonde starlet on the rise—Marilyn Monroe.

Hazel's work for Sophie Tucker did not preclude an active dating life: Her *beaux* included Richard Widmark, Victor Mature, Frank Sinatra (who "tipped" teenaged Darwin the then-astronomical sum of ten dollars for getting out of the way), and that alltime "second lead," Wendell Corey, when he wasn't emoting with Barbara Stanwyck and Joan Crawford.

As a late teenager, Darwin edited *The Miami Hurricane* at the University of Miami, where he interviewed Eleanor Roosevelt, Tab Hunter, Lucille Ball, and Adlai Stevenson. He also worked for Florida's then-Senator George Smathers, one of John F. Kennedy's best friends, establishing an ongoing pattern of picking up "Jack and Jackie" lore while still a student.

After graduation, as a journalist, he was commissioned with the opening of a bureau of *The Miami Herald* in Key West (Florida), where he took frequent morning walks with retired U.S. president Harry S Truman during his vacations in what had functioned as his "Winter White House." He also got to know, sometimes very well, various celebrities "slumming" their way through off-the-record holidays in the orbit of then-resident Tennessee Williams. Celebrities hanging out in the permissive arts environment of Key West during those days included Tallulah Bankhead, Cary Grant, Tony Curtis, the stepfather of Richard Burton, a gaggle of show-biz and publishing moguls, and the once-notorious stripper, Bettie Page.

For about a decade in New York, Darwin worked in television journalism and advertising with his long-time partner, the journalist, art director, and distinguished arts-industry socialite Stanley Mills Haggart. Jointly, they produced TV commercials starring such high-powered stars as Joan Crawford (then feverishly promoting Pepsi-Cola), Ronald Reagan (General Electric), and Debbie Reynolds (selling Singer Sewing Machines), along with such other entertainers as Louis Armstrong, Lena Horne, Arlene Dahl, and countless other show-biz personalities hawking commercial products.

During his youth, Stanley had flourished as an insider in early Hollywood as a "leg man" and source of information for Hedda Hopper, the fabled gossip columnist. When Stanley wasn't dishing newsy revelations with Hedda, he had worked as a Powers model; a romantic lead opposite Silent-era film star Mae Murray; the intimate companion of superstar Randolph Scott before Scott became emotionally involved with Cary Grant; and a man-about-town who archived gossip from everybody who mattered back when the movie colony was small, accessible, and confident that details about their tribal rites would absolutely never be reported in the press. Over the years, Stanley's vast cornucopia of inside Hollywood information was passed on to Darwin, who amplified it with copious interviews and research of his own.

After Stanley's death in 1980, Darwin inherited a treasure trove of memoirs, notes, and interviews detailing Stanley's early adventures in Hollywood, including in-depth recitations of scandals that even Hedda Hopper during her heyday was afraid to publish. Most legal and journalistic standards back then interpreted those oral histories as "unprintable." Times, of course, changed.

Beginning in the early 1960s, Darwin joined forces with the then-fledgling Arthur Frommer organization, playing a key role in researching and writing more than 50 titles and defining the style and values that later emerged as the world's leading travel accessories, THE FROMMER GUIDES, with particular emphasis on Europe, California, and the Caribbean. Between the creation and updating of hundreds of editions of detailed travel guides to England, France, Italy, Spain, Portugal, Austria, Germany, California, and Switzerland, he continued to interview and discuss the triumphs, feuds, and frustrations of celebrities, many by then reclusive, whom he either sought out or encountered randomly as part of his extensive travels.

Darwin has also written several novels, including the best-selling cult classic *Butterflies in Heat* (which was later made into a film, *Tropic of Desire,* starring Eartha Kitt), *Venus* (inspired by the life of the fabled eroticist and diarist, Anaïs Nin), and *Midnight in Savannah,* a satirical overview of the sexual eccentricities of the Deep South inspired by Savannah's most notorious celebrity murder. He also transformed into literary format the details which he and Stanley Haggart had compiled about the relatively underpublicized scandals of the Silent Screen, releasing them in 2001 as *Hollywood's Silent Closet,* "an uncensored, underground history of Pre-Code Hollywood, loaded with facts and rumors from generations past." A few years later, he did the same for the country-western music industry when he issued *Rhinestone Country.*

Since then, Darwin has penned more than a dozen uncensored Hollywood biographies, many of them award-winners, on subjects who have included Marlon Brando, Merv Griffin, Katharine Hepburn, Howard Hughes, Humphrey Bogart, Michael Jackson, Paul Newman, and Steve McQueen. He's also co-authored, in league with Danforth Prince, three *Hollywood Babylon* anthologies, plus four separate volumes of film critiques, reviews, and commentary.

In 2011, Darwin, along with co-author Roy Moseley, won a staggering total of four literary awards for *Damn You, Scarlett O'Hara—The Private Lives of Vivien Leigh and Laurence Olivier.* They included either First Prizes or Honorable Mentions from the San Francisco, Paris, and New York Book Festivals, and the coveted Grand Prize from the Beach Book Festival, which defined that title as "The Best Summer Reading of 2011," and as "the most forthright and honest biography of the Romeo and Juliet of the 20th century ever published."

Darwin is presently at work on *Frank Sinatra, The Boudoir Singer,* wherein scads of witnesses testify, often for the first time, about how 'Ol Blue Eyes did indeed do things His Way.

Darwin can be heard at regular interviews as a radio commentator discussing celebrity events, pop culture, and politics. He's also a Hollywood columnist, pouring out bi-weekly and monthly newsletters which include *Blood Moon's Dirty Laundry*, which anyone can receive without charge by registering an email address at **www.BloodMoonProductions.com**. Additionally, through South Florida's *Boomer Times Magazine*, he crafts a monthly column, *Hollywood Remembered,* about the complicated and competitive lives of modern-day players in politics and the Entertainment Industry.

✯✯✯✯✯

Danforth Prince

Danforth Prince, president and founder of Blood Moon Productions and co-author of this book, is the hottest producer and publisher of celebrity exposés in America. In 2011, a respected Hollywood consortium of literary critics and book marketers, The Beach Book Festival, defined him as "Publisher of the Year."

Publishing in collaboration with the National Book Network, he has documented some of the controversies associated with his work in more than 30 videotaped documentaries and book trailers, all of which can be watched, without charge, either on his company's website, **www.BloodMoonProductions.com,** or by performing a search on YouTube or Vimeo.com.

During his early 20s, Prince was a resident of France, studying religion at the Catholic Institute and supporting himself as a building contractor, translator, and salesman in Paris' garment district. Prince launched his journalistic career in 1976 in the Paris bureau of *The New York Times.* Since his original encounter with Darwin Porter in 1982, he has also functioned as the co-author and director of research for as many as 50 of THE FROMMER GUIDES, describing and reviewing the hotels, restaurants, nightclubs, and cultural monuments of France, England, Italy, Germany, Switzerland, Austria, Portugal, Spain, Hungary, Morocco, the Caribbean, and America's Deep South.

A graduate of Hamilton College, and proud of his Moravian roots in Bethlehem, Pennsylvania, and distant ancestral roots to Harriet Beecher Stowe, he is a resident of New York City.

The Kennedys-Index

If you liked this book, check out these other titles from

BLOOD MOON PRODUCTIONS

Entertainment About How America Interprets Its Celebrities

Blood Moon Productions is a New York-based publishing enterprise dedicated to researching, salvaging, and indexing the oral histories of America's entertainment industry. Reorganized with its present name in 2004, Blood Moon originated in 1997 as The Georgia Literary Assn., a vehicle for the promotion of obscure writers from America's Deep South.

Blood Moon's authors, administration, and staff are associated with some of the writing, research, and editorial functions of THE FROMMER GUIDES, a subdivision of John Wiley & Sons, a respected name in travel publishing. Blood Moon also maintains a back list of at least 20 critically acclaimed biographies and film guides. Its titles are distributed within North America and Australia by the National Book Network (www.NBNBooks.com), within the U.K. by Turnaround (www.Turnaround-uk.com), and through secondary wholesalers and online everywhere.

Since 2004, Blood Moon has been awarded at least sixteen nationally recognized literary prizes. They've included both silver and bronze medals from the IPPY (Independent Publishers Assn.) Awards; four nominations and two Honorable Mentions for BOOK OF THE YEAR from Foreword Reviews; and Awards and Honorable Mentions from the New England, the Los Angeles, the Paris, the New York, and the Hollywood Book Festivals.

For more about us, including free subscription to our scandalous bi-weekly celebrity dish (**BLOOD MOON'S DIRTY LAUNDRY**) and access to a growing number of videotaped book trailers, click on **WWW.BLOODMOONPRODUCTIONS.COM** or refer to the pages which immediately follow.

Thanks for your interest, best wishes, and happy reading.

Danforth Prince, President
Blood Moon Productions Ltd.

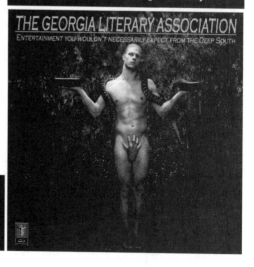

BLOOD MOON
Productions, Ltd.

Salvaging the unrecorded
histories of the Entertainment Industry's
"off the record" past

And its affiliate, the Georgia Literary Assn

THE GEORGIA LITERARY ASSOCIATION
ENTERTAINMENT YOU WOULDN'T NECESSARILY EXPECT FROM THE DEEP SOUTH

FRANK SINATRA
THE BOUDOIR SINGER

All the Gossip Unfit to Print from the
Glory Days of Ol' Blue Eyes

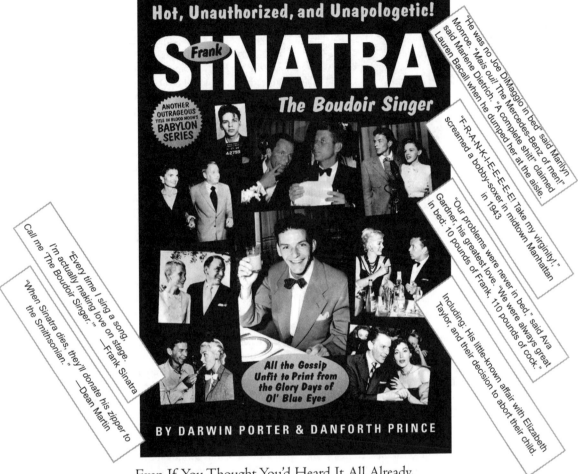

Hot, Unauthorized, and Unapologetic!

Frank SINATRA
The Boudoir Singer

ANOTHER OUTRAGEOUS TITLE IN BLOOD MOON'S BABYLON SERIES

All the Gossip Unfit to Print from the Glory Days of Ol' Blue Eyes

BY DARWIN PORTER & DANFORTH PRINCE

"He was no Joe DiMaggio in bed" said Marilyn Monroe. "Mais oui! The Mercedes-Benz of men!" said Marlene Dietrich. "A complete shit!" claimed Lauren Bacall when he dumped her at the aisle.

"F-R-A-N-K-I-E-E-E-E-E! Take my virginity!," screamed a bobby-soxer in midtown Manhattan in 1943.

"Our problems were never in bed," said Ava Gardner his greatest love. "We were always great in bed: 10 pounds of Frank, 110 pounds of cock."

Including: His little-known affair with Elizabeth Taylor, and their decision to abort their child.

"Every time I sing a song, I'm actually making love on stage. Call me 'The Boudoir Singer.'" —Frank Sinatra

"When Sinatra dies, they'll donate his zipper to the Smithsonian." —Dean Martin

Even If You Thought You'd Heard It All Already,
You'll Be Amazed At How Much This Book Contains That Never Got Published Before

Vendettas and high-octane indiscretions, fast and famous women, deep sensitivities and sporadic psychoses, suicide attempts, presidential pimping, FBI coverups, and a pantload of hushed-up scandals about

FABULOUS FRANKIE AND HIS MIND-BLOWING COHORTS!

Available September 2011

Hardcover, 425 sizzling pages with LOTS of photos
ISBN 978-1-936003-19-8 $26.95

Damn You, Scarlett O'Hara
The Private Lives of **Vivien Leigh** and **Laurence Olivier**

by **Darwin Porter** and **Roy Moseley**

HOT, SHOCKING, METICULOUSLY RESEARCHED, AND WINNER OF FOUR DISTINGUISHED LITERARY AWARDS SINCE ITS CONTROVERSIAL RELEASE IN FEBRUARY OF 2011.

Here, for the first time, is a biography that raises the curtain on the secret lives of (Lord) **Laurence Olivier**, known for his interpretation of the brooding and tormented Heathcliff of Emily Brontë's *Wuthering Heights,* and **Vivien Leigh,** who immortalized herself with her Oscar-winning portrayals of Scarlett O'Hara in Margaret Mitchell's *Gone With the Wind,* and as Blanche DuBois in Tennessee Williams' *A Streetcar Named Desire.*

Even though the spotlight shone on this famous pair throughout most of their tabloid-fueled careers, much of what went on behind the velvet curtain remained hidden from view until the publication of this ground-breaking biography. The PRIVATE LIVES (to borrow a phrase from their gossipy contemporary, Noël Coward) of this famous couple are exposed with searing insights into their sexual excess and personal anguish.

Dashing and "impossibly handsome," Laurence Olivier was pursued by some of the most dazzling luminaries, male and female, of the movie and theater worlds. The influential theatrical producer David Lewis asserted, "He would have slept with anyone." That included Richard Burton, who fell madly in love with him, as did Noël Coward. Lord Olivier's promiscuous, emotionally disturbed wife (Viv to her lovers) led a tumultuous off-the-record life whose paramours ranged from the A-list to men she picked up off the street. None of the brilliant roles depicted by Lord and Lady Olivier, on stage or on screen, ever matched the power and drama of personal dramas which wavered between Wagnerian opera and Greek tragedy. *Damn You, Scarlett O'Hara* is the definitive and most revelatory portrait ever published of the most talented and tormented actor and actress of the 20th century.

Darwin Porter is the co-author of this seminal work. Winner of numerous awards for his headline-generating biographies, he has shed new light on Marlon Brando, Steve McQueen, Paul Newman, Katharine Hepburn, Humphrey Bogart, Merv Griffin, Michael Jackson, and Howard Hughes.

Roy Moseley, this book's other co-author, was the adopted godson and intimate friend of Lord and Lady Olivier, maintaining a decades-long association with the famous couple, nurturing them through a tumultuous life of triumphs, emotional breakdowns, and streams of suppressed scandal. Moseley even had the painful honor of being present at the deathbed rituals of Lady Olivier. Moseley has authored or co-authored biographies of Queen Elizabeth and Prince Philip, Rex Harrison, Cary Grant, Merle Oberon, Roger Moore, and Moseley's long-time companion during the final years of her life, Miss Bette Davis.

DAMN YOU, SCARLETT O'HARA
THE PRIVATE LIFES OF LAURENCE OLIVIER AND VIVIEN LEIGH

by Darwin Porter and Roy Moseley
ISBN 978-1-936003-15-0   Hardcover, 708 pages, $27.95

What Pair of Famous Hollywood Sisters Refused to Forgive the Insults of their Lifelong Feud?

Of the hundreds of movie stars who flourished during the 1940s, the constantly feuding sisters, Olivia de Havilland and Joan Fontaine, outlived their contemporaries and jointly survived as the last remaining superstars of Hollywood's Golden Age. Their war with each other smoldered and flamed for more than ninety years, as they clawed at and sabotaged each other for the same roles, the same Oscar awards, and the same men. Jointly, they nurtured the movie colony's most ferocious case of sibling rivalry.

This new collaborative effort by two of the publishing industry's most respected celebrity biographers involves more than just the untold story of a primal and particularly bitter intra-sibling feud. It's a bittersweet ode to a sweeping but vanished era, with keen and startling new insights into the sisters' top-drawer colleagues and competitors, with a flooding sense of wisdom about the enduring legacy of bloodlines, no matter how blurred and complicated.

OLIVIA DE HAVILLAND AND JOAN FONTAINE
TWISTED SISTERS: TO EACH HER OWN

as relayed by

Darwin Porter and Olivia's long-time business manager, **Roy Moseley**

A Startling and Comprehensive Hardcover, with 450 pages, 125 photos, and More Scandalous Gossip than either Melanie (from *Gone With the Wind*) or the second Mrs. De Winter (from *Rebecca*) would ever have tolerated.

ISBN 978-1-936003-27-3 $27.95   Available everywhere in January of 2012

CRIMINAL ACTIVITIES AND VOYEURISTIC MANIA FROM AMERICA'S CHIEF LAW-ENFORCEMENT OFFICER

It was 1928. Into FBI Director J. Edgar Hoover's Office walked a job applicant. Clyde Tolson, fresh from America's Corn Belt. He was handsome, macho, well-built, and soft-spoken. Later, he'd be called "the Gary Cooper of the FBI."

Hoover sat up and took immediate notice of Tolson's commanding presence, especially his piercing black eyes. After an hour of chatting with Tolson, Hoover proclaimed, "Our bureau needs more men like you."

When Hoover invited Tolson to his home for dinner that night, the meal would mark the beginning of thousands served over the next forty years. Before the rooster crowed, Hoover had been nicknamed "Speed," and Tolson was called "Junior." In public, of course, Tolson referred to Hoover as "The Boss."

But as Tolson, one drunken night, told their "fag hag," Ethel Merman: "When we go home and shut the door, I'm the boss."

For their sexual amusement, but often for blackmail purposes, Junior and Speed viewed the obscene files of the FBI. Illegal wiretaps and hidden microphones were used to destroy their enemies.

"Hoover ruled as the head of America's Gestapo," claimed an angry Harry S Truman. Through nine different presidents, Hoover kept his job, even blackmailing Dwight D. Eisenhower.

The files he accumulated on "my worst enemy," Eleanor Roosevelt, silenced her opposition to him. As time went by, Hoover and Tolson opened a celebrity version of Pandora's box, learning the darkest secrets of Errol Flynn (was he a Nazi?), Marilyn Monroe, Elvis Presley, the Kennedys, Marlon Brando, Rock Hudson, and especially Martin Luther King, Jr., among countless others.

"For decades, America has been in the grip of two homosexual lovers," Lyndon B. Johnson told his pal, Florida Senator George Smathers. "And there's not a God damn thing I can do about it. He's got us by the cojones, and he'll never let go."

For nearly half a century, this peculiarly private man, who carefully guarded his own dark secrets, held virtually unchecked public power. He manipulated every president from FDR (*"Sometime, J. Edgar, we'll catch you with your pants down"*) to Richard Nixon. He used illegal wiretaps and hidden microphones to destroy anyone who opposed him. And just for fun, he and bedmate Clyde Tolson investigated Amercca's greatest entertainers, including Marilyn Monroe and Elvis Presley; its greatest scientists (including Albert Einstein), and its greated civil rights leaders.

Darwin Porter's saga of power and corruption has a revelation on every page—cross dressing, gay parties, sexual indiscretions, hustlers for sale, alliances with the Mafia, and criminal activity by the nation's chief law enforcer.

It's all here, with chilling details about the abuse of power on the dark side of the American saga.

But mostly it's the decades-long love story of America's two most powerful men who could tell presidents "how to skip rope." (Hoover's words.)

Darwin Porter has been fascinated by the American concept of fame since he worked as an entertainment columnist for The Miami Herald early in his career. Since then, he's evolved into one of the most acclaimed celebrity biographers in the world.

Coming soon from Blood Moon Productions   A mind-boggling 6" x 9" paperback, with photos

J. EDGAR HOOVER AND CLYDE TOLSON
Investigating the Sexual Secrets of America's Most Famous Men and Women

by Darwin Porter $18.95   ISBN 978-1-936003-25-9

WHAT does a man really have to do to make it in Show Biz? Finally--A COOL Biography that was too HOT to be published during the lifetime of its subject. TALES OF A LURID LIFE!

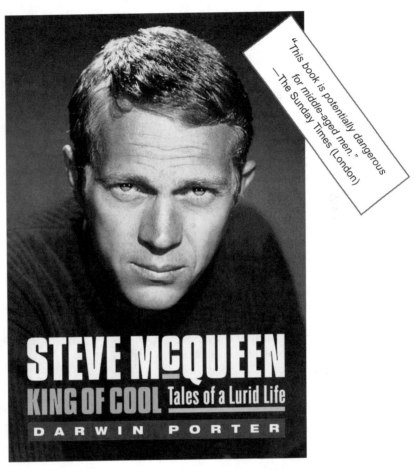

"This book is potentially dangerous for middle-aged men."
—The Sunday Times (London)

The drama of Steve McQueen's personal life far exceeded any role he ever played on screen. Born to a prostitute, he was brutally molested by some of his mother's "johns," and endured gang rape in reform school. His drift into prostitution began when he was hired as a towel boy in the most notorious bordello in the Dominican Republic, where he starred in a string of cheap porno films. Returning to New York before migrating to Hollywood, he hustled men on Times Square and, as a "gentleman escort" in a borrowed tux, rich older women.

And then, sudden stardom as he became the world's top box office attraction. The abused became the abuser. "I live for myself, and I answer to nobody," he proclaimed. "The last thing I want to do is fall in love with a broad."

Thus began a string of seductions that included hundreds of overnight pickups--both male and female. Topping his A-list conquests were James Dean, Paul Newman, Marilyn Monroe, and Barbra Streisand. Finally, this pioneering biography explores the mysterious death of Steve McQueen. Were those salacious rumors really true?

Steve McQueen   King of Cool   Tales of a Lurid Life
Darwin Porter

ISBN 978-1-936003-05-1   A carefully researched, 466-page hardcover with dozens of photos   **$26.95**

PAUL NEWMAN

THE MAN BEHIND THE BABY BLUES, HIS SECRET LIFE EXPOSED

Darwin Porter

THE MOST COMPELLING BIOGRAPHY OF THE ICONIC ACTOR EVER PUBLISHED

Drawn from firsthand interviews with insiders who knew Paul Newman intimately, and compiled over a period of nearly a half-century, this is the world's most honest and most revelatory biography about Hollywood's pre-eminent male sex symbol, with dozens of potentially shocking revelations.

Whereas the situations it exposes were widely known within Hollywood's inner circles, they've never before been revealed to the general public.

If you're a fan of Newman (and who do you know who isn't) you really should look at this book. It's a respectful but candid cornucopia of information about the sexual and emotional adventures of a young man on Broadway and in Hollywood.

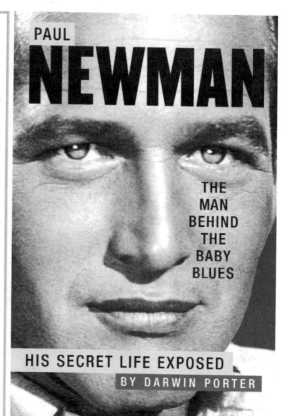

PAUL **NEWMAN**

THE MAN BEHIND THE BABY BLUES

HIS SECRET LIFE EXPOSED

BY DARWIN PORTER

PAUL NEWMAN WAS A FAMOUS, FULL-TIME RESIDENT OF CONNECTICUT. SHORTLY AFTER HIS DEATH IN 2009, THIS TITLE WON AN HONORABLE MENTION FROM HIS NEIGHBORS AT THE NEW ENGLAND BOOK FESTIVAL

This is a pioneering and posthumous biography of a charismatic American icon. His rule over the hearts of American moviegoers lasted for more than half a century. Paul Newman was a potent, desirable, and ambiguous sex symbol, a former sailor from Shaker Heights, Ohio, who parlayed his ambisexual charm and extraordinary good looks into one of the most successful careers in Hollywood.

It's all here, as recorded by celebrity chronicler Darwin Porter--the giddy heights and agonizing lows of a great American star, with revelations never before published in any other biography.

Paul Newman, The Man Behind the Baby Blues
His Secret Life Exposed

Darwin Porter
Hardcover, 520 pages, with dozens of photos.
ISBN 978-0-9786465-1-6 $26.95

"One wonders how he managed to avoid public scrutiny for so long."

MERV GRIFFIN
A Life in the Closet

Darwin Porter

"Darwin Porter told me why he tore the door off Merv's closet.......*Heeeere's Merv!* is 560 pages, 100 photos, a truckload of gossip, and a bedful of unauthorized dish."

Cindy Adams, The NY Post

"*Darwin Porter tears the door off Merv Griffin's closet with gusto in this sizzling, superlatively researched biography...It brims with insider gossip that's about Hollywood legends, writ large, smart, and with great style.*"

Richard LaBonté, BOOKMARKS

Merv Griffin, A Life in the Closet

Merv Griffin began his career as a Big Band singer, moved on to a failed career as a romantic hero in the movies, and eventually rewrote the rules of everything associated with the broadcasting industry. Along the way, he met and befriended virtually everyone who mattered, made billions operating casinos and developing jingles, contests, and word games. All of this while maintaining a male harem and a secret life as America's most famously closeted homosexual.

In this comprehensive biography--the first published since Merv's death in 2007--celebrity biographer Darwin Porter reveals the amazing details behind the richest, most successful, and in some ways, the most notorious mogul in the history of America's entertainment industry.

Most of his viewers (they numbered 20 million per day) thought that **Merv Griffin**'s life was an ongoing series of chatty segués--amiable, seamless, uncontroversial.
But things were far more complicated than viewers at the time ever thought. Here, from the writer who unzipped **Marlon Brando**, is the first post-mortem, unauthorized overview of the mysterious life of **the richest and most notorious man in television**

HOT, CONTROVERSIAL, & RIGOROUSLY RESEARCHED
HERE'S MERV! Hardcover, with photos

ISBN 978-0-9786465-0-9 $26.95

Startling New Information about Golden Age Hollywood You've Never Seen Before

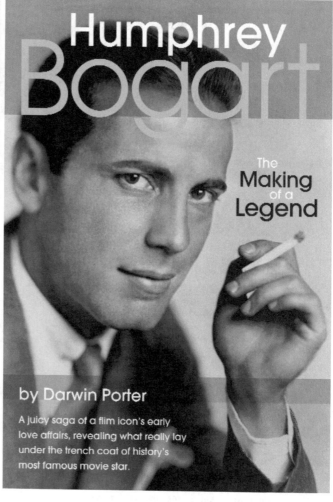

Humphrey **Bogart**

The **Making** of a **Legend**

by Darwin Porter

A juicy saga of a film icon's early love affairs, revealing what really lay under the trench coat of history's most famous movie star.

Whereas Humphrey Bogart is always at the top of any list of the Entertainment Industry's most famous actors, very little is known about how he clawed his way to stardom from Broadway to Hollywood during Prohibition and the Jazz Age.

This radical expansion of one of Darwin Porter's pioneering biographies begins with Bogart's origins as the child of wealthy (morphine-addicted) parents in New York City, then examines the scandals, love affairs, breakthrough successes, and failures that launched Bogart on the road to becoming an American icon. Drawn from original interviews with friends and foes who knew a lot about what lay beneath his trenchcoat, this exposé covers Bogart's life from his birth in 1899 till his marriage to Lauren Bacall in 1945. It includes details about behind-the-scenes dramas associated with three mysterious marriages, and films such as *The Petrified Forest, The Maltese Falcon, High Sierra,* and *Casablanca.* Read all about the debut and formative years of the actor who influenced many generations of film-goers, laying Bogie's life bare in a style you've come to expect from Darwin Porter. Exposed with all their juicy details is what Bogie never told his fourth wife, Lauren Bacall, herself a screen legend.

This revelatory book is based on dusty unpublished memoirs, letters, diaries, and often personal interviews from the women—and the men—who adored him. There are also shocking allegations from colleagues, former friends, and jilted lovers who wanted the screen icon to burn in hell. All this and more, much more, in Darwin Porter's exposé of Bogie's startling secret life.

Humphrey Bogart, The Making of a Legend
Darwin Porter
A "cradle-to-grave" hardcover, 542 pages, with hundreds of photos
ISBN 978-1-936003-14-3. $27.95

Brando Unzipped

Darwin Porter

This "entertainingly outrageous" (FRONTIERS MAGAZINE) biography provides a definitive, blow-by-blow description of the "hot, provocative, and barely under control drama" that was the life of America's most famous Postwar actor.

"Lurid, raunchy, perceptive, and certainly worth reading...One of the ten best show-biz biographies of 2006." ***The Sunday Times (London)***

"**Yummy**. An irresistably flamboyant romp of a read."
Books to Watch Out For

"Astonishing. An extraordinarily detailed portrait of Brando that's as blunt, uncompromising, and X-rated as the man himself."
Women's Weekly

"This shocking new book is sparking a major reassessment of Brando's legacy as one of Hollywood's most macho lotharios."
Daily Express (London)

"As author Darwin Porter finds, it wasn't just the acting world Marlon Brando conquered. It was the actors, too."
Gay Times (London)

"*Brando Unzipped* is the definitive gossip guide to the late, great actor's life."
The New York Daily News

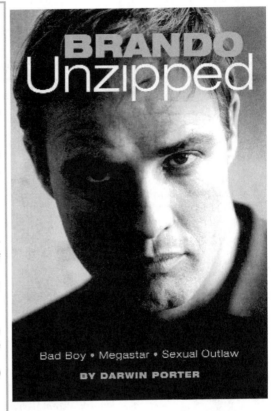

A definitive and artfully lurid hardcover with 625 indexed pages and hundreds of photos

ISBN 978-0-9748118-2-6. $26.95

This is one of our most visible and most frequently reviewed titles. A best-seller, it's now in its fifth printing, with French, Portuguese, and Dutch editions available in Europe. Shortly after its release, this title was extensively serialized by THE SUNDAY TIMES in the UK, and in other major Sunday supplements in mainland Europe and Australia.

Katharine the Great

HEPBURN

A Lifetime of Secrets Revealed

A gossippy tell-all that fans of
Old Hollywood find fascinating.

Darwin Porter
569 pages, with photos $16.95
ISBN   978-0-9748118-0-2

Katharine Hepburn was the world's greatest screen diva--the most famous actress in American history. But until the appearance of this biography, no one had ever published the intimate details of her complicated and ferociously secretive private life. Thanks to the "deferential and obsequious whitewashes" which followed in the wake of her death, readers probably know WHAT KATE REMEMBERED. Here, however, is an unvarnished account of what Katharine Hepburn desperately wanted to forget.

"Behind the scenes of her movies, Katharine Hepburn played the temptress to as many women as she did men, ranted and raved with her co-stars and directors, and broke into her neighbors' homes for fun. And somehow, she managed to keep all of it out of the press. As they say, Katharine the Great is hard to put down."

The Dallas Voice

"The door to Hepburn's closet has finally been opened. This is the most honest and least apologetic biography of Hollywood's most ferociously private actress ever written."

Senior Life Magazine, Miami

"In Porter's biography of Katharine Hepburn, details about the inner workings of a movie studio (RKO in the early 30s), are relished."

The Bottom Line, Palm Springs

Katharine
The Great

HEPBURN
A Lifetime of Secrets Revealed

Darwin Porter

"Darwin Porter's biography of Hepburn cannot be lightly dismissed or ignored. Connoisseurs of Hepburn's life would do well to seek it out as a forbidden supplement."

The Sunday Times (London)

Katharine Hepburn was the most obsessively secretive actress in Hollywood. Her androgynous, pan-sexual appeal usually went over big with movie audiences--until those disastrous flops when it didn't. This book tells the how and why of Kate Hepburn's most closely guarded secrets.

Here it is: **WHAT REALLY HAPPENED**, with answers to everything you've ever wondered about the pop star's rise, fall, and rebirth, post-mortem, as **An American Icon**

Jacko
His Rise and Fall

The Social and Sexual History of Michael Jackson

Darwin Porter.

Rigorously updated in the wake of MJ's death, this is the most thorough, best-researched, and most comprehensive biography of the superstar ever published.

ISBN 978-0-936003-10-5. Hardcover
600 indexed pages   ©2009 $27.95

"This is the story of Peter Pan gone rotten. Don't stop till you get enough. Darwin Porter's biography of Michael Jackson is dangerously addictive."
The Sunday Observer, London

"In this compelling glimpse of Jackson's life, Porter provides what many journalists have failed to produce in their writings about the pop star: A real person behind the headlines."
Foreword Magazine

"I'd have thought that there wasn't one single gossippy rock yet to be overturned in the microscopically scrutinized life of Michael Jackson, but Darwin Porter has proven me wrong. Definitely a page-turner. But don't turn the pages too quickly. Almost every one holds a fascinating revelation."
Books to Watch Out For

Winner of an Honorable Mention from the

He rewrote the rules of America's entertainment industry, and he led a life of notoriety. Even his death was the occasion for more scandal, which continues to this day.

Read this biography for the real story of the circumstances and players who created the icon which the world will forever remember as "the gloved one," Michael Jackson.

A DEMENTED BILLIONAIRE:

From his reckless pursuit of love as a rich teenager to his final days as a demented fossil, Howard Hughes tasted the best and worst of the century he occupied. Along the way, he changed the worlds of aviation and entertainment forever. This biography reveals inside details about his destructive and usually scandalous associations with other Hollywood players.

Howard Hughes
Hell's Angel
Darwin Porter

Set amid descriptions of the unimaginable changes that affected America between Hughes's birth in 1905 and his death in 1976, this book gives an insider's perspective about what money can buy--and what it can't.

"Darwin Porter's access to film industry insiders and other Hughes confidants supplied him with the resources he needed to create a portrait of Hughes that both corroborates what other Hughes biographies have divulged, and go them one better." ***Foreword Magazine***

"Thanks to this bio of Howard Hughes, we'll never be able to look at the old pin-ups in quite the same way again." ***The Times* (London)**

Winner of an Honorable Mention from the 2011 Los Angeles Book Festival
814 pages, with photos $32.95
ISBN 978-1-936003-13-6

Hughes--A young billionaire looks toward his notorious future.

"The Aviator flew both ways. Porter's biography presents new allegations about Hughes' shady dealings with some of the biggest names of the 20th century"

New York Daily News

Billie Dove--duenna of the Silent Screen. She gave him syphilis.

HOLLYWOOD BABYLON STRIKES AGAIN!

THE PROFOUNDLY OUTRAGEOUS VOLUME TWO OF BLOOD MOON'S BABYLON SERIES

"Volume Two of Blood Moon's overview of exhibitionism, sexuality, and sin as filtered through 85 years of Hollywood indiscretion.

"Monumentally exhaustive... The Ultimate Guilty Pleasure"
Shelf Awareness

Winner of the Los Angeles Book Festival's Best Nonfiction Title of 2010, and the New England Book Festival's Best Anthology for 2010.

"If you love smutty celebrity dirt as much as I do, then have I got a book for you!"
The Hollywood Offender

"These books will set the graves of Hollywood's cemeteries spinning"   **Daily Express**

Hollywood Babylon Strikes Again!

Darwin Porter and Danforth Prince
Hardcover, 380 outrageous pages, with hundreds of photos

ISBN 978-1-936003-12-9 $25.95

HOLLYWOOD BABYLON IT'S BACK!

VOLUME ONE OF BLOOD MOON'S BABYLON SERIES

From the Golden Age of beautiful bombshells and handsome hunks to today's sleaziest, most corrupt, and most deliciously indecorous hotties, this is the hottest compilation of inter-generational scandal in the history of Hollywood.

As they were unfolding, these stories were known only within Hollywood's most decadent cliques. But all of that changed with the release of this series!

"The American movie industry is always eager for the spotlight if the close-up is flattering and good for business. But Hollywood may get more than it bargained for with **Hollywood Babylon's** compendium of stories, rumors, and myths. Virtually every page features one kind of train wreck or another, usually accompanied by spectacularly lurid photographs. It provides a hair-raising list of compromises and strategically granted sexual favors as proof that some stars will do anything for a part. Try as you might, you won't be able to stop turning the pages. In revealing so many facts previously under wraps, this book, in fact, raises the question of how much more remains hidden."

Shelf Awareness/ Bookselling News

Blood Moon's Babylon Series:

Outrageous overviews of exhibitionism, sexuality, and sin as filtered through 85 years of Hollywood indiscretion.

Celebrity Psychos

"These books will set the graves of Hollywood's cemeteries spinning"   **Daily Express**

Hollywood Babylon-It's Back!

Darwin Porter and Danforth Prince
Hardcover, 408 outrageous pages, with hundreds of photos

ISBN 978-0-9748118-8-8 $24.95

OUT OF THE CELLULOID CLOSET
HOMOSEXUALITY IN THE MOVIES

50 Years of Queer Cinema--500 of the Best GLBTQ Films Ever Made

A Reference Source for Private Homes and Libraries

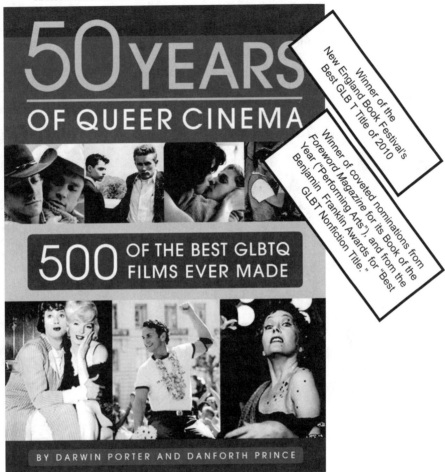

Winner of the New England Book Festival's Best GLB T Title of 2010

Winner of coveted nominations from Foreword Magazine for its Book of the Year ("Performing Arts"), and from the Benjamin Franklin Awards for "Best GLBT Nonfiction Title."

"In the Internet age, where every movie, queer or otherwise, is blogged about somewhere, a hefty print compendium of film facts and pointed opinion might seem anachronistic. But flipping through well-reasoned pages of commentary is so satisfying. Add to that physical thrill the charm of analysis that is sometimes sassy and always smart, and this filtered survey of short reviews is a must for queer-film fans.

"In part one, Porter and Prince provide a succinct "A to Z romp" through 500 films, with quick plot summaries and on-point critical assessments, each film summed up with a pithy headline: *Yossi & Jagger* is "Macho Israeli Soldiers Make Love, Not War.

"The films surveyed in part two are quirkier fare, 160 "less publicized" efforts, including—no lie—*Karl Rove, I Love You*, in which gay actor Dan Butler falls for 'George W. Bush's Turd Blossom.'

"Essays on Derek Jarman, Tennessee Williams, Andy Warhol, Jack Wrangler, Joe Gage and others—and on how *The Front Runner* never got made—round out this indispensable survey of gay-interest cinema."

An award-winning softcover, 524 pages, with substantive comments and gossip about almost 650 films, with hundreds of photos

ISBN 978-1-936003-09-9 $25.95

RICHARD LABONTÉ
BOOK MARKS/QSYNDICATE

Other Hot Film Guides from Blood Moon

These guidebooks contain essays, descriptions and reviews of hundreds of gay films released between 2007 and 2010, plus photos, special features, gossip about When Divas Clash on location, insights into intra-industry brouhahas, AND The Blood Moon Awards

Volume One   **$19.95**
ISBN 978-0-9748118-4-0

Volume Two   **$21.95**
ISBN 978-0-9748118-7-1

Hip, Funny, Informative

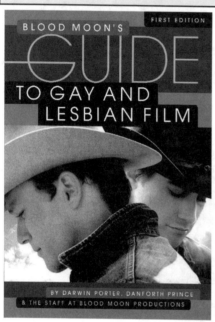

This series has won three prestigious book awards, including an Honorable Mention from the Hollywood Book Festival.

WELL-REVIEWED, SMASHING BARRIERS

"Authoritative, exhaustive, and essential, **Blood Moon's Guide to Gay & Lesbian Film** is the queer girl's and queer boy's one-stop resource for what to add to their feature-film queues. The film synopses and the snippets of critics' reviews are reason enough to keep this annual compendium of cinematic information close the the DVD player. But the extras--including the Blood Moon Awards and the commentary on queer short films--are butter on the popcorn."
Books to Watch Out For

"Startling. This exhaustive guide documents everything from the mainstream to the obscure."
HX New York

"Listing everything fabu in films, this is an essential guide for both the casual viewer and the hard-core movie-watching homo."

Bay Windows (Boston)

"From feisty Blood Moon Productions, this big, lively guidebook of (mostly) recent gay and gay-ish films is not meant to be a dust-collecting reference book covering the history of GLBT films. Instead, it's an annual running commentary on what's new and what's going on in gay filmmaking."

Mandate

Midnight in Savannah

A Horrifying, Bittersweet Novel about Sexual Eccentricities in the Deep South

Darwin Porter

A supremely entertaining paperback
that will haunt you long after your return from Georgia
498 pages **$16.95**   **ISBN 978-0-9668030-1-3**

After its publication in 2000, Darwin Porter's *Midnight in Savannah* quickly established itself as one of the best-selling gay novels in the history of the Deep South.

Eugene Raymond, a filmmaker in Nashville, writes, "Porter disturbs by showing the world as a *film noir* cul-de-sac.   Corruption has no respect for gender or much of anything else.

"In MIDNIGHT, both Lavender Morgan (at 72, the world's oldest courtesan) and Tipper Zelda (an obese, fading chanteuse taunted as 'the black widow) purchase lust from sexually conflicted young men with drop-dead faces, chiseled bodies, and genetically gifted crotches. These women once relied on their physicality to steal the hearts and fortunes of the world's richest and most powerful men. Now, as they slide closer every day to joining the corpses of their former husbands, these once-beautiful women must depend, in a perverse twist of fate, on sexual outlaws for *le petit mort*. And to survive, the hustlers must idle their personal dreams while struggling to cajole what they need from a sexual liaison they detest. Mendacity reigns. Physical beauty as living hell. CAT ON A HOT TIN ROOF's Big Daddy must be spinning in his grave right now."

"If you're not already a Darwin Porter fan, this novel will make you one!   We've come a long way, baby, since Gore Vidal's The City and the Pillar."
Time Out for Books

"An artfully brutal saga of corruption, greed, sexual tension, and murder, highlighted by the eccentricities of the Deep South. Compulsive Reading."
The Georgia Literary Assn.

"I've just booked the next flight to Savannah! Nothing like a good Georgia boy on a chilly night in Dixie!"
Out!

Wild, orgiastic nights in pre-code Hollywood

Hollywood's Silent Closet

Darwin Porter

A compelling, door stopping paperback, 7" x 10"
with 746 pages and 60 vintage photos
ISBN 978-0-9668030-2-0 $24.95

a novel by
Darwin Porter

"The Little Tramp" **Charlie Chaplin** (above) was one of the most recklessly debauched players in Hollywood.

Disillusioned In her later years, **Mary Pickford** (left) declared herself a recluse and virtually never left her bedroom.

An anthology of star-studded scandal from Tinseltown's very gay and very lavender past, it focuses on Hollywood's secrets from the 1920s, including the controversial backgrounds of the great lovers of the Silent Screen.

Valentino, Ramon Novarro, Charlie Chaplin, Fatty Arbuckle, Pola Negri, Mary Pickford, and many others figure into eyewitness accounts of the debauched excesses that went on behind closed doors. It also documents the often tragic endings of America's first screen idols, some of whom admitted to being more famous than the monarchs of England and Jesus Christ combined.

The first book of its kind, it's the most intimate and most realistic novel about sex, murder, blackmail, and degradation in early Hollywood ever written.

"The *Myra Breckinridge* of the Silent-Screen era. Lush, luscious, and langorously decadent. A brilliant primer of *Who Was Who* in early Hollywood."

Gay Times, London

A banquet of information about the pansexual intrigues of Hollywood between 1919 and 1926 compiled from eyewitness interviews with men and women, all of them insiders, who flourished in its midst. Not for the timid, it names names and doesn't spare the guilty. If you believe, like Truman Capote, that the literary treatment of gossip will become the literature of the 21st century, then you will love *Hollywood's Silent Closet.*

Millions of fans lusted after **Gary Cooper** (background) and **Rudolph Valentino** (foreground) but until the release of this book, **The Public Never Knew.**

BLOOD MOON

An Artfully Brutal Tale of Psychosis, Sexual Obsession, Money, Power, Religion, and Love.

by Darwin Porter

In 2008, this title was designated as one of the ten best horror novels ever published
in a survey conducted by the British literary club *Boiz Who Read*

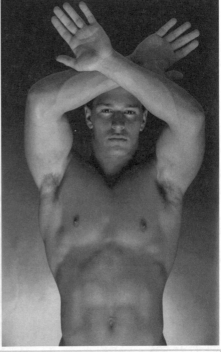

Blood Moon exposes the murky labyrinths of fanatical Christianity in America today, all within a spunky context of male eroticism. If you never thought that sex, psychosis, right-wing religion, and violence aren't linked, think again.

"In the gay genre, Blood Moon does for the novel what Danielle Steele and John Grisham have been publishing in the straight world for years."

Frank Fenton

Rose Phillips, Blood Moon's charismatic and deviant evangelist, and her shocking but beautiful gay son, Shelley, were surely written in hell. Together, they're a brilliant—and jarring—depiction of a fiercely aggressive Oedipal couple competing for the same male prizes.

*"**Blood Moon** reads like an IMAX spectacle about the power of male beauty, with red-hot icons, a breathless climax, and erotica that's akin to Anaïs Nin on Viagra with a bump of meth."*

Eugene Raymond

A controversial, compelling, and artfully potboiling paperback that describes what really happens when the Moon Turns to Blood.　　**ISBN 978-0-9668030-4-4**　　$10.99

Rhinestone Country

A Sometimes Erotic Thriller about Love and the Music Industry   Darwin Porter

All that glitter, all that publicity, all that applause, all that pain...

The *True Grit* of show-biz novels, *Rhinestone Country* is a provocative, realistic, and tender portrayal of the Country-Western music industry, closeted lives south of the Mason-Dixon line, and three of the singers who clawed their way to stardom.

Rhinestone Country reads like a scalding gulp of rotgut whiskey on a snowy night in a bow-jacks honky-tonk.
          -Mississippi Pearl

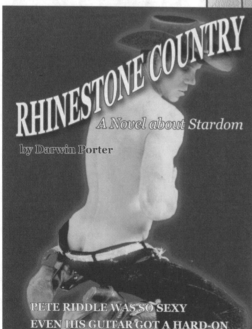

"*Beautifully crafted, Rhinestone Country sweeps with power and tenderness across the racial, social, and sexual landscapes of the Deep South. This is a daring and dazzling work about trauma, deception, and pain, all of it with a Southern accent.*"   **Peter Tompkins**

"*A gay and erotic treatment of the Country-Western music industry? Nashville has come out of the closet at last!*"
          The Georgia Literary Assn.

Softcover, with a Southern accent, some memorable men and down-home women, and a whole lot of pathos

569 pages   **ISBN 978-0-9668030-3-7** $15.99

BUTTERFLIES IN HEAT

Darwin Porter

A compellingly retro softcover expressing some eternal truths about LOVE, HATE, GREED, AND SEX

Tennessee Williams, who understood a thing or two about loss, love, and drama, had this to say about **Butterflies in Heat:**

"I'd walk the waterfront for Numie any day."

"The most SCORCHING novel of the BIZ-ZARE, the FLAMBOYANT, the CORRUPT since Midnight Cowboy. The strikingly beautiful blond hustler, Numie, has come to the end of the line. Here, in the SEARING HEAT of a tropical cay, he arouses PASSIONS that explode under the BLOOD-RED SUN."
Manor Reviews

"A well-established cult classic. How does Darwin Porter's garden grow? Only in the moonlight, and only at midnight, when man-eating vegetation in any color but green bursts into full bloom to devour the latest offerings."

James Leo Herlihy, author of
MIDNIGHT COWBOY

This title, a cult classic now in its **16th printing**, has sold steadily to a coterie of Darwin Porter fans since its inauguration in 1976, when it was the thing EVERYBODY in Key West was talking about, and the inspiration for the movie (The Last Resort/ Tropic of Desire) that EVERYBODY wanted to be in.

"Darwin Porter writes with an incredible understanding of the milieu--hot enough to singe the wings off any butterfly."
James Kirkwood, co-author of A CHORUS LINE

ISBN
978-0-9668030-9-9
$14.95

"We know from the beginning that we're getting into a hotbed that has morbid fascination for potential readers. The novel evolves, in fact, into one massive melée of malevolence, vendetta, and e-v-i-l, stunningly absorbing alone for its sheer and unrelenting exploration of the lower depths."
BESTSELLERS

BLOOD MOON's

Dirty Laundry

ALL THE GOSSIP UNFIT TO PRINT, AS AUTHORED BY DARWIN PORTER

Blood Moon maintains its ongoing commitment to a FREE twice-monthly newsletter
wherein **Darwin Porter,**

America's most literate muckraker, analyzes recent celebrity gossip.

Putting the *oooomph* back into editorial coverage of
current events and celebrity scandal,
it's Blood Moon's response to the 21st century tabloids.

SIGN UP FOR IT FREE, TODAY!

**CHEAP AND SALACIOUS CELEBRITY DISH
LIKE YOU'VE NEVER SEEN IT BEFORE. WHY?**

BECAUSE DIRTY LAUNDRY MAKES WASHDAY FUN!

The water's hot, and the soap is free, but you won't get really clean
unless you sign up for it first, FREE AND WITHOUT CHARGE,
from the home page of

WWW.BLOODMOONPRODUCTIONS.COM

SO YOU WANT TO LEARN HOW TO SWIM IN THE SHARK-INFESTED WATERS OF THE BOOK TRADES?

New and Available Now: An Updated Report Filmed at Book Expo 2011

Book Expo 2010

Blood Moon's
VIEW FROM
THE FLOOR

No other closeup has ever before captured **the heat**, **the drama**, and **the mania** of one exhibitor's *View from the Floor.* Accessorized with a cast of thousands and featuring cameo interviews from dozens of book industry bigshots. Shot on location in New York City during the mania of **Book Expo 2010.**

See it for FREE at
bloodmoonproductions.com

DIVING BACK INTO THE SHARK-INFESTED WATERS OF THE BOOK TRADES!

Book Expo 2011

Blood Moon's
VIEW FROM
THE FLOOR ❷

SEE IT NOW

In May of 2010, Blood Moon rented an $8,500 booth at **Book Expo, 2010,** the world's largest literary marketplace, and made a 75-minute movie about what happened during the maniacal goings-on that followed.

In June of 2011, we filmed a 60-minute updated version, reflecting the previous year's evolution of the thousands of events affecting the book trades.

We offer these films without charge to anyone who dreams about maneuvering his or her way through the shark-infested waters of the book trades. Watch these films, download or share them, without charge, from the home page of

www.BloodMoonProductions.com

BLOOD MOON PRODUCTIONS ANNOUNCES THE AVAILABILITY OF A PAIR OF DOCUMENTARIES AND INFO-MERCIALS it filmed at two separate instances of the world's largest literary trade fair, *Book Expo America.*

BLOOD MOON'S VIEW FROM THE FLOOR, Versions 1 and 2, represent history's first attempts to capture—close, in-your-face, uncensored, and personalized—the interactions, alliances, scandals, and dramas that explode for a small book publisher during a bookselling mega-event devoted to the marketing, pricing, and sale of its literary products.

Conceived as a means of increasing public awareness of Blood Moon's literary products, these films were developed as publicity and promotion pieces by the company's founder and president, Danforth Prince. "Book publishers operate in a state of barely controlled hysteria, especially in this economic climate," he said. "Within these films, we've captured some of the drama of how books are promoted and hawked at highly competitive events where everyone from Barbra Streisand to the Duchess of York will enthusiastically shake his or her bon-bon to sell something."

"At BEA, enemies, competitors, and authors evoke Oscar night in Hollywood before the awards are announced," Prince continued. "These films are the first attempt to depict, without charge, on video, how a small press swims in the frantic, shark-infested waters of the book trade. They document specific moments in America's mercantile history, with implications for America's reading habits and how consumers will opt to amuse and entertain themselves in the 21st century."

During the footage he shot from within and near his booths at BEA 2010 and 2011, Mr. Prince was directed by Polish-born Piotr Kajstura, winner of several filmmaking awards and grants for his work with, among others, the tourism board of South Carolina.

BOOK EXPO 2010, BLOOD MOON'S VIEW FROM THE FLOOR.
AND BOOK EXPO 2011, BLOOD MOON'S VIEW FROM THE FLOOR 2
© Blood Moon Productions, Ltd. Available now, electronically and without charge,
from the home page of **BloodMoonProductions.com**.

What Book-Industry Critics Said About the 2010 Installment of this Film:

"Blood Moon Productions, which specializes in books about Hollywood celebrity scandals of the past—many of which were hushed up at the time—offers a feature-length video on BookExpo America 2010, which aims to give "nonprofessional book people an insight into book fairs" while highlighting some Blood Moon titles. The narrator is Blood Moon president Danforth Prince, who interviews, among others, Carole Stuart of Barricade Books, Philip Rafshoon, owner of Outwrite Bookstore and Coffeehouse, Atlanta, Ga., Graeme Aitkin of the Bookshop in Sydney, Australia, Eugene Schwartz of ForeWord Reviews, and a what seems like half of the staff of National Book Network, Blood Moon's distributor."
Shelf-Awareness.com August 3, 2010 (volume 2, issue #1247)

DIVING BACK INTO THE SHARK-INFESTED WATERS OF THE BOOK TRADES!

Blood Moon's View from the Floor 2.
An updated installment filmed at Book Expo 2011
Viewable and downloadable now, without charge, from
www.BloodMoonProductions.com